P9-AFA-772

QUILTS

A LIVING TRADITION

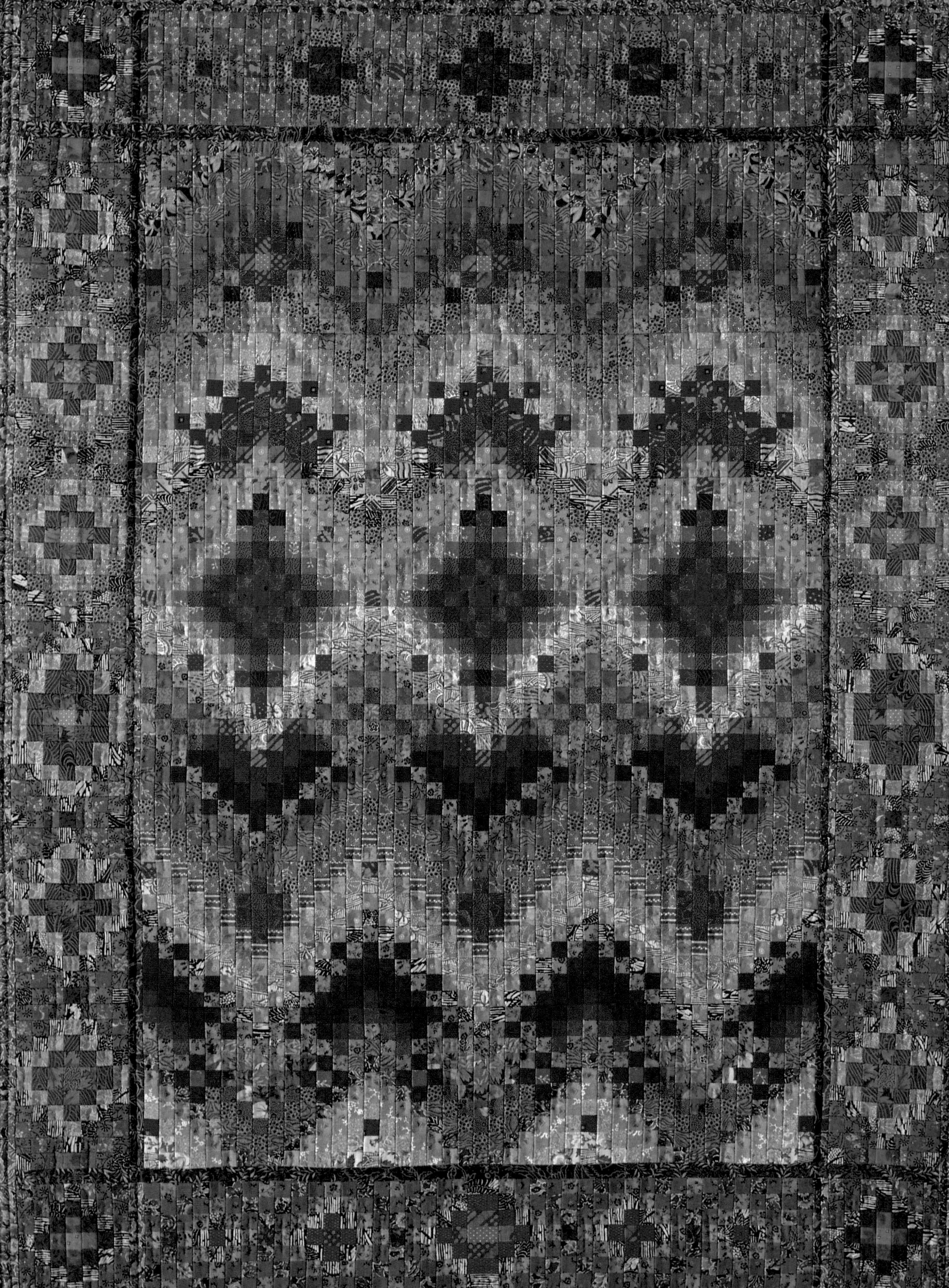

QUILTS

A LIVING TRADITION

Robert Shaw

HUGH LAUTER LEVIN ASSOCIATES, INC.

◄ **AUGUST OFFERING**

Susan Sawyer. 1990. East Calais, Vermont. Cottons; machine pieced and quilted. 45 x 34 in. Collection of David and Judith Gayer.

According to the quiltmaker, "The design, with borders and medallions, refers to Oriental rug traditions. The red shapes on blue remind me of red raspberries with light shining through or [of] pomegranate seeds. It's not the red of blood or fire, but the red of ripe, abundant fruit, hence the title."

Design by Kathleen Herlihy-Paoli, Inkstone Design
Photo research by Ellin Yassky Silberblatt
Editorial production by Deborah Teipel Zindell
Printed and bound in Hong Kong
ISBN 0-88363-395-7

Acknowledgments

This book would not have been possible without the help and generosity of many, many people. First, I want to thank the hundreds of quiltmakers who sent photographs of their work to be considered for the book. Although only a few of the thousands of quilts I looked at could be included, every one of their makers made a real contribution to my understanding of the diverse world of contemporary quilts, and I am indebted to all of them.

Ardis and Robert James generously allowed open access to their remarkable collection of antique and contemporary quilts, many of which are here published for the first time. Myron Miller ably photographed quilts from the James collection, and Stacey Epstein, curator of the collection, assisted with photography and information.

Penny McMorris, co-author of the still definitive *The Art Quilt*, offered encouragement throughout the project. Penny also put me in touch with John Walsh III, who graciously shared some of his extraordinary art quilts. Yvonne Porcella and Martha Connell helped me better understand the history and meaning of the art quilt movement. Shelly Zegart gave me complete access to her intensely focused collection, read and critiqued parts of the manuscript and made a number of helpful suggestions. Robert Cargo directed me to the work of several outstanding Southern quilters and shared great quilts from his vast collection. Joel Kopp of America Hurrah offered access to his extensive photo files and shared several fresh and wonderful quilts. Kei Kobayashi offered invaluable assistance on Japanese quiltmaking. Mr. T. Higuchi of Kokusai Art allowed use of some of his company's excellent quilt photographs. Margaret Wood helped me track down several other Native American quilters and shared information from her research into Indian quilting traditions. Carolyn Mazloomi alerted other African-American quilters to the project, as did Carole Y. Lyles and Barbara Pietila of NAAAQ. Richard Cleveland, director of the Vermont Quilt Festival, let me peruse his enormous slide library and suggested a number of quiltmakers. Julie Silber and Joe Cunningham of The Quilt Complex shared a mutual enthusiasm for maverick quilts and country blues and helped with photographs and information. Michael James and Nancy Crow shared brand new work and information about their new directions. Kate Adams, master of miniatures, put me in touch with a number of extraordinary quiltmakers, including Jonathan Shannon and Mary Glick. Elizabeth Akana unselfishly championed the work of several other Hawaiian quilters and helped arrange photography of quilts by Sharon Balai and Stan Yates. Lee Wild provided me with information and contacts throughout the Hawaiian islands. Camille Cognac sent several fat envelopes full of names, information, and enticing photographs.

Several professional colleagues deserve special thanks. Colleen Callahan of the Valentine Museum pointed out several unknown masterpieces in that great collection. Marsha MacDowell of Michigan State University helped enormously with Native American and African-American quilts. Sandra Staebell of the Kentucky Museum went out of her way to help with photographs and information. Thanks are also due to Mrs. Eric Steinfeldt of the Witte Museum, Laurann Figg of the Vesterheim Norwegian-American Museum, Zoe Perkins of the St. Louis Art Museum, Deborah Kraak of the H.F. du Pont Winterthur Museum, Dilys Blum of the Philadelphia Museum of Art, Stacy Hollander and Janey Fire of the Museum of American Folk Art, Margaret Woods of the Museum of the Rockies, Lynne Robertson, executive director of the McKissick Museum, Linda Mann, executive director of The Craftsman's Guild of Mississippi, Lisa Howorth of the Center for Studies of Southern Culture at the University of Mississippi, and Mary Lohrenz of the Mississippi Historical Museum.

Thanks also to Laurel Horton, president of the American Quilt Study Group, Susan Knobloch, executive director of Quilt San Diego, Nancy Cameron Armstrong of the Canadian Quilt Study Group, Hazel Carter of the Quilter's Hall of Fame, Mimi Handler and Jean Creznic of *Early American Life Magazine*, Carter Houck, Bets Ramsey, Dorothy Osler, Linda Carlson, Pat Ferrero, Helen Kelley, and the dozens of other people I've undoubtedly overlooked.

I am immensely grateful to Hugh Levin, who conceived this project and supported it wholeheartedly from start to finish. Michael Ruscoe did early photographic research, and project manager Ellin Silberblatt coordinated the diverse aspects of the book with her rare combination of unfailing grace and single-minded tenacity. Thanks are also due to Debby Zindell, who nimbly edited the manuscript, to long-distance designer Kathleen Herlihy-Paoli, who provided the book's beautiful layout from her new home in Montana, and to Jan Scaglia, for her fine production work.

Finally, loving thanks to my girls: my daughters, Emma and Georgia, who told me which quilts they liked best, and my wife Nancy, who, with patience, respect, and love, somehow kept us all together and moving onward.

ROBERT SHAW
Shelburne, Vermont

Contents

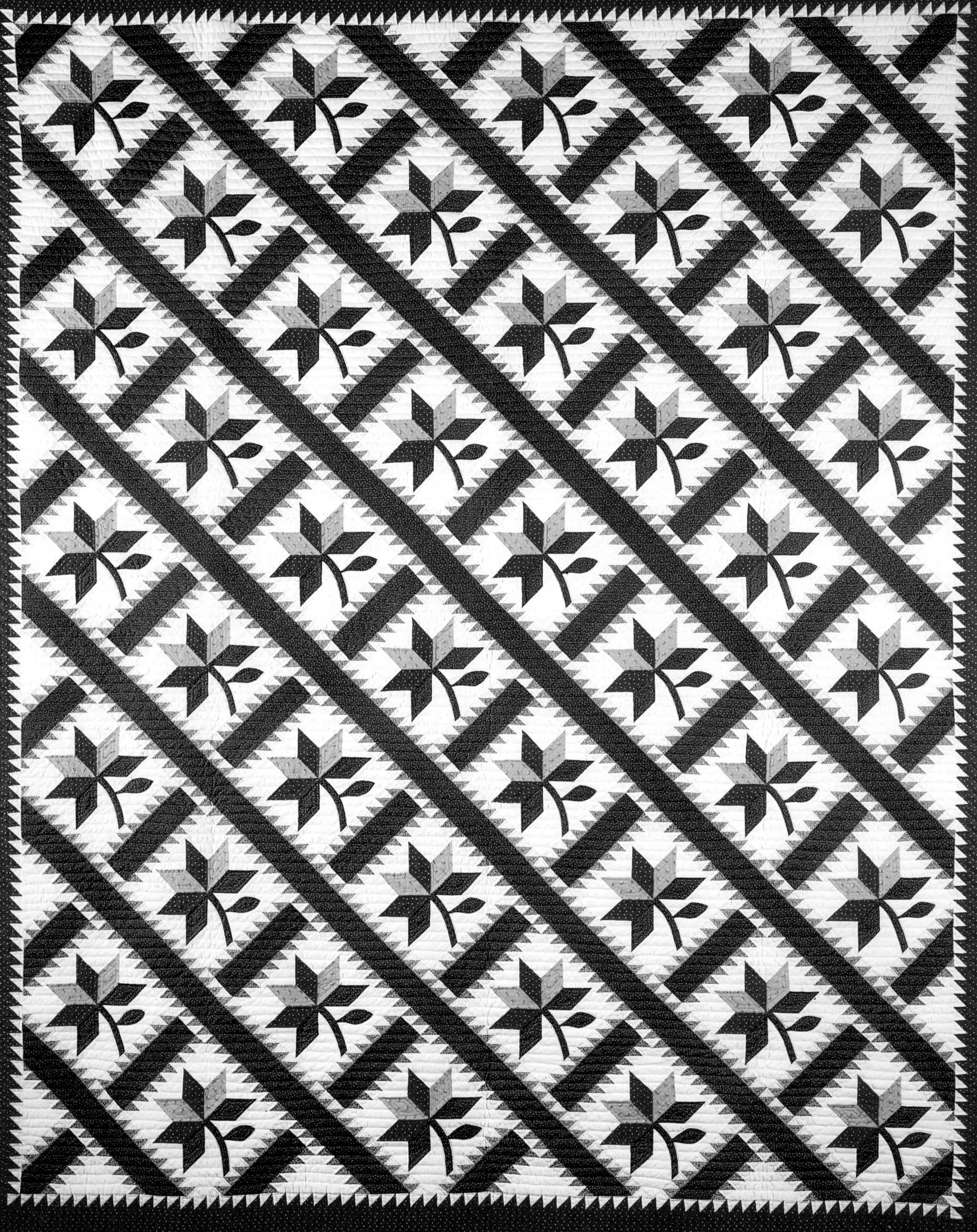

Introduction: The Democratic Art

Quilts are America's gift to the world. Like many of this country's traditions, quiltmaking's origins lie in Europe, but the germ of the Old World idea flourished in the new land, growing into something entirely and uniquely American. No other craft or art form is more closely identified with the values that define this country than quilting. Like jazz, like the cowboy, like baseball, the simple idea of quiltmaking has reached seemingly every corner of the world, taking a vision of America and the American way of life with it. Quilts represent American possibilities and opportunities: of freedom, democracy, equality, home, community, and individual expression. Almost as powerfully symbolic as the American flag (which they have sometimes imitated), quilts embody the Declaration of Independence's inalienable rights of life, liberty, and the pursuit of happiness in their bold and open designs, colorful and exuberant variety, and singular and expressive creativity. Throughout the world, quilts are symbols of America and the daily life of its people, emblems of hope infused with a host of meanings, some broad, national, and patriotic, others subtle, familial, and personal.

For Americans, quilts are objects of great affection, stirring memories of childhood, family, warmth, comfort, and safety. Quilts have been an important part of our daily life for over two hundred years. Few American lives have not been touched by quilts. They are among the most common objects that have been made by Americans and are by far the best loved of all household things. Only the flintiest curmudgeon could fail to warm to the thought of quilts; only a Scrooge could say "Bah, humbug" to their charms and associations. Hundreds of thousands of American women have made quilts and many if not most Americans have slept under a quilt, often made by their mother, sister, aunt, or grandmother. Quilts still cover and decorate millions of American beds. Paradoxically, in an age when inexpensive (and often foreign-made) quilts are offered by every homewares catalog imaginable, there are more people making quilts today than ever before in history. Although a homemade quilt functions no better than a store-bought one, many people prefer a personal touch. Untold thousands of quilts have been made in kitchens, living rooms, grange halls, and church basements across this country, where women could work their own ideas and creative expressions into the fabric of their families' bedcovers.

◄ Peony with Sawtooth Border

Mary Ghormley. 1992. Lincoln, Nebraska. Cottons; hand pieced, appliquéd, and quilted. 102 1/2 x 81 1/2 in. Collection of the artist.

Mary Ghormley is a quilt historian, collector, and traditional quilter who has made a number of copies of antique quilts since she began quilting in the 1960s. She says, "As I collect, I see myself as a conservator, saving quilts from being destroyed, lost, and unappreciated." This charming old-fashioned quilt is patterned after an original dated c. 1850 that was reproduced in a Japanese exhibition catalog.

Quiltmaking is a quintessentially democratic activity, accessible to anyone with basic sewing skills, an urge for self-expression, and an eye for beauty. Although the idea of sewing an insulating layer between two pieces of cloth is an ancient one, it was in the new and unrestricted society of nineteenth-century America that the possibilities inherent in the idea of quilting took hold and flourished. After visiting the United States in the 1830s, Alexis de Tocqueville observed in his still definitive study *Democracy in America*, "Democratic nations...will therefore cultivate the arts that serve to render life easy in preference to those whose object is to adorn it. They will habitually prefer the useful to the beautiful, and they will require that the beautiful should be useful." He might well have been writing about quilts. No other American art form so inextricably intertwines usefulness and beauty. Americans needed warm bedcoverings and found dynamic new ways to make their bedcoverings attractive to the eye. Quilts can be both functional and decorative, intimate and abstract, well crafted and artful. Quilts satisfy the basic human need for warmth. They also fulfill the desires for self-expression and for creating things of beauty. In a traditional quilt, these pairings of seeming opposites are inseparable; each informs and enhances the other. The function of the quilt allows its art to flourish; the art of the quilt allows its function to retain meaning. Even though quilts are now sometimes made as self-conscious works of art, without thought given to purpose, and as often hang on walls as cover beds, their simple, traditional function still ties them to us, grounds them, and deflates their makers' pretensions—in a sense, keeps them honest.

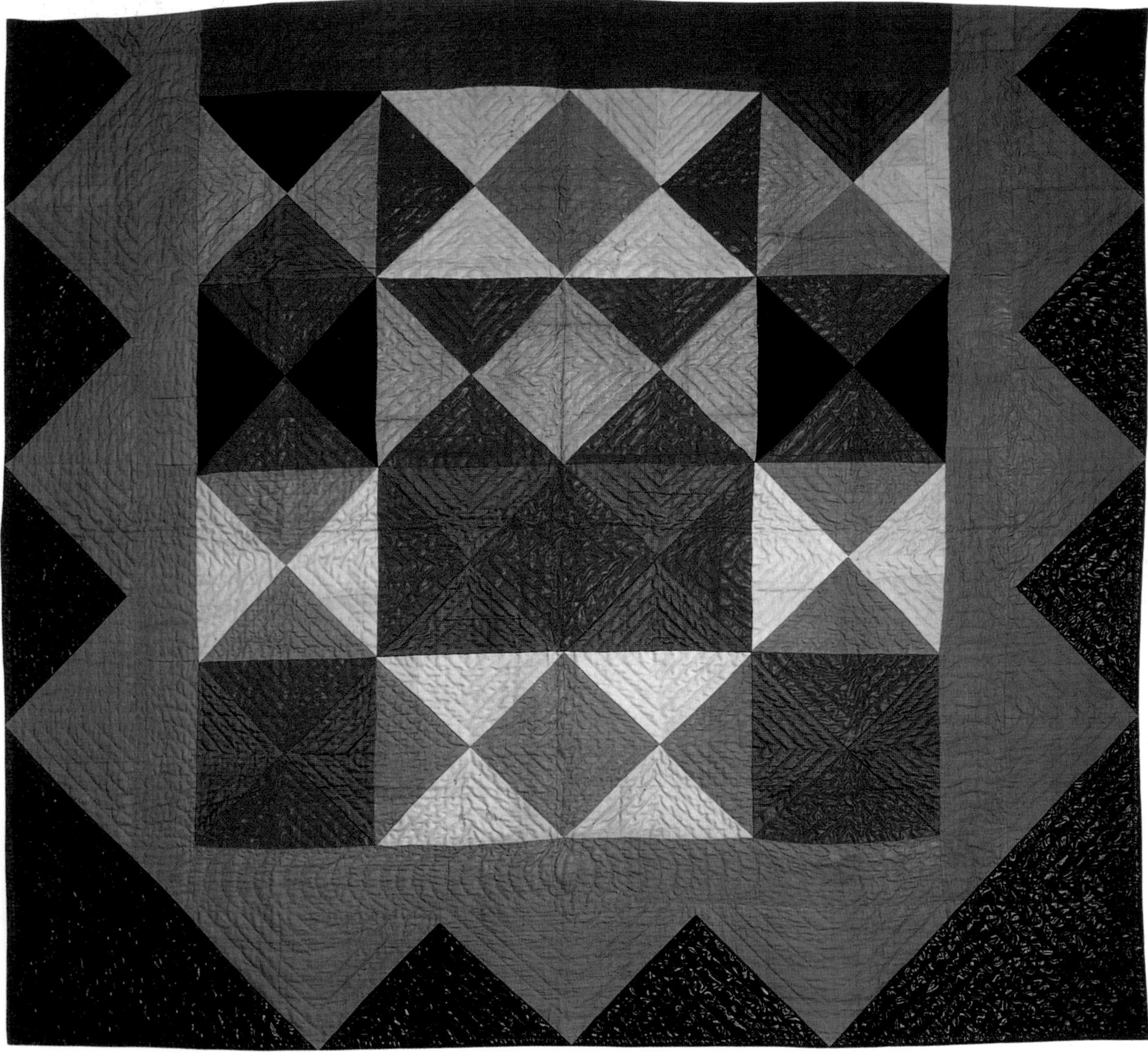

◄ **HARLEQUIN MEDALLION CALIMANCO**

Artist unknown. c. 1800–1820. New England. Glazed wools; hand pieced and quilted. 86 3/4 x 96 in. Museum of American Folk Art, New York, gift of Cyril Nelson in loving memory of his grandparents, John Williams and Sophie von Hack Macy.

This unique composition surrounds a carefully organized geometric central medallion with a powerfully jagged, triangular border. The brightly colored wool pieces are cleverly arranged to give the impression that the medallion is built with four rectangles with center diamonds, bordered on either side by squares that are made up of four triangles, but the four rectangles are actually made of mirror image squares. Bold overall quilting completes the complex surface of this masterpiece.

Log Cabin—Light and Dark ▶

Ursula Egger-Graf. 1980. Volkerswil, Switzerland. Cottons; machine pieced and hand quilted. 55 1/2 x 55 1/2 in. Collection of the artist.

This quilt was made in memory of the quiltmaker's grandmother and includes her apron among its fabrics. The thirty-six blocks are set to form rows of interlocking diamonds, arranged in a three, two, three, two, three pattern.

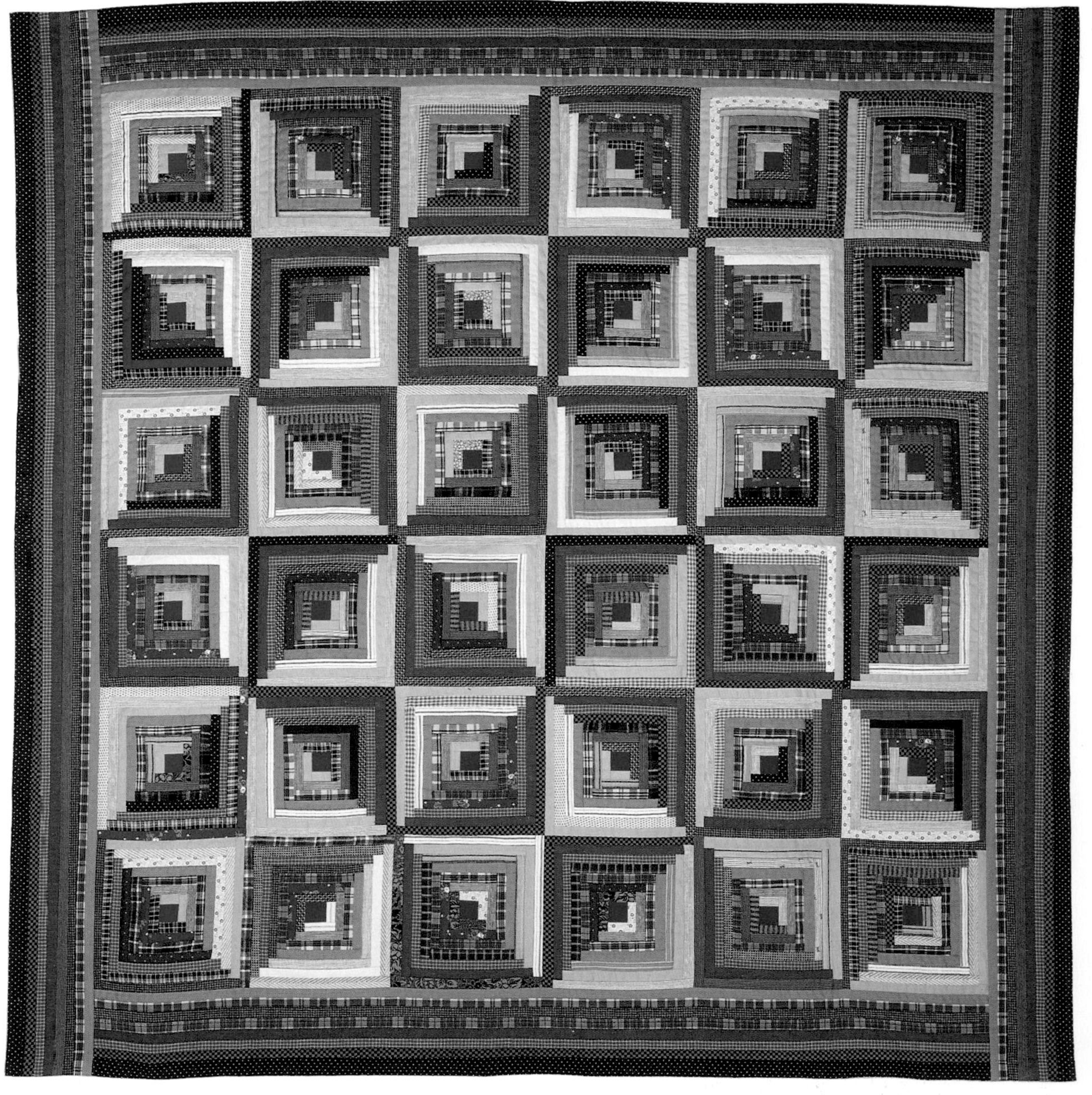

Quilts belong to American women. Although some men have been quiltmakers, the medium has traditionally been associated with and dominated by women. Women have defined quiltmaking, set its standards, outlined its parameters, and judged its accomplishments. For women, quilts have offered a means of expression and empowerment in a medium of their own making, to be shared almost exclusively with other women. For a substantial part of this country's history, quilts were virtually the only means of personal and artistic expression readily available to the average woman. Quiltmaking was something that women looked forward to after long days of farm or housework. Because women have invested so much of themselves in their quilts, quilts are often personal or family treasures, carefully and even ceremoniously passed down from generation to generation (usually by the female members of a family), and lovingly cared for and brought out for special occasions. Quilts serve as documents of the history of women in America, attesting to both personal and shared concerns, and expressing a full range of emotions and experiences. Social historians and students of the relatively new science of material culture now study quilts alongside diaries, letters, and other primary documents, including them among the most important sources of information about women's lives in earlier times. Every quilt is different; each reveals something of its maker's personality and individuality as well as her place within her community and society. Because quilts were a

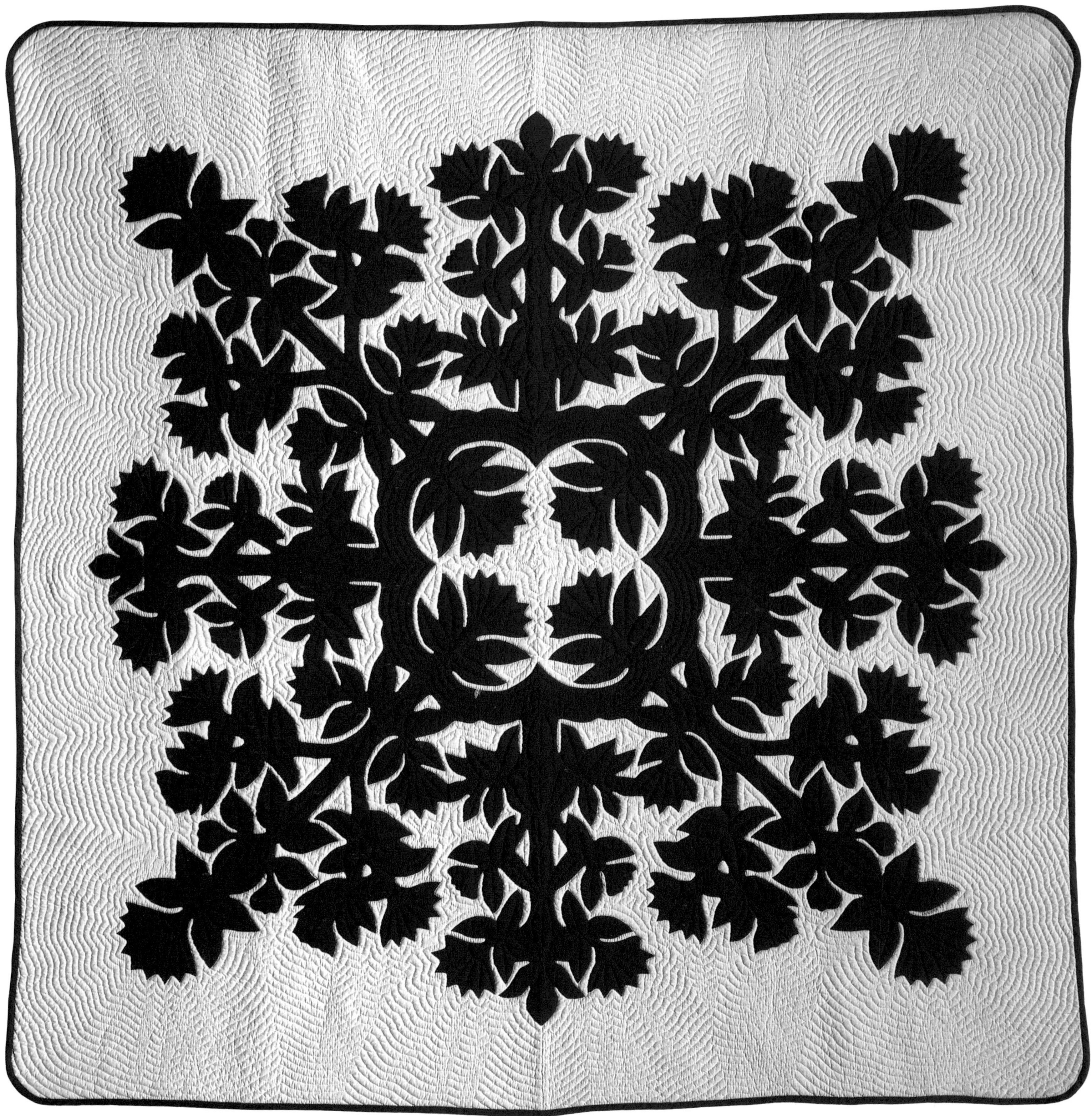

▲ **KALANA LEHUA O HAWAII**

Designed by Eleanor Ahuna, made by Annette Sumado. 1984. Island of Hawaii. Plain woven cotton; hand appliquéd and contour quilted. 88 x 88 in. Collection of Annette Sumado.

In this original design, two repeating symmetrical floral motifs surround a rounded central octagon. The four complex corner designs include flowers that fill the center of the octagon. The bright red lehua flower, which is the basis for the design, is the official flower of the island of Hawaii.

source of solace and a creative outlet for so many women, they can be especially revealing about women's feelings and perceptions of themselves, sometimes telling stories and carrying emotions that cannot be as effectively expressed by more literal means.

Quilts have always been a unifying force among women, a common creative interest to be shared, a source of both communal pride and personal accomplishment. Women have long supported each other in and through quilting, uniting periodically in formal and informal gatherings, groups, and meetings where they inevitably share each other's lives, trials, and tribulations as well as quilts in progress, and where they can encourage each other's ideas and work. Quilt groups are enormously popular today for all these reasons: one quilter wrote that "in fifteen years together our Tuesday night group has experienced three births, two deaths, and a heart transplant." These shared meanings that bind women together can be specific and personal ones that bring together a family or a group of friends or neighbors, or they can be more general and subconscious and therefore available to a broader and less clearly defined community. Unlike other needle arts, or most other handcrafts for that matter, quiltmaking lends itself to communal expression. More than one woman can easily work on the same quilt, either together or separately. A mother and her daughters might work a quilt together as the girls test their cutting, piecing, and stitching abilities before attempting the craft alone, or several neighbors or church members might collaborate on a top to give away to a friend or sell to aid a cause. Women have made quilts for each other and with each other, and have often made quilts to support local and national causes that were important to them. During the Civil War, women on both sides of the conflict made thousands of quilts which were sold to support the efforts of their husbands, brothers, fathers, and neighbors; thousands more were made for use in camps and hospitals. Women have also made quilts to support church groups, missionary work, Christian Temperance Unions, women's suffrage, the Red Cross, the civil rights movement, and dozens of other causes in which they were deeply involved. These communally made quilts provide a history of many of the issues that have concerned American women over the past two hundred years.

Quilts are powerful symbolic objects that stimulate the imagination and evoke for many a lost and innocent America of small towns, closely knit families, moral integrity, neighborly concern, and Christian charity. That this America is mythic only emphasizes the power of the quilt as symbol and metaphor. At its most superficial level this scene is a sweet, sentimental, and nostalgic one that could have been painted by a Norman Rockwell or Grandma Moses. But at its most profound, it is something quite different. Quilts touch our deepest longings for ourselves and for our children, opening direct channels to our emotions, hopes, and dreams as only great art can. They tie neighbors to neighbors, husbands to wives, parents to children, brothers to sisters, and grandparents to grandchildren, and can carry community and family memories from generation to generation. Quilts are also symbols of relationships, especially the primal and nurturing relationship between mother and child. They are the most intimate of objects, created out of love and care, metaphorically wrapping the sleeper in the warmth and concern of the maker's affection, promising comfort, protection, and peace through the night's dark uncertainties.

By their nature, quilts are understood as much through touch, the most intimate of the senses, as by sight, cradling us as we sleep and thereby receiving our dreams. We fondly recall

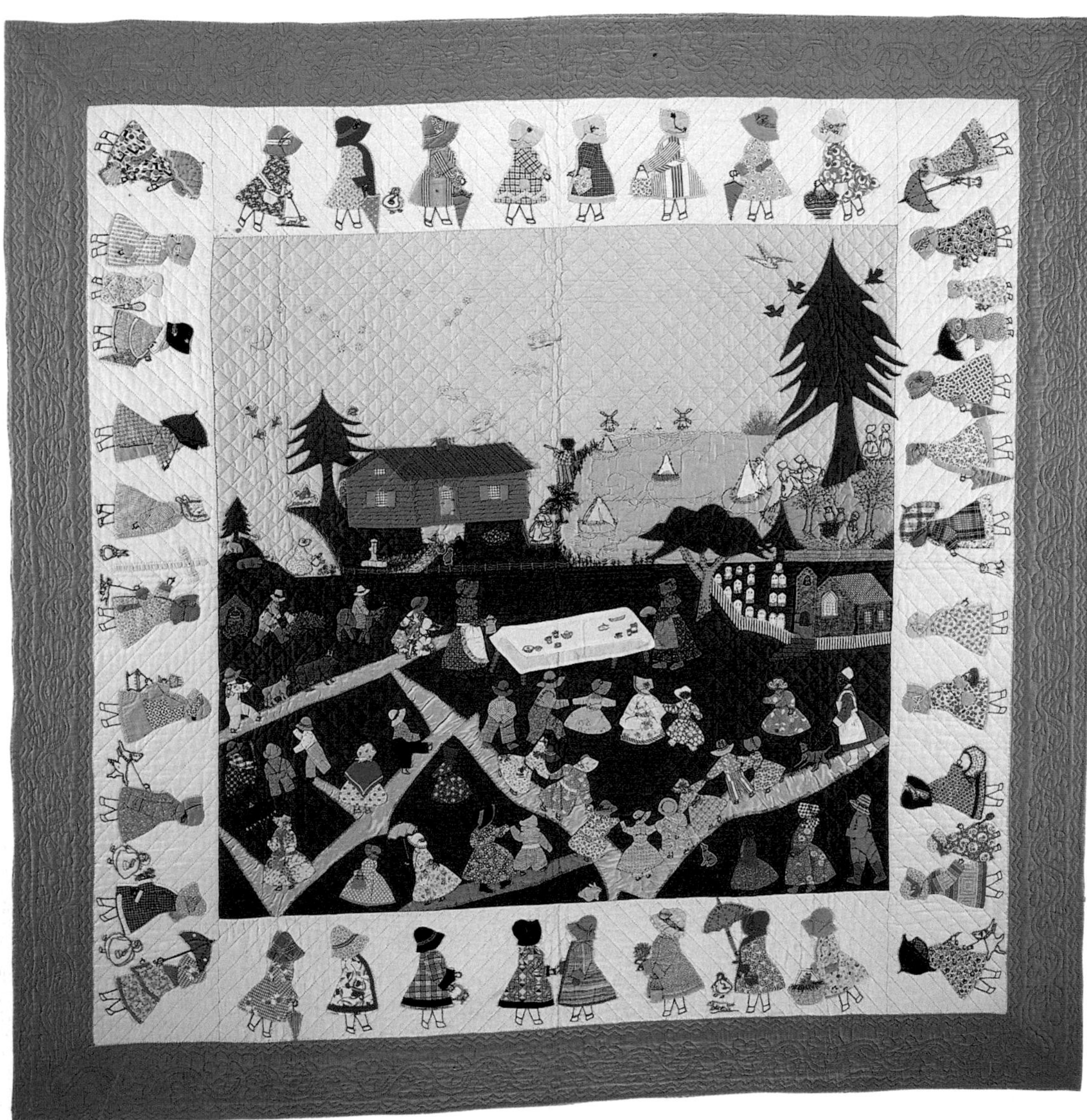

◀ **SUNDAY SCHOOL PICNIC**

Jennie C. Trein. 1932. Nazareth, Pennsylvania. Cottons; hand appliquéd and quilted. 84 x 83 in. Collection of Shelly Zegart.

Jennie Trein made her first quilt at age ten and was still quilting at eighty-five. She made more than 100 quilts and 300 rugs, played the piano, sang in her church choir for over sixty years, and took up the cornet at age forty-four. Mrs. Trein's highly personal *Sunday School Picnic* was "made and design[ed] for [her]self." In 1964 she wrote, "I can truly say. . . the Picnic Quilt is the only one in the whole wide world and therefore very special...find my mother to your right, bringing a loaf of homemade bread, which was her speciality. She is dressed exactly as I used to see her since my childhood . . . see her high button shoes. . . .To the lower right corner see our next door neighbors who never walked to church side by side, but like the geese going to water."

the soft backing and warm filling of the quilt that covered us in the dark, as well as the decorative top that was revealed in the light of day. The decorative lines of innumerable tiny, intricate quilt stitches that bind the pieces of the top together and unify all three layers of the quilt may also be felt as well as seen, their patterns traced in the dark by fingers which might discover hidden hearts, flowers, vines, and other patterns. This tactile element brings quilts even closer to us, both literally and figuratively. They can both contain and conjure the most powerful and basic human meanings simply by their physical presence. No other type of art enjoys such close and easy access to the essence of our daily lives and to the elemental mysteries of birth, sex, and death which define us and take place in the beds that quilts cover. Quilts can protect us as infants, warm and befriend us as children, clothe us while we make love, comfort us in age and sickness, and shroud us when we die.

Quilts have been made and used by Americans of every walk of life: man and woman, rich and poor, educated and unschooled, New Englander and Southerner, Anglo-American and African-American, Christian and Jew, craftsperson and artist, amateur and professional. Each has brought her or his own personal and community history to quiltmaking, expanding the boundaries and meaning of the art. Quilts embody and symbolize unity, both through the methods of their construction and their long established place in our daily lives. Like their closely stitched layers and pieces, quilts bind and connect disparate and even opposing segments of the American public into a unified whole. The quilting bee is one of our most treasured images of cooperative work and community, a romantic image of early America expounded as early as the middle of the nineteenth century. (In fact the persistent image of the quilting bee is so pleasing, powerful, and compelling to our collective national psyche that it has distorted historical truth by suggesting that most quilts were actually made at bees.) Quilts bring people together, figuratively and literally. Quilts have always been used to reflect and memorialize friendship and community. Throughout the past two centuries, women have made quilts that serve as memorials of gratitude for service, of shared activities and feelings, and of rites of passage. Church members sometimes put together a quilt to give to a respected departing minister, neighbors stitched quilts to give to friends moving to another part of the country, friends and family members made quilts to give to a young woman as she began her married life. These quilts often carried signatures of the women who made the blocks and sometimes consisted of pictorial or signature blocks with special meanings to both givers and recipient. The AIDS quilt produced in recent years by the NAMES project is the largest and perhaps the most extraordinary example in the long tradition of these cooperative memorial quilts, a massive work of public art made up of thousands of pieces of private sorrow and memory to promote awareness and understanding of a shared national tragedy.

AMERICAN HERITAGE FLEA MARKET ▶

Terrie Hancock Mangat. 1985. Cincinnati, Ohio. Cottons, cotton blends, silk, acrylic paint, color photocopying; hand appliquéd, hand and machine pieced with hand embroidery and beadwork; embellished with various ornaments, hand quilted by Sue Rule, Carlisle, Kentucky. 84 1/2 x 70 in. Collection of John Walsh III.

This colorful art quilt depicts a flea market entrepreneur holding a tacky Statue of Liberty and presiding over a wild smorgasbord of other Americana, including a table draped with the Stars and Stripes, a Coca-Cola sign, an Uncle Sam mechanical bank, a baseball, an old telephone, a Peace button, a Mickey Mouse clock, a Popeye doll, kitschy salt and pepper shakers, and much, much more. Aunt Jemima and sterotyped Japanese and Native American dolls represent the melting pot, and a picture of the King himself—Elvis Aaron Presley—completes the scene.

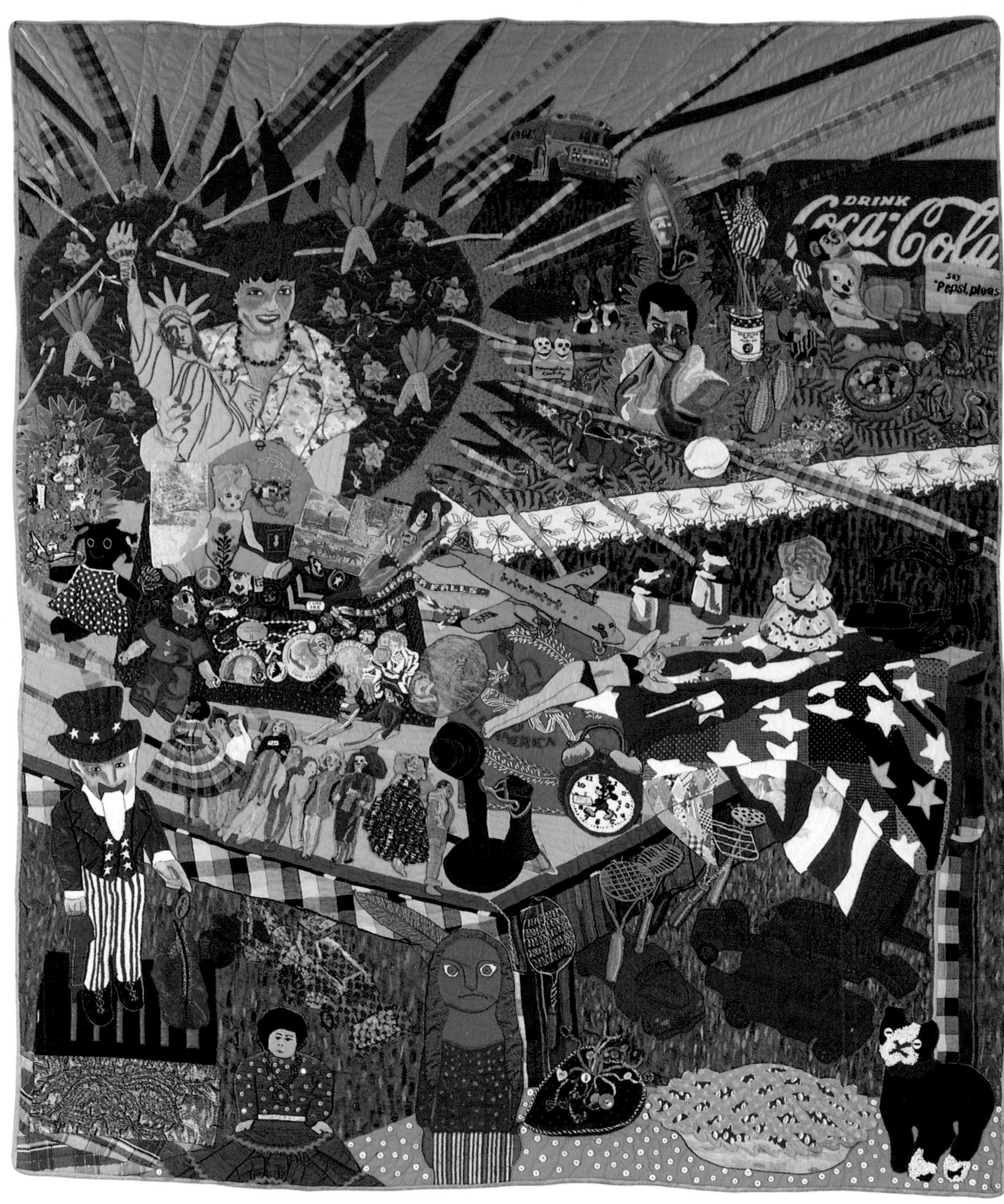

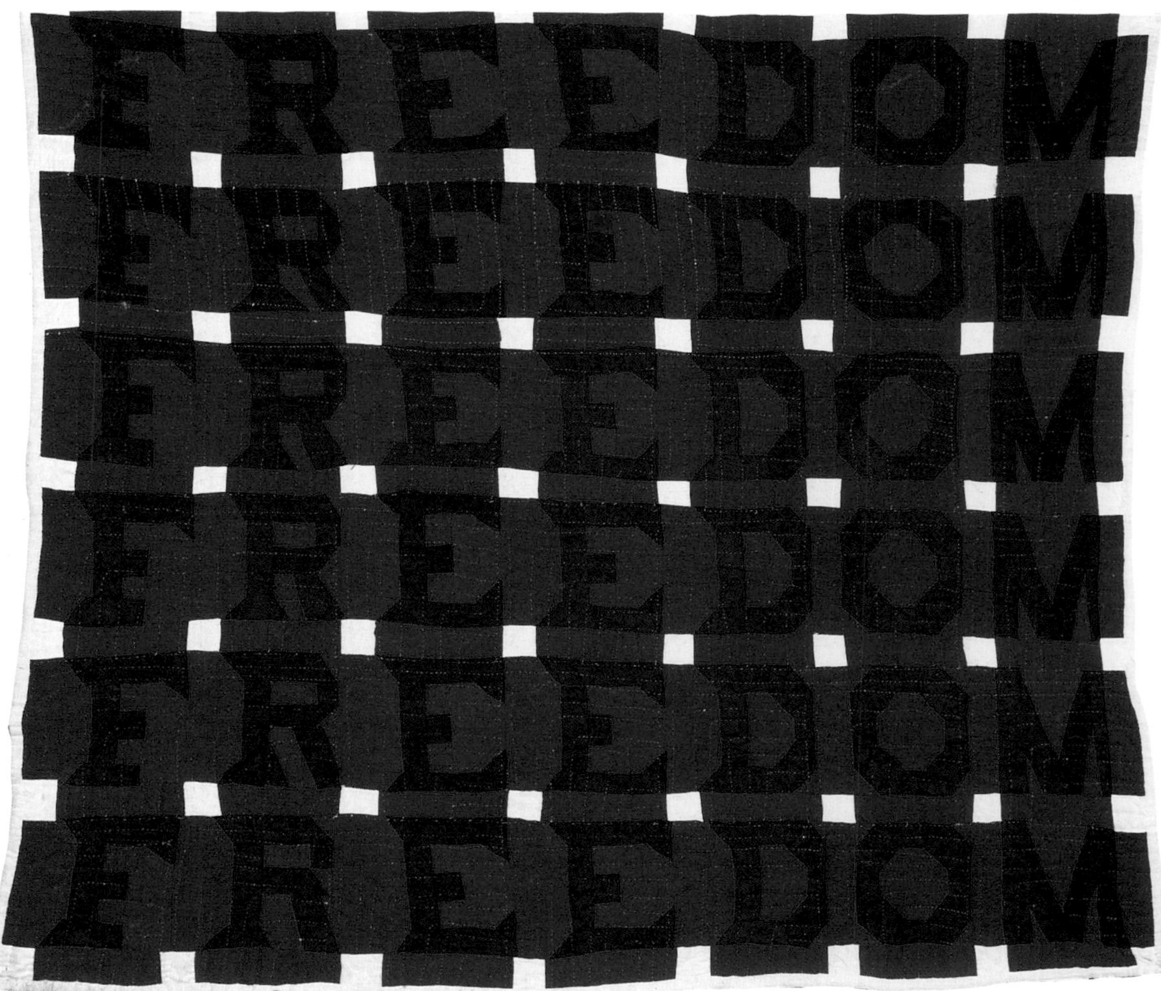

Freedom Quilt ▸

Jessie Telfair. 1980. Parrot, Georgia. Cotton and synthetic fabrics; hand pieced, appliquéd, and quilted. 73 x 85 in. Collection of Shelly Zegart.

Jessie Telfair was fired from her job of twelve years because she voted in a general election in the mid-1970s. Her patriotically colored *Freedom Quilt* is at once a celebration of her sudden independence and a statement of personal and political indignation.

Women have passed the art of quiltmaking from generation to generation. Before the invention of the sewing machine, hand sewing was an essential skill required of every girl. Women were expected to be able to attend to all the needs of the household: to make dresses and shirts, mend torn or worn clothing, darn socks, fashion curtains, and fabricate bedcovers. Mothers taught daughters how to sew and, when they had become proficient enough, how to design and fashion quilts. Nineteenth-century women freely shared patterns and techniques with each other. They could also follow patterns for quilts published in popular ladies magazines such as *Godey's Lady's Book*. Quilt contests became a regular feature of many church and county fairs and offered further opportunities for sharing and learning, challenging quilters to new heights of creativity. During the Depression years, mail-order quilt kits advertised in women's magazines allowed quilters to copy favorite patterns designed by master craftspeople.

In today's information age, student quilters can choose from a vast array of learning opportunities and teaching materials. They can join a local quilt guild, which often pools talent to help less advanced quilters and acts as a support and critique group for its members. They can attend classes with master quilters, buy their videos, watch their TV shows, and read their books. Quilt shows around the country offer a chance to look at others' work, to meet fellow quilters, and to purchase supplies, designs, and teaching methods. Museum and gallery exhibitions explore quilt history or help define the state of the art. Hundreds of how-to books have been published in recent years, on subjects ranging from the most basic techniques to sophisticated color design and fabric choices. And the computer has allowed quilters to further explore the possibilities of geometric construction and to design complex new pieced patterns. Quiltmakers around the world come on-line with each other, networking and sharing their ideas and techniques.

Other traditional handcrafts, such as weaving, blacksmithing, basket making, cabinetmaking, woodcarving, and pottery-making, require far greater technical knowledge and ability than quiltmaking and were therefore often left to trained professional craftspeople within the community. Quiltmaking, however, was never a medium reserved for specialists. It was and is available to everyone, young and old, highly skilled and technically inept alike. A successful quilt does not require particular technical skill; there are many splendid, visually successful quilts of average or even poor workmanship. Craftsmanship then is but one aspect by which a quilt may be judged. The overall impact of a quilt top often obscures or even overwhelms the clumsiness of its fine details. Art takes precedence over craft.

The quilt top gave American women a blank canvas, an arena for self-expression totally protected within the domestic environment, where they could safely indulge their creative imaginations and dare to attempt conceptual solutions to artistic problems not even dreamed of by painters of the time. Although the sometimes striking resemblance between abstract quilt de-

NEON ON FALLING SNOW ▶

Mimiko Misawa. 1990. Kumamoto Prefecture, Japan. Cottons; hand pieced and quilted with silver thread. 75 x 68 in. Collection of the artist.

This very clever quilt uses printed fabrics set in geometric patterns to brilliant effect. Each of the six large five-patch blocks, which are variants on the old American Double Sawtooth pattern, is a successful little quilt in its own right. By setting the squares off with two strips of black, gray, and white fabric and placing all against a heavily quilted field of blue, the artist has created an overall composition full of shifting, sparkling color and light.

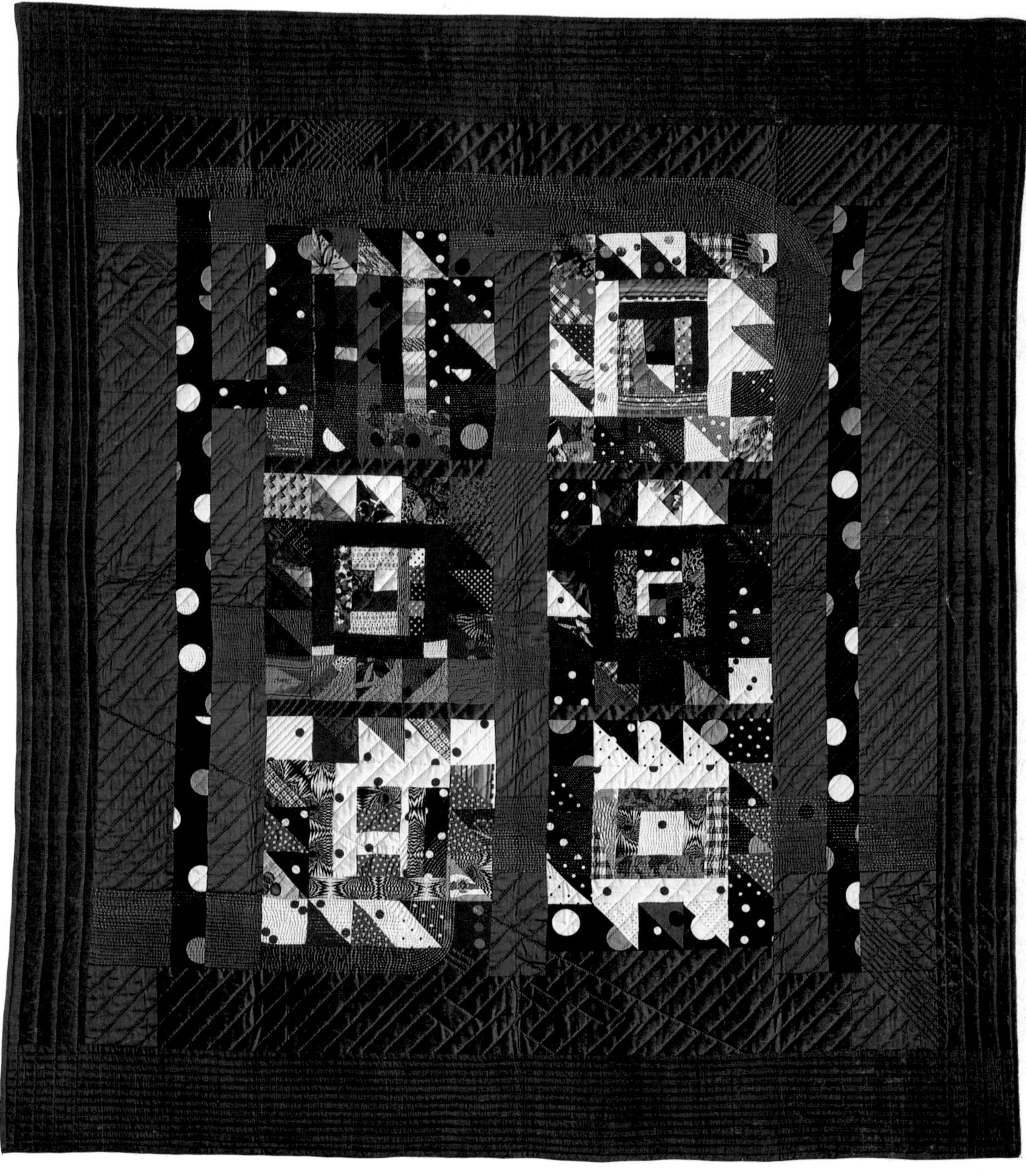

signs and modern art is purely coincidental, the dazzling optical effects sometimes achieved by such graphically compelling pieced patterns as Tumbling Blocks, Rob Peter to Pay Paul, Ocean Waves, or the various Log Cabin variations can still take the most sophisticated viewer completely by surprise. The ultimately restrictive geometry of pieced quilting of course encouraged and even forced some of these experiments. Appliqué quilts, like premodern painting itself, generally demanded a more conventional and conservative approach, representational and pictorial rather than geometric and abstract. Appliqués were usually made "for best," as pieces designed to be decorative and often brought out only for company. They also demanded a finer attention to technique than pieced quilts and sometimes tended toward fussiness at the expense of power of expression. However, because the appliqué method allowed the quiltmaker considerably more design freedom, appliqués are often more personal than pieced quilts, and the most remarkable examples, such as Harriet Powers's *Bible Quilt* or Jonathan Shannon's *Amigos Muertos*, can be packed with the most vibrant and intensely private meaning, or, like the Burdick/Childs family Centennial album quilt or Suzanne Marshall's *Adam and Eve*, shine with charm and wit.

Because they are so familiar to us, quilts, no matter how abstract or personal their design, have none of the intimidating qualities of a painted canvas. Quilts are, we believe, made by everyday people for everyday reasons. The art of the quilt belongs to all of us because it is not generally perceived as something made by artists, by people who are not one of us. Americans have always known quiltmakers, openly embraced their creations, and applauded their achievements. Quiltmakers have always been seen as our peers, not our betters. These biases and attitudes have been a double-edged sword for quilts, until recently keeping them from being taken seriously by historians and scholars and from receiving the recognition they have deserved as artistic works of considerable merit and cultural importance. Today's studio art quilters also struggle against the hoary and homey notion of the quilt as domestic artifact rather than object of art. This struggle is often compounded by prejudices of those who do not recognize quilts as art or women as artists.

Unlike most other American craftspeople such as cabinetmakers, metalsmiths, and weavers, who worked at their craft for economic reasons, very few quiltmakers made quilts specifically for sale. The few who did more often sold patterns and designs than fully worked quilts, thereby offering ideas and aid to less skilled or imaginative quilters. The democratic availability and personal meaning of quiltmaking kept quilts largely out of the marketplace throughout the nineteenth century. It was at once more economical, more meaningful, and more pleasing to fashion one's own. Few nineteenth-century women would consider buying another woman's quilt and fewer still would consider selling something so heavily invested with personal meaning. Because the quiltmaker and user were most often one and the same, or at least related to one another, the outside pressures imposed on the craftsperson by the marketplace and the need for economy in time and materials were not significant driving factors in the fabrication of most quilts. Since she was working for herself, the quiltmaker was largely free to indulge her own taste and inclinations, choose her own designs and cloth, and set her own schedule for completing the work at hand. This remains true today, and many people

▼ Finn

Pauline Burbidge. 1983. Nottingham, England. Cottons; machine pieced and quilted. 95 x 93 in. Collection of Ardis and Robert James.

Like many of Pauline Burbidge's quilts, *Finn* explores a flat, geometric pattern that creates an illusion of depth. To plan the design, the artist cut cardboard models and placed them in front of mirrors. The resulting pattern resembles receding steps.

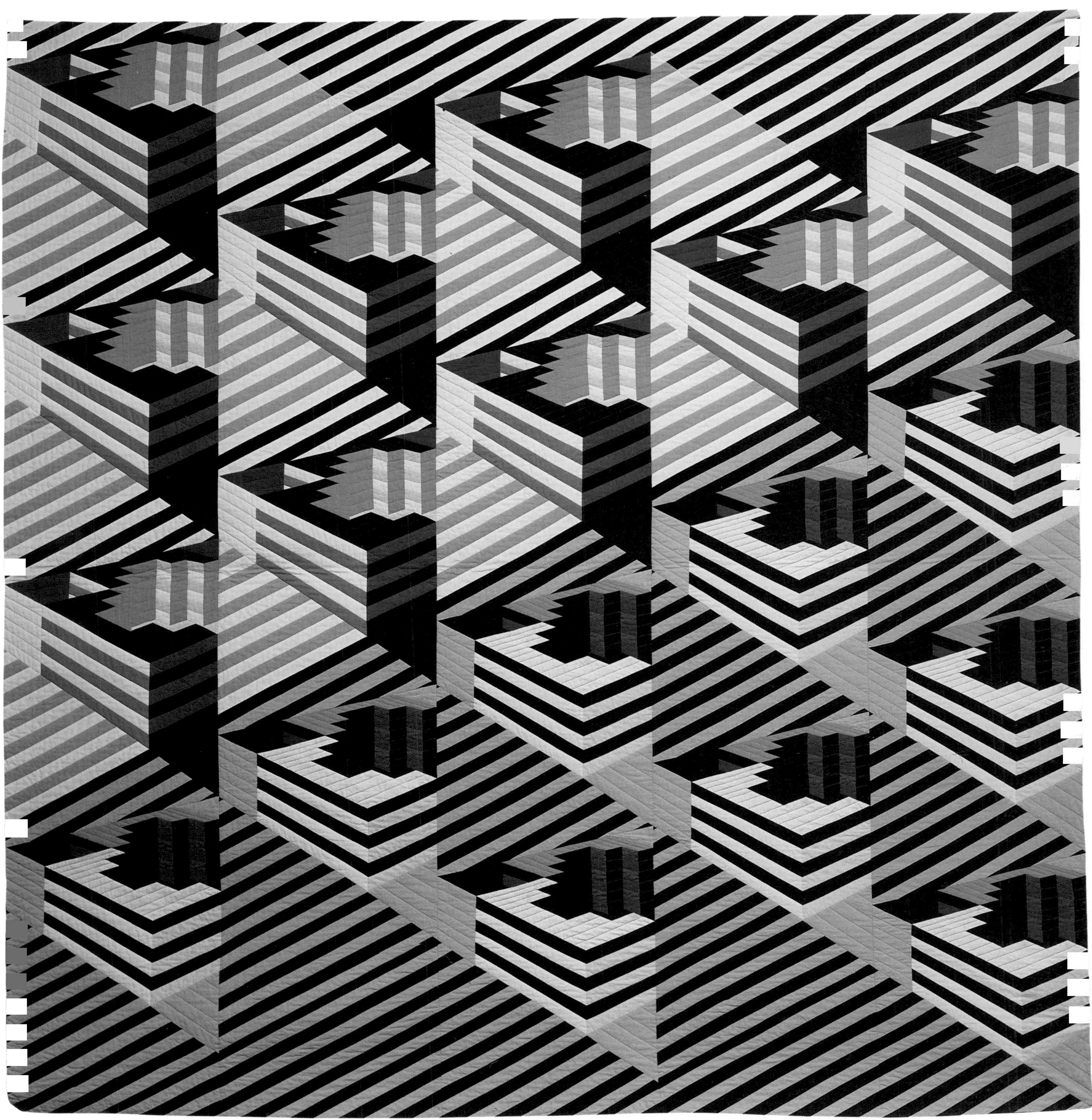

have turned to quiltmaking in the past two decades as a creative outlet, supported by broad public interest and the fact that quiltmaking continues to satisfy an essential domestic need.

In our advanced consumer society, quiltmaking is still by far the most widely practiced of all traditional handcrafts. Necessity is no longer much of a factor; few women need to make quilts because they cannot afford to buy them. Although quilts are now widely available in the marketplace—inexpensive imported Chinese quilts flood department stores and fashion and homewares catalogs, and professional and part-time craftspeople around the world offer their quilts in local craft centers, shows, and sales—millions of people choose to make their own. The democratic impulse has carried quiltmaking around the world: to Hawaii, Japan, Scandinavia, Russia, Australia, New Zealand, and beyond. Wherever the idea of quiltmaking has traveled, it has taken root and flourished, absorbing the enriching mixture of local traditions and taking new shape and energy from the talents and concepts of individual quilters.

This study will attempt to trace the continuum of quilting traditions as they have evolved from the earliest traceable manifestations of the eighteenth century to the present day. In particular it will explore the diverse and ever expanding world of quiltmaking in the mid-1990s, examining the work of living quiltmakers in the United States and around the world. The rich and unique traditions of Amish, African-American, Native American, and Hawaiian quiltmaking is reflected here in both historic and contemporary quilts from each of these important cultural groups. A broad overview of the many specialized facets of today's quilts encompasses new quilts made following traditional patterns as well as those of distinctly modern design. The book includes quilts made by textile artists and quilts made by everyday women for everyday use. A section on quilts in Japan, a country now obsessed with quiltmaking, will show some of the exciting new ways that Japan's ancient textile traditions are being combined with the traditions of the American quilt.

The selection of illustrated quilts is by necessity personal and somewhat arbitrary; there are enough extraordinary quiltmakers at work today to fill a volume like this one several times over without significant diminution in quality or variety. Quiltmaking has grown tremendously in the past twenty-five years, encompassing a vast array of traditional approaches as well as a host of new techniques, fabric choices, and design alternatives. Rarely in history has so much creative energy been concentrated within a single medium; rarely have so many different craftspeople approached a single set of artistic goalposts from so many diverging, although not necessarily mutually exclusive, points of view. Many of the women (and men) currently making quilts choose to work within traditional formats, finding new ways to express themselves within the time-tested parameters of the pieced and appliqué quilt. Others, many of them trained studio artists drawn to the special tactile and visual properties of fabric, are purposefully pushing the boundaries of the art, making textile "paintings" and collages that test our notions of what a quilt is and what it should and can mean. All derive their inspiration from a common source and a shared tradition; each has something important to add to the ever broadening historical panorama of quiltmaking.

The history of the quilt began beyond America's shores and will surely now develop beyond them as well. As quiltmaking has spread from America around the world, it has also traveled back to this country. Its creative origins are reinterpreted and reinvigorated by their reflection in the traditions and ideas of other cultures. The quilt seems capable of infinite change and variety, equally able to decorate and warm a bed or hang on an office or gallery wall, to carry a variety of meanings to people of widely differing cultures and classes and to unite them all in the common understanding and appreciation of a shared medium. Quiltmaking is the art of democracy, a simple, powerful, and empowering idea that has spread across the world at the grassroots level, passing in the folk tradition from one person to the next, changing slightly with each movement, taking a new but somehow familiar shape no matter where it travels and who it touches. The idea and practice of quiltmaking now echo around the world. Everyone who is touched by quiltmaking becomes a part of it, adding to its rich and broad meanings, sharing in its comforting and healing traditions. We all have become part of the great democratic community of the quilt. It continues to grow and cover us all.

Central Square in a Diamond ▶

Kristin Miller. c. 1850. Ontario, Canada. Hand-pieced wool. 77 x 60 in. National Museums of Canada, Canadian Museum of Civilization, Ottawa, Ontario.

This rough but powerful gem was made from handspun and handwoven wool, probably shorn from sheep raised by the quiltmaker. By the time the quilt was made, its central medallion style and careful border-by-border method of assembly were considered hopelessly old-fashioned. Nevertheless, the quilt has an honesty and integrity that complement its simple and direct aesthetic perfectly.

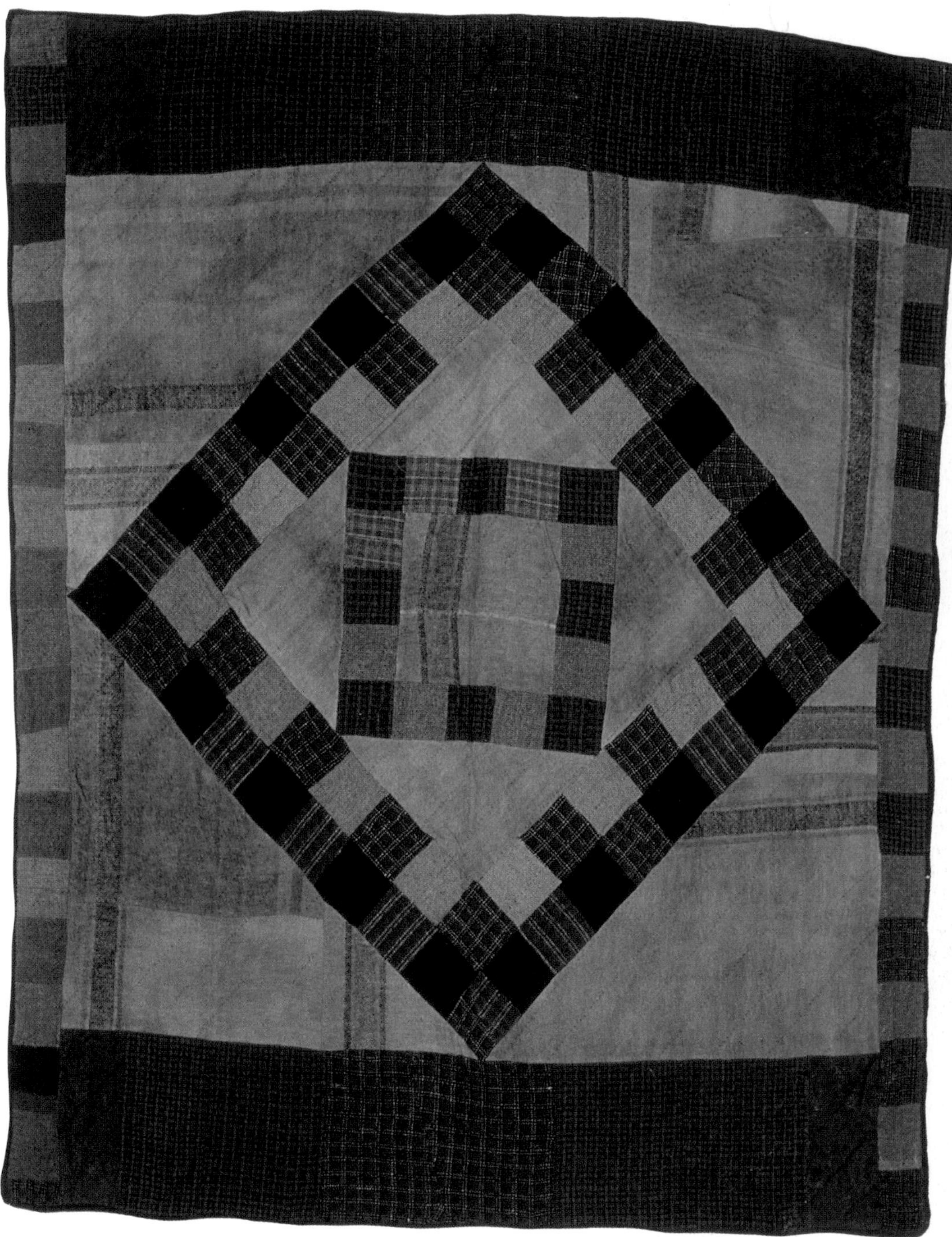

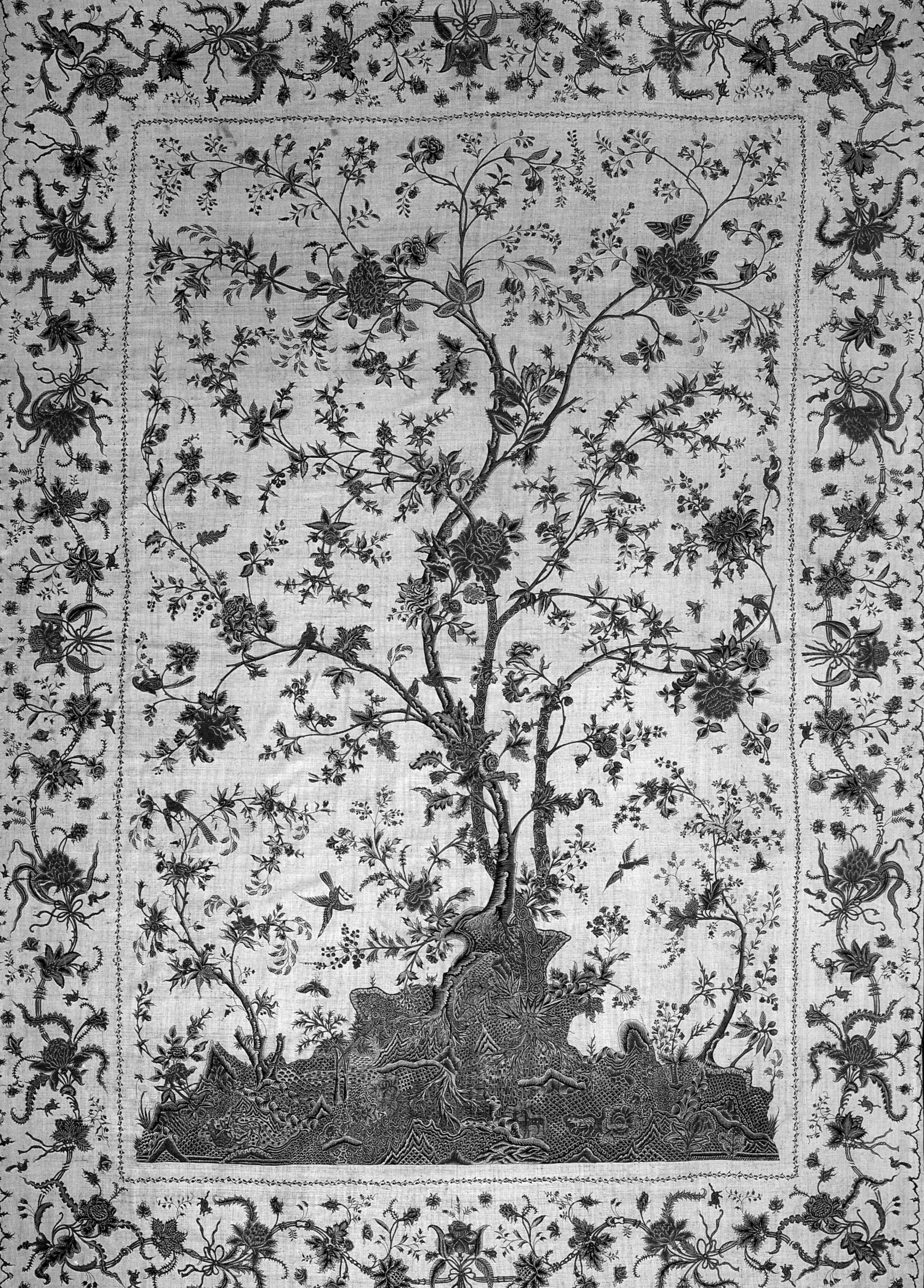

The Evolution of the American Quilt

Establishing the Tradition (1760–1860)

The concept of quilting or sewing an insulating layer of cloth or fiber between two layers of cloth is an ancient one. Textile workers of many different cultures in many lands have recognized the advantages of sewing cloth in layers. First, the layers of cloth reinforce each other's strength, producing a textile that is much more durable than a single layer. Second, an insulating layer sewn between two pieces of cloth can provide warmth and, if thick and tight enough, can also provide protection against piercing objects, both natural and manmade. Third, a layered textile is much easier to patch than a single layer of cloth and is also somewhat less susceptible to tearing.

Quilting was most often used in clothing in early societies. Evidence of quilted clothing exists in representations of Egyptian monarchs dating three thousand years before the birth of Christ. The concept of quilting may have been brought to Europe by the Crusaders. Tightly quilted clothing, like that worn by the Muslim Saracens who defeated the Christians, was used widely in medieval Europe as part of a soldier's protective armor. Several references to decoratively quilted clothing, which apparently became quite fashionable, can be found in English literature of the seventeenth and early eighteenth centuries. Quilted drapes and bed hangings were also used in Europe during this period.

The bed quilt as we know it today seems to have had its real beginnings in Europe in the mid-1700s, since very few quilts survive that can be dated with any degree of confidence to this period. The quilt began to gain favor during the last decades of the eighteenth century: a number

◂ **Palampore**

Artist unknown. c. 1760. India. Cotton; painted and dyed. 124 x 84 in. Private collection.

Made for export to the American or European market, this Indian palampore epitomizes the unparalleled sophistication of that country's cottons at mid-century. The unquilted palampore features the Tree of Life motif, with graceful, flowering branches and numerous birds perched on the limbs. A variety of animals play on the rocky mound, out if which two smaller trees grow. A border of meandering floral vines is decorated with bouquets of flowers tied with bows.

of extant textiles that we would readily identify today as quilts were made between 1770 and 1800 in Holland and Great Britain. Immigrants carried the concept across the Atlantic, executing similar-looking textiles in America at about the same time.

Quilts were not common until the middle decades of the nineteenth century. By that time a wide variety of commercial fabrics were available to many women, a fact which dispels the romantic myth of the early quilt being painstakingly pieced together out of common rag-bag scraps. Also contrary to popular belief, most surviving early quilts were made in upper-class rather than poor households and were created more for show than for warmth. The earliest patchwork quilts of the late 1700s did employ scraps, but again, they were crafted in the homes of the upper class and the scraps were pieces of chintz left over from making high-style dresses and other fancy clothing. In addition, many of these early quilts were thinly lined or left unlined to show off their fine quilt stitching. Quiltmaking is not then a humble craft that was born of necessity and flowered artistically as it grew, but appears rather to have been an art from the beginning, born of women's desires to be creative and expressive and to fashion objects of beauty. Patchwork quilts made of more common rag-bag scraps were certainly made by poor women in later years, but quilting's origins do not appear to stem from simple, make-do roots.

Quilts are dual purpose bedcovers, made to cover and provide warmth to the sleeper and to decorate the bed when not in use. They are usually made of three layers: a backing, which is typically made of a single piece of plain fabric; a top, which because of its visibility is usually decorated in some fashion; and a middle layer of insulating material, typically cotton or wool fiber. The layers of the quilt are joined together with thread, which also serves to hold the insulation in place and can be employed as a decorative element of the quilt top as well.

Quilts can be broken into three broad categories based on the makeup of the top: whole cloth, appliqué, and pieced. Whole cloth quilts, which are the earliest form, employ a single piece of plain or printed fabric as the top, although occasionally the top may be constructed of several large joined pieces of the same fabric or even alternating, contrasting strips. In appliqué quilts, a plain top is usually decorated by sewing small pieces of cut cloth onto a single piece of fabric. In pieced quilts, the top layer is made from many small pieces of fabric, which are usually cut into uniform shapes and then assembled in geometric patterns and sewn together to form a whole.

Among the earliest quilts on both sides of the Atlantic were whole cloth palampores, made from large single pieces of Indian cotton and chintz. These choice fabrics were imported by the Dutch and English East India companies, both founded around 1600. Europeans had long coveted and imported Indian textiles, which were among the finest, most exotic and sophisticated of their time. Palampores (the name comes from a Hindu word for bedcover) were hand painted and resist dyed to produce a stunning array of color and design. Their beautiful floral designs were very popular among those who could afford them. Upper-class English and

Dutch women bought palampores already quilted in India, but these ladies also made quilts from the decorative pieces of cloth themselves. A large branching Tree of Life surrounded by a broad floral border was the most common design choice because it gave a central focus to the quilt. The cloth was quilted all over, usually in a geometric pattern of chevrons or squares that added texture to the top but did not compete visually with the large, colorful, strikingly beautiful designs of the textile.

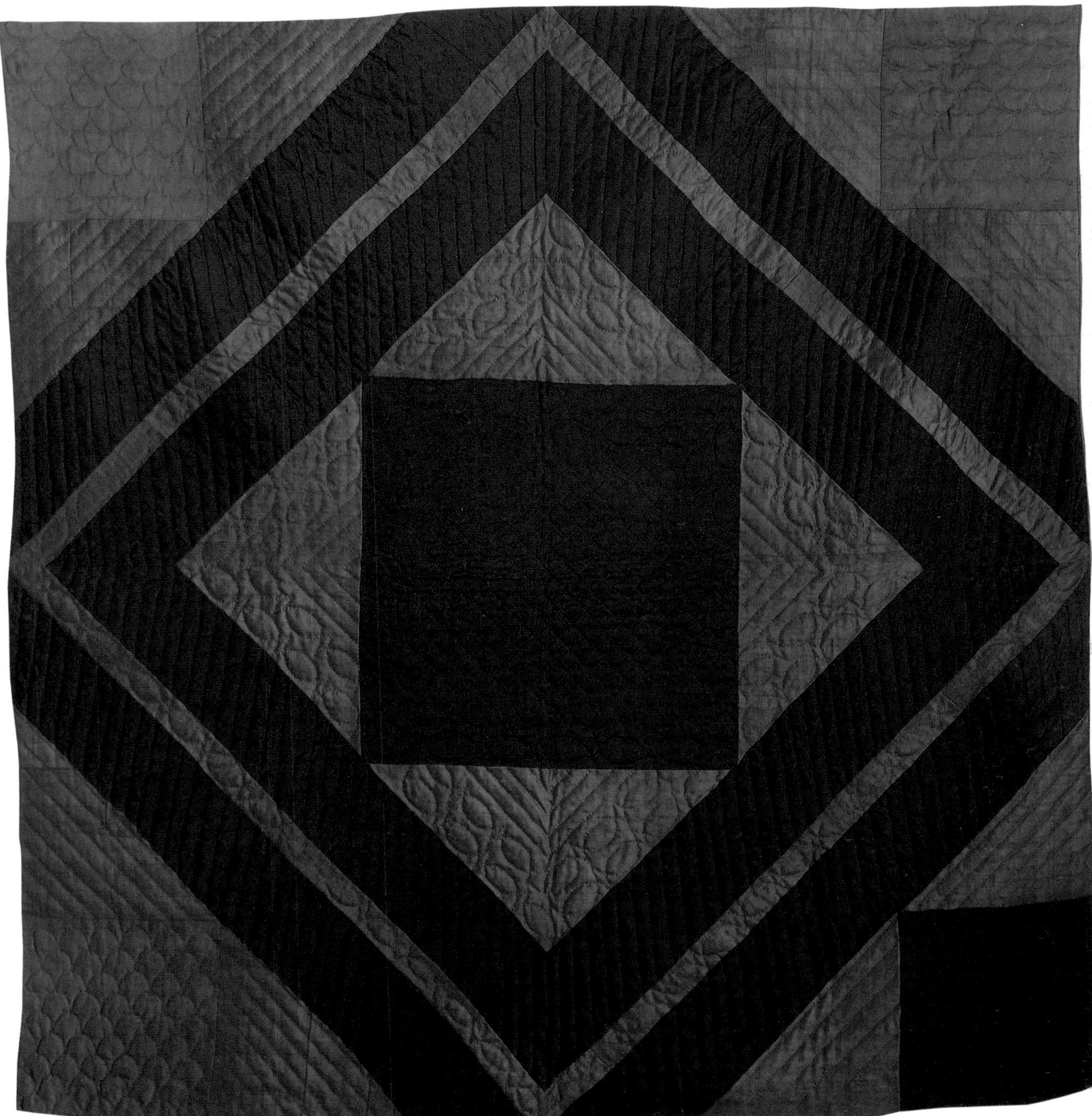

▲ **Center Square-in-Diamond**

Artist unknown. c. 1820–1840. New York State. Glazed and worsted wools; hand pieced and quilted. 78 x 76 in. Collection of Ardis and Robert James.

The dark brown central square of this unusual quilt is contained within two diamonds of the same fabric. A third, raspberry-colored diamond is formed around the square and a fourth diamond is defined between the two brown borders. The outer diamond's dimensions are greater than those of the quilt top and the incomplete corners that result give the quilt an explosive, outward energy which is further emphasized by the single dark brown corner square. Elaborate diamond, chain, leaf, and shell quilting covers the entire top.

◄ **Whole Cloth Calimanco**

Artist unknown. c. 1780–1800. Possibly New York State. Glazed wool; hand quilted. The Metropolitan Museum of Art, Rogers Fund, 1958.

Calimanco was a commercially manufactured glazed wool fabric popular for clothing and quilts in both England and America from the mid-1700s through the first decades of the nineteenth century. Most calimanco quilts, like this one, were made of solid-colored whole cloth and elaborately decorated with quilted designs. The embroidered initials *L M & W D* that are inscribed here under the central medallion are probably those of the quilt's owners.

Solid-colored whole cloth quilts, usually made from wool, were the most common quilt form in both Britain and America from the 1770s to the 1820s. Wool was, of course, abundant in both countries, and its well-known insulating qualities made it a natural choice for fabricating bedcovers. The top layer of wool fabric was typically dyed a deep, rich color, most often dark blue, rusty orange-brown, or red, and was glazed in a commercial pressing and heating process to give it an overall sheen that shimmered and glinted in the low light of the bedchamber, reflecting the soft glow of the room's candles. Intricate decorative quilt stitching of vines, shells, and other motifs covered the top of the quilt and held the insulating layer in place between the top and the backing. The tight stitching pinched the fibers of the filling layer to produce raised, three-dimensional textures that were often striking when set against the plain background of the cloth. Stitching was done using thread of the same color as the top, which also enhanced the effect of the quilted designs.

Whole cloth quilts were usually backed with rough, homemade wool and filled with carded wool fiber. During the late 1700s and early 1800s, American quilters imported calimanco, a fancy glazed English wool, to use for their tops, as well as some completed quilts made by professional English needleworkers. The whole cloth quilt remained popular in Great Britain long after it had fallen out of fashion in the United States. Quilters in Northumbria and Wales in particular kept the tradition of highly decorated whole cloth quilts alive throughout the nineteenth and early twentieth centuries, although only a few are being made today.

The elegant white-on-white quilt, another form of whole cloth quilt, was very popular in the early decades of the nineteenth century. Many were apparently made by professional seamstresses as part of a bride's dowry. These quilts, backed with linen and topped with pure white cotton usually seamed from several closely matched pieces, were sometimes lined with a very thin layer of finely combed wool or cotton; more often they were left unlined. The layers were joined and decorated with elaborate needlework designs using a variety of advanced needlework techniques. In addition to the customary floral motifs of wandering vines, leaves, flowers, fruits, and trees, some white-on-white quilts exhibit figural designs, including ships, animals, and people. White-on-whites were extremely labor intensive, prized for the quality of craftsmanship required in their making. Trapunto, or stuffed work, was one of the most time-consuming decorative techniques employed on these extraordinary textiles. After completing the needlework, the quilter used a bodkin to pull the coarser threads of the backing just far enough apart to push small pieces of filling through the fabric, thereby raising the quilted patterns. The best needleworkers demanded that the top and the backing be virtually indistinguishable and that the average eye be unable to see where the backing had been separated.

Trapunto Whole Cloth Crib Quilt ▸

Artist unknown. c. 1835. Possibly Colebrook, Connecticut. Cotton; hand quilted. 58 x 45 1/2 in. Henry Ford Museum and Greenfield Village, Dearborn, Michigan.

This masterpiece of decorative quilting was probably made as a christening gift. The entire top is covered with a variety of extremely fine quilted designs worked at eighteen to twenty stitches per inch. The diamond-shaped center medallion contains a basket or urn full of flowers and is surrounded by a series of borders decorated with quilted lines, diamonds, stars, and floral motifs. The outer edge is finished with macrame and bell tassels.

The most prevalent format for both pieced and appliqué quilts in the late eighteenth and early nineteenth centuries was the central medallion, which, as the name implies, was built around a dominant central motif surrounded by decorative borders that served as frames. In the simplest medallion designs, the central medallion was plain or printed cloth, although in most cases a dominant central design, often a star, formed the focal point of the quilt. The central motif could be framed in a circle, square, diamond, or rectangle, but the other borders were typically squares. By changing the size and shape of the center motif, its frame, and the width and number of the framing borders, quiltmakers could arrange dozens of variations on a theme.

Most central medallions were appliqués, "made for best." Using a technique that in the mid-nineteenth century came to be called *broderie perse*, quilters carefully cut intricate floral designs from printed Indian or English chintz and sewed them to the quilt top. *Broderie perse* is French for Persian embroidery, which the floral designs resembled. Many *broderie perse* tops were left unbacked and unquilted to serve as lightweight, decorative summer bedspreads; others were made into warm three-layered quilts and were covered with decorative geometric and floral stitching that complemented the appliquéd designs.

The pieced quilt, long considered the earliest quilt type to evolve, was actually the last to come to prominence. Although a couple of earlier British examples made of silk are known, pieced quilts do not appear in any numbers until the last decades of the eighteenth century. Surviving late eighteenth-century English, Dutch, and American pieced quilts look very much the same; the technique apparently originated in England and traveled from there to Holland and America. All early extant examples are made of cotton and are built of triangular pieces sewn together to form squares.

The increased availability of cotton fabric is directly responsible for the tremendous growth of quiltmaking in nineteenth-century America. Cotton transformed the patchwork quilt from a minor sewing art to the dominant folk art of American women, becoming by far the preferred material in the making of American quilts. No other material lends itself so readily to quiltmaking in ease of manufacture and use, affordability, availability, and variety of color and pattern. Cotton was first brought to America from the West Indies in the 1770s and was thereafter grown extensively in the southern United States. The invention of the cotton gin by Eli Whitney in 1793 revolutionized the processing of cotton by drastically reducing the amount of time needed to remove seeds from the raw material, thus opening up new possibilities for manufacturers of cotton cloth both in America and Great Britain. Before Whitney, one person could laboriously pick the seeds from only one pound of cotton a day; using the gin, that same worker could process five hundred pounds in the same amount of time. The patchwork quilt is a child of the cotton gin and of the Industrial Revolution: the new technology reduced the cost of cotton dramatically and made it widely available to the growing American middle class. Indeed, it can be argued that the quilt as we know it today was born in 1793.

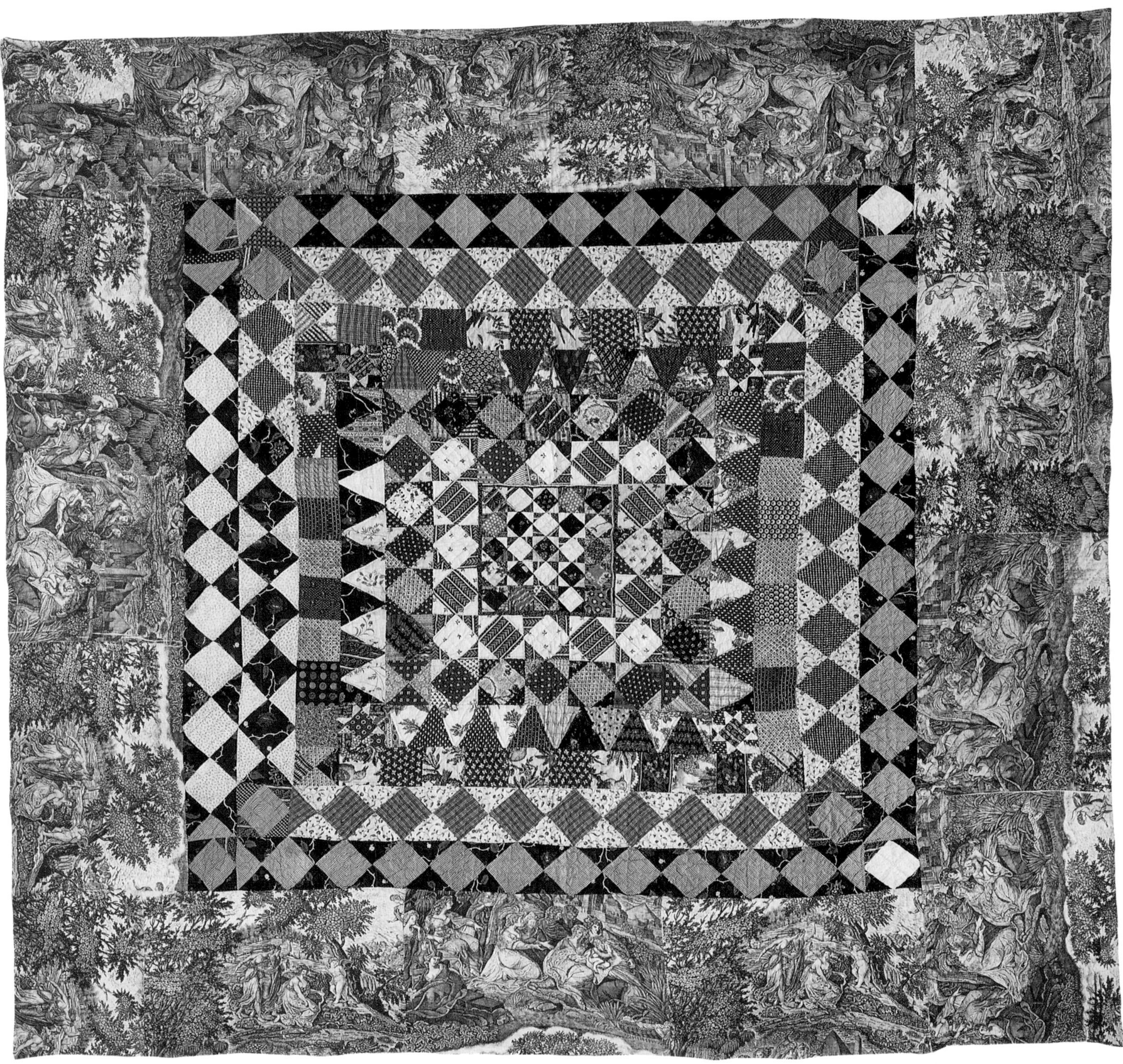

▲ **Central Medallion with Toile Border**

Artist unknown. c. 1780–1810. England. Cottons; hand pieced. 98 x 104 in. Private collection.

This classic central medallion quilt exemplifies the style. It is built entirely from pieced triangles and diamonds, moving border by border from the small central square to the expansive outside edge of printed cotton toile, which would have draped down the sides and over the foot of the bed.

Cotton processing technology grew quickly in response to the enormous amount of resource material made available by Whitney's gin, and by 1825 the industry was fully and firmly established in the United States. Nineteenth-century American women enjoyed an unparalleled variety of choices of dyed and printed cotton fabrics produced by the new mills of the burgeoning industrial giant. Then, as now, the full range of available fabric is reflected in the quilts that were created. Today's quilts represent the virtually unlimited range of materials available to the contemporary quilter, who can choose modern or antique fabric from any country of the world or, if she wishes, dye her own.

The textile industry led the Industrial Revolution in both Britain and the United States. The "Satanic mills" that English poet and prophet William Blake railed against for their literal and figurative exploitation and oppression of the human spirit were textile mills that produced printed cotton fabric, much of it for the American market. Likewise, the gigantic mills of such Merrimack River factory towns as Lowell and Lawrence, Massachusetts, were also textile mills. These mills fueled the New England economy in the early decades of the 1800s and brought thousands of young women into the workforce. Most of these girls were twelve- to eighteen-year-old daughters of farmers, and were recruited from the New England countryside with the promise of steady wages, which they usually laid aside as a dowry against their wedding day. A typical workday for a mill girl was a tedious and sometimes grueling fourteen hours long, starting at the crack of dawn and continuing until long after dark during the winter months. The mills ran every day except Sunday. It seems ironic that the American patchwork quilt, so closely identified with romantic notions of the lost values of early American life, is a product of the same Industrial Revolution that supposedly helped to destroy those values.

Changes in American society also had a profound influence on the development of quilting. The election of Andrew Jackson in 1828, the first common man to lead the new nation, made explicit the meaning of democracy in America. Unlike Washington, Jefferson, Monroe, and the Adamses, Jackson was not an aristocrat, but was, rather, an uneducated and relatively unsophisticated man from an undistinguished and decidedly unprosperous family. Jackson's election made it clear to all that every American could not only aspire to his dreams, but might realize them as well. As Ralph Waldo Emerson, the country's leading man of letters, put it, "Ours is a country of beginnings, of projects, of vast designs and expectations. It has no past. All has an onward and prospective look."

In the years between Jackson's election and the outbreak of the Civil War, a virtually unlimited, if often naive, sense of national pride and personal opportunity led the country to turn from the established models of Europe towards artistic expression that reflected American values and ideals. Some of America's most confident and enduring works of art were created during this period: Emerson's *Nature* (1836) and *The American Scholar* (1837); Nathaniel Hawthorne's *Scarlet Letter* (1850); Herman Melville's *Moby Dick* (1851); Henry David Thoreau's *Walden* (self-published in 1854); Walt Whitman's *Leaves of Grass* (self-published in 1855); John James Audubon's *Birds of America* (self-published between 1827 and 1838) and George Catlin's *Lives of the North American Indians* (1844); George Caleb Bingham's *Fur Traders* and Edward Hicks's *Peaceable Kingdom* (both series painted in the mid-1840s); the vast landscapes of Thomas Cole and the dignified folk portraits of Erastus Salisbury Field and Ammi Phillips. These works, and many more as important, defined something entirely new—what it meant to be American.

In his introduction to *Leaves of Grass*, Walt Whitman summed up what he believed was new about America and Americans. With grace and eloquence he provided a catalog of what made the country and its people different:

> *Here are the roughs and beards and space and ruggedness and nonchalance that the soul loves... it must indeed own the riches of summer and winter, and need never be bankrupt while corn grows from the ground or the orchards drop apples or the bays contain fish... Other states indicate themselves in their deputies... but the genius of the United States is not best or most in its executives or legislatures,... but always most in the common people. Their manners speech dress friendships—the freshness and candor of their physiognomy—the picturesque looseness of their carriage... their deathless attachment to freedom—their aversion to anything indecorous or soft or mean... the fierceness of their aroused resentment—their curiousity and welcome of novelty—their self-esteem and wonderful sympathy—their susceptibility to a slight—the air they have of persons who never knew how it felt to stand in the presence of superiors... their good temper and openheartedness—the terrible significance of their elections—the President's taking off his hat to them not they to him.*

All these attributes and more defined the proud and independent new American spirit and set it apart from that of any previous civilization.

Just as the literary and visual arts shook loose their European models, so quilts became for the first time something distinctly American. The block-style quilt began its rise to dominance, leaving the European influenced center medallion format behind and forging a new and decidedly American method of organizing the quilt top. And the elegant Baltimore style album quilt, which took advantage of that port's access to a vast array of newly imported English cotton fabrics as well as the full panoply of American-made textiles, was the style that brought the art of appliqué to a pinnacle of unparalleled refinement and technical achievement during the 1840s and 1850s.

Block-style quilts can be constructed of either appliquéd or pieced units, or a combination of the two. The popular album quilts of the 1840s and 1850s, which were often made by women belonging to a particular church, fraternal, or social group, are examples of block-style appliqué organization. As in pieced block style, the same appliqué block might be repeated many times to form the top. Unlike the central medallion style, the block pattern top lacks a central focus and instead democratically emphasizes the whole as the sum of its equal parts. Each block carries the same importance—all blocks are created equal—and together they make up a union stronger than any of the individual components.

The block pattern top embodies American aesthetics and democratic inclinations in a variety of ways. As a convenient and economical means of making and organizing the top, it allows the quilter to craft one square at a time rather than having to work on the entire top. The quilt frame required to assemble a central medallion top occupied a good deal of space and had to stay in place for the duration of the quilt's making, whereas with block style a woman could work on the individual blocks in her lap and then assemble them into a top when all were completed. This method of reducing the quilt top to small and manageable units also lends itself to communal quiltmaking, thereby gracing a single quilt with the artistry of several women. Block quilting also

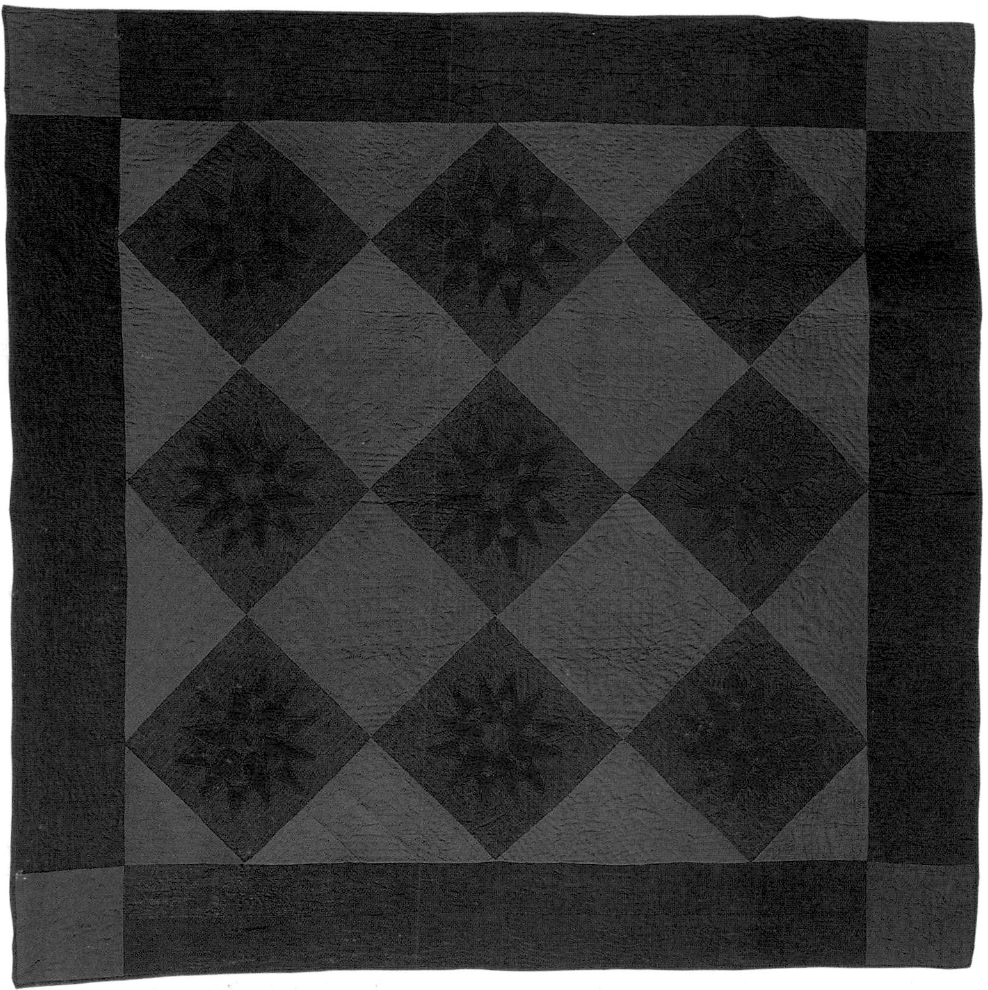

◂ **Snowflake**

Unknown Quaker artist. c. 1850. Lancaster County, Pennsylvania. Wools; hand pieced and appliquéd, with hand quilting. 85 x 85 in. Collection of Ardis and Robert James.

The nine red snowflake blocks are set on point, alternating with plain chestnut brown colored blocks and an inner border of chestnut half and quarter blocks. The wide outermost border of black is cornered with chestnut squares, and the entire top is intricately quilted.

encourages sharing (or copying) of patterns, and quilters were quick to learn from each others' design solutions. Block style is a natural outgrowth of the democratization of quilting in America, as women of all classes became increasingly able to afford commercially manufactured, store-bought cloth, and to spend considerable amounts of time crafting decorative and useful quilts for their families, either on their own or with friends and neighbors.

The patterns developed by nineteenth-century American quilters were much more open than the busy mosaic piecework that remained popular in Britain and Holland. The earliest of the American pattern units were probably simple organizations of squares, such as One-Patch, Four-Patch, and Nine-Patch, or triangles, such as Wild Geese Flying or Birds in the Air. More complex patterns evolved and spread quickly, taking on different names and a host of subtle variations as they passed from region to region and quilter to quilter. New and popular magazines for women such as *Godey's Lady's Book,* which began publication in 1830 as a sort of fluffy, sentimental literary magazine for women, offered printed block patterns and instructions for those interested in quilting. *Godey's* became a particularly important and influential publication for women. Sarah Josepha Hale, *Godey's* editor from 1837 until shortly before her death in 1879, was an early and ardent feminist who proclaimed that the magazine was "expressly designed to mark the progress of female improvement." By 1850 *Godey's* circulation had grown to 150,000. Under Mrs. Hale's direction the monthly magazine brought the latest high-style Continental fashions into homes all over America and became a dream book for American women of all stations. It also carried a column by Mrs. Hale in which she championed a wide array of women's causes and railed against the myriad injustices of America's developing society. Frequent advice about quiltmaking and instructions on particular techniques were an integral part of her chronicle of "female improvement" that reached hundreds of thousands of women.

Nineteenth-century quilters' experiments with the geometric possibilities of block piecing led them to discover patterns that could interlock to form optically deceptive overall designs such as Tumbling Blocks, Rob Peter to Pay Paul, Shoo Fly, and the various Log Cabin formulations. All of these relatively simple patterns rely on the tonalities of color in the choice of textiles for their effectiveness; if fabric colors are well chosen and arranged, visual rhythms larger than a single block emerge and the eye either shifts back and forth from single blocks to larger elements, or simply cannot isolate the building blocks of the quilt.

As a group, Baltimore album quilts are the most technically sophisticated of all American quilt types. Their craftsmanship is unmatched. The quilts coincide with Baltimore's greatest period of prosperity and prominence—from the mid-1840s to the early 1850s—during which it was the leading American seaport, the nation's third largest city, and the center of the burgeoning American textile industry. The popularity of Baltimore album quilts seems to have coincided with the growth of Methodist congregations and Masonic fraternal organizations in the greater Baltimore area; signatures on individual blocks have been traced to Methodist congregations, and many of the quilts include Masonic symbols.

The makers of these quilts, some of whom were apparently professional seamstresses, had total mastery over their chosen media of cloth and thread. The finest Baltimore album quilts exhibit an ability to choose and manipulate fabric that is matched only by the best of today's quilters. Baltimore album quiltmakers took the technique of cutting and assembling appliqués from printed cloth and then applied it to a block-style album quilt format. Quilts of twenty or twenty-five blocks were typical, with each block usually presenting a separate decorative design. Flowers, baskets, wreaths, birds, flags, buildings, and cornucopias were the most common elements of the blocks, although some included human and animal figures. The blocks were usually framed individually with a simple box, and the whole was surrounded by an elaborate border of twining and trailing vines, swags, flowers, leaves or even birds. Several dozen different pieces of fabric might be used in a single block to achieve specific results. The quilts were so technically complex that the contemporary scholar and Baltimore album quiltmaker Elly Sienkiewicz has estimated that a single Baltimore album might have taken a talented professional needleworker a full year or more of forty-hour weeks to complete. Because so many of the quilts exist, it is clear that a large number were made as group efforts, with several talented craftswomen contributing blocks to a project. Block designs were apparently shared and copied as well, and similar or even identical blocks appear in many of the quilts.

Baltimore album quilts fell from favor as quickly as they had risen to prominence as styles changed and the country's economic center shifted from Baltimore to New York City. The genteel, highly skilled, and labor intensive Baltimore album style disappeared amidst the sweeping technological and societal changes of the nineteenth century. America was growing at a staggering pace, expanding its boundaries, absorbing hoardes of new immigrants and cultures, forever changing the way the society was organized, worked, played, and developed. A shattering Civil War lay ahead, as did a revolution in the way goods and services were made and distributed. The quilt would change and develop too, reflecting the great new country's continued efforts to define itself.

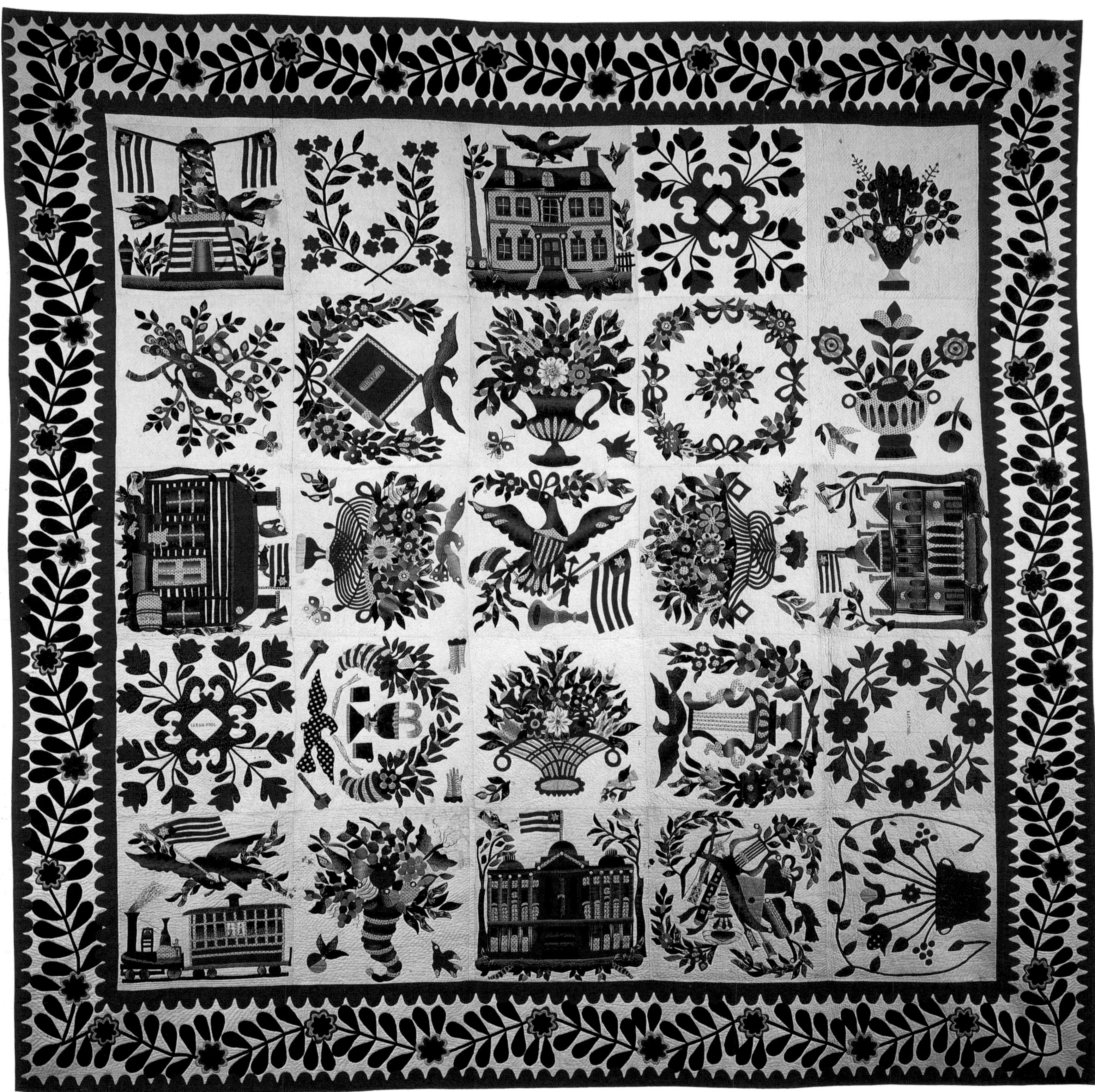

▲ **BALTIMORE ALBUM (DETAIL ►)**

Signed Sarah Pool and Mary J. Pool. c. 1840s. Baltimore, Maryland. Cottons; hand pieced and appliquéd; pen and ink inscriptions. 106 x 107 1/8 in. Private collection.

This quilt is a tour-de-force of high technical accomplishment. Each of the twenty-five blocks, meticulously crafted from many small pieces of plain and printed fabric, presents a different pictorial or floral motif. Among the designs are a log cabin with two beavers on the roof, a locomotive pulling a passenger car, two impressive civic buildings, the Baltimore Monument, several floral wreaths, trophies with musical instruments, and overflowing cornucopias. The blocks are surrounded by a meandering border of vines and flowers and are set between two scalloped red borders.

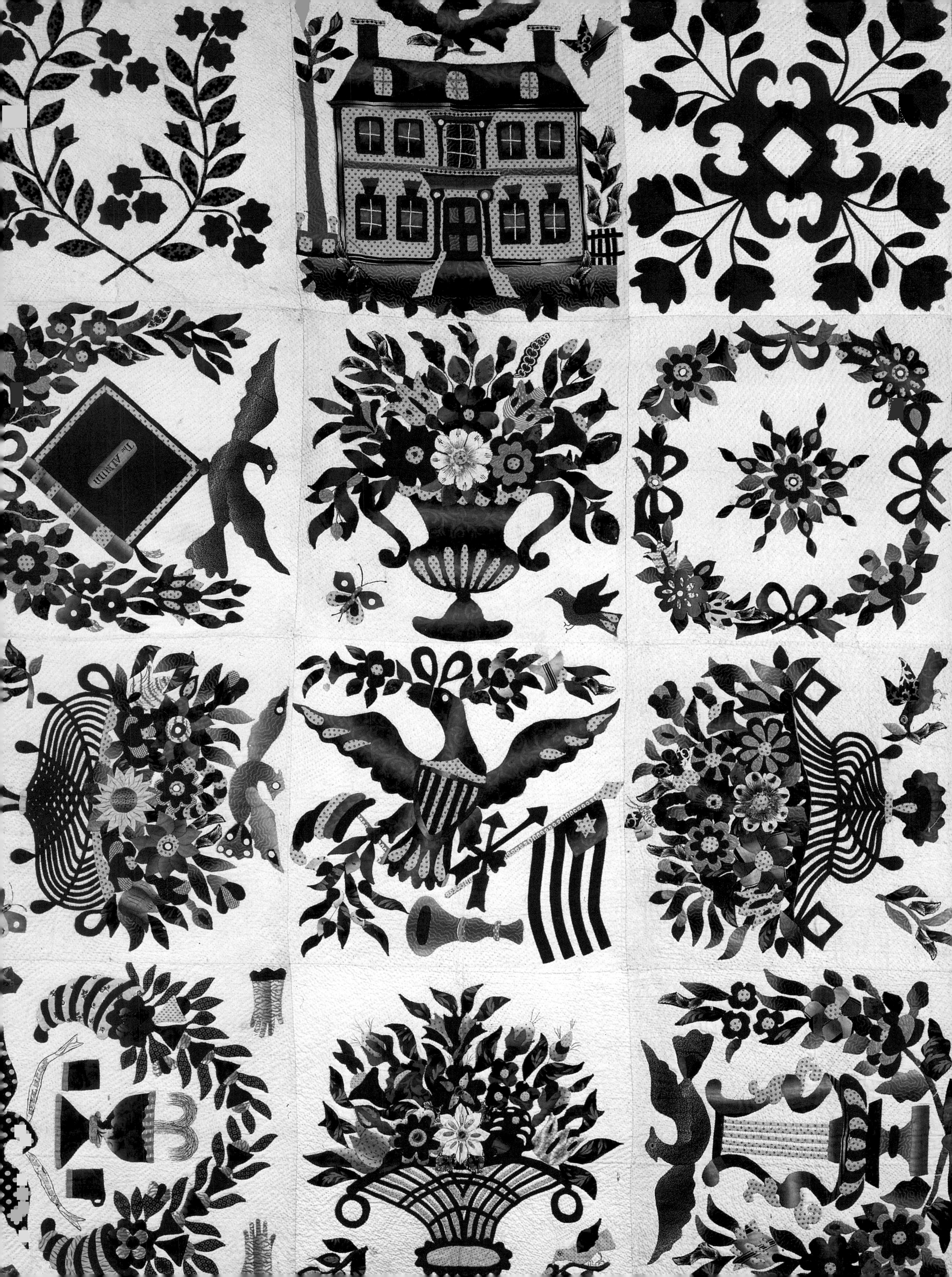
The Album

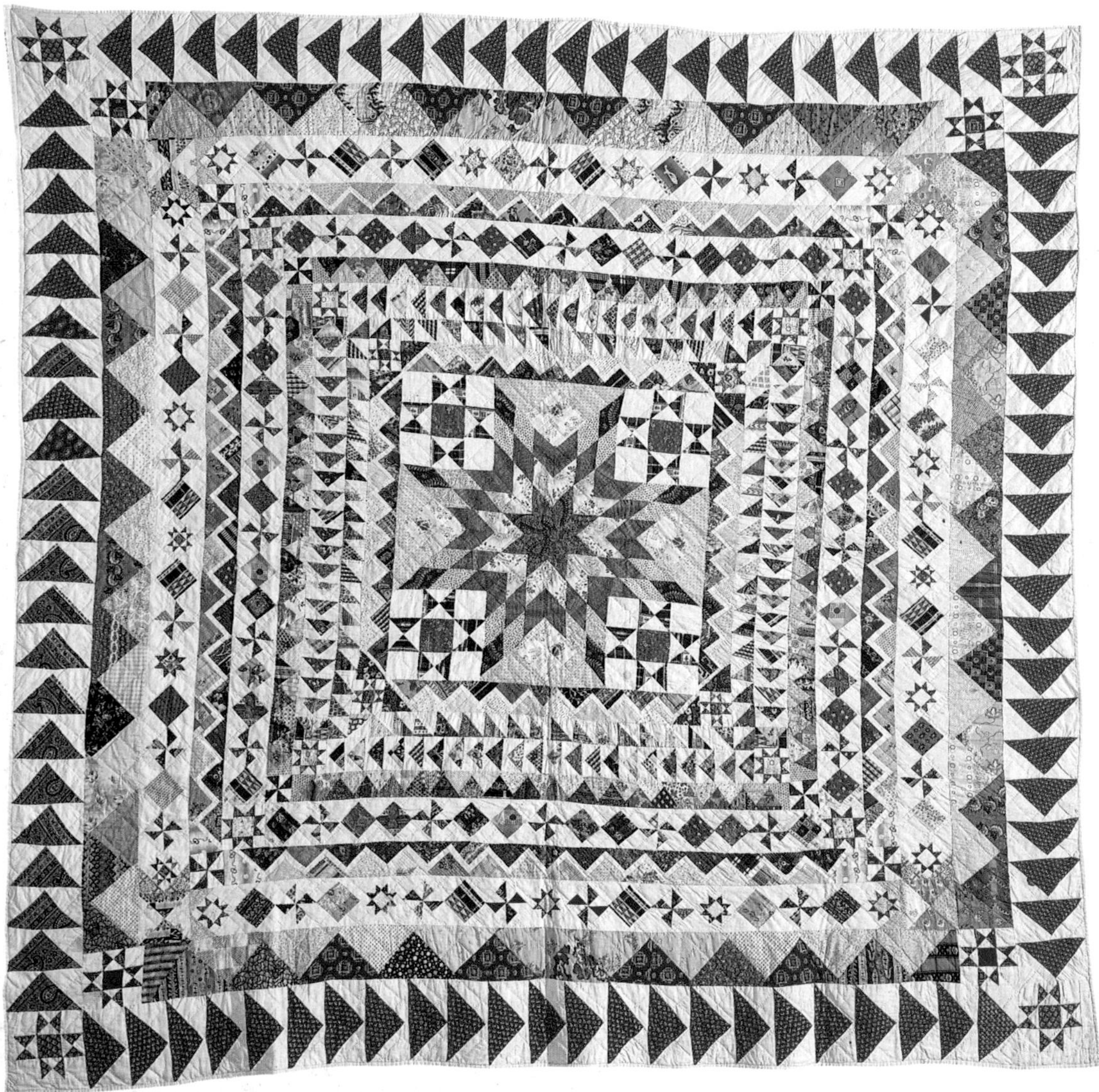

◄ **Medallion Star**

Artist unknown. c. 1830. Eastern United States. Cottons; hand pieced and quilted. 90 x 90 in. The Shelburne Museum, Shelburne, Vermont, gift of John Wilmerding.

In this resourcefully pieced quilt, a large star surrounded by four smaller variable stars forms the central medallion, which is framed by nine borders that increase in width from the center to the edge of the quilt. Moving from the inside out, the border patterns provide an encyclopedia of early pieced designs: zigzag with variable star corner blocks; sawtooth; flying geese; triangles; diamonds and pinwheels with variable star corner blocks; zigzag with pinwheel corner blocks; diamonds, pinwheel, and variable stars with hourglass corner blocks; triangles with variable star corner blocks; and flying geese with variable star corner blocks.

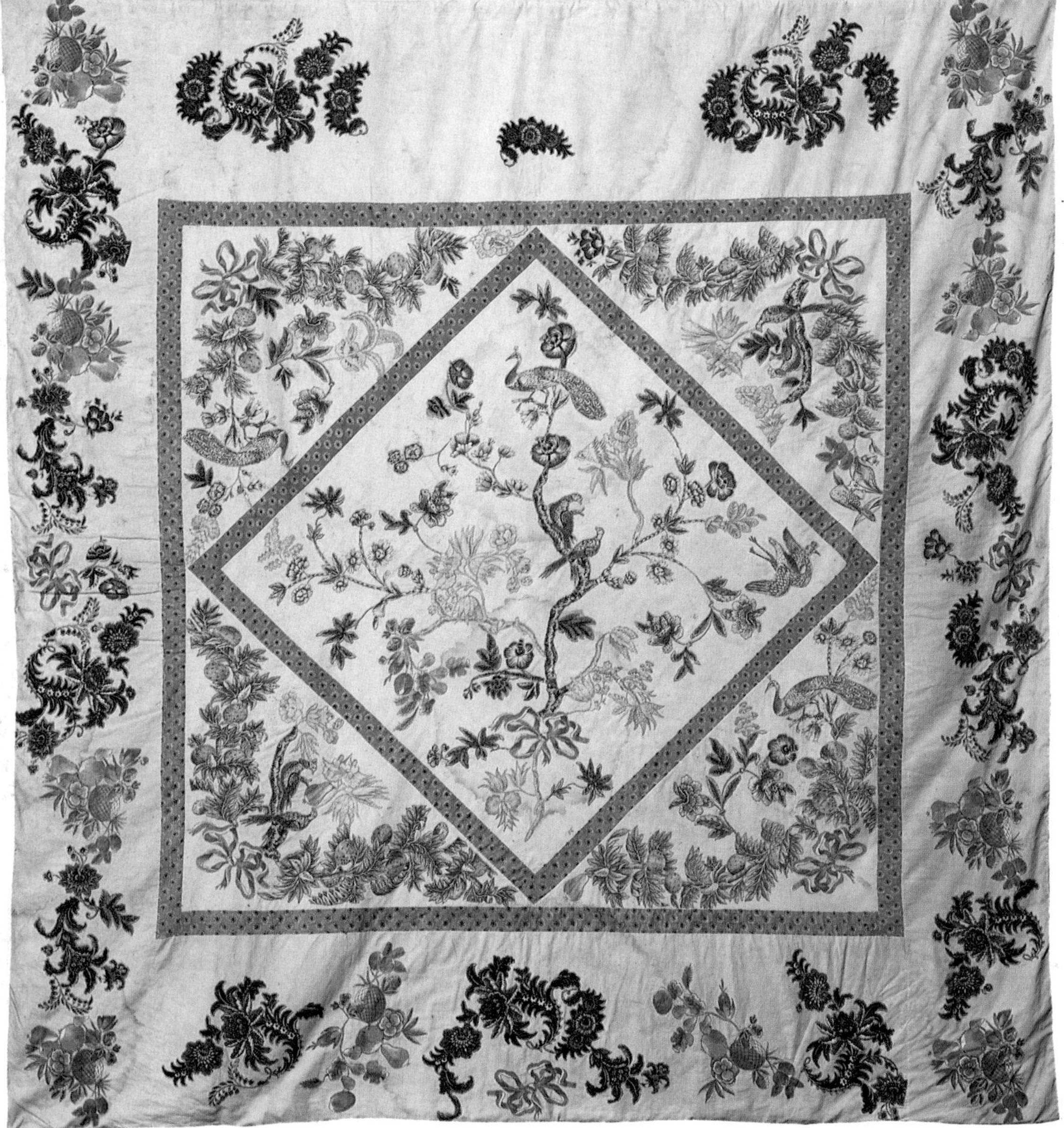

◄ **Tree of Life Coverlet**

Sarah Willis Hayes. c. 1785–1800. Gloucester County, Virginia, and Warren County, North Carolina. Cottons; hand appliquéd. Museum of Early Southern Decorative Arts, Winston-Salem, North Carolina, gift of Mrs. Elmo D. Sparks in memory of Sarah Elizabeth Hartwell.

This decorative summer spread is neither backed nor lined and is unquilted. The floral and Tree of Life appliqués were cut from printed English and French fabrics. According to family history, Mrs. Hayes started the spread while living in Virginia but did not finish it until after her move to North Carolina. The fabrics, which date over a fifteen-year span, lend support to the oral history of the coverlet's staggered composition.

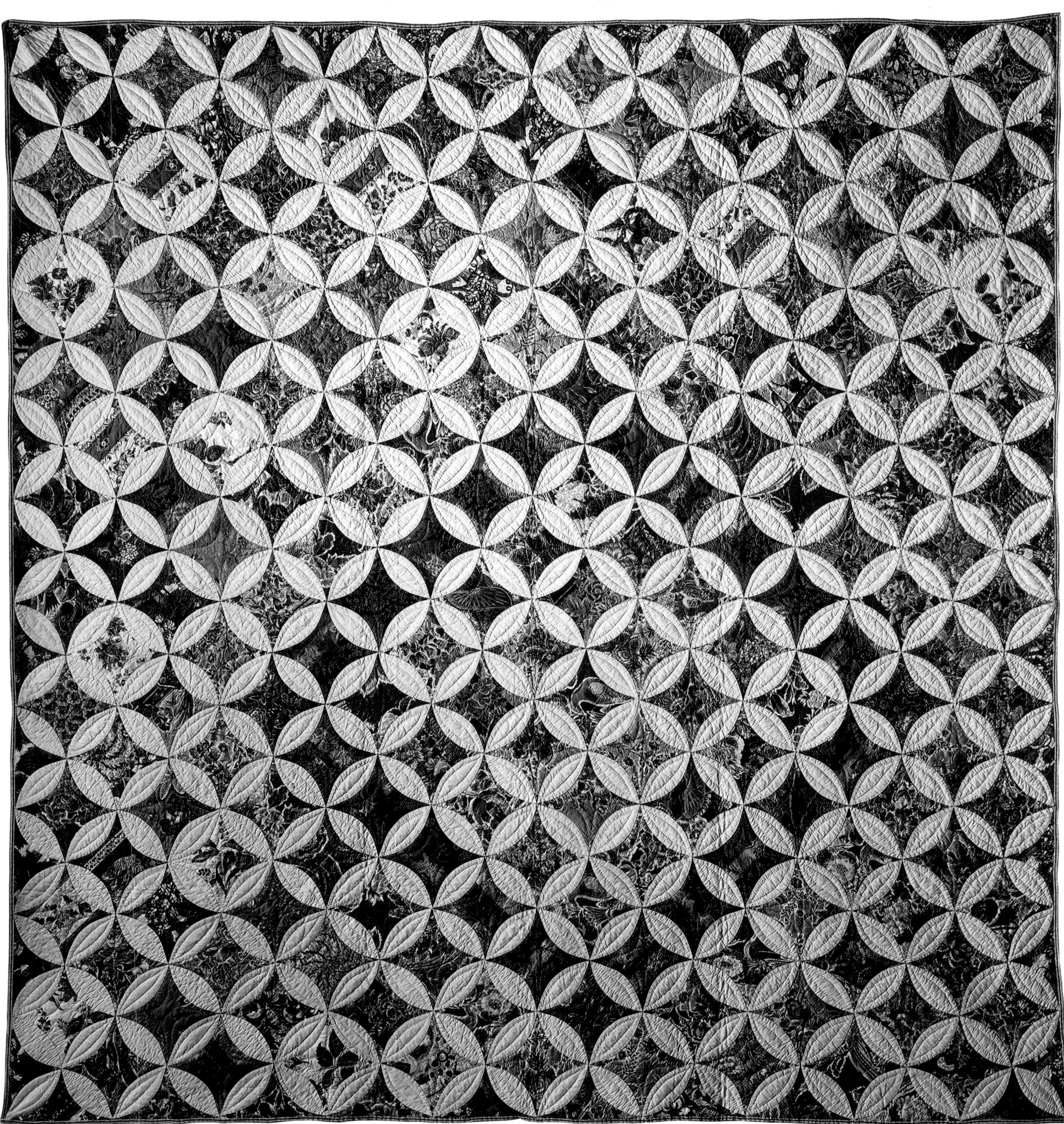

▲ **Reel or Pin Cushion**

Artist unknown. c. 1820–1830. Probably New England. Cottons; hand pieced and quilted. 92 x 90 in. Private collection.

Pieced quilts utilizing curved elements are quite rare, since it requires enormous patience and skill to fit rounded seems together tightly without having them pucker. This deceptively simple design of intersecting circles leads the eye restlessly back and forth between its white four-petaled flowers and the rich array of pin cushion–shaped printed fabrics that they encircle.

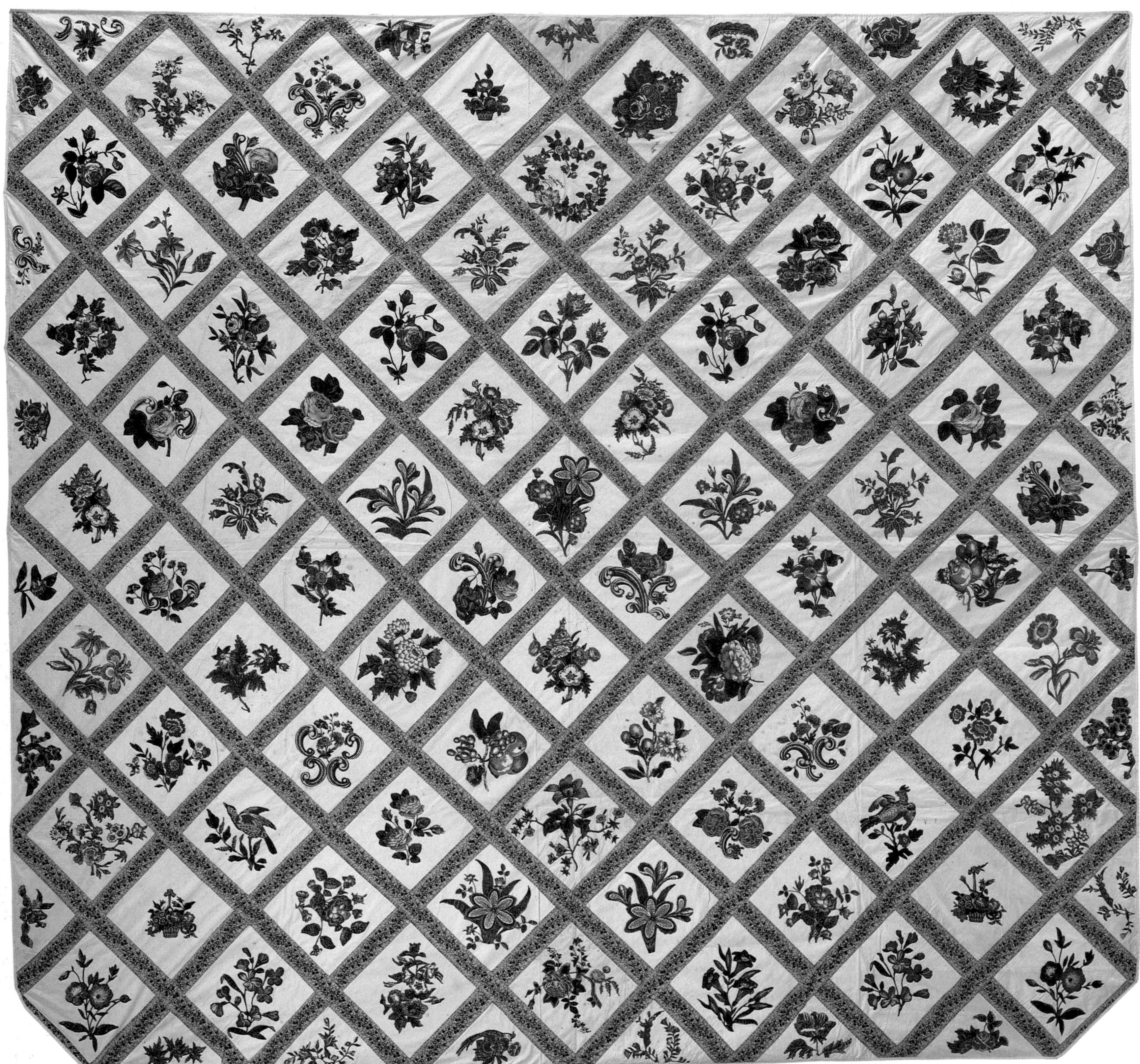

▲ **"BRODERIE PERSE" FLOWERS**

Lily and Lydia Corliiss. 1842–1843. Probably Maryland. Chintzes; hand pieced and appliquéd. 96 x 104 in. Private collection.

Each one of the appliquéd blocks here is assembled from a variety of chintz motifs, resulting in a series of original floral compositions within which no two are alike. The seventy-eight diamond-shaped blocks are separated by a lattice framework of floral printed fabric and bordered by twenty-five half blocks.

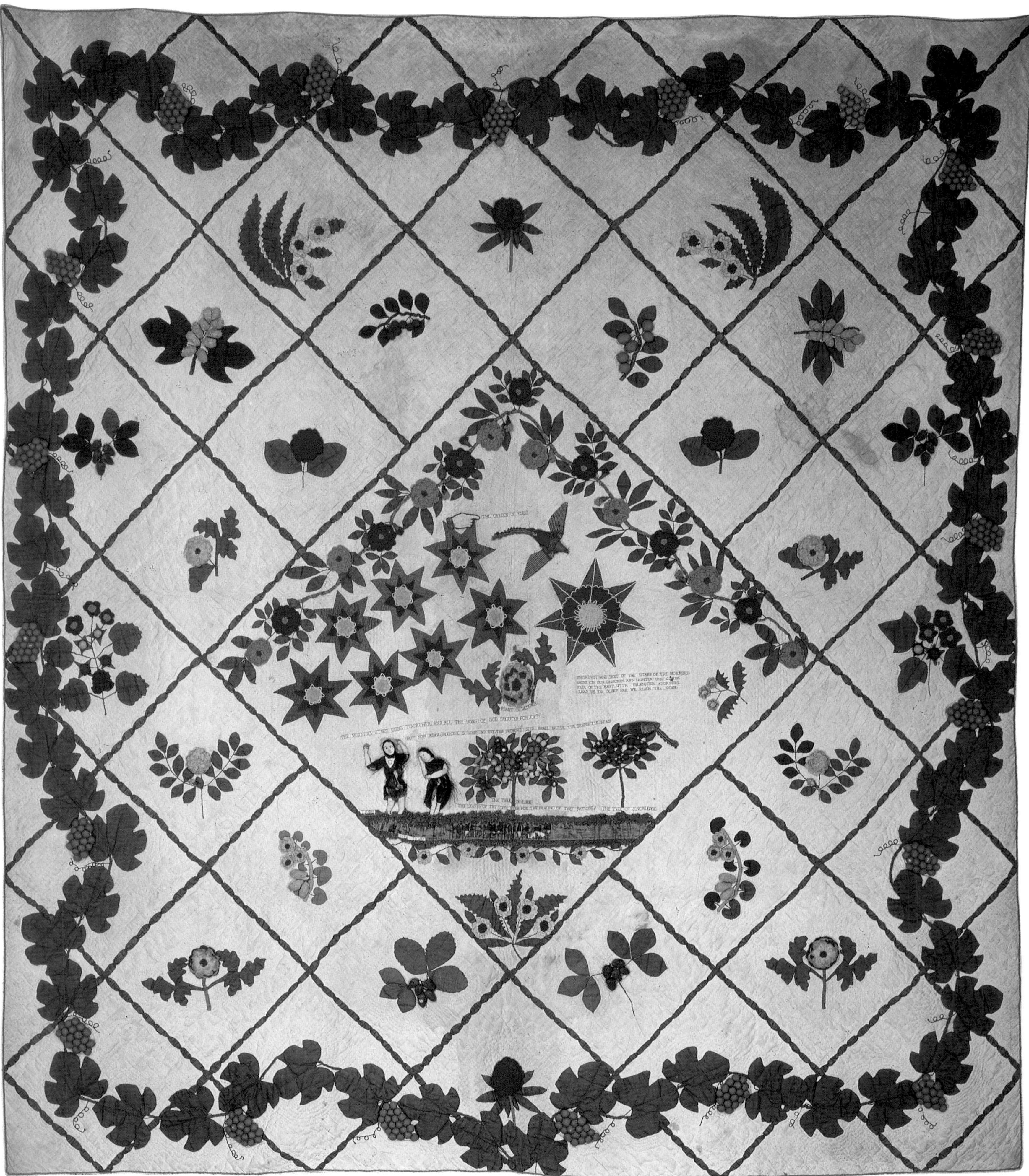

▲ THE GARDEN OF EDEN

Olive Batchelor Wells. c. 1842. Painesville, Ohio. Cotton, wool, and silk; pieced, appliquéd, embroidered, stuffed, gathered, beaded, and quilted. 85 1/2 x 76 in. Spencer Museum of Art, University of Kansas, Lawrence, gift of C. Wells Haven.

Olive Batchelor (1822–1893) is believed to have made his quilt shortly before her marriage to Leonidus Wells in 1843. The figures of Adam and Eve, as well as the bunches of grapes, the apples of knowledge, and other fruits and flowers, are stuffed so as to raise them from the quilt's surface. The fallen Adam and Eve wear silk clothing over their formerly innocent nakedness. A verse from the old hymn "Brightest and Best" is embroidered under the largest star: "Brightest and Best of the Sons of the Morning/Shine on Our Darkness and Lighten Our Gloom./Star of the East, with Splendour Adorning/Lead Us to Glory Ere We Reach the Tomb."

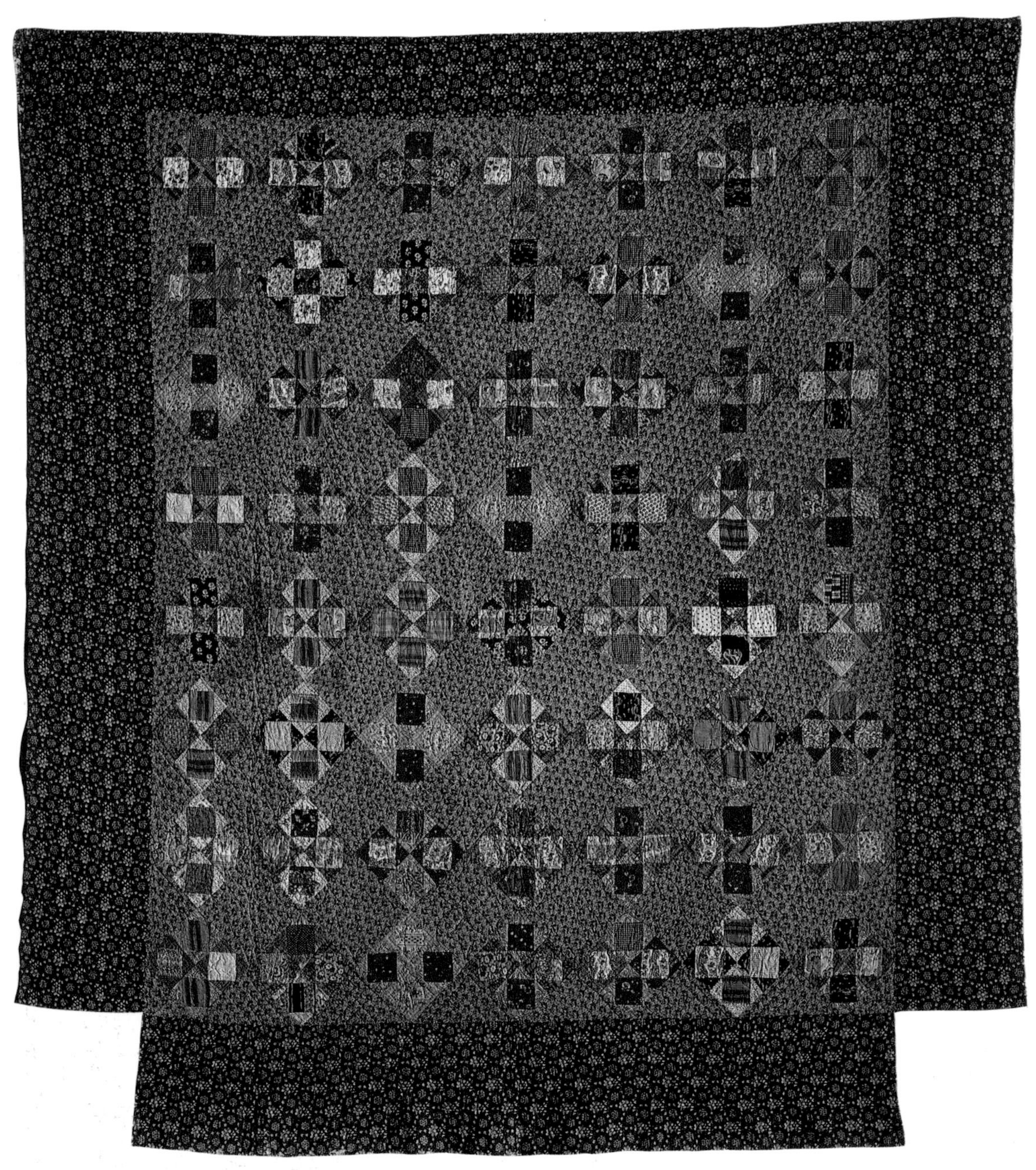

◄ Four-Patch

Artist unknown. c. 1825–1840. Eastern United States. Cottons; hand pieced and quilted. 100 1/8 x 89 3/4 in. Spencer Museum of Art, University of Kansas, Lawrence.

This early block-style quilt was made to fit a four-poster bed. The quilt is made from a combination of English and American cotton fabrics, probably pulled from the family rag bag. The diamond-shaped blocks are built around a square pieced from four equal triangles and surrounded by whole cloth squares set within four triangles of matched fabric. Each row of pieced blocks is set off by a row of light brown whole cloth diamonds. The blocks are bordered by triangles cut from the light brown print and a wide sash of darker brown printed fabric.

Sunflower or Compass ►

A member of the Bordon family. c. 1835. Rhinebeck, New York. Cottons; hand pieced and quilted. 88 x 78 in. Private collection.

A richly hued array of blue, red, and brown fabrics makes up this quietly elegant country quilt. The pieced compasses or sunflowers are interlaced with a network of square-centered X or star-shaped designs, and a border of half forms surrounds the entire quilt.

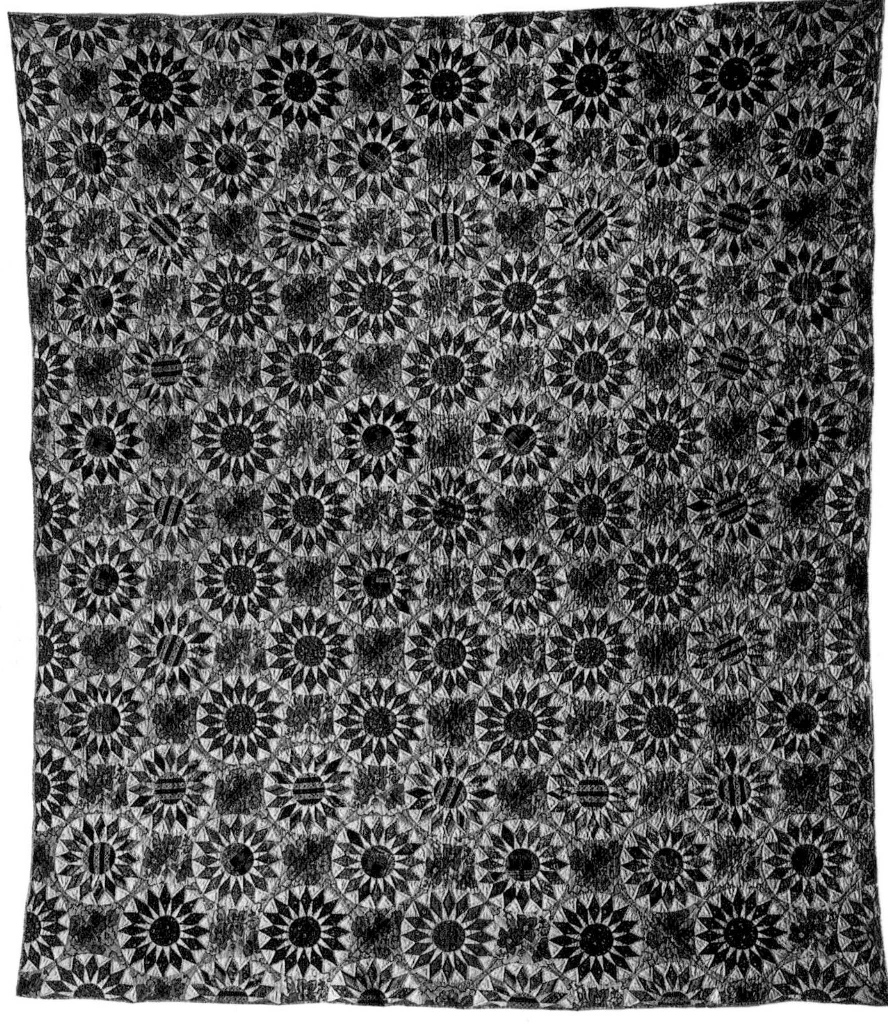

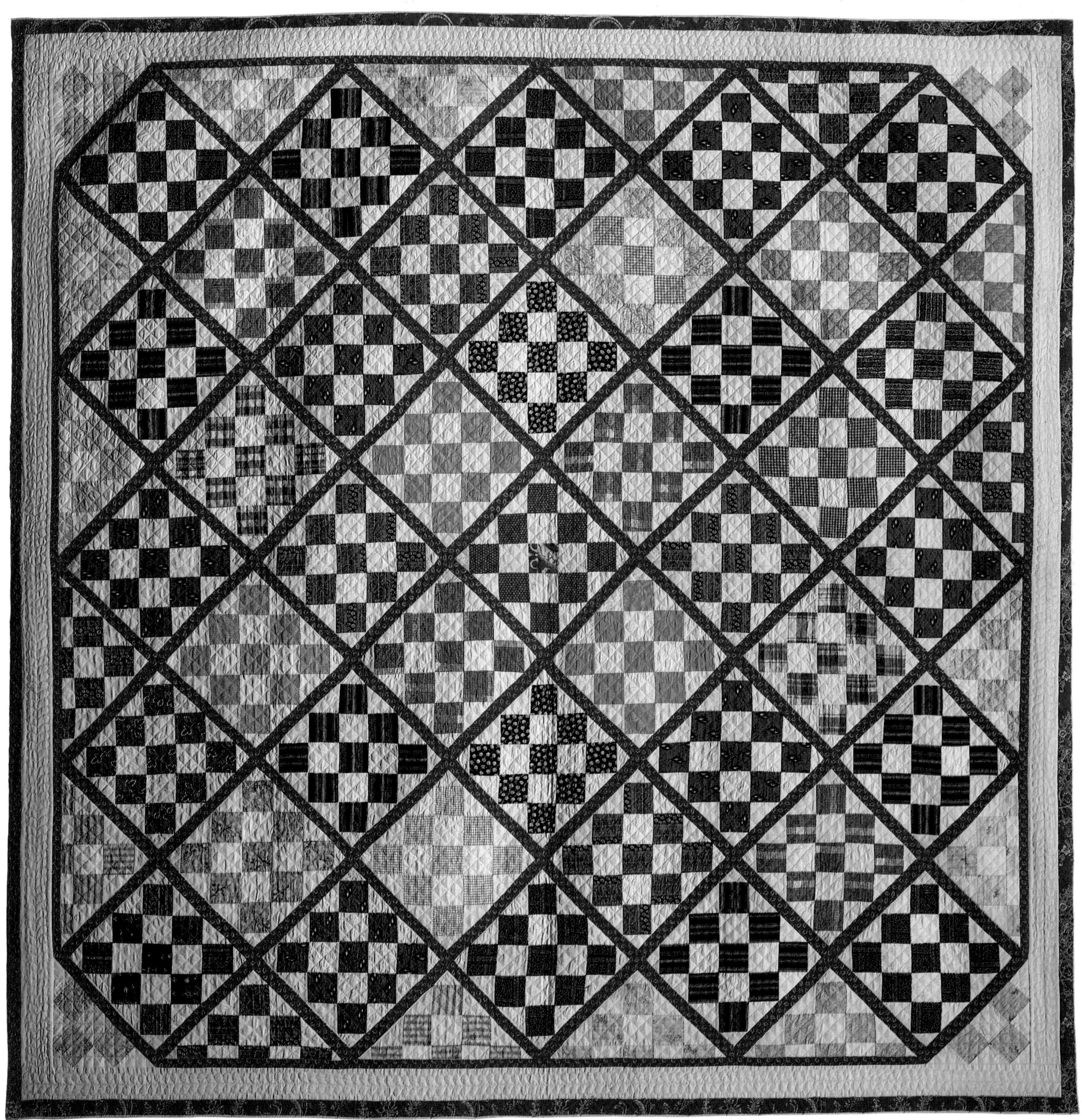

▲ **NINE-PATCH VARIATION**

Rebecca Davis. c. 1846. Eastern United States. Cottons; hand pieced and quilted. 83 3/4 x 82 3/4 in. The Metropolitan Museum of Art, gift of Mrs. Andrew Galbraith Carey, granddaughter of the maker.

Made of newly imported English printed cottons, this handsome quilt is one of three by the same maker in the collection of the Metropolitan Museum. All three include pieces of the same fabric, which may have been purchased as dress material. Each one of the diamond-shaped units of this quilt is built around a central nine-patch with a square added at each side. There are thirteen full-sized squares in each unit, four of them white and nine of them made of colored fabric.

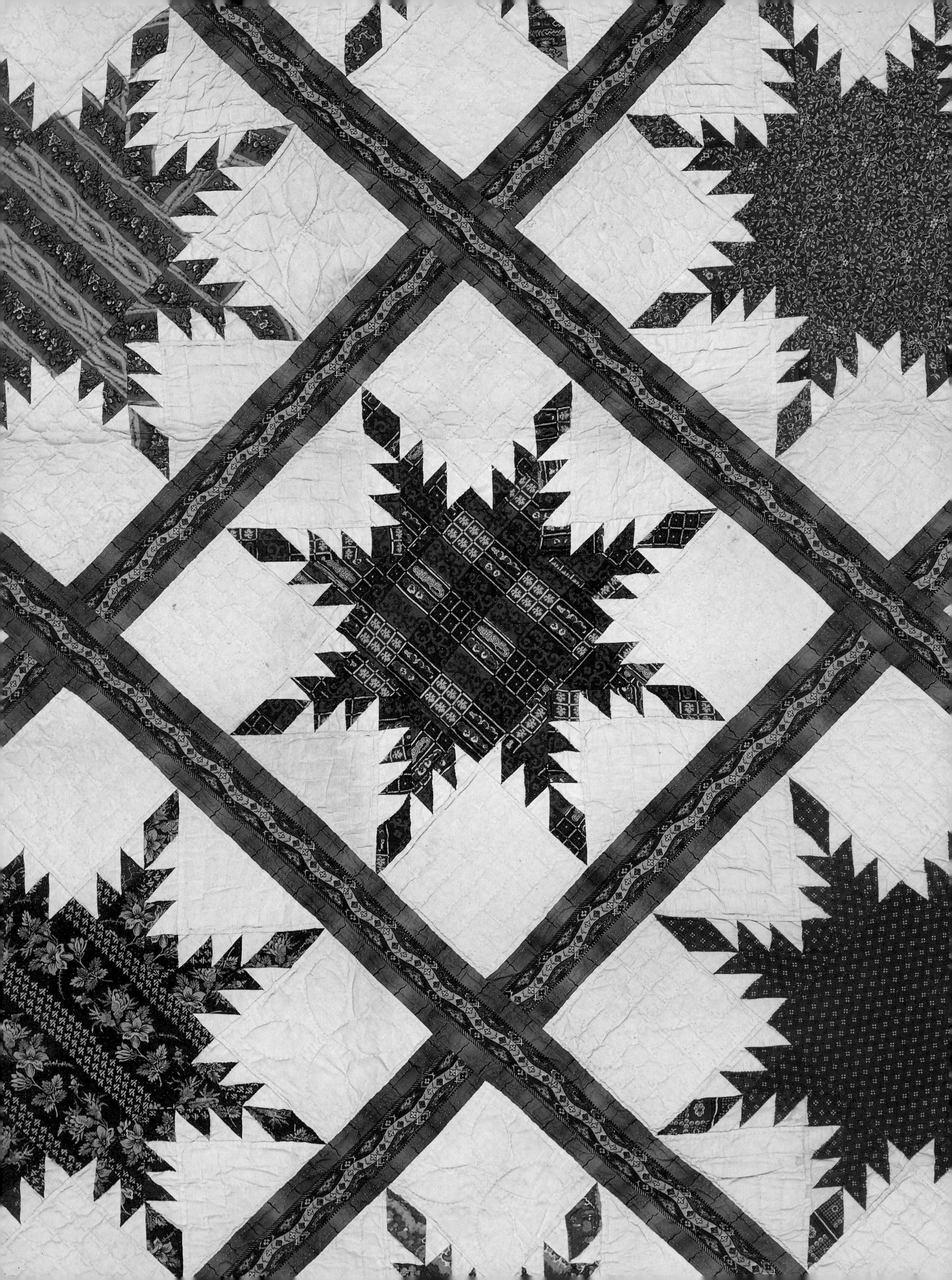

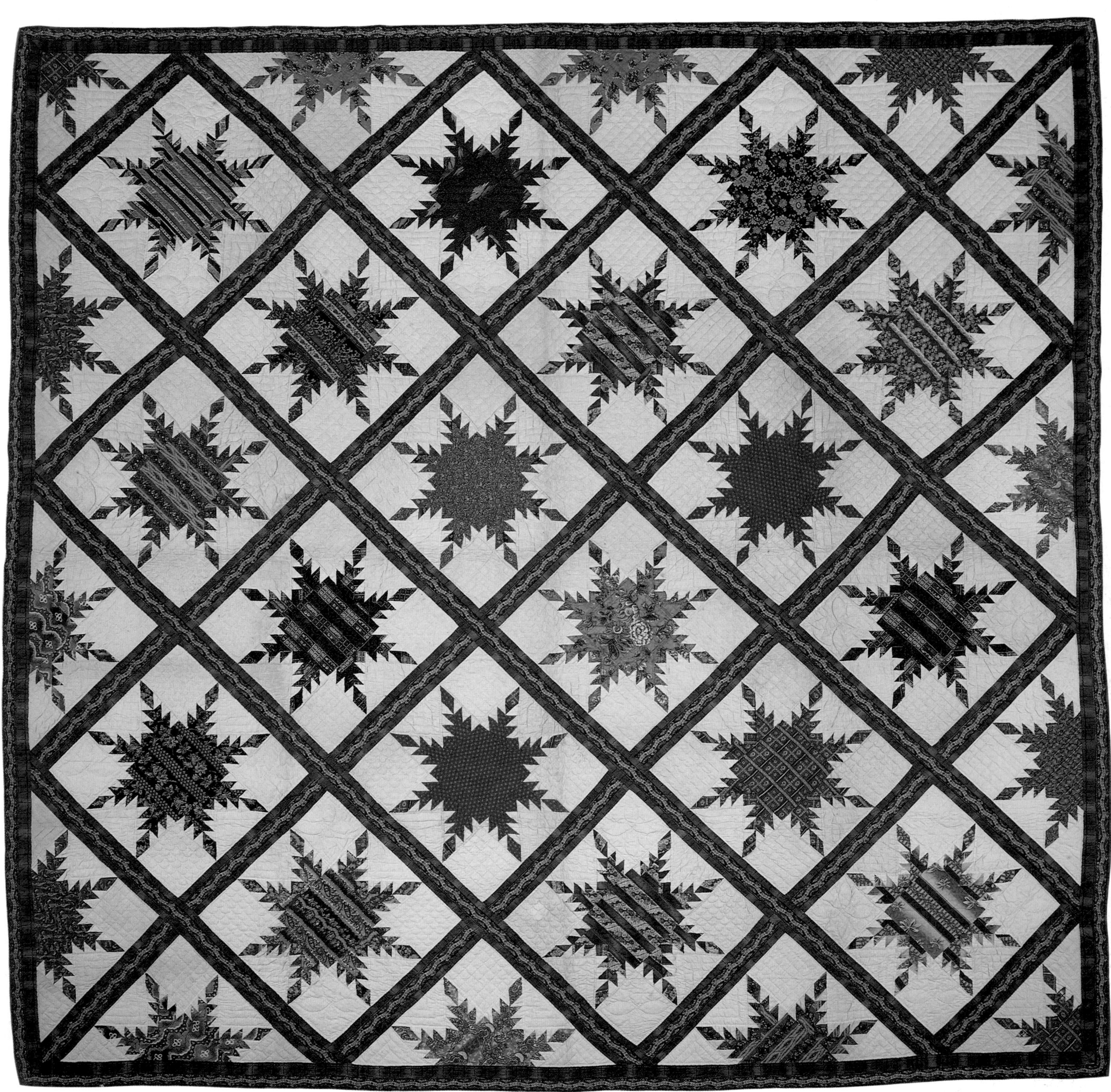

▲ **FEATHERED STAR** (◄ **DETAIL**)

Artist unknown. c. 1825–1840. Monmouth County, New Jersey. Cottons and chintzes; hand pieced and quilted. 90 x 90 in. Private collection.

This stunning quilt's fourteen full, twelve half, and two quarter blocks show off a marvelous selection of early printed fabrics. The intricately pieced star blocks are framed by a lattice of striped fabric, and the quilt is bordered by the same fabric, cut so that the stripe lies close to the edge of the quilt.

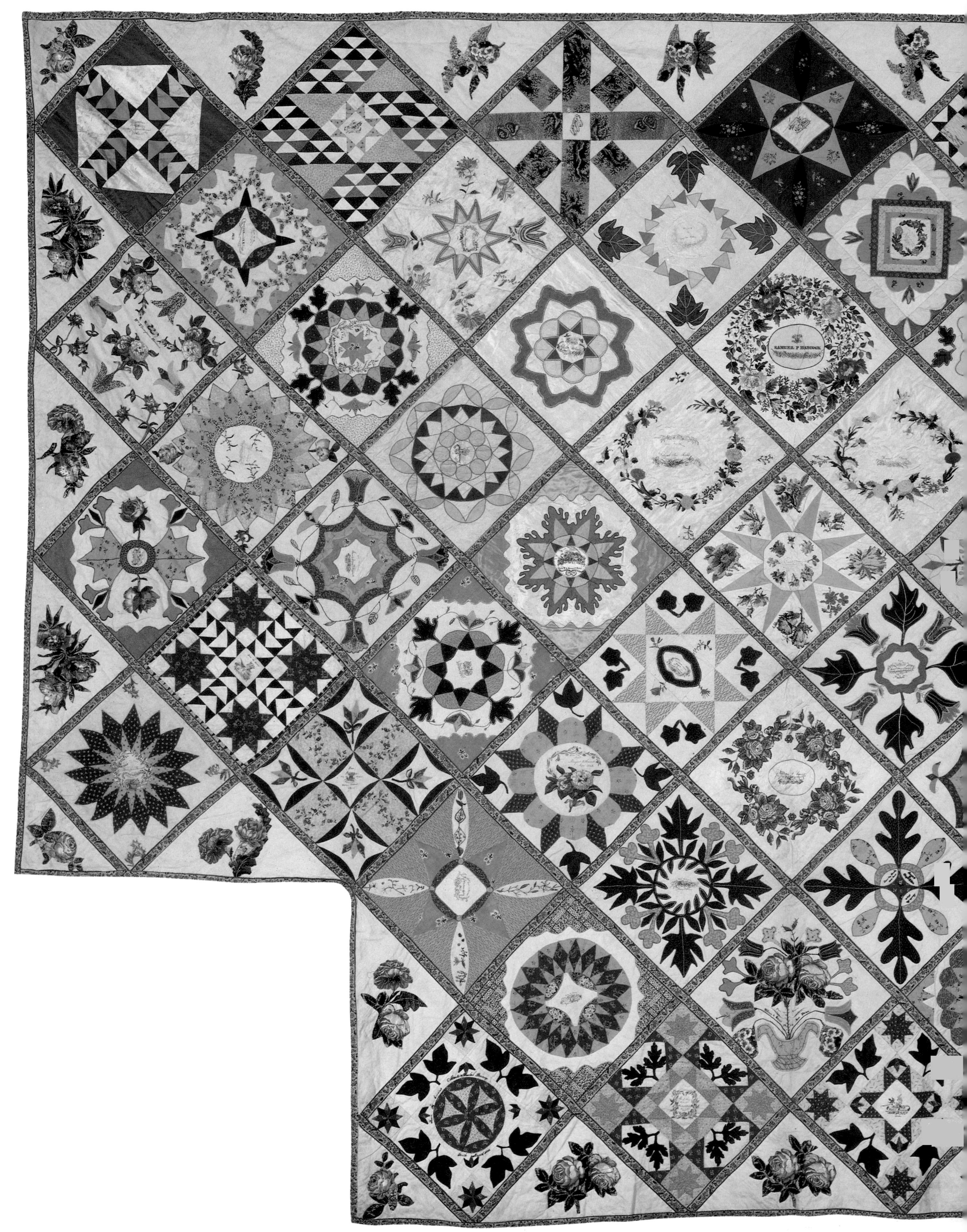
SAMUEL P HANCOCK

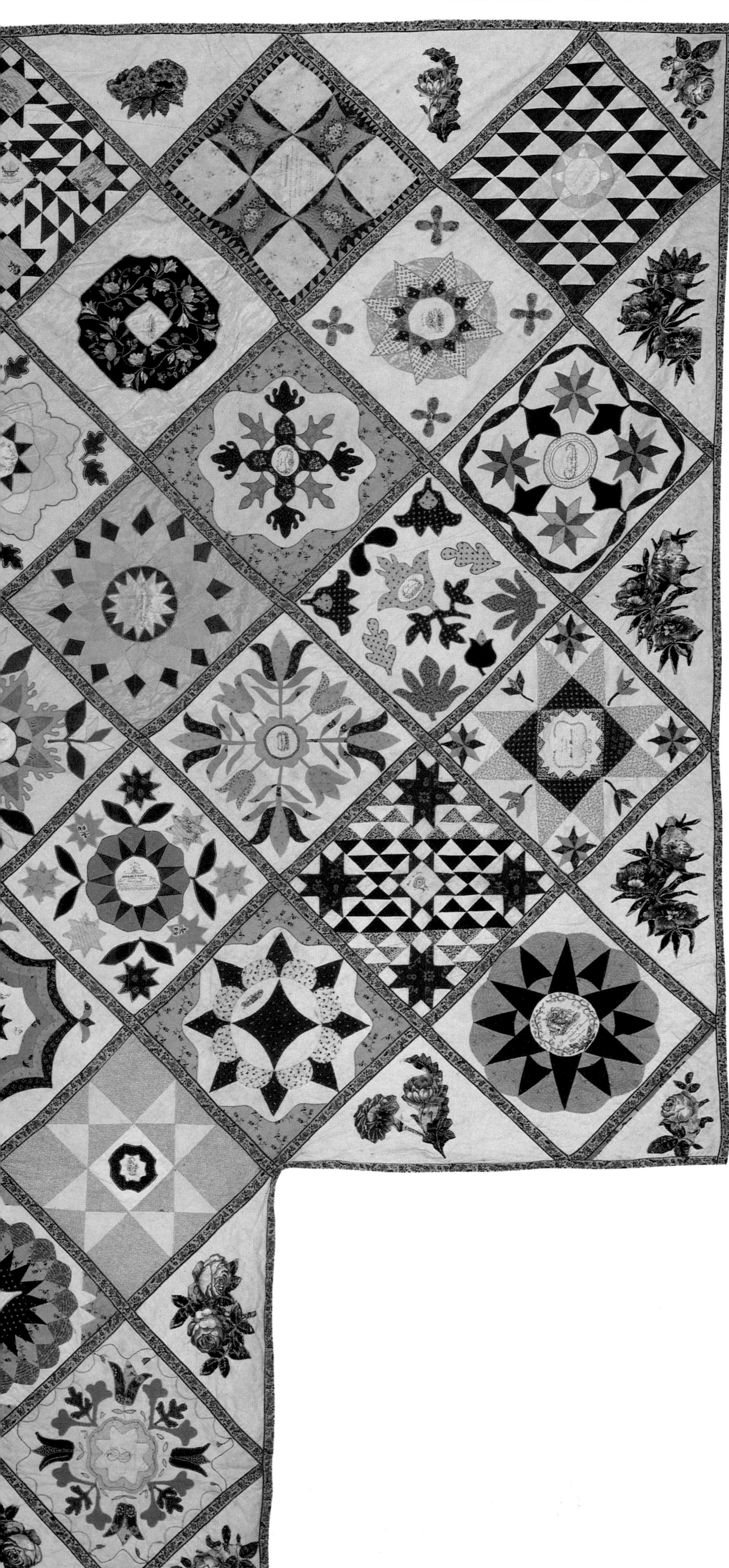

◄ **WEDDING ALBUM**

Charlotte Gillingham. 1842–1843. Philadelphia, Pennsylvania. Cotton with block- and roller-printed cotton, silk appliqué and pieced work; silk with silk embroidery; intersecting diagonal quilting; drawings, inscriptions, and signatures in ink. 97 x 126 in. Philadelphia Museum of Art, gift of the five granddaughters of Samuel Padgett Hancock: Mrs. Levis Lloyd Mann, Mrs. H. Maxwell Langdon, Mrs. George K. Helbert, Mrs. Nelson D. Warwick, and Mrs. Granville B. Hopkins.

This fabulously intricate quilt was probably made as a wedding present for Samuel Padgett Hancock by Charlotte Gillingham, his fiancée. The couple, both from prominent Philadelphia Quaker families, were joined in marriage on February 22, 1844. The fifty-seven blocks are all different and display a highly unusual combination of techniques, including *broderie perse* appliqué, pieced work, and fancy needlepoint embroidery. Roses cut from roller-printed chintz border the quilt on all sides of its four-poster bed shape.

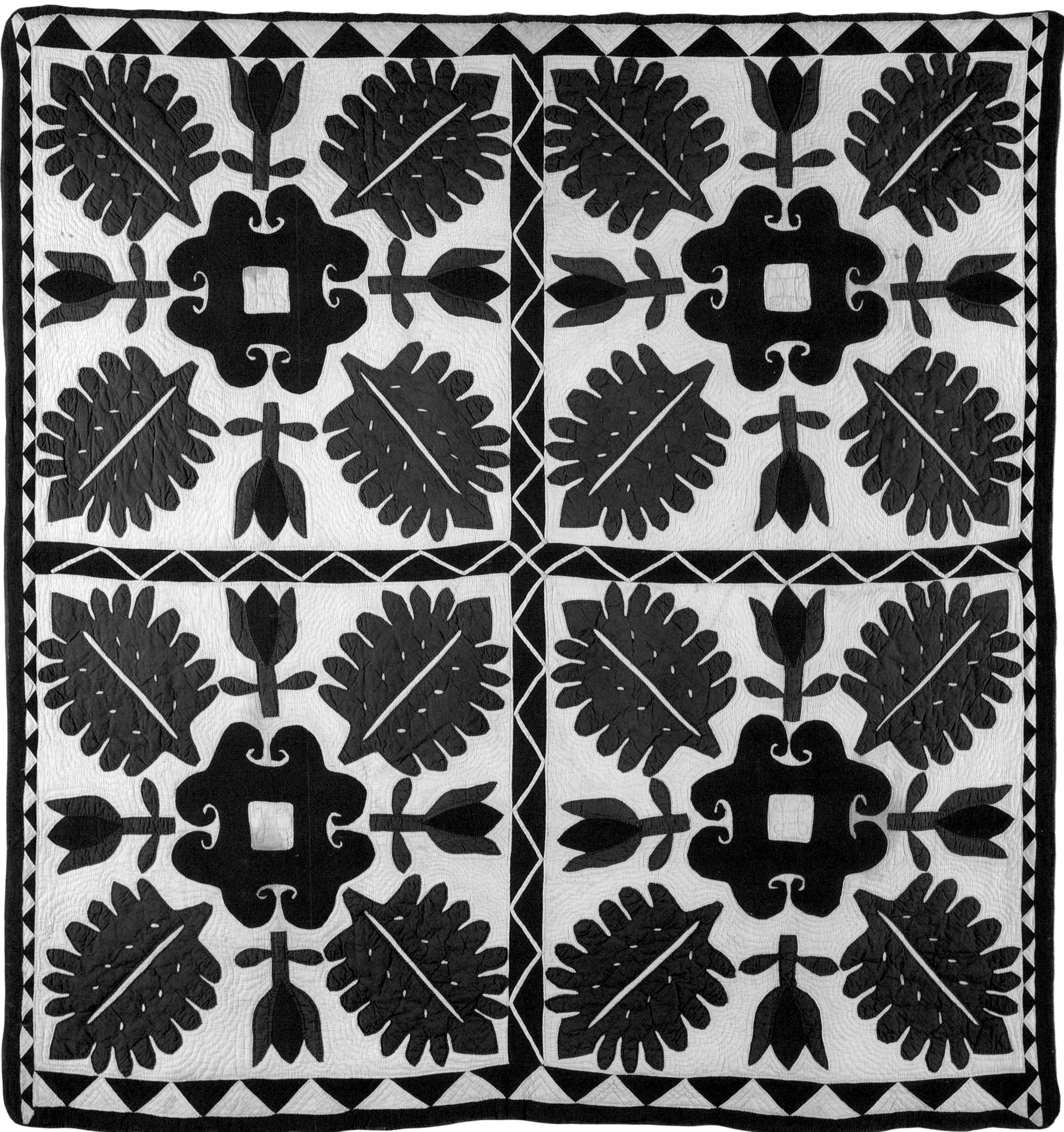

▲ **TINKER'S TOBACCO LEAF AND TULIP**

Artist unknown. c. 1850. Kentucky. Cottons; hand appliquéd and quilted. 77 1/2 x 74 in. Collection of Linda Carlson.

According to Linda Carlson, who has done extensive research on the four-block form, four-block quilts originated in Pennsylvania German communities in the 1840s, about the same time that the multiple block quilt became popular. This example of the four-block form is distinguished by its unusual combination of motifs, the appliquéd lightning streaks on the sashing, and the paired borders of large and small triangles.

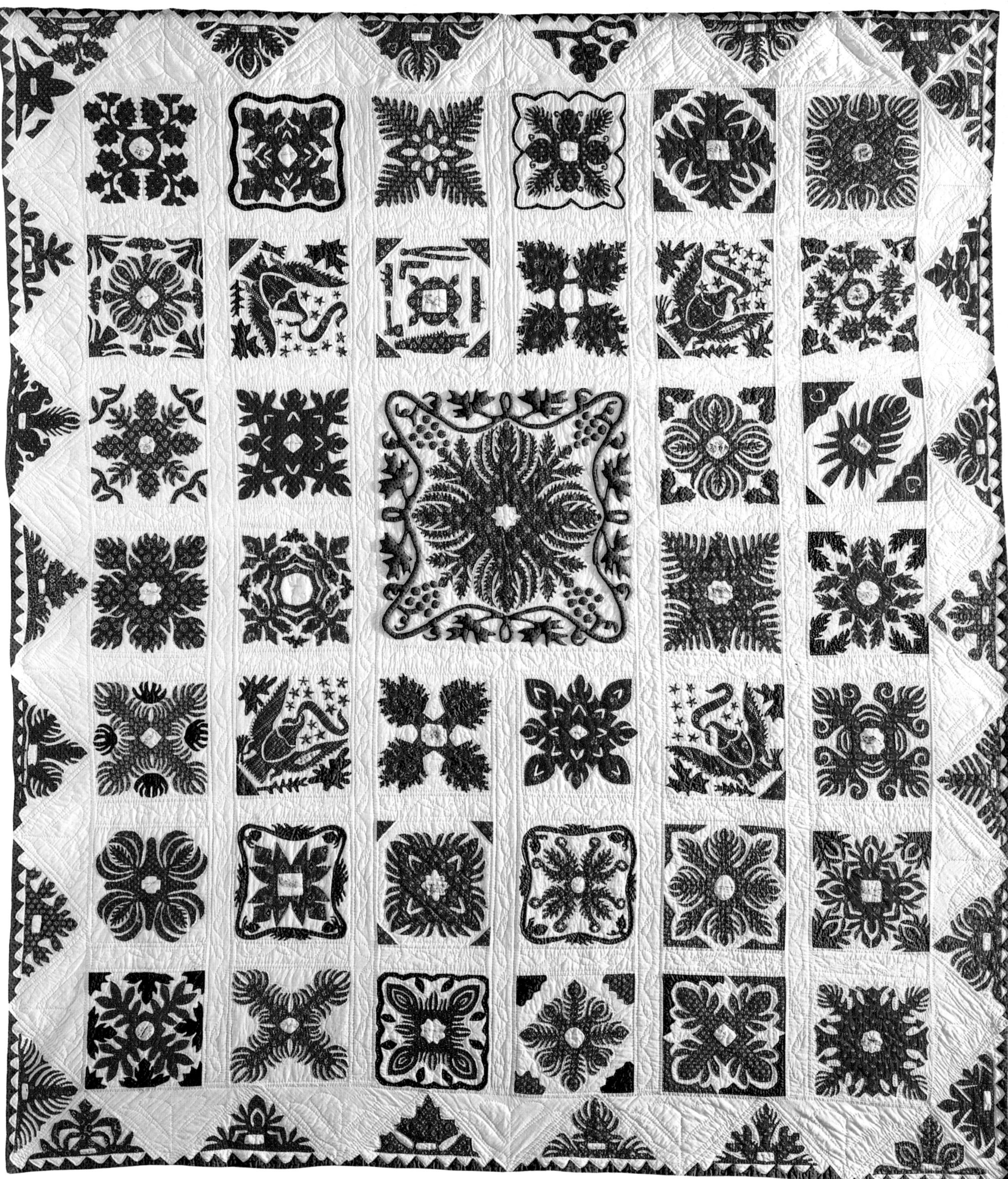

▲ **"SCHERENSCHNITTE" ALBUM**

Martha Ann James. c. 1845. Chester County, Pennsylvania. Cottons; hand appliquéd; hand quilted by Effie Belle James Pringle, Helen Pringle Anderson, and Jean Pringle Swanson. 84 x 72 1/2 in. Collection of Jean Pringle Swanson.

This is one of two elaborate quilt tops believed to have been made as marriage quilts that are still owned by the family of the maker. Martha Ann James's granddaughter and great-granddaughter began quilting the top in the late 1940s; the quilting was completed by another great-granddaughter in the 1980s. Most of the thirty-eight blocks were created from abstract paper designs using the Pennsylvania German technique of folding and cutting known as *scherenschnitte*. Many of the blocks are signed, suggesting that the quilt was made for a commemorative purpose, although all the appliqué blocks appear to be the work of one hand. The central medallion is cornered by four shield-bodied eagle blocks and bordered by a unique block representing carpenter's tools including a saw, a plane, a rule, an axe, and a pair of pliers.

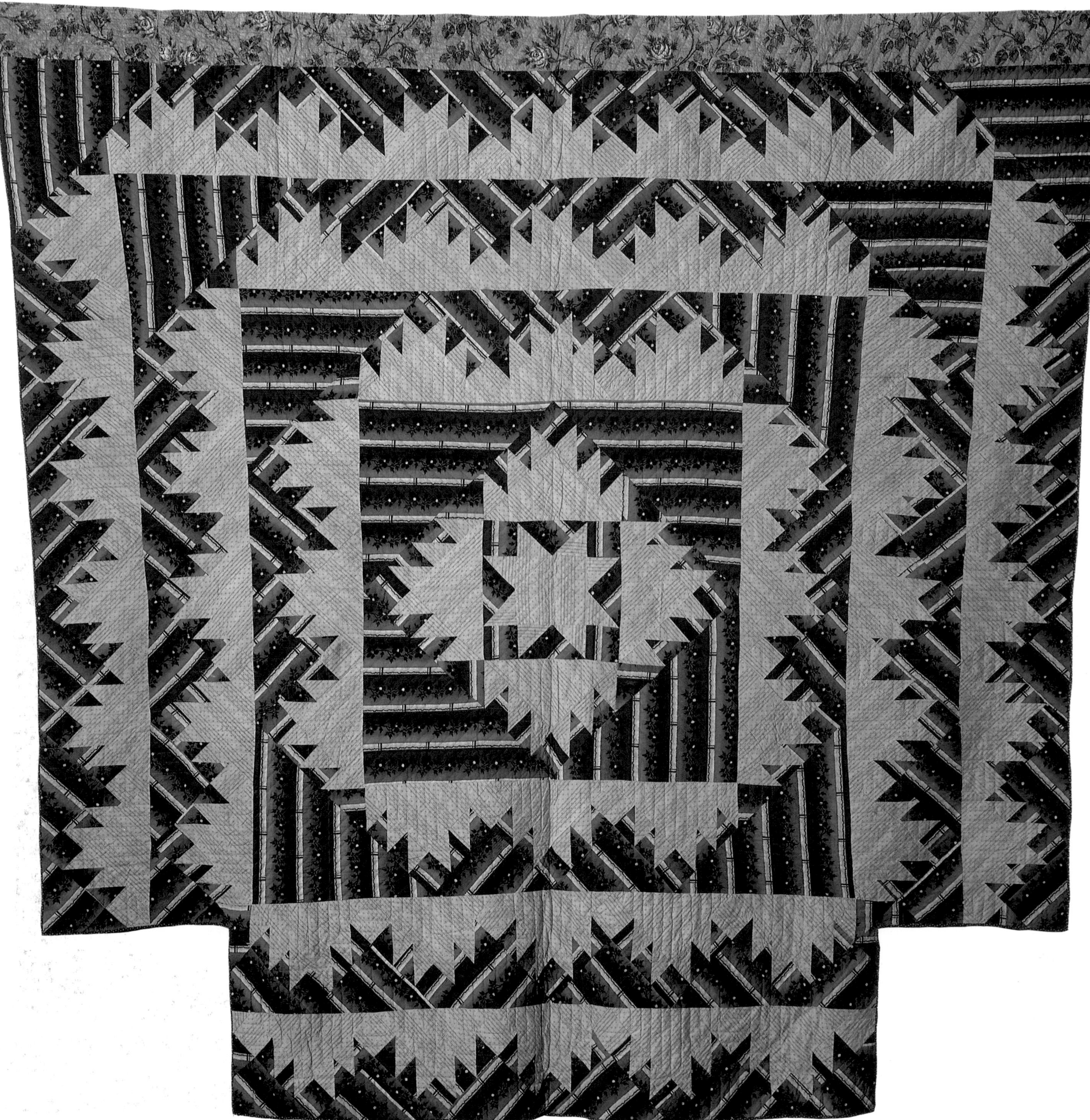

▲ Delectable Mountains

Artist unknown. c. 1840. Probably New England. Cottons; hand pieced and quilted. 92 x 88 in. Collection of Ardis and Robert James.

The name of this popular pattern derives from John Bunyan's allegory *Pilgrim's Progress*, a book found in many early American homes. From that text: "They went then till they came to the Delectable Mountains . . . behold the gardens and orchards, the vineyards and the fountains of water." The quilt is cut for a four-poster bed. An eight-pointed star forms the central medallion, and the whole is enclosed by multiple borders.

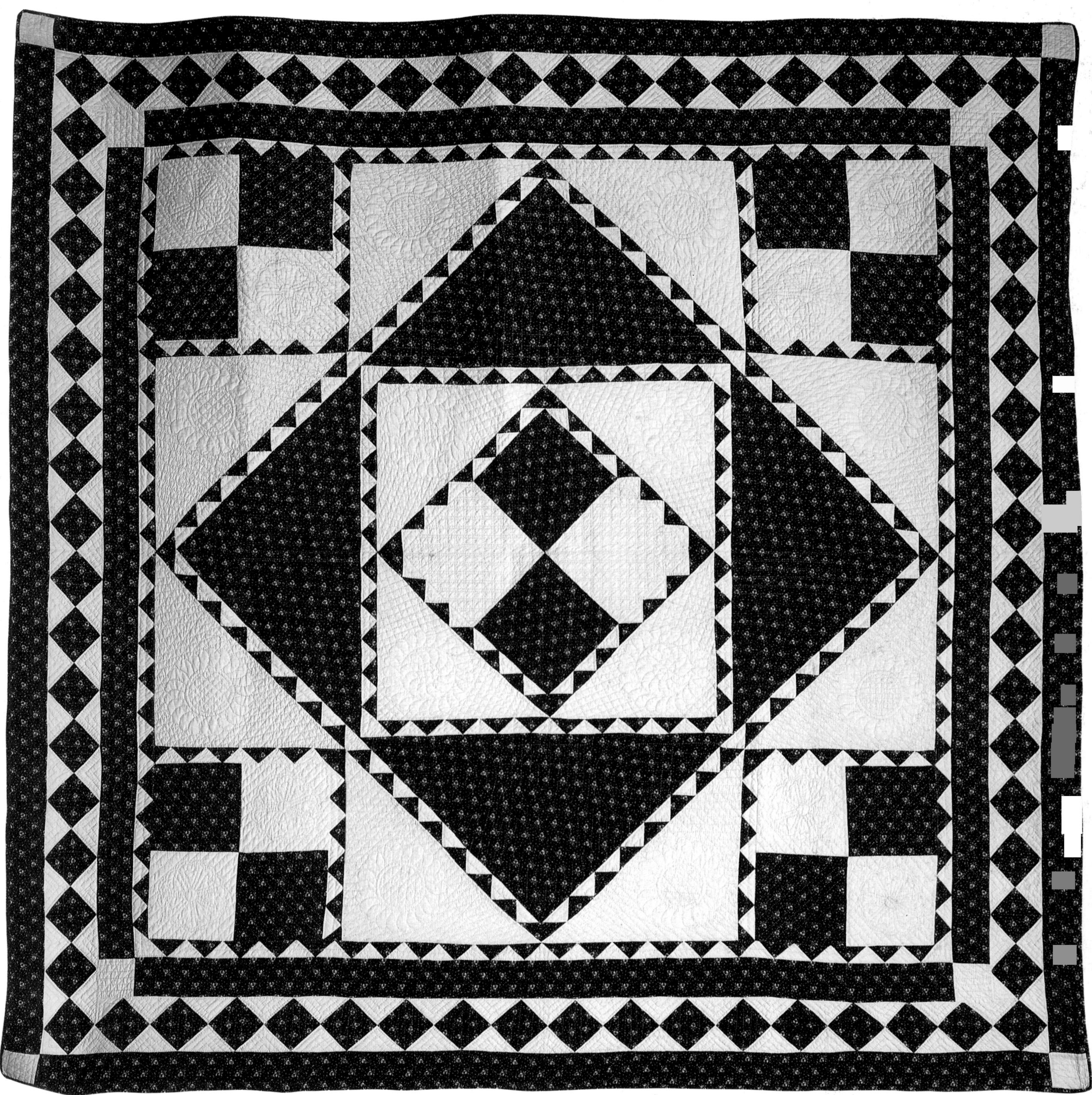

▲ **Four-Patch Diamond in the Square**

Artist unknown. c. 1840–1860. Pennsylvania. Cottons; hand and machine pieced, hand quilted. 85 x 85 in. Collection of Ardis and Robert James.

This powerful minimalist exploration in dark blue calico on white turns the four-patch center diamond on its side to create the four corner squares, and effectively borders all the center geometrics with sawtooth triangles. Small white squares corner the dark outer border, a rhythm negatively echoed by the broken corners of the inner border.

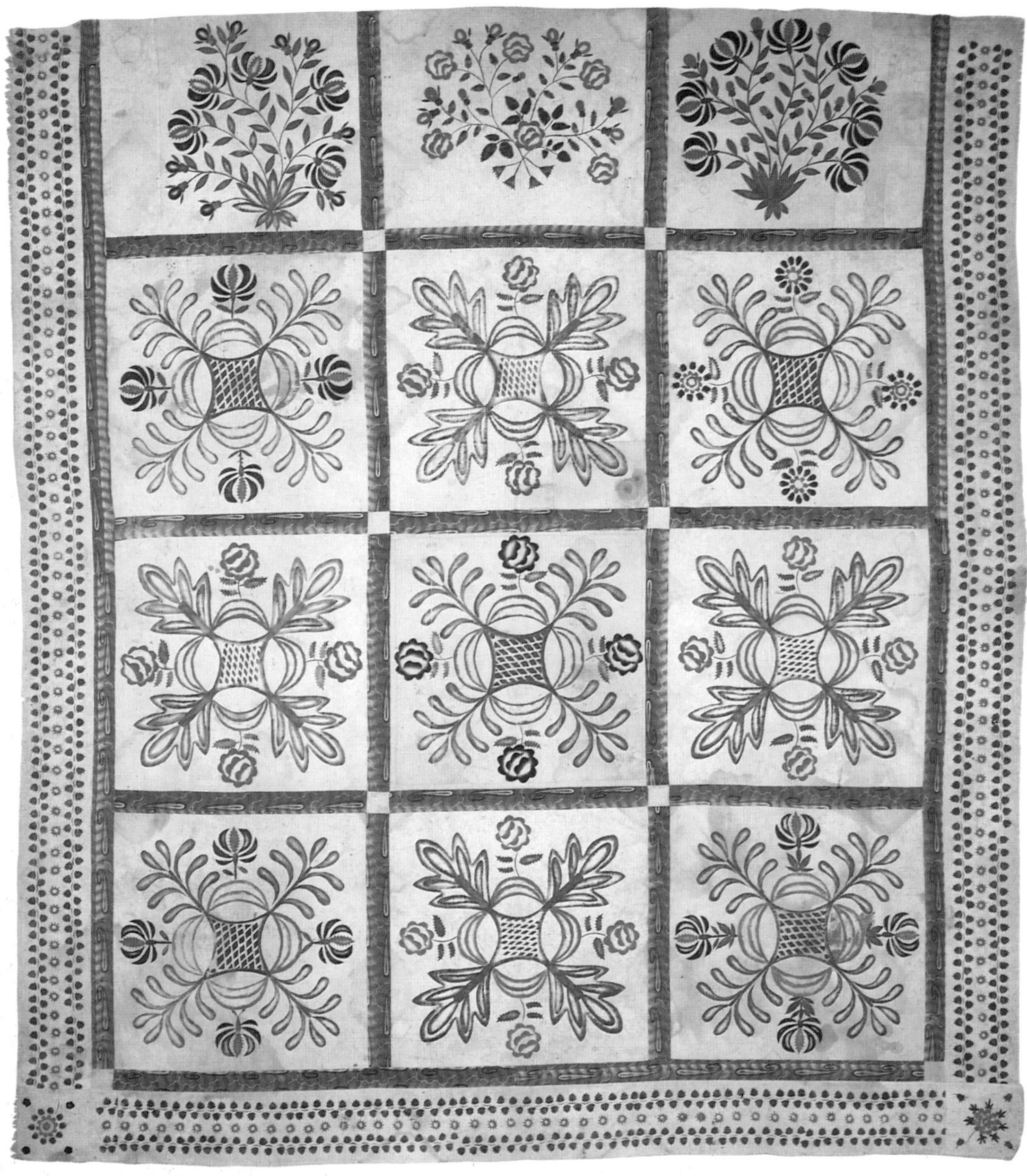

◂ STENCILED SPREAD

Possibly Sara Massey. c. 1825–1840. Possibly Watertown, New York. Cotton, paint. 88 x 76 1/4 in. Museum of American Folk Art, New York, gift of Dr. Robert Bishop.

Painted stenciled designs were extremely popular in the second quarter of the nineteenth century. During this period, itinerant decorators carried kits of precut stencil designs throughout the northeastern states and applied them to the walls of homes and taverns. Stencils were also sometimes used to decorate trunks, chair backs, tinware, and other household objects, including a few summer bedspreads such as this one.

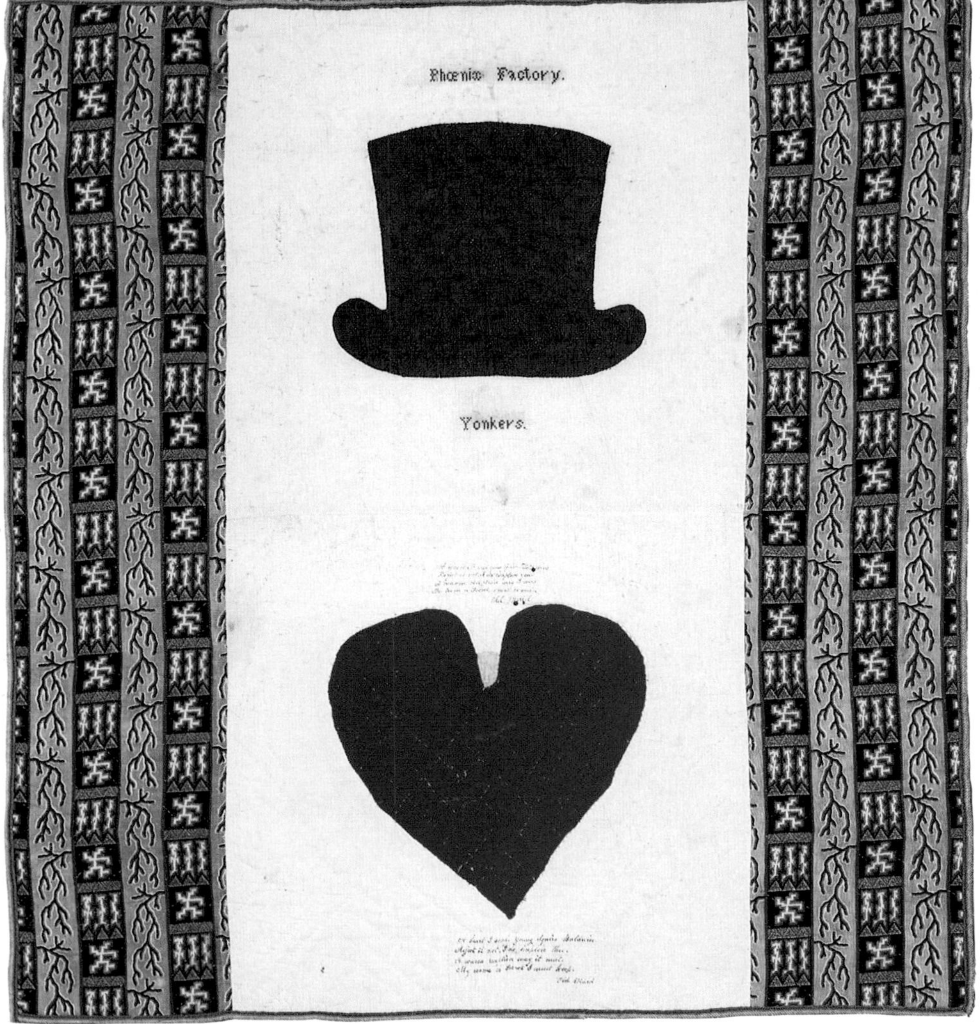

◂ THE HAT AND HEART QUILT

Probably made by E.K. Storrs for Anson Baldwin. c. 1847. Yonkers, New York. Cotton and wool; appliquéd, embroidered, and quilted, with ink inscription. 35 x 33 in. Baltimore Museum of Art, gift of Irwin and Linda Berman, St. Simons Island, Georgia.

This charming but mysterious little quilt bears virtually identical ink inscriptions above and below the appliquéd heart. One reads, "A heart I send, Young Squire Baldwin/Reject it not, I do implore you./A warm reception may it meet./My name a secret I must keep./Old Maid." Quilt scholar Sandi Fox has speculated that the quilt is a valentine made for the Reverend Anson Baldwin by his wife, and that the "Phoenix Factory" inscription is a symbolic reference to a new factory built by Baldwin and his business partner after their previous one had burned in 1844.

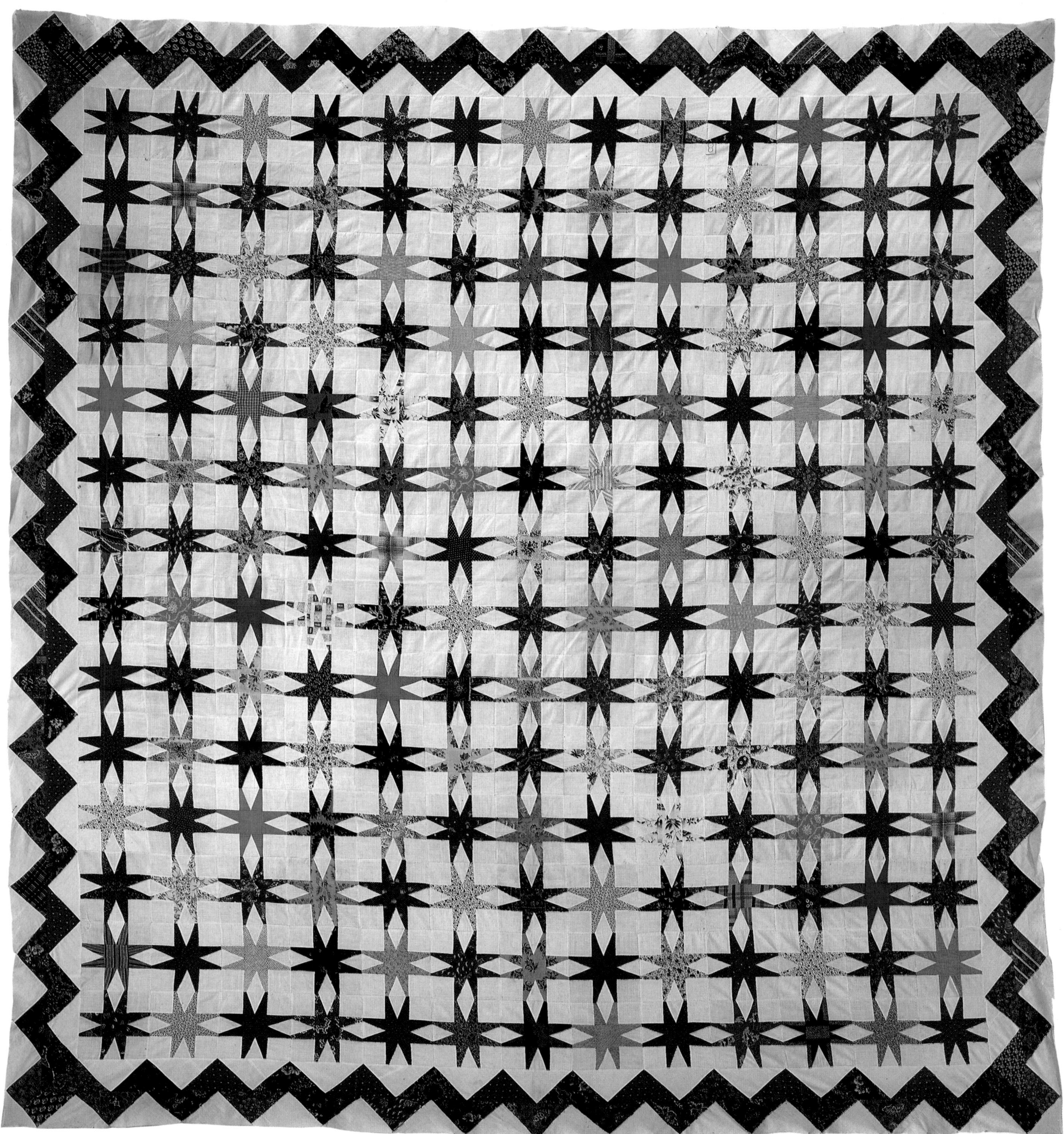

▲ **Darting Minnows**

Artist unknown. c. 1845. Northeastern United States. Cottons; hand pieced. Private collection.

This unquilted top was made from scraps that had been saved for at least two decades. The calicos in the jagged border date from the 1840s, when the quilt was made. The pattern is aptly named: the eight-pointed stars of colored fabric intersect to form negative lozenge-shapes and create a surface that moves with the constant, restless energy of a pool of darting minnows.

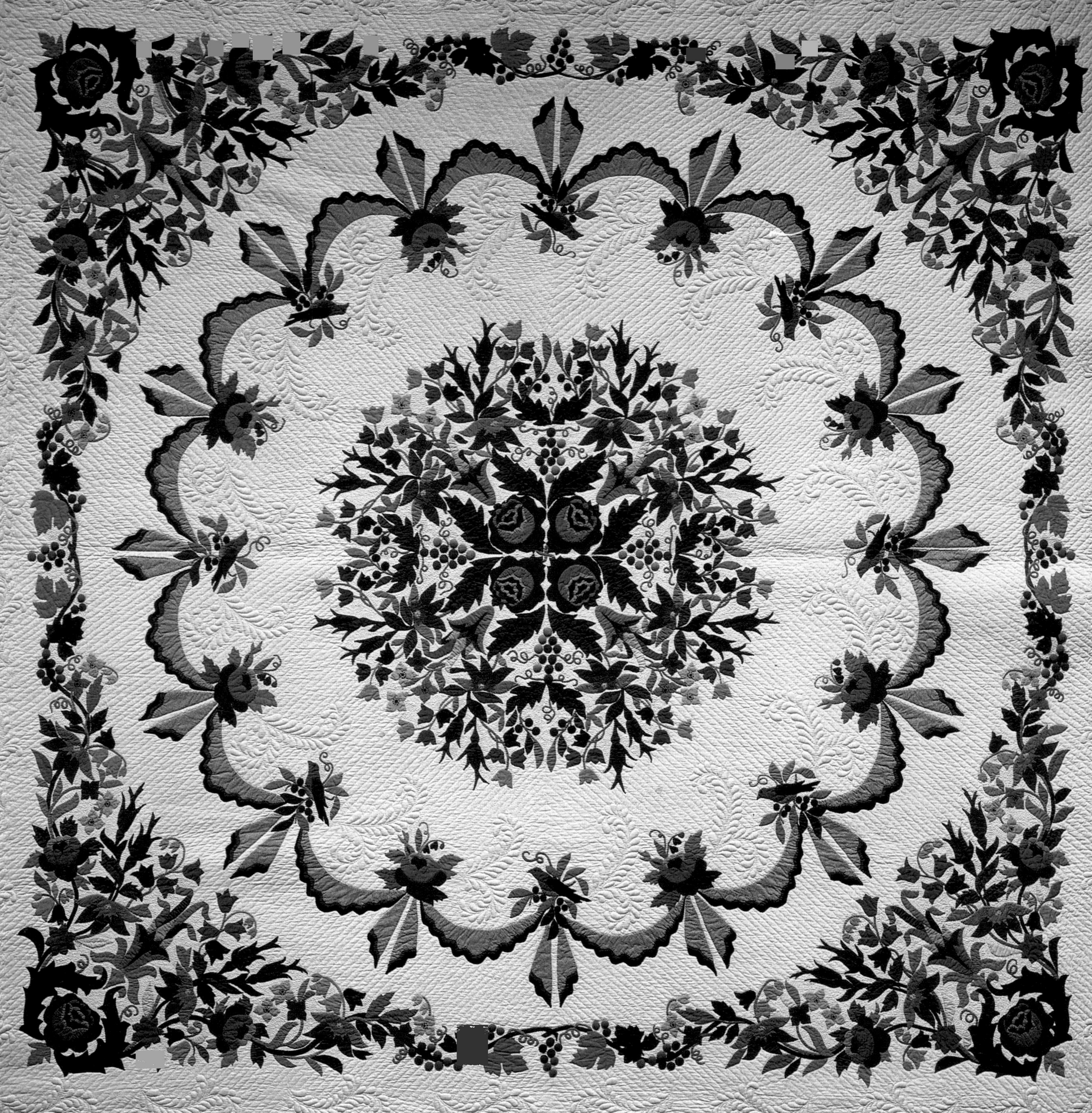

The Development of Quiltmaking in America (1860–1970)

American quiltmaking grew to full maturity in the second half of the nineteenth century, its development mirroring the country's rapid expansion and economic growth. The years between the beginning of the Civil War and the turn of the new century were the most productive and creative in the history of quiltmaking. As America became a world power, so too American quiltmaking became a world folk art and one of this country's greatest artistic achievements. Quiltmaking's domestic roots would, however, keep its importance largely hidden and unrecognized for another century.

America's rich cultural mix and unswerving dedication to freedom of expression contributed greatly to the widespread growth of quiltmaking. Thirty-five million people seeking personal and religious freedom as well as economic opportunity emigrated to America from Europe between 1815 and 1915. As migration pushed steadily westward, a host of different religious and ethnic groups settled the newly opened lands of the west, from Ohio to Texas to California, bringing with them their own beliefs and traditions, all of which became part of the country's identity. New England Yankees, Southern Quakers, Scotch-Irish, Welsh, German Protestants, Swiss Mennonites, Scandinavian Lutherans, and French-Canadian Catholics all traveled west. Each group made quilts that reflected their own centuries-old aesthetic traditions. Germans, for example, often favored vibrant color combinations, while Yankees preferred more subdued palettes; floral appliqués and four-block patterns were popular among German mainstream Protestants, while Mennonites made pieced quilts with blocks set within plain borders. As time passed, these diverse cultural groups coalesced and became part of new, larger, and more homogeneous communities. Only a few groups (most notably the Amish) remained separate; most eventually interacted, bringing fresh ideas and inspiration to each other's traditions, while still retaining much of their own distinct cultural identities.

Dramatic and far reaching changes in technology also influenced the craft of quiltmaking. The expanding textile industry offered more and more choices to American consumers. Commercial aniline dyes, introduced in the 1850s, drastically changed the palette of fabric color

◂ **Paradise Garden**

Rose Good Kretsinger. 1946. Emporia, Kansas. Cotton; appliquéd; reverse appliquéd with stuffed quilting by an unknown quilter. 93 x 94 in. Spencer Museum of Art, University of Kansas, Lawrence, gift of Mary Kretsinger.

Rose Good Kretsinger (1886–1963), co-author of *The Romance of the Patchwork Quilt in America* and one of the leading quiltmakers of her time, studied design at the Art Institute of Chicago and worked as a professional jewelry designer in Chicago before her marriage.

available to the average quilter. Aniline dyes, which derived from chemicals, were generally much brighter and sharper than the comparatively soft-hued natural dyes derived from plant and mineral sources which had preceded them. Roller-printed fabrics became obtainable in a wide range of designs, and any single design could be printed in many different colors. By the 1870s, over twelve hundred different printed fabric colors gave American women a wealth of creative choices.

The sewing machine, also introduced in the 1850s, ultimately contributed to a decline in the quality of hand stitching, once the standard of quilt craftsmanship. The sewing machine was a great leveler; it thoroughly democratized quiltmaking by making it possible for virtually anyone to sew layers of cloth together with some precision. The new machine caught on quickly; by the 1870s, nearly three quarters of a million were being made annually. Use of the sewing machine completely changed the way Americans dressed, making possible a clothes-making industry that had largely eliminated homemade clothing by the turn of the twentieth century. As early as 1867, *The Atlantic Monthly* observed that "the sewing machine is one of the means by which the industrious laborer is as well clad as any millionaire need be, and by which working-girls are enabled to gratify their women's instinct of decoration." Quiltmaking responded as well to the widespread availability of dress fabrics and the use of the new machine which could stitch these fabrics together; all but the lowest classes of women could now make similarly complex and attractive quilts of store-bought fabrics, and make them much more quickly.

Twentieth-century collectors have identified as many as four thousand different quilt patterns, the great majority of which were conceived during the second half of the nineteenth century. Appliqué and pieced patterns were disseminated through women's magazines, through church and community groups, at country fairs, and from neighbor to neighbor. Pat-

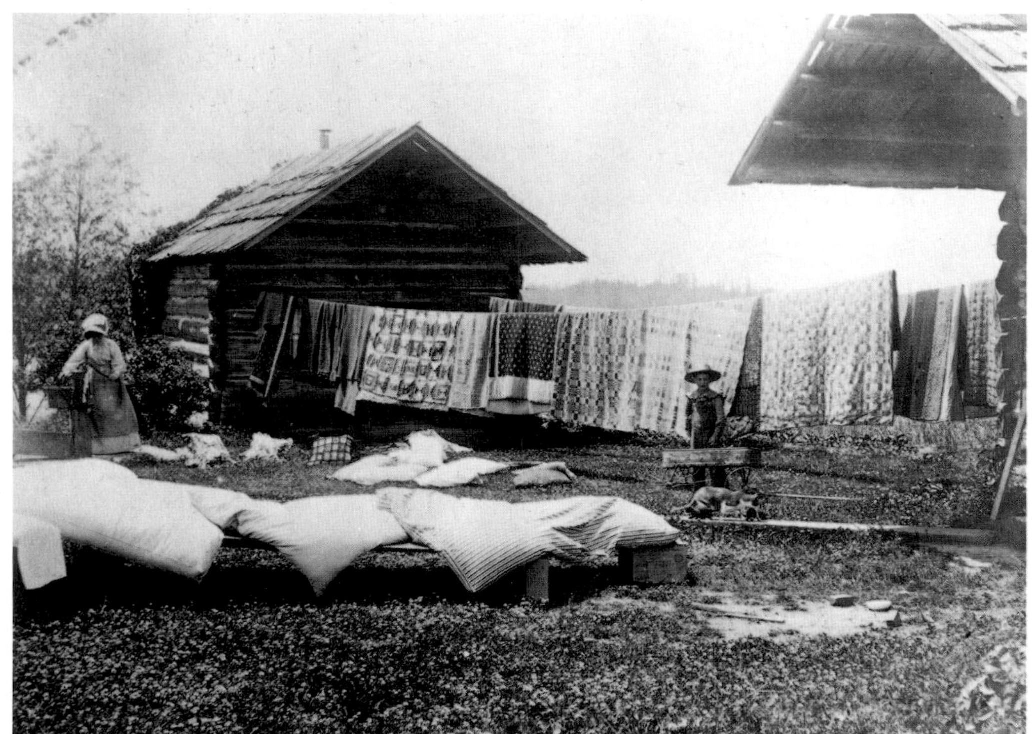

◀ *A woman and her son are seen airing quilts and bedding outside their home in Seattle, Washington, in this c. 1890 photograph. Among the quilts hanging on the line is a Log Cabin, at far left. Special Collections Division, University of Washington Libraries, Seattle.*

▼ *This proud-looking group of women gathered for a quilting bee in Mehama, Oregon, c. 1905. Oregon Historical Society, Portland.*

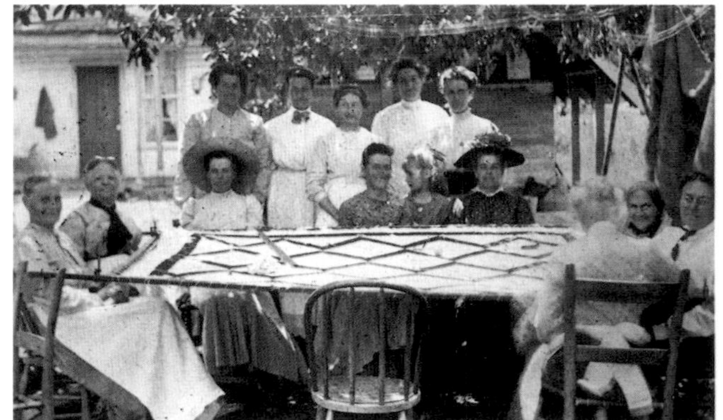

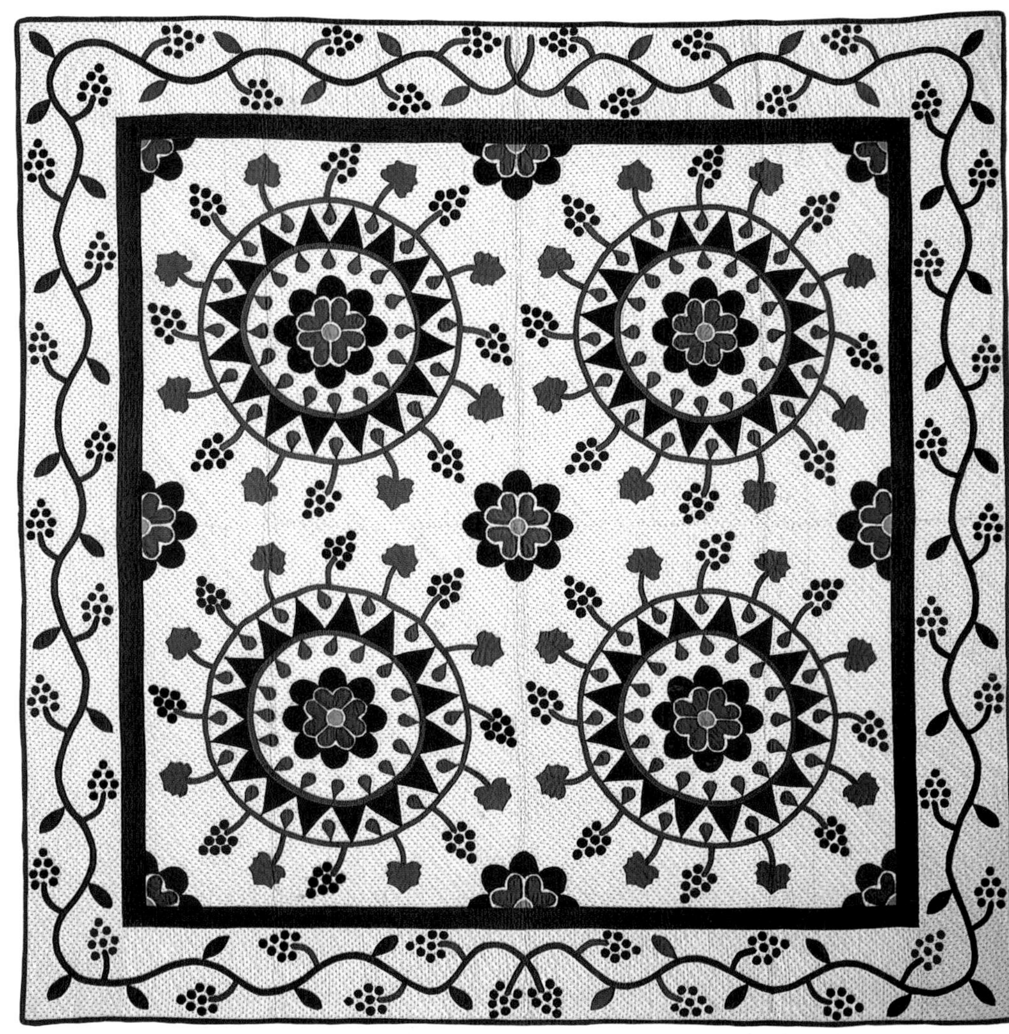

FLOWERS, GRAPES, AND SAWTOOTH WHEELS ▸

Artist unknown. c. 1870–1900. Pennsylvania. Appliquéd cottons; hand quilted. 82 1/2 x 82 1/2 in. Collection of Ardis and Robert James.

This colorful floral quilt is a triumph of original appliqué design. The design is built around five flowers, one standing alone in the center of the quilt with four others uniformly spaced and set within sawtooth wheels. Half flowers edge the four central points of the wide surrounding border, and one third flowers appear in each of its four corners.

terns incorporated and synthesized native American flora and fauna, religious, fraternal, and ethnic motifs, and patriotic symbols, as well as hundreds of clever geometric combinations. Pattern names, which changed as the patterns moved from region to region and quilter to quilter, offer a rich sampling of the American language and frame of mind: Rocky Road to Kansas, Underground Railroad, Peony and Prairie Flower, Bread Basket, Hit and Miss, Tippecanoe and Tyler Too, World without End, Square Deal, Lone Star, Puss in the Corner, Carpenter's Square, Bearpaw, Old Maid's Ramble, Indian Puzzle, Drunkard's Path, Zigzag, and Sawtooth.

The two most popular pieced patterns of the late nineteenth century, the Log Cabin and the crazy, are actually families of patterns rather than single design ideas. Each sets up a broad conceptual base upon which a seemingly infinite number of variations can be built. Both groups of patterns first appeared soon after the Civil War, and their origins may be linked to the effects of the war, popular mythology, and the polar extremes of the divided country's zeitgeist. In a sense, the Log Cabin may be seen to represent a longing for simpler times, while the crazy embodies the frenzied complexity of the modern age.

If there is a quintessential American quilt it is probably the Log Cabin, a pieced quilt organized in block style that forms an overall visual pattern and carries many symbolic connections. Log Cabins present a fascinating window into the continuum of American quilting, always reflecting the times in which they are made but also remaining true to their origins and historical meanings. Log Cabins have remained popular for well over a century; seemingly every generation and cultural group has been attracted by the Log Cabin and found ways to make it contemporary. Late Victorian-era quilters made Log Cabins from the same fancy dress silks they used for crazy quilts, early twentieth-century Amish quilters used wool in startlingly original color combinations, and Depression-era women employed the quiet pastel fabrics that were popular at the time.

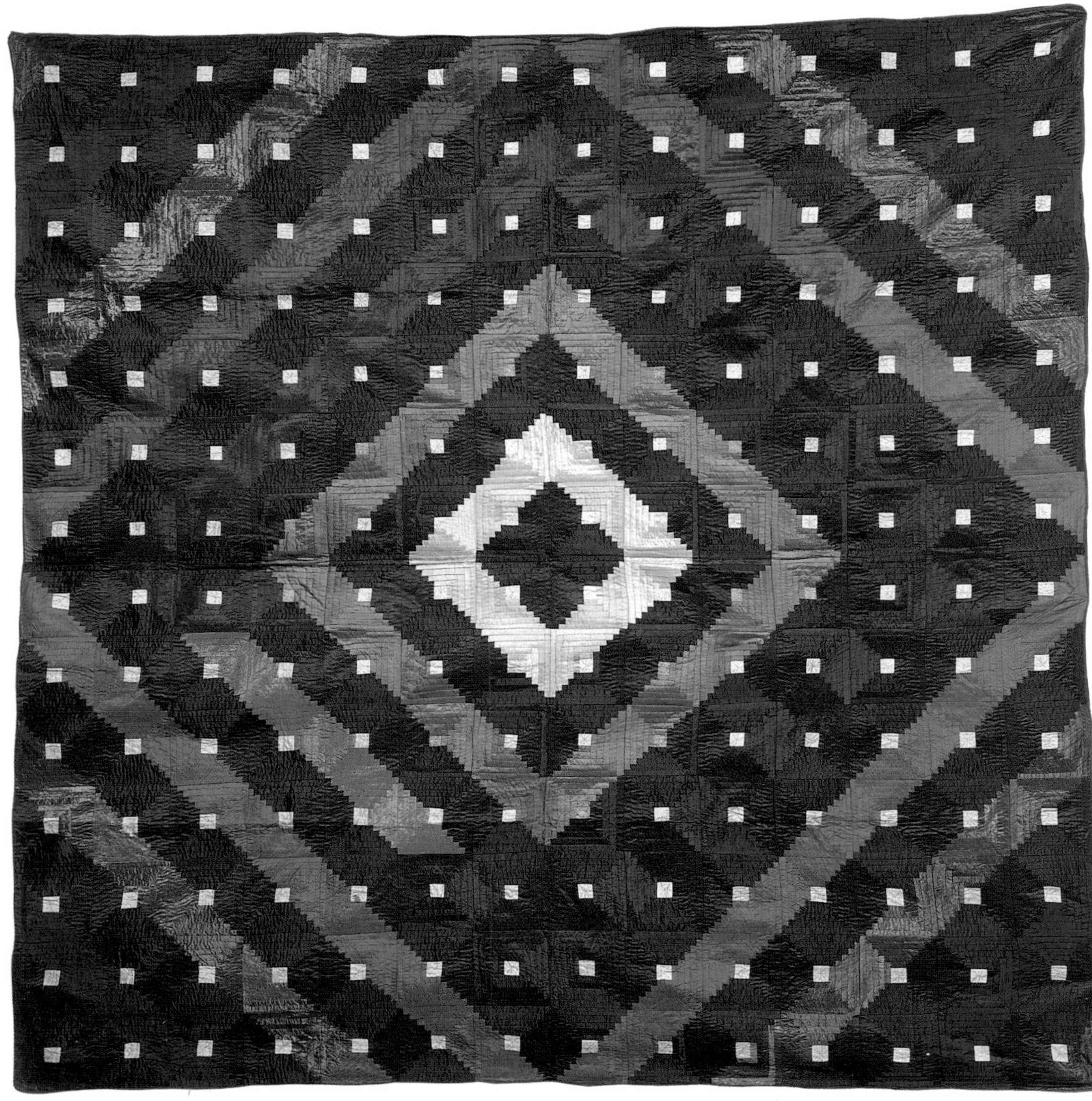

◄ **Log Cabin—Barn Raising Variation**

Artist unknown. c. 1870. Eastern Pennsylvania. Silk top with wool paisley backing; hand pieced and embroidered. 82 x 82 in. Collection of Ardis and Robert James.

The white centers of the blocks of this quilt each carry a hand-stitched star. This quilt's use of white for the block centers and its rather odd overall color palette set it apart from less inventive Log Cabin designs. The Barn Raising variation of the Log Cabin was so named because its alternating dark and light pattern resembles a barn's post-and-beam framework.

Today's quiltmakers continue to find fresh ways to reinterpret these timeless patterns, incorporating contemporary fabrics and design influences. The Log Cabin is a favorite of some modern African-American quilters, whose slightly off-kilter variations on the theme have in turn inspired some art quilters to reexamine the pattern. Art quilters such as Nancy Crow and Liz Axford, who achieve extraordinary results with geometrically configured patterns, have explored the seemingly limitless resources of the Log Cabin design through the use of intense and unexpected color combinations, varied block sizes, and carefully orchestrated fabric choices. The Log Cabin seems indefatigable, destined to remain fresh as long as there are imaginative quiltmakers to play with its possibilities.

The Log Cabin evokes the spirit of Abraham Lincoln, who successfully mythologized his own beginnings to suggest his ties to the simple pioneering values of frontier America—honesty, hard work, humility, and liberty. In a sense, every Log Cabin quilt represents a keeping of faith with the martyred Lincoln, the Union he preserved, and the American values he came to represent in the popular mind. Indeed, the carefully stacked logs and predictably repeating blocks may be seen as hopeful metaphors for the rebuilding of the Union itself.

All Log Cabin quilts are organized in repeating block formats. Each block is built around a small central square of material, which is often made of red cloth to symbolize the warm glow of the "cabin's" hearth fire. The color chosen for the central square is almost always repeated throughout the quilt as a unifying element. Working from the center of the block, strips, or "logs," of graduated length are laid down tightly side by side to form the block. Most Log Cabins are not strictly pieced but, rather, sewn to a ground of muslin or other backing using a combination of pieced and appliqué methods called pressed piecing. After the center block is laid, each succeeding rectangle is hemmed on one side, laid on top of the neighboring piece, and sewn to the ground. This overlapping system, which requires careful measuring so that the edges match, is continued until the block is complete. Most Log Cabin quilts employ cotton, although some quilters have used wool, silk, velvet, and satin. Log Cabins are rarely quilted because the many seams of the tightly constructed blocks do not require the extra structural support.

The size of the individual blocks can vary enormously from quilt to quilt. And, depending on how the logs and blocks are organized, with the resulting patterns of light and dark colors, a virtually endless number of design variations can be achieved. The Log Cabin family of patterns contains a number of subsets, simply and evocatively named for the way the blocks are organized to form the overall visual pattern: Light and Dark, Barn Raising, Straight Furrow, Courthouse Steps, Clocks, Streak of Lightning, and Windmill Blades or Pineapple.

If the Log Cabin pattern exemplifies order, simplicity, and union, the crazy, on the other hand, represents a Lewis Carroll–like image of disorder, complexity, and dissolution. Crazy quilts offered a perfect counterpart to the late Victorian taste for opulently furnished and lavishly comfortable interiors, full of heavily ornamented furniture, taxidermic mounts, Oriental rugs, richly patterned wallpaper, exotic potted plants, and assorted bric-a-brac. Although some crazies are organized in block format, essentially grouping a number of miniature crazies into a whole, most are random compositions that cover the entire quilt top. Crazy quilts allowed women to give absolutely free rein to their imaginations, combining fabrics, colors, piece sizes and shapes, fancy embroidery stitches, and even paint in designs of sometimes wild, freely associated complexity. Although the arrangement of elements may appear haphazard, many crazies, if not most, were carefully planned. At the height of their popularity in the 1880s, crazy quilt patterns were even included in some popular magazines. Crazies flourished largely because of the vast array of manufactured cot-

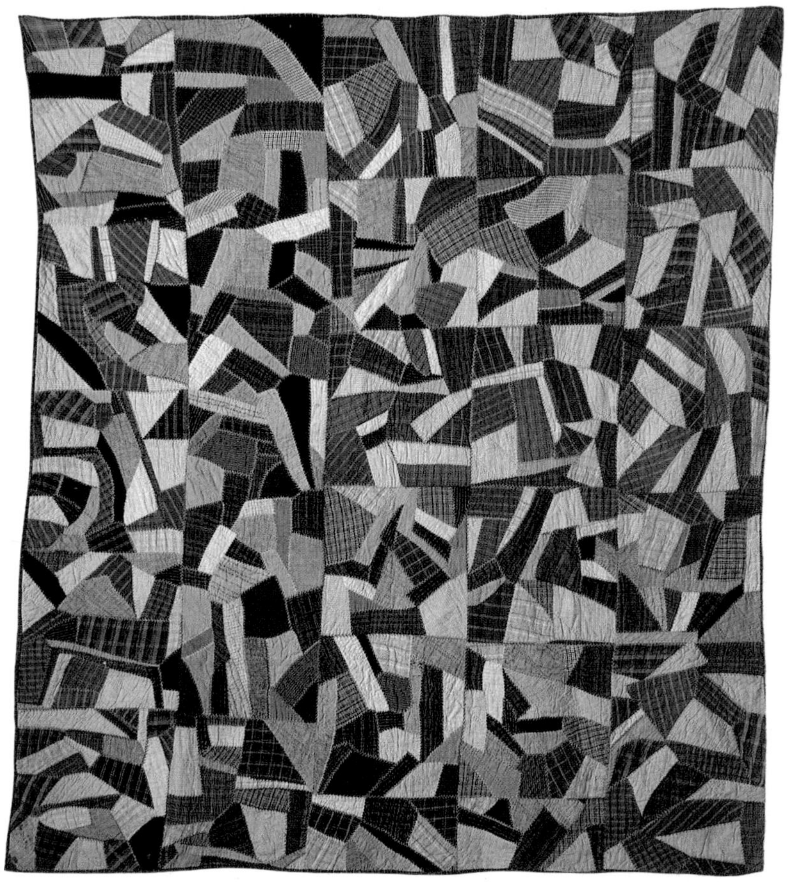

FLANNEL CRAZY ▶

Artist unknown. c. 1900. Minnesota. Cotton flannels; hand pieced and quilted. Collection of Ardis and Robert James.

The subdued, even somber, palette and patterned flannels of this crazy give it a very different feel from those made with brightly hued and more exotic fabrics.

tons and especially fancy silk dress fabrics available in the late nineteenth century. Quiltmakers reveled in the abundance of fabric choices, and every wild and crazy quilt was the joyful expression of that liberating freedom.

To Victorians the word *crazy* not only meant wild, mad, or insane, as is generally true today, but it also suggested crazed, meaning broken or splintered, as with glass or china. The description thus appropriately reflected both the quilts' irregular designs and their prominent decorative embroidery stitches, which joined the crazy pieces with jagged, spidery patterns. Contemporary magazines naturally delighted in playing on words, warning quilters not to be driven "crazy" by the complexity of the work.

Like Log Cabins, crazy quilts were rarely actually quilted. Indeed, the majority of them are unfilled tops rather than quilts in the strictest sense of the word. When they were lined, the layers were usually tied rather than quilted together. Most crazies were made strictly as decorative pieces or throws and were not intended to function as bedcovers. Crazies are generally relatively small in size, made to cover only a sofa back, table top, or lap. In addition, the use of fragile silks made fine quilt stitching extremely difficult and everyday use impractical.

Overtly nostalgic and sentimental, crazy quilts can serve as scrapbooks, recalling specific historical or family events, beloved family pets, heroes, holidays, and celebrations. They can incorporate and preserve bits of fabric drawn from family and friends, a piece of this family member's dress or that one's tie, lace collar, or apron. Embroidered names or verses can also add to the complex surface of the crazy. Many crazy quilts represent unique and often highly personal visions. They are small worlds of their own, created as stays against the powerfully divisive forces of the outside world.

Crazy quilts also reflect late Victorian society's new fascination with Japan and its traditional arts. The Japanese Pavilion was one of the greatest hits of the 1876 Centennial Exposition in Philadelphia, attracting nearly ten million visitors. Americans who had no previous exposure to Japan and its culture were mesmerized by the highly sophisticated objects they encountered at the exposition. Articles in popular magazines fueled interest in Japan, and Japanese clothing, fans, paper lanterns, and other trademark artifacts were quickly appropriated by American advertisers, designers, and entrepreneurs. Japanese prints, ceramics, textiles, lacquered wooden work, and other arts and crafts became extremely popular. The asymmetrical, off-balance look of many Japanese prints exerted tremendous influence on artists as diverse as Winslow Homer and Edgar Degas in the final decades of the century, opening up and validating new design approaches. Japanese design had a similarly liberating effect throughout the general population, who found it fresh, exotic, and exciting. Quilters no longer felt restricted to the use of regularly shaped and evenly spaced pieces as required by conventional block piecing; the rigid, rational geometry of the West was for a time replaced with the perceived mystery and irregularity of the Orient.

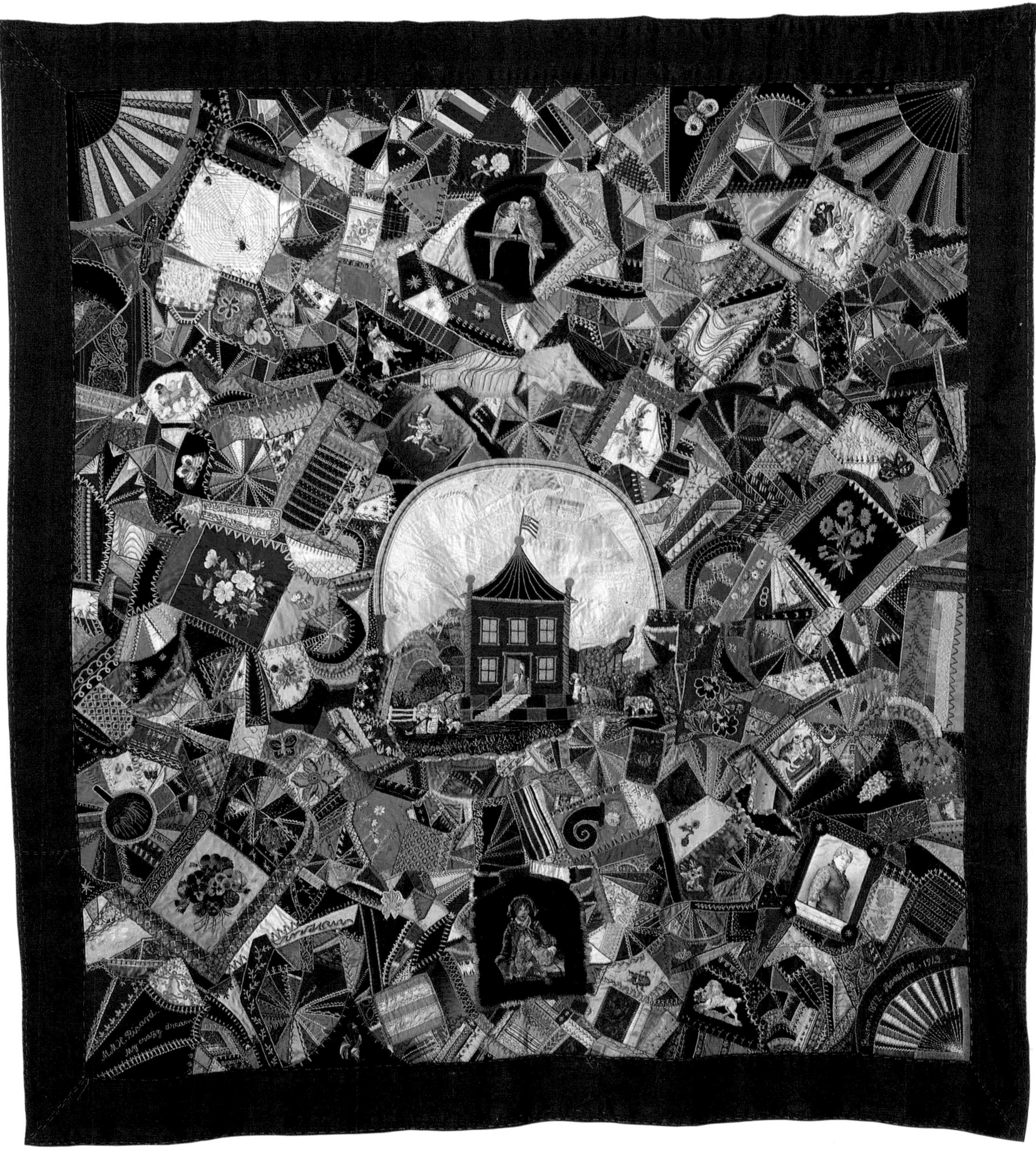

▲ **My Crazy Dream**

M.M. Hernandred Ricard. 1877–1912. Boston and Haverhill, Massachusetts. Embroidered silks. 65 x 60 in. Collection of Ardis and Robert James.

This quilt's dates span the crazy quilt era. M.M. Hernandred Ricard included a picture of herself in the lower right corner of her marvelously free and roiling composition and signed and titled the quilt in embroidery stitch at bottom left.

The Centennial Exposition marked a milestone not just for crazies, but for all quilts and quilters. Hundreds of quilts were exhibited at the fair. Never before had so many American women gathered in one place and never before had they admired each others' work on so vast a scale. For the first time, American women were able to realize collectively, albeit unconsciously, that quilts were a connecting thread between them, and to appreciate the quilt as a hallmark of their ordinary but nonetheless meaningful lives. The Centennial Exposition's exhibits elevated pride in America, American invention, American technological advances, and American workmanship to unprecedented heights. These forces, combined with the availability

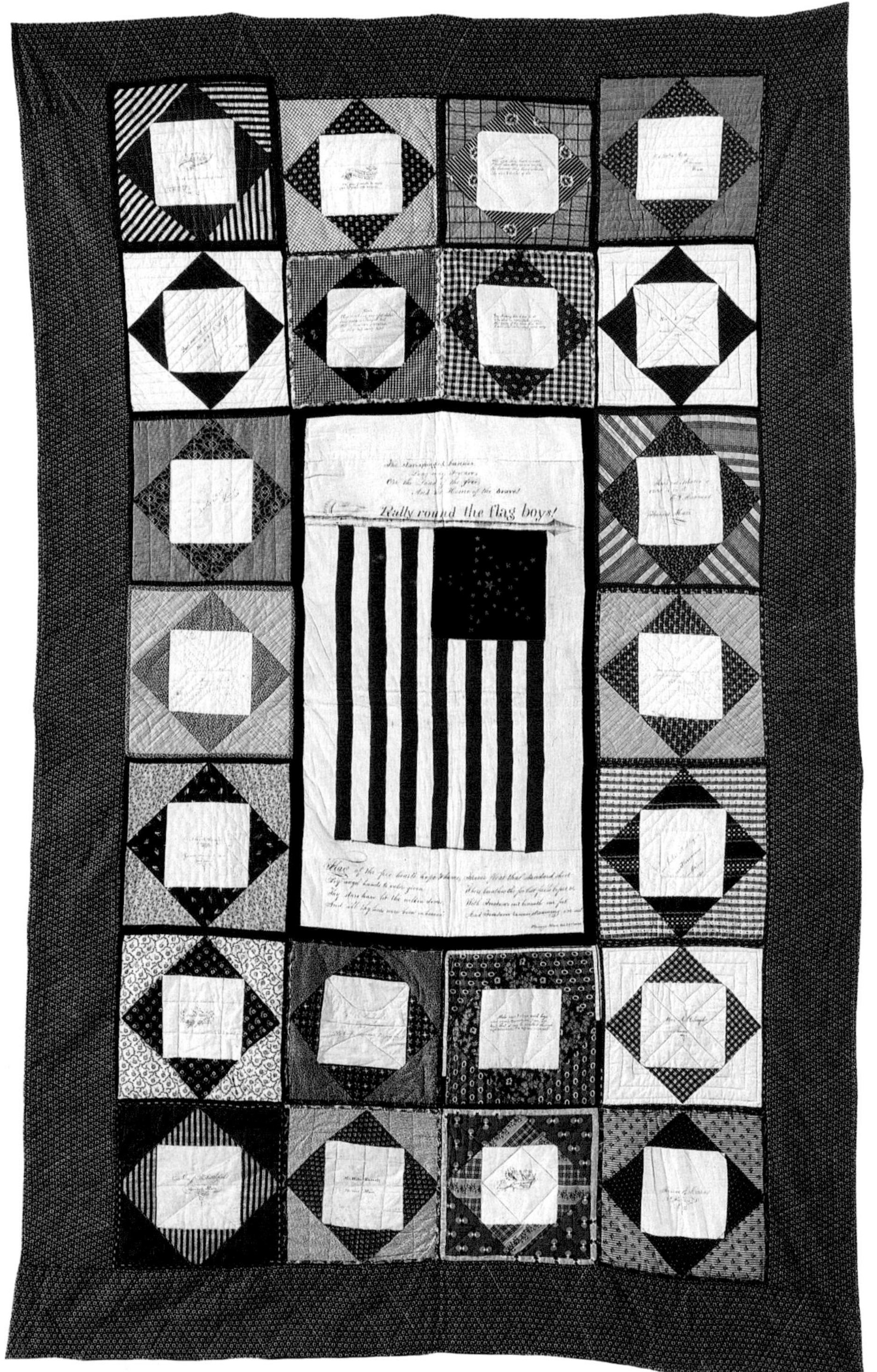

◂ **Civil War Veteran's Quilt**

Artist unknown. c. 1865. Florence, Massachusetts. Hand-pieced cottons; inked inscriptions. 85 x 53 in. Private collection.

This patriotic quilt, made to fit a soldier's narrow cot, was one of thousands made by women during the Civil War for use on the field or in hospitals. Inscribed above the flag is the last verse of "The Star Spangled Banner"—"The star spangled banner/Long may it wave/O'er the land of the free/And the home of the brave"—and entered in larger letters, "Rally Round the Flag Boys."

of the sewing machine and the enormous range of fabric choices, helped to launch an era of creativity and invention in the last quarter of the nineteenth century so remarkable that many quilt historians see this period as the Golden Age of American quiltmaking.

Social reform also exerted a powerful influence on the direction and importance of quiltmaking. Throughout the second half of the nineteenth century and into the the early years of the twentieth century, quilts were associated with the full range of women's social reform activities, including abolition, Civil War relief, fund-raising for benevolent causes, missionary work, and temperance. Beginning in the 1830s, women sponsored fairs to raise money for the abolitionist cause and sold quilts as well as baked goods and other homemade products to support their belief in the anti-slavery movement. Throughout the nineteenth century women also gathered together in church groups to make fund-raising quilts to support missionary work among the "heathen," while missionaries taught quiltmaking and other domestic skills to newly converted African-Americans, Hawaiians, and American Indians. During the Civil War, Ladies Aid and Sewing Societies in both the North and the South provided thousands of quilts to soldiers and hospitals in need of bedcoverings. In the northern states women organized great Sanitary Fairs in major cities to raise money in support of hospital relief, and quilts were a cornerstone of these highly successful fund-raisers. The sale of quilts also benefitted the Women's Christian Temperance Movement, founded in 1874 and by far the largest and best organized women's movement of the nineteenth century. Its empowering solidarity led directly to the battle for suffrage and other women's rights in the early twentieth century, and it gave women the courage to make themselves, rather than some outside party, the cause.

By the beginning of the new century, however, interest in traditional handcrafts had waned and quiltmaking, so much an integral part of the success of the early women's movements, fell from favor as a creative activity. Quilts were considered old-fashioned and were associated with an earlier, more rural America; the majority of women who could do so bought their bed-coverings in stores. When they were discussed, quilts were often romaticized and identified as a quaint, make-do art of "our great-grandmothers." Such influential suffragettes as Abigail Duniway of Oregon saw quilts and other needlework as symbols of the old order and the oppression of women. Innovation came to a standstill as most quiltmakers looked nostalgically back to the past for their inspiration. Patterns, which were published in such glossy new women's magazines as *Women's Home Companion* and *The Modern Priscilla*, became simpler and more formulaic. However, rural and poor women all over the country continued to make fresh and creative quilts. And within culturally isolated groups like the Amish of Pennsylvania and the Midwest, quilting remained a highly valued art.

A renewed, more practical interest in quiltmaking—as a way of saving money— resulted from the calamitous economic downturn toward depression of the late 1920s. Quiltmaking enjoyed a tremendous creative revival during the depression years of the 1930s. Many traditional patterns were reinterpreted and given a fresh look when they were worked in the light, breezy pastel colors fashionable at the time. Newspapers and women's magazines, designed to appeal to thrifty and resourceful homemakers, printed patterns that could be cut out or copied, and a number of companies offered do-it-yourself quilt kits, complete with fabric marked with the proper shapes ready to be cut and sewn. Many new patterns were also devised. Decorative and often elaborate floral appliqués featuring realistically rendered contemporary flowers such as morning glories, irises, and pansies were especially popular. Other designs incorporated such symbols of the modern age as airplanes, automobiles, and even Mickey and Minnie Mouse, or reflected the clean, abstract, machine-age geometry of the Art Deco style.

The Chicago World's Fair of 1933, held in the midst of the Great Depression, was the site of the largest quilt show ever held.

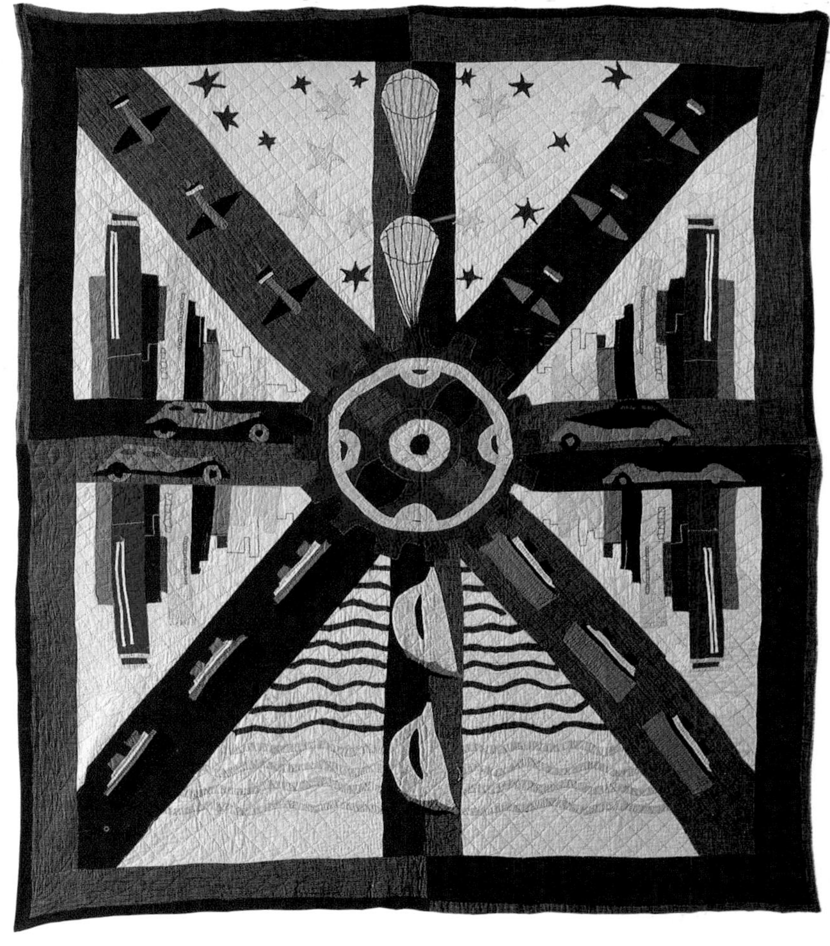

The Century of Progress ▶

Artist unknown. c. 1933. Ohio. Cottons; appliquéd and quilted. 84 x 74 in. Private collection.

This quilt follows the theme of the 1933 Chicago World's Fair with representations of automobiles, airplanes, ocean liners, parachutes, and other advances in modern transportation. Air travel is represented in the upper half of the quilt, while cars drive across its center, and images of water transportation fill the bottom half.

Sears, Roebuck and Company, the country's leading retailer, organized a contest and offered $7,500 in prize money; $1,200 was to be awarded to the finest quilt entered. Over 25,000 women submitted quilts to local and regional contests around the country, and the thirty finalists were put on exhibit in the Sears pavilion at the fair. The 1933 fair also celebrated the city of Chicago's centennial and was billed as "The Century of Progress Exposition." Quiltmakers were encouraged to create quilts on this theme and, in addition to the many traditional patterns that were displayed, many "modern" designs which reflected contemporary notions of industrial progress appeared among the entrants. About 125 of the quilts entered in the Sears contest have been rediscovered in recent years, and these surviving quilts provide a fascinating glimpse at the tastes and ideas of the time.

Commercialism and mass marketing also effected profound changes in quiltmaking in the 1930s, broadening its audience tremendously. A year after the World's Fair, Stearns and Foster, a leading retailer of cotton batting, sent a booklet called *The Romance of Quilt-Making Sales* to its retailers around the country. It began:

> *Today quiltmaking has a universal appeal.The best evidence of this is in the editorial content of the magazines and newspapers which women read. Four years ago it was only the small town magazines which published quilt articles. Today, these small town magazines are equalled, if not surpassed, in the quilt material published by great national women's magazines and metropolitan newspapers with millions of aggregate circulation. Recent surveys show that at least 400 metropolitan newspapers are publishing quilt material regularly. A Gallup survey in six large cities shows further that the quilt article is the most popular Sunday feature—32% of the women reading it. Many of these newspapers have sponsored quilt shows and had attendances numbering in the tens of thousands. This past summer even witnessed the First National Quilt Show with quilts entered from all states of the Union. [This was, of course, the Sears contest at the Chicago World's Fair.]*

The first broad public stirrings of scholarly and collector interest in American antiques and folk art began in the 1920s. The so-called Colonial Revival championed and popularized the early American look in home decorating, and Americans began to fill their homes with antique and reproduction Windsor chairs, hooked rugs, and hand-blocked wallpapers. *The Magazine Antiques* published its first issue in 1922 and provided a forum for historians and collectors. The Metropolitan Museum opened its American wing in 1924, formally validating the interest in things American. The first public exhibition of folk art also occurred in 1924, when Juliana Force, director of the Whitney Studio Club (forerunner of the Whitney Museum) and herself an avid collector of folk art, invited the painter Henry Schnackenberg to organize *Early American Art* at the club. The exhibition piqued interest, and later that year the prominent Boston antiques dealer Isabel Carleton Wilde began marketing folk art along with New England furniture and glass. In 1930 Newark Museum curator Holger Cahill curated *American Primitives* at Newark, an exhibition of folk paintings. In 1931 he followed with *American Folk Sculpture: The Work of 18th and 19th Century Craftsmen.* Late in 1932 Abby Aldrich Rockefeller, acting anony-

Basket of Flowers with Grapes ▶

Artist unknown. c. 1920. Hamburg, Pennsylvania. Cottons; appliquéd, folded, and embroidered on cotton sateen; hand quilted. 77 x 69 in. Collection of Ardis and Robert James.

The dozens of grapes in the border of this delicious example are each meticulously stuffed to add a three-dimensional effect to the bunches.

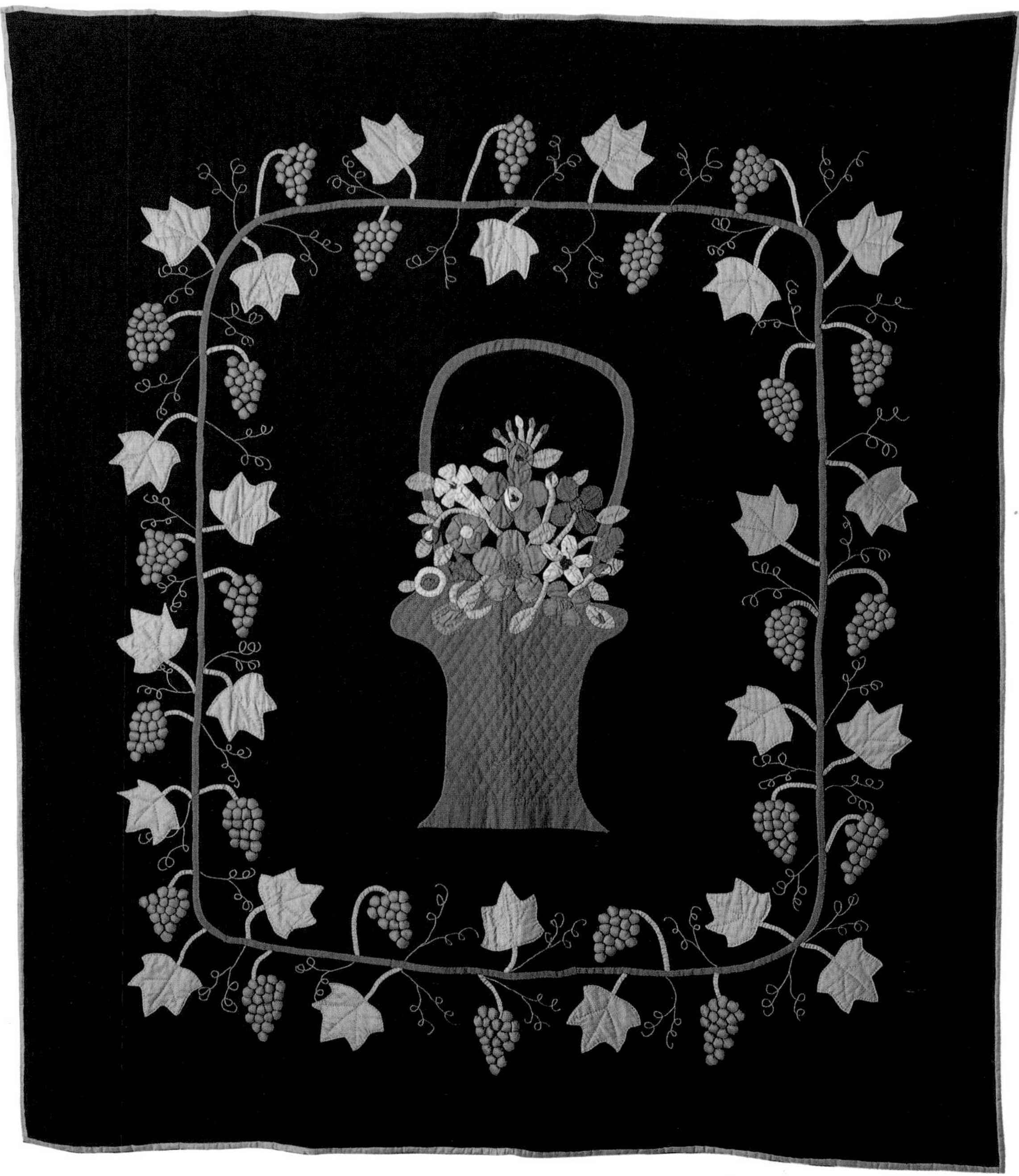

mously, loaned 174 objects from her collection to the Museum of Modern Art for *American Folk Art: The Art of the Common Man in America*, also curated by Cahill, who was serving as acting director of the museum. In 1933 and 1934 this exhibition exposed many to folk art for the first time as it traveled to six other institutions, including the Pennsylvania Museum of Art in Philadelphia, the Museum of Fine Arts in Boston, and the Rhode Island School of Design in Providence. At the same time, the WPA organized and funded the Index of American Design, which sent unemployed artists into the countryside to render examples of American crafts and folk arts, quilts among them.

Perhaps because they were still such a vibrant and evolving part of American life—still very much a living art—quilts lagged behind other American textiles such as hooked rugs and samplers in garnering attention from collectors and scholars. Relatively few people collected quilts until the late 1930s, and there were no quilts included in any of the seminal folk art shows mentioned above. Books on quilt history and art were far outnumbered by how-to books, and they still are. Perhaps the ratio between the two types of books can be read as an index of the relative health of the tradition. Two seminal books, Marie Webster's *Quilts, Their*

Story and How to Make Them, published in 1915, and Ruth Finley's *Old Patchwork Quilts and the Women Who Made Them*, published in 1929, set the early standards for quilt scholarship and remain basic books in any quilting library. Both authors made some mistakes, however; their educated guesses about the origins of patchwork are now known to have simply prolonged some romantic myths. Of course, only recently have these old assumptions been challenged by researchers who have access to many more quilts and much more data. For their time, both books were remarkably well researched. Books focusing on patterns, such as Ruby Short McKim's *One Hundred and One Patchwork Patterns*, first published in 1931, and Rose Kretsinger and Carrie Hall's *The Romance of the Patchwork Quilt in America*, published in 1935, fueled that decade's intense interest in traditional quilt patterns and their history. Kretsinger and Hall's book, for example, offered over seven hundred historic patterns gathered in the Midwest.

Beginning in the 1930s, a few pioneering collectors of Americana and folk art began to collect outstanding quilts. Among the most important early folk art collectors and by far the most important of early quilt collectors was Electra Havemeyer Webb, who later founded the Shelburne Museum in Shelburne, Vermont. In 1955 she wrote in *Art in America*:

My interpretation is a simple one. Since the word folk in America means all of us, folk art is that self-expression which has welled up from the hearts and hands of the people. The creators can be kin or strangers and they can be rich or poor, professional or amateur, but in America, and particularly in Vermont and all of New England, they are still known as "folks." Their work can be exquisitely wrought or it can be crude. We are apt to differ in our ideas as to whether it is truly art, and to what degree it is artistic. But

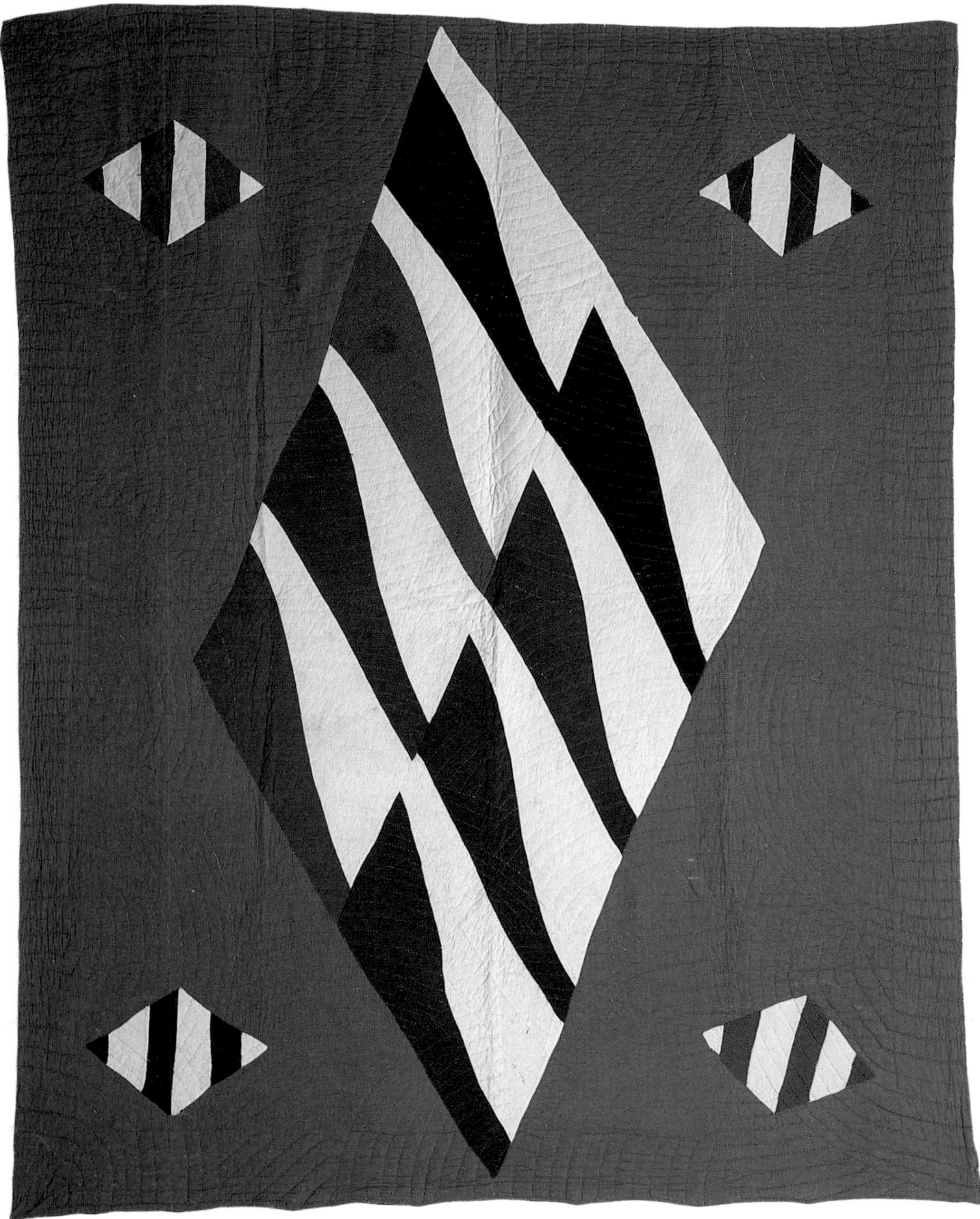

◄ **Abstract Diamonds**

Artist and region unknown. c. 1936. Cottons; hand pieced, appliquéd, and quilted. 86 x 70 in. Collection of Ardis and Robert James.

This simple pattern of pieced elongated diamonds reflects the influence of modern industrial design in its stripped-down, elemental abstraction. The quilt is dated by the inclusion of a Republican seal promoting the candidacy of Alf Landon, who ran unsuccessfully against Franklin D. Roosevelt in the presidential election of 1936.

Electra Webb (right), early quilt collector and founder of the Shelburne Museum, examines part of the museum's collection with her assistant, Lilian Baker Carlisle, c. 1957. ▶

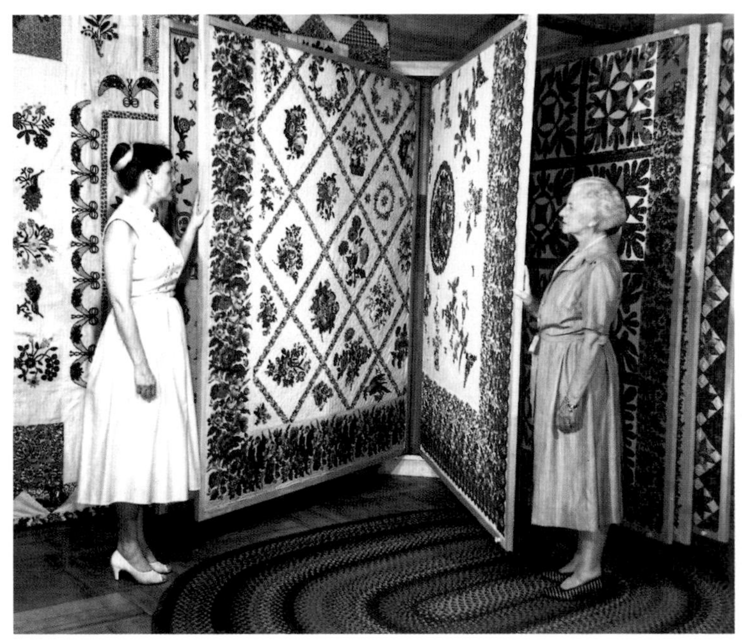

we must sense in all of the work properly identified as folk art the strong desire on the part of the people to create something of beauty. When our forefathers created it, they were expressing themselves and they were trying to transmit that feeling to the work itself. Perhaps the creators did not think of it as art, but I am one who has thought so for approximately fifty years.

Mrs. Webb, whose parents had been major collectors of European paintings, largely ignored the primitive paintings that had so captivated other early folk art collectors and instead concentrated her efforts on sculpture and textiles. She maintained a close personal and professional relationship for many years with the quilt collector, dealer, and author Florence Peto, from whom she purchased many fine quilts. Peto, the author of *Historic Quilts* (1939) and *American Quilts and Coverlets* (1949) and herself a quiltmaker of considerable talent, served as Mrs. Webb's principal quilt advisor throughout the 1940s and 1950s and helped build her remarkable collection of over four hundred historic bedcovers. Mrs. Webb's Shelburne Museum opened to the public in 1952 and from the beginning offered by far the largest and finest ongoing public exhibition of quilts available anywhere in the world. Shelburne served as a focal point for scholars and collectors of quilts throughout the 1950s and 1960s, and its excellent 1957 catalog *Pieced and Appliqué Quilts at Shelburne Museum* was one of the first museum publications on the subject.

Despite the efforts of people like Mrs. Webb, quiltmaking again fell from favor after World War II and remained largely an underground phenomenon until the 1960s. Thousands of women continued to make quilts though the 1950s, of course, but the great economic prosperity and material gains of the post-war years made handcrafted quilts once again undesirable, unnecessary, and unfashionable, and they were relegated to the lower and needier classes who could not afford to buy bedcovers. America stood alone, a towering economic giant, and its people's unprecedented material comfort and standard of living were the envy of the world. Interest in quiltmaking escalated again in the 1960s as the counterculture rejected the status quo and, in an effort to search for basic American values and ways to live, looked back to earlier times. With the nation's bicentennial on the horizon, the greatest and most sustained revival of all was gathering force. Quilts were about to become one of the key threads that would tie American women's search for the past and hopes for the future together.

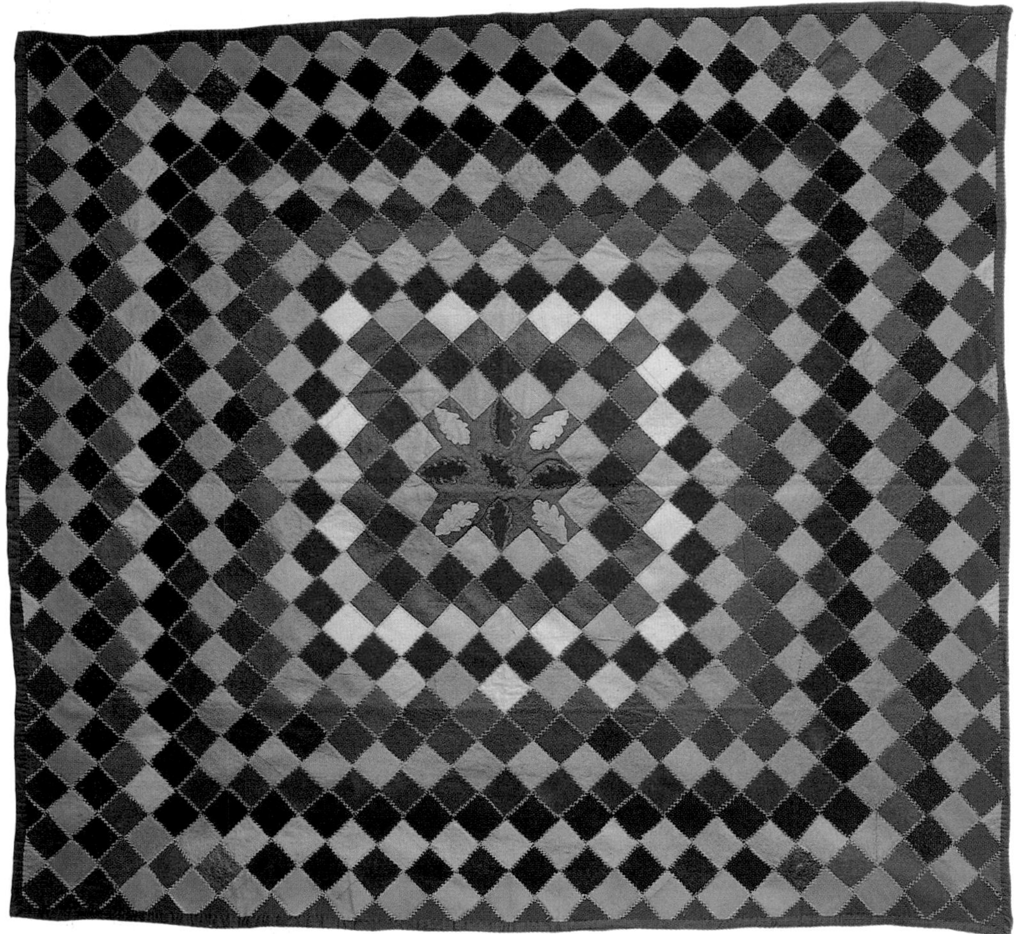

◄ Diamond Patch

Artist unknown. c. 1860. Possibly Ontario. Wool felts; hand pieced with blanket stitching, hand appliquéd with buttonhole stitching. 68 x 75 in. Collection of Ardis and Robert James.

Nine red and yellow appliquéd leaves are set on a bright green field at the center of this quilt and are surrounded by multiple borders pieced of solid-colored diamonds. The quilt is brightest at its center and becomes darker hued with each succeeding row.

Feathered Star and Oak Leaves ►

Mary A. Purdy. 1869. Springfield Center, New York. Cottons; hand pieced, appliquéd, and quilted. 90 x 74 in. The Shelburne Museum, Shelburne, Vermont.

Mary Purdy created a unique composition by extending the border motif of appliquéd oak leaves into the usually negative spaces between the pieced feathered star blocks. The bright yellow and green print fabric from which the leaves were cut contrasts sharply with the subdued brown stars. The oak, common to New York, has long been a symbol of quiet and abiding strength, longevity, and remembrance.

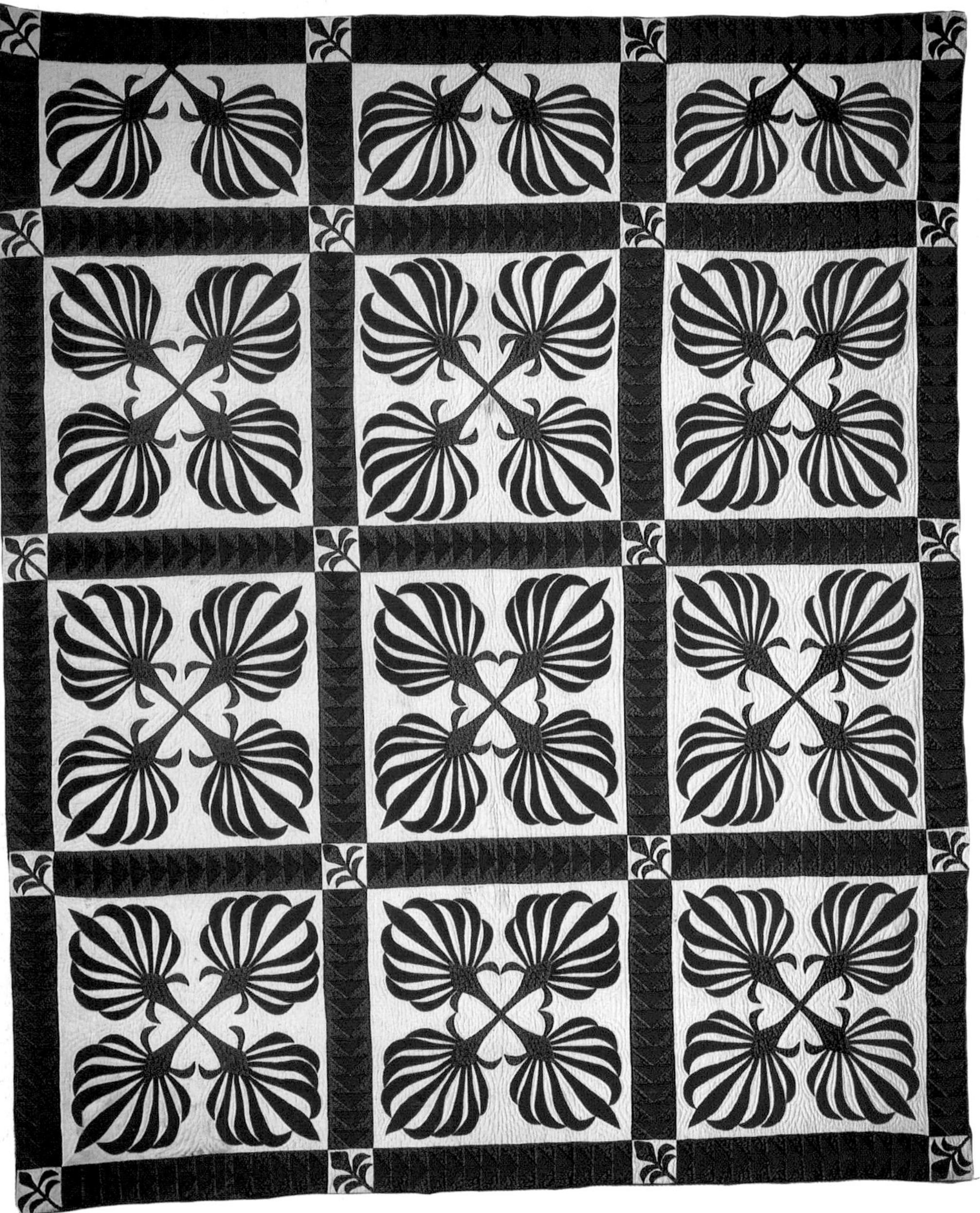

◄ Cotton Boll

Frances Johnston. c. 1860. Cherry Hill, North Carolina. Cottons; hand pieced, appliquéd, and quilted. 106 x 89 in. North Carolina Museum of History, Raleigh, North Carolina.

This richly colored and proudly defiant quilt, made by an elderly Southern woman near the beginning of the Civil War (Frances Johnson was born in 1782 and died in 1872), employs the cotton boll as its dominant motif. Cotton was, of course, the South's main crop and the crop upon which slavery was built. Ironically, the cotton harvested by the clearly undemocratic institution of slavery was essential to quiltmakers, who used it to create a uniquely democratic American art form. For reasons known only to the maker of this quilt, one of the rosebuds used in the corner blocks was deliberately turned in a different direction from the others.

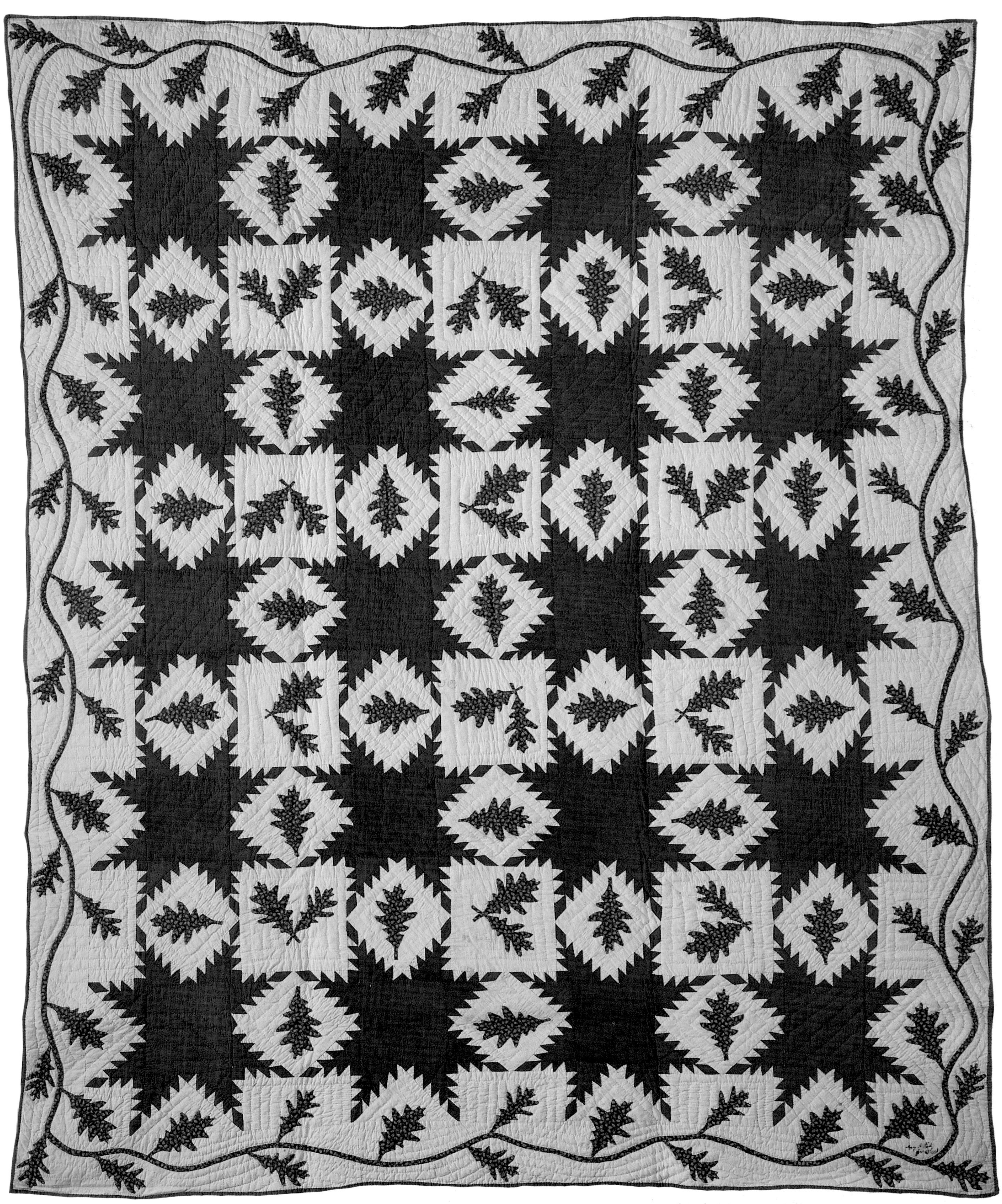

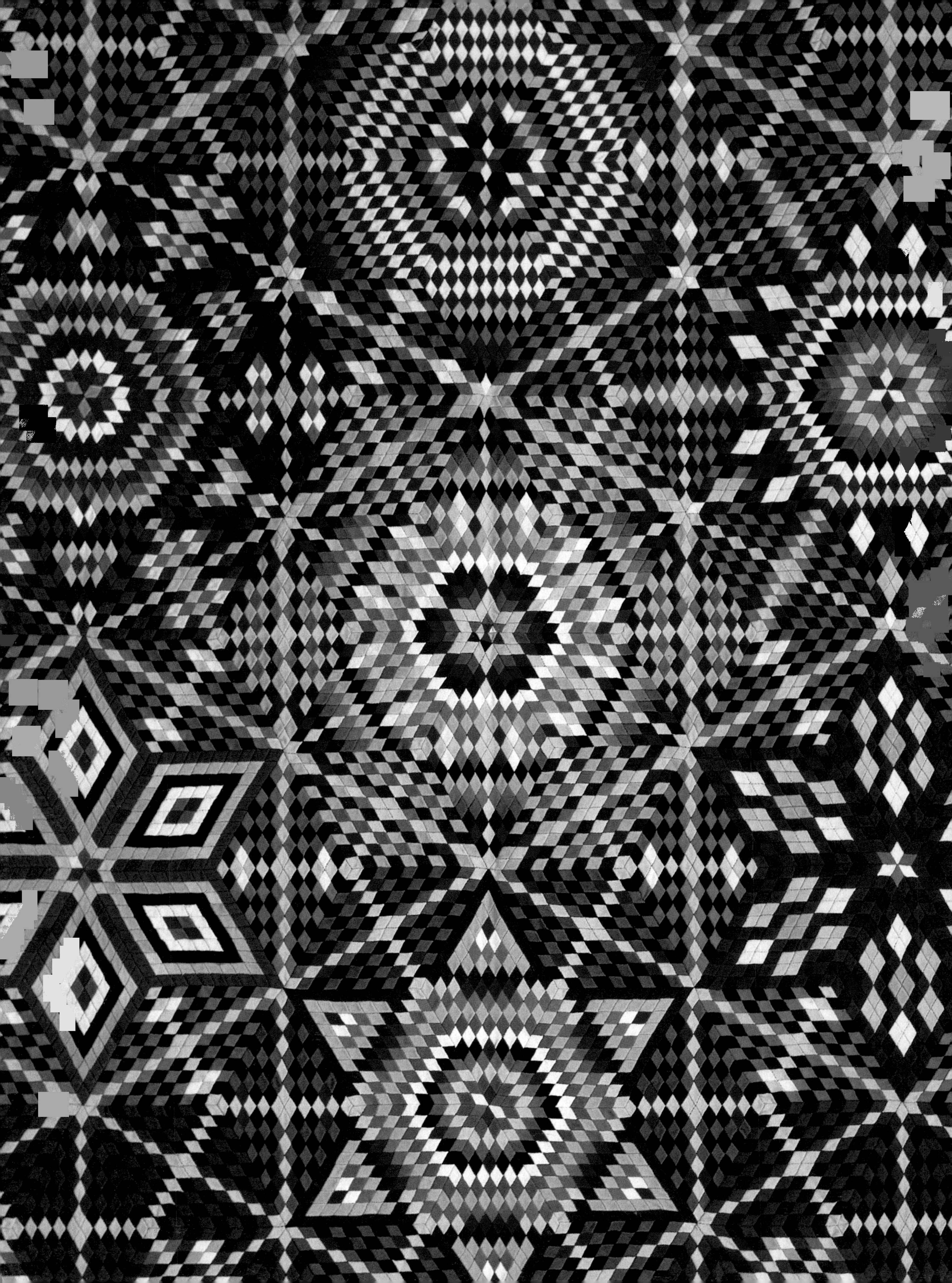

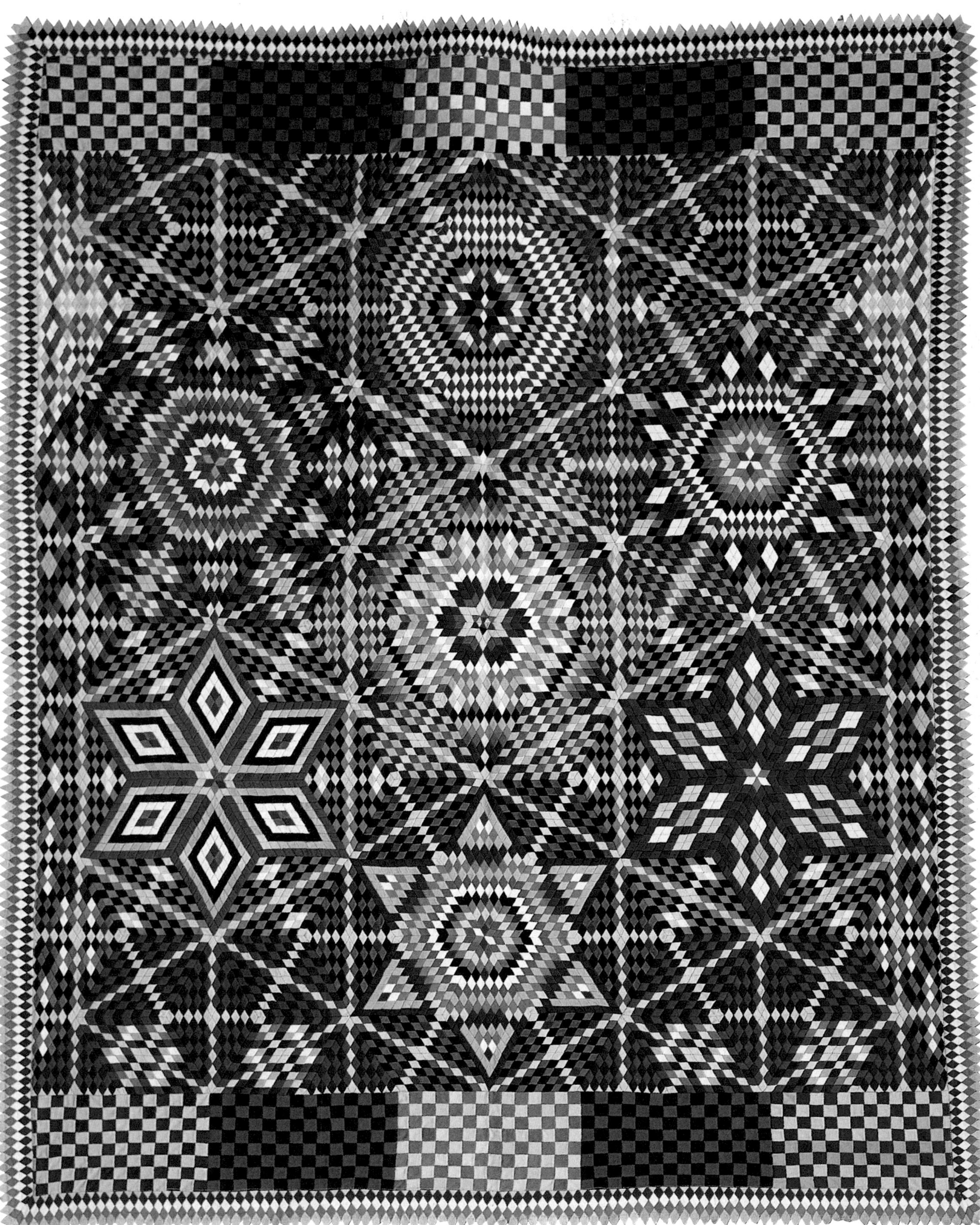

▲ STAR MOSAIC (◄ DETAIL)

Artist unknown. c. 1870. Found in Germantown, Pennsylvania. Wool flannels; hand pieced. 77 x 62 in. Collection of Ardis and Robert James.

Seven different large star designs form the center of this unusual and complex quilt, which is far more carefully organized than first impressions might suggest. The entire quilt top is made of tiny diamonds of flannel in a variety of colors. Hexagonal grids enclose the large stars, and the entire center of the quilt bustles with the activity of numerous small symmetries. Checkerboard patterns make up the top and bottom of the quilt, and the whole is framed with borders built from alternating rows of colored diamonds.

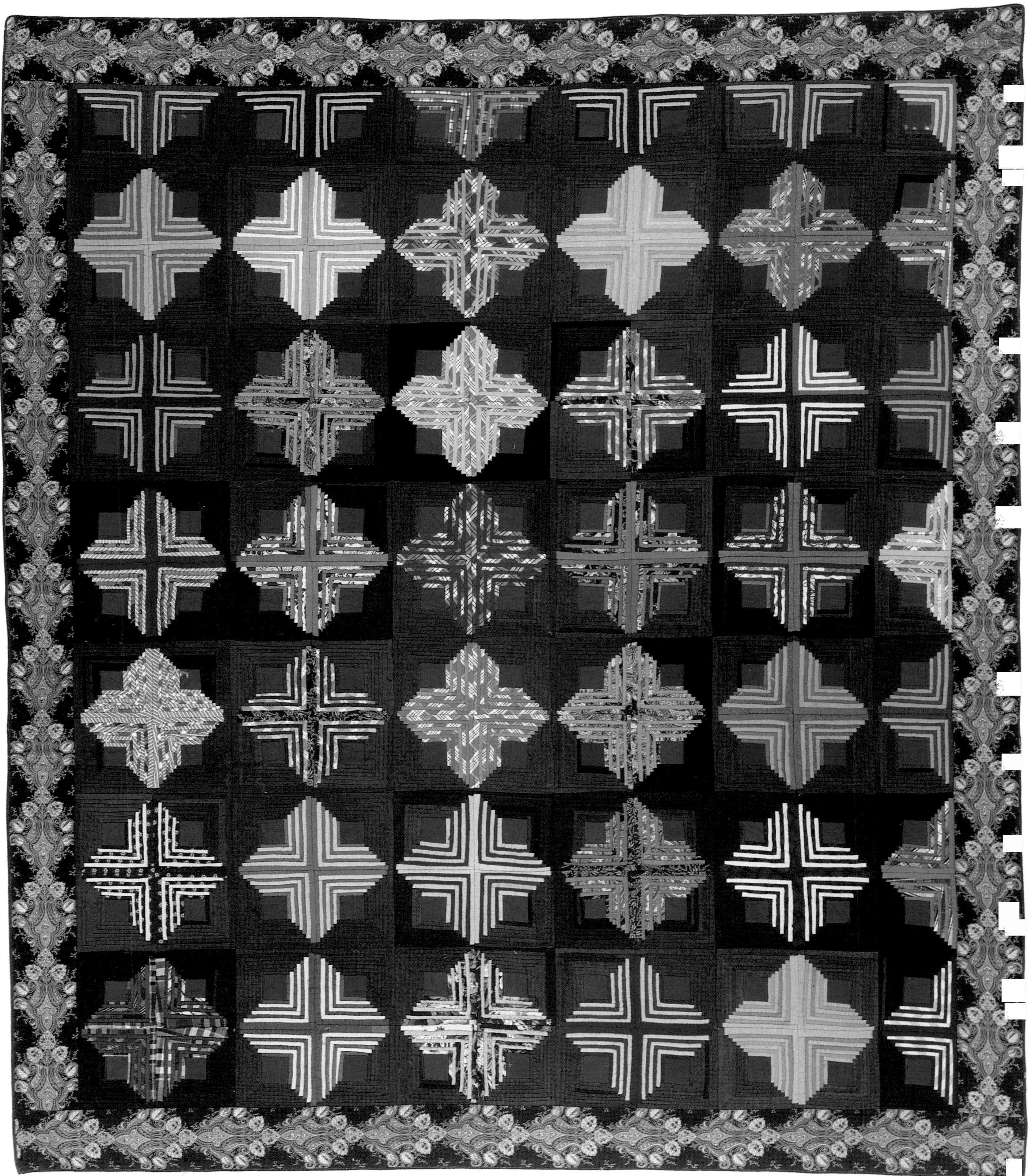

▲ **Log Cabin—Light and Dark Variation**

Artist unknown. c. 1875. Virginia. Wools and alpacas; hand pieced and quilted. 92 x 80 in. The Valentine Museum, Richmond, Virginia, gift of Mrs. Robert T. Barton, Jr.

The wide paisley print border that surrounds this dramatic Log Cabin variation is unusual but effective. Wool was not often used in Victorian-era quilts.

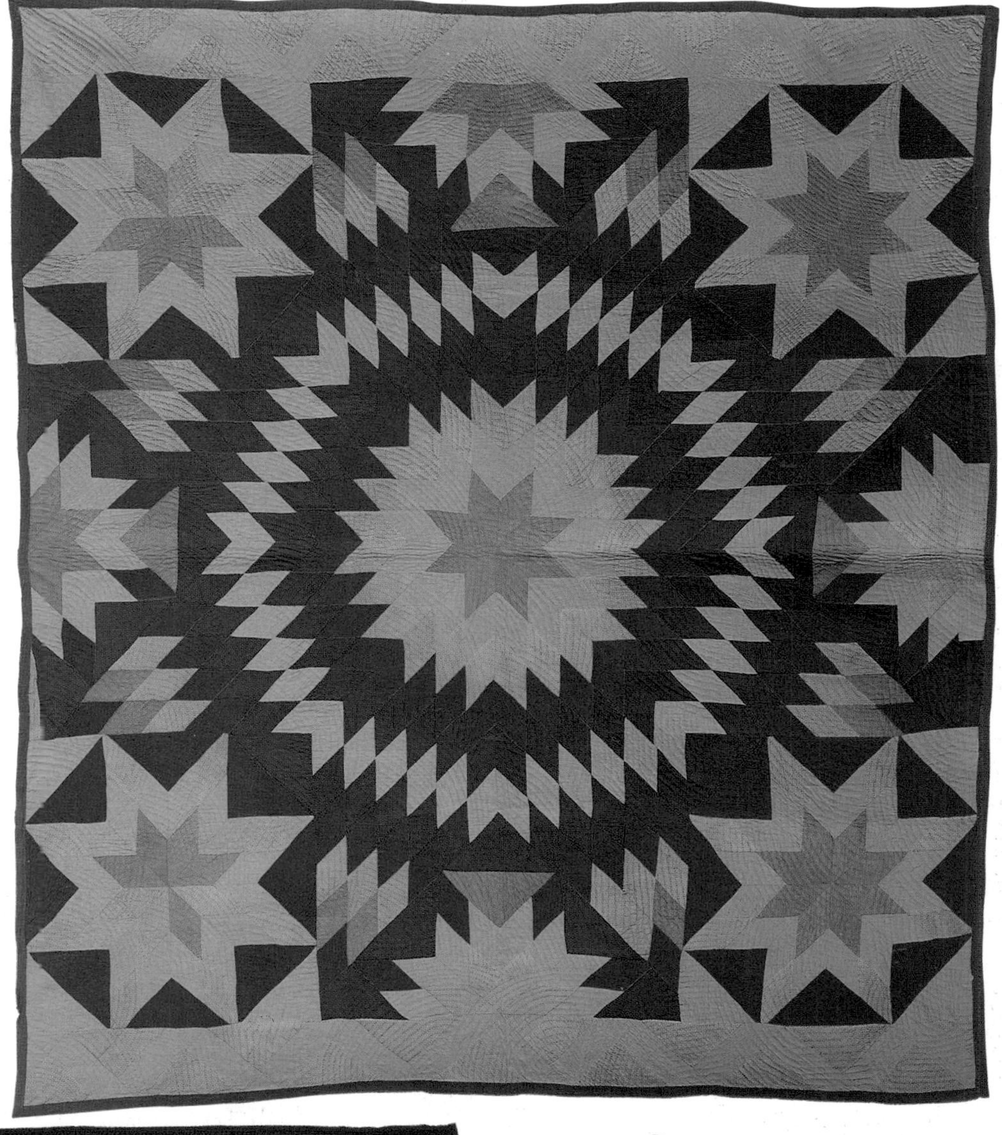

Blazing Star ▶

Artist unknown. c. 1880. Missouri. Cottons; hand pieced and quilted. 94 x 84 in. Collection of Ardis and Robert James.

The large star at the center of this dramatic quilt is cornered by four smaller eight-point stars set against red, and four half stars set against black. There is a blue and yellow zigzag border at top and bottom, and the whole explosive composition is contained within a narrow strip of red binding.

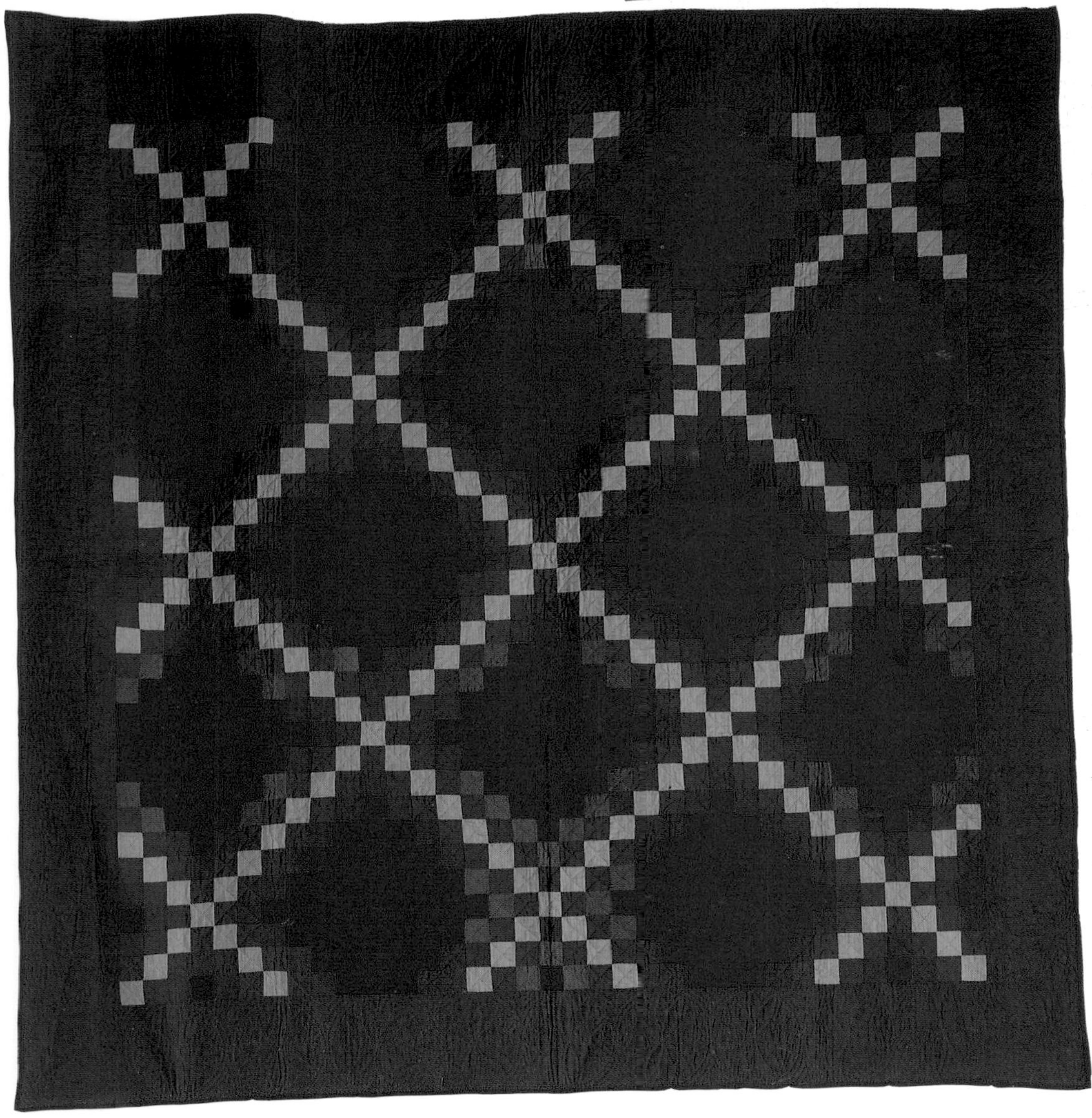

◀ Triple Irish Chain

Unknown Old Order Mennonite artist. c. 1870. Mifflin County, Pennsylvania. Cottons; hand pieced and quilted. 83 x 84 in. Collection of Ardis and Robert James.

This intensely colored quilt combines deeply saturated red, deep blue, deep green, and gold to spectacular effect. The unusual green color used here was achieved at home by dying cloth in a solution of walnut hulls.

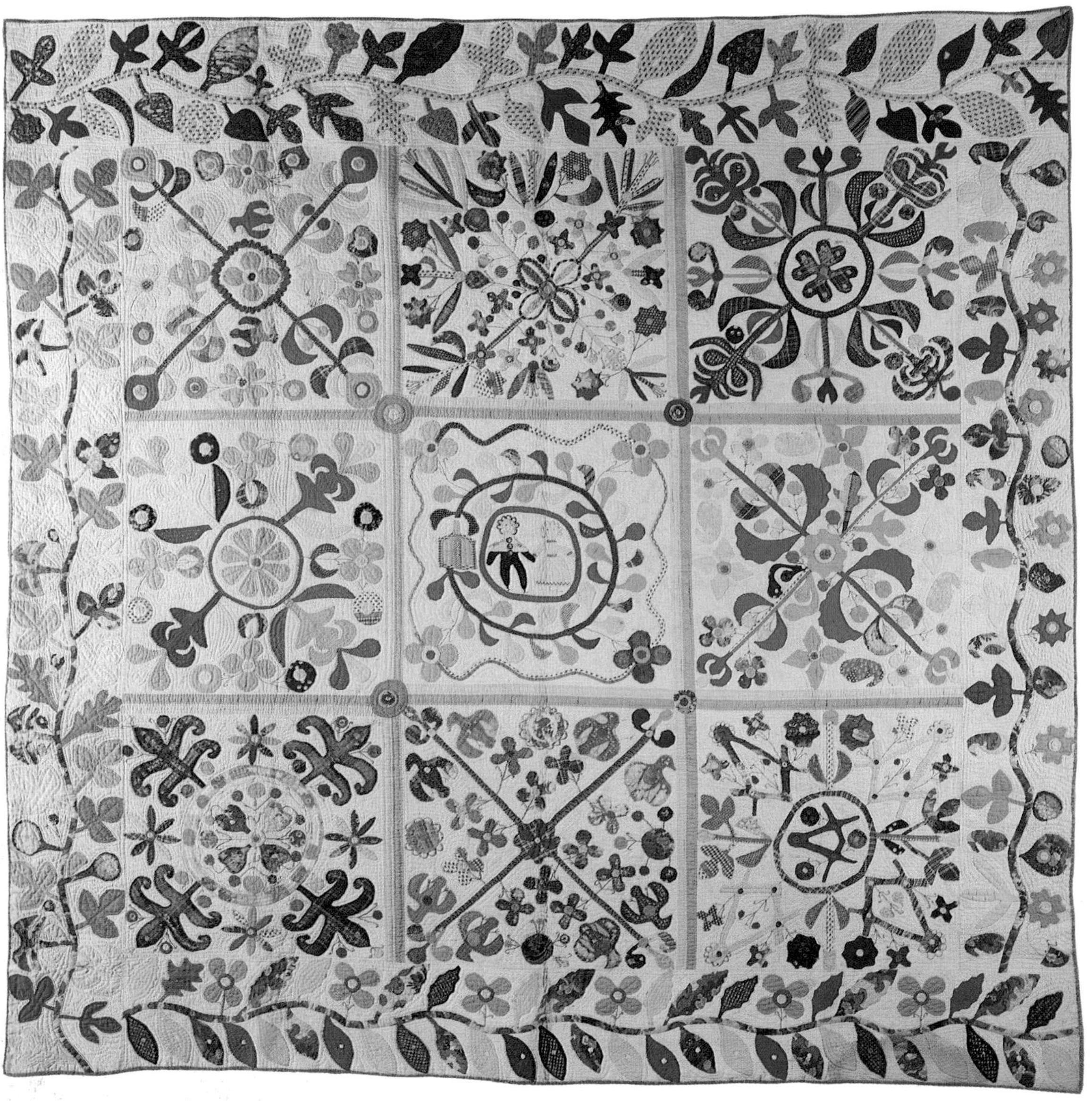

◄ **THE MARRIAGE QUILT**

Artist unknown. c. 1865. Staunton, Virginia, area. Cottons; hand appliquéd, embroidered, and quilted. 94 x 92 1/2 in. The Atlanta History Center, Atlanta, Georgia.

The five squares and five compasses depicted in the lower right-hand block of this complex appliqué quilt are symbols closely associated with Freemasonry, one of the most prominent of nineteenth-century America's many secret societies. Many, if not most, nineteenth-century American men were members of such fraternal organizations as the Masons, the Odd Fellows, and the Improved Order of Red Men. The stylized couple and church in the center block suggest the quilt was made to commemorate the marriage of an unidentified Lodge member.

◄ **ONEIDA ALBUM**

Members of the Oneida Community. 1873. Oneida, New York. Appliquéd cottons; embroidery, ink. 89 x 84 in. Collection of the Oneida Community Mansion House.

Oneida was a utopian community founded in 1847 by Vermonter John Humphrey Noyes. Like the Shakers, members of the Oneida community held all property in common. Unlike the celibate Shakers, however, they extended their communism to their sexual relations, practicing what Noyes called "Complex Marriage," a sort of regulated promiscuity. In 1873 community members, urged by Noyes's wife, made two album quilts. The community's newsletter reported on this member effort in March 1873: "Those who used to be active at 'quiltings' forty or fifty years ago say they never heard of a quilt like this. It is an 'album-bed-quilt' with the wildest variations, and we imagine that half a century hence it will be an interesting memorial of the industries and aspirations of the year 1873."

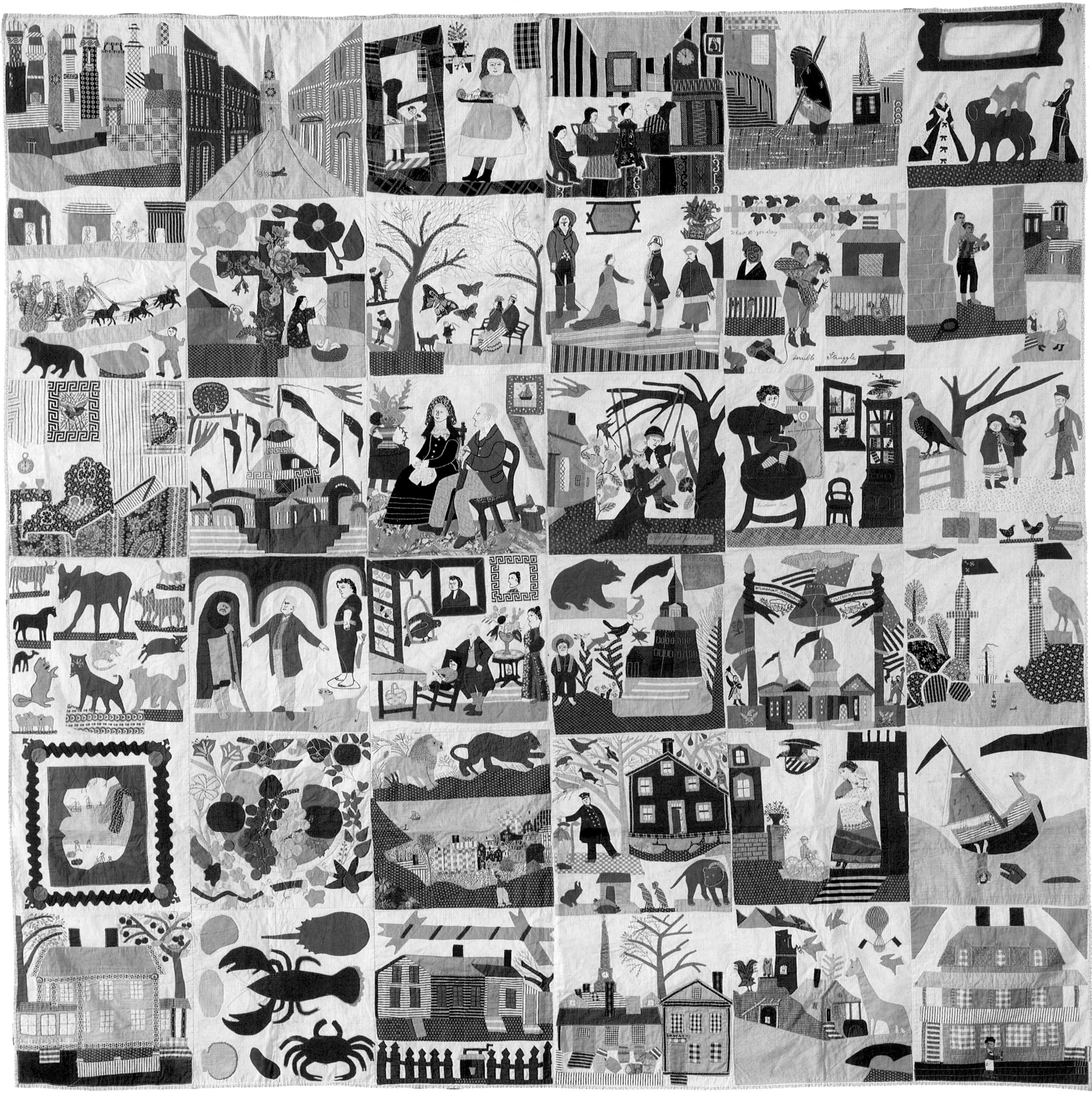

▲ **CENTENNIAL ALBUM**

Members of the Burdick/Childs family. c. 1876. North Adams, Massachusetts. Appliquéd cottons. 78 1/2 x 79 1/4 in. The Shelburne Museum, Shelburne, Vermont.

The thirty-six blocks of this remarkable album quilt can be broken into three main groups. People and stories make up the largest group, buildings along with three representations of the Philadelphia Centennial Exhibition of 1876 comprise the second group, and animals the third. The quilt is clearly the work of more than one hand and probably was made as a family project, perhaps after a visit to the Centennial Exhibition, an event that was attended by millions of Americans. The two "animal" blocks are much simpler and cruder than the others and were most probably done by a child. The quilt abounds with fun and good humor: amusing juxtapositions of scale appear within many of the blocks, and several of the story blocks carry titles such as "The Tiresome Boy," "My First Proposal," and " My Last Proposal." The fabrics are also cleverly chosen to suggest the textures of building materials, landscapes, picture frames, and clothing.

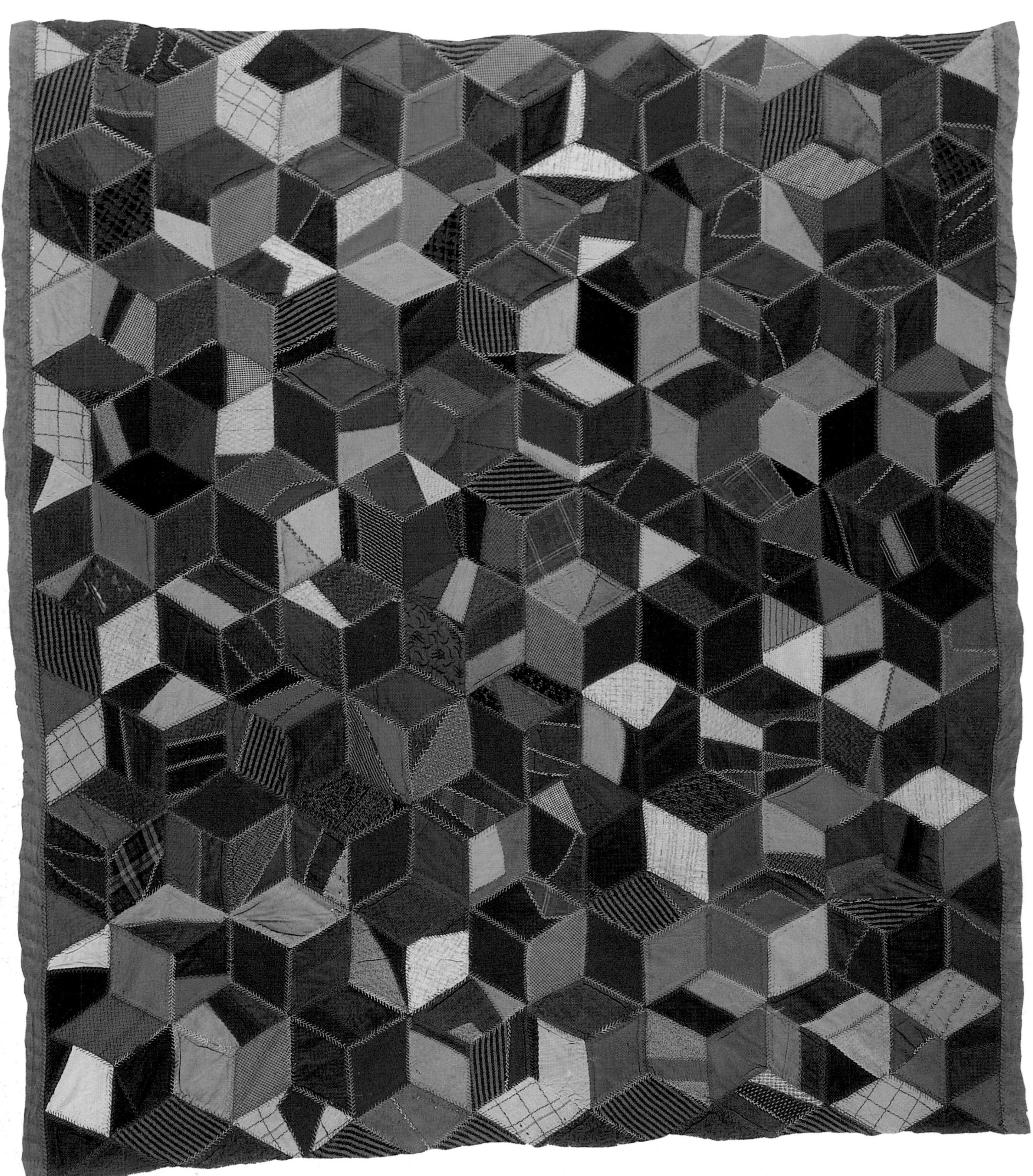

▲ **Crazy Tumbling Blocks (Detail ▶)**

Mary Noe Anderson. c. 1870. Logan County, Kentucky. Wools; hand pieced and embroidered. 83 x 74 in. The Kentucky Museum, Western Kentucky University, Bowling Green, Kentucky, gift of Mary Anderson Henry.

The Kentucky Museum owns nine quilts that, according to family members, were made by Mary Noe Anderson, who lived from 1844 to 1881. This unorthodox quilt combines traditional piecework with such typical elements of the crazy quilt as patterned fabric, oddly shaped pieces, and seams of prominent embroidery stitches.

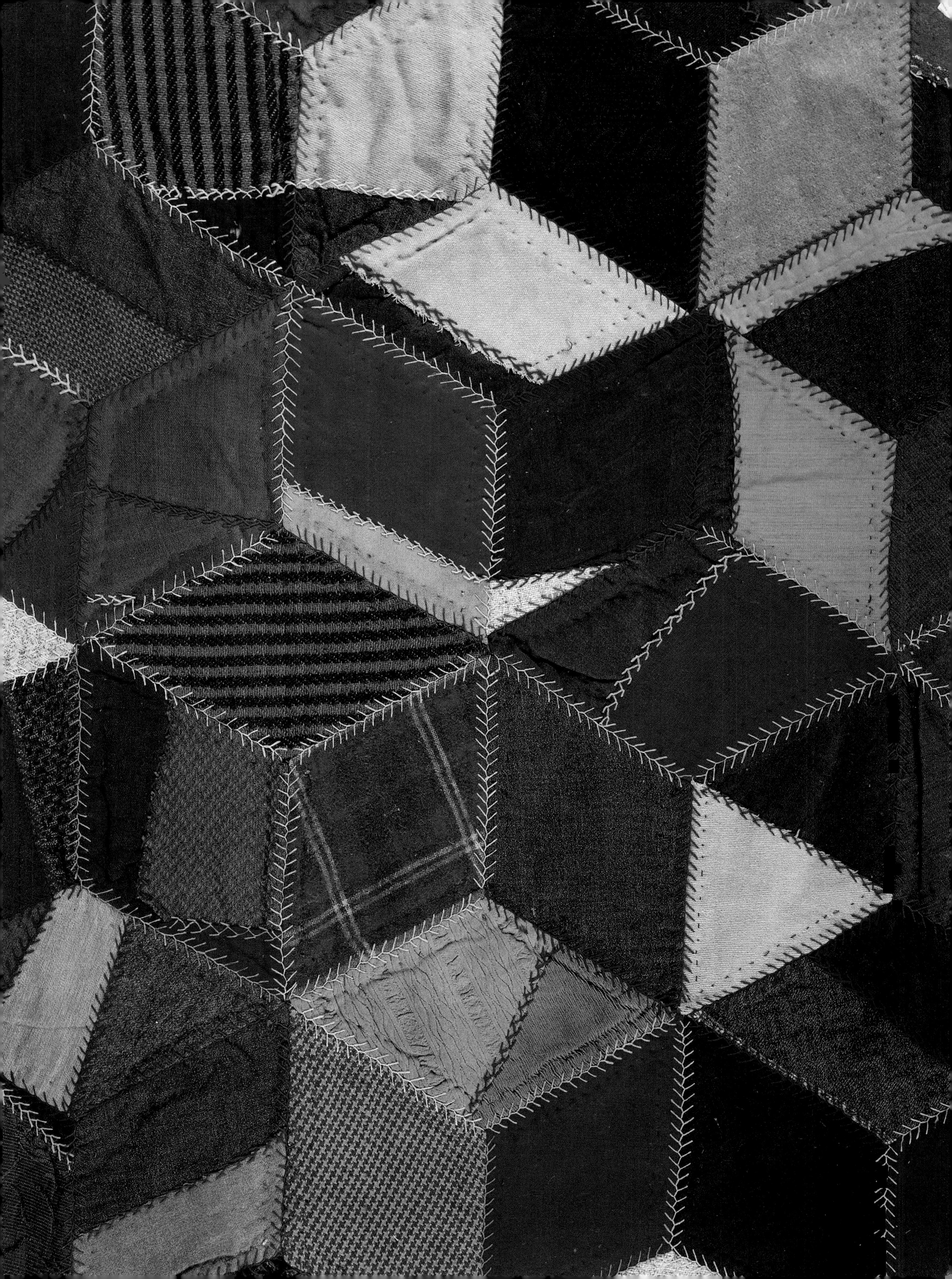

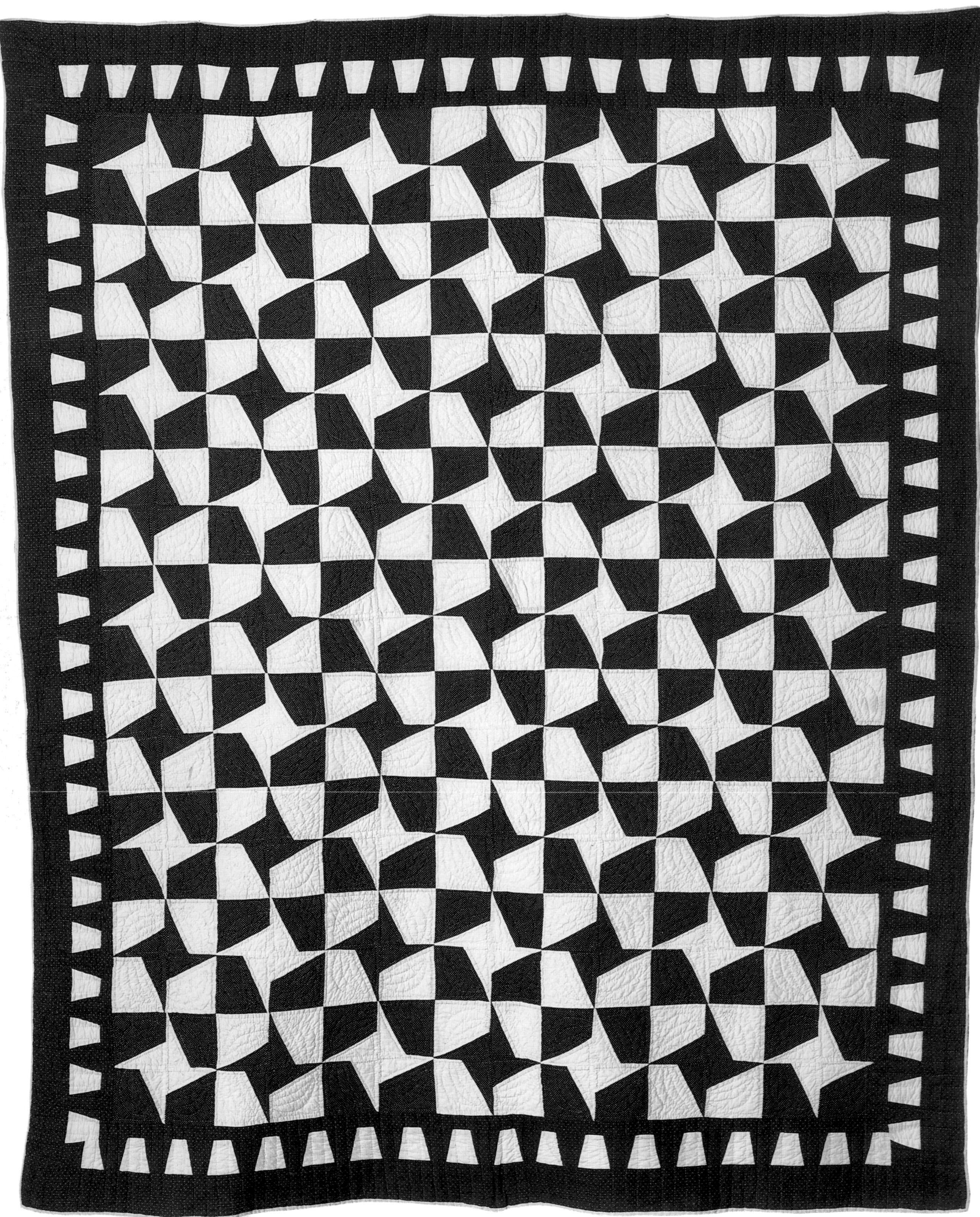

▲ **FOUR-POINT STAR**

Artist unknown. c. 1880. Indiana or Ohio. Cottons; hand pieced and quilted. 87 x 73 in. Collection of Ardis and Robert James.

The sixty-three blocks here reverse images in alternating dark blue and white fabric to create a very powerful positive/negative rhythm. The wide, seven-inch border is made up of a slightly lighter blue pin dot material with an inner border of pieced white cone shapes.

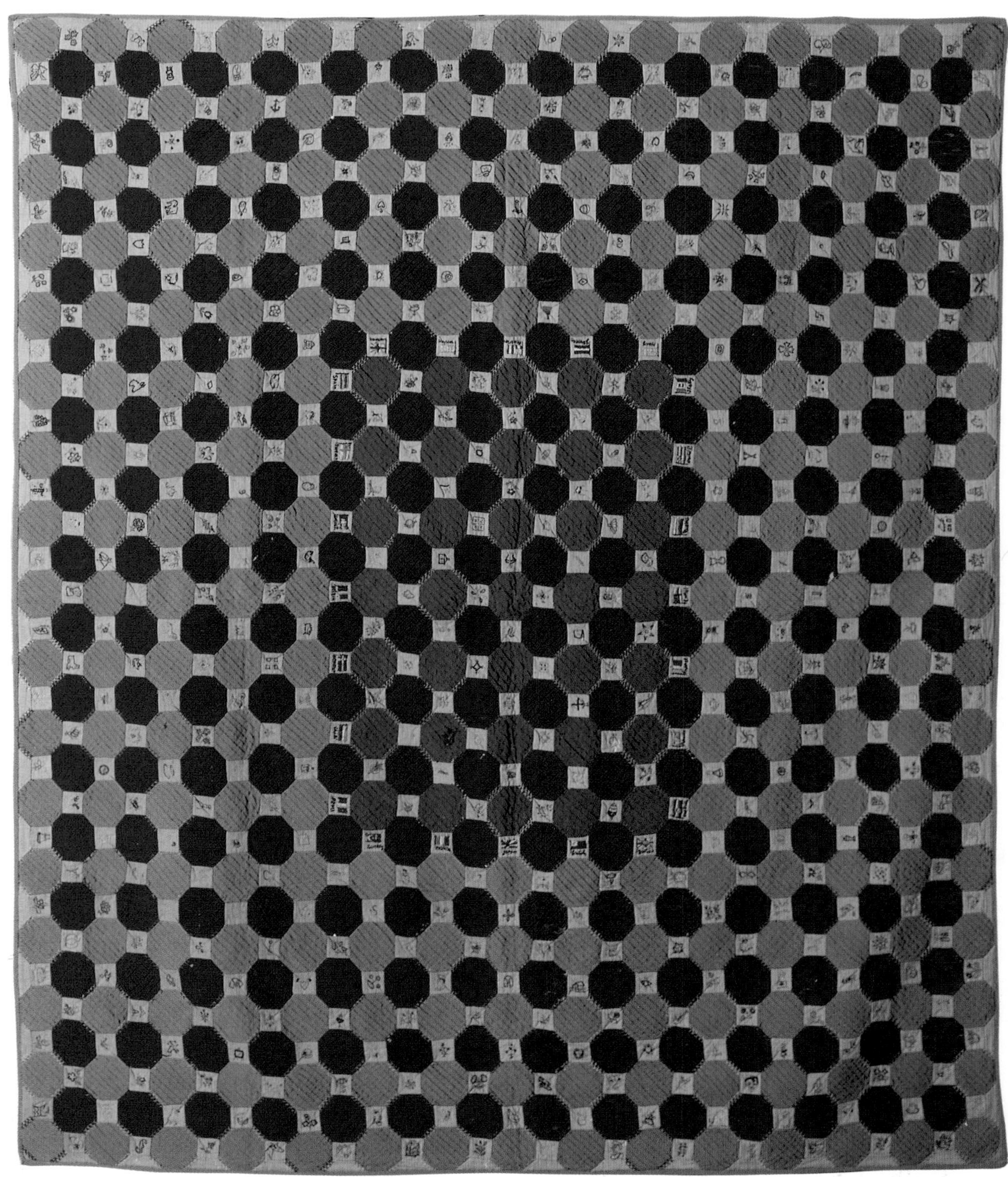

Log Cabin—Courthouse Steps Variation ▸

Artist unknown. c. 1885. Indiana. Wool top with cotton sateen backing; hand pieced and embroidered. 67 x 58 in. Collection of Ardis and Robert James.

The bright yellow centers of the blocks of this quilt are embroidered with tiny figures. By clever manipulation of the four fabric colors used in the quilt (red, teal, light green, and yellow), the maker has created a tantalizing visual illusion that is almost impossible to deconstruct. Teal is used exclusively at the center of the quilt to create a rectangular focus.

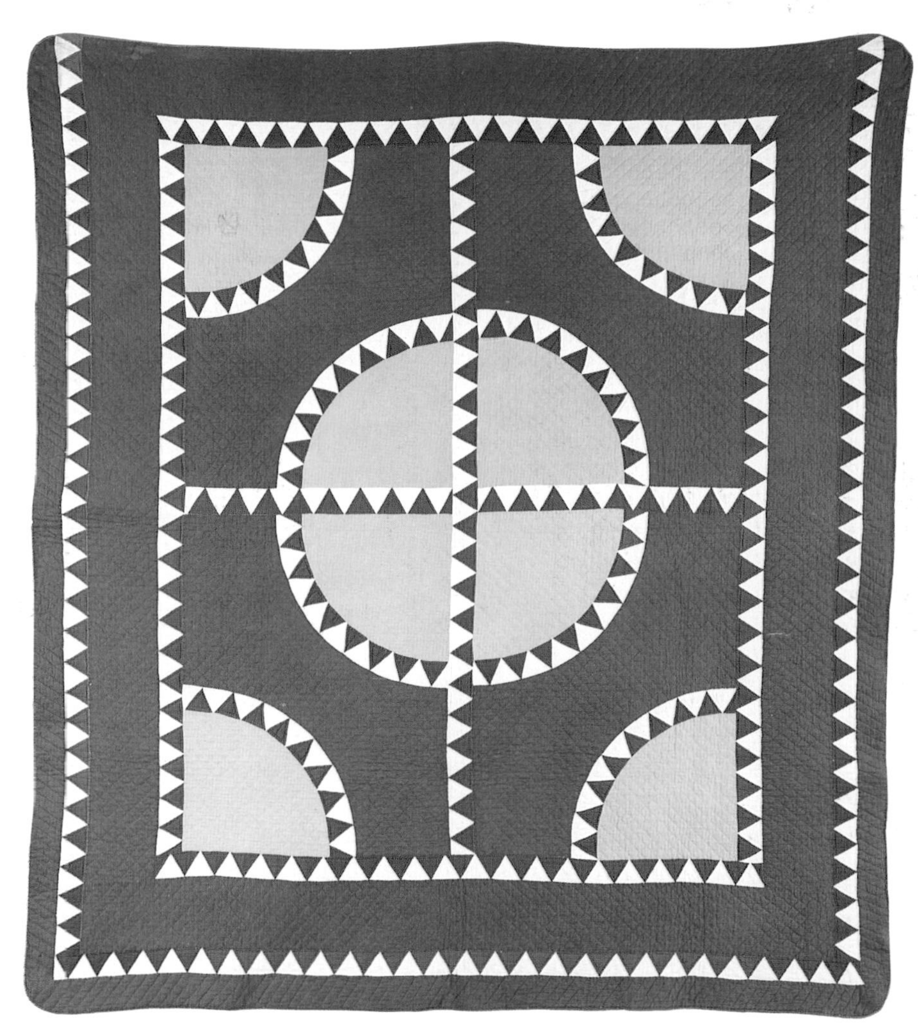

Four-Block Sunburst ▸

Artist unknown. c. 1880. Kentucky. Cottons; pieced and quilted. 77 x 67 in. Collection of Shelly Zegart.

The unusual orientation of this original design seems to place the viewer inside a room, looking through a huge four-pane window full of brilliant sunshine. The deceptively simple four-block pattern is made up of equal squares with quarter circles of yellow placed in two of the opposite corners, and is set off by square frames, semicircular rays of light brown triangles on white, and fields of deep sky blue.

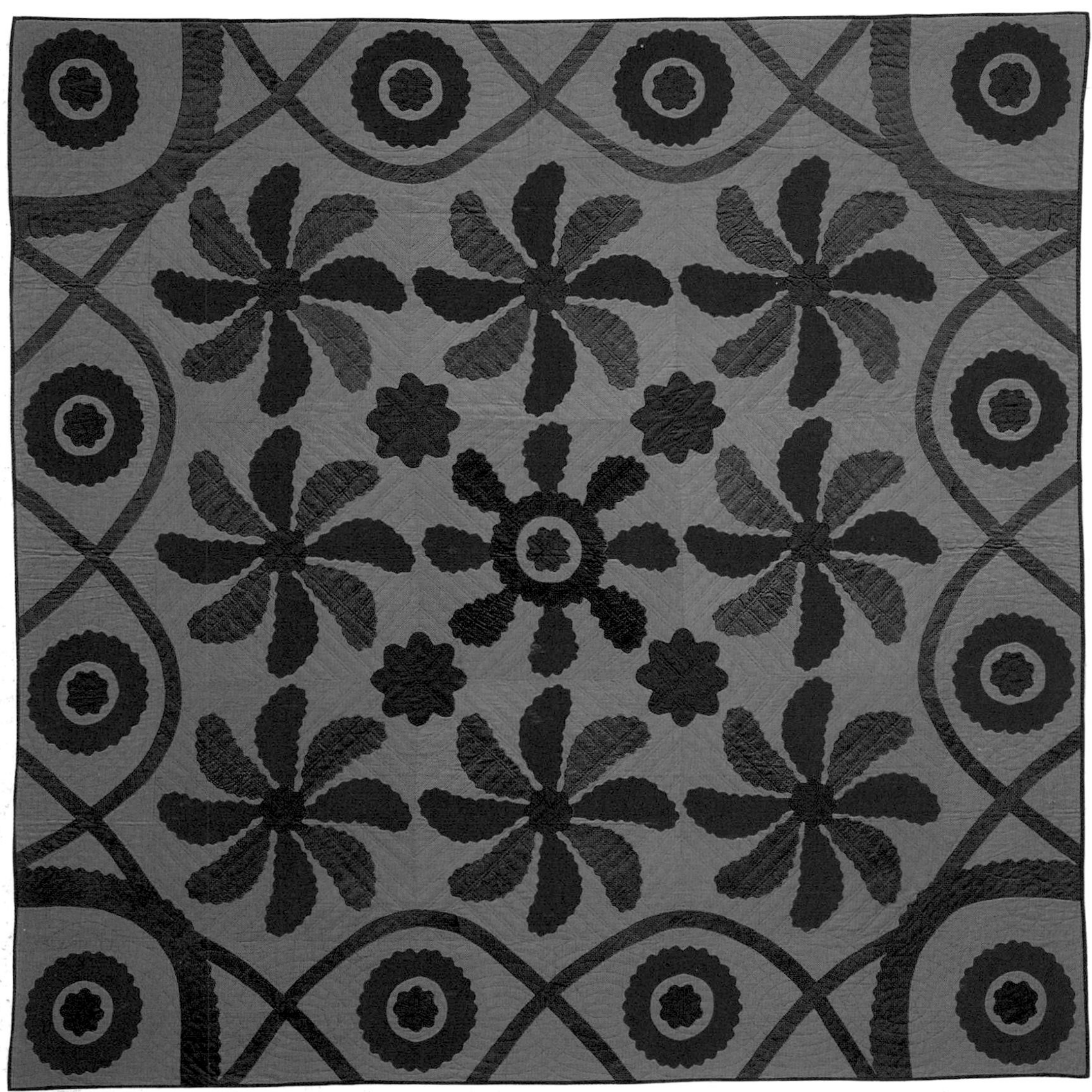

PINE TREE ▶

Artist unknown. c. 1885. Warwick House, Lititz, Pennsylvania. Cottons; machine pieced and hand quilted. 89 x 75 in. Collection of Ardis and Robert James.

The vast forests of virgin pine encountered by colonists provided one of this country's earliest and most enduring symbols. This Victorian version of the popular pattern sets teal trees against a rich red background.

▲ PRINCESS FEATHER VARIATION

Unknown Mennonite artist. c. 1890. York County, Pennsylvania. Cottons; hand appliquéd and quilted. 84 x 84 in. Collection of Ardis and Robert James.

This quilt is a dizzying explosion of color that whirls outward from the center feathered blossom to four blue stars, eight spinning princess feathers, and borders of looping blue bands and red and blue blossoms that echo the center. All are set against a vivid orange field.

JULY FOURTH ▶

Artist unknown. c. 1885–1910. Pennsylvania. Hand appliquéd cottons; unquilted. 88 x 80 in. Collection of Ardis and Robert James.

Forty-nine identical blocks of an original graphic pattern appliquéd in one-inch-wide strips of red fabric against a light blue print make up this unique quilt. A row of half blocks forms one end of the quilt. The overall pattern is a square within a diamond within a square, with bars running from the center of each side of the diamond to the corners of the outermost square.

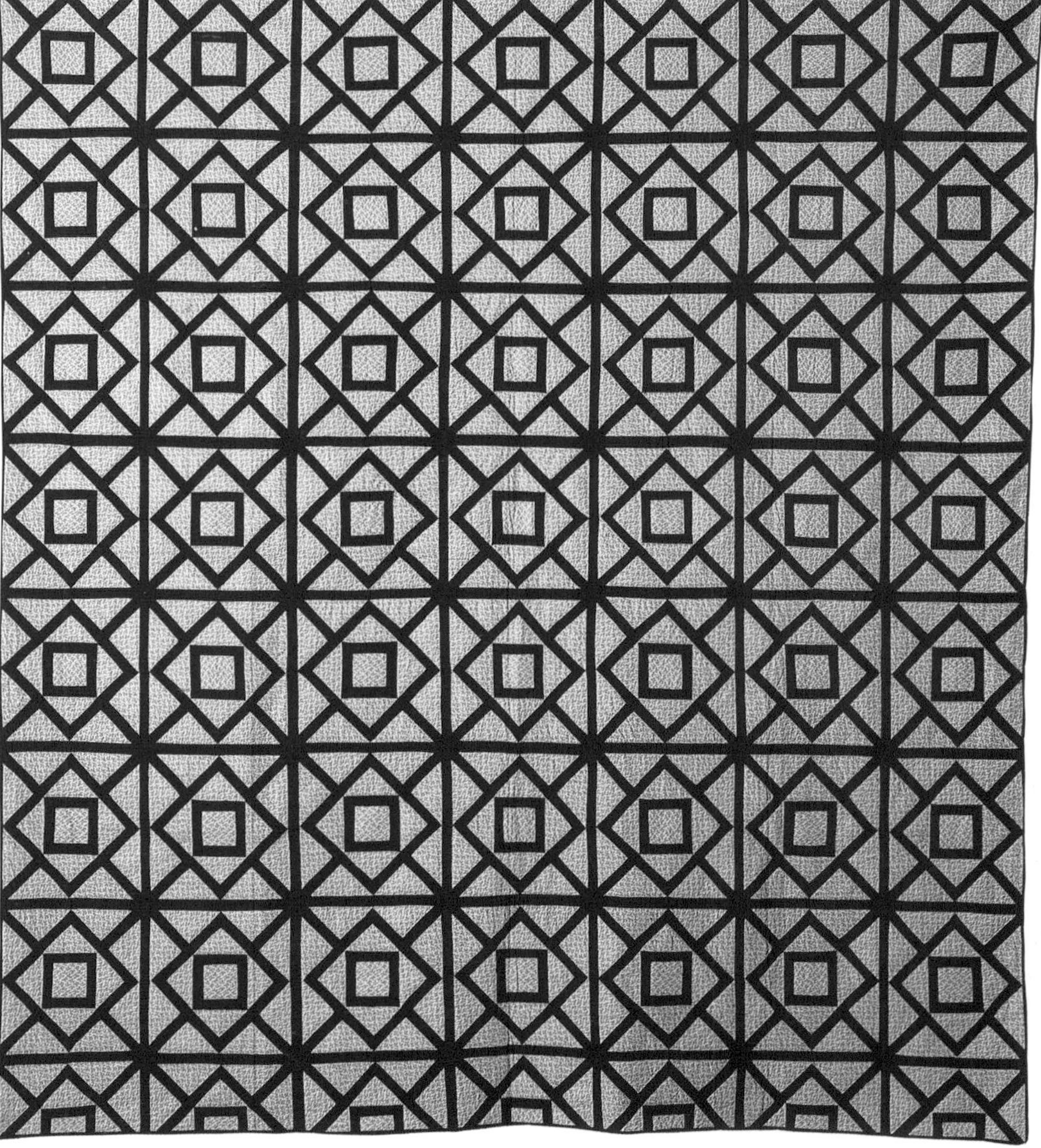

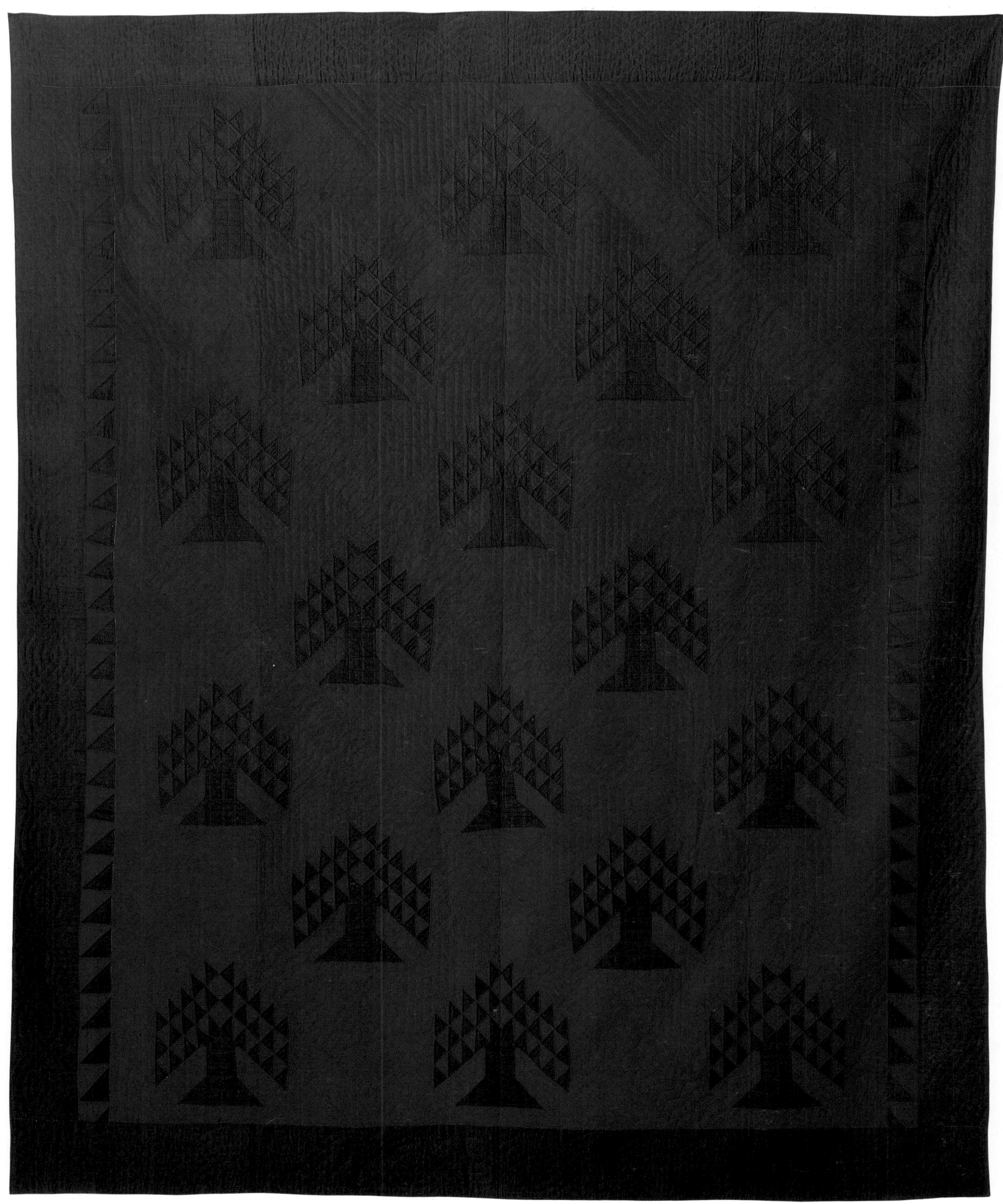

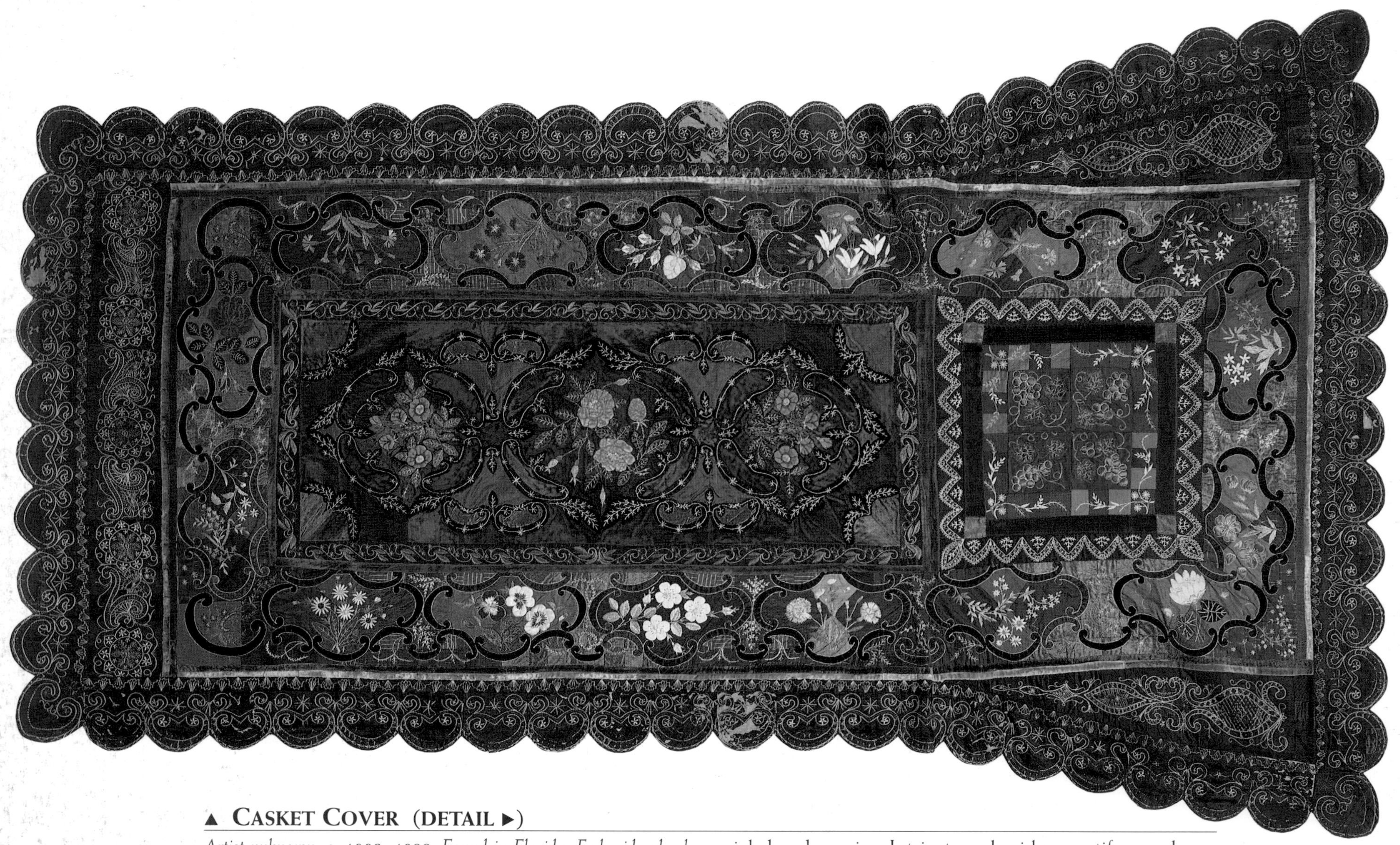

▲ **Casket Cover (detail ▶)**

Artist unknown. c. 1880–1900. Found in Florida. Embroidered velvet, silk, and satin. 47 x 98 in. Collection of Ardis and Robert James.

This ornately decorated piece was apparently made to drape over the top of a casket during a wake and/or memorial church service. Intricate embroidery motifs sewn by an expert hand cover the entire piece, which, apart from its unusual shape and function, is reminiscent of the richly embroidered crazy quilts of the late Victorian era.

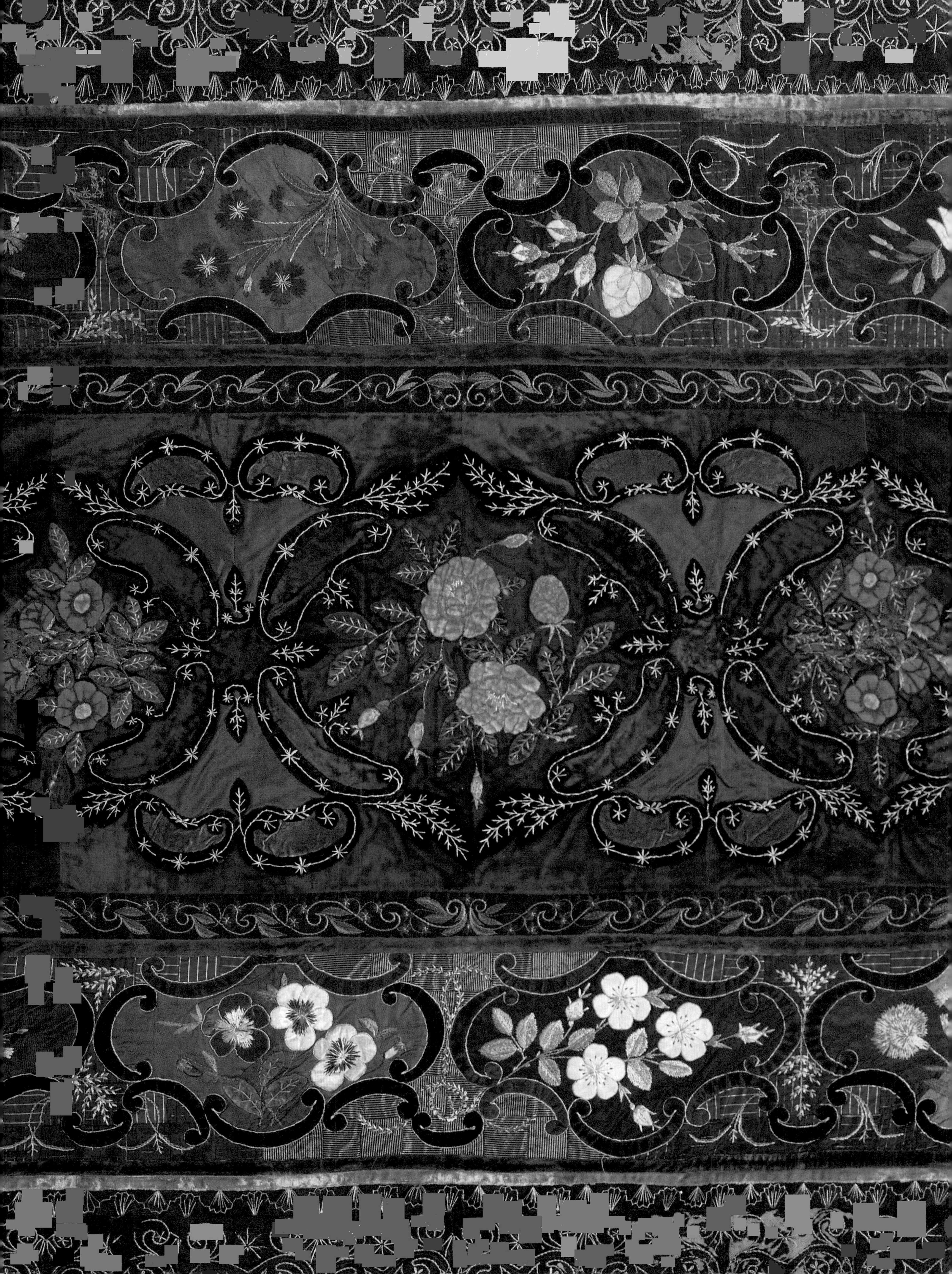

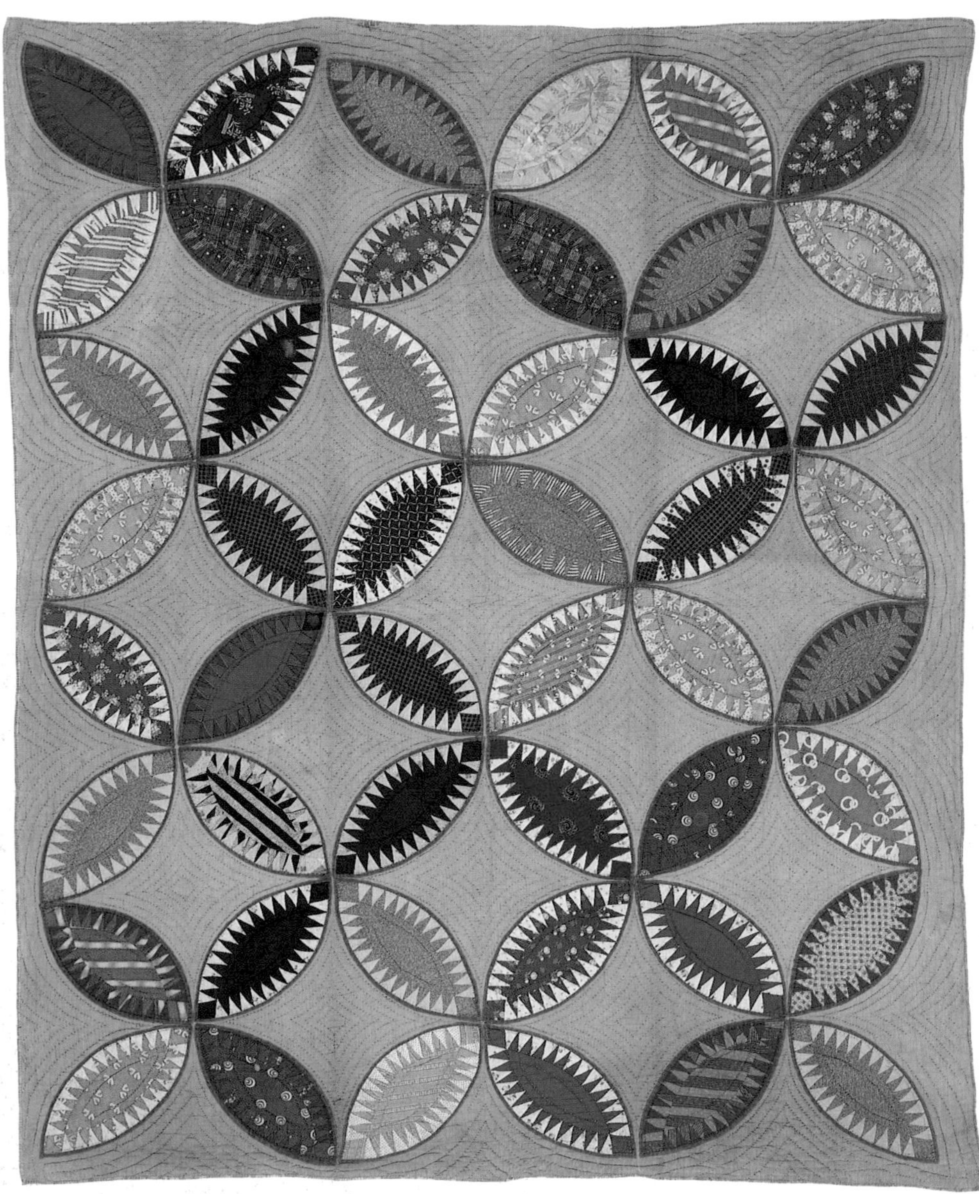

Stars, Moon, and Comet ▶

"Grandma" Carpenter. 1892. Lincoln, Pennsylvania. Cottons; appliquéd and embroidered, hand quilted. 95 x 86 in. Collection of Ardis and Robert James.

"Grandma" Carpenter made quilts, some of them quite similar, for fourteen of her grandchildren, one of whom was the well-known folk artist Miles Carpenter. This quilt was made for Mrs. Carpenter's daughter Frances's first child, Elsie, who was born in 1884. The quilt, which was apparently known in the family as *God's Nighttime Sky*, was put away as a memorial when Elsie died in 1894. The eight-inch gold border is filled with quilted grapes and vining leaves.

▲ Tobacco Leaves

Mary Norvell Guerrant. c. 1895. Buckingham County, Virginia. Cottons; hand pieced. 88 x 71 in. The Valentine Museum, Richmond, Virginia, gift of Mrs. Thomas F. Foster.

This unusual pattern, more commonly known as Pickle Dish, is a forerunner of the Double Wedding Ring, which was one of the most popular patterns of the 1920s and 1930s.

The "Sacret Bibel" Quilt ▶

Possibly by Susan Arrowood. c. 1895. Possibly West Chester, Pennsylvania. Cottons; appliquéd, embroidered, and tied; ink inscriptions. 90 x 72 in. Museum of American Folk Art, New York, gift of Amicus Foundation, Inc., and Evelyn and Leonard Lauder.

A series of ink inscriptions, crudely written and poorly spelled, identify some of the scenes depicted as "Jesus on the monn/tain sending his de/siples threw the/world to preach," "John baptizing Jesus/in the river off/Jorden," "Jesus crucif on the cross," "The angel/guarding the sleeping man," and "Adam an eav in/the Garden." Another inscription reads, "Susan Arrowood/Sacret bibel quilt," thus possibly identifying the quilt's maker. The somewhat haphazard composition and indifferent, slap-dash craftsmanship only reinforce the quilt's intensely personal power of expression.

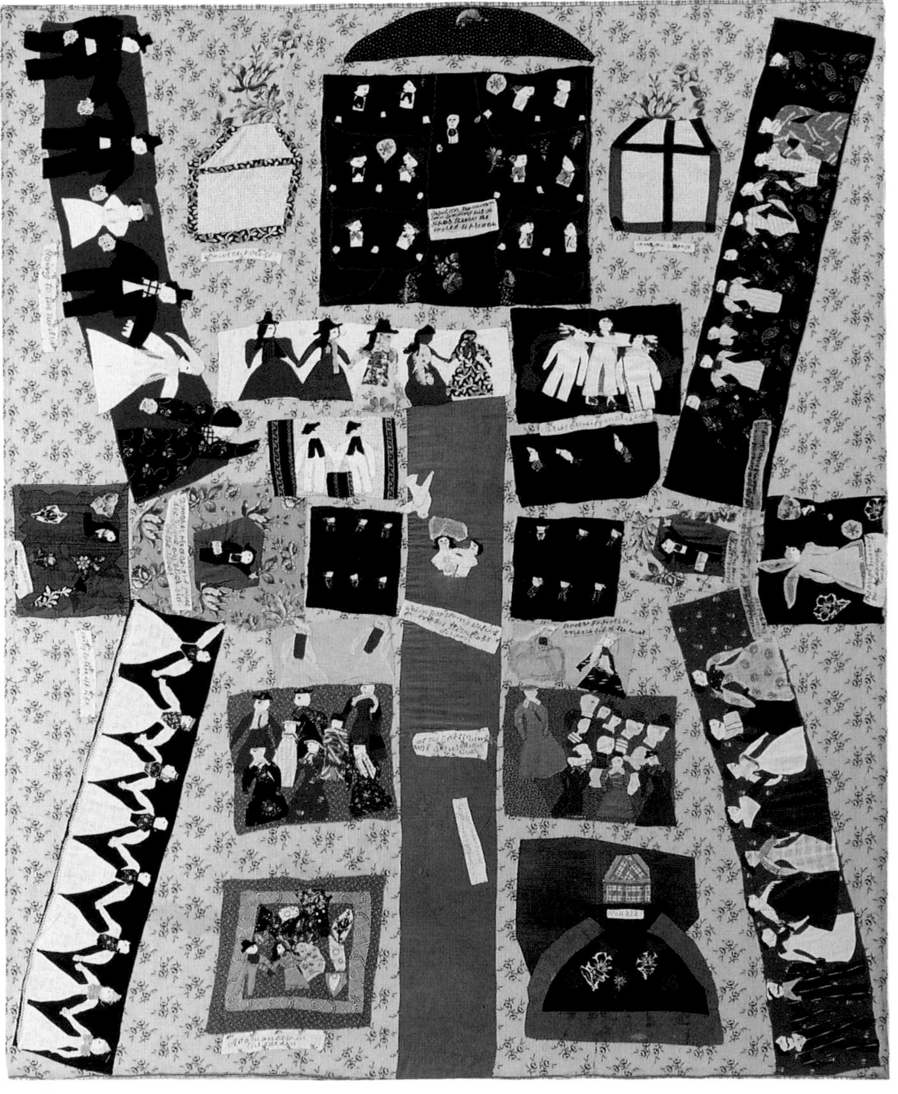

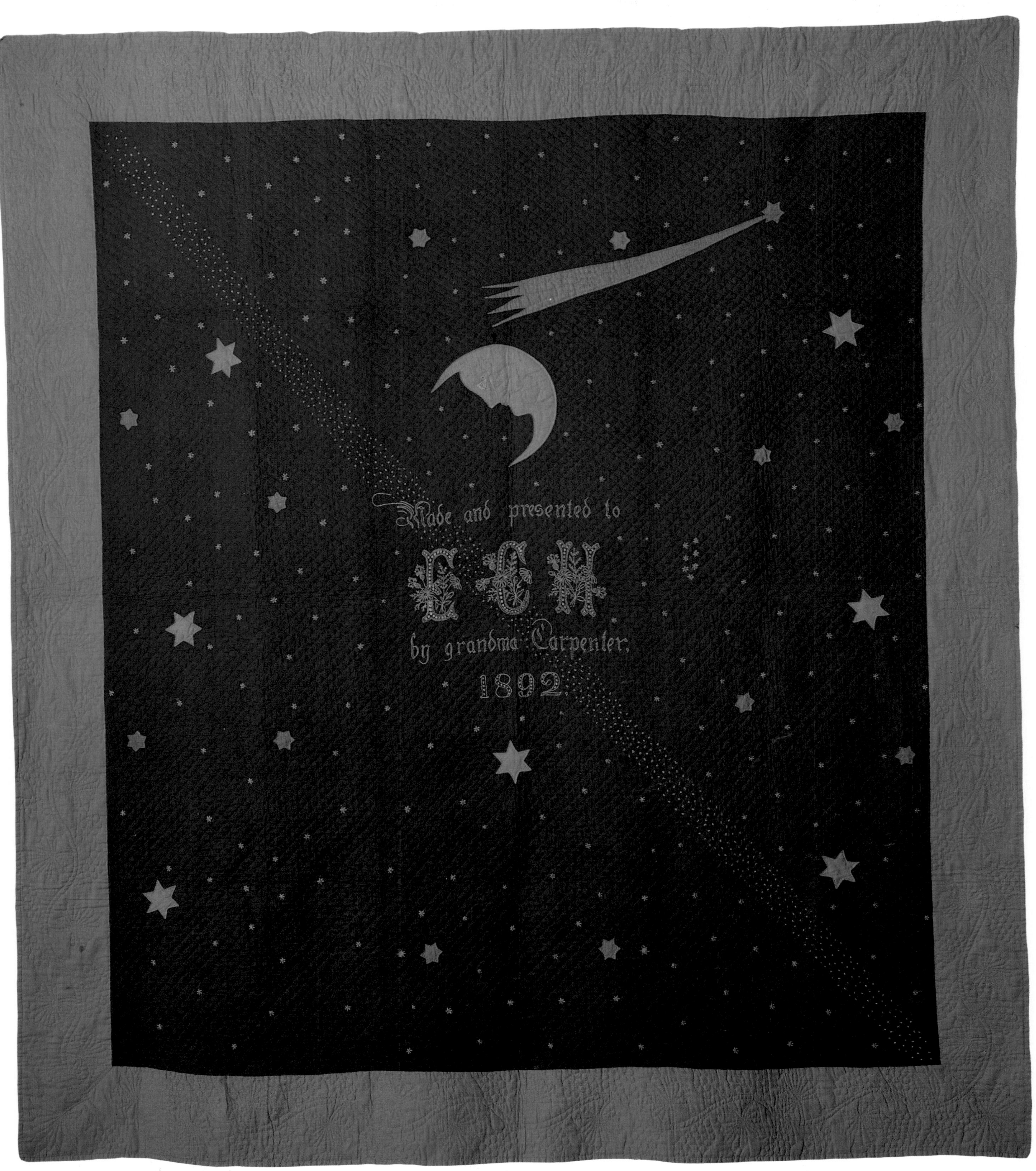
Made and presented to
ECH
by grandma Carpenter.
1892.

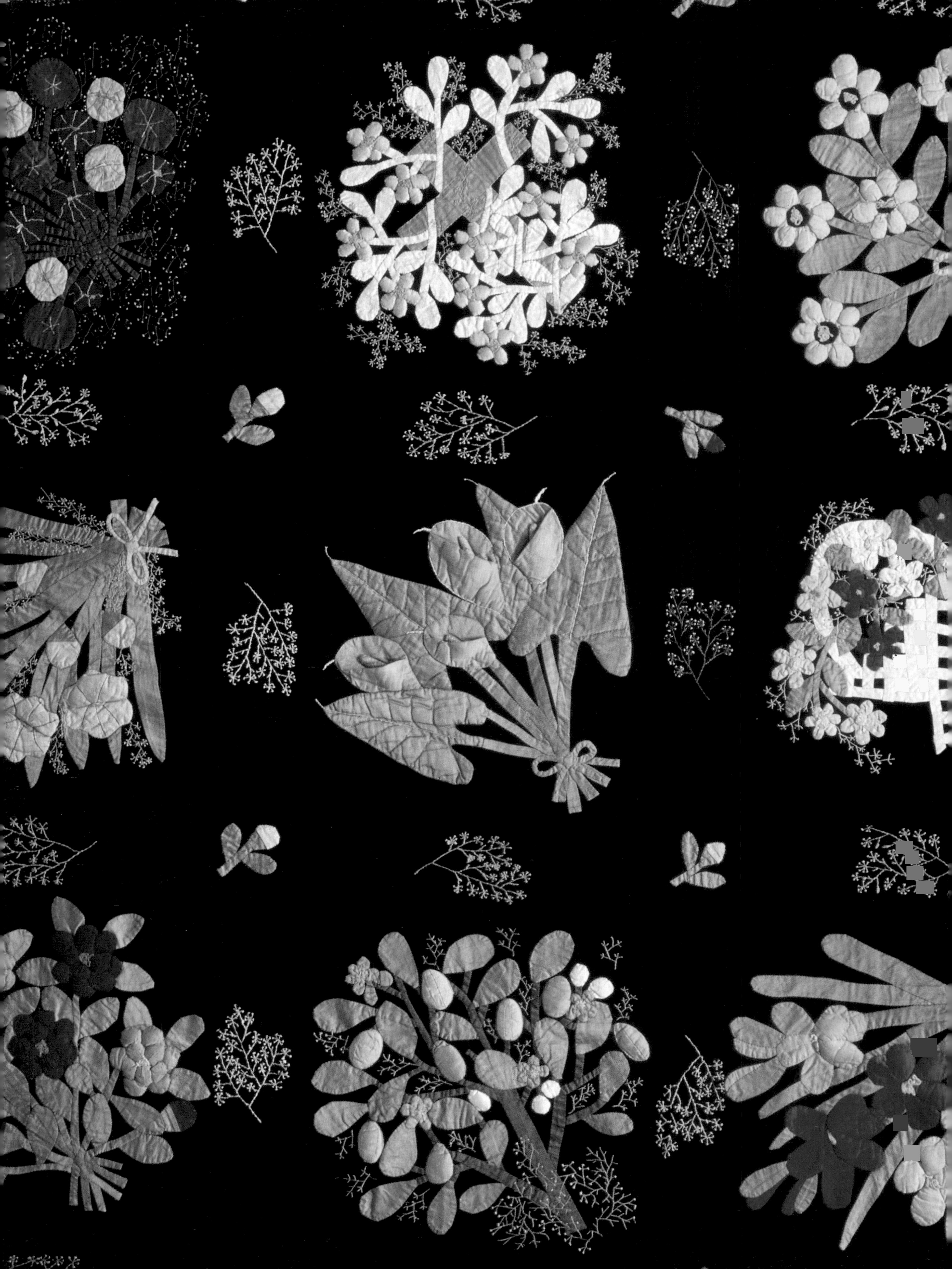

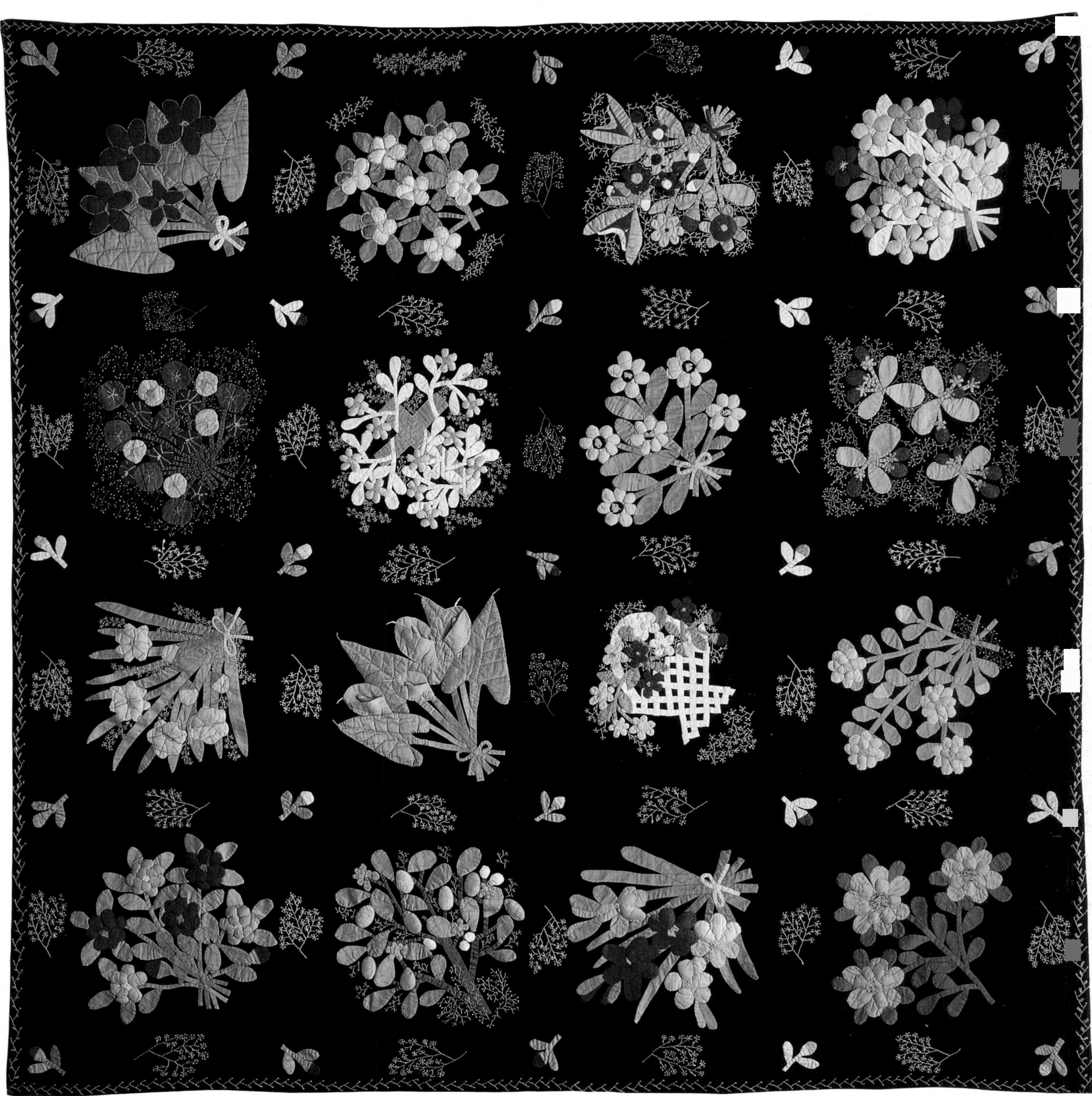

▲ FLORAL ALBUM (◄ DETAIL)

Artist unknown. c. 1880–1900. Probably eastern Pennsylvania. Cottons; hand appliquéd, embroidered, and quilted. 87 1/2 x 88 in. Collection of Ardis and Robert James.

This sumptuous Victorian album quilt offers sixteen different bouquets, including calla lilies and nasturtiums. The carefully rendered appliquéd floral arrangements are complemented with embroidered sprigs of baby's breath and surrounded by an embroidered border. The quiltmaker must have been a gardener or florist who knew (and loved) her flowers well.

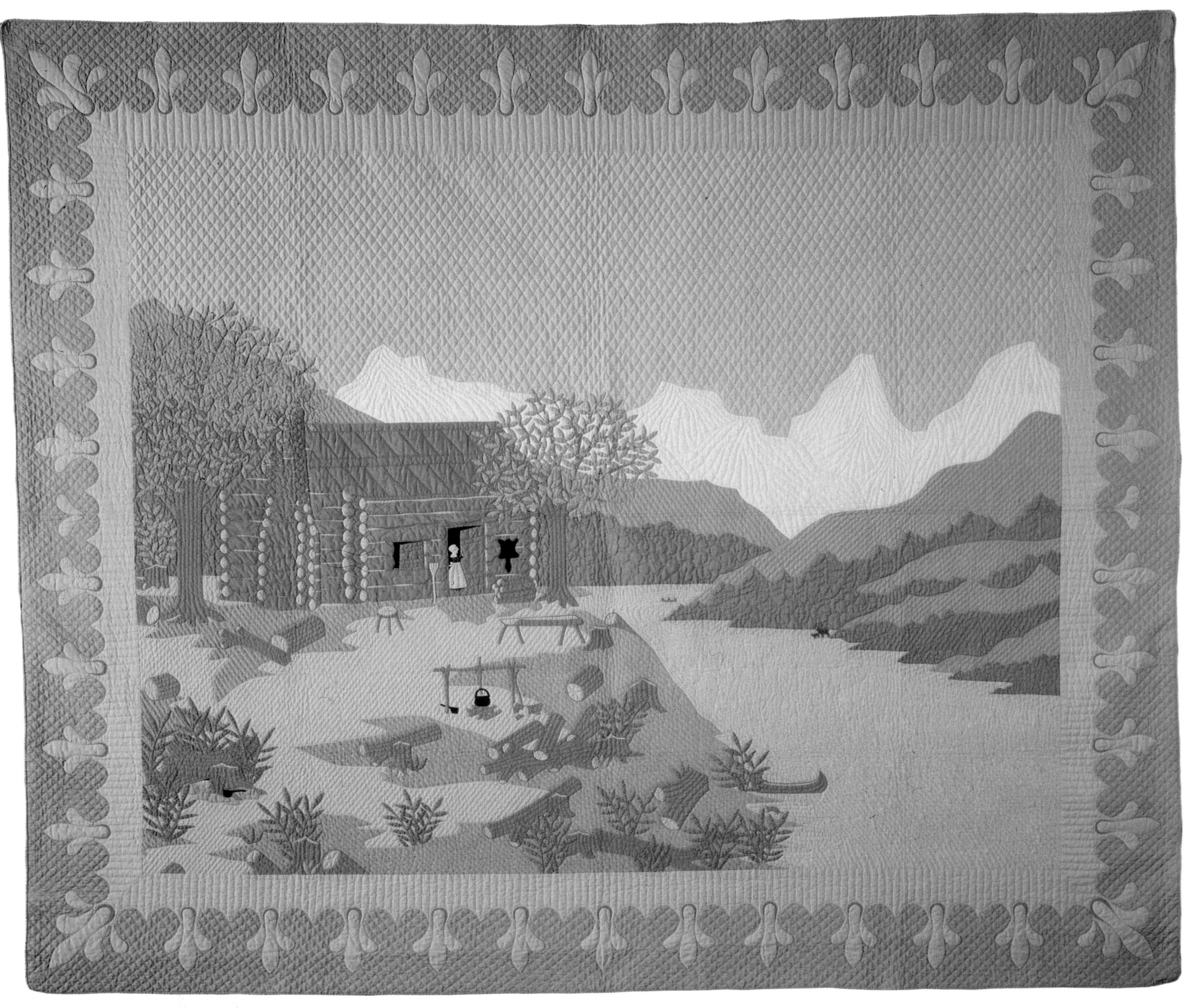

▲ Log Cabin and Mountain Landscape

Artist unknown. c. 1920s. Possibly Quebec. Cottons; hand appliquéd and quilted. 77 x 94 1/2 in. The Shelburne Museum, Shelburne, Vermont, gift of George Frelinghuysen.

This remarkable early twentieth-century textile painting includes an inner border that deliberately imitates a picture frame. Although the quilt was found in upstate New York, the beaver pelt hanging on the cabin wall and the fleurs-de-lis that decorate the outer border suggest that the quiltmaker may have been French Canadian.

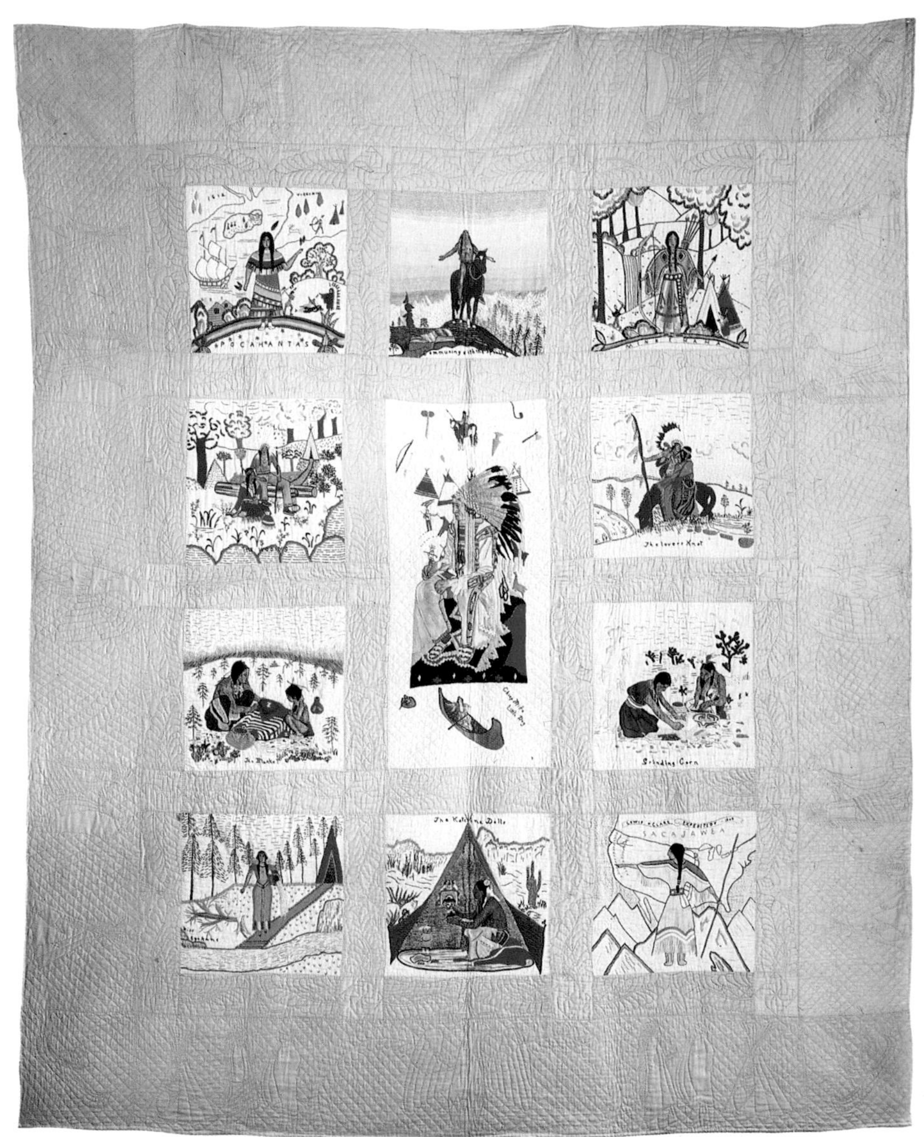

INDIAN SCENES ▶

Belle, Irma, and Ralph Wright. c. 1910. Wenona, Illinois. Cottons; hand pieced, appliquéd, embroidered, with some hand painting. 102 x 84 in. Collection of Shelly Zegart.

Ralph Wright designed this detailed pictorial quilt, while his mother Belle and Aunt Irma did the needlework. Among the famous Indians represented are Pocahontas, Minnehaha, and Sacajawea; tribal scenes include vignettes depicting Sioux, Hopi, and Navajo customs and artifacts.

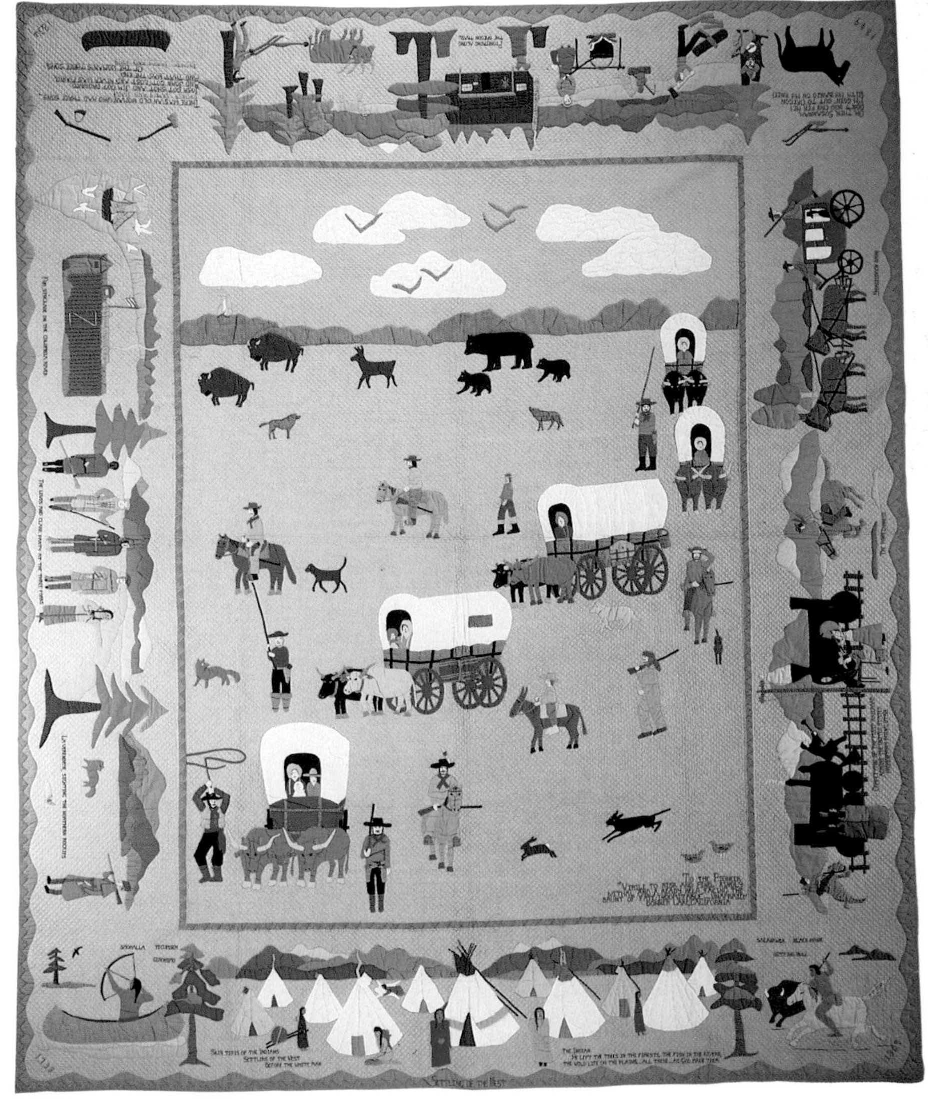

SETTLING THE WEST ▶

Mildred Jacob Chappell. Started March 1931, completed September 1932. Yuma, Colorado. Cottons; pieced, appliquéd, embroidered, machine quilted. 103 x 83 in. Collection of Shelly Zegart.

Inscribed on the back of this quilt is the following statement: "I, Mildred Jacob Chappell, made this quilt as a labor of love. Love for the 'Old West' as I have known it in history and books. Love of the 'New West' as I have known it in travel. Love of the Indian before the white men invaded his kingdom . . . My only regret is that I could not have lived one hundred years earlier." *Settling the West* was successfully entered in "The Century of Progress" competition sponsored by Sears Roebuck at the 1933 Chicago World's Fair.

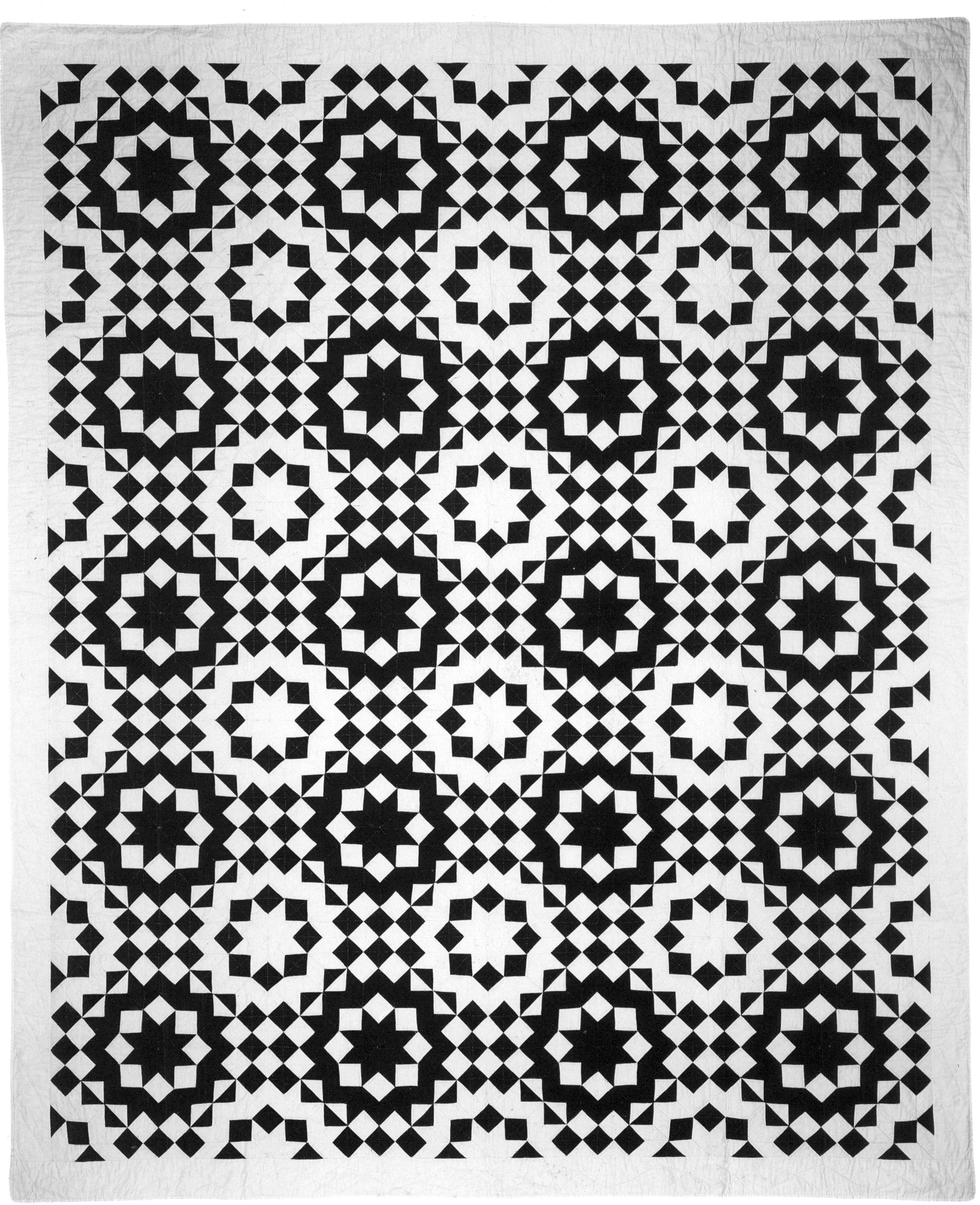

◄ **Carpenter's Wheel**

Artist unknown. c. 1900. Ohio. Cottons; pieced and quilted. 96 x 78 in. Collection of Shelly Zegart.

This two-color quilt is organized into a vibrant, pulsating light and dark composition of intersecting positive/negative wheels. The Carpenter's Wheel or Broken Star pattern surrounds a central star that is pieced from eight diamonds with another star pieced of eight squares and an exploded outer star of diamonds. The blocks are completed with a border of triangles and four corner squares and are set on point against each other to make up the top.

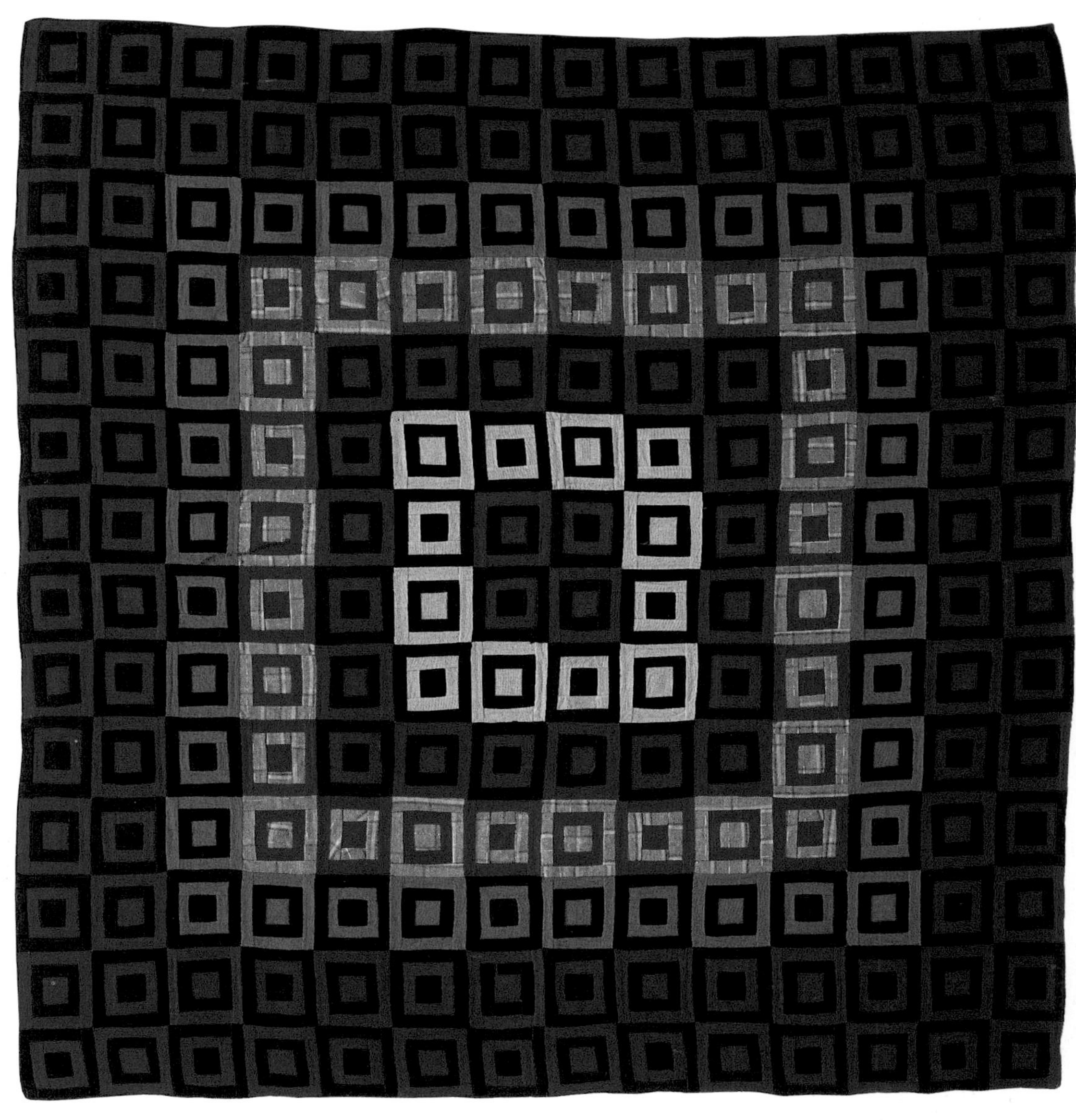

▲ **Square-Within-Square**

Unknown Mennonite artist. c. 1930. Pennsylvania. Wools; hand pieced and quilted. 68 x 68 in. Esprit Quilt Collection, San Francisco, California.

This mind-bending optical color exercise is built from precisely pieced, paired positive/negative blocks. The overall composition, which is created solely through the manipulation of color, is a four-block central medallion surrounded by four borders and a double outer row of red and black blocks.

◄ **Embroidered Denim Scrap Quilt**

Artist unknown. c. 1920. Alabama. Hand-pieced cotton denim with hand embroidery. 84 x 76 in. Collection of Robert Cargo.

This unique quilt was made from scraps of denim, probably leftovers gathered from an overall factory, that are pieced to form a top and are covered with lines and stars of white embroidery. The highly visible white selvedges of many of the scraps combine with the embroidered work to form a spidery network of fragmented lines.

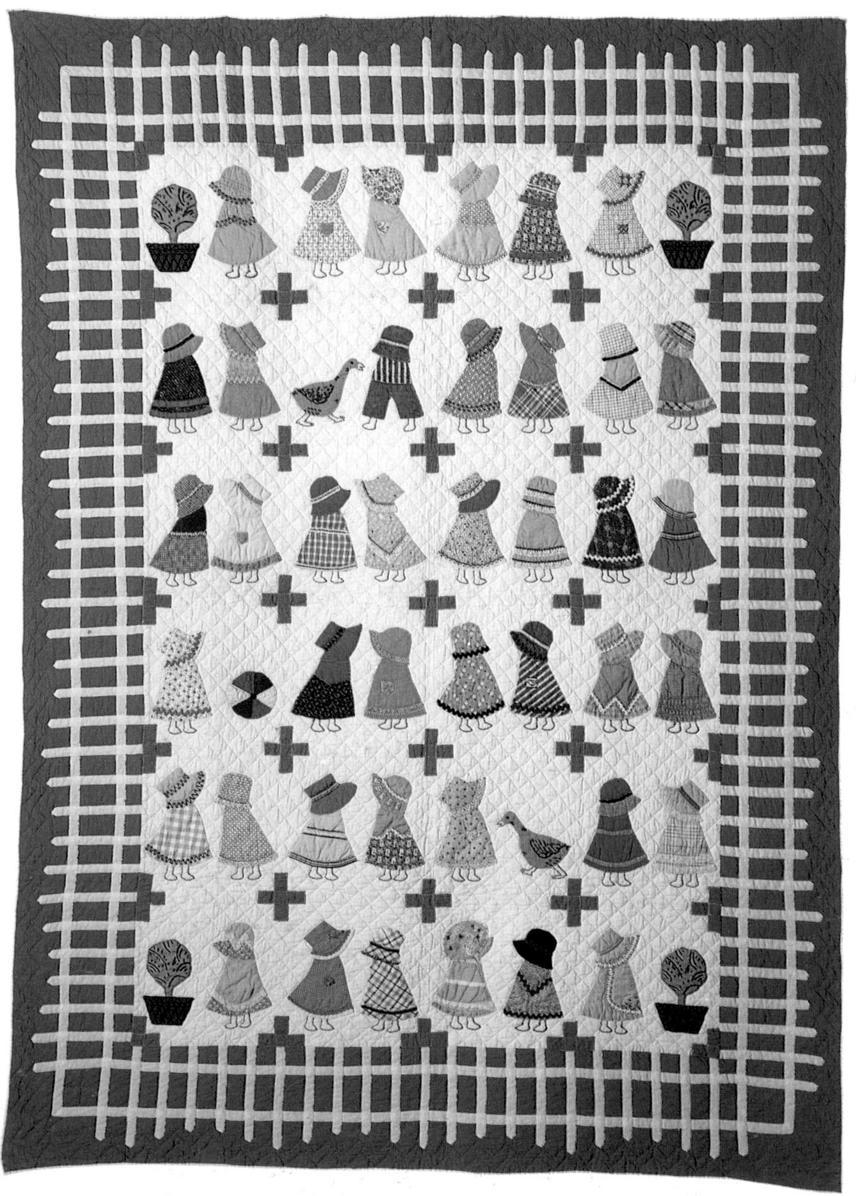

Crazy Neckties ▸

Artist unknown. c. 1930–1935. Anderson, Indiana. Silk neckties; hand peiced, sewn, and embroidered. 91 x 69 in. Collection of Ardis and Robert James.

The resourceful maker of this exuberant and amusing Depression-era crazy must have had open access to a tie factory or haberdashery.

◂ Sunbonnet Sue

Artist and region unknown. c. 1940–1950. Cottons, embroidery, ribbon, lace; hand appliquéd, machine quilted, hand embroidered. 86 x 63 in. Collection of Ardis and Robert James.

Although Sunbonnet Sue has become perhaps the ultimate quilting cliché, this charming and imaginative variation of the widely distributed and overused pattern helps explain its enormous popularity. The traditional bonneted figures, each wearing a different costume, are set in pairs, seemingly in conversation with each other. Single bonneted figures interact amusingly with marching geese, potted plants, and a beach ball. All are surrounded by a decidedly one-dimensional white picket fence set against a field of lavender fabric to create a scene irresistible to all but the most jaded viewer.

God Bless Our Home ▸

Mary Dora Kreyenhangen. c. 1945. Cincinnati, Ohio. Cottons; pieced and quilted. 102 x 84 in. Collection of Shelly Zegart.

The quiltmaker's mother ran a dry goods store where Mary Kreyenhangen chose the fabrics used in this nostalgic World War II–era quilt. Kreyenhangen, who was also a painter, depicted herself at work at an easel in the upper corners of the quilt.

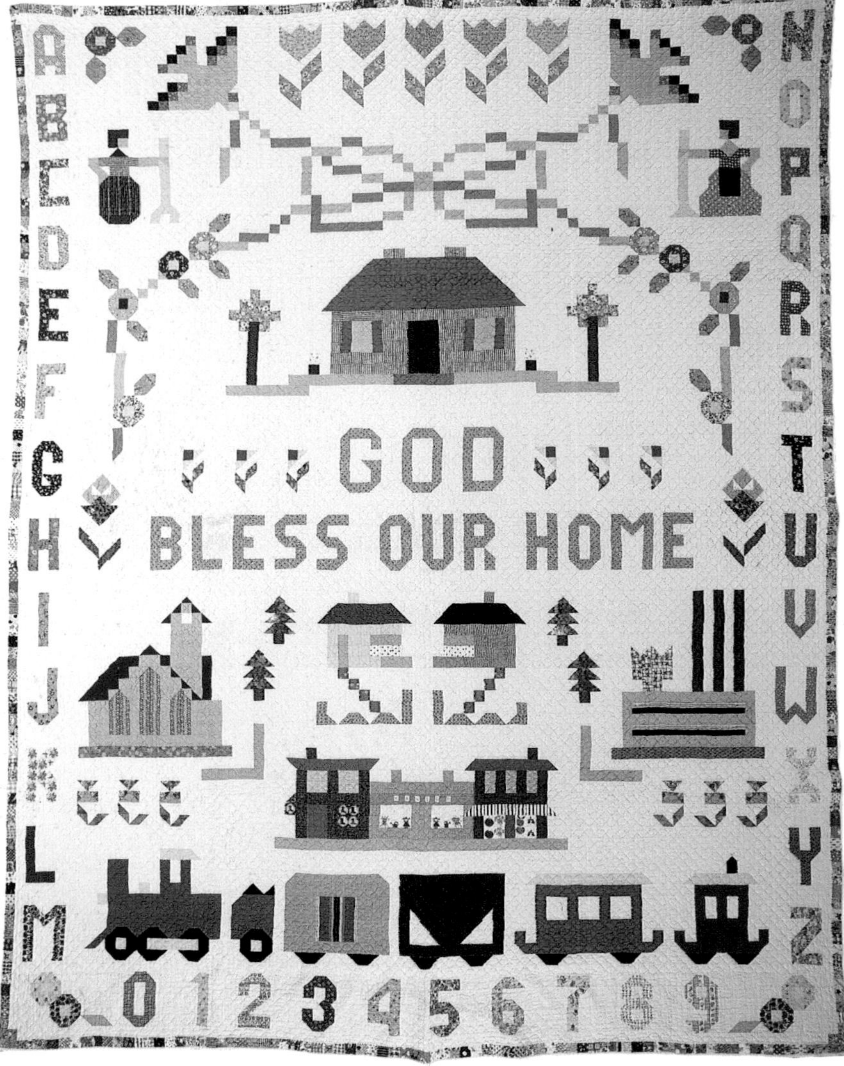

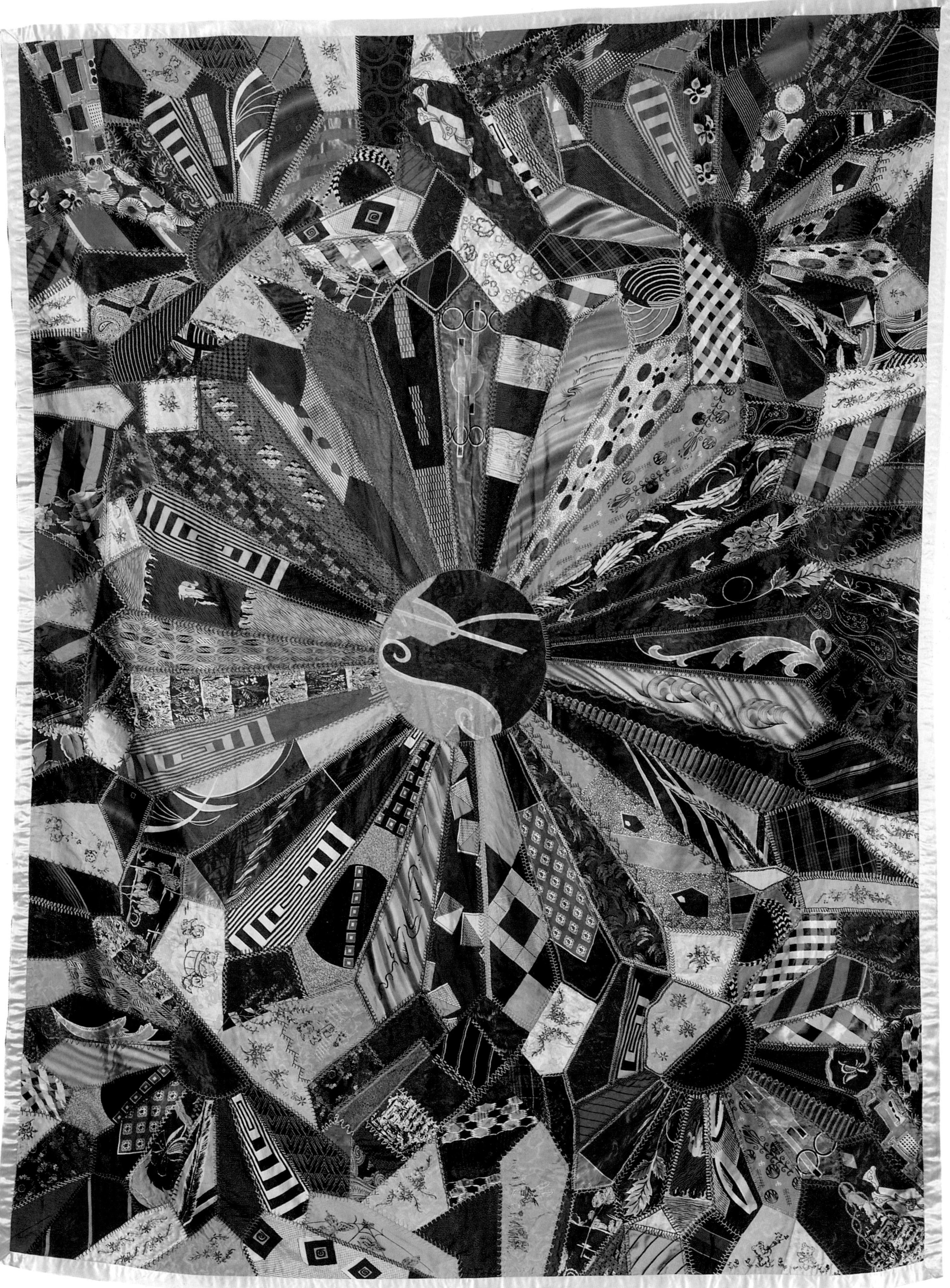

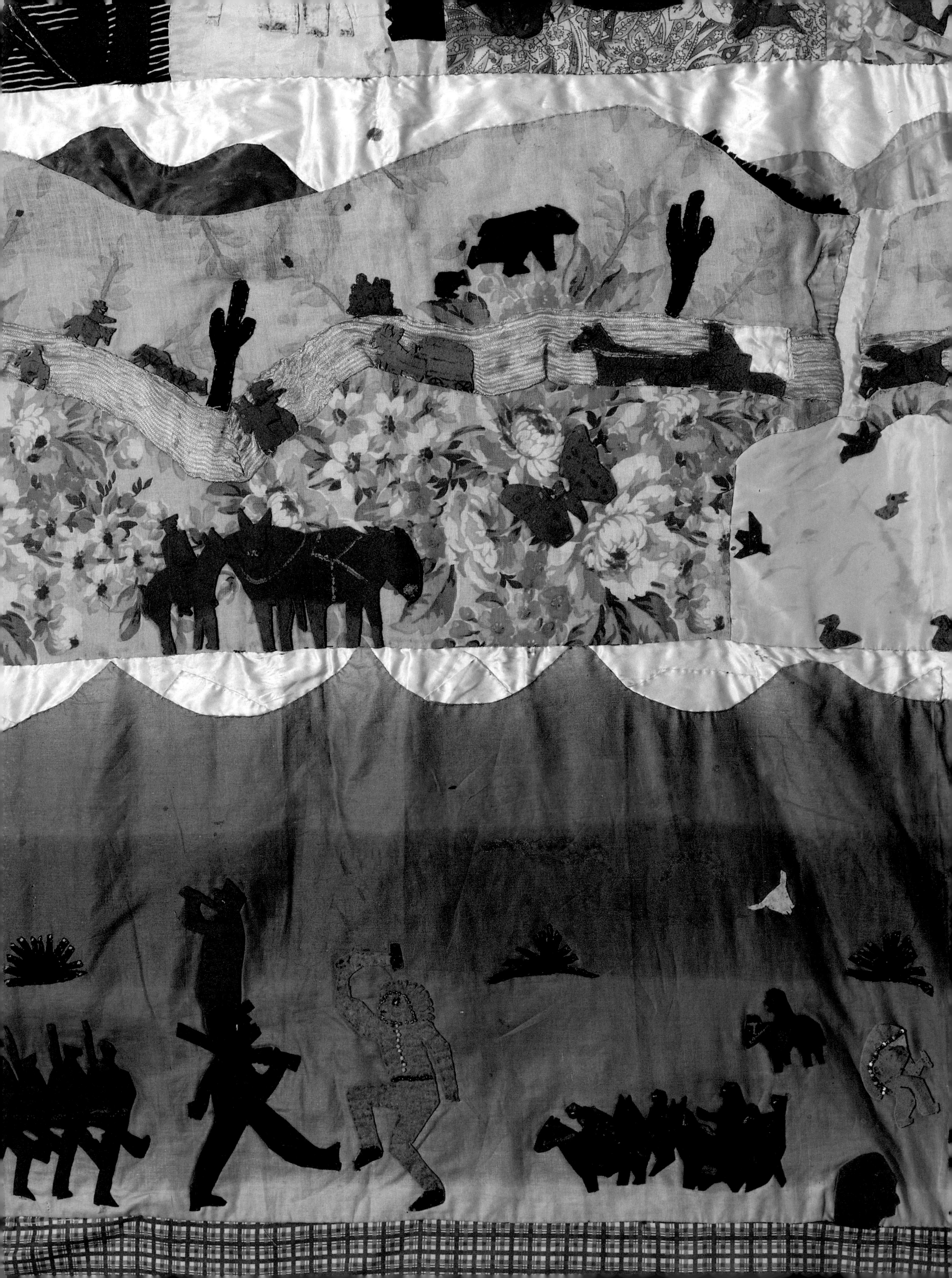

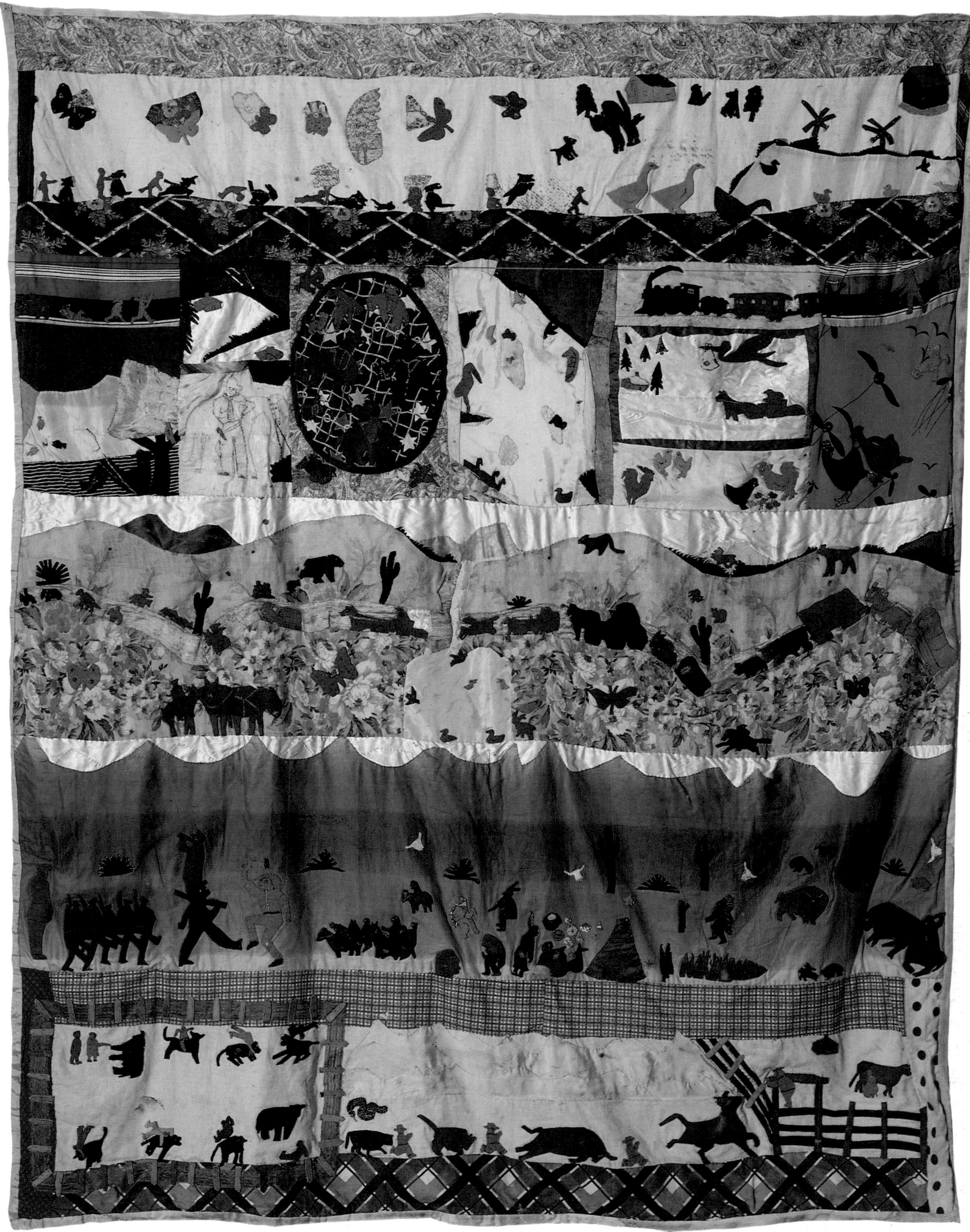

▲ UNCLE CLINT'S QUILT (◄ DETAIL)

Clinton R. Hamilton. c. 1940. Washington, D.C. Felts, rayon blends, pen and ink; hand appliquéd. 74 x 62 in. Private collection.

Clinton R. Hamilton (1865–1962) claimed that he ran away from home at age nine and lived with the Sioux in South Dakota until he was fourteen. He later fought in the "Indian Wars" and was wounded at the infamous Battle of Wounded Knee. Hamilton was ashamed of the treatment given the Indians and learned Native American languages and crafts. He also wrote a considerable amount of light verse, becoming known as the poet laureate of the Soldier's Home in Washington where he spent his last years. Among the many vignettes included in his quilt are depictions of a stagecoach pursued by Indians, two women watching a corral scene of red-eyed bulls and riders, a stork bearing a baby in a sling racing a doctor in his horse and buggy to a snow-bound house, a cowboy with gun and bandana standing next to his tethered horse, a woman milking a cow, a group of oxen-drawn covered wagons set against a mountain landscape, a fisherman sleeping under a tree, an Indian village, and a buffalo hunt.

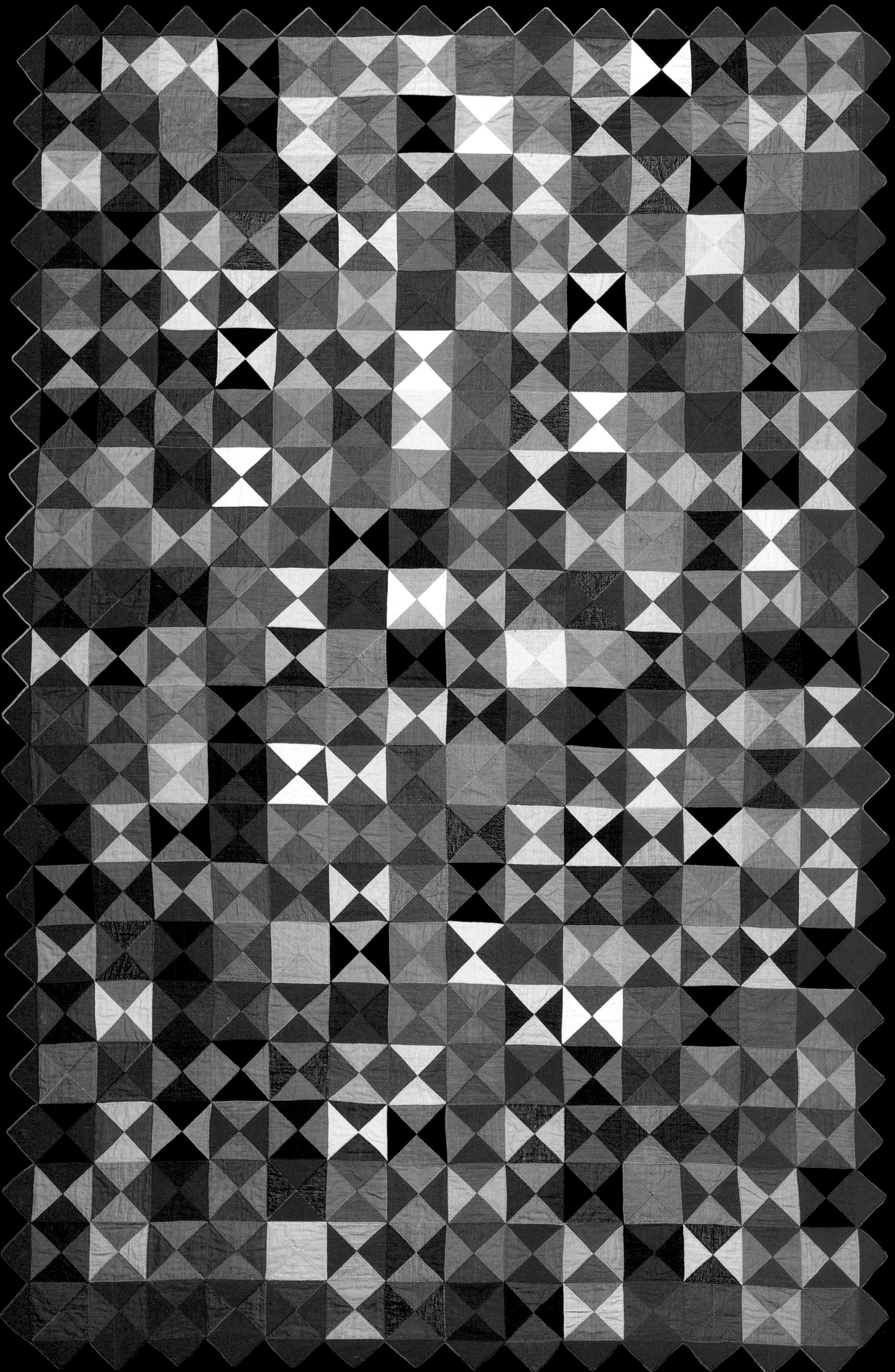

QUILTS TODAY: 1970 AND BEYOND

A GREAT REVIVAL

Interest in quilts and quilting, which began as a groundswell in the 1960s, burgeoned in the 1970s as America, looking forward to its 200th birthday, turned its attention to its past. A public unsure of its present after the revolutionary changes of the turbulent '60s—the civil rights movement, the assassinations of Medgar Evers, Malcolm X, John Kennedy, Robert Kennedy, and Martin Luther King, women's liberation, the sexual revolution, the divisive war in Vietnam—increasingly looked back, searching for core American values and achievements. In the early 1970s, the widely acknowledged failure in Vietnam and the humiliating public disgrace of Richard Nixon brought American morale and national pride to a low ebb. The Bicentennial gave us a reason to celebrate and to reexamine our history, both personal and communal. We found much to be proud of when we looked to America's past.

The renewed interest in quiltmaking had begun in the 1960s as young people disillusioned with the values of the society around them turned to other cultures, religions, and eras for instruction. "We are as gods and might as well get good at it," declared former Merry Prankster Stewart Brand in his first *Whole Earth Catalogue*, the bible of the back-to-the-land movement. "So far remotely done power and glory—as via government, big business, formal education, church—has succeeded to the point where gross defects obscure actual gains. In response to this dilemma . . . a realm of intimate, personal power is developing—the power of the individual to conduct their own education, find their own inspiration, shape their own environment, and share the adventure with whoever is interested." Traditional American crafts and folk arts were studied closely, many of them for the first time. All over the country, young Americans took up forgotten handcrafts such as weaving, pottery, stained glass, furni-

◄ **YES AND NO**

Marilyn Neuhart. 1977. Hermosa Beach, California. Hand-pieced Mexican cottons; hand quilted. 91 x 60 in. Collection of the quiltmaker.

This jaunty quilt is made up of 308 blocks of paired triangles (the central element of the traditional Broken Dishes pattern). The quiltmaker has used deeply saturated contemporary colors and unexpected color combinations for the two pairs of triangles that make up each block, and the whole composition is bordered with a unifying fence of hot red triangles. The vibrant ying/yang, push/pull of the colorful interlocking hourglass shapes gives the quilt its name and its almost frantic, pulsating energy.

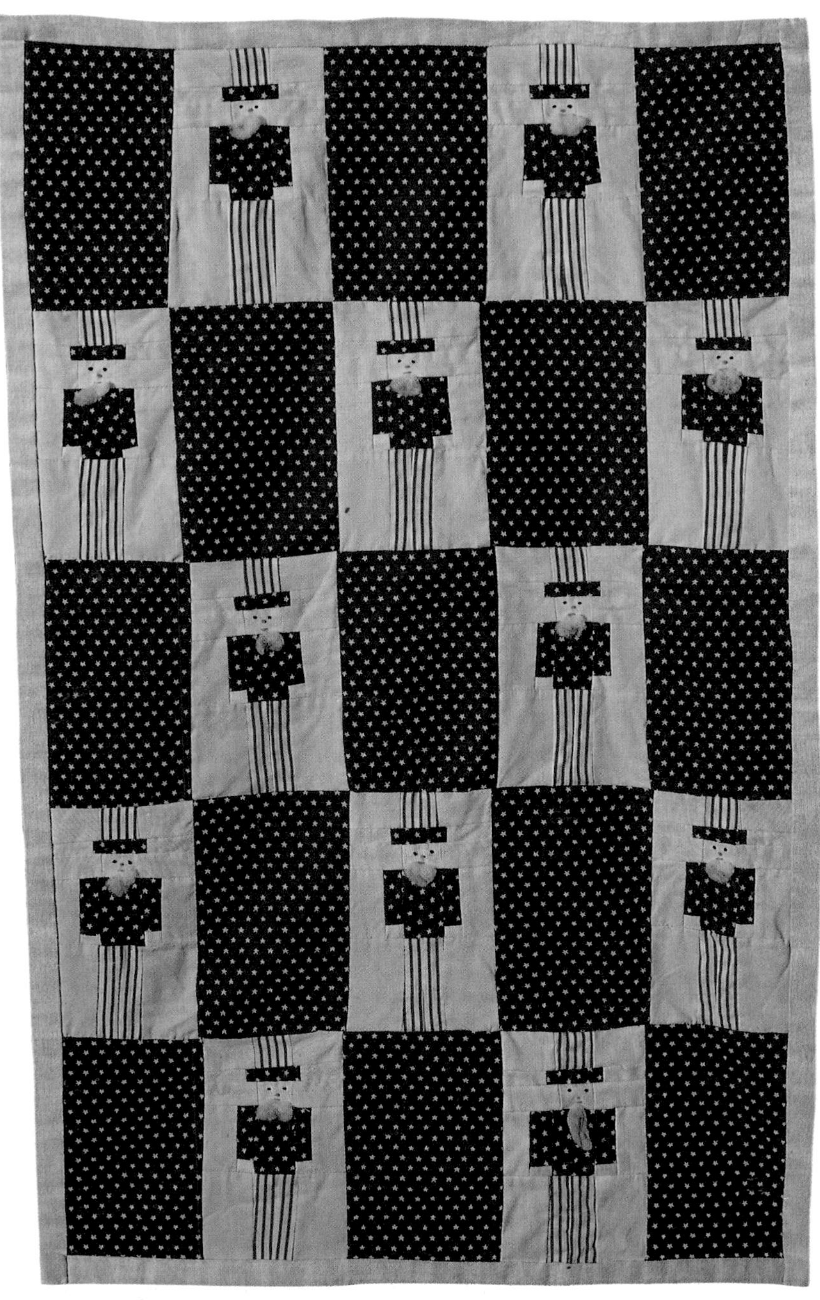

◀ **UNCLE SAM**

Artist unknown. c. 1985. Tennessee. Hand-pieced cottons, cotton batting. 33 x 20 in. Collection of Ardis and Robert James.

This charming little quilt is made of rows of tall rectangular blocks of navy and white star print fabric alternating with pieced Uncle Sams that have French-knot eyes and noses, batting beards, and wear red striped hats and pants, with shirts and hat brims of the star print. The top is tied to the back with red thread rather than quilted, but, although a simple and somewhat crude method of assembly, it only adds to the overall appeal of the piece.

ture making, and quiltmaking. Folklorists, collectors, and students sought out older and often rural craftspeople who could still teach these crafts and thus provide connections to traditions obscured by neglect. They researched traditional forms and techniques, brought older books back into print, and wrote a flotilla of how-to books.

Ruby Short McKim's venerable *One Hundred and One Patchwork Patterns*, a staple of the Great Depression years that was first published in 1931, was reprinted by Dover Publications in 1962, presaging the movement, and has sold thousands of copies over the years. Pioneer quilt artist Jean Ray Laury was instrumental in making quiltmaking accessible to thousands of American women through her simple and appealing modern designs, published throughout the 1960s and 1970s in widely read magazines such as *Better Homes and Gardens* and *Family Circle*. Laury's equally influential books, including *Appliqué Stitchery* (1966) and *Quilts and Coverlets: A Contemporary Approach* (1970), offered quilters a fresh and exciting range of clearly presented techniques and design ideas. Another of the most original and influential books of the great quilt revival that began in the mid-1960s was Beth Gutcheon's 1973 *Perfect Patchwork Primer*, which outlined the basic techniques of the craft for a new generation of enthusiasts eager to discover its history and create their own quilts. The jacket copy for Gutcheon's book describes the obsessive passion of the time for homemade handcrafts:

> *Newest craft to catch fire on the do-it-yourself scene, the very American art of patchwork quilting, is a living, vivid activity deeply rooted in our country's history and, most particularly, the history of its women. . . . Ms Gutcheon brims with ideas. She tells how to make money at quiltmaking, how to organize quilting parties . . . She also gives plans for more than 70 projects to make with patchworks—tote bags, wall hangings, coasters, mats, hot pads, skirts, vests, pillows, playpen liners, coffee-pot cozies, bibs, floor furniture (!), a traveling board game, cookbook covers, and other gifts, wearables and usables.*

Museums were also beginning to pay attention to this textile art form. In 1971 the Whitney Museum of American Art exhibition *Abstract Design in American Quilts* marked a turning point in quilt history. The exhibition was organized by Jonathan Holstein, who, with Gail van der Hoof, had assembled a collection of historic pieced quilts based solely on their aesthetic merits. *Abstract Design in American Quilts* presented quilts as works of fine art that hung on the walls of one of the country's most prestigious museums of contemporary art and were favorably compared with the paintings hanging in other galleries. Displaying quilts on walls was not without precedent. Electra Havemeyer Webb, founder of the Shelburne Museum in Vermont and perhaps the most prominent early quilt collector, had removed some of her many quilts from beds and hung them since the mid-1950s, but they were presented in a homey context of American history and antiques, not as works of art hung in a stark, well-lit gallery setting. Like her colleagues at Williamsburg, Historic Deerfield, Old Sturbridge Village, and other "outdoor" museums that were created to represent life in early America, Mrs. Webb also presented quilts within historic room settings.

The Whitney exhibition was novel in that it purposefully took quilts out of any sort of historical context and looked at them strictly as works of abstract art. Holstein's catalog begged the question, pointing out the quilts' similarities to modern abstract painting and noting how their makers had found design solutions that would not be "discovered" by artists until a century later. Where previous collectors had often emphasized the craft of quilting, valuing technical accomplishment and focusing on beautifully worked appliquéd quilts, Holstein looked at the power and expression of the overall design. Eschewing appliqué quilts, which were often made as decorations "for best," Holstein favored everyday utilitarian pieced quilts, sometimes overlooking sloppy workmanship for the impact of the design viewed as a whole. He was also one of the first collectors to bring attention to the brightly colored quilts of Pennsylvania's German immigrants, particularly the Amish and Mennonites, who had often used color in astonishingly fresh and painterly ways.

Over the course of the next five years versions of Holstein's exhibition traveled extensively in the United States, Europe, and Japan. The exhi-

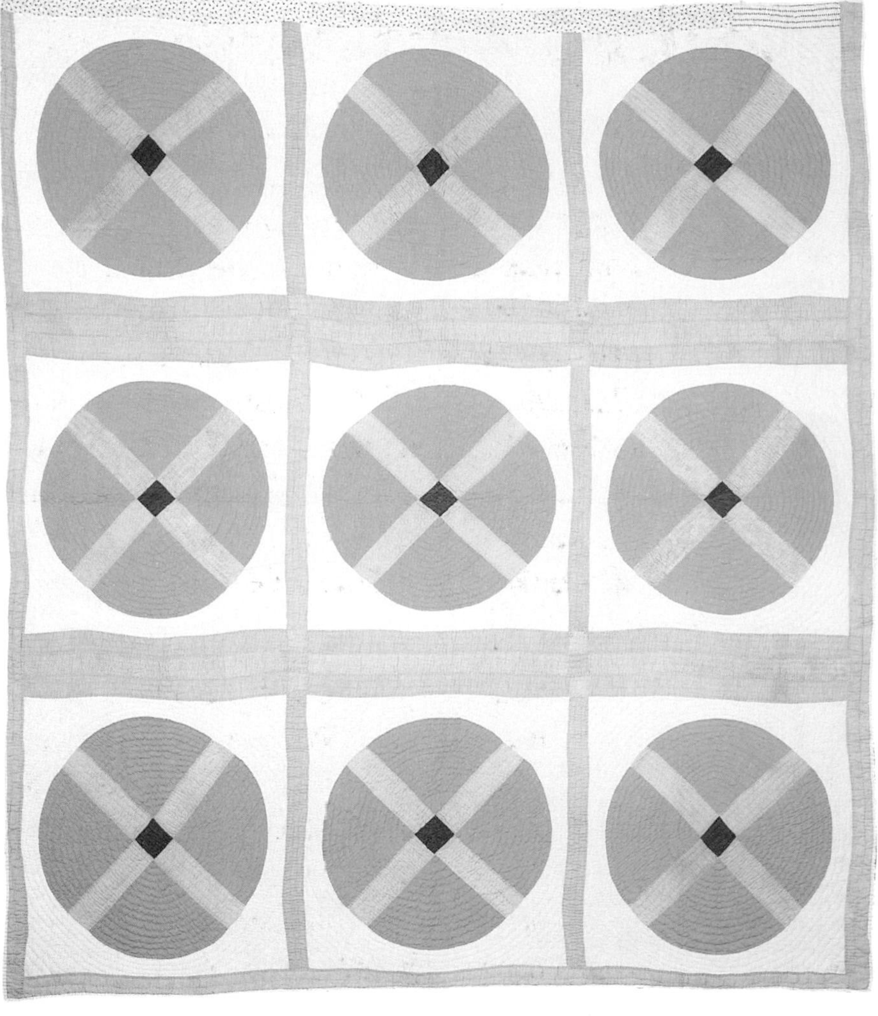

Circles and Crosses ▸

Artist unknown. c. 1890. Colorado. Cottons; pieced and quilted. 84 1/2 x 75 1/2 in. Collection of Jonathan Holstein.

This unique original design was the signature quilt for the seminal exhibition *Abstract Design in American Quilts*, which opened at the Whitney Museum in New York in 1971.

bition turned heads wherever it was seen and is cited by many of today's quilters and textile artists as the event in their lives that both introduced them to quilting for the first time and suggested its artistic possibilities. Holstein's exhibition was successful beyond anyone's expectations. It changed the way people looked at quilts, lifting them out of the domestic environment and giving them a new validity and vitality. Influential art critics raved about the Whitney show, finding a freshness in these decades-old and somewhat unintentional works of art that was often found lacking in the contemporary art world of the early 1970s. The country's most respected and influential art critic, Hilton Kramer of *The New York Times*, wrote, "The suspicion persists that the most authentic visual articulation of the American imagination in the last century is to be found in the so-called 'minor' arts,—especially in the visual crafts that had their origins in the workaday functions of regional life. . . . For a century or more preceding the self-conscious invention of pictorial abstraction in European painting, the anonymous quilt-makers of the American provinces created a remarkable succession of visual masterpieces that anticipated many of the forms that were later prized for their originality and courage."

Quilt collecting, which had been a relatively quiet pursuit in the 1960s, began in earnest in the 1970s. Collectors began to seek things American actively, finding artistic, cultural, and spiritual, as well as monetary value in objects that had previously been passed over in favor of "higher" (European or classically based) arts. Young dealers and collectors scoured the countryside, buying quilts for themselves and for a public increasingly hungry for pieces that could provide a link to their own newly discovered past. As more—and wealthier—collectors entered the marketplace, supply eventually lagged behind demand and prices for choice pieces began to escalate substantially. This trend, of course, continues to the present day, and masterpiece quilts that twenty-five years ago sold for at most a few thousand dollars can now occasionally bring well into six figures. Masterpiece quilts in museums and private collections were identified and ambitious and covetous collectors began "counting the bodies," antiques trade slang for keeping tabs on the ownership of key pieces. Dozens of outstanding private quilt collections have been formed

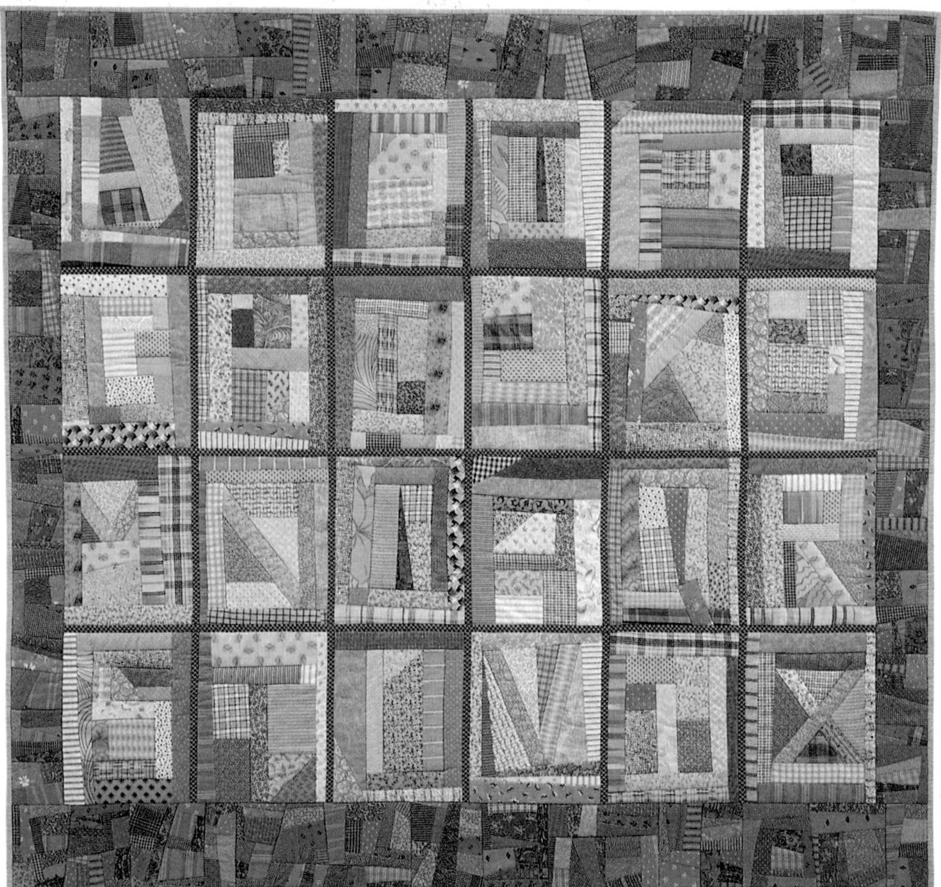

◂ **XYZ**

Judy Hopkins. 1992. Anchorage, Alaska. Cottons; machine pieced and quilted. 54 3/4 x 57 1/2 in. Collection of the artist.

This scrap alphabet quilt was inspired by an improvisational alphabet quilt by Joanne May. The last three letters of the alphabet are superimposed in the twenty-fourth block, hence the title. Judy Hopkins is a professional quiltmaker and teacher, and has authored or co-authored five instructional and pattern books for quilters.

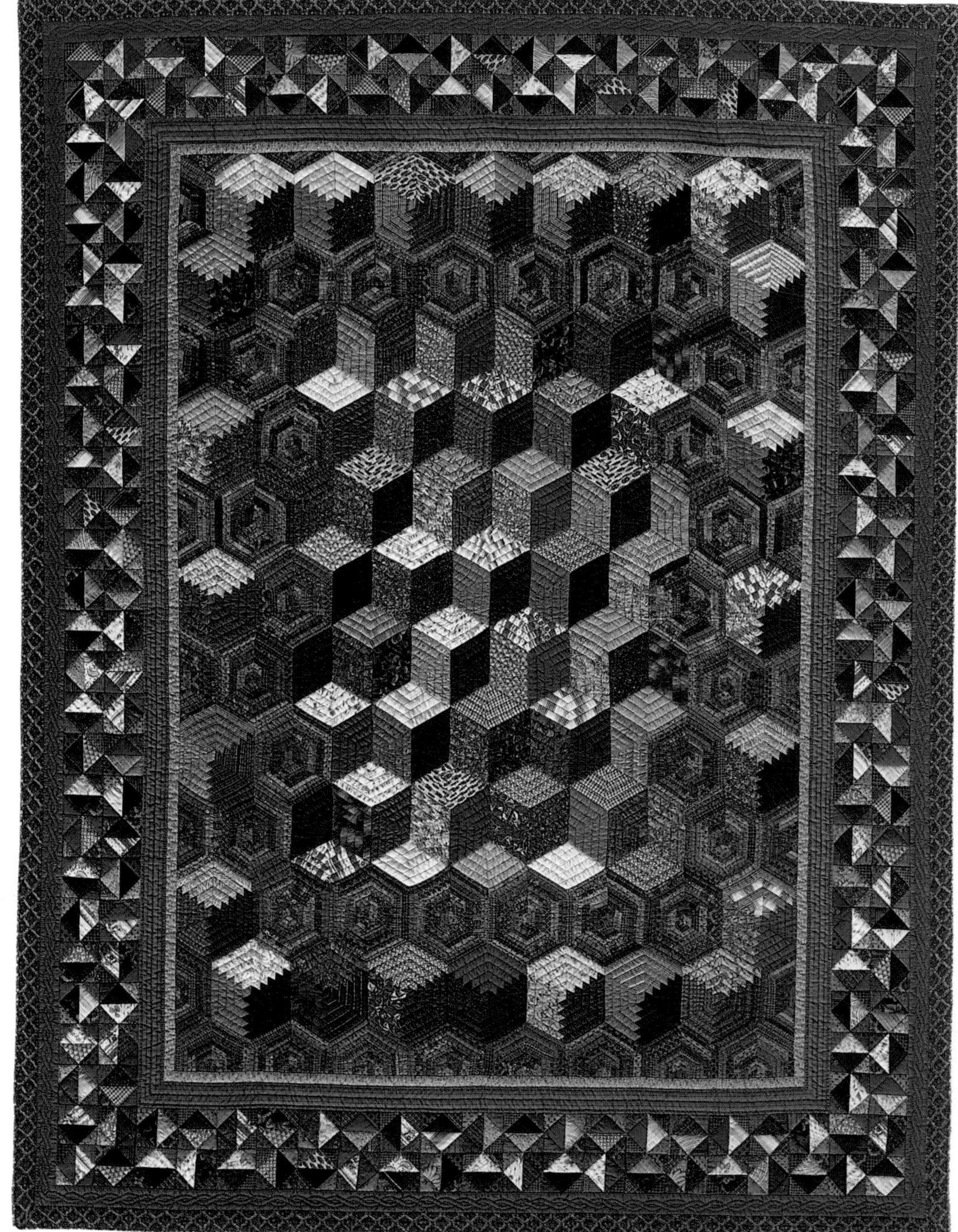

TUMBLING BLOCK LOG CABIN ▶

Flavin Glover. 1991. Auburn, Alabama. Cotton and cotton/polyester blends; machine pieced and hand quilted. 113 x 87 in. Collection of the artist.

In addition to quilts, Flavin Glover also designs and makes quilted clothing. Here, she has combined two of the favorite illusionistic patterns of the nineteenth century.

in the past thirty years and thousands of remarkable quilts rescued from neglect or even destruction by private and institutional collectors.

In response to the awakening interest of collectors and museums, the 1970s also brought the first truly comprehensive and well-researched overviews of quilt history. Jonathan Holstein's provocative *The Pieced Quilt: An American Design Tradition*, published shortly after his exhibition opened, was the first book to look seriously at quilts as works of art, and, like the exhibition, championed utilitarian quilts that most previous authors had largely ignored. *Quilts in America*, by Patsy and Myron Orlofsky, first published in 1974, set a new standard for careful and thorough scholarship in the field, while Carlton Safford and Robert Bishop's *American Quilts and Coverlets*, also published in 1974, offered a rich pictorial survey of historic bedcovers, from bed rugs and woven coverlets to quilts of every sort. Pat Ferrero, Linda Reuther, and Julie Silber's 1981 exhibition and catalog *American Quilts: A Handmade Legacy* balanced Holstein's art historical approach by drawing attention to the social history of quilting and placing quilts within the context of women's lives. Dozens of other historical studies followed these seminal works. Each new book or exhibition inspired researchers to dig deeper and explore different aspects of quilt history; each added pieces to the puzzle, filling in parts of the highly complex overall story.

The sheer volume of quilts existing today is staggering. A 1987 survey of museum and corporate collections in the United States and Canada conducted by the American Folklife Center at the Library of Congress identified over 25,000 quilts in public hands, a number that grows each year. The great majority of historic quilts remain in private hands, however. There are thousands of private collections of quilts of widely varying size and quality in the United States, Europe, Japan, and other countries. Many of these private collections include hundreds of pieces and a few have grown to contain one thousand or more quilts. Dozens of antique dealers across the country specialize in quilts, and such major auction houses as Christie's and Sotheby's regularly feature quilts in their sales of Americana and folk art.

In addition, forty-eight states have conducted or are in the process of conducting statewide quilt searches, far-reaching endeavors which have examined and documented over 140,000 historic quilts. Many of the state searches have mounted special exhibitions after completing their field work, and several, including Kentucky, New York, Ohio, Arizona, Texas, Illinois, and Vermont, have published books picturing and discussing at least a portion of the quilts surveyed. Quilts from Kentucky traveled nationally under the auspices of the Smithsonian Institution Traveling Exhibition Service, SITES. In addition to those in the United States, quilt surveys have also been conducted recently in England, Ireland, Canada, and Australia.

The Kentucky Quilt Project, Inc., organized in 1981, provided the model and the impetus for other state searches, which together have become an interlocking set of initiatives that has been called the largest grassroots movement in the decorative arts since the Index of American Design was compiled during the Great Depression. Like the Index of American Design, a WPA effort that recorded craft objects throughout the country, the state quilt projects have not only made a huge body of material available for study; they have also redefined understanding of the objects surveyed. The documentation of so many quilts has furnished quilt scholars with new insights, causing them to question some of the most basic and commonly held tenets of quilt history. Among these is the commonly accepted belief that pieced quilts were most often made from rag-bag scraps. While this may have been true for some hard pressed and frugal quilters, it now appears certain that the majority of quilters bought fabric specifically for their quilts and only used scraps from the rag bag to supplement. Necessity could indeed be the mother of invention, but it apparently did not dictate the choices of most quilters.

▼ The Vermont Quilt Festival, held each July since 1981 in Northfield, Vermont, draws thousands of quilt enthusiasts from all over the United States.

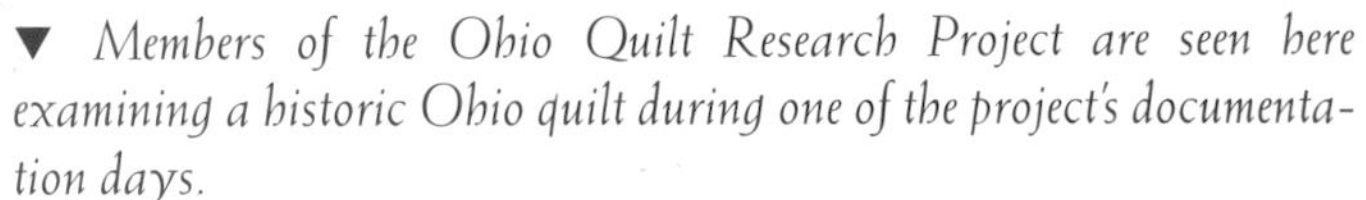

▼ Members of the Ohio Quilt Research Project are seen here examining a historic Ohio quilt during one of the project's documentation days.

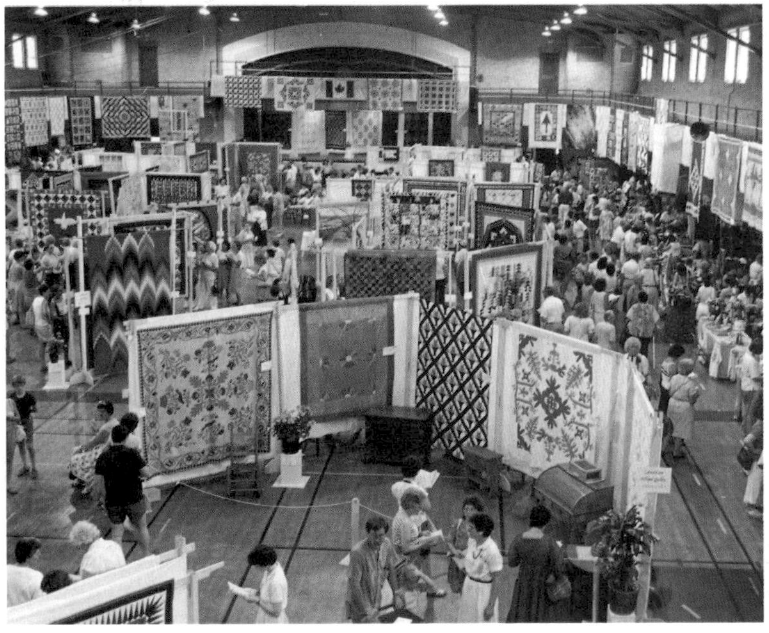

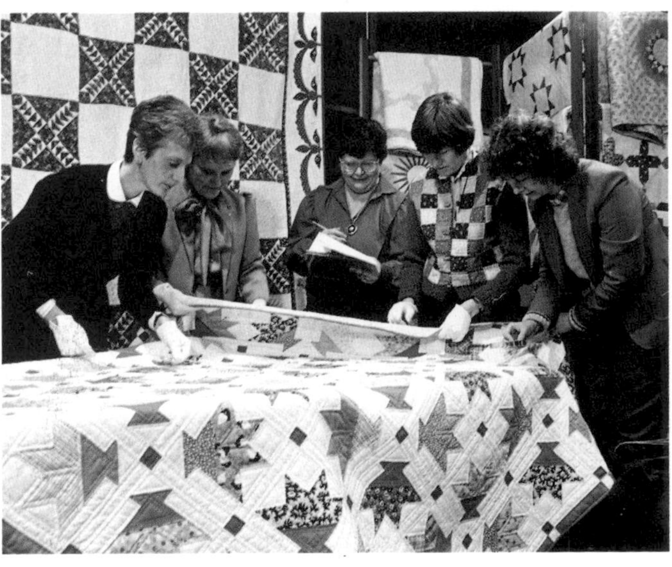

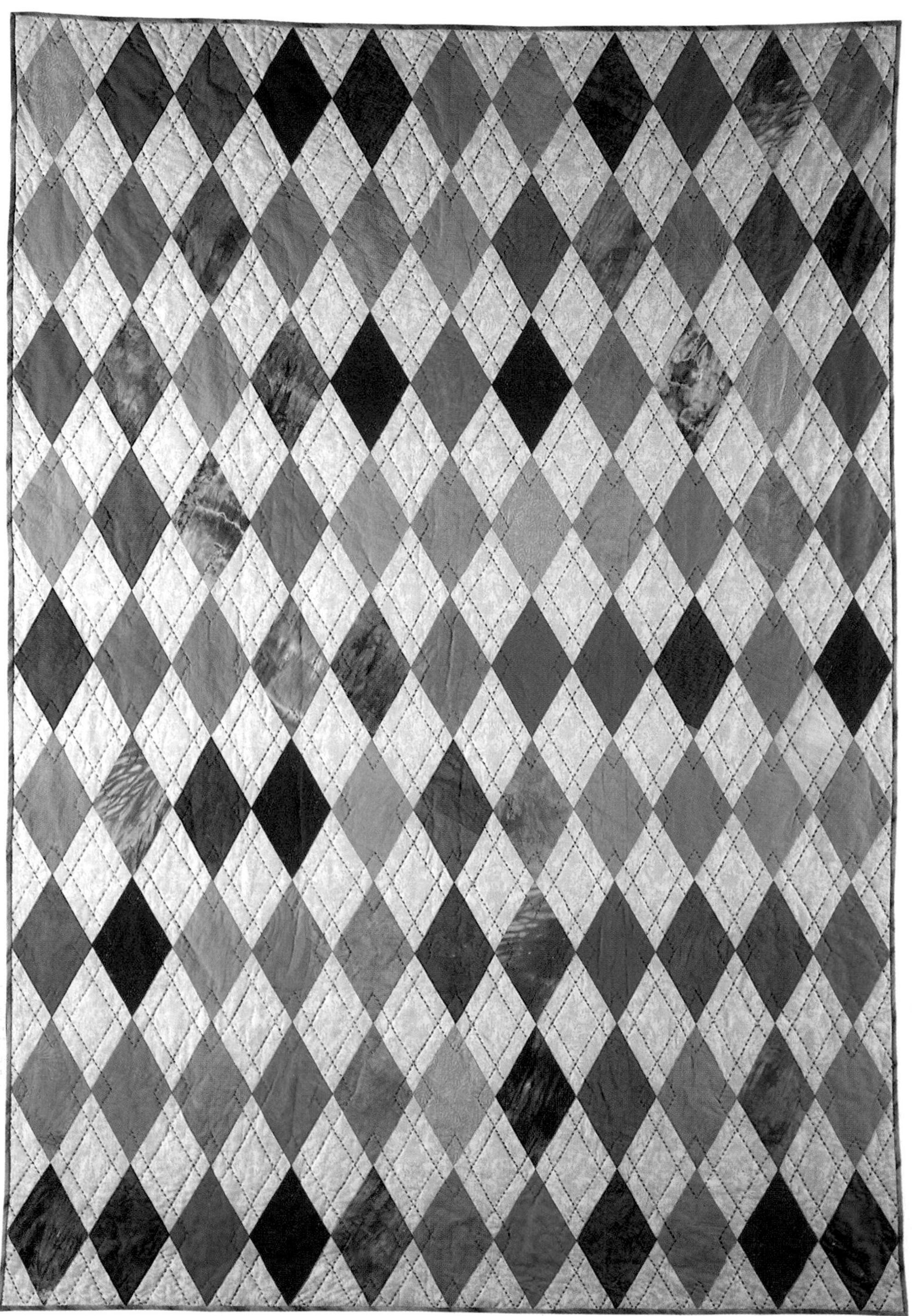

Harlequin ▸

Jo Walters. 1992. Miami, Florida. Cottons; machine pieced and hand quilted. 81 x 57 in. Collection of the artist.

This one-patch mosaic of diamonds was inspired by an antique harlequin marionette dressed in the motley traditionally associated with fools. The piece is quilted with an original technique developed by Jo Walters that she calls "BigStitch."

The Kentucky Quilt Project organized twelve quilt days in locations across the state and advertised widely through women's groups, local museums, and historical societies. Newspaper stories helped spread the word, which traveled by word of mouth from one family to the next. The organizers were met with an overwhelming response. Family treasures were unearthed and over one thousand quilts were examined and documented during the quilt days. Project directors urged quilters to preserve their heritage, and several of the finest quilts discovered during the project have since been donated to state museums where they can be enjoyed by all Kentuckians.

The state surveys have been tremendously positive experiences for organizers and quilt owners alike, creating a shared sense of pride in quiltmakers' achievements. Pat Moore, chairperson of the Historical Documentation Committee for the Colorado Quilting Council, summed up her involvement with the Colorado project this way: "So many times this year there has been an elderly lady who brought in her quilts for us to document, not knowing what it is that we do. We put the quilt up on the frame to photograph it and she sees that quilt in a whole new way and for a few minutes her quilt is the star of the show. I believe we honor all women, all quiltmakers, past and present, when we take the time to pay attention and make a record of the quilts we document."

Ralph Waldo Emerson once said, "Properly speaking, there is no history, only biography." The new, context-oriented approaches to history inaugurated in the 1960s took him at his word and tried to balance the picture painted by studies limited to great events and powerful individuals by exploring the lives of everyday people. These new methods of looking at the past affected the way in which quilts were perceived. Quilts were finally recognized as functional objects with fascinating and revealing stories to tell about their times as well as aesthetic masterpieces with an important place in the history of American craftsmanship, art, and design. Like facets of a diamond, the different aspects of a quilt enhance its appeal, offering a variety of ways to view and appreciate its significance, the whole always being more than the sum of the parts.

The women's movement of the 1960s had a profound influence on quilt study and quiltmaking. The role of women in the shaping of American society had, up to this point, been largely ignored by historians (most of whom were men) and feminist scholars sought to broaden and refocus the lines of inquiry. Women's history became an important part of the curriculum at many centers of higher learning. Women's studies, which examined, valued, and validated women's lives, helped to dignify the quilt, lifting it from mundane domestic obscurity. Quilts eventually came to be recognized as windows into the lives of the everyday women who had made them and as critical documents of earlier times and experiences. Quilts provided a unifying thread, a shared creative activity that illuminated nineteenth- and early twentieth-century women's lives as no other artifact could. By studying quilts, researchers and scholars (most of whom, not surprisingly, have been women) discovered that they could learn not only about the craft itself but also about the complex emotions and situations of the craftswomen themselves, thereby filling in some of the enormous blanks in the historical record of women.

The importance of quilts as social documents, as well as their basis as functional objects, has often seemed at odds with an appreciation of their aesthetic significance. Studies of material culture, the things made and used by people living at a certain period of time, emphasize the contexts within which artifacts were made rather than their individual artistry or craftsmanship. Material culture, which values process over product, has often fought a pitched either/or battle with art history, which studies aesthetics and creativity. Folklorists who resist taking quilts out of their social context and art historians uncomfortable including such concerns in a discussion of aesthetic merit have complicated attempts at dialogue that might bridge the two camps. Both sides of the argument, which has been waged over the "folk" arts since the term was coined, have valid points, but they need to be seen as complementary rather than contradictory or mutually exclusive.

Quilt study has been furthered but also complicated by the enormous, ongoing creative energy of quiltmakers, some of whom are transforming the medium through their innovative work. An estimated seven million Americans are now making quilts, as are millions of other women (and men) around the world. Over one thousand books on quilts and quiltmaking are currently available in English. The great majority of these are instructional, offering technical assistance and support to the legions of home quilters eager to expand their knowledge of historic and contemporary methods and skills. More than any other craft or art form, the art

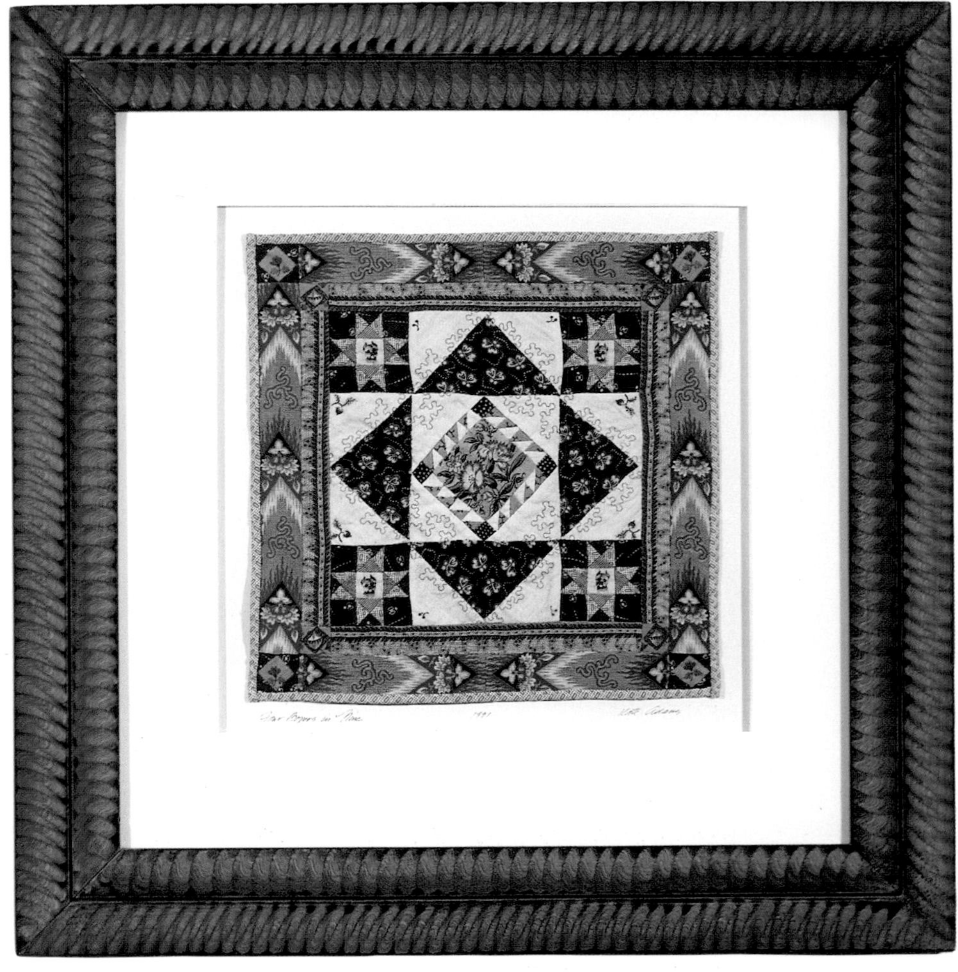

Four Boxers in Nine (Miniature Medallion Quilt) ▸

Kate Adams. 1991. Kennebunkport, Maine. Historic cottons; hand pieced and quilted. Wooden frame; hand painted by James Hastrich. Quilt: 8 3/4 x 8 3/4 in.; frame: 14 x 14 in. Collection of the artist.

Kate Adams is a professional quiltmaker who specializes in miniature adaptations of traditional patterns rendered on a one inch = one foot scale. This tiny central medallion quilt is named for the conversation print used in the center of the stars, which are nine-patch blocks. The quilt is made entirely from scraps of historic fabric which date from 1830 to 1900. Adams is particularly drawn to the central medallion style, because, she says, "It allows . . . a lot of spontaneity in the design."

of quiltmaking seems to be picking up momentum rather than slowing down, and scholars and researchers struggle to keep up with all the developments in the field.

Quilt teaching has become a mini-industry in its own right and dozens of well-known quiltmakers earn a large portion of their income traveling and teaching classes. Teachers are usually known through their books, which often focus on a particular type of quilt or approach to quiltmaking. Although much contemporary instruction inevitably teaches technical skills, and many students are satisfied to make quilts just like their master's, some teachers try to tap the creative process and challenge their students' resourcefulness and imagination. Quiltmaker and teacher Joe Cunningham, for example, sometimes asks class members to bring twelve pieces of scrap material to class with them. Students invariably bring carefully chosen pieces that they have already mentally formed into a design or pattern. Cunningham confounds their plans and expectations by putting all the pieces together in a hat and then asking each quilter to draw twelve out and make a square using what she or he has found. Quilters are thus forced to feel the frustration and hard-won satisfaction of finding their own solutions.

The number of people involved with quilts, quilt study, and quiltmaking continues to grow exponentially. Houston's seventeen-year-old International Quilt Festival and Market, which bills itself as "The Nation's Trade Show for the Quilting Industry," attracts over 45,000 quilters each year, while the American Quilter's Society annual convention in Paducah, Kentucky, draws over 30,000. The Houston show, which is the world's largest quilt festival, is a "consumer show, sale and quiltmaking academy" that has grown to fill a 100,000-square-foot convention hall with vendors, dealers, teachers, and special invitational and juried exhibits. Over 75,000 quilters belong to the American Quilter's Society, which maintains a museum of contemporary quilts in Paducah dedicated to showing "the accomplishments of today's quilters." The society offers several quilt exhibitions each year and publishes dozens of catalogs and how-to books for quilters as well as a magazine, *American Quilter*. The 1995 AQS show offered $80,000 in cash prizes, and over one hundred lectures and classes by thirty-nine instructors. The leading American quilting periodical, *The Quilter's Newsletter*, which has been published monthly since 1969, reaches over 170,000 subscribers, and quilts and especially quiltmaking are the focus of at least a dozen other magazines. A quick glance through any of these publications will reveal the variety of small industries that have sprung up to supply the ever increasing market for quilter's tools, supplies, and instructional aids ranging from needles and thread to patterns, kits, books, seminars, tours, and even "quilt cruises."

A network of quilt guilds now covers the country and is spreading around the world. There are over 1,500 quilt guilds with some 225,000 members in the United States, and dozens, if not hundreds, of others in Canada, Japan, Western Europe, Australia, and New Zealand. Guilds range in size from local groups with a handful of members to regional and international organizations with hundreds or even thousands of members. There are guilds in virtually every state in the union and many states support dozens of different groups. Guild names such as Thread Benders, Stitch and Gab, Silver Thimbles, or Piece Corps sometimes belie the seriousness with which these groups approach their common interest. The ten-member Hands of Friendship Quiltmakers group of Ascension Parish, Louisiana, for example, notes that:

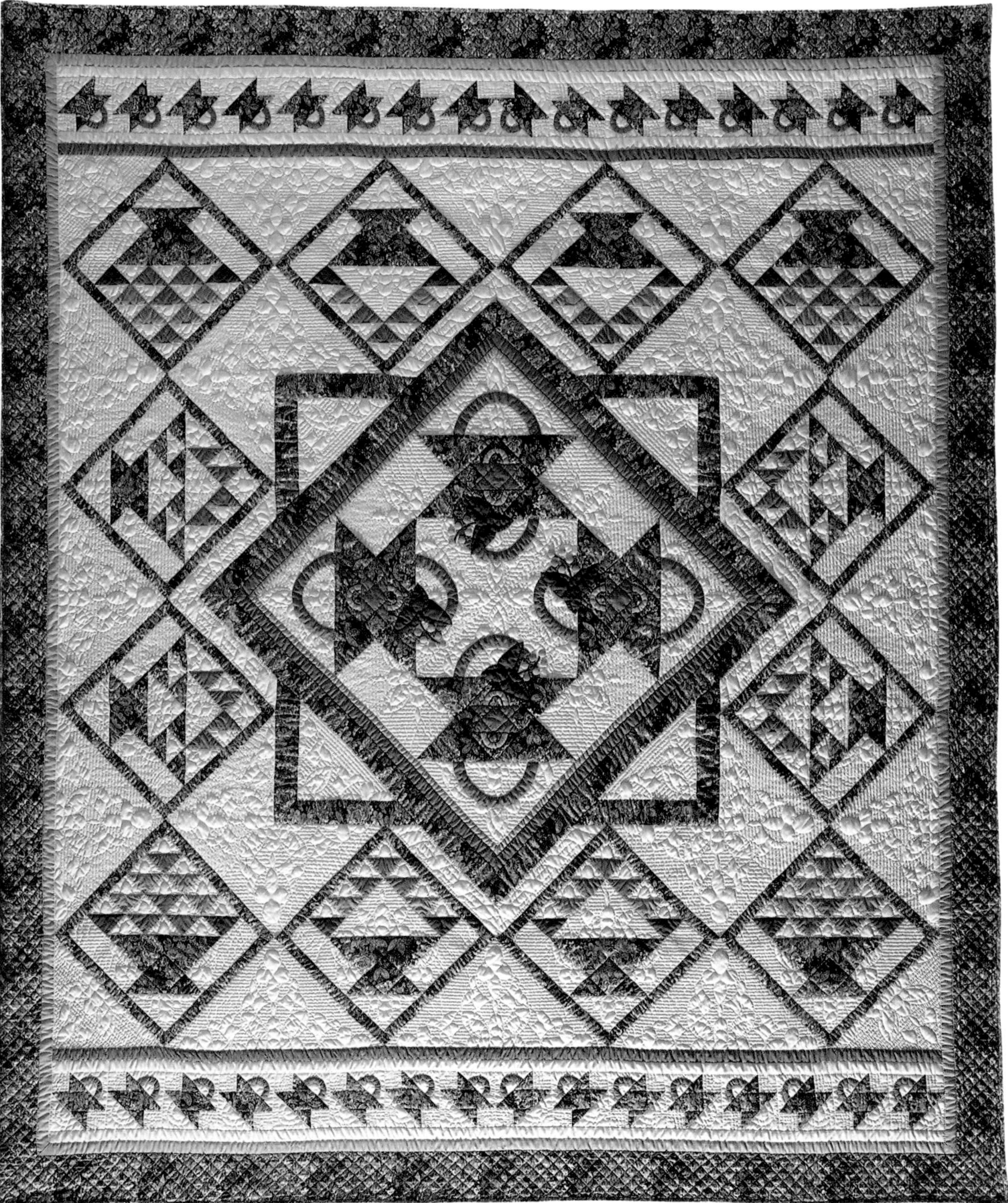

◂ **BASKET MEDALLION**

Donna Hanson Eines. 1987. Edmonds, Washington. Cottons; hand appliquéd, pieced, and quilted. 100 x 83 in. Collection of the artist.

This original design uses four different basket patterns and includes borders of tiny baskets at top and bottom. The wide variety of basket forms is complemented by intricate and elaborate hand quilting, so tightly stitched that the portions of the piece left unquilted appear to be stuffed.

We purposefully want to keep our group small. In this way, we can maintain personal, intimate and friendly relationships. . . . Our group is composed of loyal, dedicated, motivated members. Quiltmaking is our only business and we get right to the business-at-hand in our twice-monthly, all-day "quilt-ins"' . . . We learn individually through personal research and as a group through demonstrations and workshops. We are committed to sharing our knowledge with others so that our "best" quilting will constantly become "better." We put our knowledge and skills to work. . . . We organized a local quilt day which resulted in locating 110 old quilts [and] . . . also provide demonstrations and workshops about quiltmaking and quilt history. Our members have donated books to the local library and have made lap quilts for nursing homes, pillows for abused children and crib quilts for babies with AIDS.

Despite the current popularity of quilts and quiltmaking and the size of the quiltmaking community, it remains in many ways a closed and sometimes surprisingly insular system. The next phase of its growth is already demanding more interaction with the worlds of the academy and the art and antiques marketplace, both of which are imposing their own high and complex standards of scholarship and connoisseurship on the previously accepted norms of the quilt community. Growing pains are inevitable in this relatively youthful and exuberant grassroots movement. Quilt scholarship remains in its infancy, and many new theories are being developed and tested by the hundreds of amateur and still relatively few professional researchers who are gathering quilts and pieces of quilt history and sifting through the dramatically increased universe of data. As more professional historians and art scholars begin to look at quilts seriously, a clearer understanding of their enormous importance to the story of American life, social history, and artistic achievement is emerging.

The American Quilt Study Group, founded in 1980 by quilt scholar Sally Garoutte, has played a particularly important role in raising the level of scholarship within the quilting community. The AQSG's goal is to "develop a responsible and accurate body of information about quilts and their makers." The group's mission statement continues, "A reliable history of quiltmaking provides insights into the lives and times of quiltmakers, and connects women with their heritage and their place in creative art. The American Quilt Study Group is dedicated to preserving the story of quiltmaking—past, present and future." The AQSG, which now has over 750 members, holds a seminar each year in a major city, where a number of papers on different aspects of quilt history are presented. The papers are published in an annual volume called *Uncoverings*. The 1994 conference in Birmingham, Alabama, for example, included a keynote address by art quilter Nancy Crow called "What's Happening in Quiltmaking Today," as well as papers on such diverse topics as Scotch-Irish quilts in West Virginia, Baltimore album quilts, and Toni Morrison's novel *Beloved* seen as a metaphoric crazy quilt.

Among the many other organizations and forums presenting new information and interpretations of the history and meanings of quilts and quiltmaking are: the Oral Traditions Project of Pennsylvania, coordinated by folklorist Jeanette Lasansky, a lecturer at Bucknell University; *The Quilt Journal: An International Review*, recently founded, directed, and edited by

Shelly Zegart and Eleanor Bingham Miller of the Kentucky Quilt Project, and quilt scholar Jonathan Holstein; and *Quilts in Santa Fe,* a new conference directed by quilt author and former Los Angeles County Museum associate curator Sandi Fox. These types of conferences and networks will undoubtedly continue to proliferate as inquiry into quilts, quiltmaking, and quiltmakers intensifies and diversifies, incorporating approaches and methodologies drawn from a variety of academic disciplines.

Perhaps because they have worked so hard to reclaim it, quilters are fiercely protective of their heritage and respond to any perceived threat to its integrity in a manner totally peculiar to this craft. The Smithsonian Institution caused a furor when it recently licensed Chinese-made reproductions of several quilt masterpieces from its collection, including Harriet Powers's *Bible Quilt.* Enraged American quilters organized a strong and compelling public protest against the move, arguing that the Smithsonian was doubly wrong in sending the work overseas, thereby, as they saw it, falsifying the quilt's history and unfairly competing against the work of American craftspeople. The debate helped galvanize public discussion and awareness about the continuing importance of quilts as documents and expressions of the experience of American women. More than 25,000 quilters signed petitions of protest that were presented to the Smithsonian, a lobbying group was formed, and a panel of major figures in the American quilt world went to Washington to meet with Smithsonian officials. The Smithsonian, caught completely off guard, countered with its own economic argument, explaining that it was carrying out its educational mission by making the quilts widely available at an extremely reasonable price. The Institution has since worked to assuage the feelings of still angry quilters by seeking their input, limiting the museum's Chinese contract, awarding further quilt reproductions to American quilt cooperatives such as Cabin Creek Quilters Co-Op of West Virginia, authorizing an American-made line of high quality fabrics for quilters based on historic cloth found in its quilt collection, and licensing kits and a book of patterns adapted from Smithsonian quilts.

Quilt cooperatives like Cabin Creek have played an important economic role in rural communities for many years. Co-ops, particularly in the South, have provided outlets for craftspeople's work for decades and have also been instrumental in keeping traditional crafts alive. The idea was fostered in Appalachia by Dr. William Goodell Frost, president of Berea College in Kentucky and a key figure in the revival of handcrafts in the early twentieth century. Beginning in the 1890s, Dr. Frost recognized the cultural and economic value of the traditional handcrafts of the region and encouraged what he dubbed the "fireside industries," holding annual fairs at Berea, helping weavers and other craftspeople market their products, and ultimately establishing a crafts curriculum at his college. Throughout the early decades of this century, the idea spread throughout the rural South, to places like Penland, North Carolina, and Pleasant Hill, Tennessee, where craft schools were established which, in the words of Penland's early promotional literature, "grew first out of a dream to revive and perpetuate the native arts and crafts of a mountain community, and secondly, out of a desire to provide for the people of this mountain community an opportunity of supplementing the products of their small farms with a little cash income." A number of quilting cooperatives were established in the 1930s, and today there are over one hundred craft cooperatives in Appalachia, virtually all of them offering quilts made by local artisans which are then marketed outside the region by the co-op.

Although quilters have always competed with one another, both consciously and unconsciously, and quilt competitions have been a feature of fairs since the mid-1800s, competitions have exerted a particularly strong influence over quiltmaking in recent years. Hundreds of quilt shows are held all over the world each year, many with cash prizes. Quilts entered in these contests are separated into different categories, which can be as simple as bed quilts and wall hangings, or as complex as the American Quilter's Society's traditional pieced, innovative pieced, appliqué, other techniques, and wall quilts, each category divided into a professional and amateur division. Each category in a competition is judged separately and a best of show is also awarded. The contests typically have complex and highly standardized methods of judging, which attempt to balance artistic and technical evaluations. The seventeen-year-old Vermont Quilt Festival, held annually in Northfield, Vermont, has, for example, developed a one hundred-point system. Each quilt can be given up to fifteen points for overall impact, forty points for design, and forty-five points for craftsmanship. When considering design, judges may award up to twenty points for use of pattern and design, ten points for effectiveness of color, five points for suitability of materials, and five points for border treatment. Under craftsmanship, up to twenty points are available for the precision of the work on the quilt's top and back, twenty points for the quality of the quilting and/or other needlework, and five points for the binding and edging. Such stringent rules, of course, help ensure fair and equitable standards for all entrants, but can also enforce a certain uniformity among entries by tending to lead quiltmakers to look to the rules rather than their own creative instincts when fashioning pieces for competition. Real innovation and originality can be out of place in such a climate, and technique can be valued over aesthetic quality, discouraging quilters whose craftsmanship does not match their artistic abilities.

As this study can only begin to suggest, the world of contemporary quiltmaking is diverse in the extreme, with approaches as complexly varied as the women and men who inhabit it. Some quilters, such as Martha Skelton of Mississippi and Mary Ghormley of Nebraska, still follow strictly traditional methods and patterns and produce quilts that can be virtually indistinguishable from pieces made a hundred or more years ago. Other quilters, such as Laurel Horton of South Carolina and Suzanne Marshall of Missouri, produce original pieced and/or appliqué designs that extend the range and vocabulary of traditional quiltmaking in ways familiar to all quiltmakers, by incorporating contemporary colors, fabrics, design motifs, and images into their work.

Still other modern quiltmakers, such as Carol Gersen of Maryland and Jonathan Shannon of California, are obscuring the boundaries between traditional and art quilting by creating pieces intended to be viewed as works of art but which are made primarily using traditional methods. These quilters and others, like Velda Newman of California and Ruth McDowell of

Massachusetts, have created consistent bodies of work that straddle the middle ground between quilt as craft and quilt as art; their quilts seem to beg the question of what is traditional and what is art. An increasing number of quiltmakers move back and forth between both worlds, creating traditional pieces and art quilts that often share little or no visual common ground. Julia E. Pfaff of Virginia, for example, has made a number of colorful traditional pieced quilts that employ Middle Eastern embroidery techniques; she also makes uniquely constructed art quilts that reflect her love of printmaking and her profession of archaeology. Certainly, all of these innovative quiltmakers are helping to expand and redefine quilting through their work and the question of labels is ultimately irrelevant.

All facets of quiltmaking are being explored, not least the countless specialized techniques that attract many quilters. Some advocates of the art of appliqué, for example, have concentrated on Baltimore style album quilts, carefully analyzing the techniques and patterns found in historic examples of the genre and designing their own blocks and overall compositions based on their findings. Other quilters have become masters of machine piecing, *broderie perse*, trapunto, Seminole strip piecing, reverse appliqué, Batik and Ikat dyeing, stenciling, and other, sometimes arcane, techniques. Still others have taken original approaches to design in an effort to express their own interests and perspectives on the world. Teresa Barkley of Astoria, New York, for example, has carried her knowledge and love of postage stamps into her quiltmaking, creating a series of witty quilts whose designs resemble the issue of some erudite and slightly surreal post office. Yvonne Foreman, who lives outside New York City, has made a number of intricate geometric quilts based on decorative subway tile mosaics, while Texan Judy Cloninger makes quilts based on classic Oriental carpet designs. A few quilters, such as Tina Gravatt of Philadelphia and Kate Adams of Kennebunkport, Maine, specialize in miniature quilts, making precisely accurate, diminutive versions of historic patterns that defy traditional expectations of scale. Gravatt often exhibits her quilts on doll beds which represent the era of the quilt's popularity, thereby giving the quilts an added historic visual emphasis, while Adams, who collects and uses remnants of historic fabric for an authentic effect, sets her

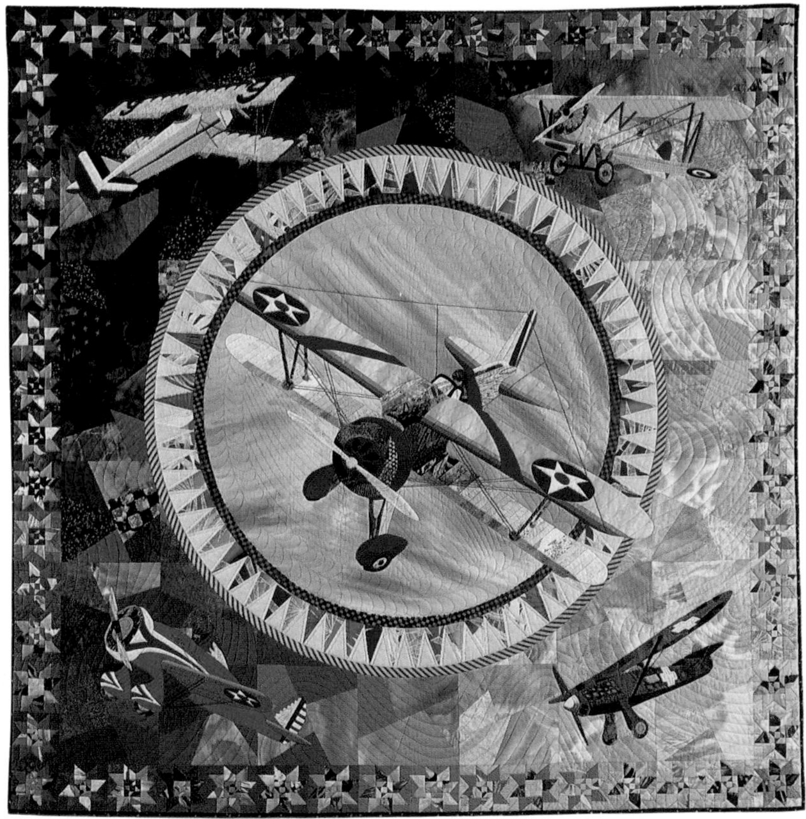

AIR SHOW ▸

Jonathan Shannon. 1992. Belvedere, California. Cottons; hand pieced, appliquéd, and quilted. 81 x 81 in. Museum of the American Quilter's Society, Paducah, Kentucky.

Jonathan Shannon has worked as an advertising director and fashion designer. He took up quilting in 1988 and says, "Quiltmaking combines my artistic training with my love of textiles into a medium which gives me intense pleasure and creative satisfaction." Shannon's quilts combine modern imagery with a complete mastery of traditional techniques and craftsmanship. "Tradition is how we anchor ourselves to other people," he states. "Tradition is respect for others. Even though I want my quilts to be . . . an expression of my individuality, I also want them to tie me to the history of quiltmaking. I want to be part of that stream of effort across time." *Air Show* won Best of Show at the 1993 American Quilter's Society contest.

IO'S DREAM ▶

Joe Cunningham and Gwen Marston. 1984. Michigan. Cottons; hand pieced and quilted. 45 x 35 in. Private collection.

Using a combination of large blocks of solid color and intricate hand quilting, *Io's Dream* shows the influence of Amish quiltmaking. The quilting represents a series of Zeus's metamorphoses during his lengthy pursuit of Io: he appears as a fog, the sea, a peacock's tail, and, most prominently, a bull.

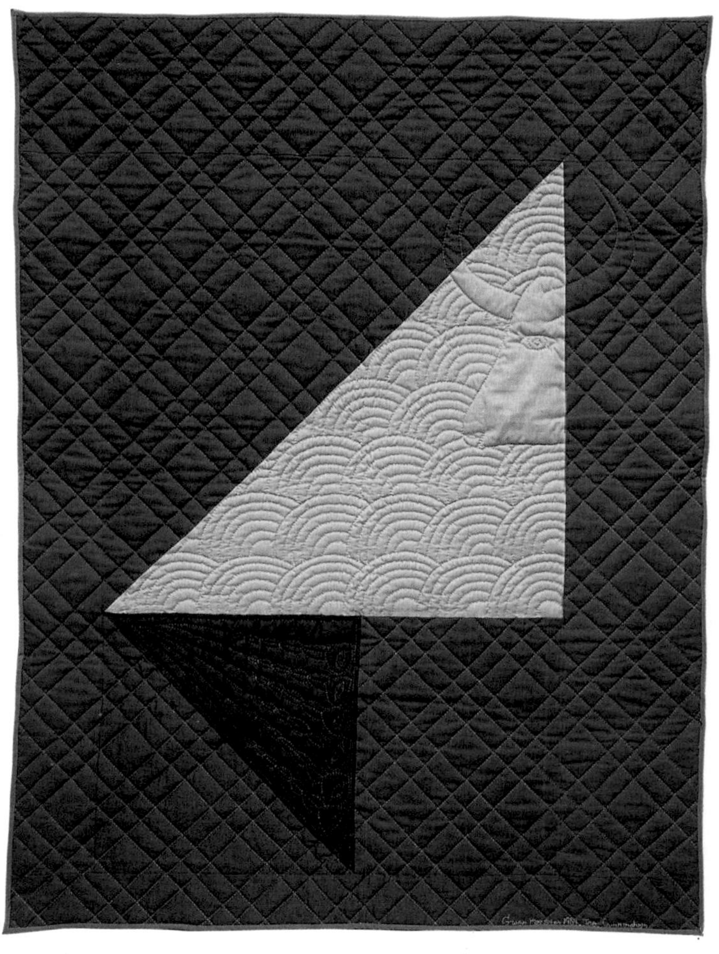

quilts in grain-painted frames, intending them to be hung on the wall and viewed as small works of art.

Quilts, which workers and visitors alike find a cheerful and pleasing alternative to modern art, also have become a staple of corporate boardrooms, offices, and such public spaces as banks, hospitals, and airports. Esprit de Corp., a San Francisco-based manufacturer of women's apparel, set the standard in the early 1970s by decorating the walls of its open, warehouselike corporate headquarters with portions of a remarkable collection of Amish quilts gathered by founder Doug Tompkins and his advisor Julie Silber, who became curator of the collection in 1982. Esprit's offices have long been a required stop for quilt enthusiasts. In recent years, the company, now under the direction of Susie Tompkins, has set an entirely new corporate tone with its growing collection of "maverick" quilts—one-of-a-kind utility quilts that often break conventional rules of craftsmanship or composition but succeed brilliantly as quirky and utterly original aesthetic statements. Dozens of other corporations, including AT&T, IBM, General Foods, Philip Morris, Levi-Strauss, and The Chase Manhattan Bank, also include quilts in their art collections and public exhibit areas. These and many other businesses of all sizes have found that quilts make people more comfortable in the workplace by softening an often cold, impersonal, and generic feel.

Public appreciation of quilts also derives from their role in commemorating significant events and focusing attention on important causes. From the Civil War on, quilts have remained a staple of women's relief and charitable organizations. They have been sold to support efforts from disaster relief to the prevention of child abuse, and are also donated to children's service organizations, hospitals, and other worthy causes. Thousands of quilts were made to celebrate the Bicentennial. Many of these were group efforts, albums put together by members of church, school, scout or other social and community organizations. In 1986 the Museum of American Folk Art in New York presented The Great American Quilt Festival, which included a contest in honor of the Statue of Liberty's 100th anniversary and drew entries from each of the fifty states. In 1989, over 7,000 North Dakotans celebrated the centennial of their state's entry into the Union by contributing to a massive 85 x 134-foot commemorative quilt. But this effort is dwarfed, both in size and number of contributors, by the AIDS memorial quilt organized by the NAMES Project, which, by October of 1992, when it was spread on the mall in Washington, D.C., covered thirteen acres.

The AIDS memorial quilt was conceived in 1985 by Cleve Jones, a longtime gay rights activist from San Francisco. Jones had asked marchers in an annual candlelight parade to write down names of people they knew who had died of AIDS. The names were taped on the walls of the Federal Building in San Francisco, and the sight brought Jones an epiphany: "Suddenly the names looked like a patchwork quilt, and that idea evoked such warm old memories of comfort. I had been consumed with rage and fear. Most of my old friends were dead. I felt that we lived in this little ghetto on the West Coast that would be destroyed without . . . the rest of the world even noticing. I knew we needed a memorial." Since 1986, when Jones made the first panel for the quilt in honor of his best friend, over 20,000 lives have been memorialized by friends, lovers, and family members as part of this ongoing project, which is at once a healing exercise, a public protest and consciousness raiser, and a way to honor the victims of the most pernicious scourge in our country's history. In November 1994, twenty-eight prominent fashion designers, including Bill Blass, Giorgio Armani, Ralph Lauren, Donna Karan, and Calvin Klein, took out a full-page ad in *The New York Times* to announce that they were supporting the NAMES project by creating and displaying "a magnificent series of designer panels" for the quilt and asked readers to "join us in our grand design to illustrate the impact of AIDS." Sadly, the quilt continues to grow and now is so large that it must be shown in pieces.

As quiltmaking enters the information age, quilters literally have the world at their fingertips. They can avail themselves of techniques, textile traditions, and design ideas drawn from the entire history of quiltmaking both here and around the world. An American quilter can, for example, be influenced by Japanese art as she designs a pictorial quilt, while a Japanese quilter can use kimono silks to fashion his version of a traditional American Log Cabin pattern. As regional and ethnic traditions break down under the homogenizing weight of mass culture, their peculiar innovations and techniques are admired, studied, assimilated, and absorbed by other quilters. A number of quiltmakers from outside the traditions are making Amish or Hawaiian style quilts, for example, sometimes reproducing historic examples, but more often using the traditional concepts and examples as a starting point for their own creative ideas. In this way the traditions are transformed, perhaps losing some or all of their original ethnic purity, but, on the other hand, extending their range of expression and accessibility and remaining viable.

Unlike previous revivals of interest in quiltmaking, the great revival that began in the 1960s shows no sign of faltering. Instead, it seems to grow stronger and more vital year by year. The act of quiltmaking seems a mirror in which virtually anyone can find her or his own reflection. The medium's elastic and unshakeable malleability, its ability to absorb multiple influences and vast cultural differences without losing its own identity, help ensure its continued vitality. Quilts are now, finally, both a widely accepted and appreciated part of the panorama of American history, and a part of the fabric of modern daily life, made, used, and enjoyed by millions of people around the world. At the same time that quilting's past is being explored in new and exciting ways, its future is being assured by creative individuals who are finding myriad ways to enliven and extend its varied traditions into the twenty-first century.

Quilts tie the varied threads of our history and experience together, telling us who we are, where we have come from, and what we carry into our future. Both as metaphor and creative act, the binding and empowering energy of the quilt will undoubtedly continue to work its magic as long as people seek to warm and comfort each other, and to express themselves.

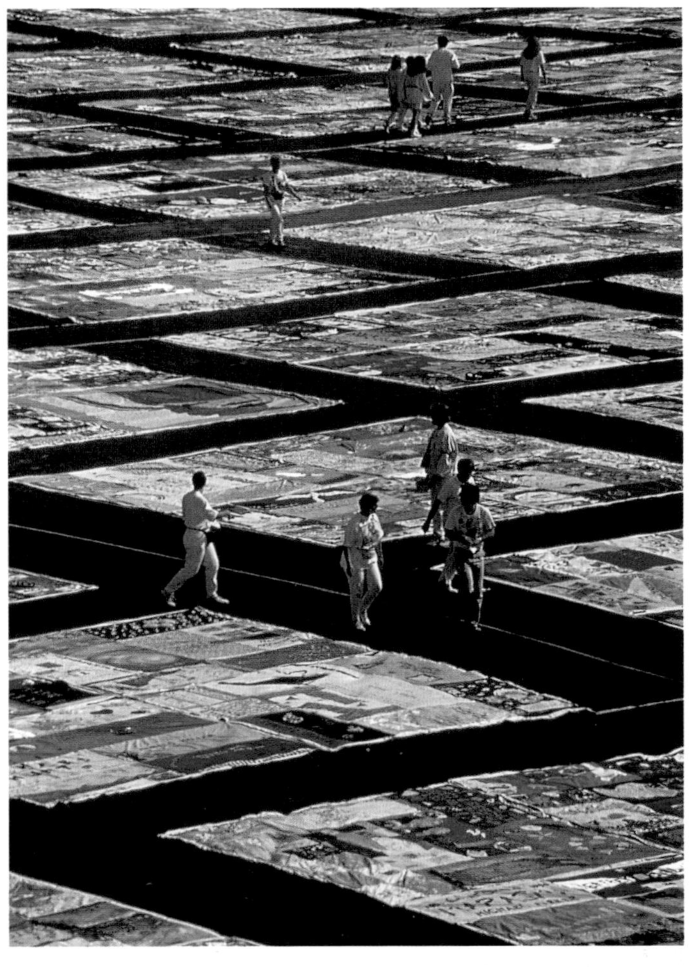

▼ **THE AIDS MEMORIAL QUILT (DETAIL ▶)**

1985–1992.

Begun in 1985, this tragic document has grown to include over 20,000 panels, each memorializing someone who has died from AIDS. The assembled quilt is seen here exhibited on the Mall in Washington, D.C., along with a closer view of some of the panels that were made in remembrance of departed loved ones.

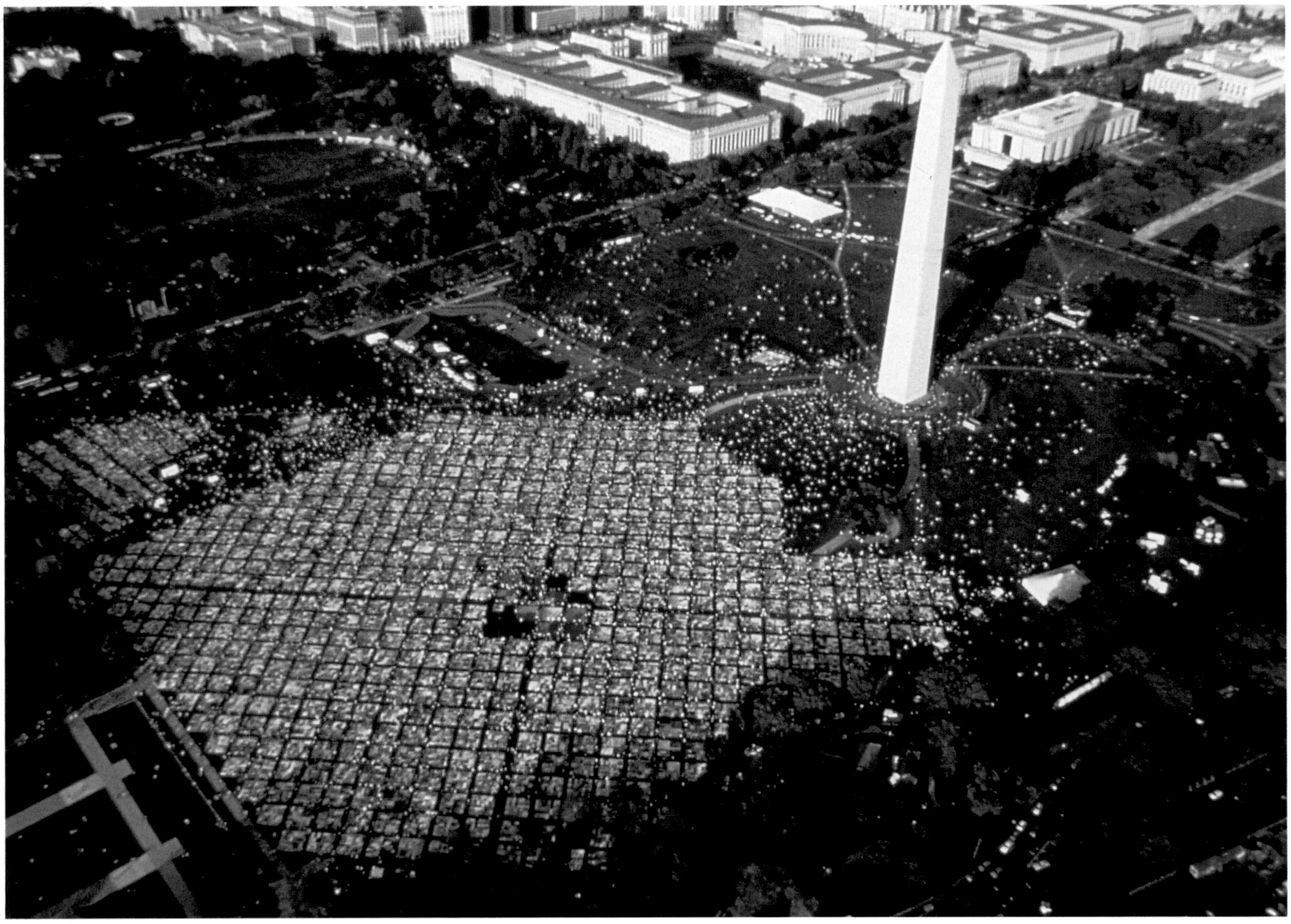

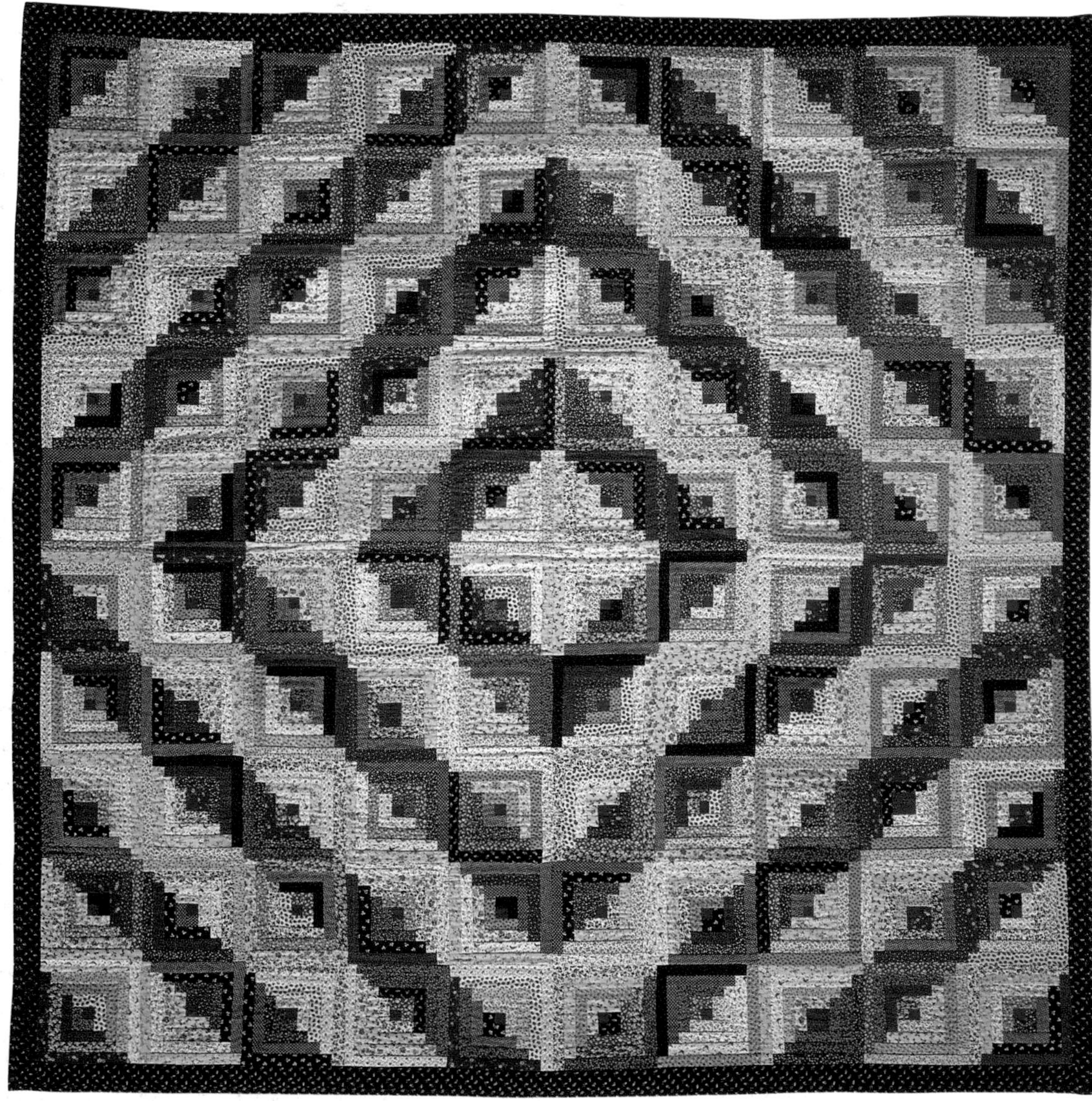

◄ **MOUNT SAINT HELEN'S QUILT (REVERSIBLE LOG CABIN—BARN RAISING)**

Louise Owens Townsend. 1980. Denver, Colorado. Cottons; machine pieced with hand appliqué. 87 x 86 in. Collection of the artist.

This reversible quilt was made during the powerful spring 1980 eruption of Mount Saint Helen's volcano in Washington State. The side with intense yellow, orange, and red represents the fiery inner core of the volcano, while the lighter brown and rust side represents the forested mountainside that was decimated in the cataclysm. Louise Townsend was the managing editor of *Quilter's Newsletter Magazine* for a number of years.

MOUNT SAINT HELEN'S QUILT (REVERSIBLE LOG CABIN—BARN RAISING) (DETAIL) ►

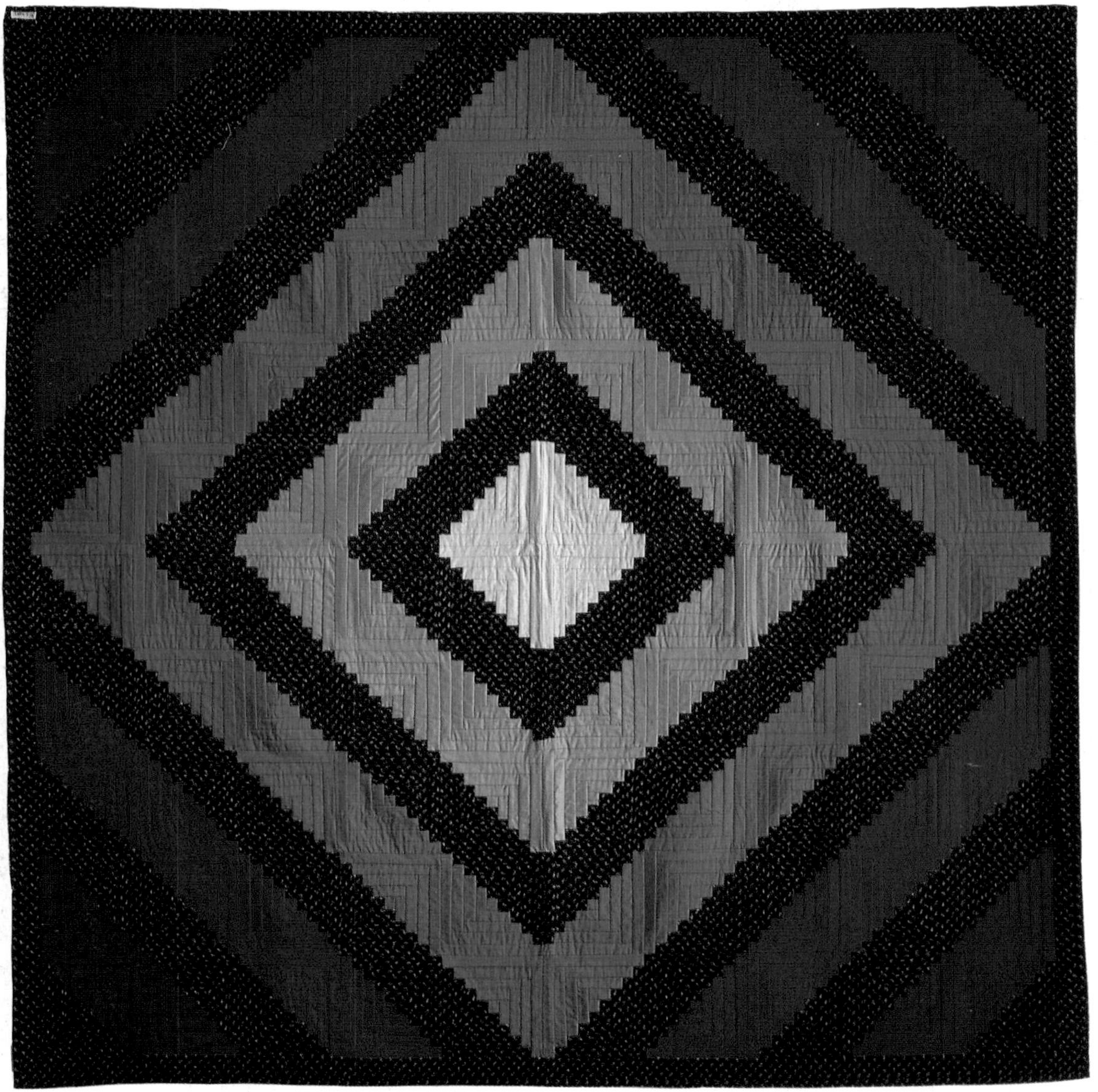

◄ **MOUNT SAINT HELEN'S QUILT (REVERSIBLE LOG CABIN—BARN RAISING) (REVERSE)**

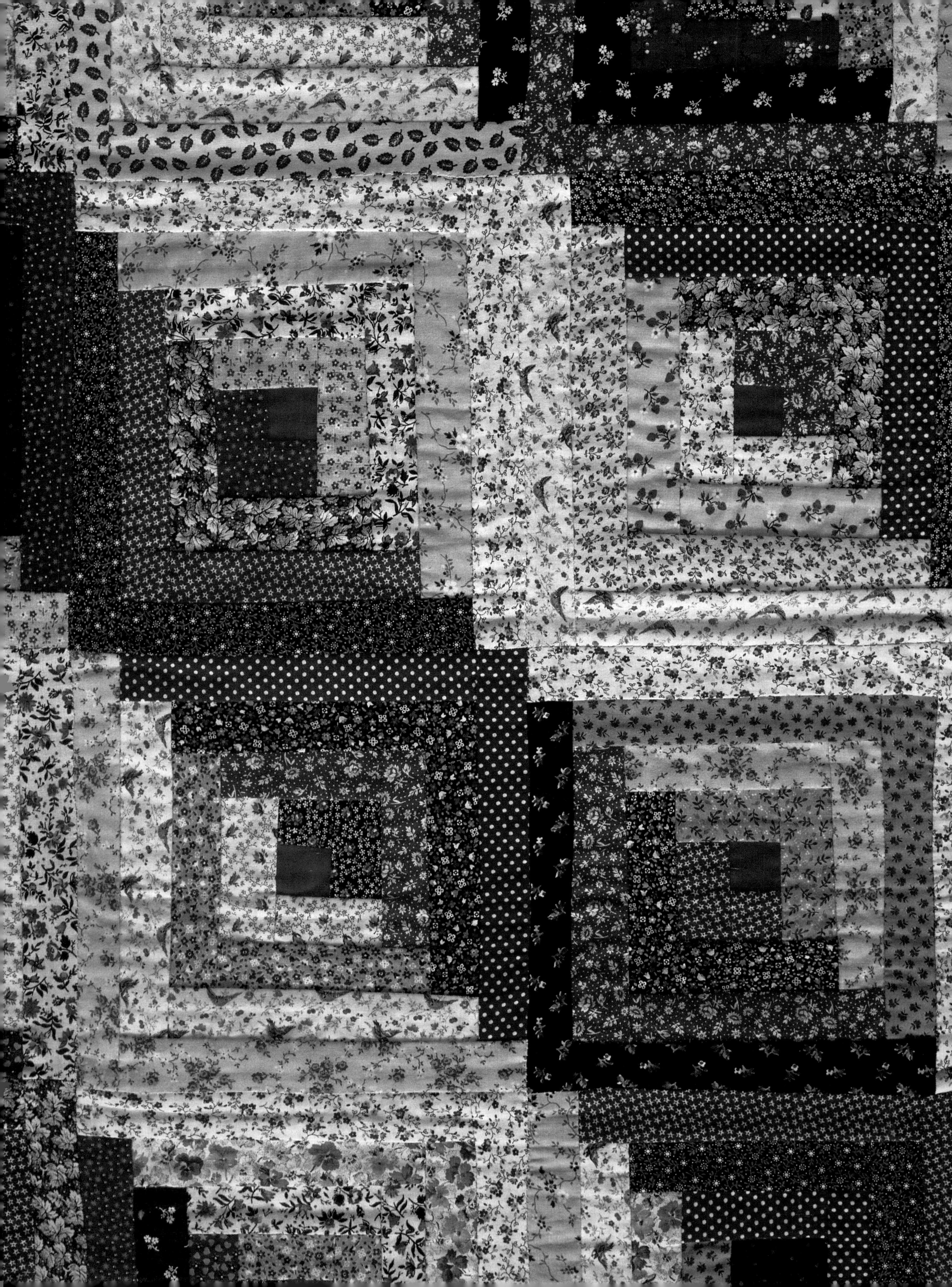

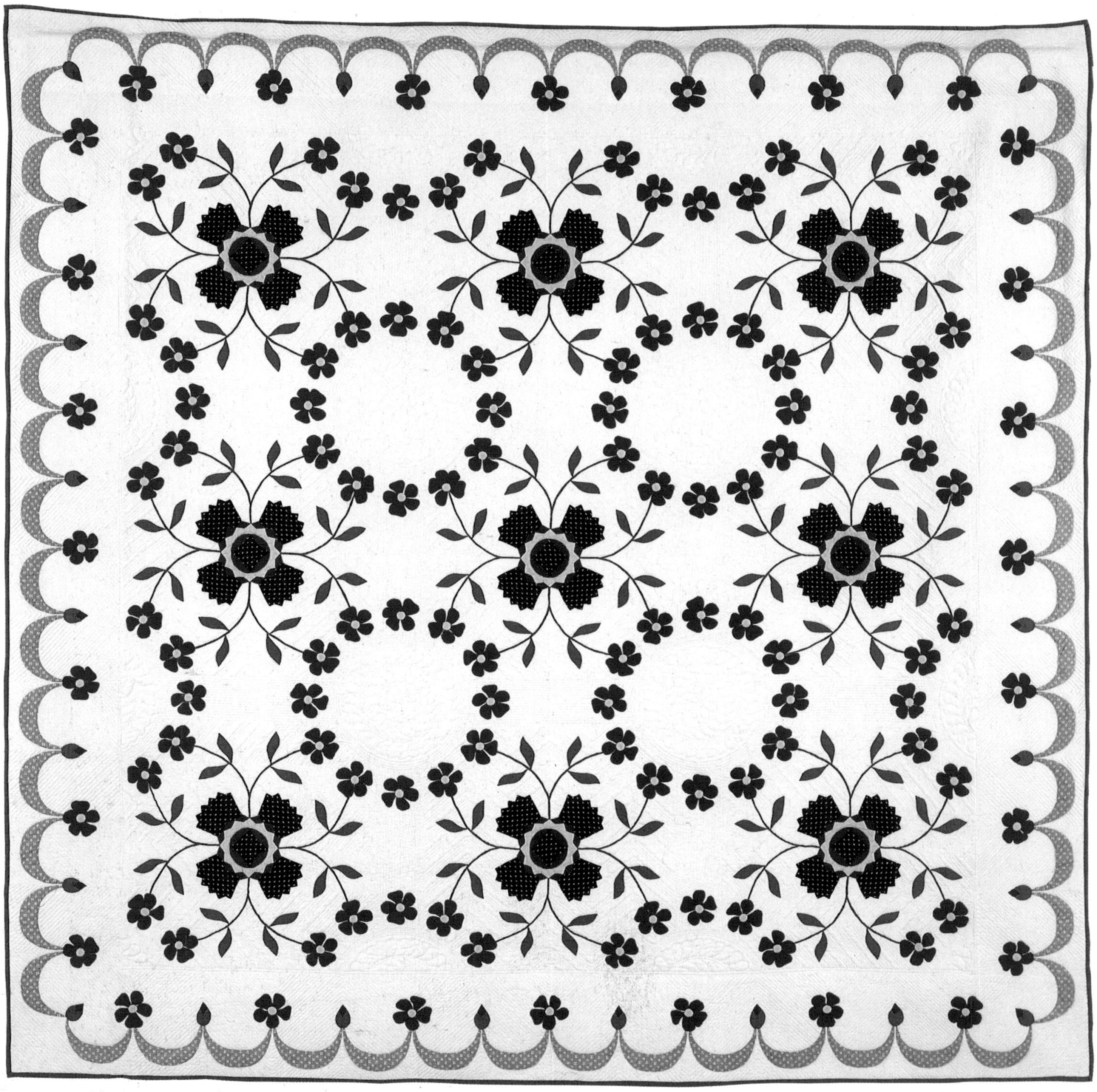

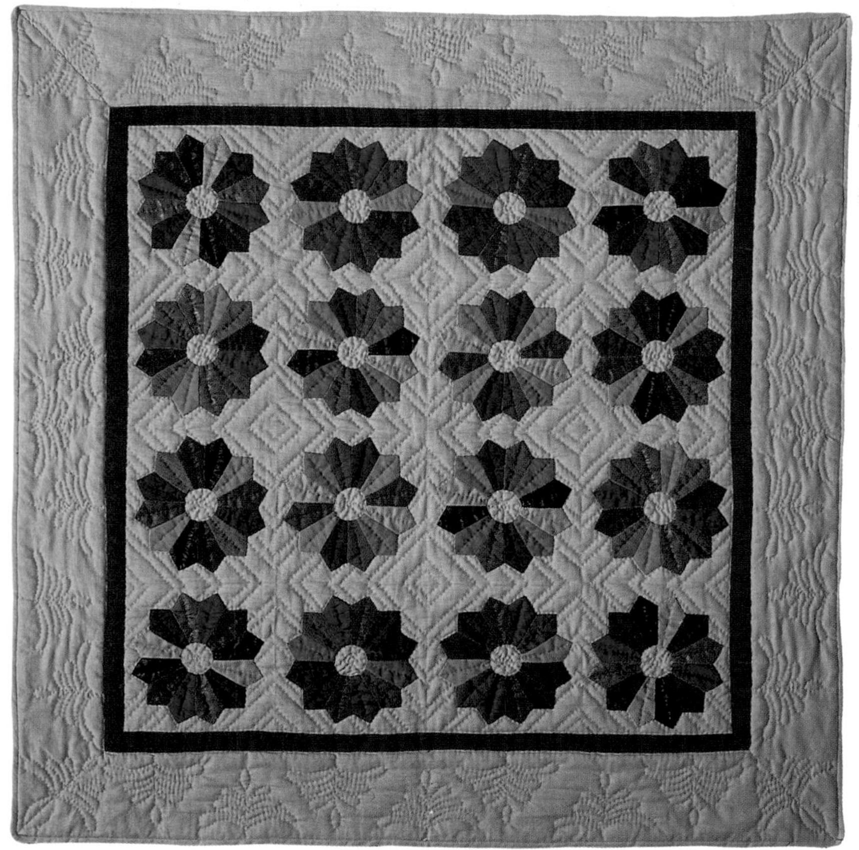

▲ WILD ROSE

Fay Pritts. 1994. Mount Pleasant, Pennsylvania. Cottons; hand appliquéd and quilted. 90 x 90 in. Museum of the American Quilter's Society, Paducah, Kentucky.

This sweet old-fashioned appliqué quilt won Best of Show at the 1994 American Quilter's Society contest. The design is based on an antique quilt partially destroyed in the Great Chicago Fire of 1871.

◄ MINIATURE DRESDEN PLATE

Tina M. Gravatt. 1993. Philadelphia, Pennsylvania. Cottons; hand pieced, machine pieced, hand quilted. 24 x 24 in. Collection of the artist. © 1993 Tina M. Gravatt.

This piece was inspired by a c. 1910 Amish quilt from Holmes County, Ohio. The plates are 4 inches in diameter and the blocks 4 1/2 inches; there are a total of 217 pieces of fabric in the tiny quilt. Tina Gravatt is a quiltmaker, teacher, lecturer, and author who concentrates on historically accurate miniatures. She has completed over 125 miniature quilts representing styles from over two hundred years of America's quilting heritage and recently began a new series of European quilts in miniature.

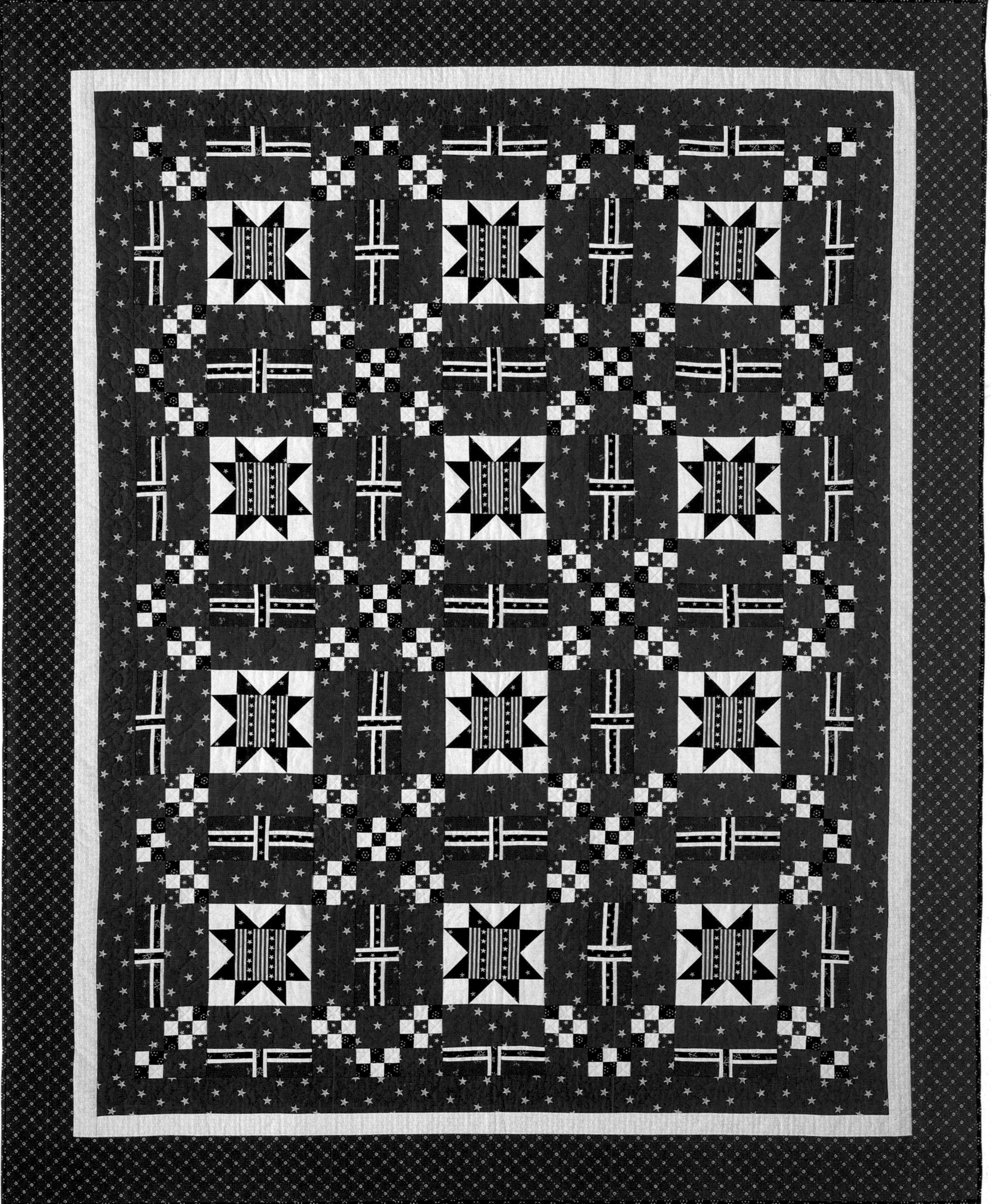

▲ I Pledge Allegiance To . . .

Helen White. 1991. Ukiah, California. Cottons; machine pieced and quilted. 80 x 68 in. Collection of the artist.

The quiltmaker says, "I was born and raised in Norway, without a quilting tradition (we knit you know), and have embraced this wonderful craft fully since my discovery in the late '70s. My quilt *I Pledge Allegiance To . . .* was meant to convey the struggle of having your heart belong to two nations. The quilt depicts American and Norwegian flag facsimiles, using a traditional block pattern as a base."

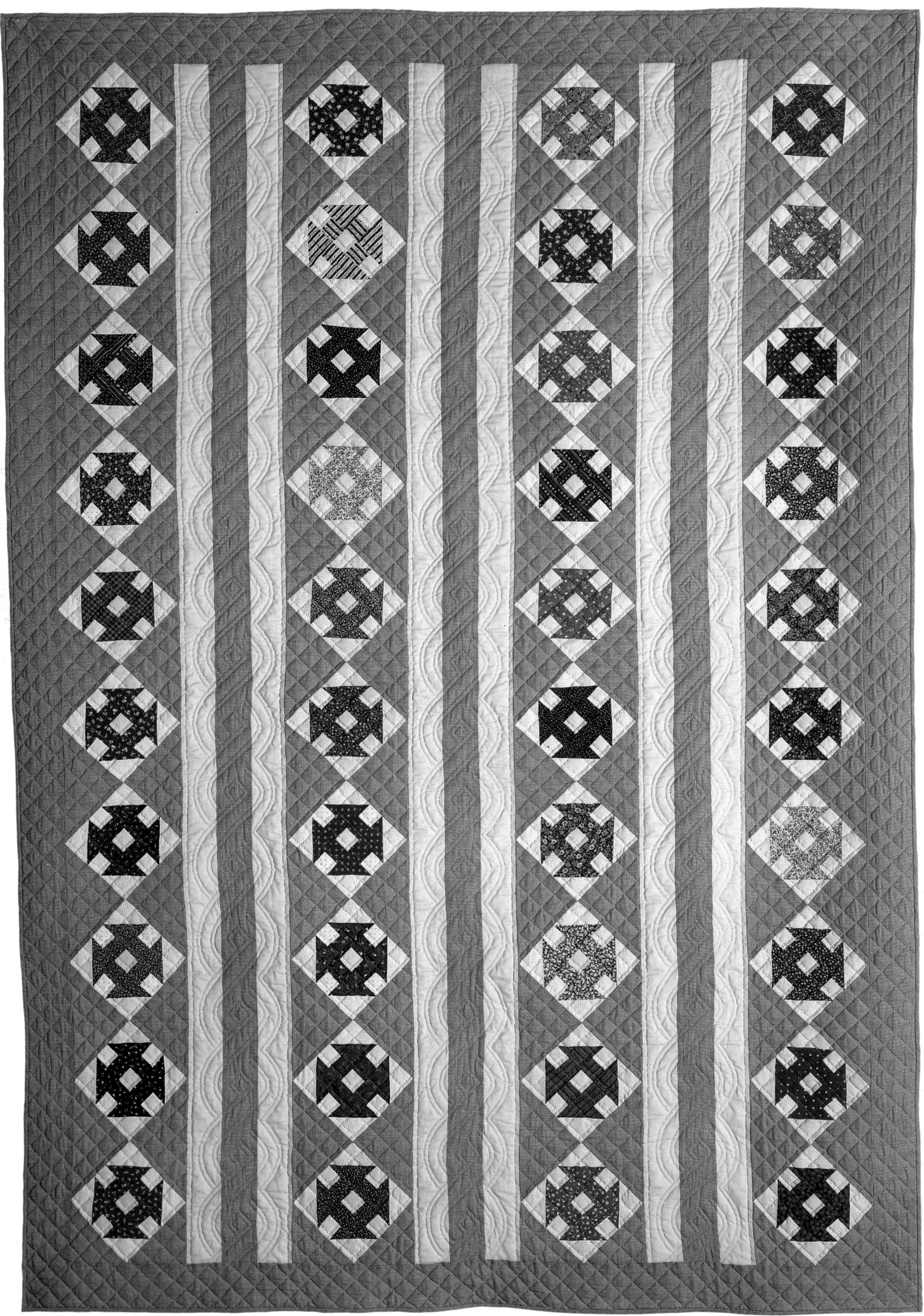

◀ Strippy Shoo-Fly

Ollie Jean Lane. 1993. Yazoo City, Mississippi. Cottons; hand pieced and quilted. 92 x 64 in. Collection of the artist.

Ollie Jean Lane makes traditional Southern quilts, working primarily from scraps. This example of her work is pieced in strips, with three rows of shoo-fly blocks divided by narrow strips of white and pink fabric. The Shoo-Fly pattern is an old Southern favorite.

Winding Road ▶

Mrs. Clara Mae Potts. 1988. Fayette County, Alabama. Synthetic knits; hand pieced and quilted. 78 x 67 in. Collection of Robert Cargo.

Like many of Mrs. Potts's quilts, this one was made entirely from material salvaged from a garment factory. The powerfully graphic pattern is aptly named.

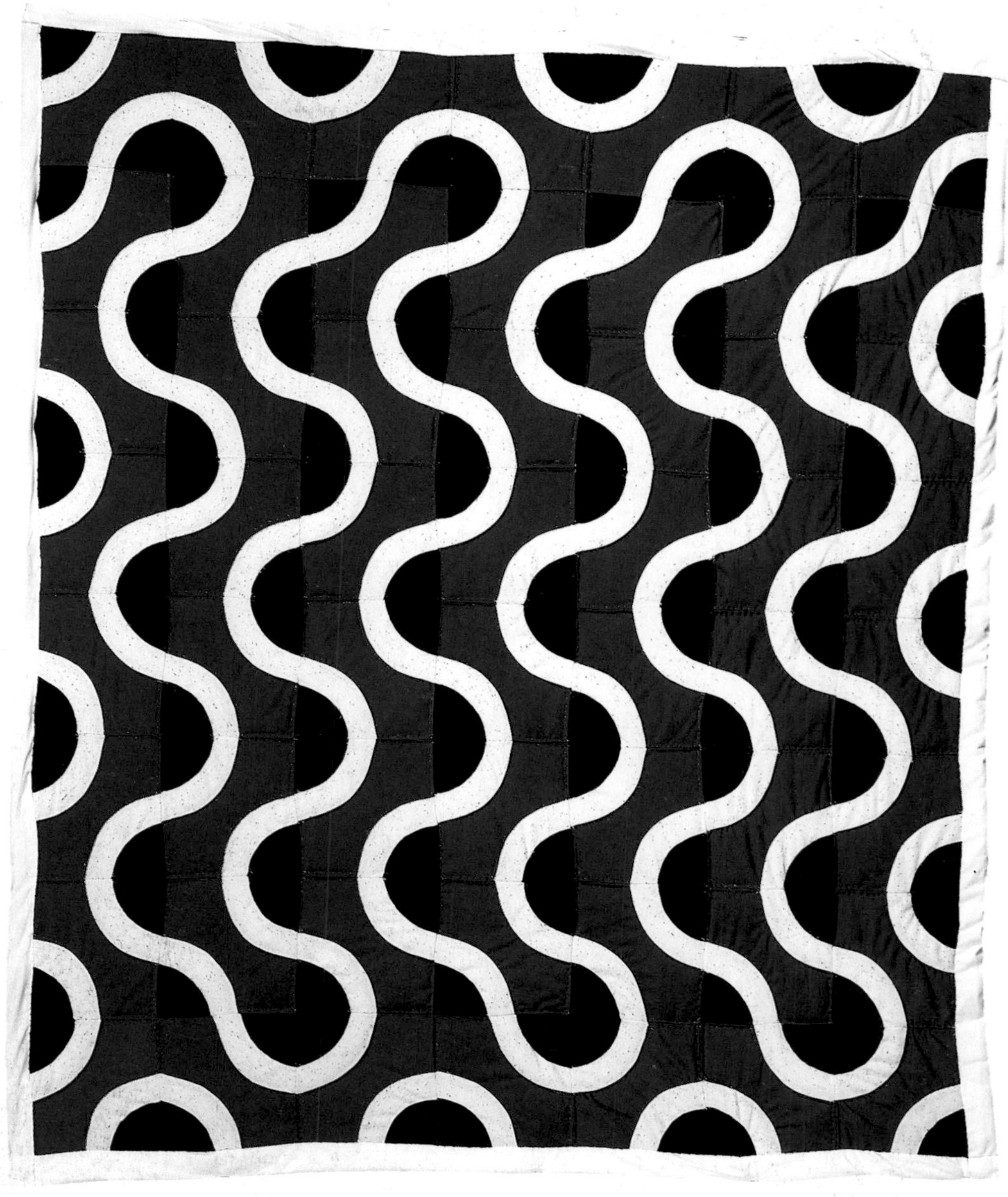

◀ Dresden Plate

Mabel Murphy. 1980. Fulton, Missouri. Cottons; hand pieced, appliquéd, and quilted. 117 x 86 in. International Folk Art Foundation Collection at The Museum of International Folk Art, Santa Fe, New Mexico.

Mabel Murphy, who made her first quilt in 1915 at the age of eight, was honored as a National Heritage Fellow by the National Endowment for the Arts, Folk Arts Program, in 1987. Her quilts are models of conservative, traditional workmanship, impeccably designed and executed.

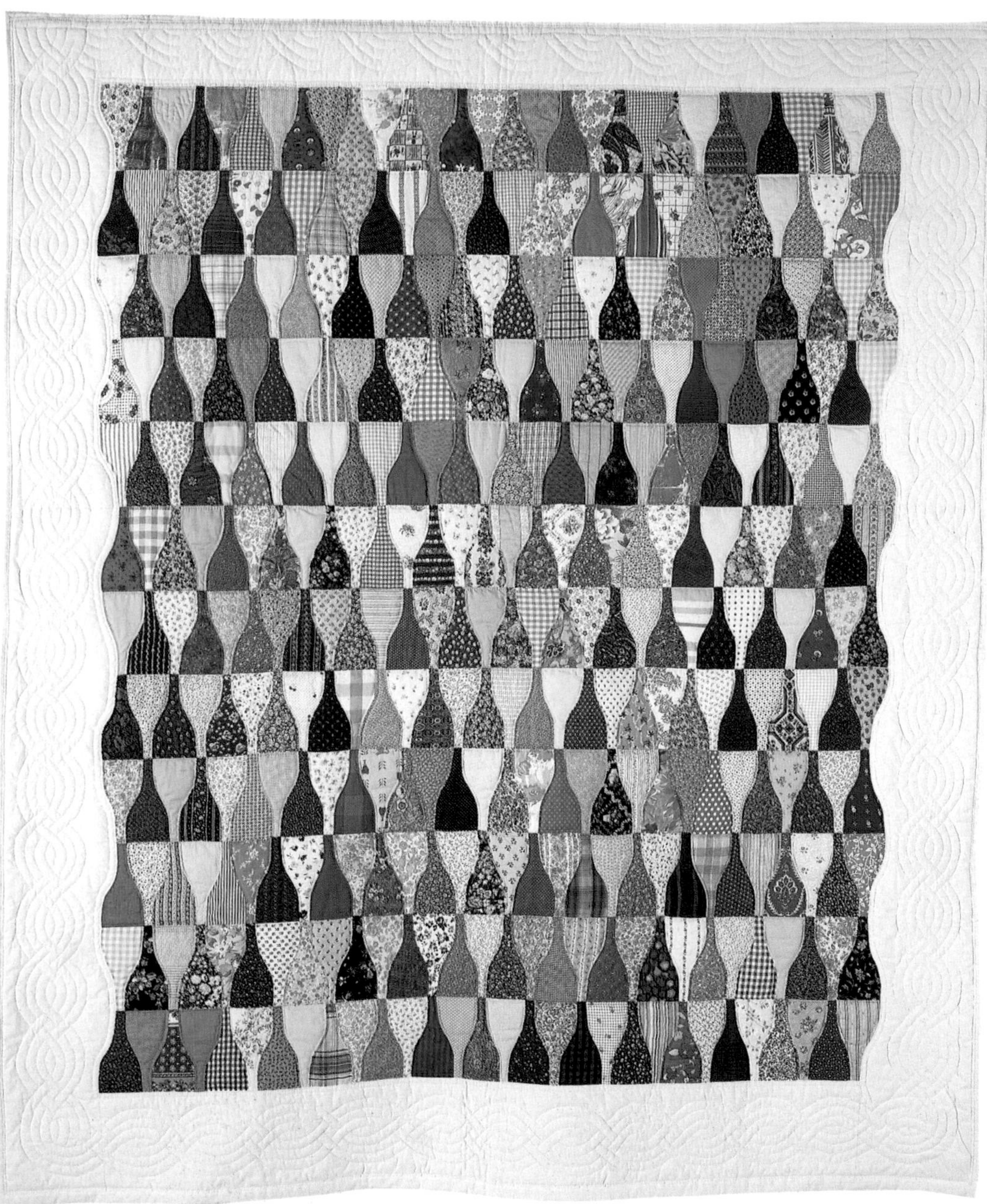

◄ **SOUTHERN CHARM**

Bets Ramsey. 1987. Chattanooga, Tennessee. Cottons; hand pieced and quilted. 94 x 78 in. Collection of the artist.

Charm quilts are built entirely from identically shaped pieces of fabric, with no two fabric patterns the same. This example of the style follows an original pattern by Bets Ramsey. Ramsey, who was co-director of the Quilts of Tennessee documentation project, was a board member of the American Quilt Study Group from 1980 to 1989 and writes a weekly quilt column for *The Chattanooga Times*.

QUILT OF QUILTS ►

Carol Doak. 1990. Windham, New Hampshire. Cottons; machine pieced, appliquéd, and quilted. 82 x 82 in. Collection of the artist.

This clever composition is a celebration of the art of quiltmaking; it depicts a universal washday, with a host of quilts hung out on clotheslines to dry. The blocks alternate between pieced and appliqué work, and each of the tiny three-inch quilts represents a different pattern. Carol Doak is the author of four books on quiltmaking.

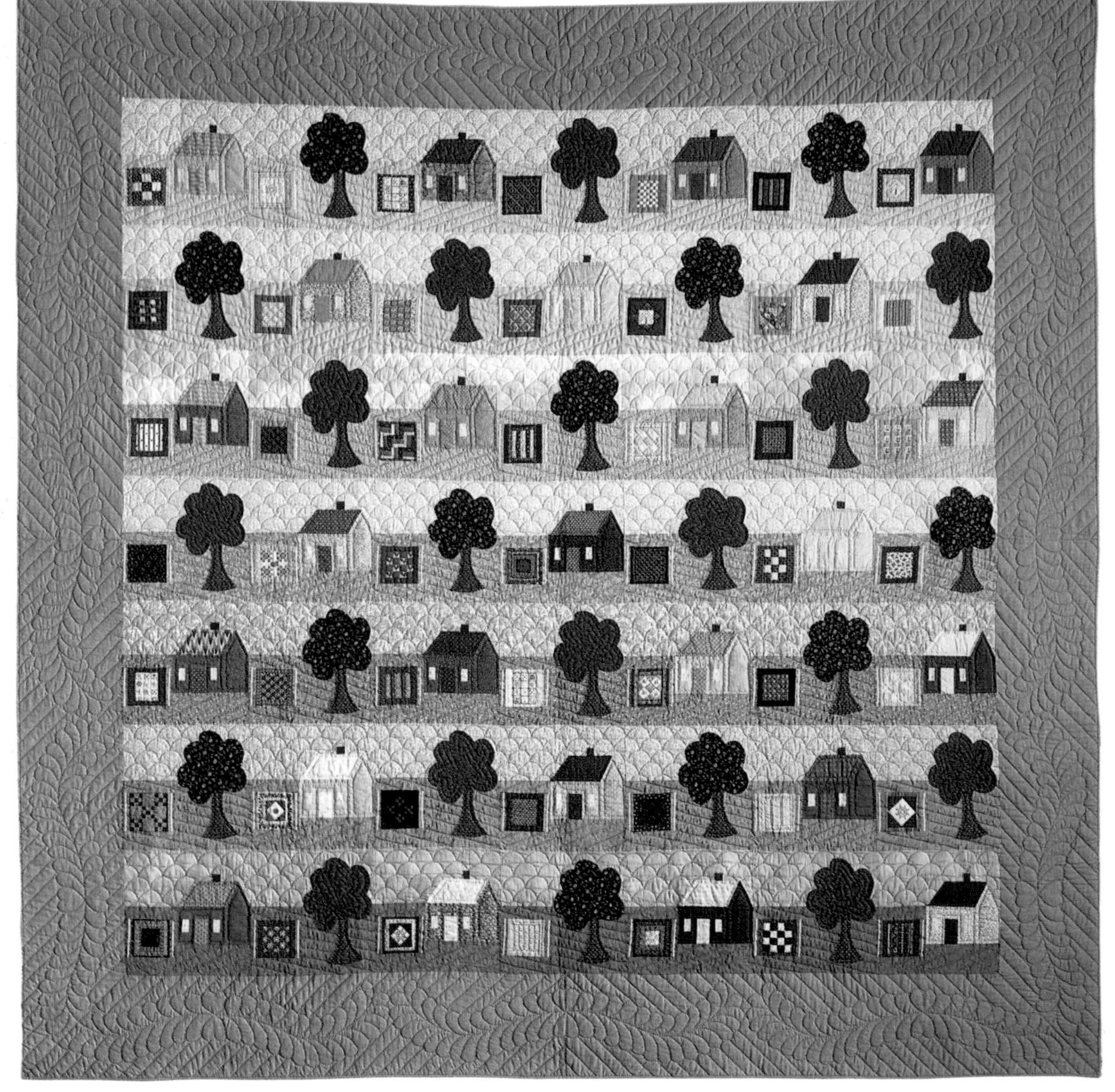

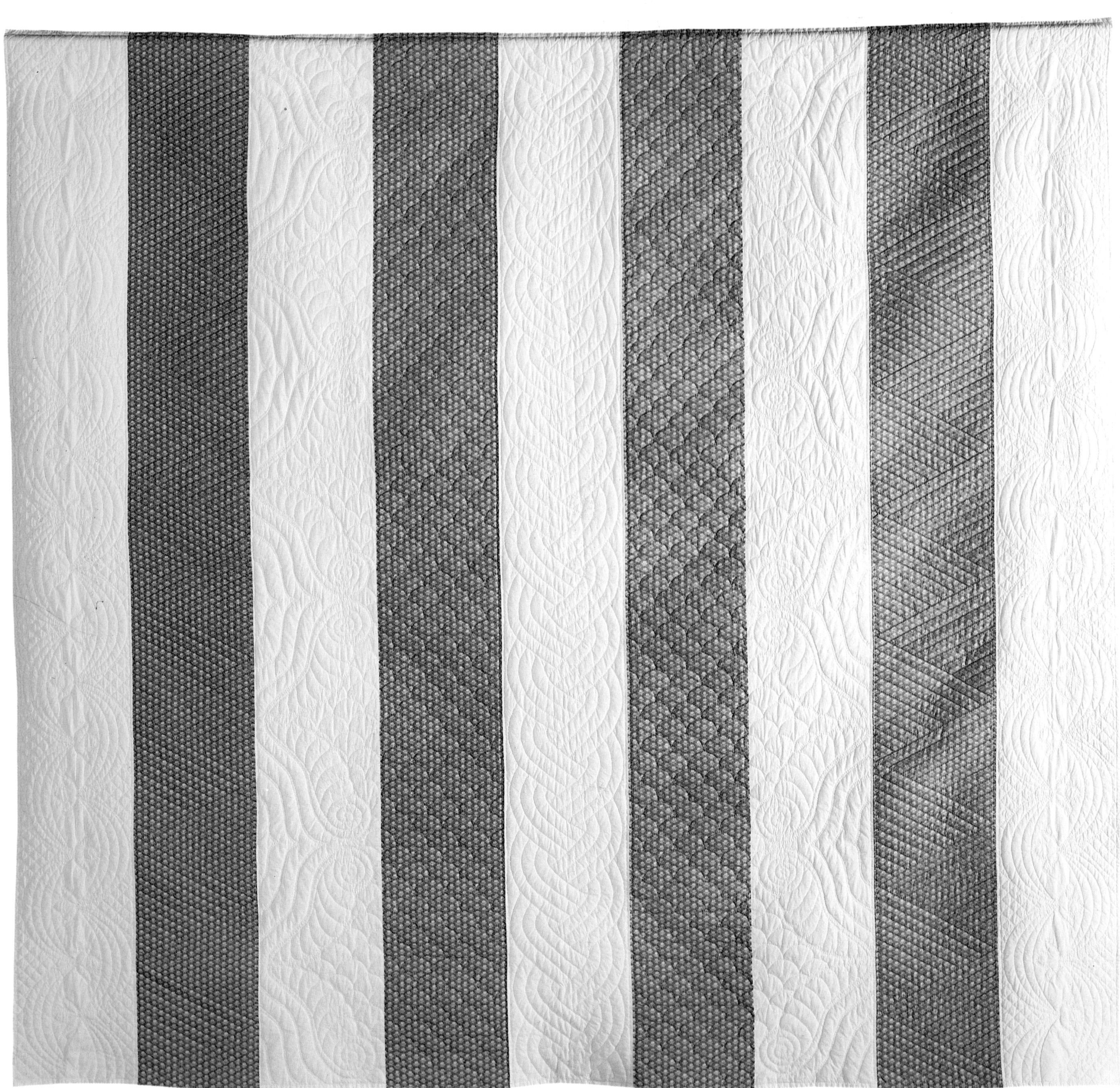

▲ Stripped Green

Dorothy Osler. Newcastle-upon-Tyne, Great Britain. Cottons; hand pieced and quilted. 90 x 84 in. Collection of the artist.

Dorothy Osler is the author of *Traditional British Quilts* and is one of a handful of English quiltmakers still working in the old style. According to Ms. Osler, "All too often 'English' quilting is associated with intricate mosaic patchwork coverlets, whereas the real strength of British quilting lies in the regional traditions where quilting (per se) in intricate and regionally distinctive patterns was the more important element of the surface design." Made of an odd number of strips in two colors, and quilted in different patterns, *Stripped Green* is typical of traditional English strip quilting in the northeastern region of the country. The quilting patterns repeat symmetrically on either side of the white central strip, thus balancing the odd number of strips.

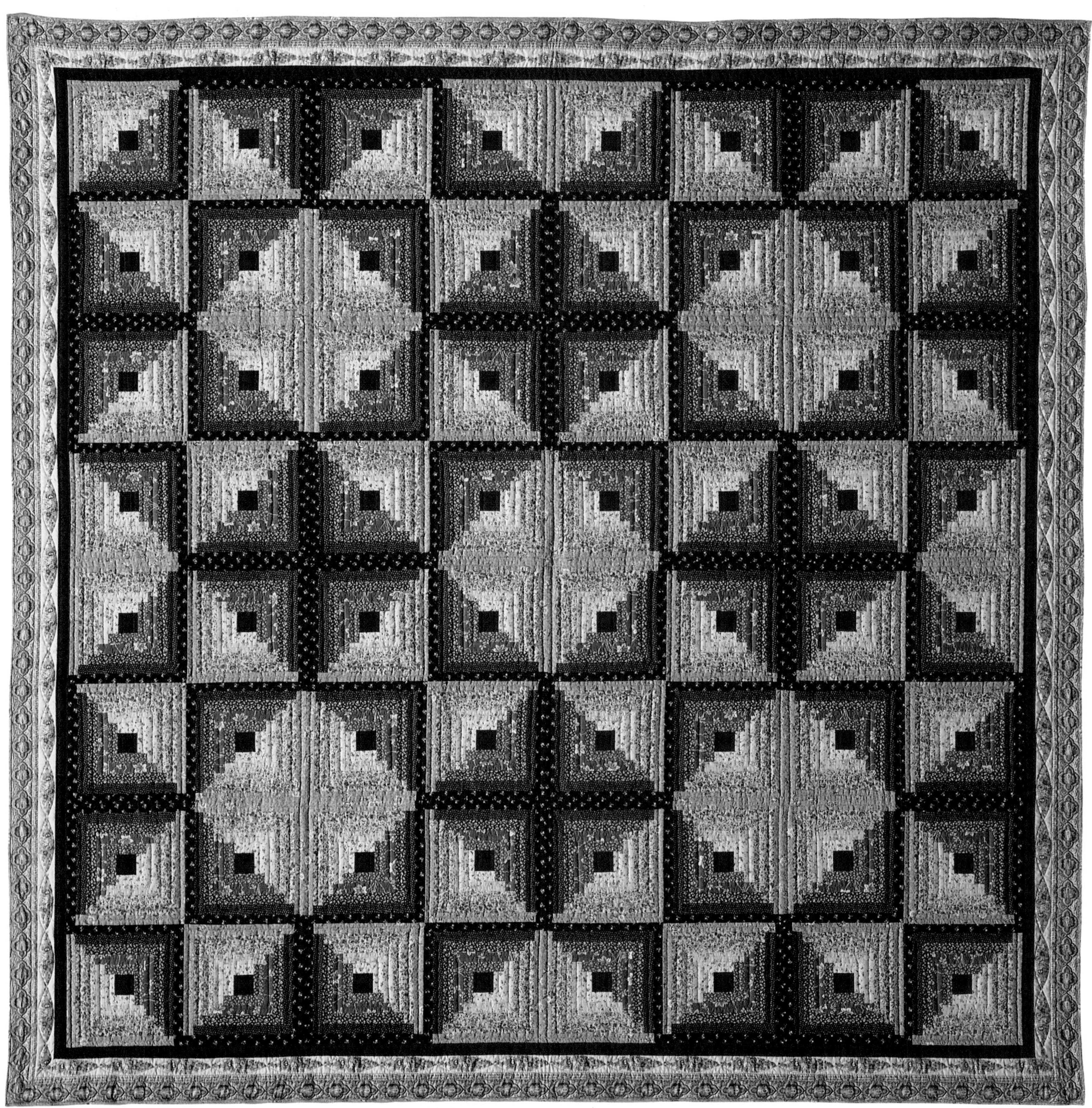

▲ Roses on the Fence

Dorothy Jenstad Pedersen. 1982. Seattle, Washington. Cottons; machine pieced and hand quilted. 90 x 90 in. Collection of Margaret Anne Pedersen Myers.

This Light and Dark Log Cabin variation is cleverly organized. The sixty-four half light, half dark blocks are set in an unusual 8 x 8 pattern to form nine large diamonds-in-squares surrounded by a border of single blocks; the light-colored portions of the blocks also form five large eight-pointed stars, one at the quilt's center and another in each quadrant of the quilt. The quilt is named after the delicate rose print that forms its outside "fence."

Broken Star ▸

Kyle Elizabeth Redente. 1987. Fort Collins, Colorado. Cottons; hand pieced and quilted. 96 x 86 in. Collection of the artist.

The Broken Star pattern was a favorite among early twentieth-century quiltmakers in the mid-West. It was often worked by Amish quilters, who typically used a palette of bright, glowing colors, often set on a black ground. This subtly colored modern example, which sets earth-toned rusty reds, browns, and gray-blues against a tan background, took four weeks to piece but two years to quilt.

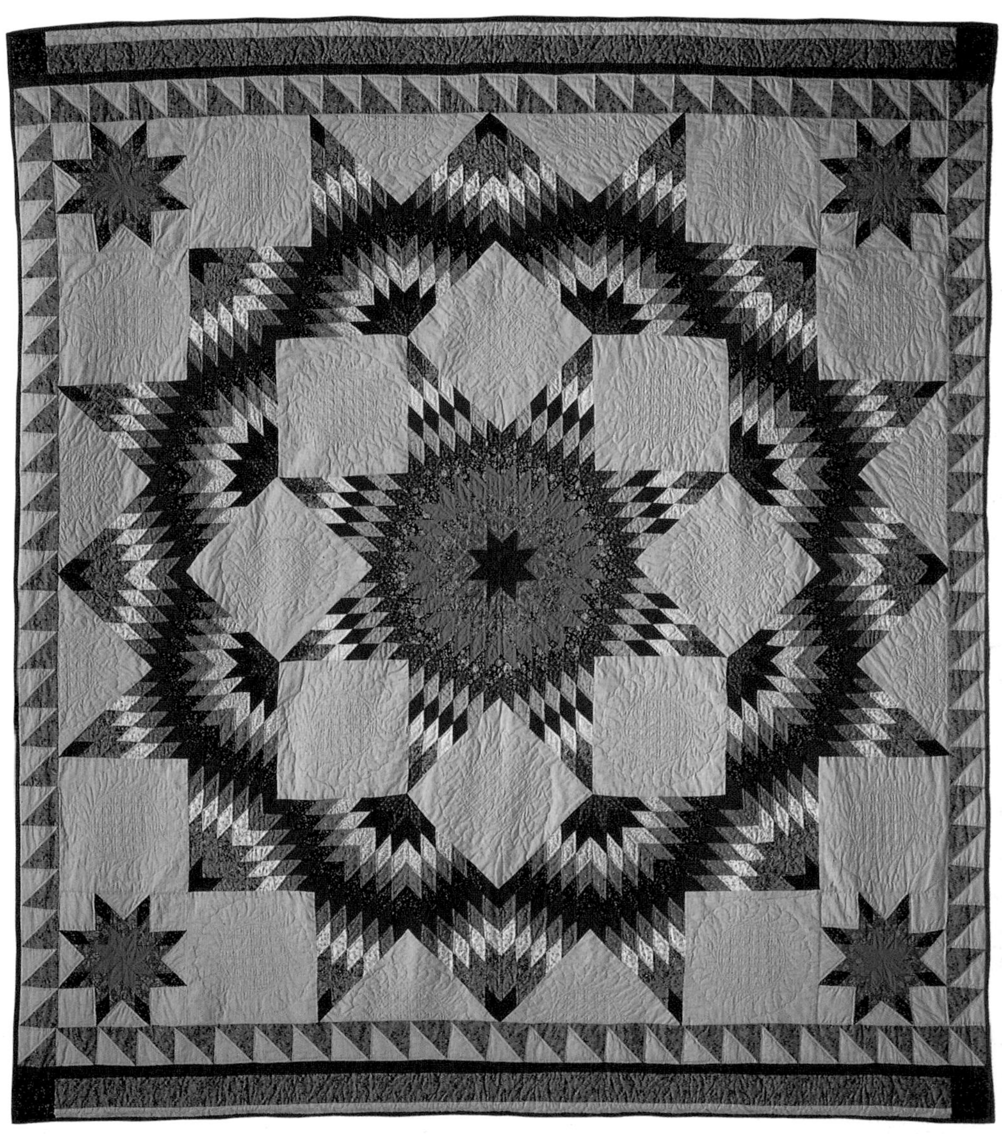

Log Cabin Variation ▸

Dena Canty. 1991. Piedmont, California. Cottons; machine pieced, hand quilted by Mary Hershberger. 66 x 66 in. Collection of the artist.

Dena Canty is a member of East Bay Heritage Quilters. Her unique Log Cabin variation arranges the light and dark patterns of the twenty-five squares to form a series of jagged, angular parallel forms.

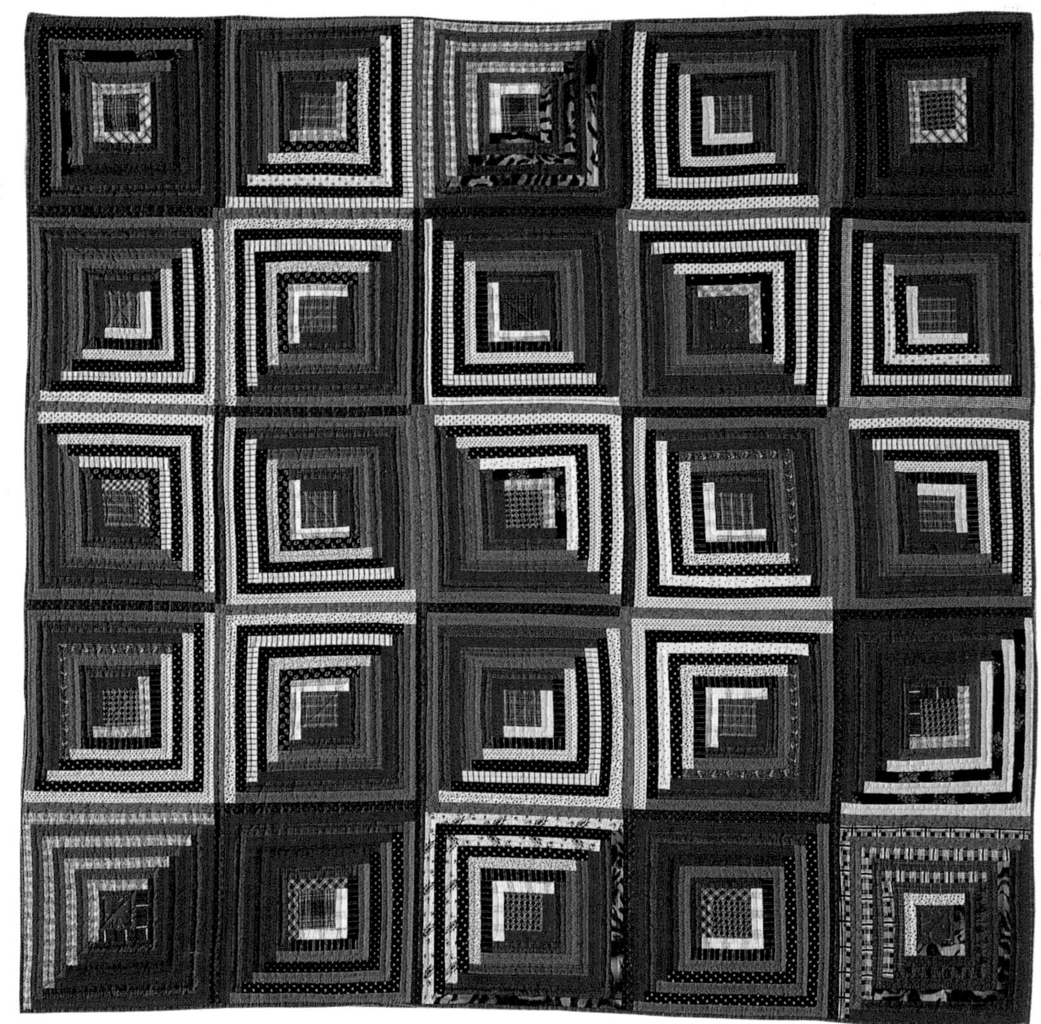

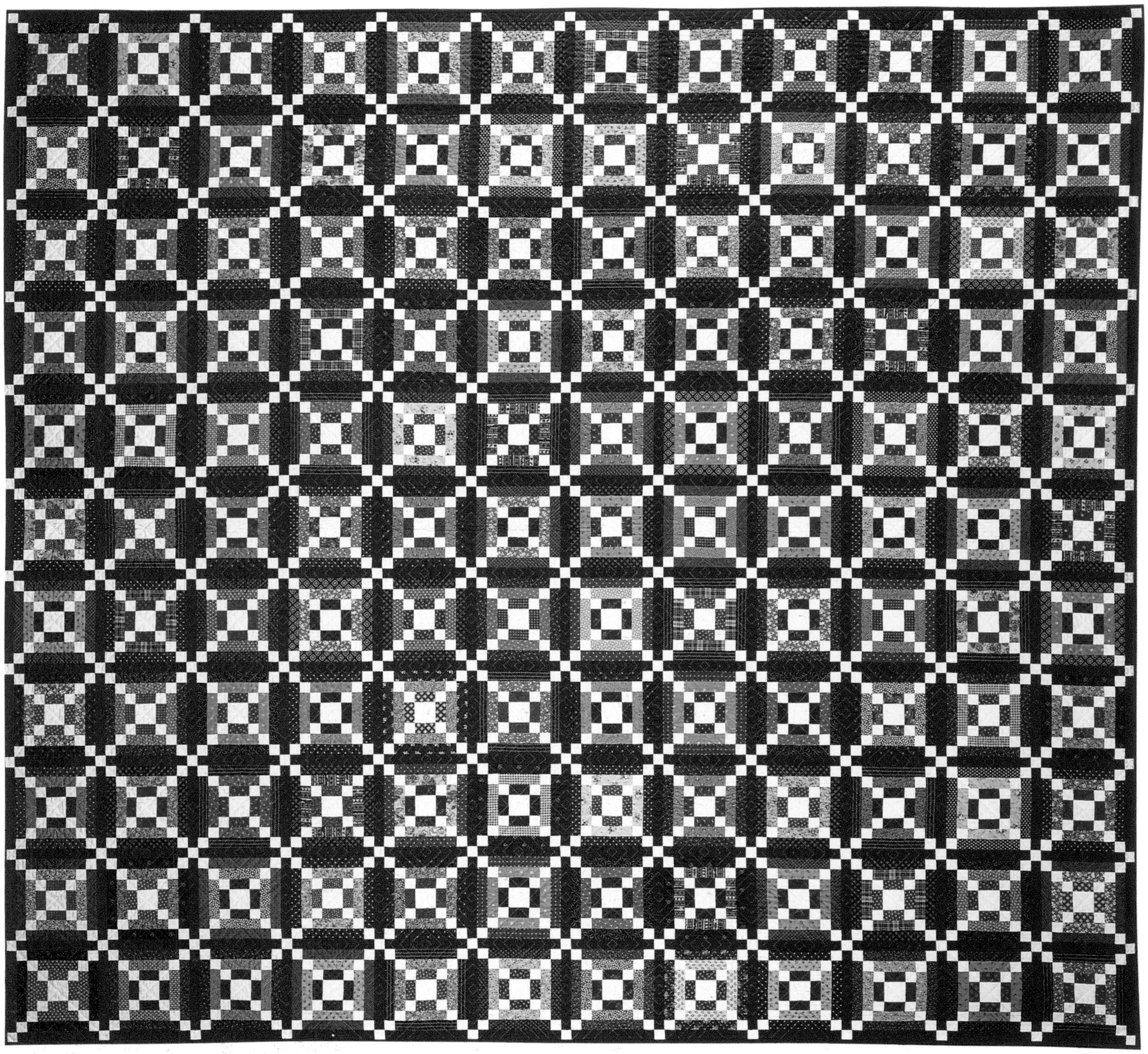

▲ Chimneys and Cornerstones

Carol Shaffer Dunklau. 1989. Lincoln, Nebraska. Cottons; hand pieced and quilted. 98 x 106 in. Collection of the artist.

This "scrap" quilt is made up of 132 blocks, each with its own unique combination of fabrics. It won Best Quilt at the 1989 Nebraska State Fair; six of Dunklau's works have received that honor since she began making quilts in the mid-1970s.

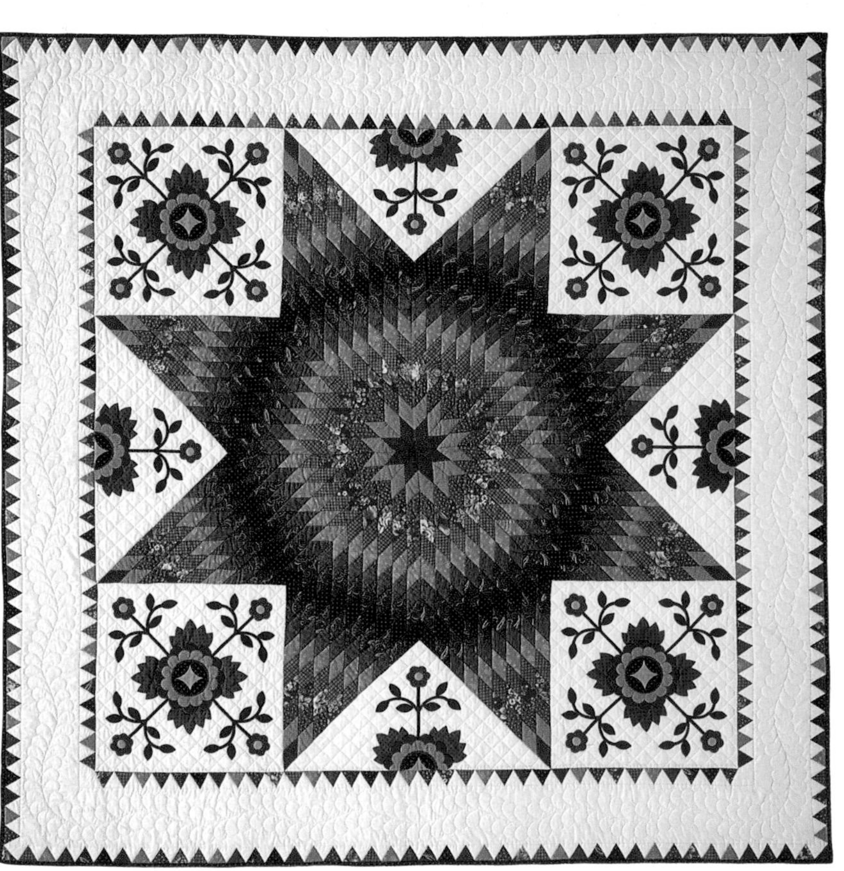

Whig Rose Star ▶

Helen Young Frost. 1993. Tucson, Arizona. Cottons; hand pieced, appliquéd, and quilted. 86 x 86 in. Collection of the artist.

Helen Young Frost and her mother Blanche Young have been writing books on quiltmaking for fifteen years. All of their books concentrate on newer and quicker ways to make time-tested traditional patterns. Frost says, "Unlike many of today's quiltmakers, I have no interest in designing new patterns; I would much rather explore the old ones, trying new colorations, fabric combinations, [and] techniques."

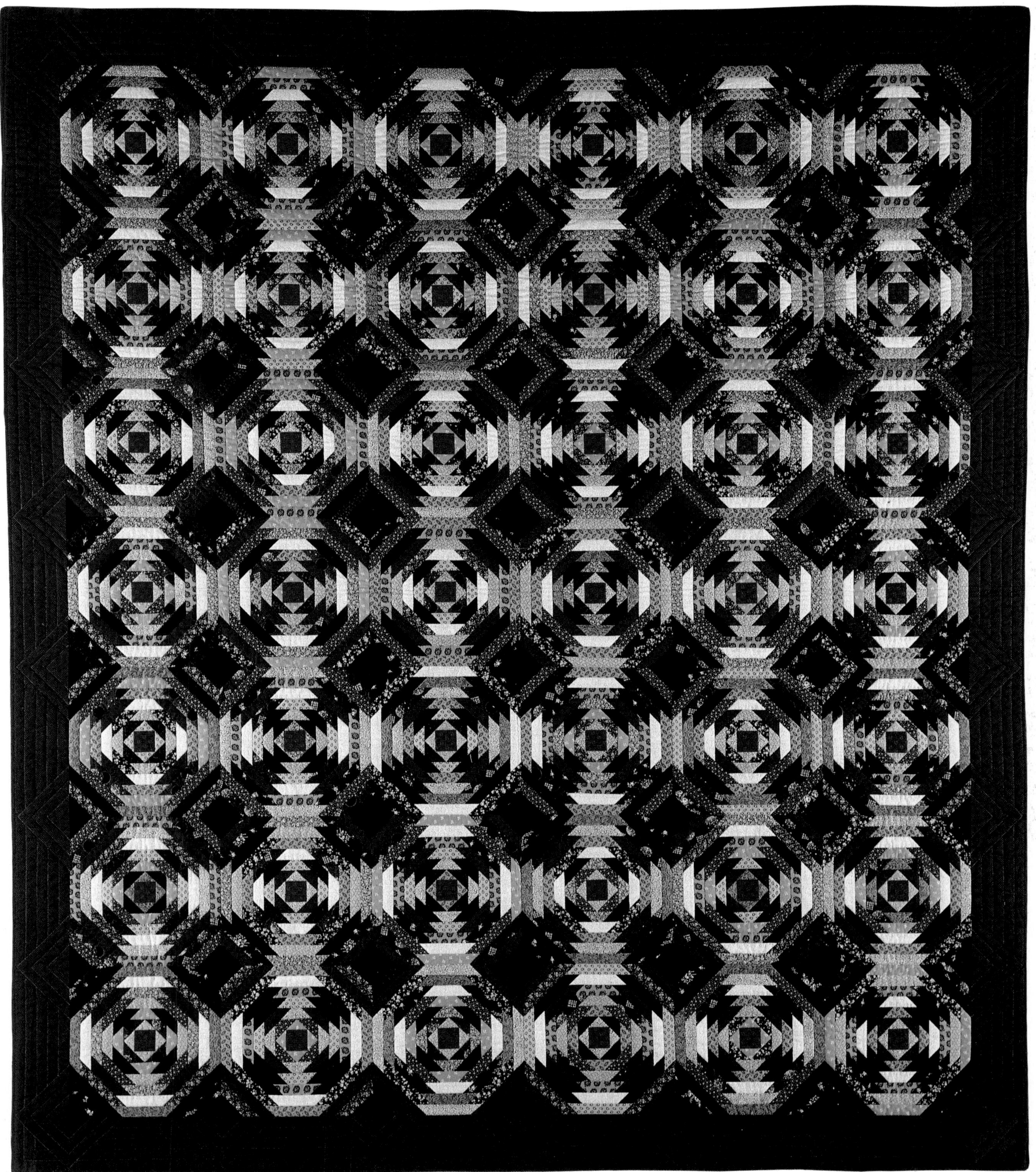

▲ BLACK PINEAPPLE LOG CABIN

Carol Shaffer Dunklau. 1982. Lincoln, Nebraska. Cottons; machine seamed, hand pieced and quilted. 106 x 83 in. Collection of the artist.

After Carol Dunklau decided to make a "non-Amish black quilt," she scoured midwestern fabric shops in search of black cotton prints, a rare commodity at the time. The diverse fabrics she found are here contrasted with a group of tan prints that form the pineapples. The deeply saturated red centers of the pineapples set the whole quilt in motion. Meticulous, nine-stitch-per-inch quilting runs in parallel lines close to the seams. *Black Pineapple* was named Best Quilt and Best of Show at the 1983 Nebraska State Fair.

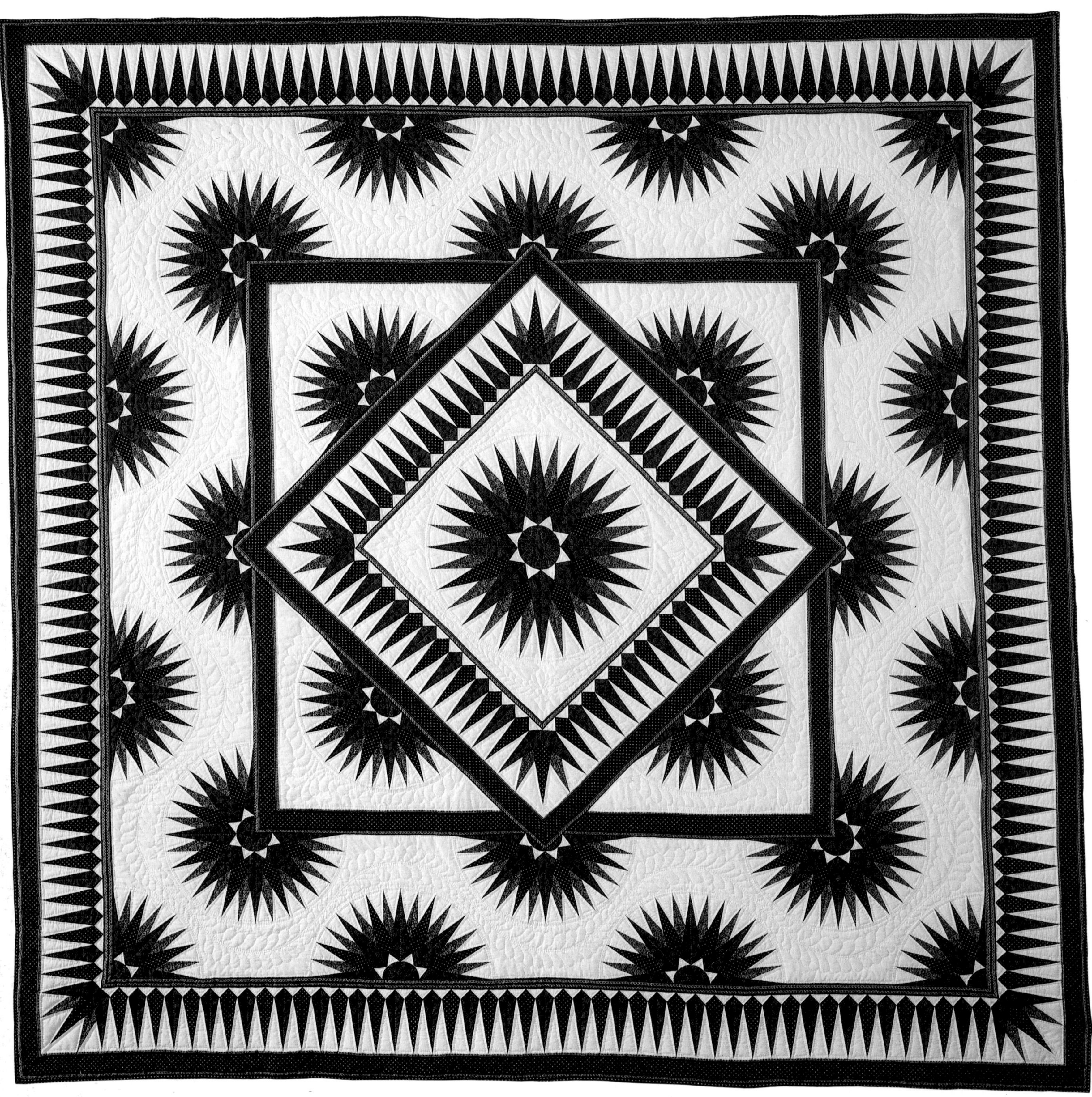

▲ MARINER'S COMPASS (DETAIL ▶)

Mary K. Ryan. 1987. Rutland, Vermont. Cottons; machine pieced; hand quilted by Merial Liberty. 96 x 96 in. Collection of Michael and Joanna Evans.

This striking adaptation of the traditional Mariner's Compass design was originally made as the raffle quilt for the 1987 Vermont Quilt Festival. In addition to traditionally based quilts such as this one, Mary Ryan also creates quilts with paisleys and border-printed fabrics that reflect her passion for Oriental rugs.

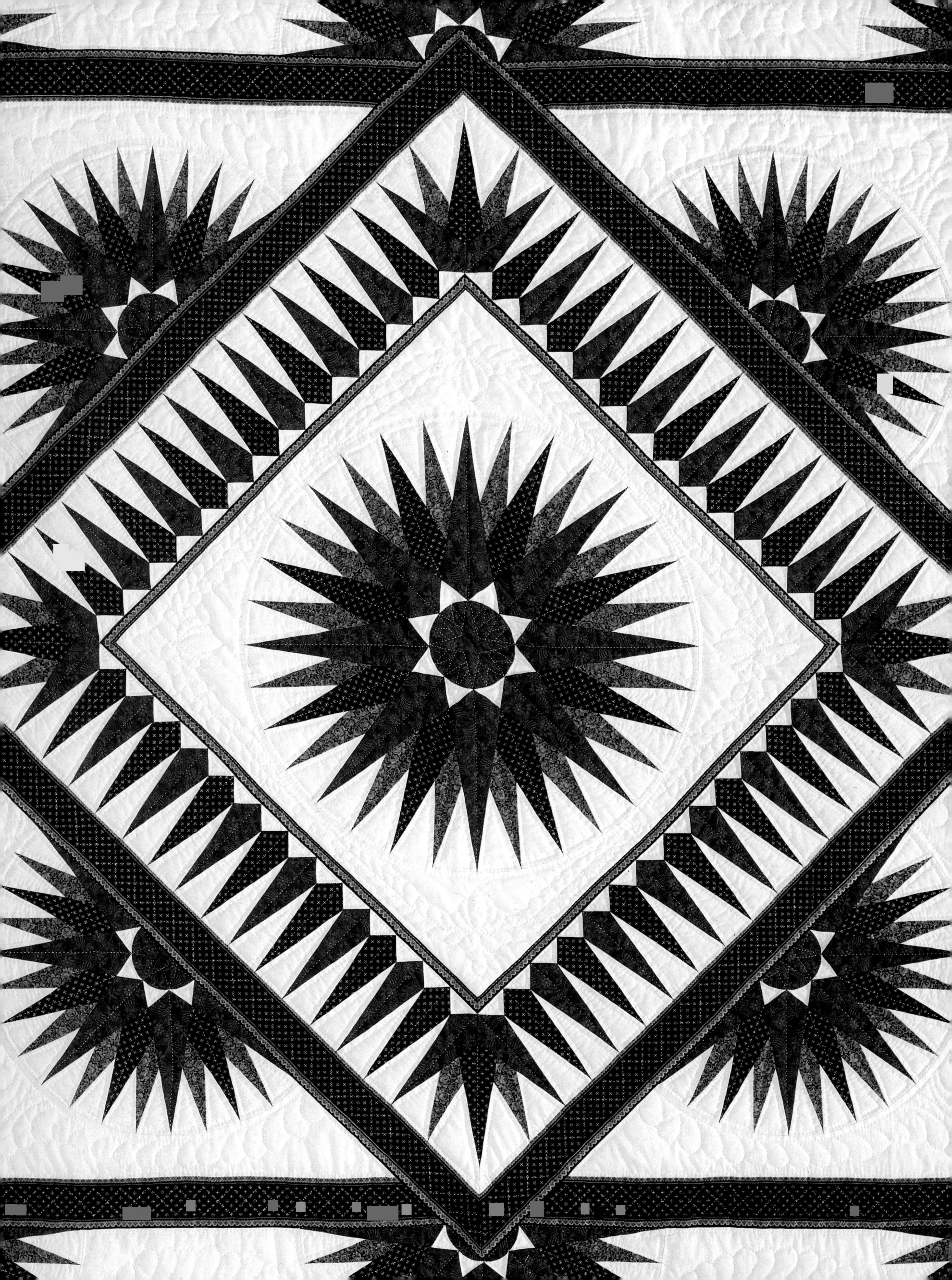

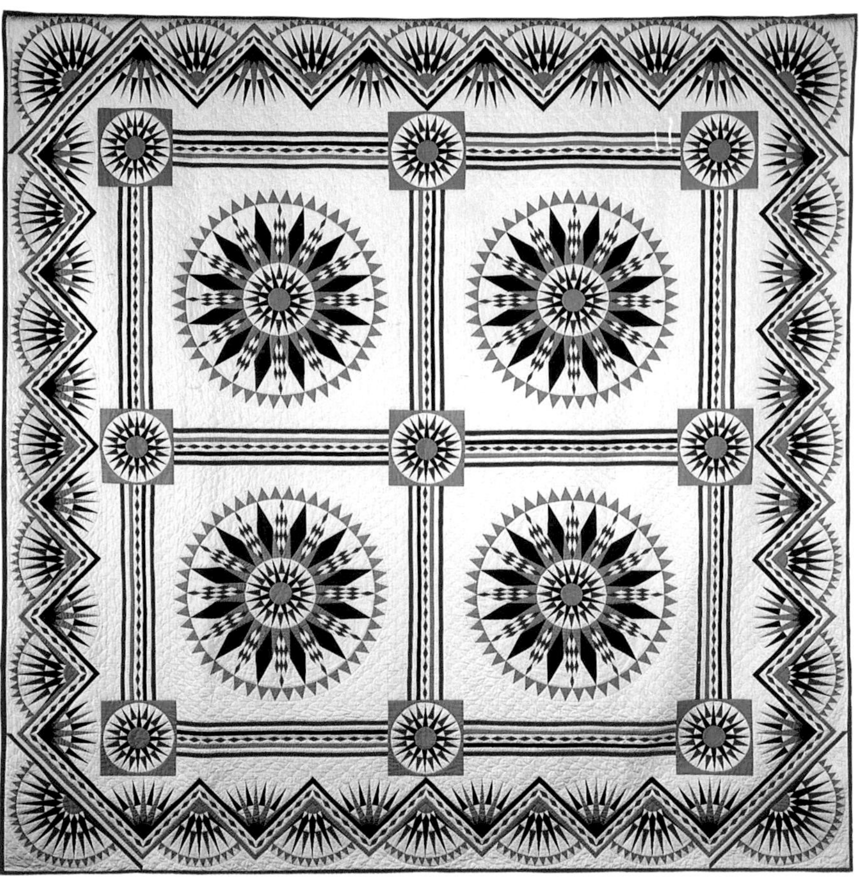

◂ **DANDELION WINE**

Debra Christine Wagner. 1992. Cosmos, Minnesota. Cottons, some hand-dyed; machine pieced and quilted. 92 x 90 in. Collection of the artist.

This imaginative variation on the traditional Mariner's Compass pattern employs an unusual palette of colors dominated by subdued golds to create a rich and graphic effect. The four large compasses at the center of the composition are complemented by nine smaller ones as well as a border of divided compasses. All of the compasses are precisely cut and pieced, and the surface is enhanced by intricate machine quilting.

Debra Christine Wagner

Debra Christine Wagner of Cosmos, Minnesota, is widely considered the finest machine piecer in the world. Her quilts, which she says reflect her obsession with mid-nineteenth-century textiles, combine powerful, graphic designs made from a deliberately limited palette of colors with highly technical and complex machine piecing and quilting. Wagner considers herself a traditionalist in design who uses time-saving, modern technology to achieve an old-fashioned look. She says, "To me, combining antique design and modern methods seems like the best of both worlds." She is especially fond of the use of tiny triangles as a design element, finding them at once graphically compelling and technically challenging, and is a master of machine trapunto quilting, perhaps the most difficult and visually impressive of traditional hand-sewing techniques.

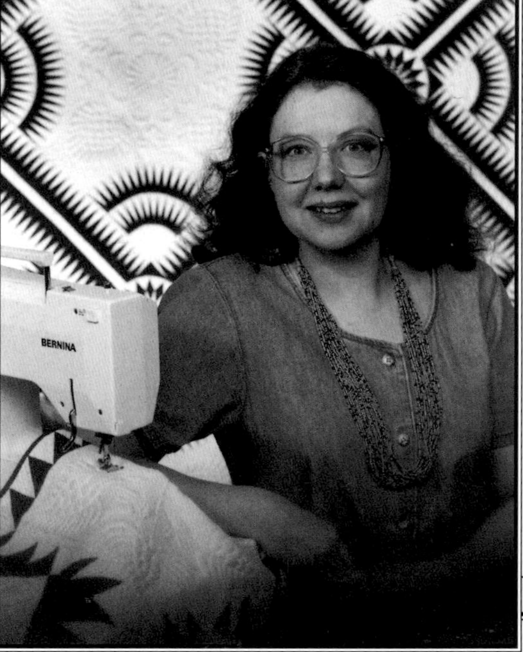

Wagner holds a Bachelor of Science degree in clothing, textiles, and design from the University of Wisconsin. She comes to her use of the sewing machine naturally: her parents have been sewing machine dealers since the mid-1960s and she took up machine embroidery just a few years after they started their business. After developing a national reputation for her prize-winning embroidery work, Wagner took up quiltmaking in 1987, applying her expertise on the sewing machine to the technical problems of this new medium. She now quilts and teaches the machine sewing techniques she has developed full-time. Two of her quilts, *Floral Urns* and *Ohio Bride's Quilt*, are in the collection of the Museum of the American Quilter's Society.

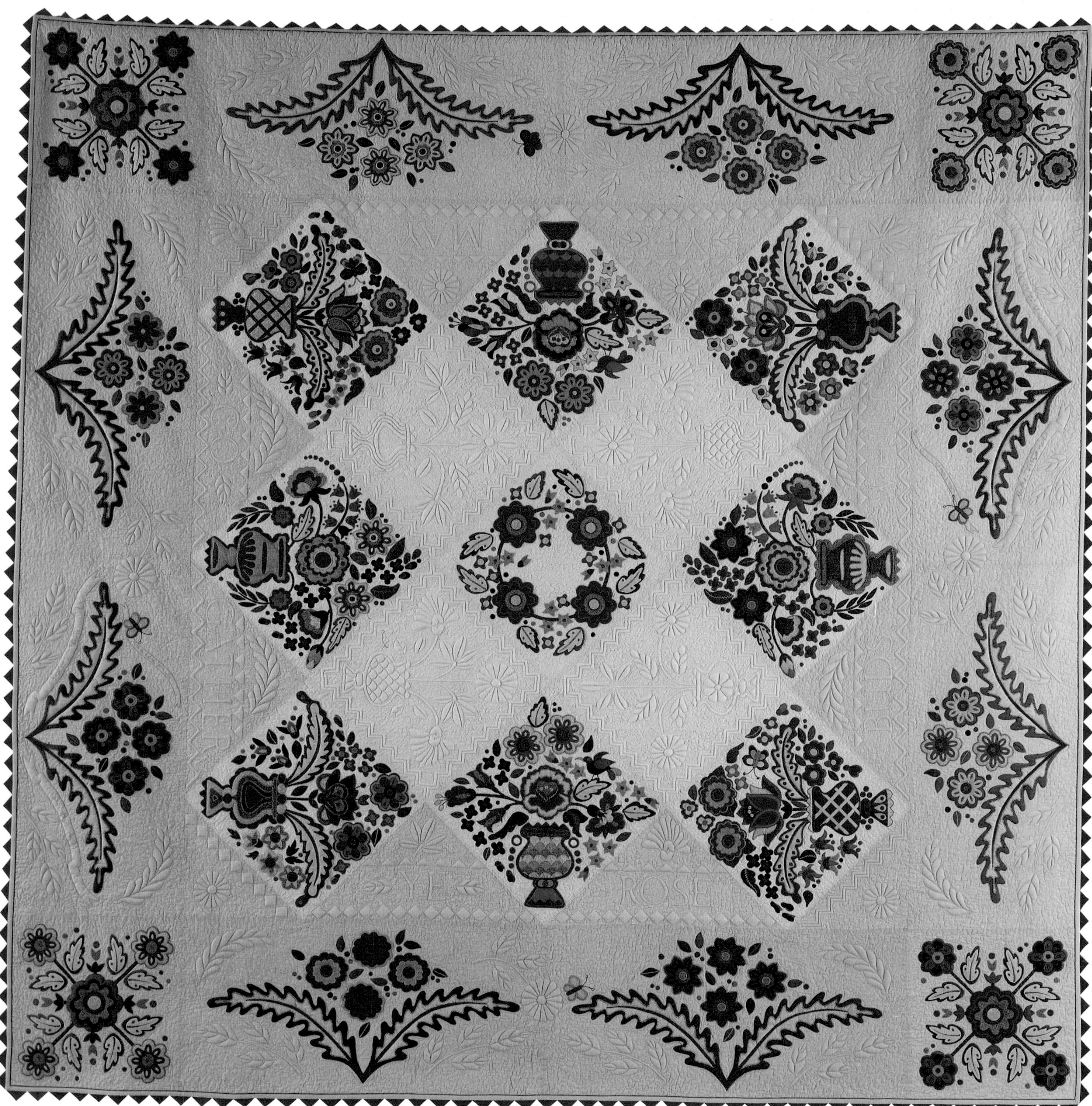

▲ **Floral Urns**

Debra Christine Wagner. 1992. Cosmos, Minnesota. Cottons; machine pieced, appliquéd, and embroidered. 90 x 90 in. Museum of the American Quilter's Society, Paducah, Kentucky.

The dense machine quilting here echoes the appliqués with trapunto leaves, swags and blossoms, and urns full of flowers. Also included is the quilted inscription "Go gather ye rose buds while ye may," a reference to the poem "To the Virgins, To Make Much of Time" by the seventeenth-century English poet Robert Herrick, which begins, "Gather ye rosebuds while ye may,/Old time is still a-flying:/And this same flower that smiles today/Tomorrow will be dying."

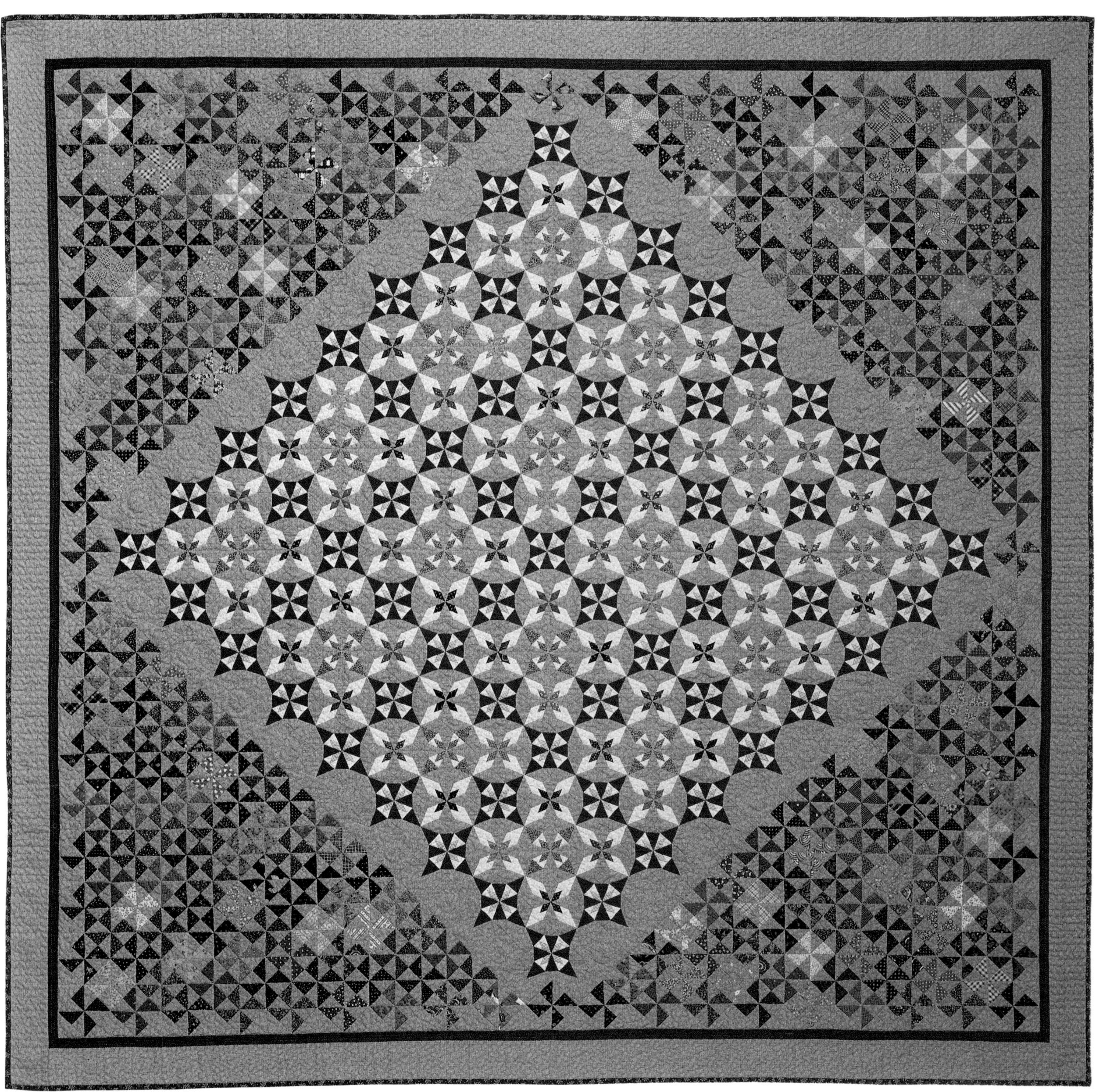

▲ **The Exchange**

Nancy Johnson-Srebo. 1990. Tunkhannock, Pennsylvania. Cottons; machine pieced; quilted by Debbie Grow. 78 1/2 x 77 1/2 in. Collection of the artist.

Nancy Johnson-Srebo is known for her precision piecing of miniature quilts. She has developed a number of special cutting and sewing techniques to achieve the accuracy needed for this kind of work. This quilt is an original melding of the Kaleidoscope and Pinwheel patterns. It is a full-sized "miniature" quilt; each of the 761 blocks measure 2 3/4 inches, and the entire quilt contains over 8,000 rotary-cut pieces and two hundred different shades of blue. The blue fabrics were collected from friends and students all over the United States. The quilt measured 84 square inches before it was quilted by Debbie Grow.

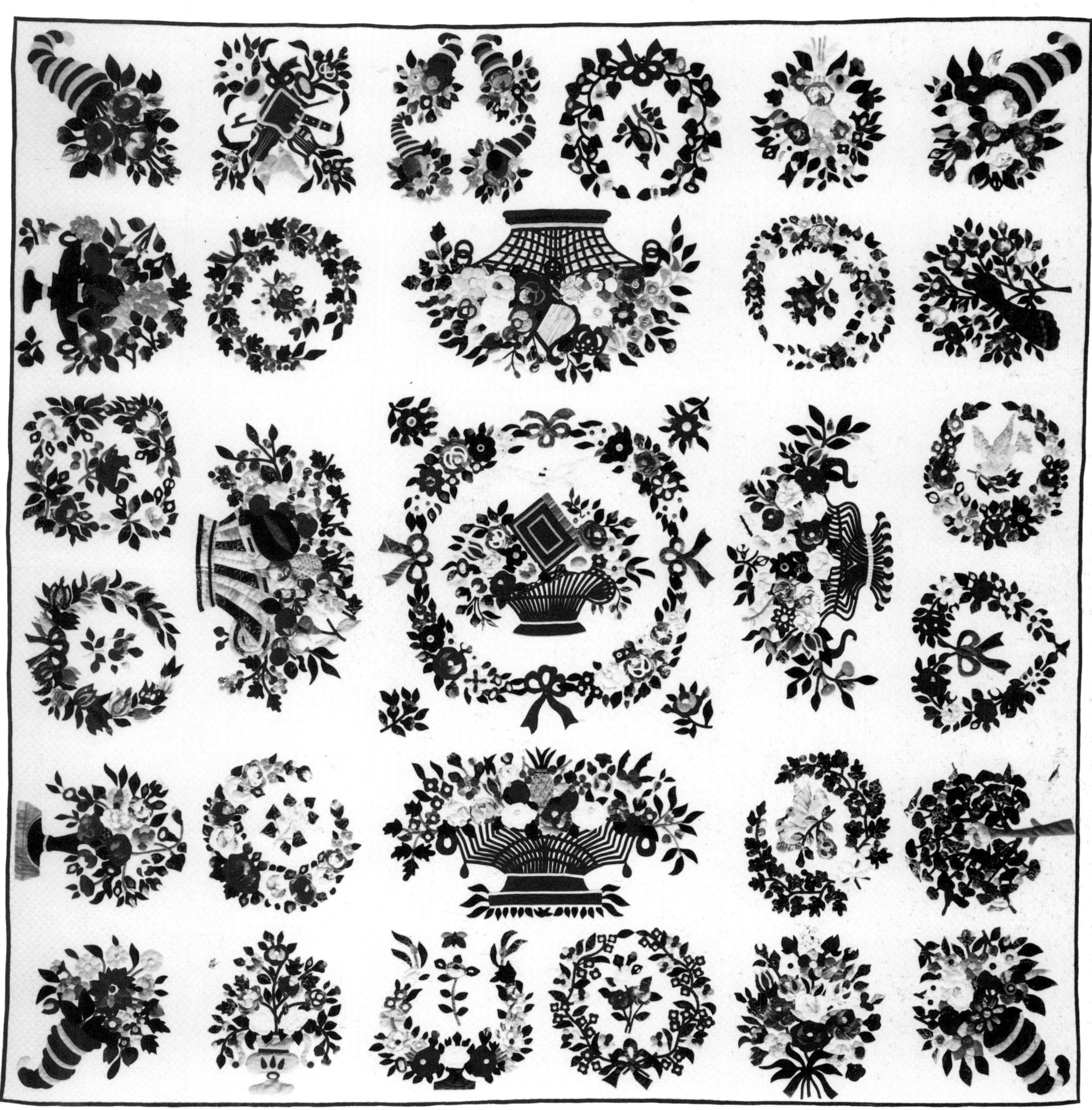

▲ **BALTIMORE ALBUM**

East Bay Heritage Quilters, designed by Adele Ingram. c. 1986. Albany, California. Cottons; hand appliquéd and quilted. Collection of East Bay Heritage Quilters.

This group effort was designed from an antique Baltimore album quilt made in the 1840s. East Bay Heritage Quilters is a very active San Francisco area group with many highly accomplished quilters as members.

WYNKEN, BLYNKEN, AND NOD ▸

Martha Skelton. 1975. Vicksburg, Mississippi. Cottons; hand appliquéd and quilted. 50 x 38 in. Private collection.

This child's quilt, made for the artist's granddaughter, was inspired by the beloved Eugene Field poem. Martha Skelton depicts the three little fishermen sailing on a quilted, moonlit sea of blue. "Wynken, Blynken and Nod one night/Sailed off in a wooden shoe—/Sailed on a river of crystal light,/Into a sea of dew . . . Wynken and Blynken are two little eyes/And Nod is a little head,/And the wooden shoe that sailed the skies/ Is a wee one's trundle-bed/So shut your eyes while mother sings/Of wonderful sights that be./And you shall see the beautiful things/As you rock on the misty sea,/Where the old shoe rocked the fishermen three/ Wynken, Blynken and Nod."

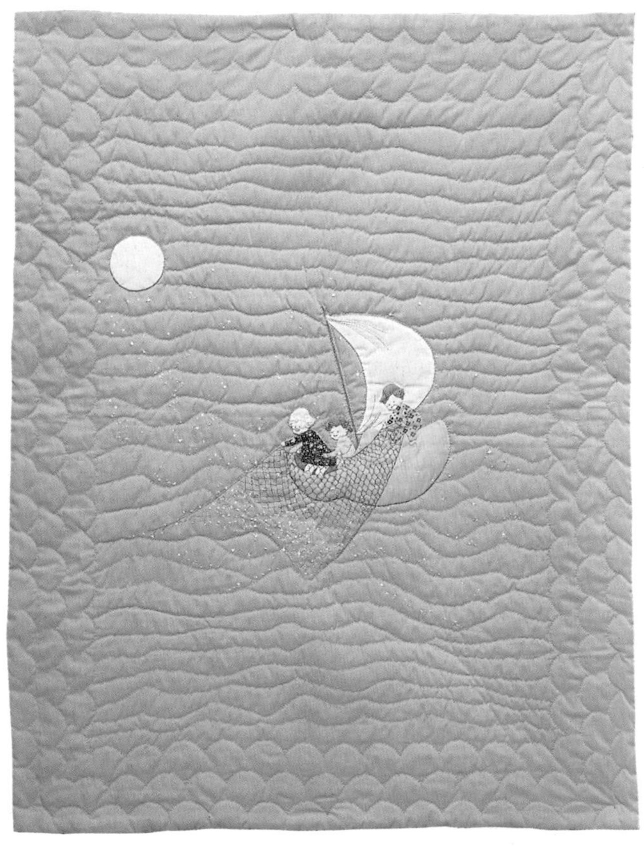

Martha Skelton

Martha Skelton of Vicksburg, Mississippi, who is considered the doyenne of Mississippi quilters and teachers, began quilting at the age of fifteen. She was born in West Virginia, grew up in Missouri and Oklahoma, and moved to Mississippi in 1947. She has studied and made traditional quilts everywhere she has lived. Skelton focuses on functional quilts, usually following traditional patterns and doing most of the piecing and quilting by hand. She often works from old fabric saved from past projects to help achieve a conservative, traditional look. She says, "My quilts are made to be used, loved, enjoyed, shared, washed and, yes, used up, worn out."

Skelton has been teaching quiltmaking since the early 1970s, when she left her job as a high school librarian. She is universally admired by her students and associates for her warmth, modesty, and generosity. According to Barbara Newman, President of the Mississippi Quilt Association, "It is almost impossible to find a quilter in Mississippi who has not taken a quilting class from Martha Skelton. Her influence and gentle encouragement have been the main reasons quilting has grown at a rapid rate in our state. When Mississippi quilters get together, sooner or later you will hear these words, 'Martha said do it this way.' We believe Martha is the ultimate authority, and, like E.F. Hutton, when Martha speaks, everyone listens." Skelton's friend and student Susan Schutt adds, "Mississippi quilters are indebted to Martha for spreading her enthusiasm and knowledge to us as gracefully as she covers the beds in her home with colorful, wonderful quilts."

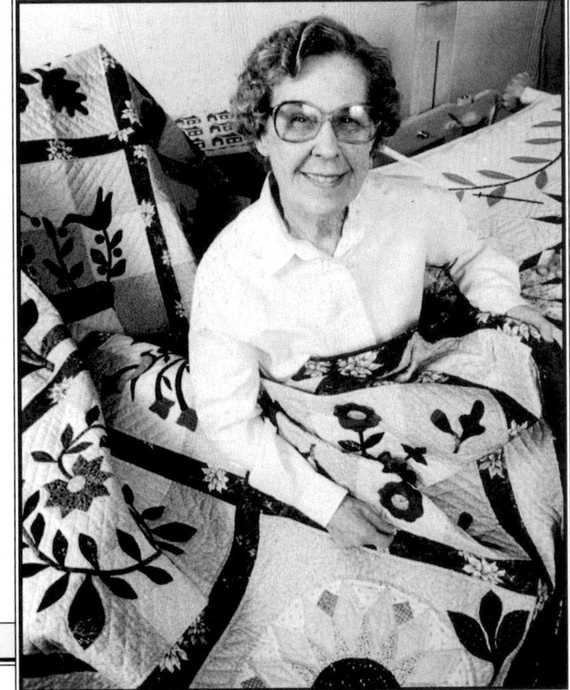

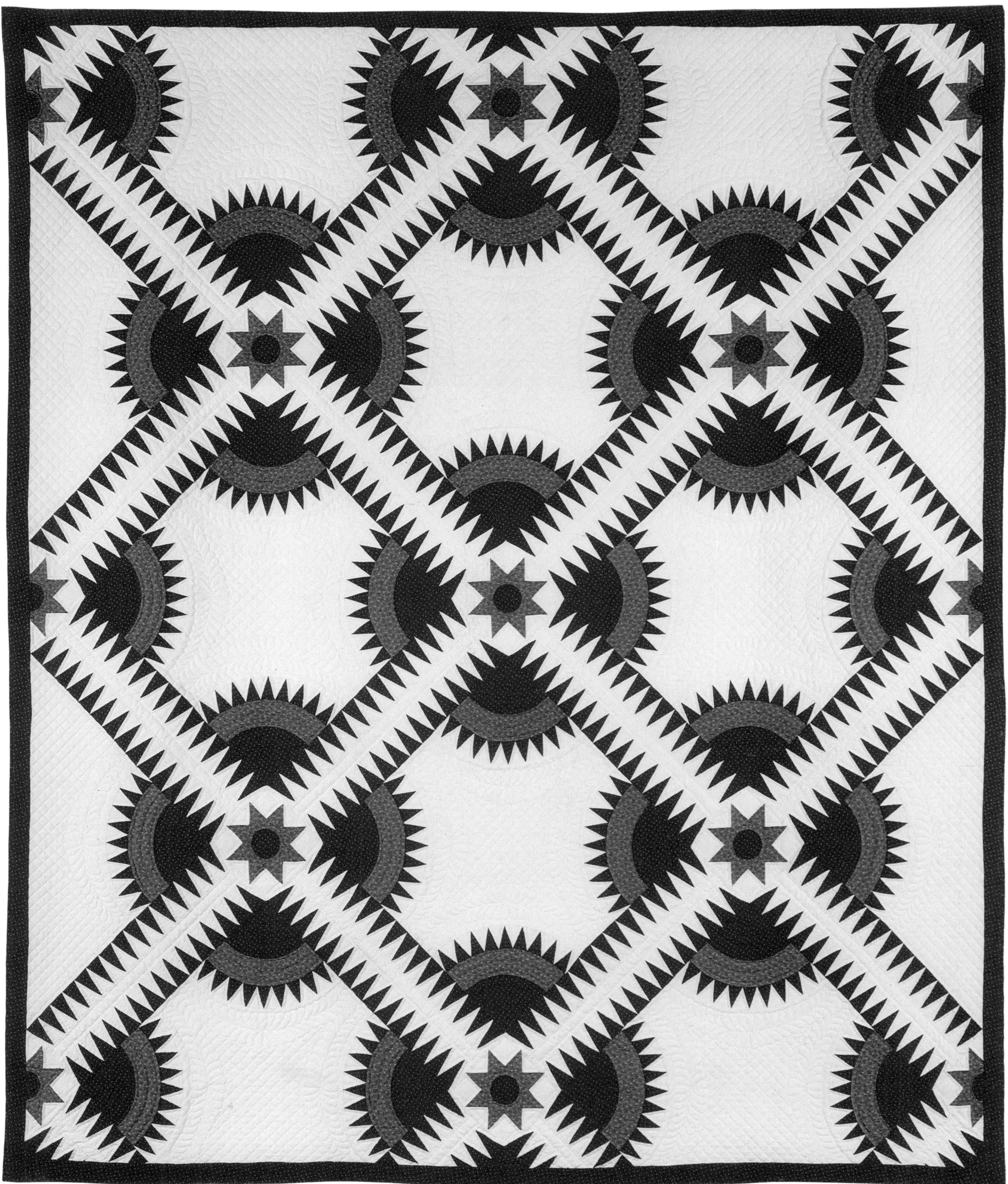

▲ NEW YORK BEAUTY

Martha Skelton. 1986. Vicksburg, Mississippi. Cottons; hand pieced, machine pieced, hand quilted. 90 x 77 in. Museum of the American Quilter's Society, Paducah, Kentucky.

Like its cousin the Mariner's Compass, which also employs a host of finely pointed triangles, this classic pattern dates to the early decades of the nineteenth century and requires mathematically precise cutting and piecing. The early quilt author and historian Florence Peto dubbed these pattens "post-graduate work" for quiltmakers.

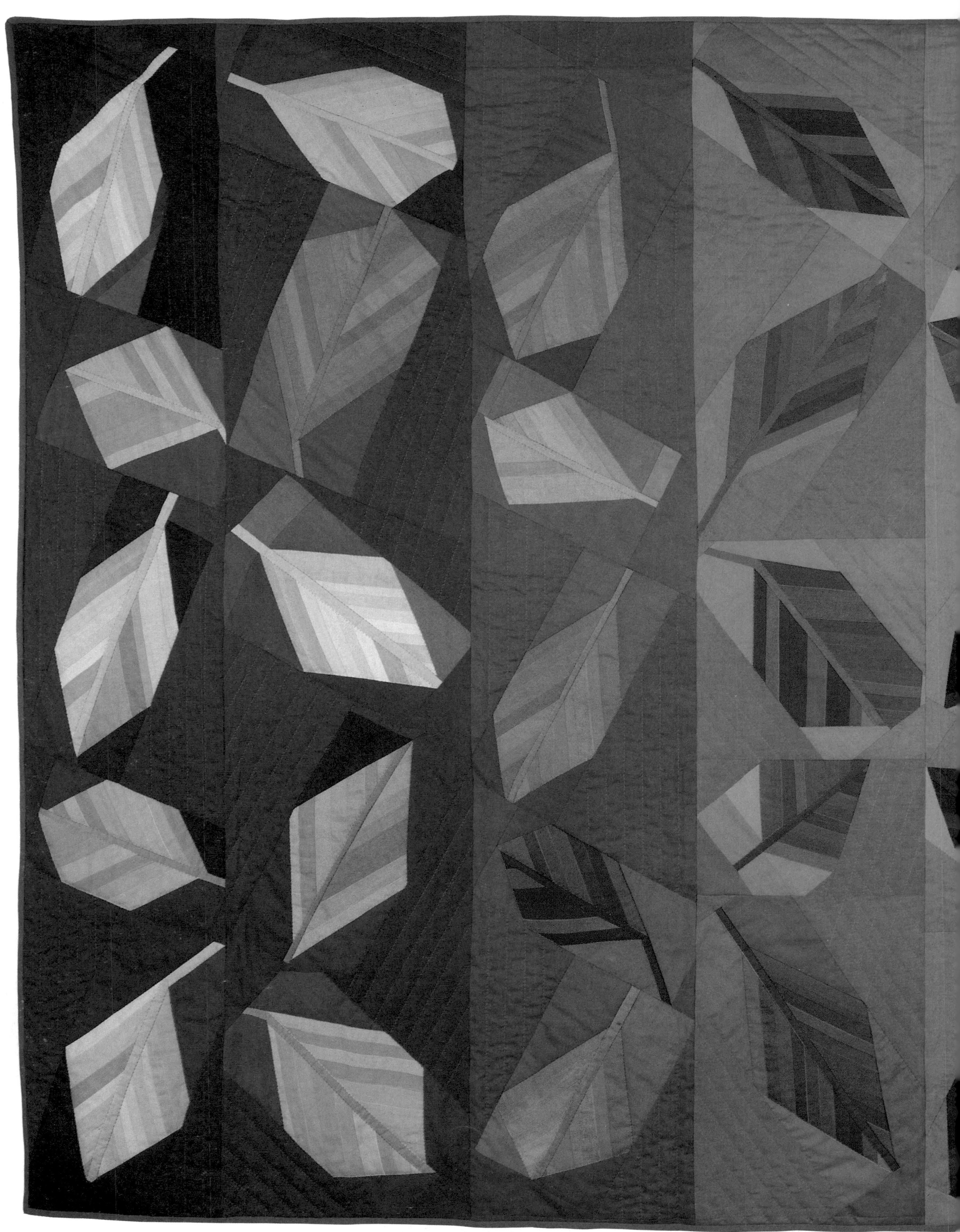

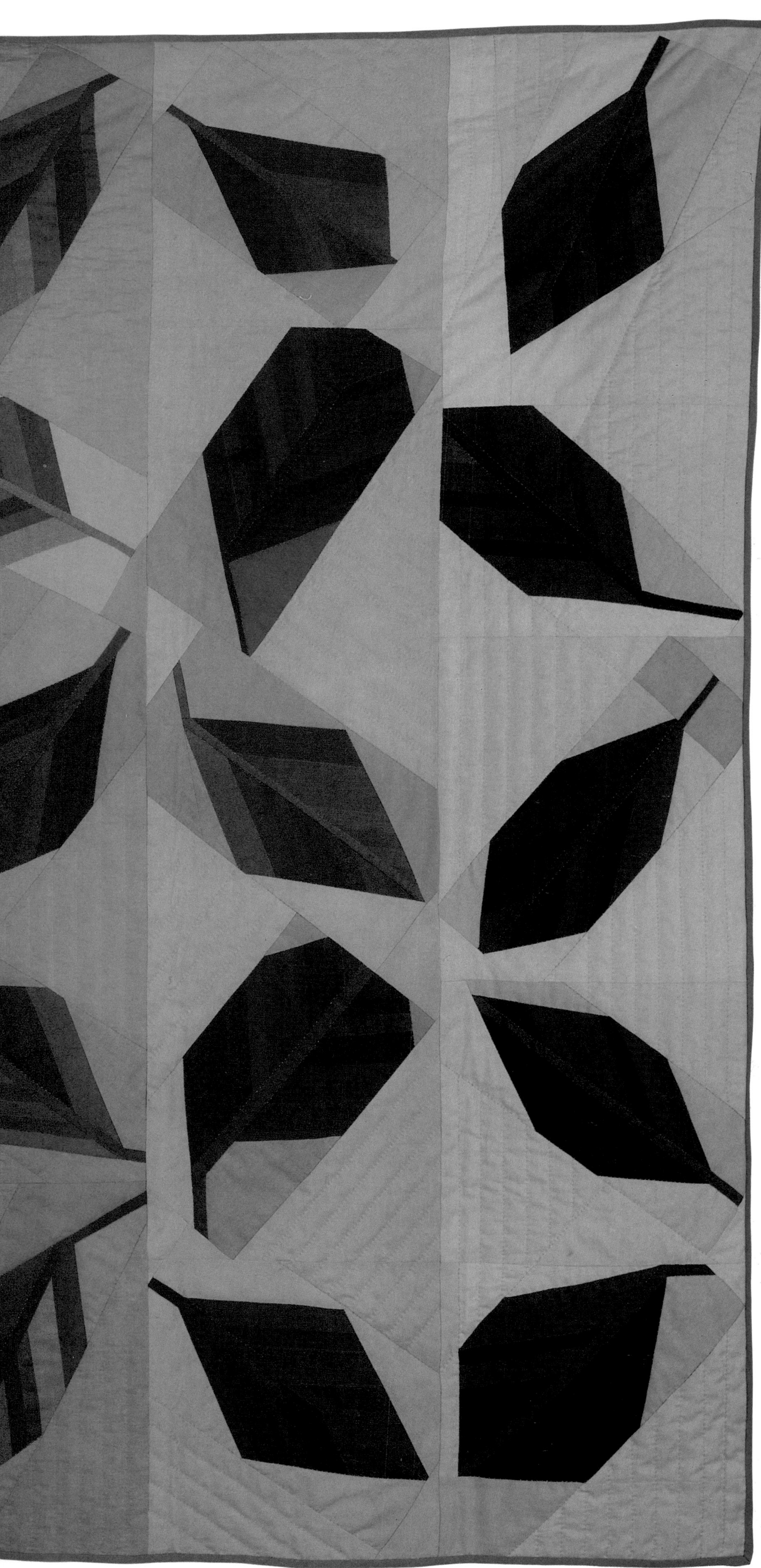

◂ **Leaf Fall**

Carol Hemphill Gersen. 1993. Boonsboro, Maryland. Hand-dyed cottons; machine pieced and hand quilted. 55 x 73 in. Collection of the artist. © 1993 Carol Hemphill Gersen.

Carol Hemphill Gersen makes pieced art quilts based on traditional American patchwork patterns. Her use of simple shapes and designs allows color and value to dominate her work, and her own hand-dyed fabrics provide the quilt's superior light fastness and unlimited color range. This recent quilt explores the rich hues and pleasing shapes of late fall leaves set against a backdrop of vivid sky to midnight blues. The tree represented is a chestnut just outside the artist's studio.

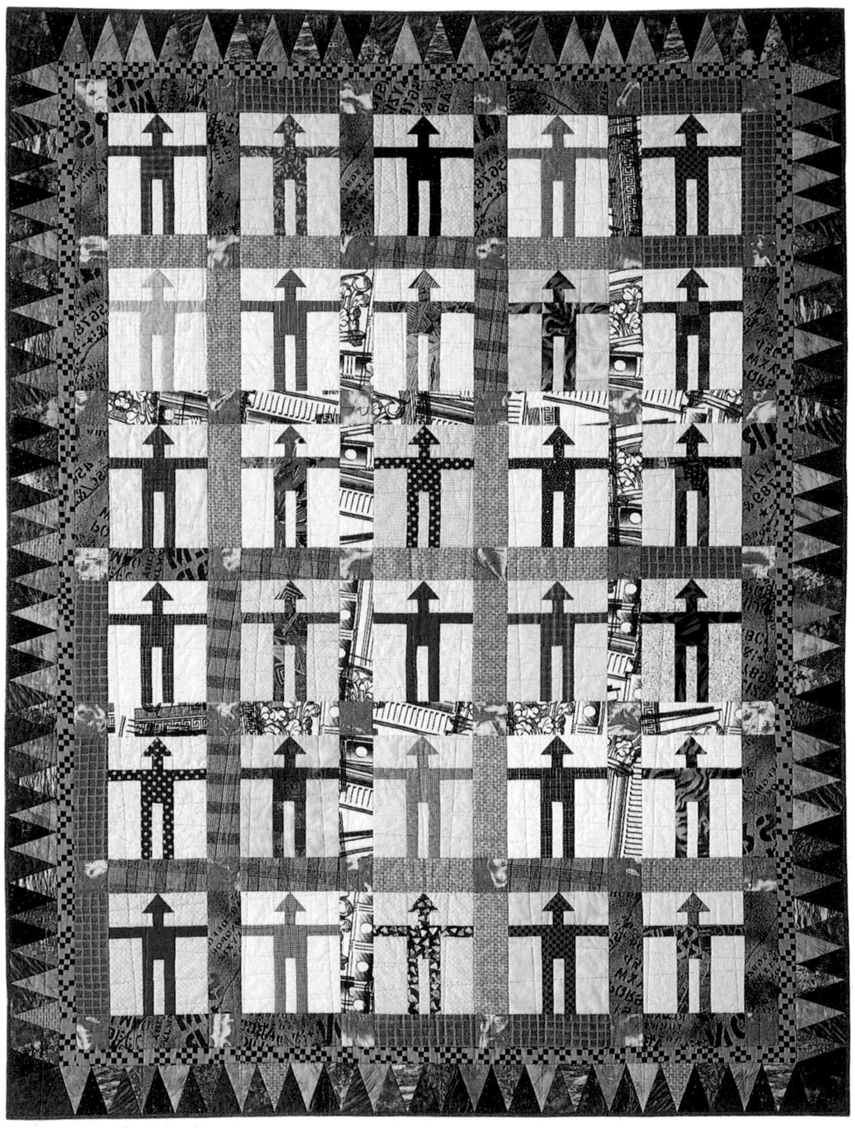

◄ Collective Conditioning

Rebecca Rohrkaste. 1994. Berkeley, California. Cottons; machine pieced and quilted. 97 x 73 1/2 in. Collection of the artist.

Rebecca Rohrkaste attended the Rhode Island School of Design and was introduced to quiltmaking in 1977. This quilt was inspired by an antique quilt that contains similar figures. Rohrkaste pieced a number of blocks of the figures before planning the quilt. She played with the arrangement of the blocks while listening to news reports of the world population conference and found the figures "had their own intentions. I gave them a traditional setting, lined up and stacked on top of each other, divided by walls, conforming to expectations even in their diversity. I felt they represented our conditioning to accept what are becoming intolerable social and environmental conditions . . . which we are all responsible for."

Hot Dogs with Mustard ►

Laurel Horton. 1990. Seneca, South Carolina. Cottons; hand pieced, screen printed, hand quilted. 62 x 48 in. Collection of the artist.

This quilt was inspired by a dream in which someone showed Laurel Horton fabric with these stylized dogs printed on it. She took a screen printing class so she could reproduce the dream fabric herself and here juxtaposed the dogs she envisioned with string-pieced blocks.

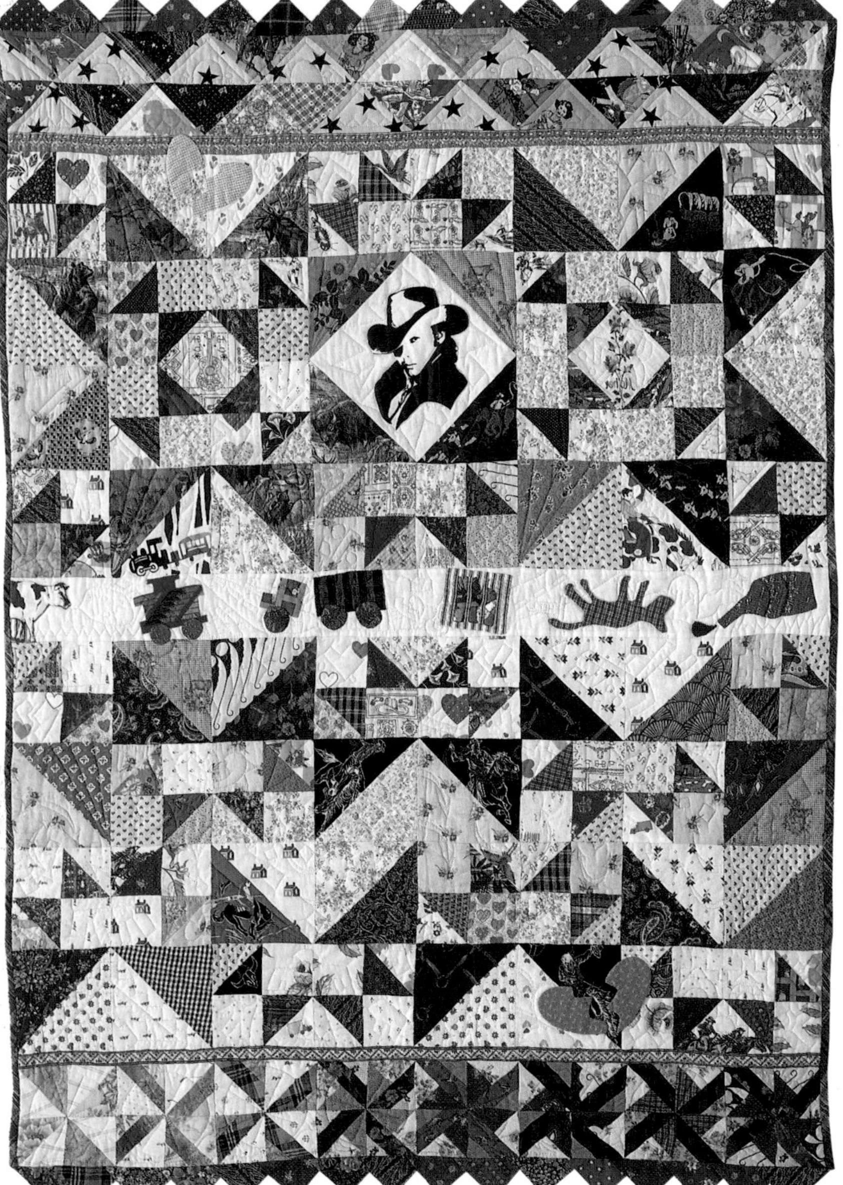

◄ I Want To Ride in the Car Hank Died In

Nina Antze. 1988. Sebastapol, California. Cottons; machine pieced and hand quilted. 66 x 48 in. Collection of the artist.

On January 1, 1953, on his way to a gig in Ohio, the legendary country singer and songwriter Hank Williams (author of such immortal songs as "Hey, Good Lookin'," and "I'm So Lonesome I Could Cry") died in the backseat of his new powder-blue Cadillac, probably of a combination of drugs and alcohol. He was twenty-nine. Nina Antze says, "When I announced to my quilt group that I wanted to make a quilt with all the elements of good country music (which are—according to Steve Goodman—mother, prison, farms, trucks, trains, Christmas, dead dogs like Old Shep, and getting drunk), they literally gave me the shirts off their backs. So there are many wonderful and varied fabrics in the quilt, including a genuine Dwight Yoakam bandana and a handkerchief my daughter gave me for Mother's Day."

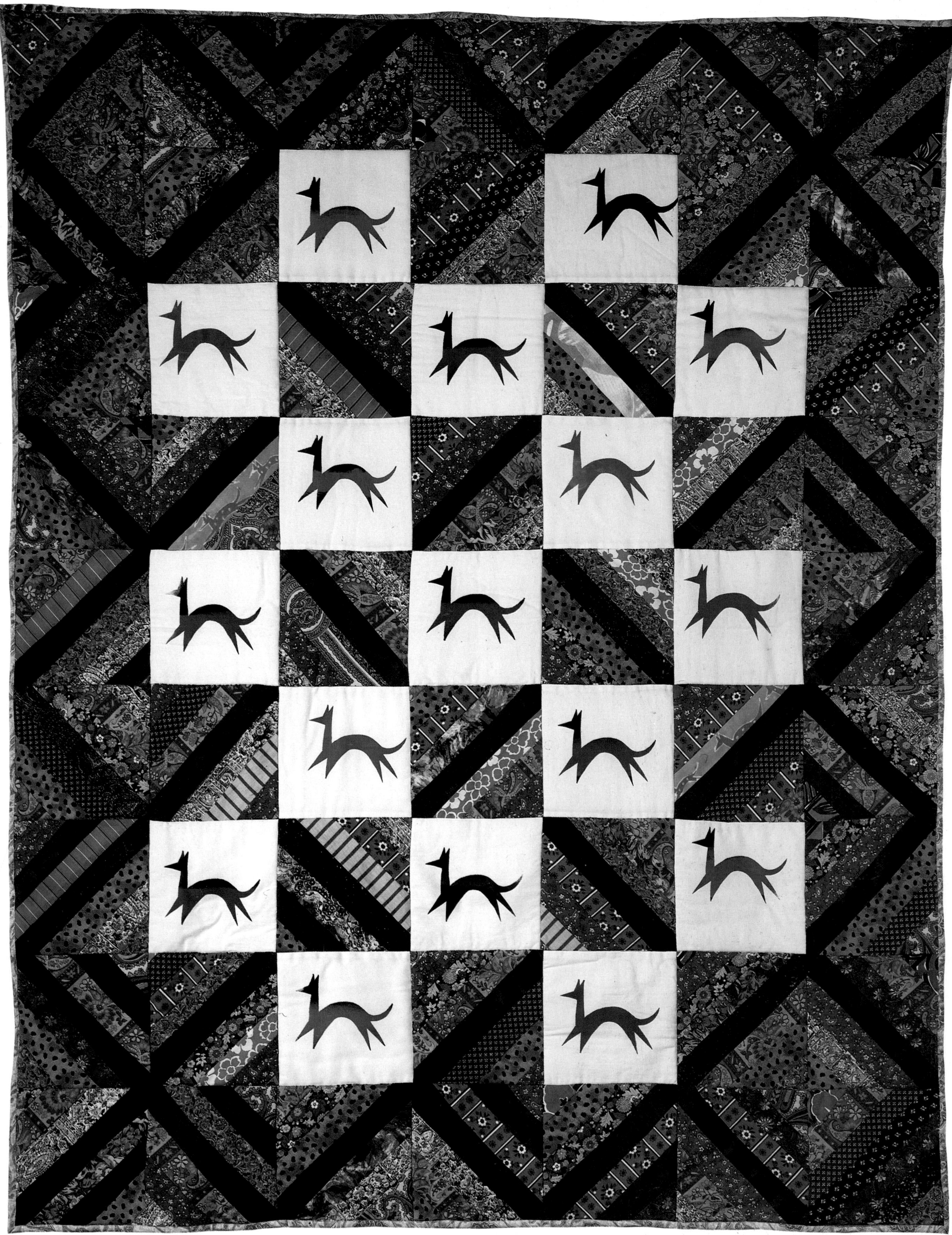

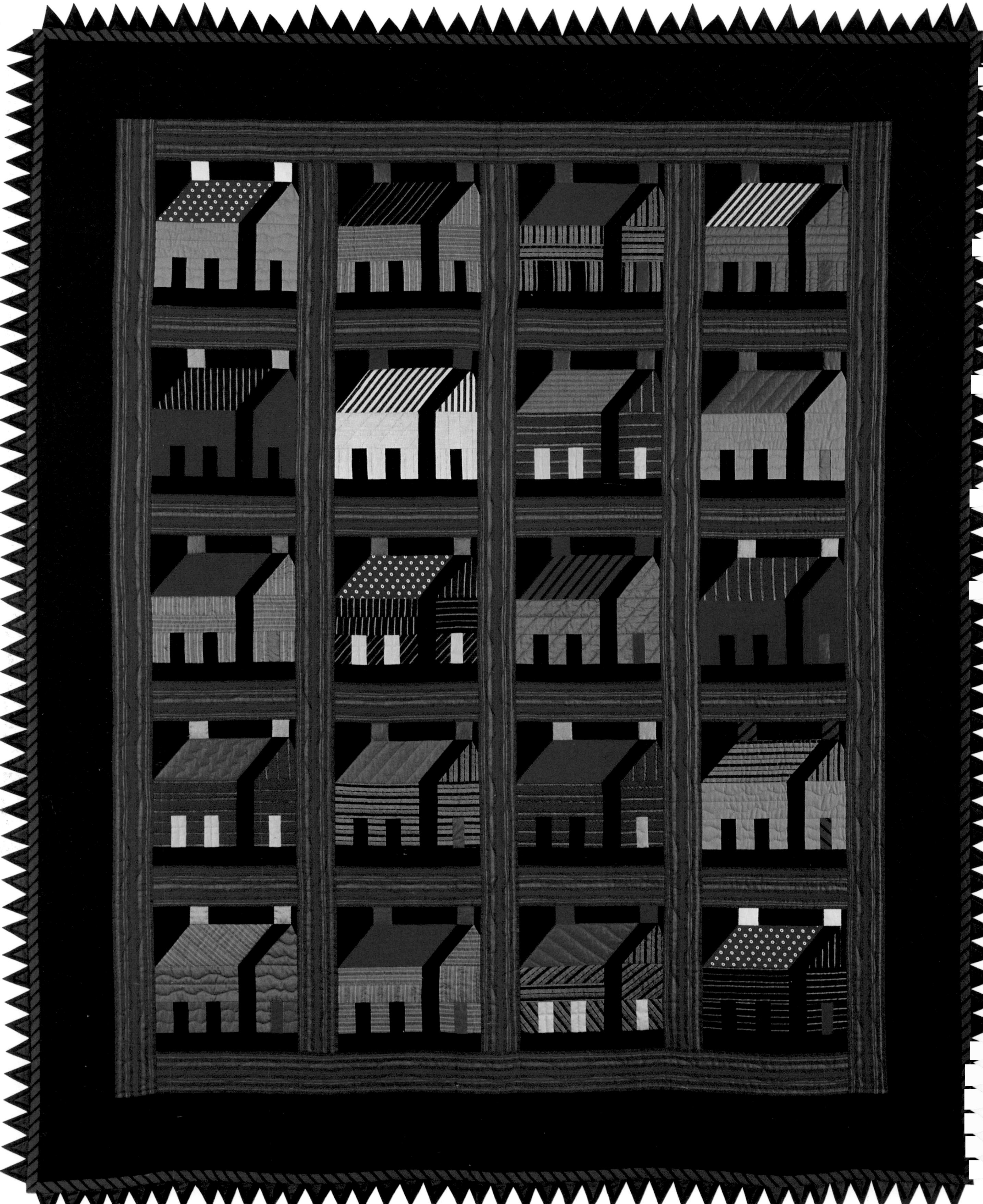

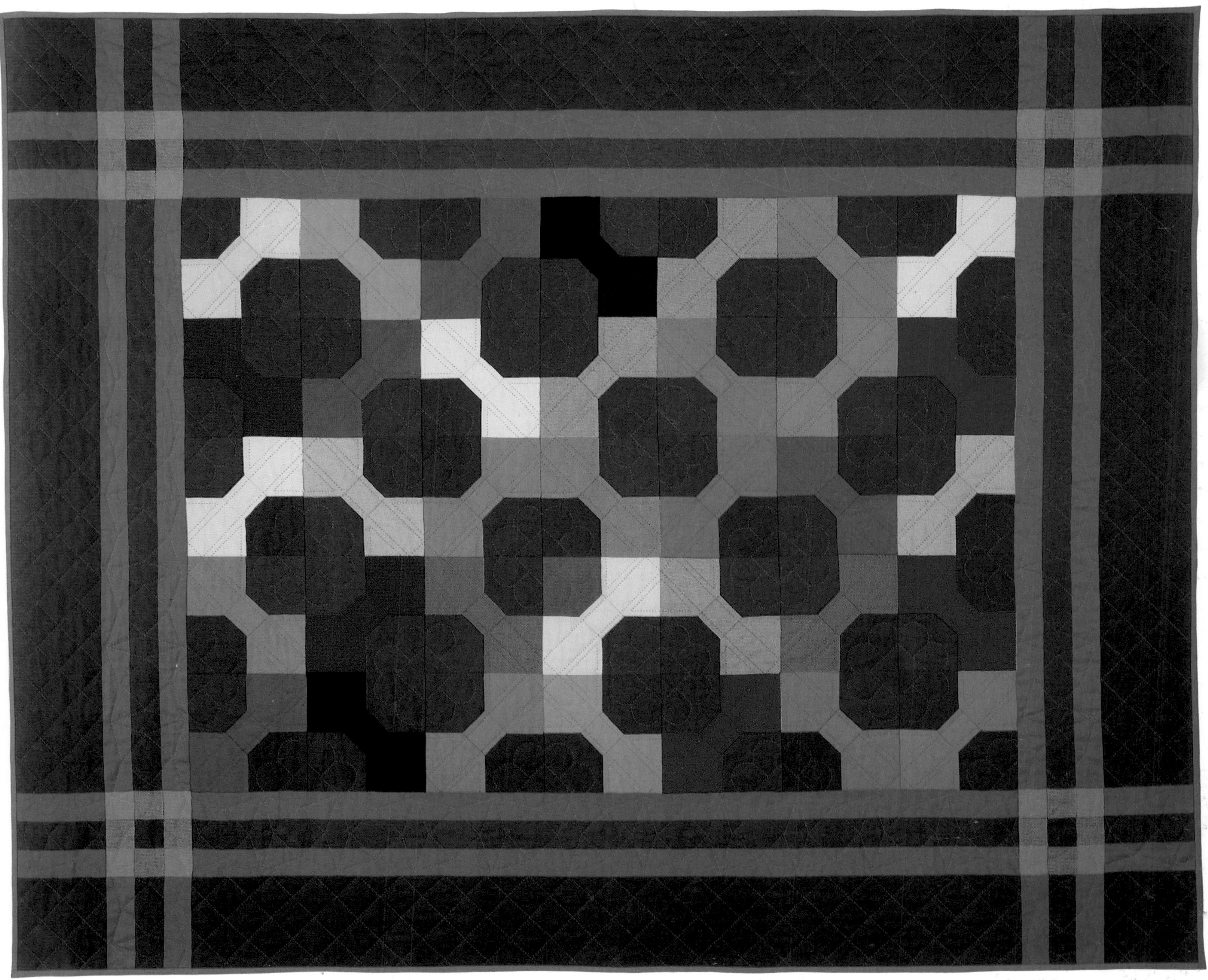

◄ BROWN COUNTY LOG CABINS

Linda Karel Sage. 1985. Morgantown, Indiana. Cottons; hand pieced. 93 x 87 in. Museum of the American Quilter's Society, Paducah, Kentucky.

Working from a commercial pattern, Linda Karel Sage used her own distinctive palette of fabrics, colors, quilting, and finishing details to make this quilt unique. The wavy lines of the quilting soften the hard-edged geometry of the houses and lattice frame, as do the wide outer border and pointed edging.

▲ BOWTIES OPEN

Judy Speezak. 1994. Brooklyn, New York. Cotton; hand pieced and quilted. 48 x 60 in. Collection of the artist.

Judy Speezak is a professional quiltmaker and teacher who specializes in traditional-style quilts. She writes, "I completed my first Bowties quilt in 1991. Having enthusiastically rotary cut more pieces than I needed, I was left with one dark green and sixty-nine dark blue pentagons when I was done. That was exactly enough to make the background on thirty-five more blocks, which worked out to a very pleasing five-by-seven-block configuration. Thus, the size of *Bowties Open* was decided for me. I paired the dark green and blues with other solids, both dark and bright, and chose to work with a slightly different block setting in this second piece just to keep it interesting."

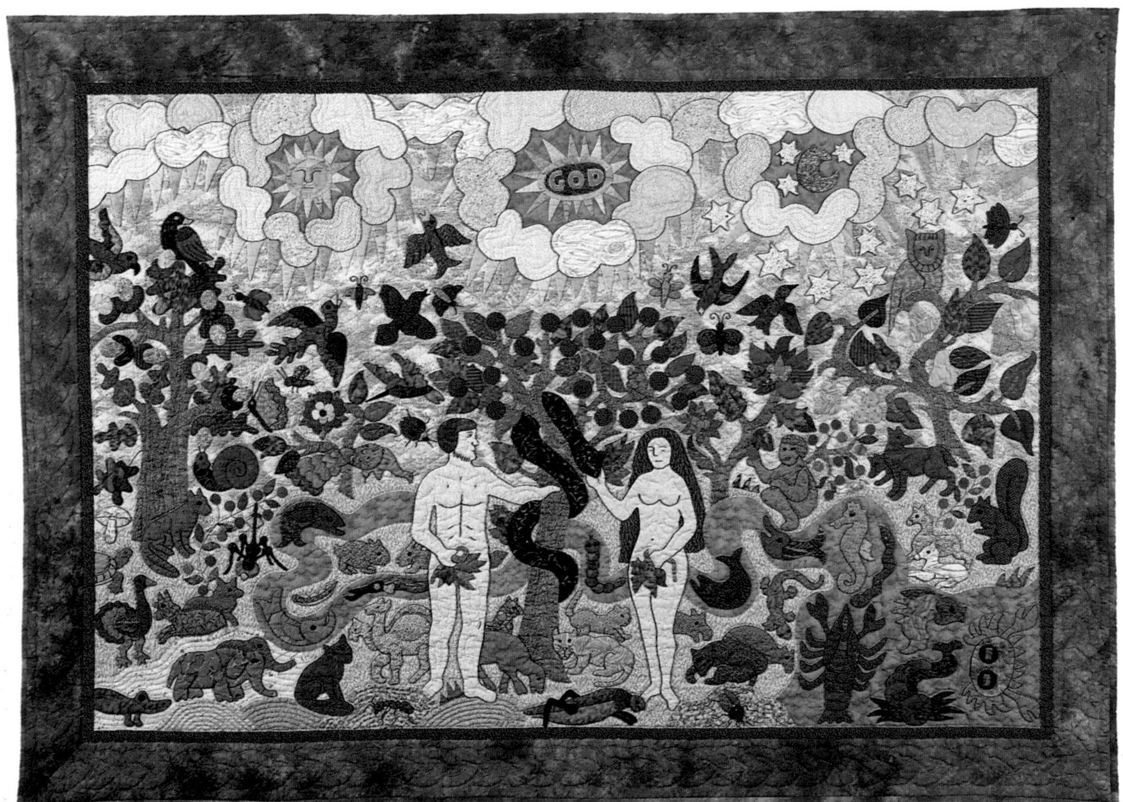

◄ **ADAM AND EVE**

Suzanne Marshall. 1994. Clayton, Missouri. Cottons; hand appliquéd and quilted. 49 x 68 in. Collection of the artist.

In this modern look at the Garden of Eden, Adam and Eve are surrounded by a host of creatures great and small. Among the appliquéd menagerie are, in addition to the requisite snake, an owl, a peacock, a pair of elephants, a crocodile, a monkey, a snail, various birds, bugs, and butterflies, and a sea-going contingent that includes a crab, a sea horse, a lobster, and a whale.

Suzanne Marshall

Suzanne Marshall of Clayton, Missouri, is a master of the art of appliqué who began to design her own work in the mid-1980s. She was, however, no stranger to textiles, having previously made many of her own clothes as well as traditional utilitarian quilts for her family for a number of years. A former elementary school teacher, she taught herself how to quilt from books. She says the quilts which she made for her family increased in size as her children grew, providing an ideal step-by-step learning experience.

Marshall's intricate quilt designs are full of small and often humorous touches. Her punningly titled *Bed Bugs* quilt, for example, places sixteen different groups of beetles at the centers of identical wreaths and surrounds them all with a border crawling with still more beetles. Marshall often spends nine months to a year working on one of her complex quilts. Each is an individual labor of love, usually differing dramatically in style and design from previous work. She works in both album and overall appliqué formats and has also made a few complex pieced quilts. She works entirely by hand, meticulously sewing each element herself. Because of the time and individual attention she devotes to each quilt, Marshall chooses not to sell her work, but instead often designates them as gifts for family and friends. She has entered her quilts in competitions since the mid-1980s, and one of her recent quilts, *Toujours Nouveau*, is in the collection of the Museum of the American Quilter's Society.

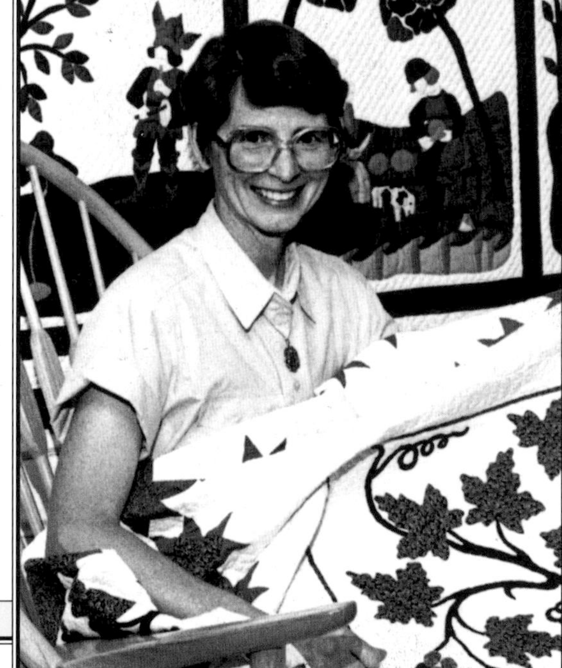

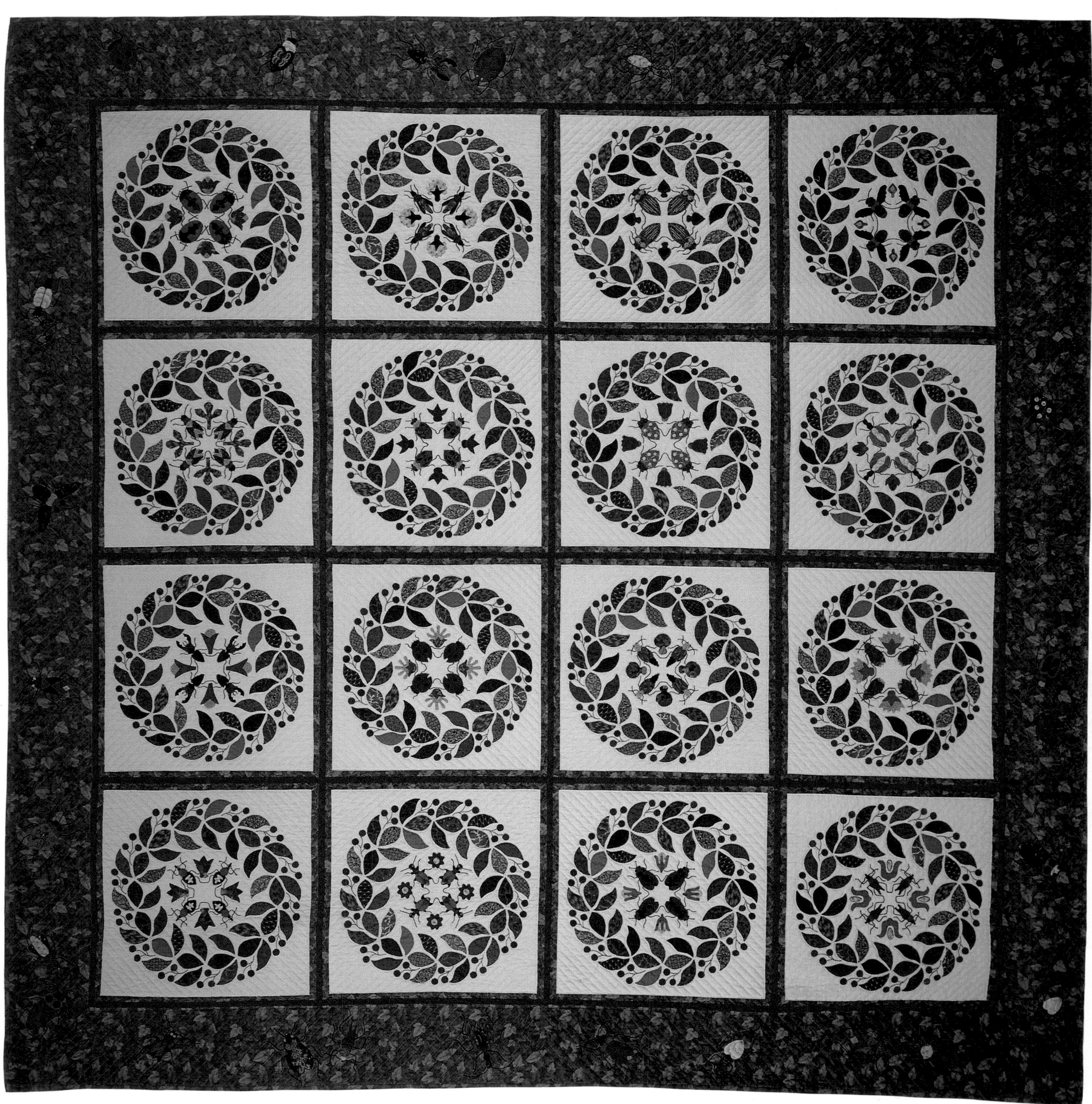

▲ **Bed Bugs**

Suzanne Marshall. 1992. Clayton, Missouri. Cottons; hand appliquéd and quilted. 92 x 92 in. Collection of the artist.

This delightful quilt makes bed bugs pleasures rather than unwelcome guests.

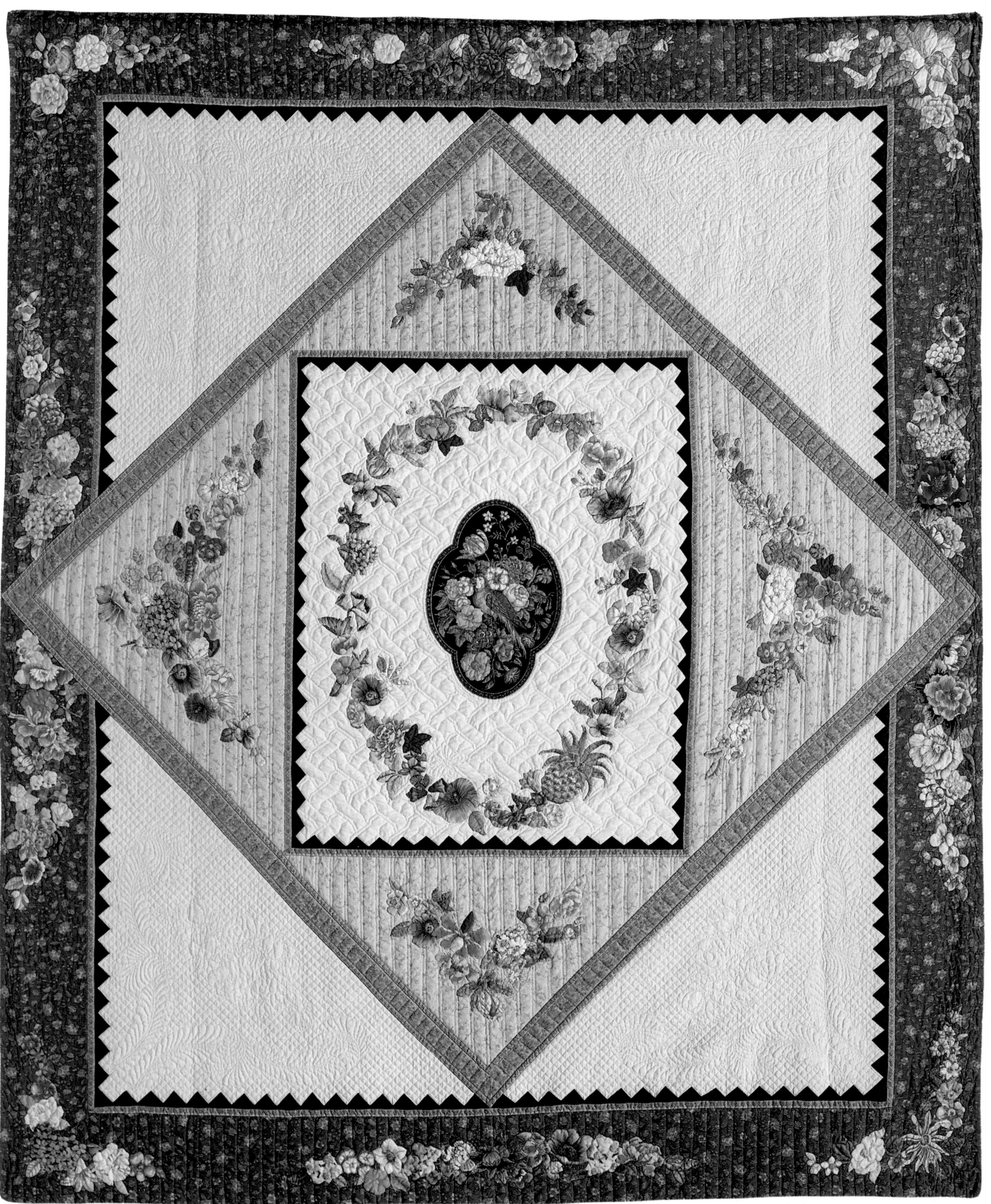

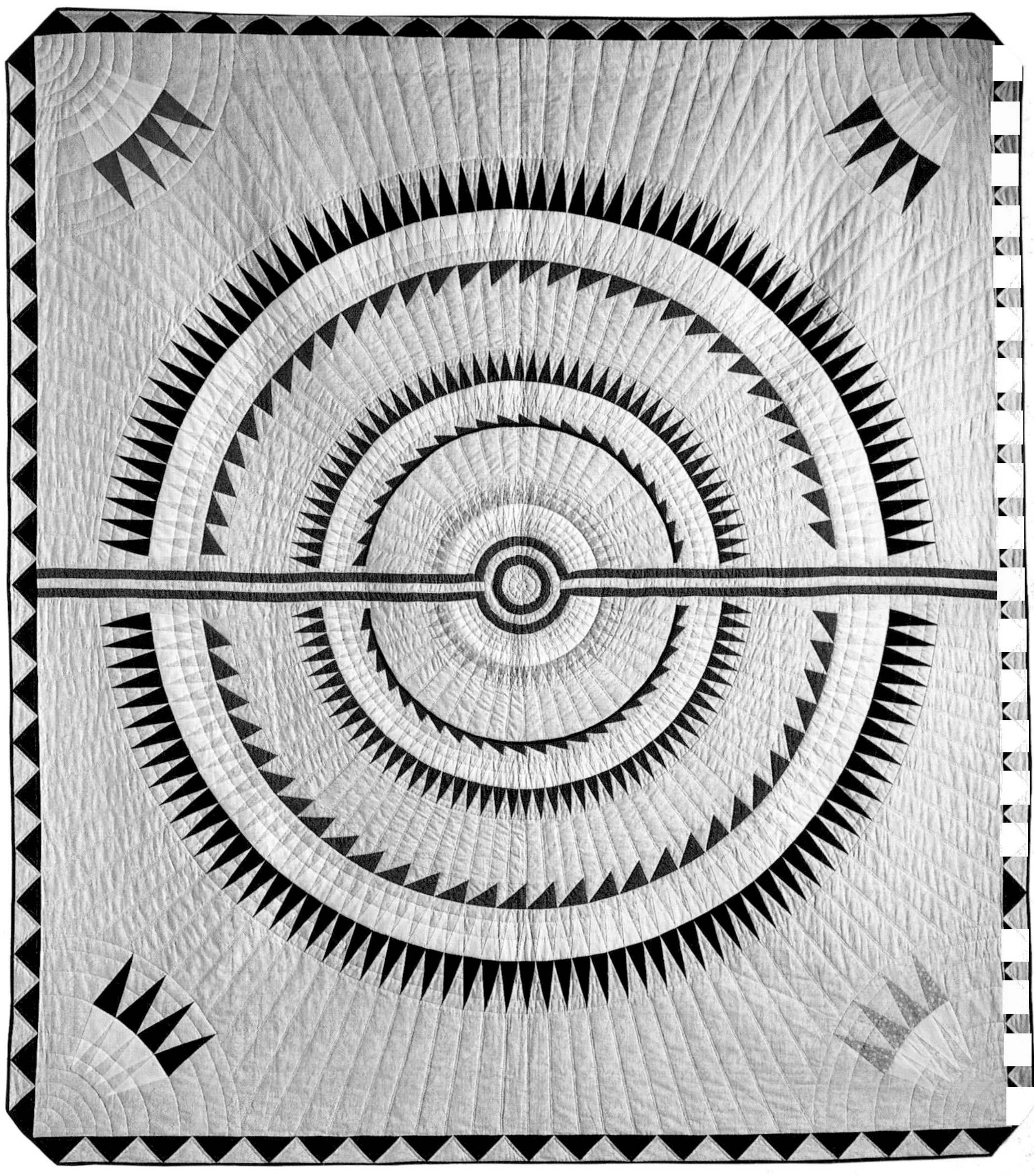

◄ Chintz Medallion

Nan Tournier. 1990–1994. Mt. Pleasant, South Carolina. Chintzes; hand appliquéd and quilted. 100 x 82 in. Collection of the artist.

As a volunteer working at the Charleston Museum, Nan Tournier has carefully studied the early nineteenth-century *broderie perse* quilts of the South Carolina lowcountry and has made several examples of these chintz appliqué quilts. This delicate quilt, which took four years to complete, is her largest and most elaborate to date.

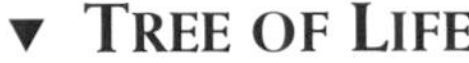

▼ Tree of Life

Barbara W. Barber. 1993. Westerly, Rhode Island. Cottons; hand appliquéd, hand stipple quilting and trapunto. 63 x 55 1/2 in. Collection of the artist.

This delicate *broderie perse* Tree of Life is complemented by trailing vines of raised trapunto quilting and framed by a wide border of subtly printed fabric.

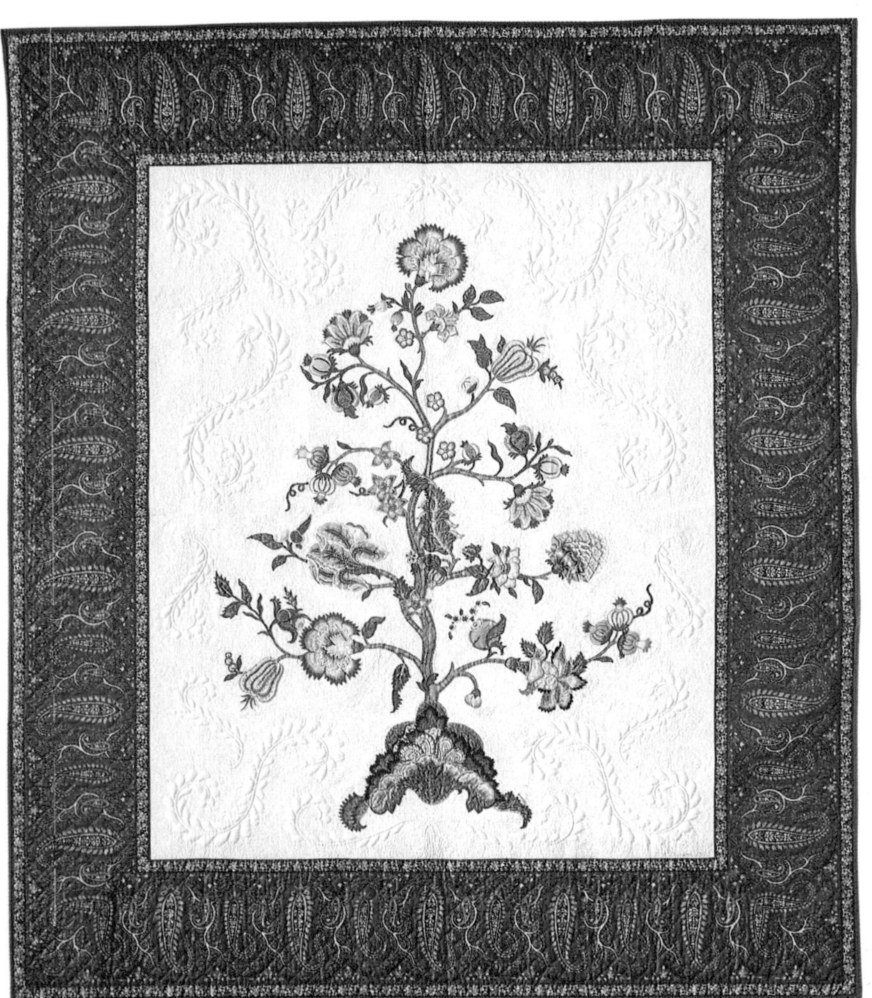

▲ Feathered Sun

John Flynn. 1993. Billings, Montana. Cottons; machine pieced and hand quilted. 96 x 80 in. Collection of the artist.

John Flynn has many stories to tell about the special difficulties of being a male quiltmaker. "I am a bearded 6'2" and the reception I got when I [first] entered a fabric store was less than cordial. A lady with rhinestone encrusted cat-eyes hanging around her neck . . . followed me everywhere to make sure I didn't break any of the fabric. If I paused for even a moment, she whipped the glasses on, looked over them, and asked if she could help me find anything particular. I said I wasn't sure what I was looking for and she said, 'Didn't she give you a list?'" Since that encounter, Flynn, who was trained as a civil engineer, has built a national reputation for his hand-quilted works, many of which feature extensive trapunto and hand stippling. He also has published five quiltmaking workbooks and founded a quilt frame company to market some of his inventions. *Feathered Sun* was inspired by Native American designs.

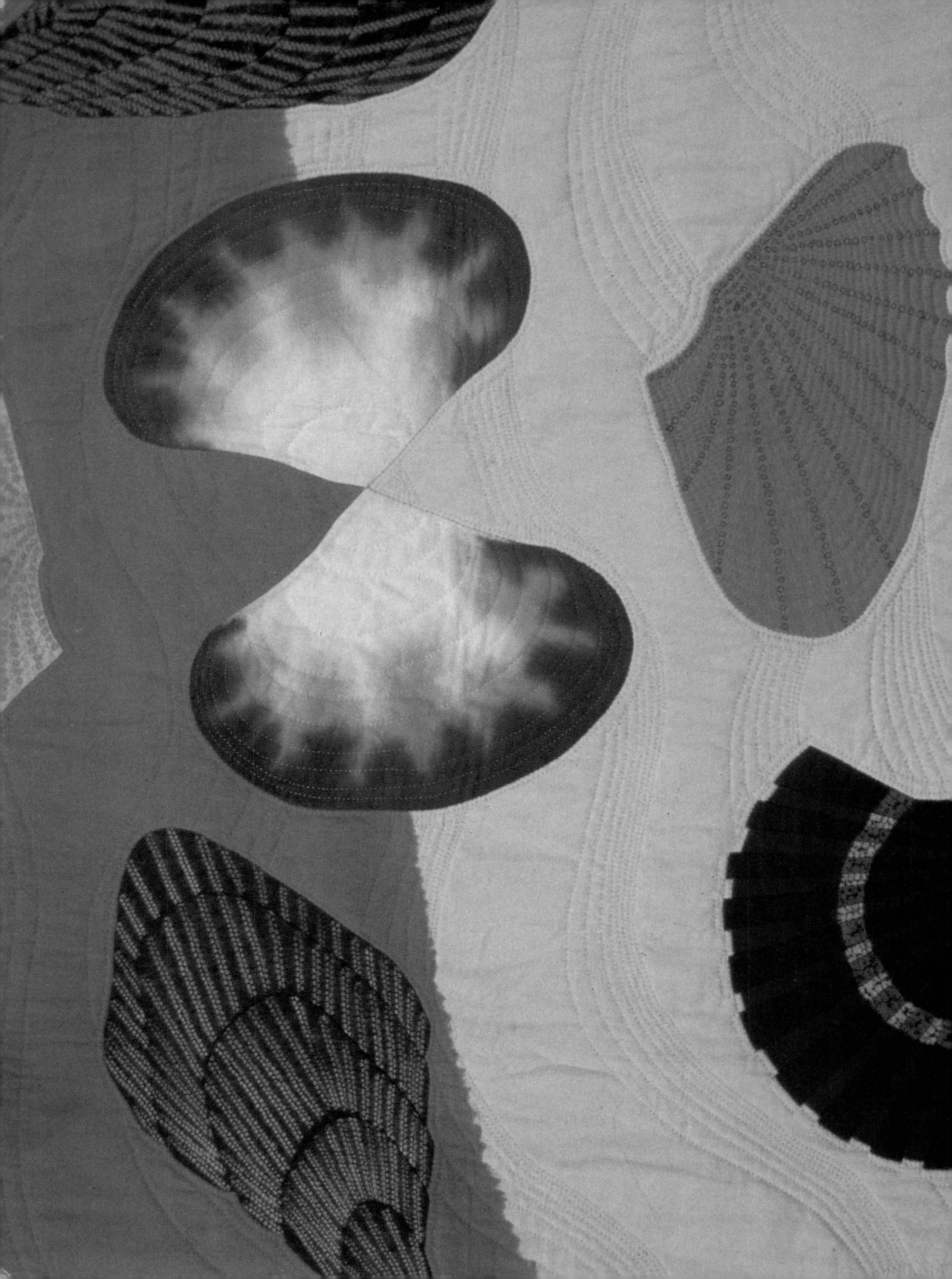

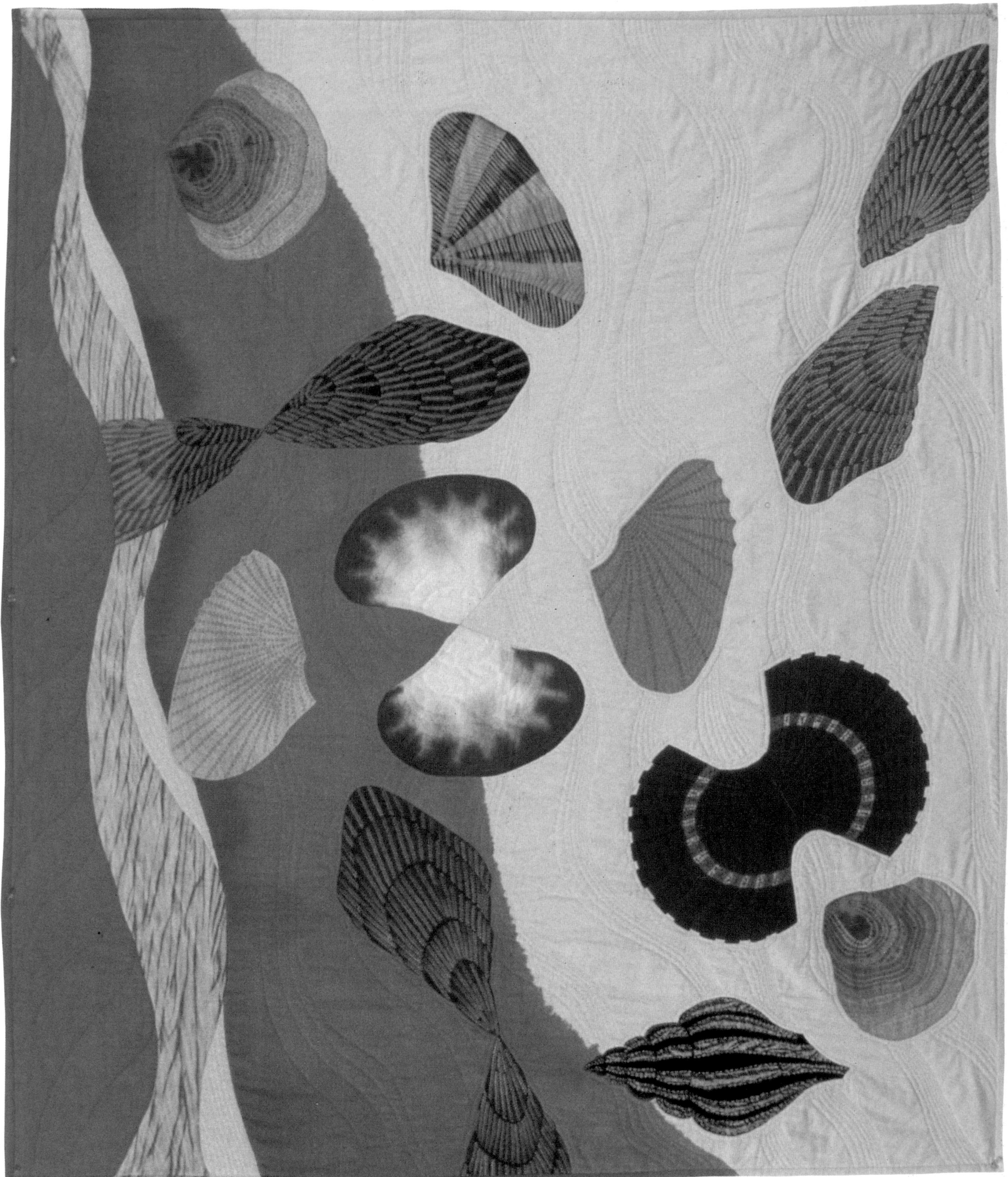

▲ "Shibori" Shores (◄ detail)

Carol Anne Grotrian. 1988. Cambridge, Massachusetts. Cottons; hand dyed, hand pieced, appliquéd, and quilted. 65 x 56 in. Collection of the artist.

This quilt depicts a beachcomber's view of an ocean edge strewn with beautiful shells. The quilt is named after the ancient Japanese resist technique *shibori*, which Carol Anne Grotrian used to dye fabrics that would then suggest the incredible range of color and texture found in seashells. In *shibori* dyeing, fabric is stitched, knotted, pleated, bound or pole-wrapped to keep dye out of certain areas and to form a pattern. Each color generally requires an hour-long dye bath.

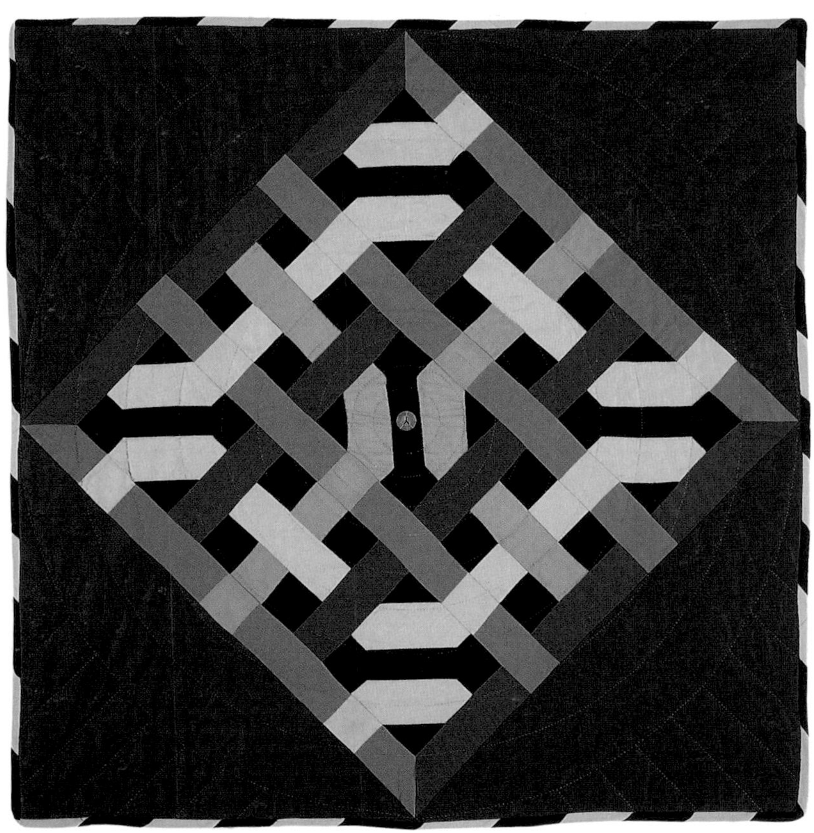

▲ **TRACKWORK**

Vikki Berman Chenette. 1992. Jersey City, New Jersey. Cottons with New York subway token; hand and machine pieced, hand quilted. 36 x 36 in. Collection of the artist

The quiltmaker's husband, who maintains track for the New York City subway system, drew the original design from which this quilt was developed.

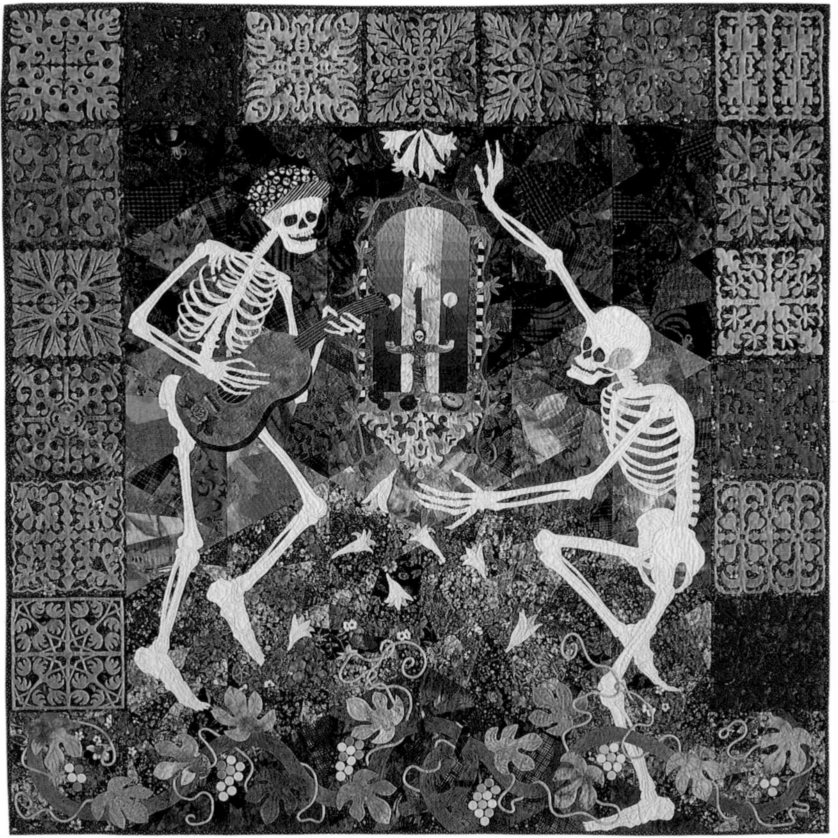

▲ **AMIGOS MUERTOS ("DEAD FRIENDS")**

Jonathan Shannon. 1993. Belvedere, California. Cottons; machine pieced, hand appliquéd and quilted. 89 x 89 in. Collection of the artist.

Jonathan Shannon made this quilt as a tribute to friends and fellow artists who had died of cancer and AIDS. *Amigos Muertos* won the 1994 National Patchwork Championship in Great Britain.

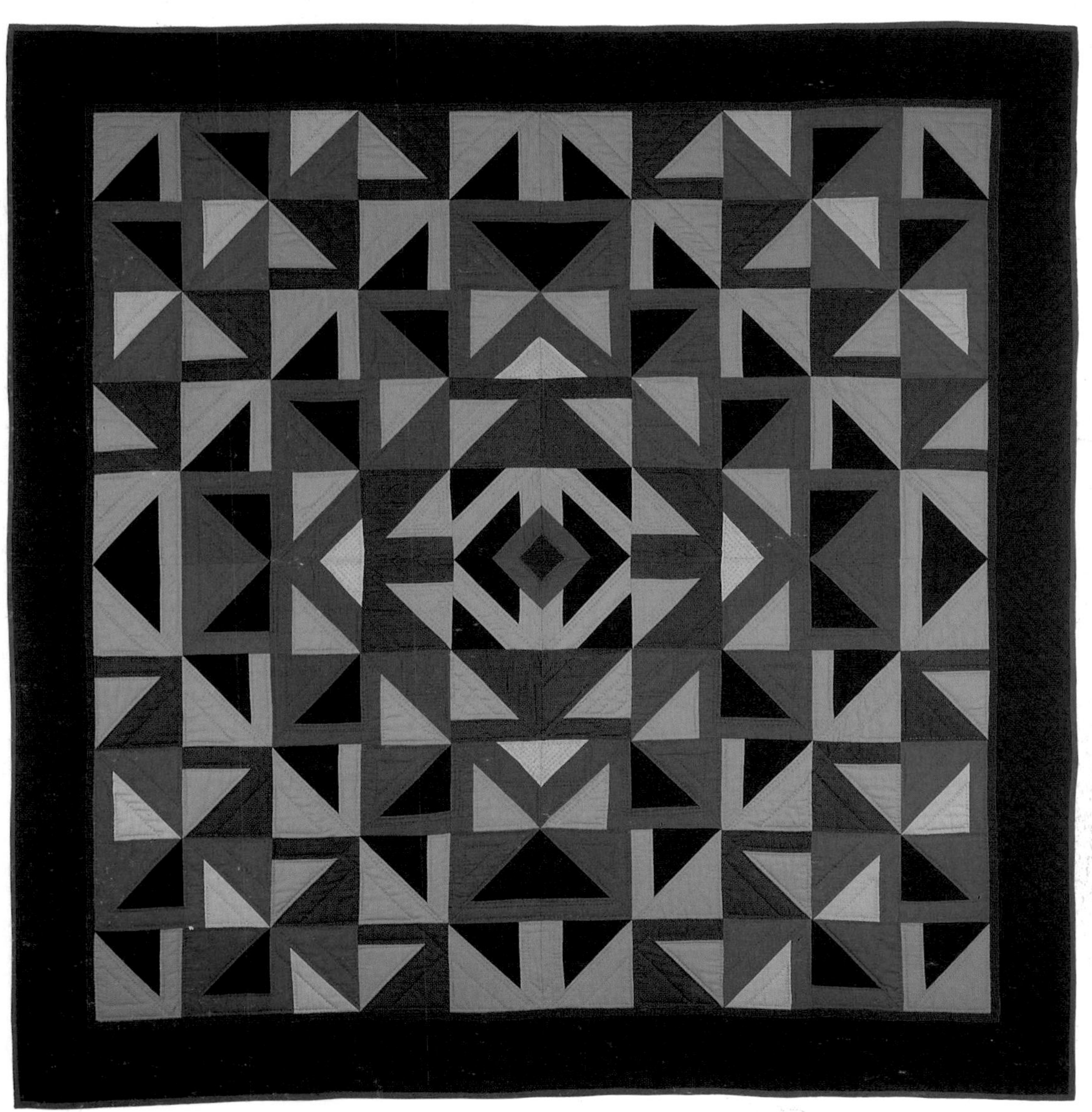

◄ **UNSEASONABLY COLD**

Stephanie Santmyers. Greensboro, North Carolina. Cottons; machine pieced and hand quilted. 59 x 59 in. Collection of the artist.

This complex but traditional-looking design is built of precisely symmetrical units, which echo from the central red and blue diamonds to the outer border. The intense but predominantly cool colors are accented by the red center and thin red outer border.

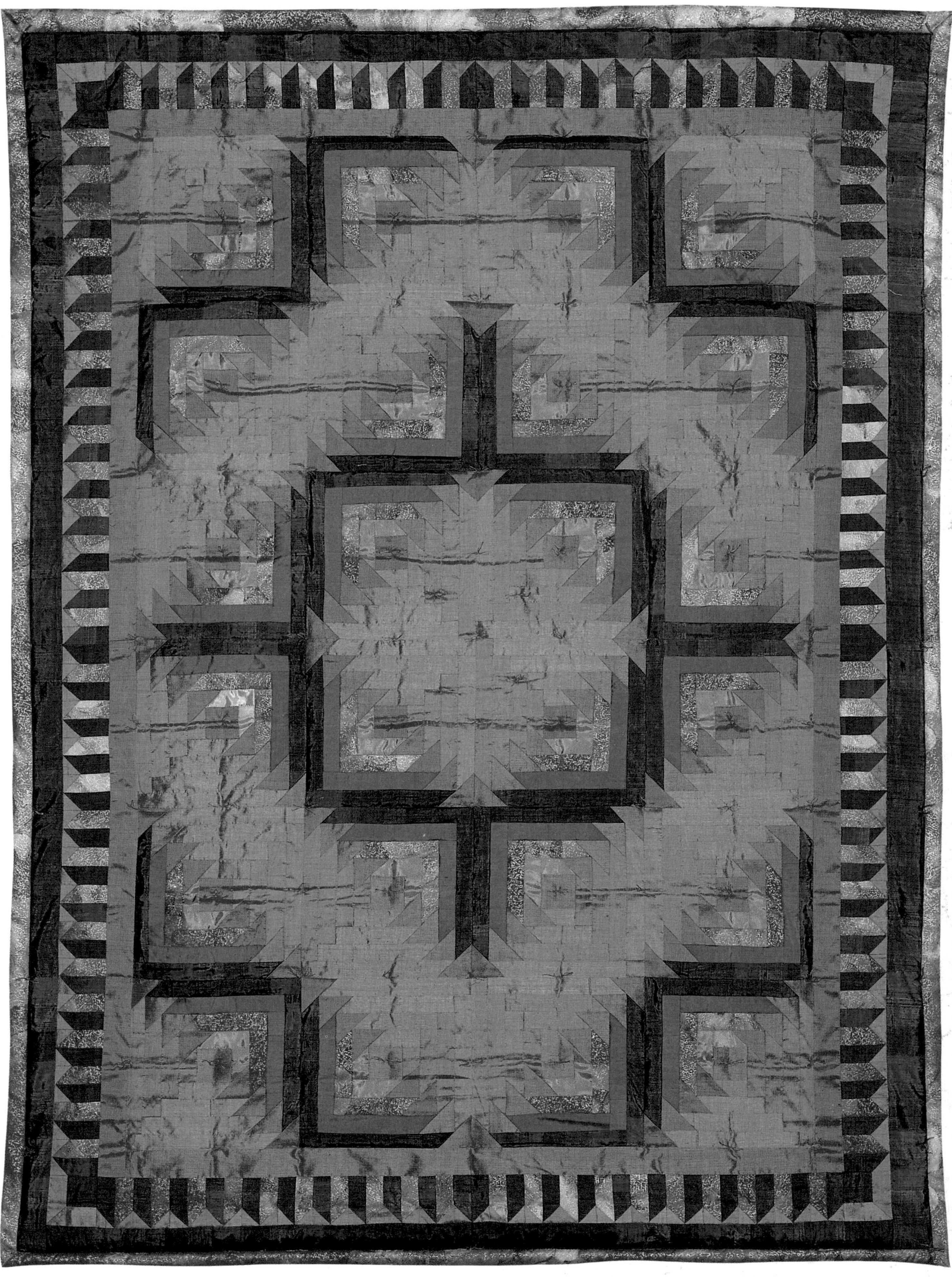

▲ **Aztek**

Liesbeth Spaans-Prins. 1991. Saint-Brice de Cognac, France. Silks tied with silk embroidery floss. 70 3/4 x 51 1/4 *in. Collection of the artist.*

This original Log Cabin variation is made of silks, many of them brought back from India and Singapore by the quiltmaker's husband, a former ship's officer. According to Liesbeth Spaans-Prins, the quilt began with "finding this crazy fabric I used as backing, but in each block as well," and received its name because it reminded her of South American designs. Spaans-Prins trained as a weaver but turned her attention to quilts beginning in the late 1980s.

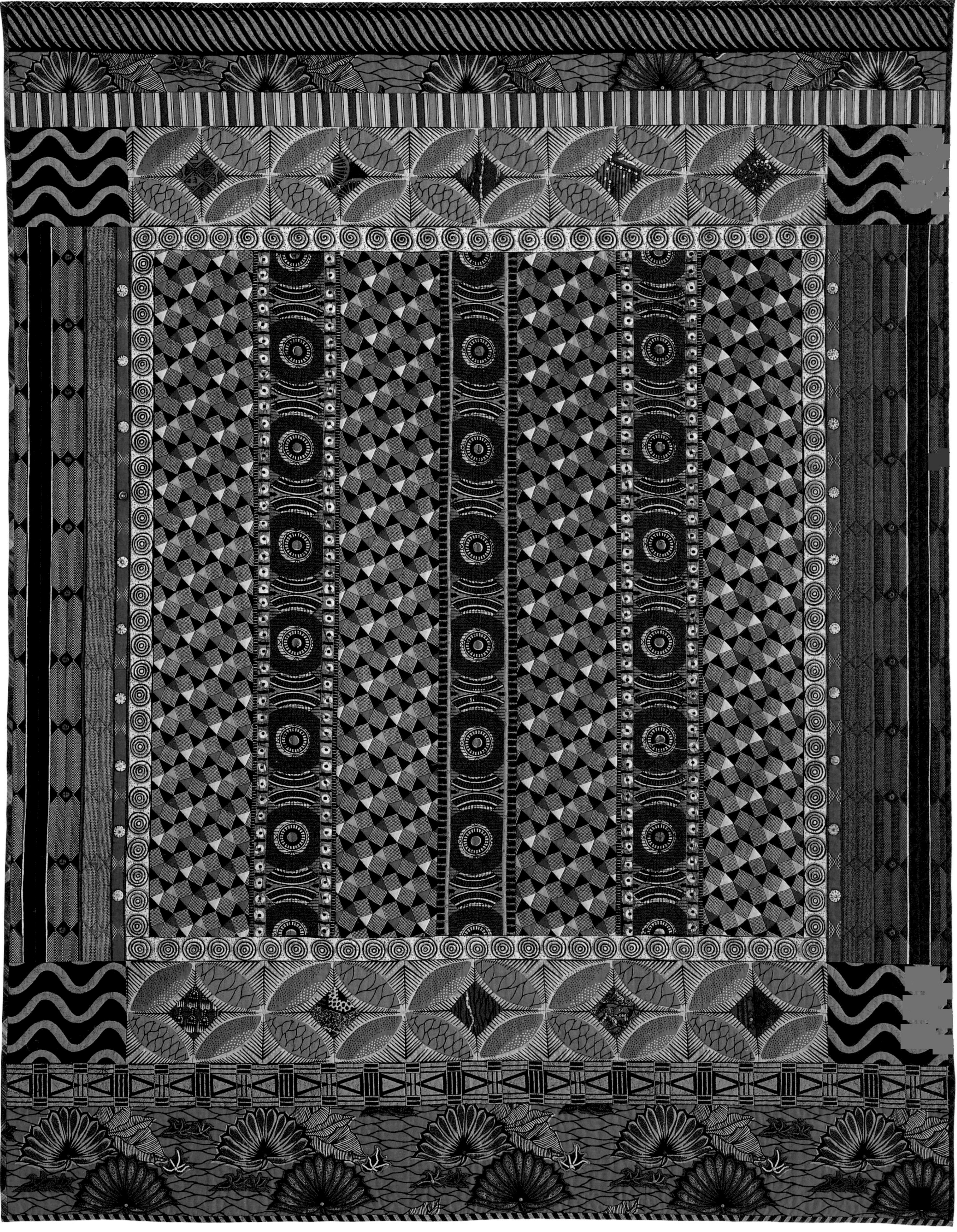

BOW TIE VARIATION ►

Tom Cuff. 1989. New York. Cottons; hand pieced and quilted. 36 1/2 x 28 in. Collection of the artist.

Tom Cuff's small quilts, influenced by Amish design, are precise and elegant variations on simple traditional patterns, often worked in printed fabric.

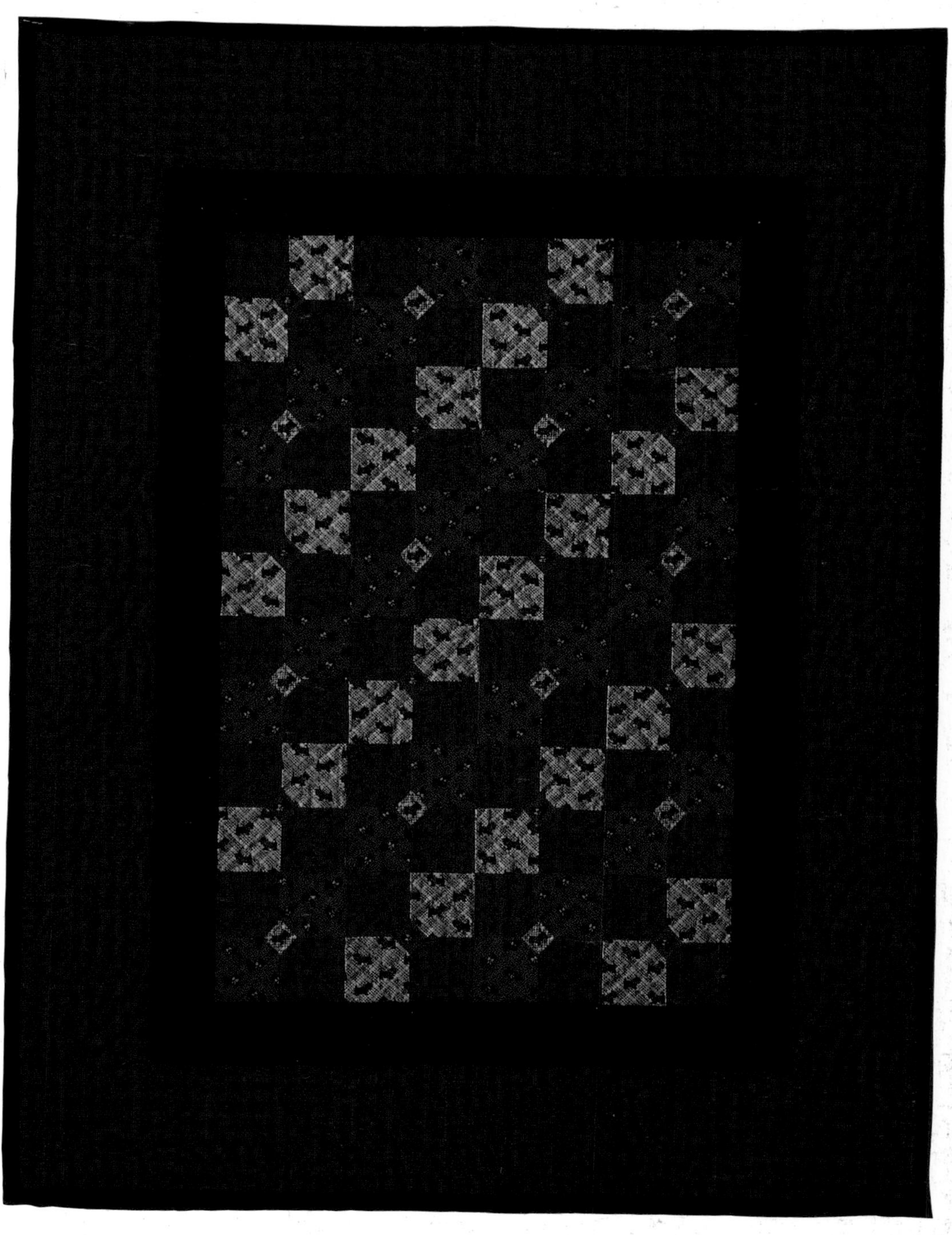

◄ ISHMAEL'S REVISITED

Roberta A. Horton. 1992. Berkeley, California. Cottons. 72 1/2 x 56 1/2 in. Collection of the artist.

Fabric Makes the Quilt is one of well-known quiltmaker and teacher Roberta Horton's four books. *Ishmael's Revisited,* which is made up entirely of African fabrics, demonstrates her point by allowing the choice of fabric to define the composition and impact of the piece.

◄ DJAKARTA

Marjorie Claybrook. 1994. Augusta, Georgia. Cottons, some hand-dyed, sateens, and sequins; hand pieced, appliquéd, and embroidered. 64 x 64 in. Collection of the artist.

Marjorie Claybrook says, "I incorporate . . . storytelling in my work . . . Primitive symbols of hands, snakes, birds, insects, fish, leaves . . . suggest . . . 'stories' to the viewer. These simplified images possess . . . universal meanings which reveal themselves to the subconscious . . . The viewer writes . . . the story in his mind—two different viewers, two different stories, neither of which may be the story I intended to tell." This goldfish quilt is one of a series that incorporates from three to six layers of transparent and translucent material into a traditional quilt format.

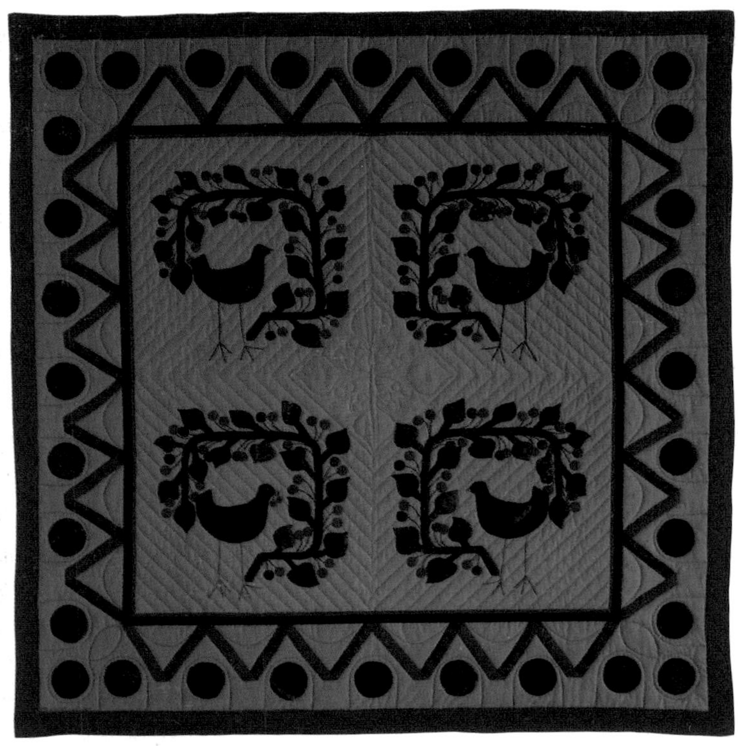

◂ Four Black Birds

Kristina M. Becker. 1992. Pleasanton, California. Cottons; appliquéd and quilted. 61 x 61 in. Collection of the artist.

Kristina Becker is a self-taught quilter who was born in Sweden and tries to "get the feeling of Sweden" into her work. She notes, "Sweden's quilt research only started a few years ago, so I cannot say that has influenced me too much. More so the colors of the embroideries and wallpaintings."

▾ Winter Cheer

Linda Roy. 1993. Neenah, Wisconsin. Cottons; machine pieced, hand appliquéd and quilted. Collection of the artist.

Made as a holiday wall quilt, *Winter Cheer* won Best of Show at the 1993 Vermont Quilt Festival. Linda Roy used a variety of reds and greens on three different white backgrounds, and avoided typical Christmas designs in order to give the quilt a broader framework.

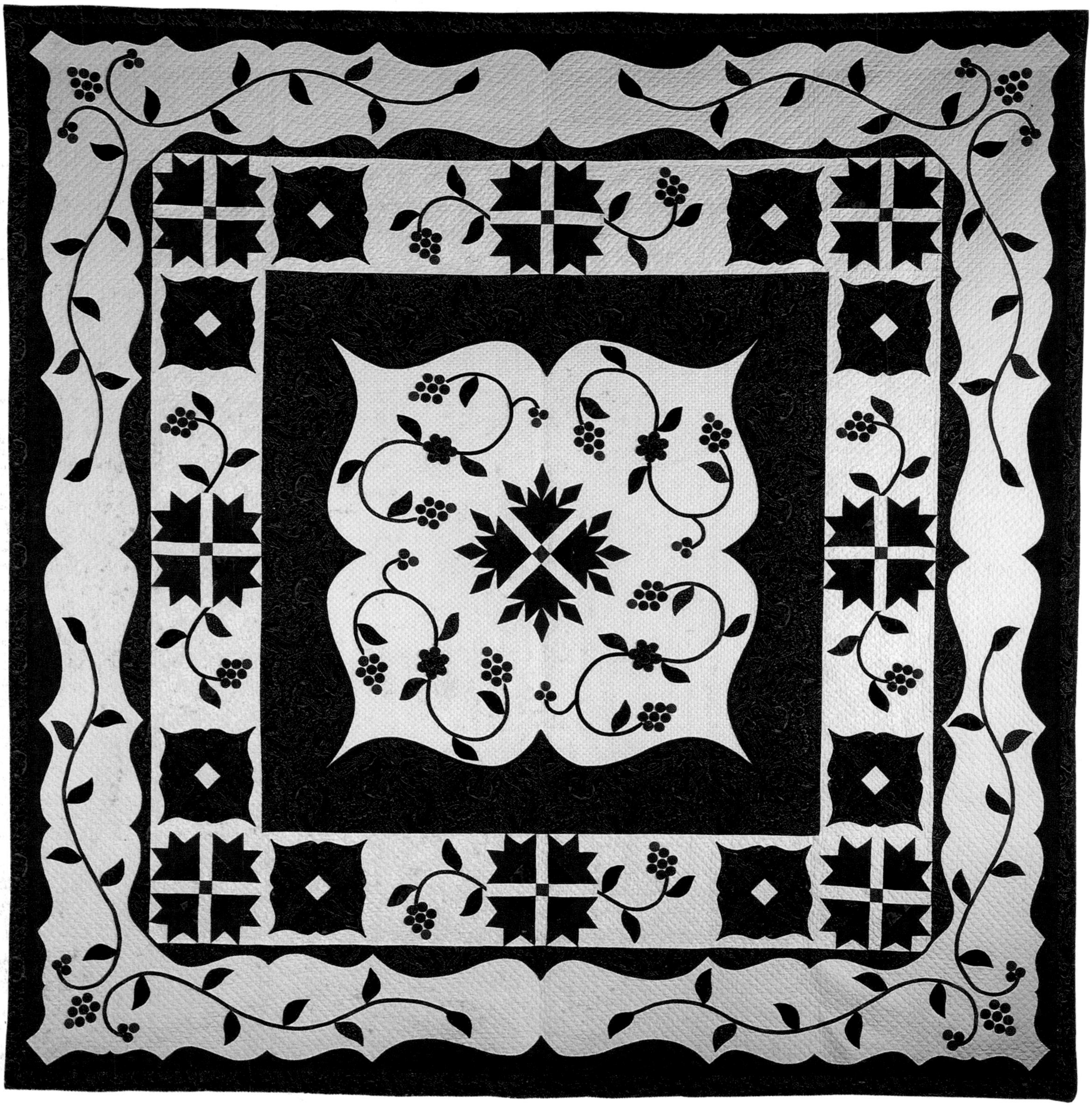

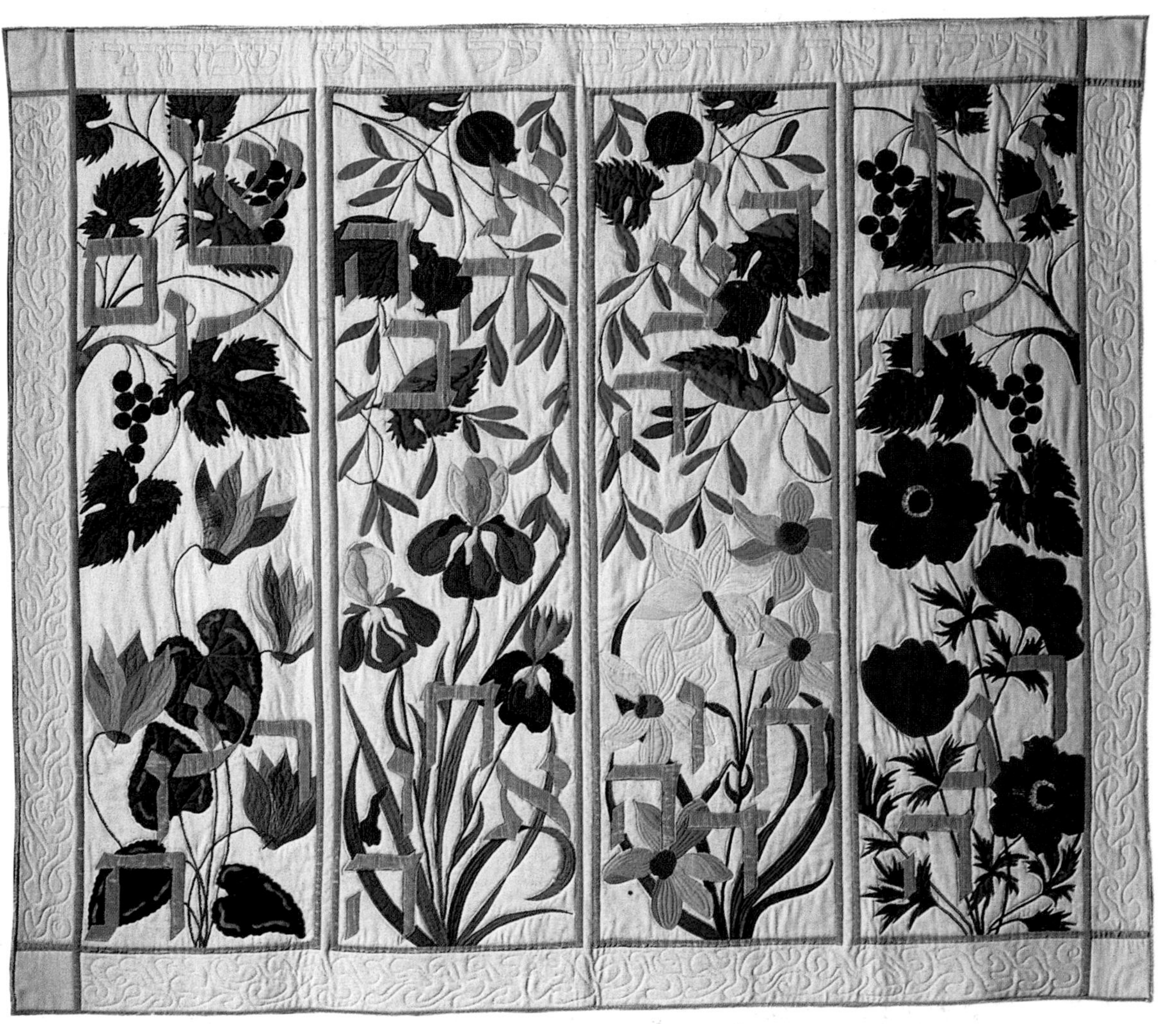

The Seventh Blessing ▶

N. Amanda Ford, fabrication and quilting; Tamar Fishman, design. 1993. Cabin John, Maryland. Silk, linen, and cotton; machine stitched and appliquéd; reverse appliqué for the Hebrew letters within each panel. 65 x 75 in. Collection of Rabbi Sam and Tamar Fishman.

A *chuppah* is a canopy under which the bride and groom stand during a Jewish wedding. This *chuppah*, made by the quilter for her son's wedding, represents the last of the seven blessings that are sung at the ceremony. It thanks God for bringing "mirth and glee, pleasure and delight, love and brotherhood, peace and good fellowship" to the couple. Each panel shows flowers found in Israel, grapes representing sanctification, and pomegranates representing fruitfulness. The Hebrew quotes across the top are from Psalm 137, which reminds us to remember Jerusalem during any happy occasion.

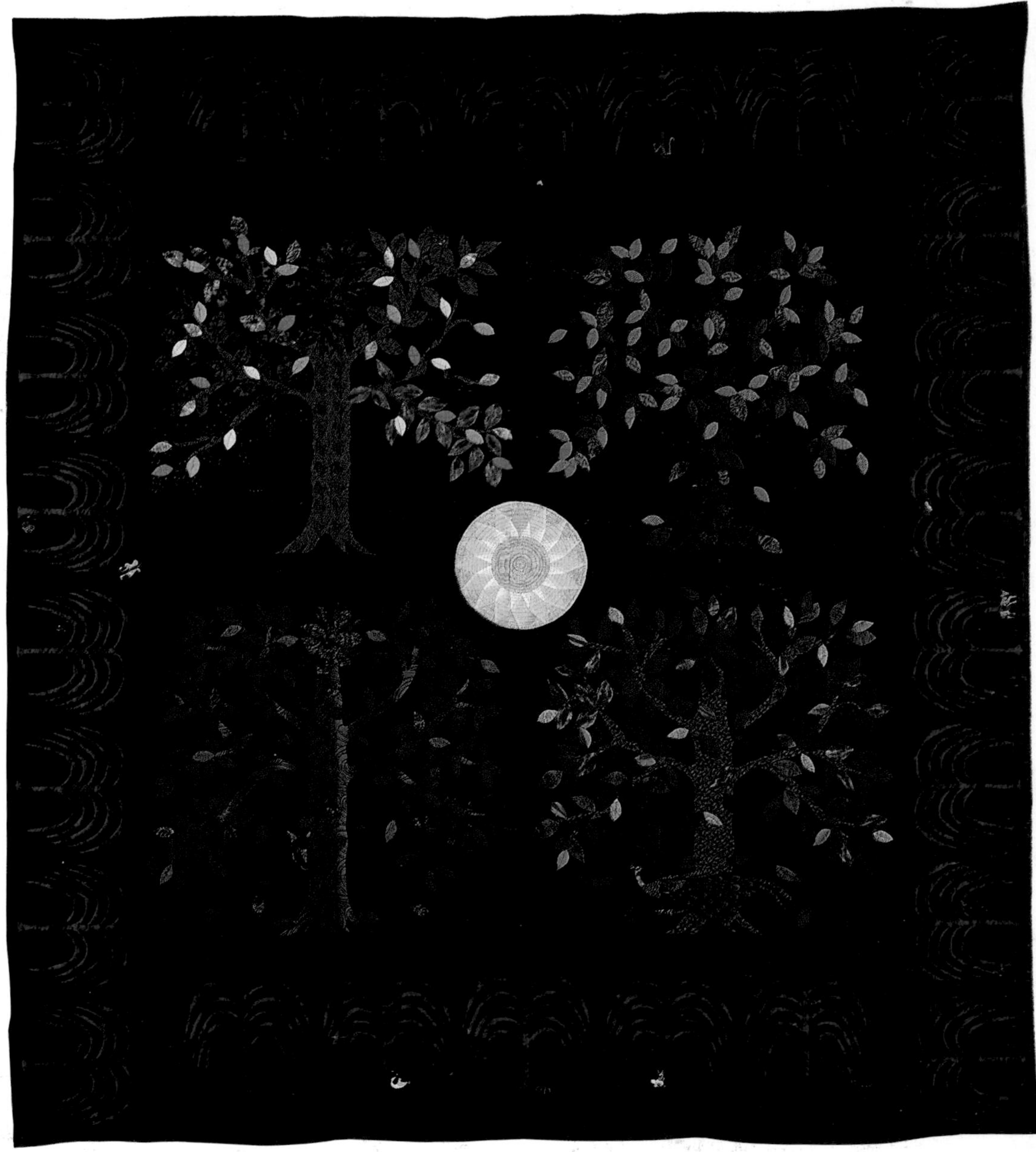

Meredith's Tree of Life at Midnight ▶

Linda Carlson. 1993. Mexico, Missouri. Cottons; hand appliquéd and quilted. 92 x 80 in. Private collection.

This stunning quilt is Linda Carlson's interpretation of one of the most common four-block patterns found during her research into the form. Named for her daughter, it includes all of her daughter's favorite animals within the blocks as well as her favorite tree, the willow, a traditional symbol of grief, in the borders. The four tree blocks are set around a full central moon. Linda Carlson's father died suddenly while she was working on the quilt, so it became at once a catharsis for her and a memorial to him. Tombstones for her father and four grandparents occupy the quilting in the border, while the back of the quilt records her loved ones' personal histories and epitaphs.

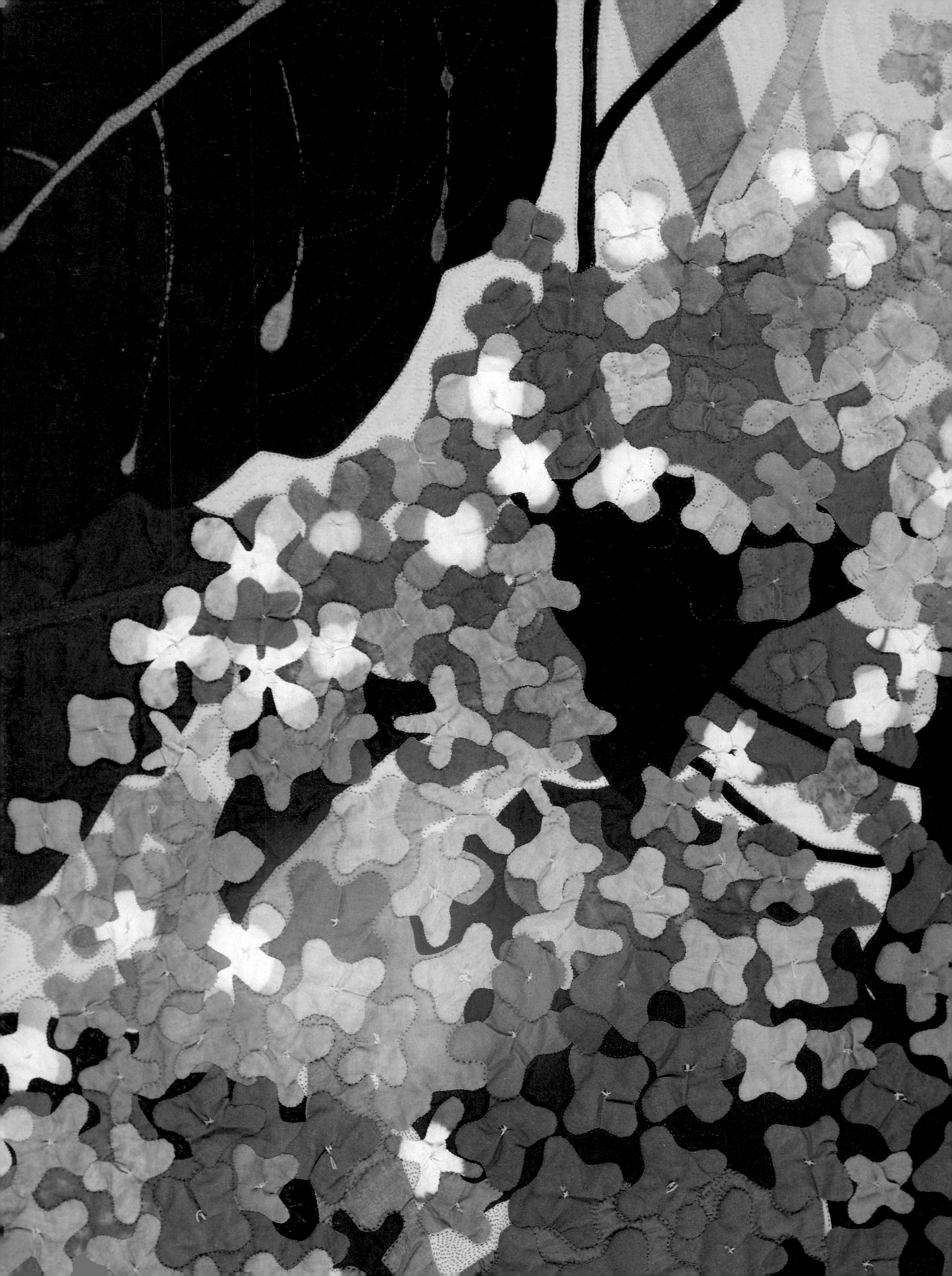

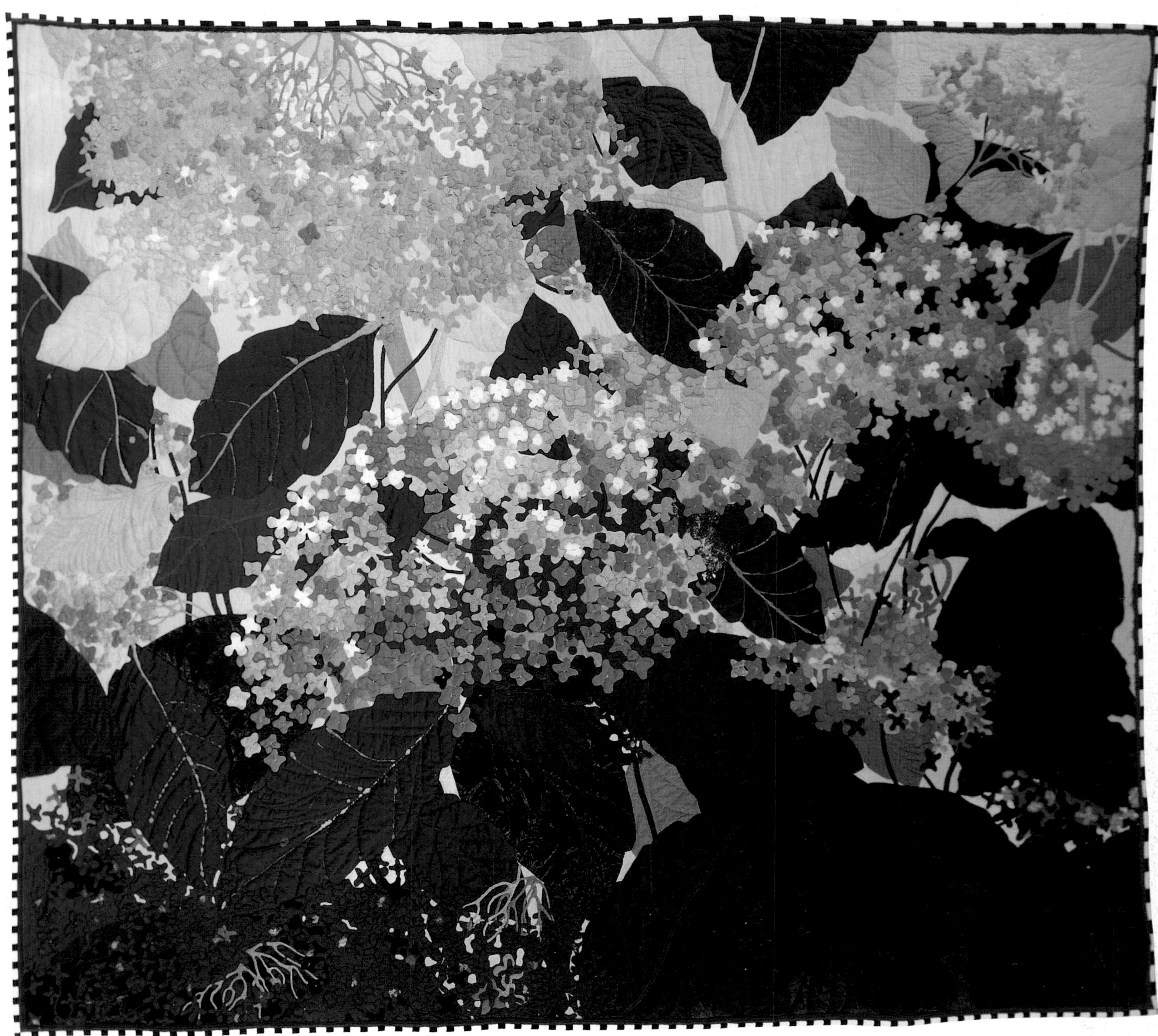

▲ **Hydrangea** (◂ **detail**)

Velda E. Newman. 1989. Cottons; hand dyed, appliquéd, and quilted. 97 x 100 in. Collection of John Walsh III.

Velda Newman prepares her enormously oversized floral appliqués by first drawing the design full-size on graph paper and dying fabric to the exact colors she needs. After the appliqué is in place, she uses free-form quilting as a second design to add texture and pattern to the leaves and flowers.

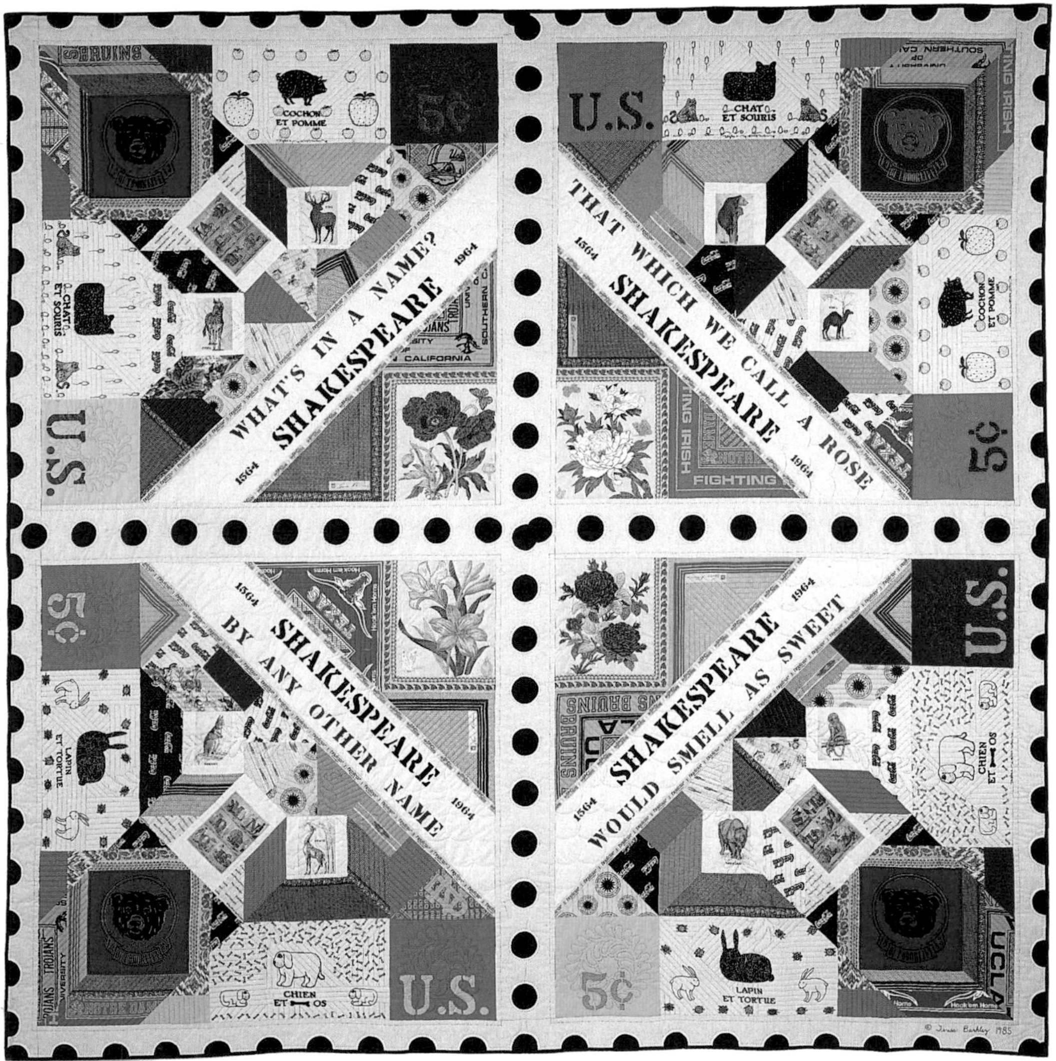

◂ THE SHAKESPEARE STAMP QUILT

Teresa Barkley. 1985. Astoria, New York. Cottons and cotton blends; machine pieced and hand appliquéd; hand painted, with printed scarves, linen tea towels, and pages from two antique linen children's books; hand quilted. 102 x 102 in. Collection of the artist.

Teresa Barkley combines "found" materials such as commemorative handkerchiefs and linen children's books with modern fabrics in her quilts. She says, "I consider quilts an art form, which, like poetry, becomes much more than the sum of its parts. While paintings or ceramics require a blending of different materials, scraps of fabric, like words, retain their original character while achieving a new meaning by virtue of their juxtaposition."

◂ SUBJECTIVE VIOLET

Stan Book. 1990. Upland, California. Cottons; machine pieced; hand quilted by Mary Stoner, Mifflintown, Pennsylvania. 54 x 51 in. Collection of the artist.

Stan Book is a fine artist who has adopted the quilt as his medium of choice. As a painter, he was drawn to pre–World War II Amish quilts, which he found important to his study of pattern and color interaction. His quilts build on the Amish tradition by incorporating the conscious influence of such modern artists as Cezanne, Klee, Albers, and Rothko. Book, who teaches art in public schools, designs, sews, and marks the quilts for quilting; the fine hand quilting (typically nine to twelve stitches per inch) is done by skilled needleworkers. Although the nine narrow violet bars in this quilt are perceived as three sets of three different shades, all these bars are actually the same color, hence, *Subjective Violet*.

▲ 42nd Street

Yvonne Forman. 1986. Hastings-on-Hudson, New York. Cottons; hand and machine pieced; hand quilted by Grace Miller. 84 x 76 in. Collection of the artist.

Yvonne Forman's series *Quilts from the NY Subways* seeks to translate the subway system's beautiful terra cotta mosaic tiles and bas reliefs from hard to soft materials, thereby bringing their beauty to a wider audience. She says, "The challenge has been to convert these beloved landmarks from ceramic to fiber without compromising the integrity of either the mosaics or the traditional quilt."

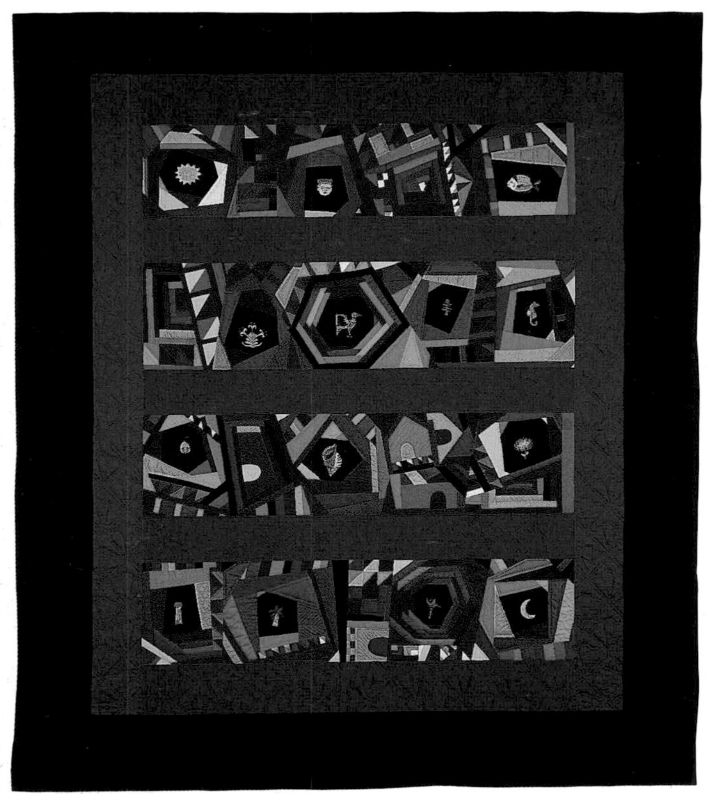

◄ #71, Peggy's Quilt— Crazy Bar Variations II

Julia E. Pfaff. 1992. Richmond, Virginia. Machine-pieced cottons with satin hand embroidery; hand quilted. 89 x 79 in. Private collection.

This piece was commissioned by a college professor who collects finely crafted functional objects. The detailed satin-stitched embroideries begin in the upper left corner with the sun and end with the moon, a progression that signifies the passing of daytime between nighttimes, when the quilt is used.

#38, Three, Four, Close the Door ►

Julia E. Pfaff. 1988. Richmond, Virginia. Cottons with satin hand embroidery; hand quilted. 54 x 44 1/2 in. Collection of the artist.

This quilt recalls happy childhood memories. Among the images Pfaff presents are Dusty, a beloved cat who grew up with her and lived seventeen years, summer fishing trips with her father, and vegetables from the family's garden.

Julia E. Pfaff

Julia E. Pfaff of Richmond, Virginia, began quilting as a child. She always wanted to be an artist and says she began her career in art at an early age, drawing on the undersides of her family's furniture. "My parents thought they had a cuckoo in the nest," she recalls.

The Ontario-born Pfaff later earned a Bachelor of Arts degree in art history from the University of Toronto and an Master of Fine Arts in textiles from Virginia Commonwealth University.

In 1980, an archaeology professor saw one of her drawings and asked her if she would like to go to Egypt to do technical drawings of objects found on a dig. She now divides her time between quiltmaking, teaching, and spending from two to six months annually working as an archaeological artist in Greece, Egypt, and Jordan.

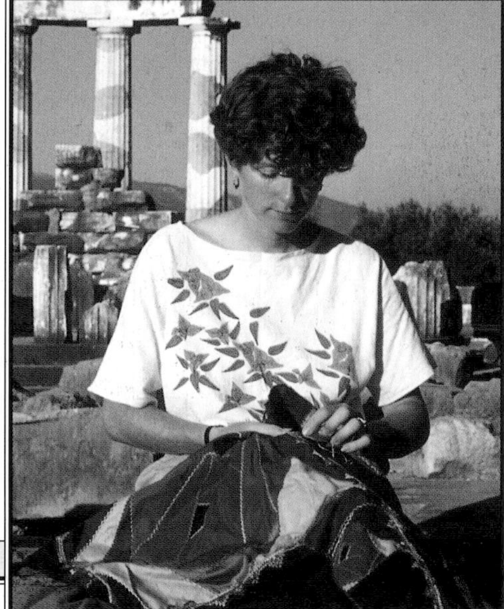

Her field work not only affords her unique experiences, but has also provided inspiration for her quilts. Her use of brightly colored cross-stitch embroidery in some of her earlier work, such as *Peggy's Quilt*, is an adaptation of Bedouin garment decoration she first saw while working in Egypt in 1981. Pfaff's current art quilts also draw on her archaeological experiences. These begin with foundation piecing to create layers of fragments and suggestions of chambers and landscapes based on her knowledge of archaeological sites. To these she adds precisely rendered images of vessels, architectural fragments, and human remains, which are transferred to fabric by such printing techniques as etching, lithography, and silk-screen. Pfaff hand paints and dyes all the fabrics for her art quilts to achieve subtle earth, stone, and sky textures and colors.

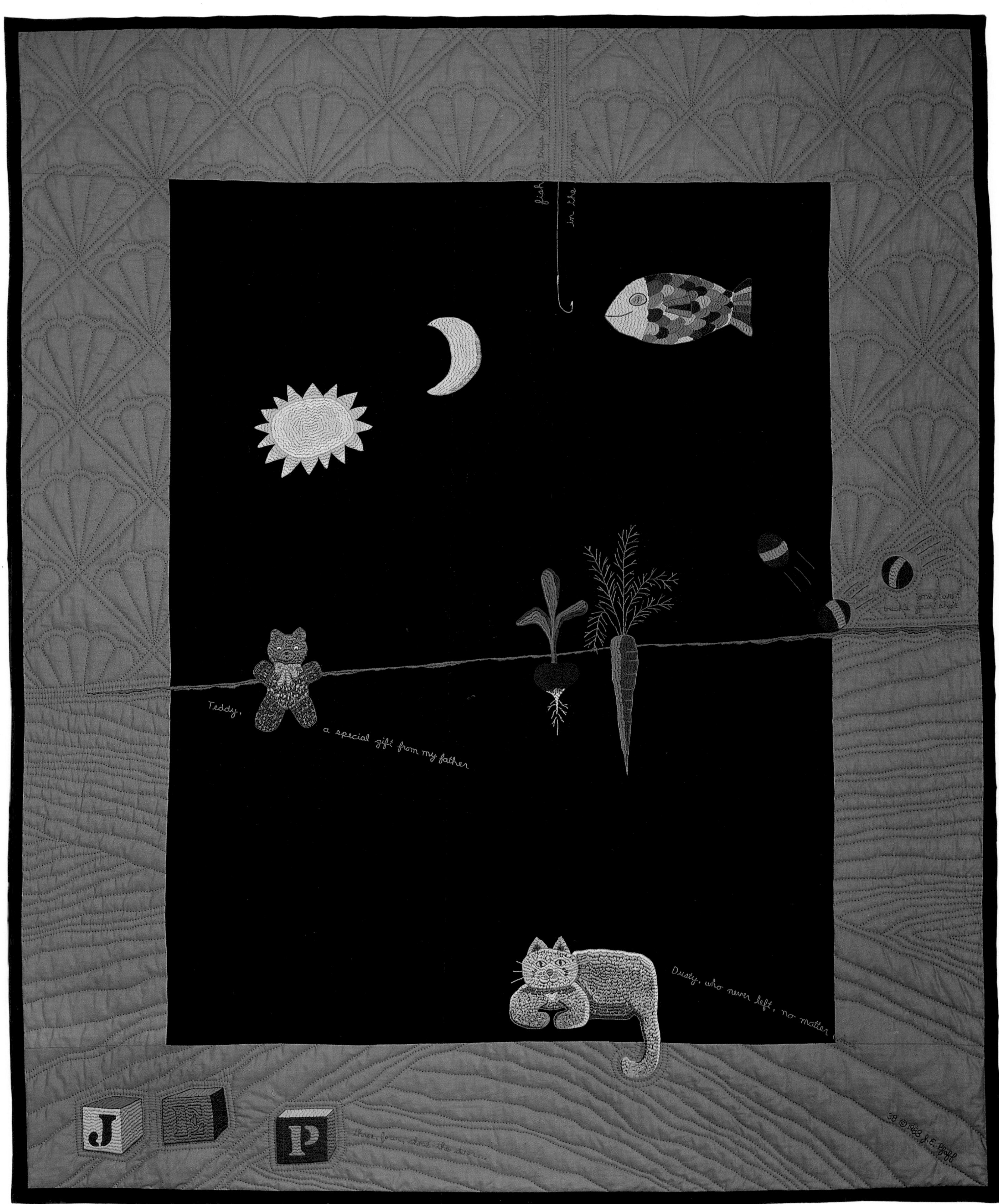
Teddy,
a special gift from my father
Dusty, who never left, no matter

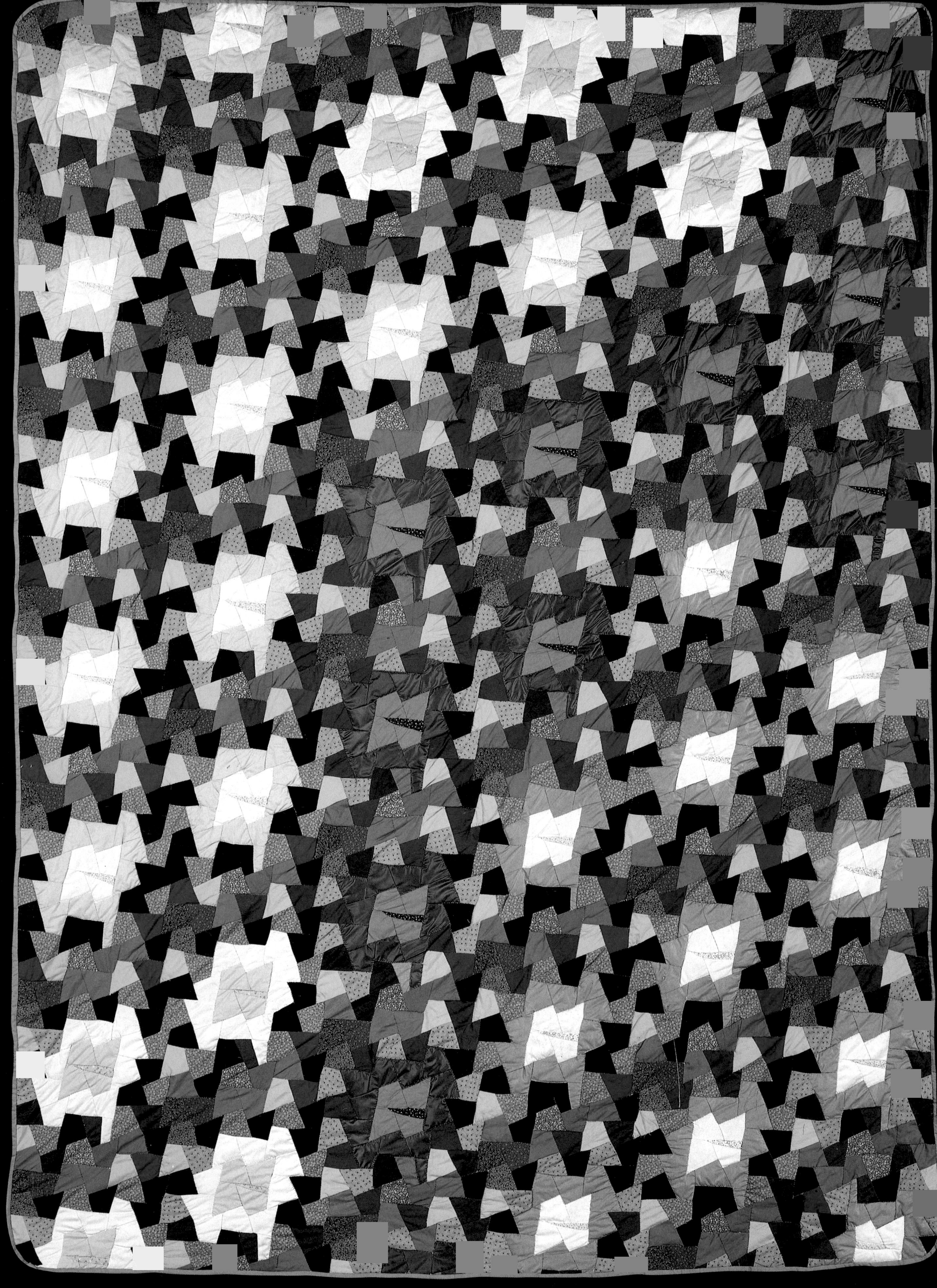

JAPANESE QUILTS: AMERICA INSPIRES A NEW TRADITION

The great quilt revival that began in America in the 1960s spurred the spread of the American quilt to a number of other countries, including France, Germany, Switzerland, Sweden, Norway, Denmark, and even Russia. But it is in Japan that the American quilt has taken by far its most striking and original form. The Japanese, a people keenly interested in America, have embraced the art of quiltmaking eagerly, but also, more than the women and men of any other country, the Japanese have taken the American idea of the quilt to heart and reimagined it. They are now giving it back to America, in still recognizable form, but full of vibrant new energy and ideas that reflect the time-honored values and traditions of their own culture as well as those of the United States.

Japan alone among the countries of the world has a truly new quilting tradition in the making. Although Japan boasts some of the richest and most ancient textile and handcraft traditions in the world, the bed quilt has never been one of them. Japan is a conservative country with deep regard for its own history and traditions. This respect for tradition extends to the historic cultural values of other countries. Pottery, basketry, paper making, woodworking, clothing design, and other traditional arts are all recognized by the Japanese as among their country's greatest aesthetic achievements, and master craftspeople are designated as "living national treasures" by the Japanese government. Japan, secure enough in its own traditions to welcome outside influence freely, was fertile ground for the seeds of America's powerful quilting traditions.

Interest in the American quilt and the art of quilting has exploded in Japan in the past two decades. Nearly a million Japanese women are now believed to be making quilts, and at least a quarter of that number consider themselves serious quilters. Exhibitions of American quilts draw enormous crowds in Japanese museums and exhibition halls, dozens of books on quilts and quiltmaking have been translated into Japanese or printed by Japanese publishers, and Japan publishes three widely read glossy quilt magazines. The Japanese excitement about quilts and quiltmaking is palpable and manifest in the work of Japanese quilters, a phenomenon all the more extraordinary since quilts were virtually unheard of in Japan merely twenty-five years ago.

◄ **MONET'S WATER-LILIES**

Teruko Inoue. 1990. Tokyo, Japan. Japanese cottons and synthetic fabrics; hand pieced and quilted. 98 1/2 x 76 3/4 in. Collection of the artist.

This cleverly pieced jigsaw puzzle of a quilt, which is built from five basic interlocking shapes, uses color to create an impressionistic surface full of the movement of light. The long narrow triangle of contrasting printed fabric that bisects the center of each "lily" is a particularly effective touch. The artist says, "This quilt was inspired by Monet's masterpiece, *Water-Lilies*. Thank you, M. Monet!"

Japan first encountered American quilts in 1976, when Jonathan Holstein's *Abstract Design in American Quilts* toured the country. This seminal exhibition was followed in the early 1980s by shows of classic American quilts from the collections of the Shelburne Museum and the Denver Art Museum. Kei Kobayashi, who organized the Shelburne Museum exhibition, is a former fashion designer who has been instrumental in linking American and Japanese traditions. She has written quilt books in both languages and her 1990 exhibition *Made in Japan: American Influences on Japanese Quilts* was the first to bring Japanese quilts to the United States. One of the most prominent Japanese quilt promoters is Kokusai Art, a Tokyo-based exhibition and publication company which sponsored the Denver Museum show and has continued to mount high quality exhibitions of American quilts over the years, including shows of quilts from the Ardis and Robert James collection, from Hawaiian museums and private collectors, and from the Indiana Museum's remarkable collection of Indiana Amish quilts. Kokusai has also organized an exhibition of outstanding Japanese quilts that has traveled to a number of American museums in recent years.

Other efforts are underway that are intended to enhance communication between American and Japanese quiltmakers. Nihon Vogue Ltd. of Tokyo, publisher of the magazine *Quilts Japan* and other needlecraft magazines and books and sponsor of an annual juried exhibition of Japanese quilts, recently announced the *Quilts Japan* Prize. Nihon Vogue will, in alternating years over the next decade, bring a juried art quilter from the highly regarded Quilt San Diego and Quilt National competitions to Japan for lectures. According to the sponsor, "The objective of the *Quilts Japan* Prize is to express gratefulness for the continued growth of the Japanese quilt, which is due greatly to American quilters, and to pay respect to the predecessors of quiltmaking. Nihon Vogue hopes to play a role in the development of quiltmaking by helping to link the ties between Japanese and American quiltmakers." Quilt San Diego director Susan Knobloch notes, "While Nihon Vogue's purpose for awarding this prize is to honor the American tradition of quiltmaking, Quilt San Diego in turn wishes to recognize and appreciate the interest Japanese quiltmakers have in this craft and art form. The *Quilts Japan* Prize provides a valuable step in the recognition that we are one earth, one people."

Since its defeat in World War II, Japan has become increasingly receptive to the influence of Western culture. Although America has been perceived through the distorted lenses of Hollywood and Madison Avenue, Japanese quiltmakers have often been able to look past the popular images and myths to extract essential elements of the American way of life. The quilt has offered women in Japan a chance to learn about American women and their lives firsthand. Through quiltmaking Japanese women can explore traditional American culture and reexamine and preserve their own at the same time. Since Japan is still very much a closed and hierarchical culture, controlled and dominated by men, Japanese women have fewer opportunities than do their counterparts in the United States. As it did for nineteenth- and early twentieth-century American women, quiltmaking thus also provides many Japanese women with an outlet for their otherwise somewhat constrained creativity and imagination.

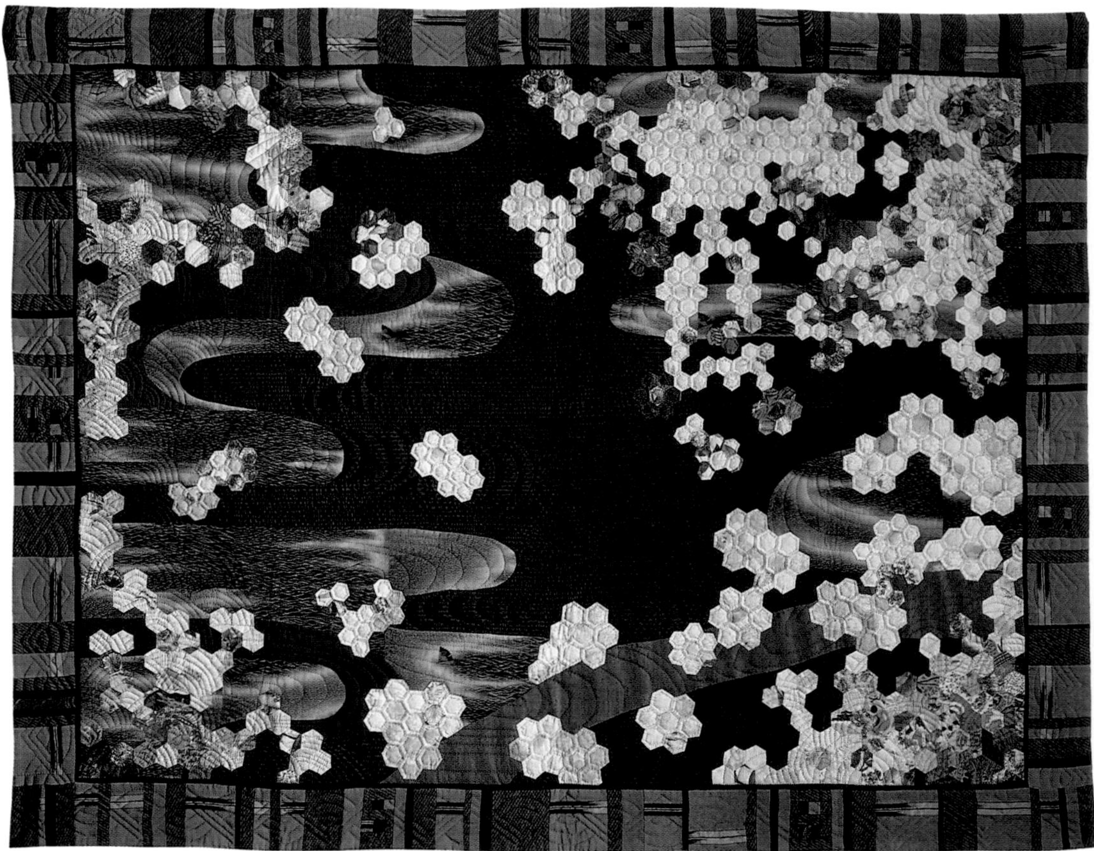

CHERRY BLOSSOMS ▶

Junko Himeno. 1990. Tokyo, Japan. Kimono silks; hand pieced, appliquéd, and quilted. 65 x 73 in. Collection of the artist.

Made from kimono fabrics, this pictorial quilt reflects the influence of traditional Japanese landscape painting. The "painting" of cherry blossoms falling into water is set within a fabric picture frame. Curved contour quilting accentuates the impression of moving water in the picture, while the frame is quilted with geometric diamond shapes.

Japanese society differs most profoundly from American society in its emphasis on group activity. In America, the individual is paramount and individualism is honored. Japanese society, on the other hand, encourages and honors submission of the self to the group will, and discourages individual achievement that does not further a group objective. Japanese quilters are thus much more group oriented than Americans. Belonging to a Japanese quilt group confers status on the member, and the social pressure to belong is enormous. Unlike Americans, most Japanese quilters learn in groups. Many attend traditional and rigidly hierarchical schools, which are tightly controlled by master teachers. Students learn to follow the master's style closely and are proud to produce quilts that closely resemble the instructor's. Individual creative expression is discouraged, as is the influence of any other school's or master's teaching. Indeed, the system is a closed circle. On graduation, students can become teachers of the school's methodology, licensed to establish their own franchise schools. These branch schools are often set up within fabric stores owned by the parent company, and new students are required to purchase a certain amount of fabric from the store. A few independent schools now exist that follow American teaching models and encourage individual creativity, but they are the exception rather than the rule. Perhaps the greatest gift that American quiltmakers can offer to Japanese craftspeople is the celebration of individual creativity and expression. It is to be hoped that the influence of those Japanese schools that champion personal expression will eventually become widespread.

The Japanese love of precision makes the craft of quiltmaking an ideal foil for many Japanese craftspeople. Contemporary Japanese quilts are executed with meticulous care, often constructed with thousands of carefully cut and assembled pieces and quilted with the tiniest and most perfectly spaced stitches. Japanese observers admire technical achievement and are quick to fault some American quilts for their less than perfect or even sometimes sloppy craftsmanship. However, at least one Japanese author and curator has suggested that Japanese quiltmakers sometimes err on the side of complexity and that they might profit by considering the artistic merits of many American quilters' successful use of negative, open space in their designs.

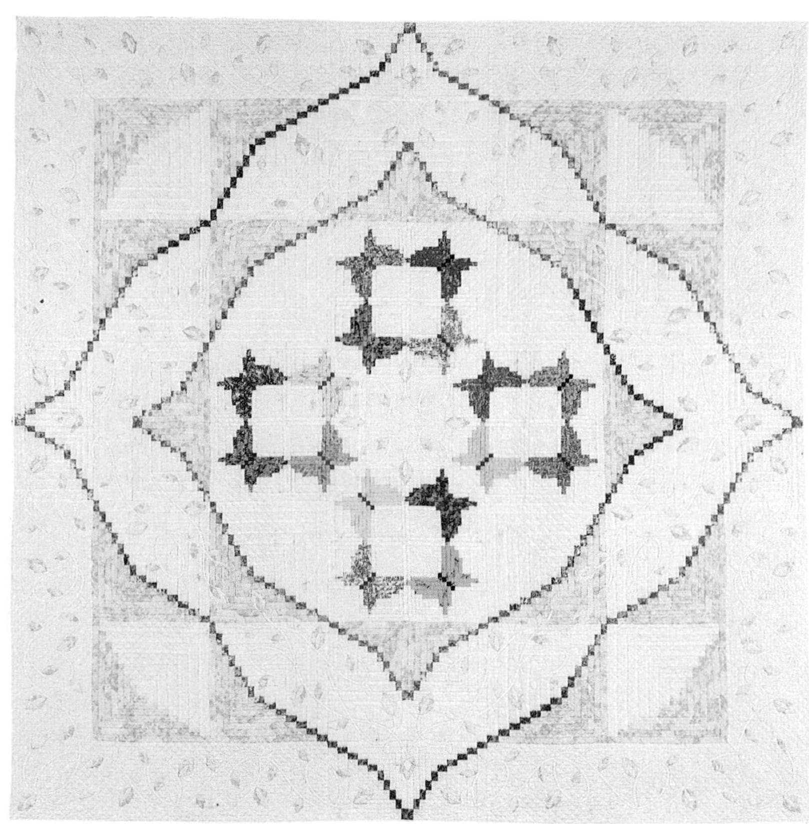

◄ **BUTTERFLY LOG CABIN**

Tomoko Fujioka. 1990. Tokyo, Japan. Japanese cottons; hand pieced, appliquéd, and quilted. 78 3/4 x 78 3/4 in. Collection of the artist.

The central grid of this predominantly white Log Cabin variation is made up of a five-by-five set of Light and Dark pattern blocks. The undulating overall tandem "butterfly" shapes extend into the otherwise all-white outer border. The "butterfly" in the center was created by changing the width and length of the logs.

One way that Japanese quilters express their own country's traditions is through the use of historic textiles such as kimono silks and indigo-dyed cottons. While most Americans simply use fabric, the Japanese honor it. Japanese tradition holds that the highest honor that can be bestowed on a fabric is to reuse it. Thus, to the Japanese quiltmaker the rag bag is where to find venerated materials, and is not, as is common in America's throw-away culture, the place of last resort. Silk is, of course, the national textile of Japan, just as cotton is America's dominant textile product. Kimono silks, used to make high status ceremonial robes, have been treasured and handed down for generations, and a wide array of antique silks are available in Japanese markets. Many beautiful contemporary silks are also being made, and Japanese quiltmakers use all to advantage. Silk is notoriously difficult to work with, and, except during the crazy quilt era of the late Victorian Age when handwork was in part influenced by things Japanese, this delicate fabric was largely avoided by American quilters. Japanese needleworkers have brought traditional methods of dealing with silk to quilting with considerable success, creating quilts that show off the fabric to stunning effect. They have also made wonderfully subdued quilts of blue and white indigo-dyed cottons, some of which have traditionally been used for Japanese farmers' and fishermen's clothing. These indigo quilts may employ many shades of blue of extremely close values, which are almost indistinguishable to Western eyes not used to such carefully orchestrated chromatic interplay. Among American quiltmakers, only the Amish have used color with such subtlety.

Japanese quiltmakers tend towards asymmetrical designs, which are traditional in Japanese arts and crafts, but rare in European and American quiltmaking, where linear geometry reigns. Although many Japanese quilters adapt American block patterns, they often find ways to throw the repeating, symmetrical rhythms off balance, by shifting the color emphasis to one side or twisting the orientation of some of the blocks, for example. Looking at these quilts can be eye opening and somewhat unsettling to Western viewers, since although the inspiration is clearly American, the result is decidedly Japanese. The use of the color white in Japanese quilts is also distinctly not American. In American quilts white is often used as a background color, a neutral color against which "real" colors are arrayed. The Japanese, by contrast, see white as a strong, vibrant color in its own right and use it in their quilts with value absolutely equal to the primary colors of blue, red, and yellow, and their subtler divisions around the color wheel. This unexpected equality of white can be one of the most startling aspects of Japanese quilts to Western eyes.

Some Japanese quiltmakers are also experimenting with designs based on origami, the ancient Japanese art of paper folding. Designer and quilt author Kei Kobayashi discovered that origami techniques could be used as an alternative to graph paper (or the computer) as a design tool for pieced quilts. By folding and coloring paper squares, she was quickly able to create a universe of over five hundred possible patchwork designs, some traditional in nature, others totally new. The origami method offers seemingly limitless possibilities, and a number of Japanese quilters have used the technique to design fresh geometric patterns that have resulted in distinctly original piecework quilts. Some other quilters have added a prominent design element by incorporating a traditional Japanese method of decorative hand stitchery known as *sashiko*, which employs boldly patterned and relatively widely spaced stitches using thread that contrasts with the primary colors of the quilt top.

The energy and enthusiasm of Japanese quilters is contagious. The Japanese have discovered much about the American way of life through quilts and quiltmaking, while at the same time they have preserved their own country's equally rich textile and craft traditions. Because American and Japanese quilters work out of widely divergent aesthetic approaches deeply rooted in their respective cultures, they have much to learn from each other. The future promises many exciting developments as Japanese quilting matures.

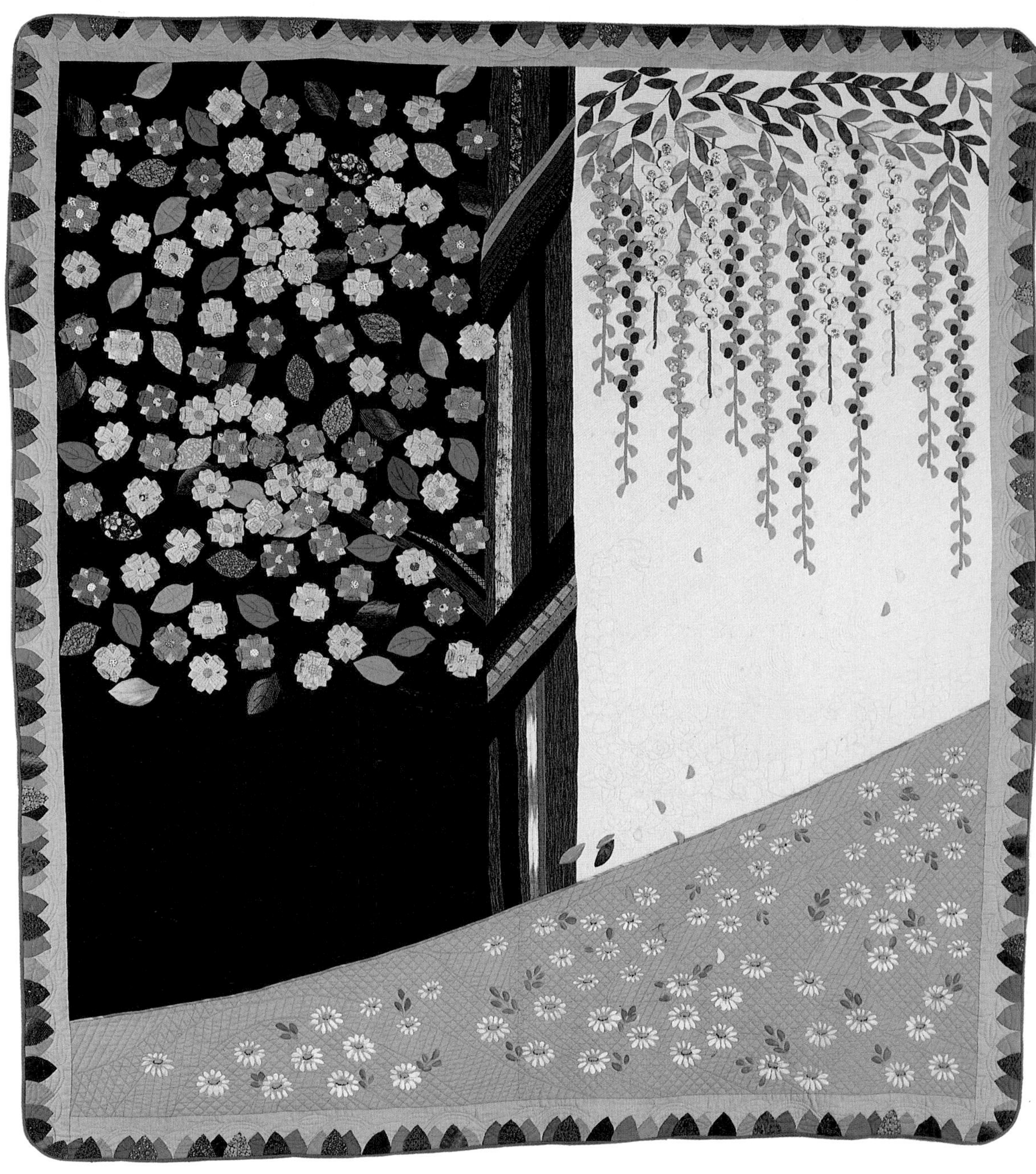

FALLING IN LOVE WITH FLOWERS ▸

Haruyo Matsuzaka. 1990. Tokyo, Japan. American and Japanese cottons, acrylic paint; hand appliquéd, pieced, and quilted. 80 3/4 x 74 3/4 in. Collection of the artist.

This quilt's unusual color combinations create a serenely inviting composition. Intricate hand quilting enhances the textures of the three broad color fields on which the flowers are placed. The quiltmaker says, "I love flowers. [This quilt recalls] the unforgettable beauty of the flowering dogwood in Virgina . . . The combination of American flowers and Japanese wisteria reflects my thoughts."

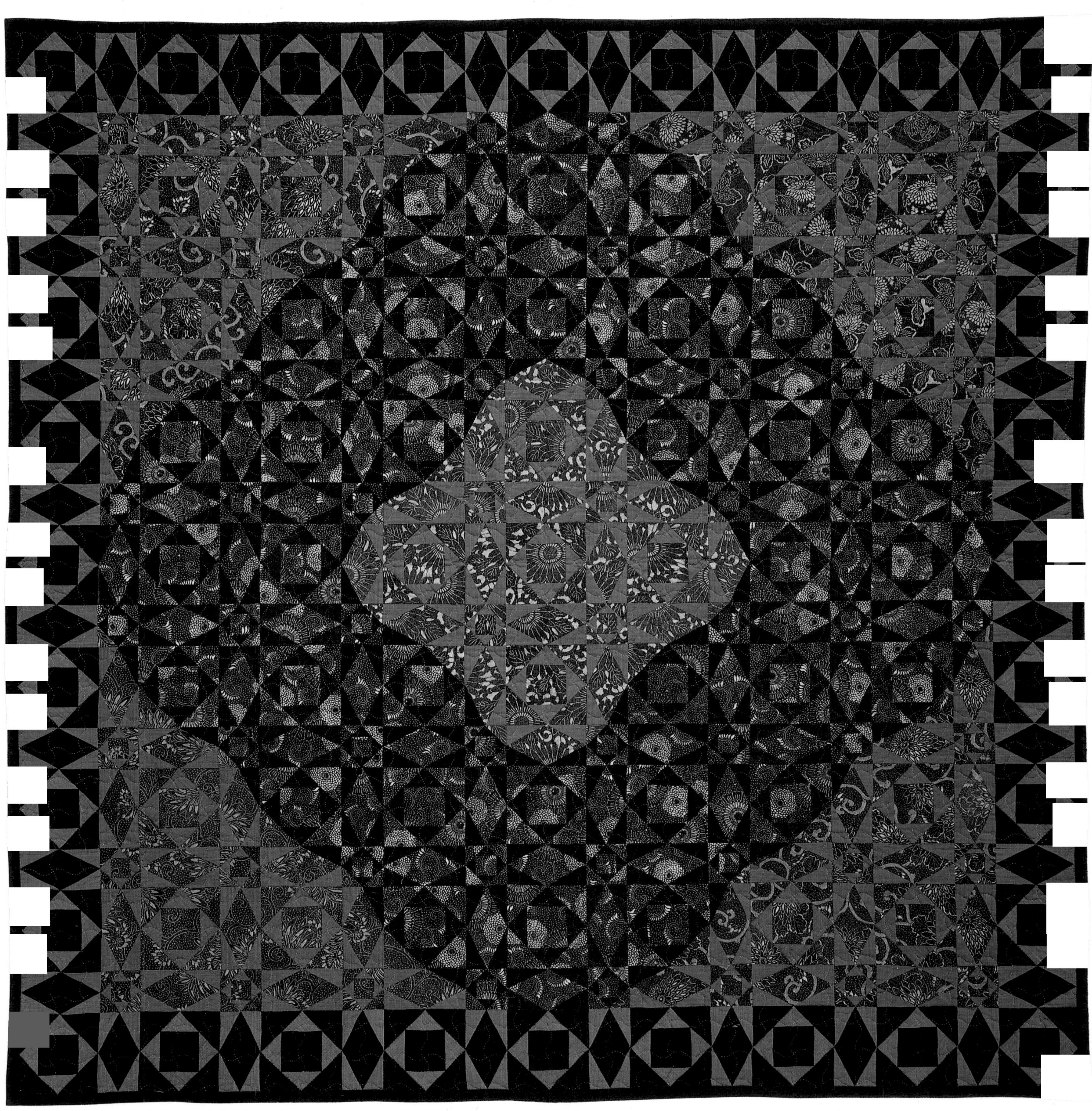

▲ **CALM SEA**

Rimiko Sato. 1990. Hokkaido, Japan. Indigo dyed cottons; hand pieced and quilted. 79 x 79 in. Collection of the artist.

Although the original pattern from which this quilt was made is called Storm at Sea, the use of closely valued indigo-dyed cottons here gives a peaceful, subdued feeling to the composition, full of gently swaying motion. The dark regular geometric outside border reinforces the impression of calm and order.

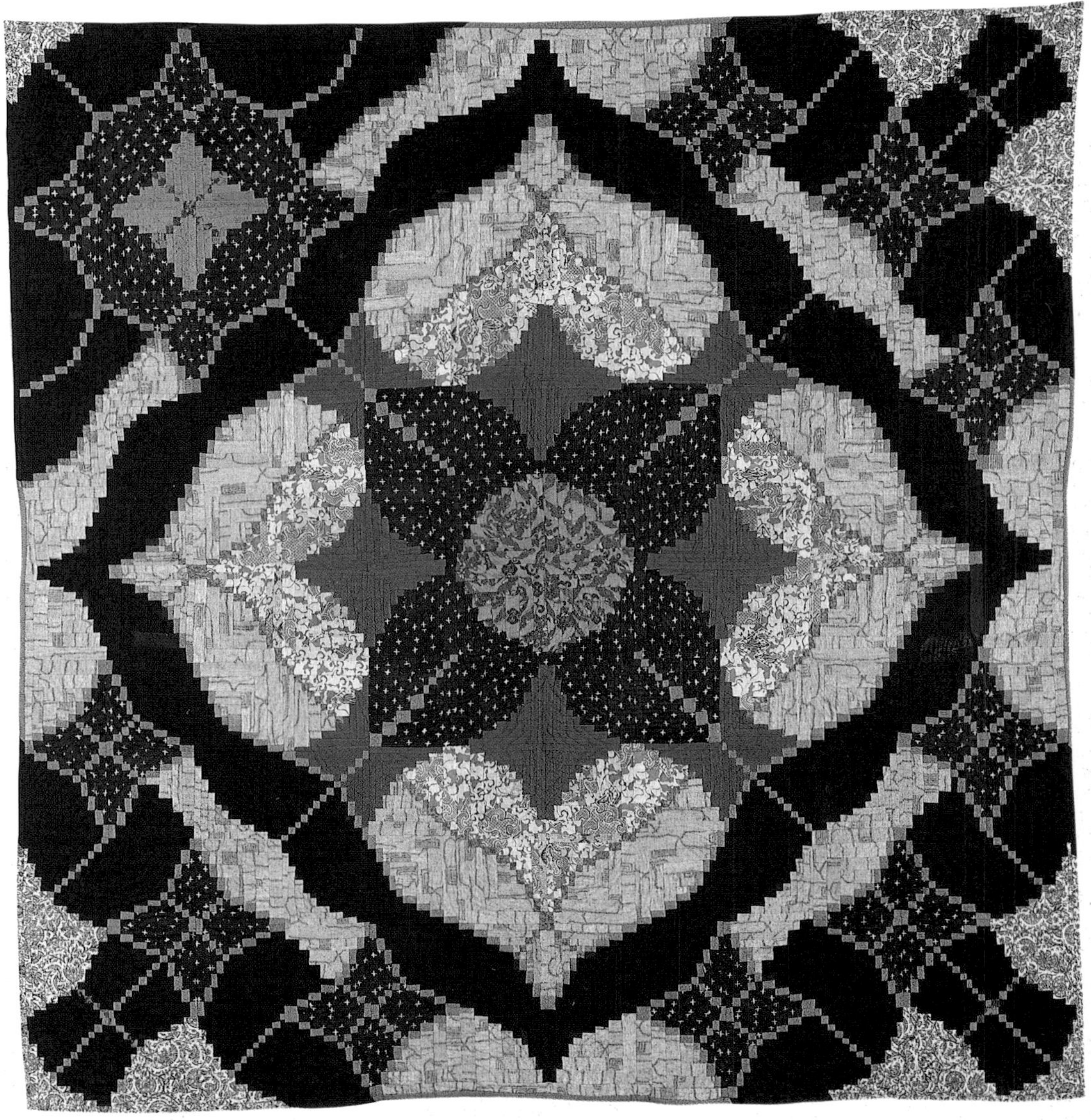

Moon Light Log Cabin ▸

Toyoko Fujisaki. 1990. Sapporo, Hokkaido, Japan. Antique Japanese cottons, silks, and linens; hand pieced and quilted. 90 1/2 x 90 1/2 in. Collection of the artist.

This quilt, which the artist says "attempts to express the texture of various moonbeams, the brightness, opaqueness, and intensity of the light," is based on a traditional motif of the Ainu people native to the island of Hokkaido. The quilt's otherwise symmetrical organization is broken in the upper left quadrant.

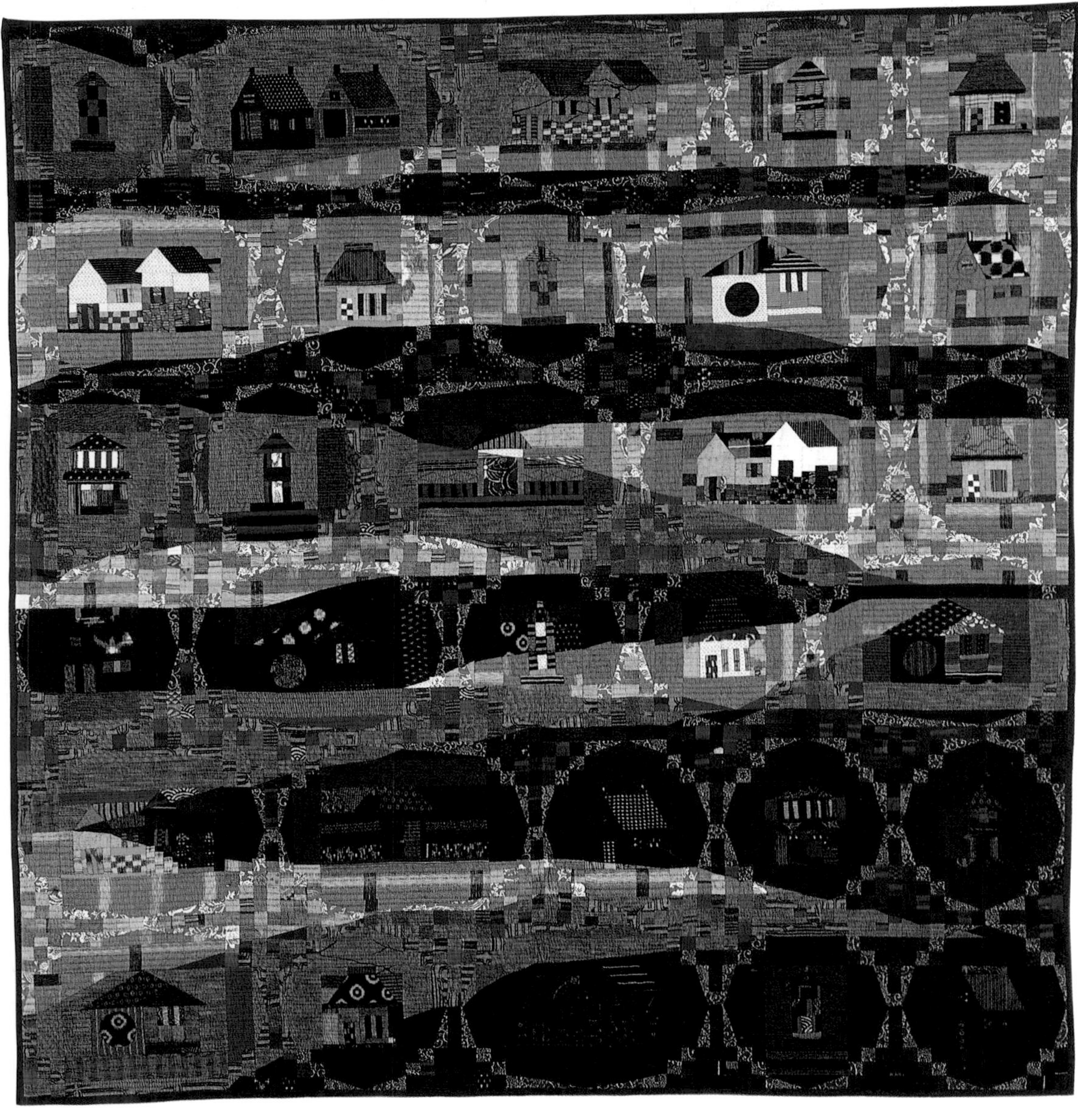

◂ Little Village

Kiyomi Shimada. 1990. Kikuchi, Japan. Japanese cottons and silks; hand pieced and quilted. 78 3/4 x 77 1/4 in. Kumamoto Museum, Japan.

Pieced houses of various architectural types appear at the center of the blocks of this inventive and playful quilt, which recalls the old American School House pattern. The artist describes this, her first quilt, as, "My fairy tale world of dark forests, shining river flows, [and] glistening window panes of my childhood. Houses large and small of a small village from my memories."

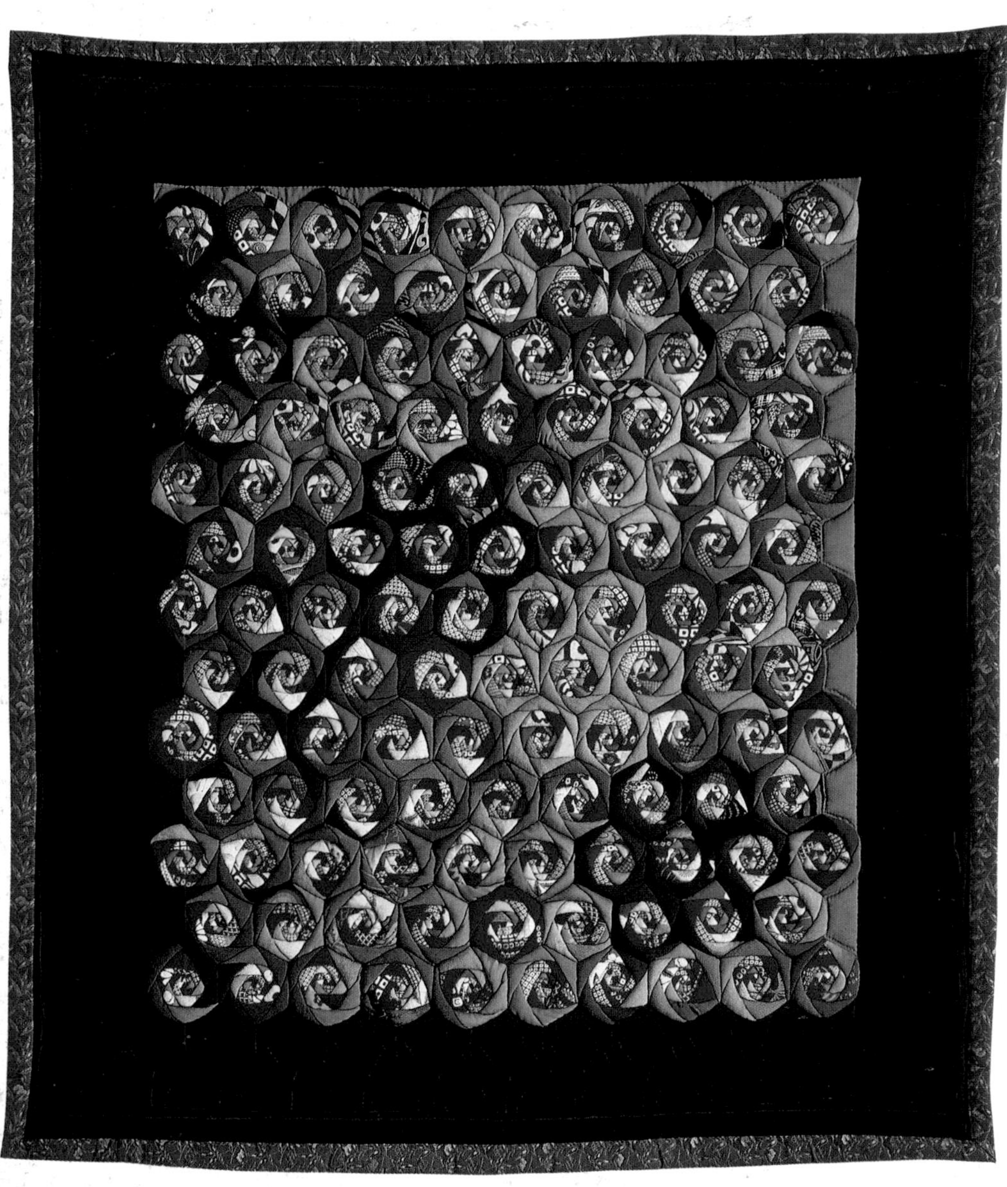

CHEST OF DRAWERS ▶

Keiko Takahashi. 1990. Tokyo, Japan. Japanese cottons; hand pieced and quilted. 91 x 71 in. Collection of the artist.

This original design was created through the use of origami. The powerful illusion of three dimensions, similar to a Tumbling Blocks pattern in its effect, was achieved through the careful use of repeating fabric colors. Setting the "drawers" at an angle increases the illusion of depth.

▲ "CHIRIMEN" FLOWERS

Kazuko Domoto. 1990. Kagoshima, Japan. Old kimono silks; hand pieced and quilted. 53 x 47 in. Collection of the artist.

Chirimen means silk crepe. This tightly packed garden of vibrant, multicolored, roselike flowers is framed by a wide, dark border and neutrally colored edge.

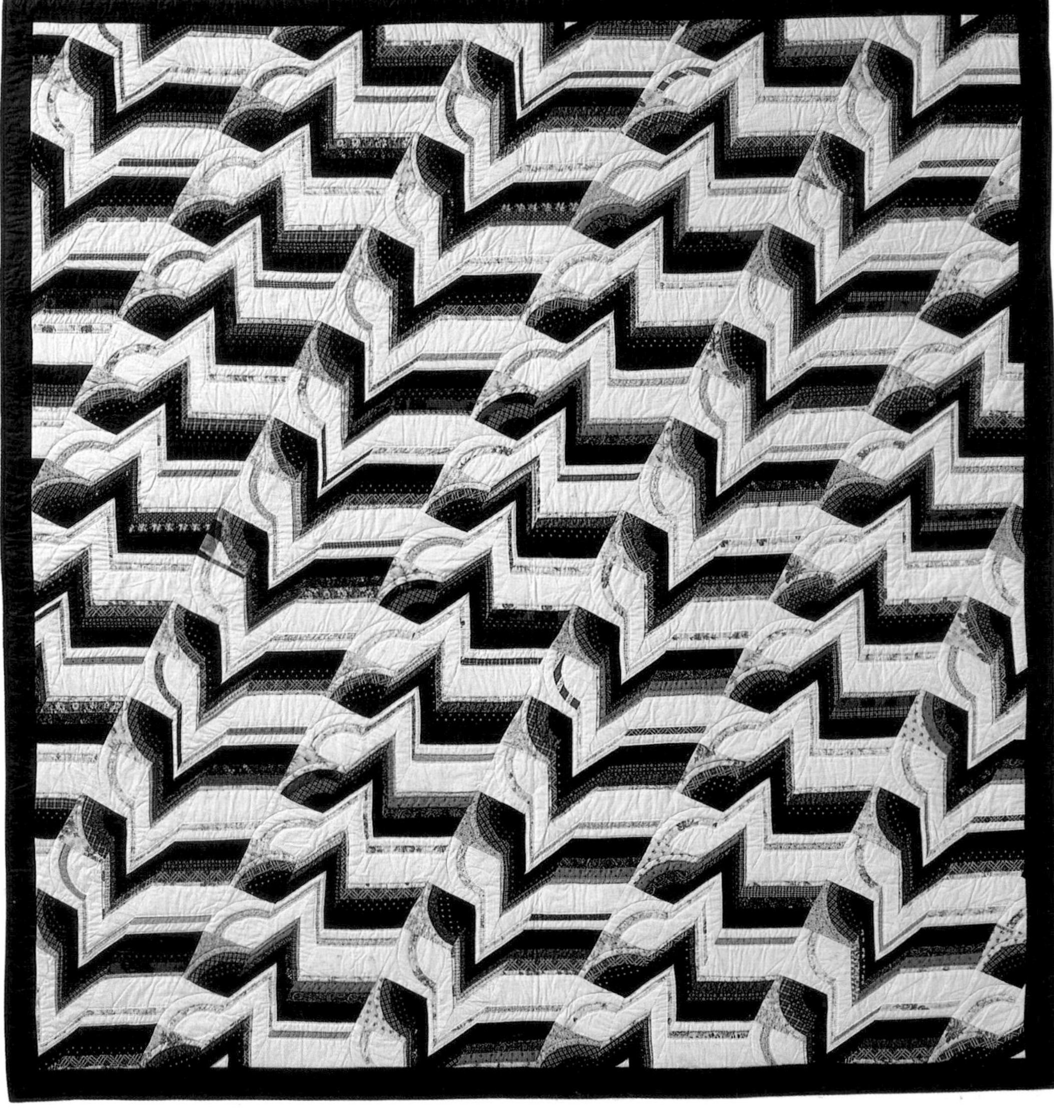

SEA GULL ▶

Katsuko Tazaki. 1993. Mito, Japan. Cottons; hand pieced and quilted. 80 3/4 x 76 in. Collection of the artist.

Sea Gull is built from a birdlike shape that alternates in opposite directions in the slanted vertical rows and repeats in positive and negative colors to form a composition full of compressed, flapping energy.

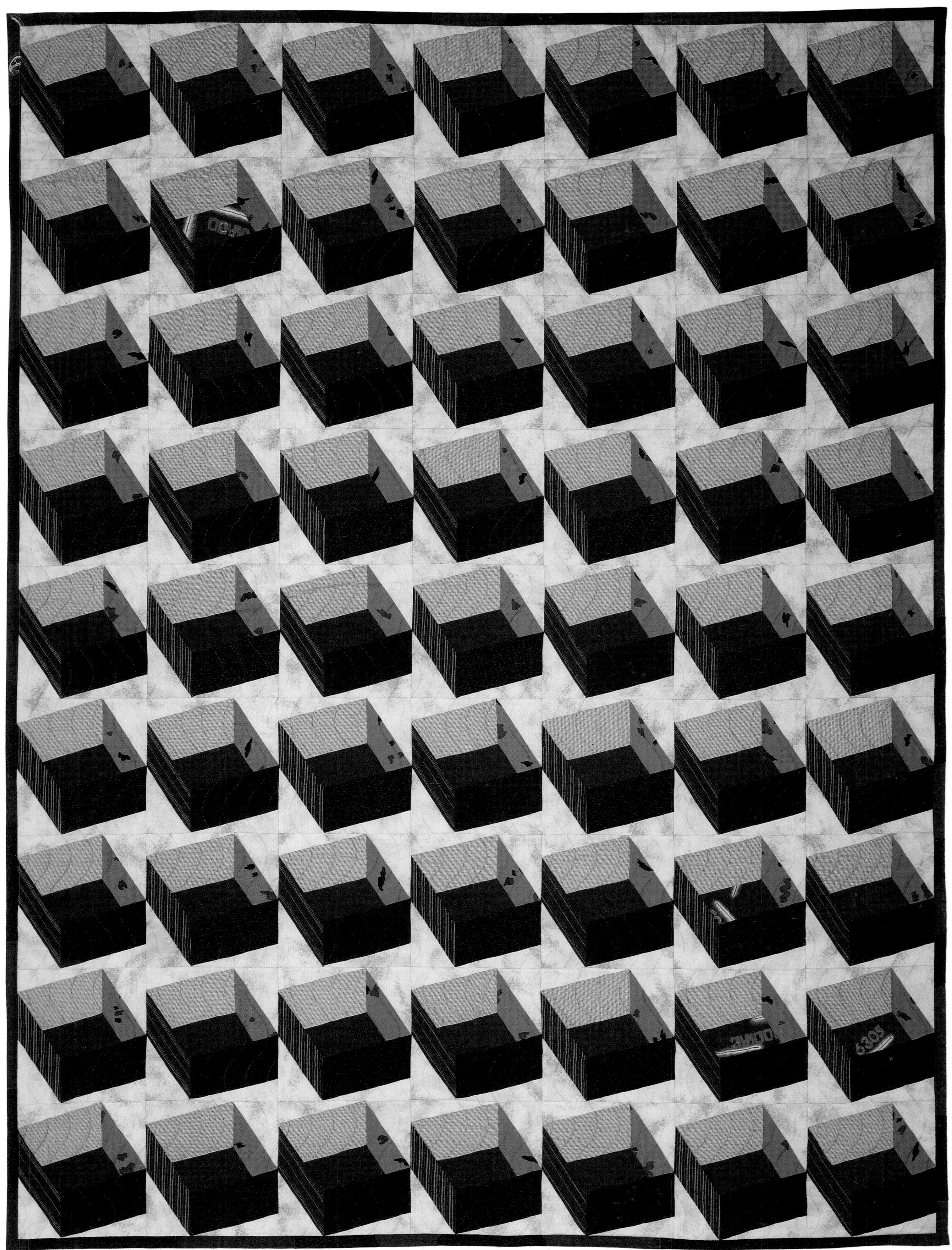

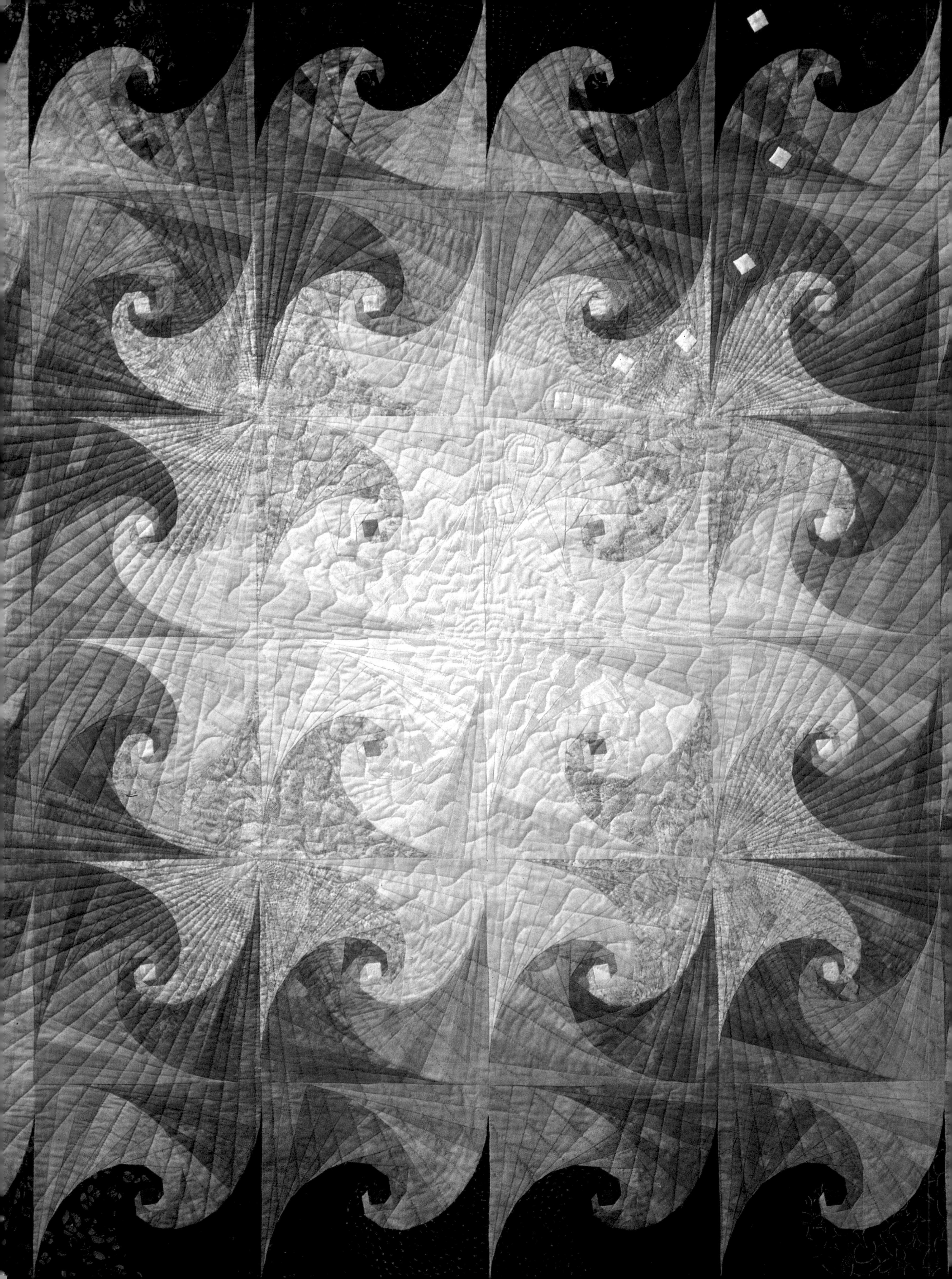

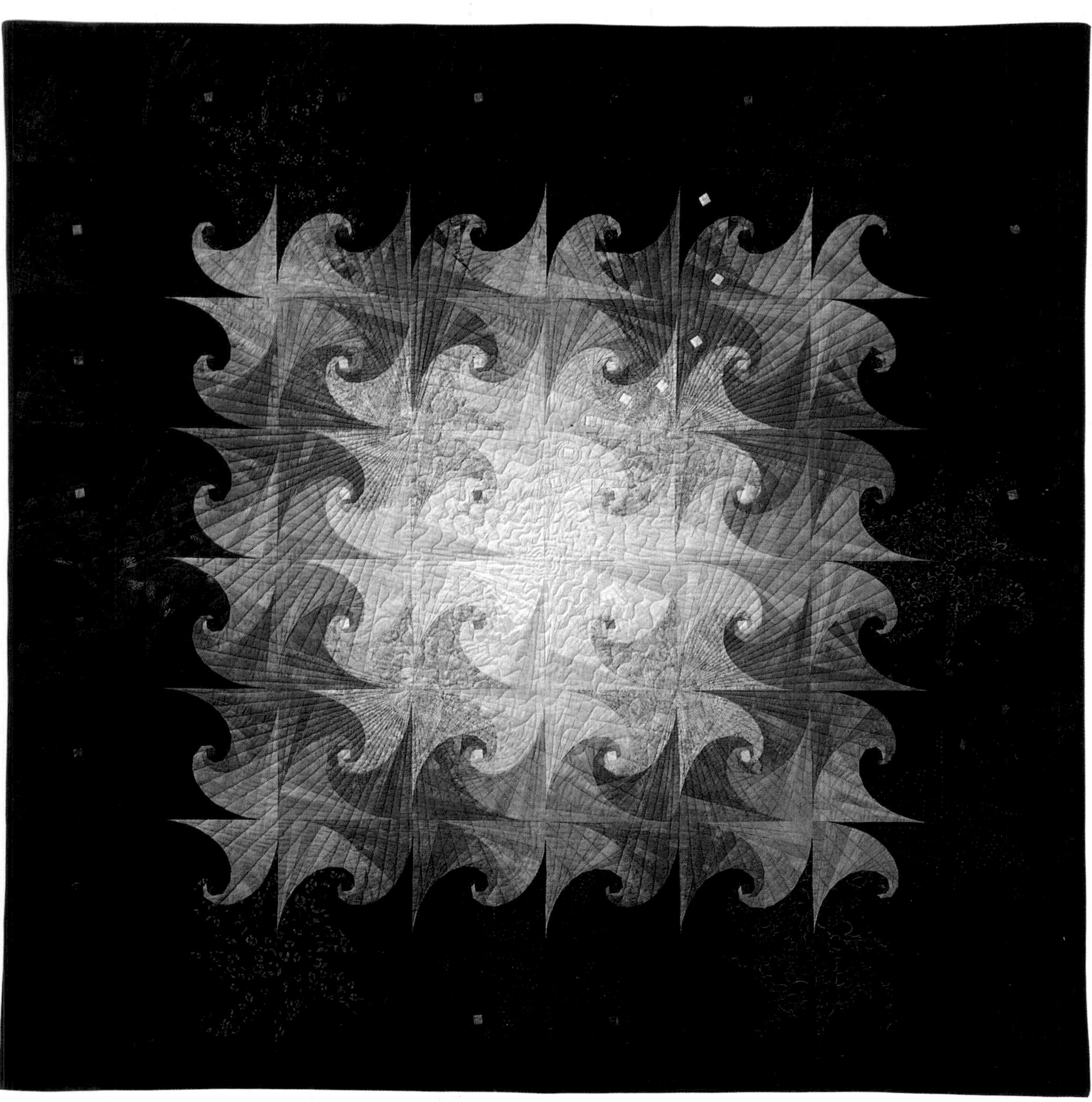

▲ PEACEFUL OCEAN (◄ DETAIL)

Mariko Nakata. 1993. Hirosaki, Japan. Indigo-dyed cottons; hand pieced and quilted. 93 3/4 x 93 3/4 in. Collection of the artist.

This graceful quilt won Grand Prize in the third annual exhibition of Quilt Nihon in 1993. The central composition is built from a single shape which resembles a cresting wave. Four of the wave shapes are joined back to back to create a revolving image that is superimposed in subtle color variations.

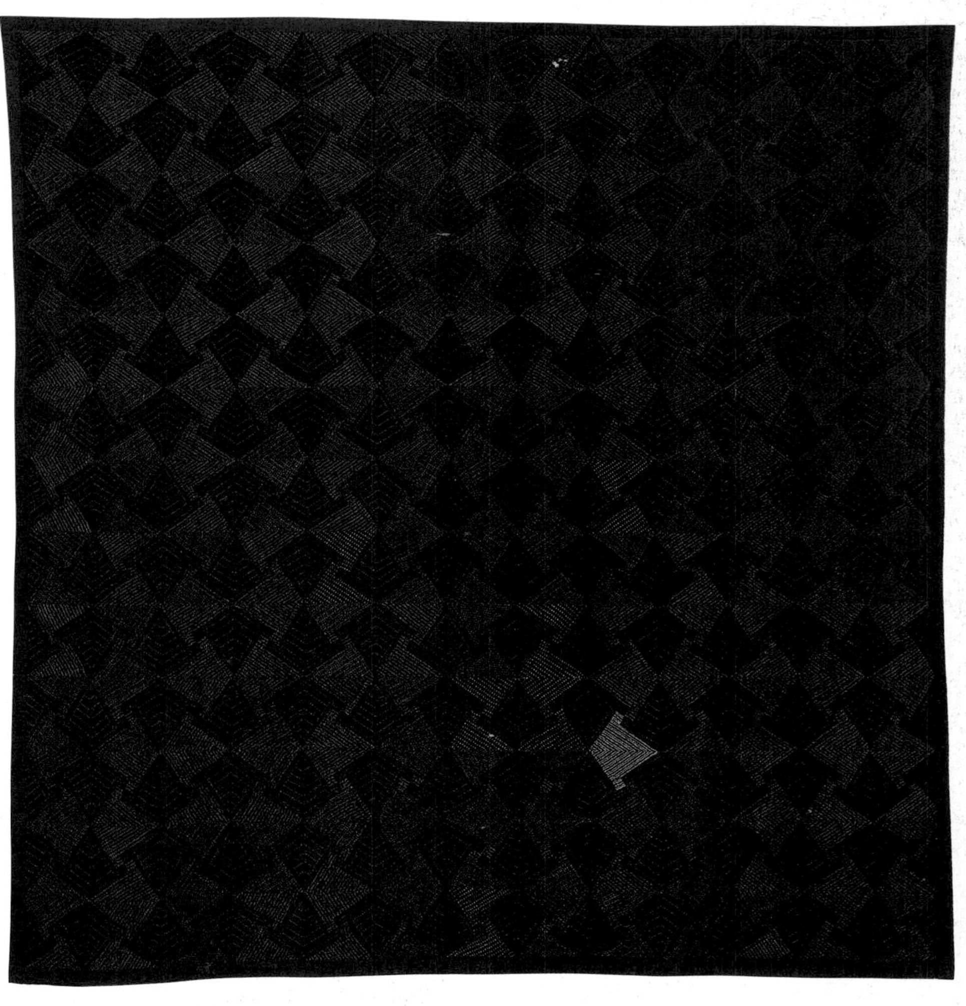

SEA OF JAPAN IN WINTER ►

Shizuko Kuroha. 1983. Tokyo, Japan. Hand-pieced and quilted cottons. 78 x 78 in. Collection of Ardis and Robert James.

Some of the fabrics used in this quietly dynamic quilt are taken from men's kimonos dating from the 1930s. The repeating shape that makes up the quilt suggests interlocking fish or water bugs swimming through cold winter water, moving toward each other, away from each other, back and forth. The alternating dark and light "fish" are made of dark blue and gray pinstriped fabric, with a shift to plain chalky blue forms in the upper right. A single gray-white form appears in the bottom right of the quilt.

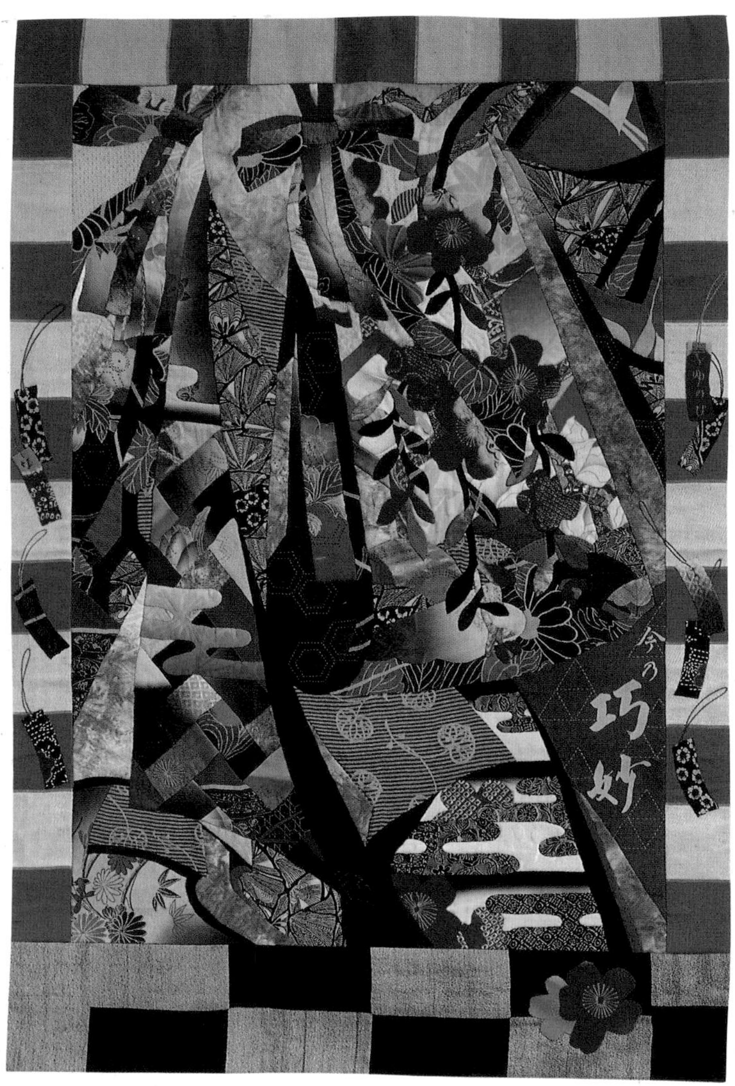

◄ KIMONO (CRIB QUILT)

Kumiko Sudo. 1989. Eugene, Oregon. Cottons; hand pieced, appliquéd, and quilted. Museum of American Folk Art, New York.

Although Kumiko Sudo grew up surrounded by textiles (her mother was a dressmaker), she first encountered American quilts in 1970 on a trip to California. She gained a reputation for her work as a textile artist before moving to the United States in 1985 and is the author of *East Quilts West*, a book of original patterns. Sudo is known for her use of a particularly wide-ranging and eclectic palette of fabrics.

BRILLIANT ►

Kayoko Oguri. 1990. Tokushima Prefecture, Japan. Cottons; hand pieced and quilted. 78 x 61 1/2 in. Collection of the artist.

This quilt employs folk weavings called *shijira-ori*, which are products of the island of Shikoku. The blocks, which vary in size by row to create an asymmetrical composition, are each made up of two pairs of equal-sized triangles. The large cross, which is built primarily of red fabrics, is also set off-center both horizontally and vertically.

MOON OVER THE MOUNTAINS ►

Ritsuko Shino. 1990. Ryugasaki, Japan. American and Japanese cottons; hand pieced and quilted. 82 x 72 in. Collection of the artist.

This original and aptly named design, which is created through the use of origami, superimposes four large triangles on a central circle to form its basic block. The use of a wide range of solid-colored and printed fabrics draws attention away from the geometric regularity of the seventy-two blocks.

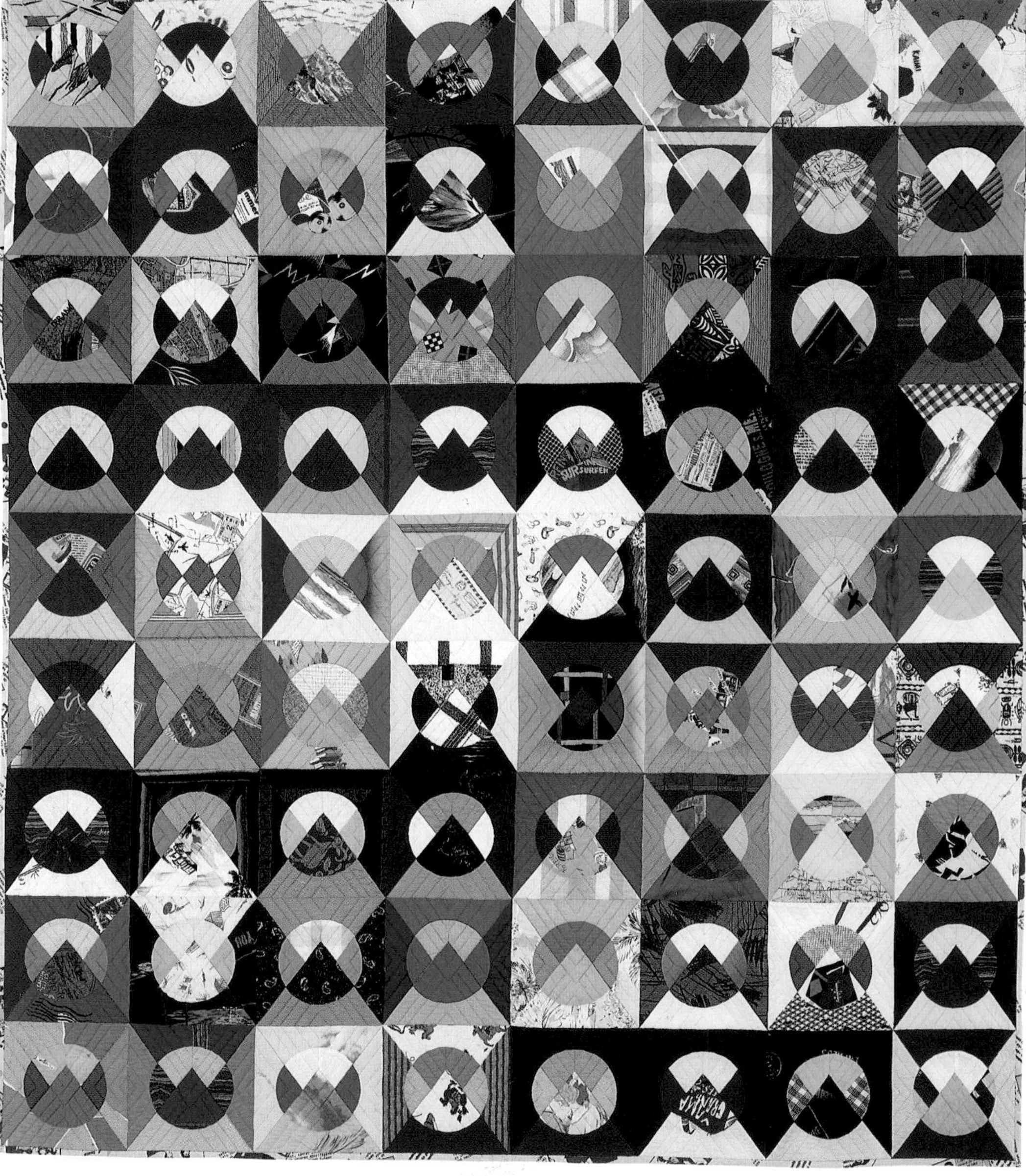

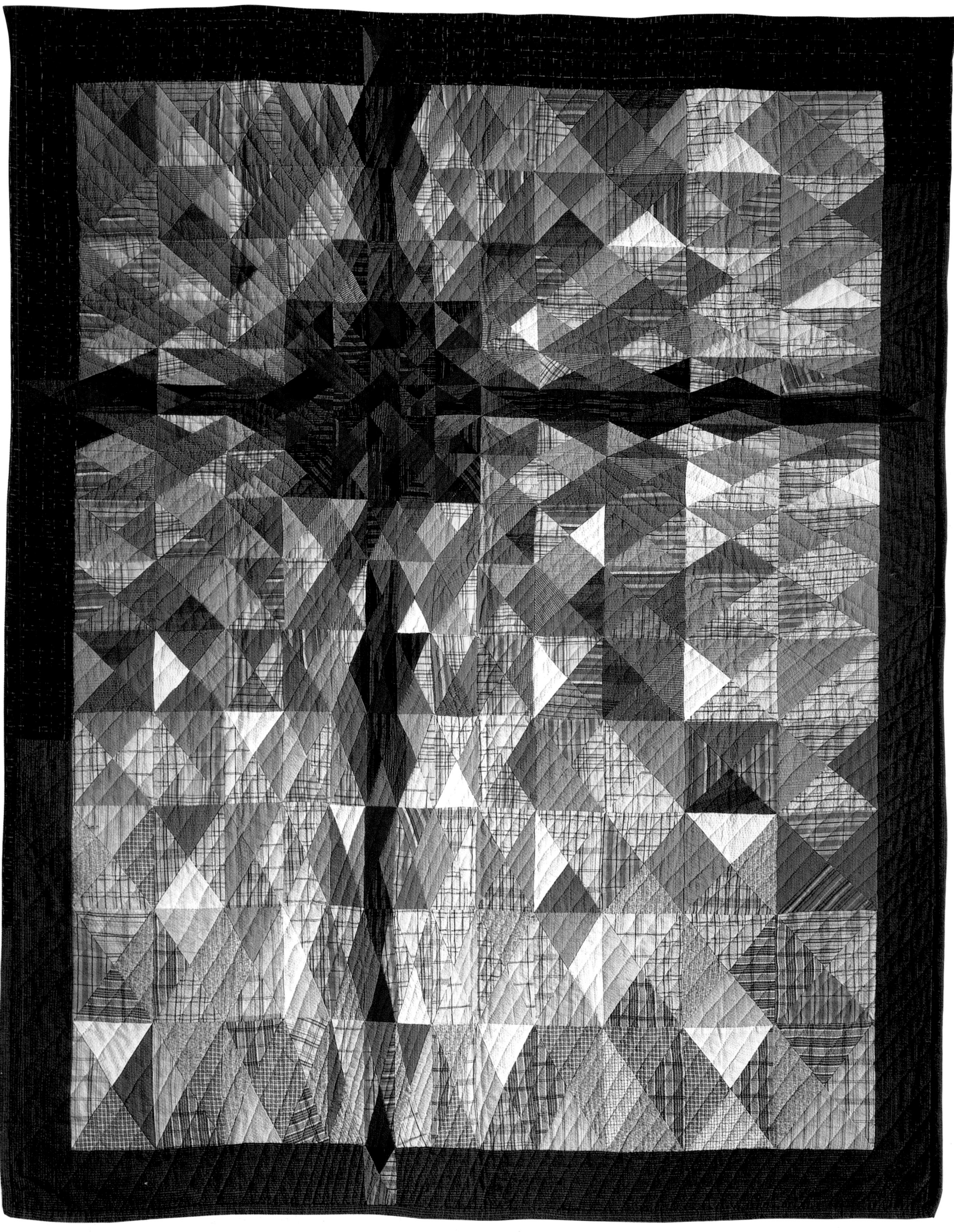

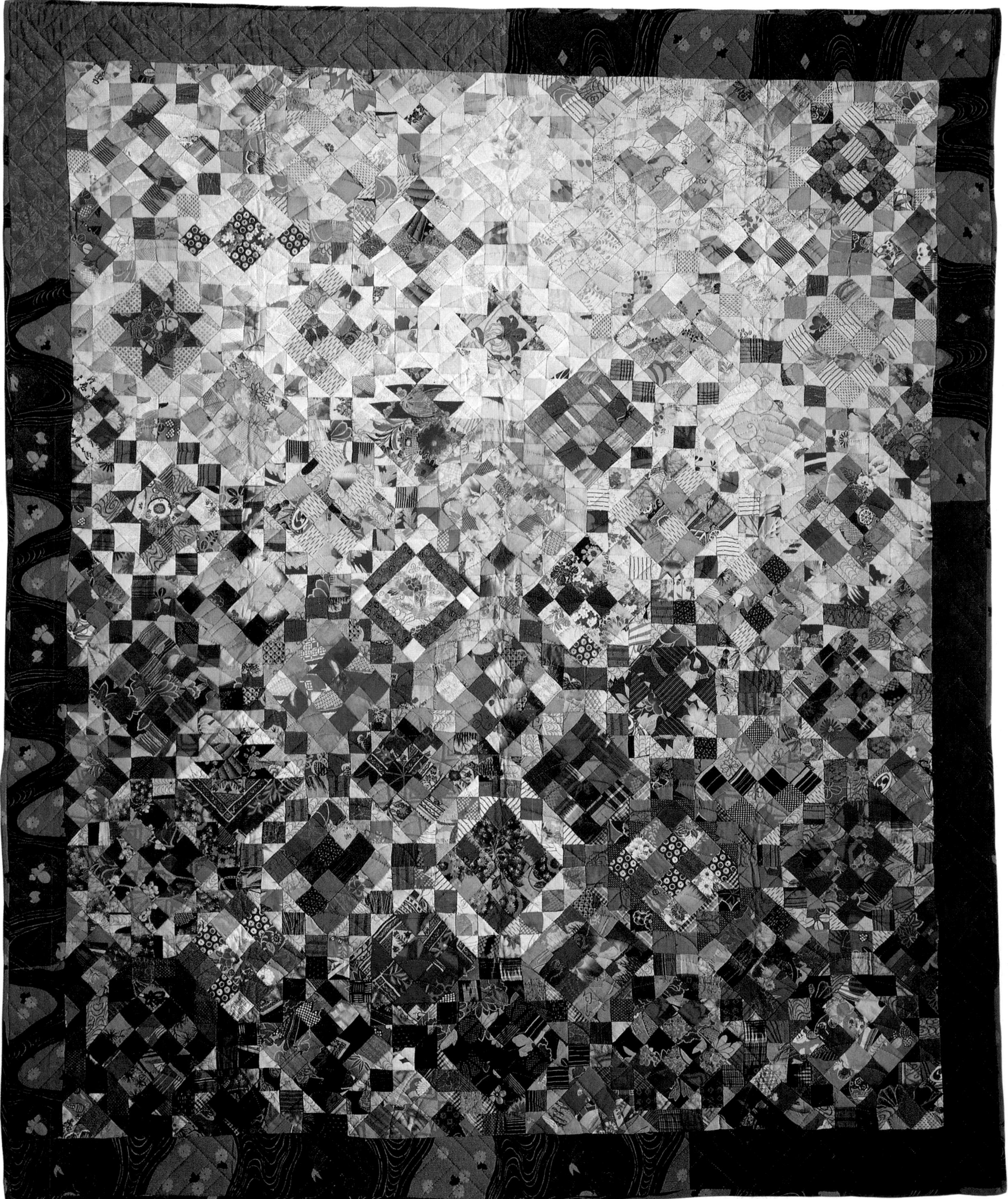

▲ OKUMINO—PAST AND PRESENT (DETAIL ▶)

Michiko Shima. 1990. Gifu Prefecture, Japan. Kimono silks; hand pieced and quilted. 80 x 67 1/2 in. Collection of the artist.

This quilt embodies two defining aspects of Japanese quiltmaking: the use of historic fabric and the preference for asymmetrical design. Japanese quilters venerate traditional fabrics and, unlike their American counterparts, hold the rag bag in high esteem. This quilt is made from old kimono fabrics. By carefully weighting the color groupings, with lighter fabrics at the top of the quilt and darker fabrics below, the quiltmaker has drawn visual attention away from the individual blocks and pulled the geometric pattern completely out of balance. An asymmetrical border frames the composition. Another characteristic of Japanese quiltmaking seen here is the use of white as an equal color, rather than as a background.

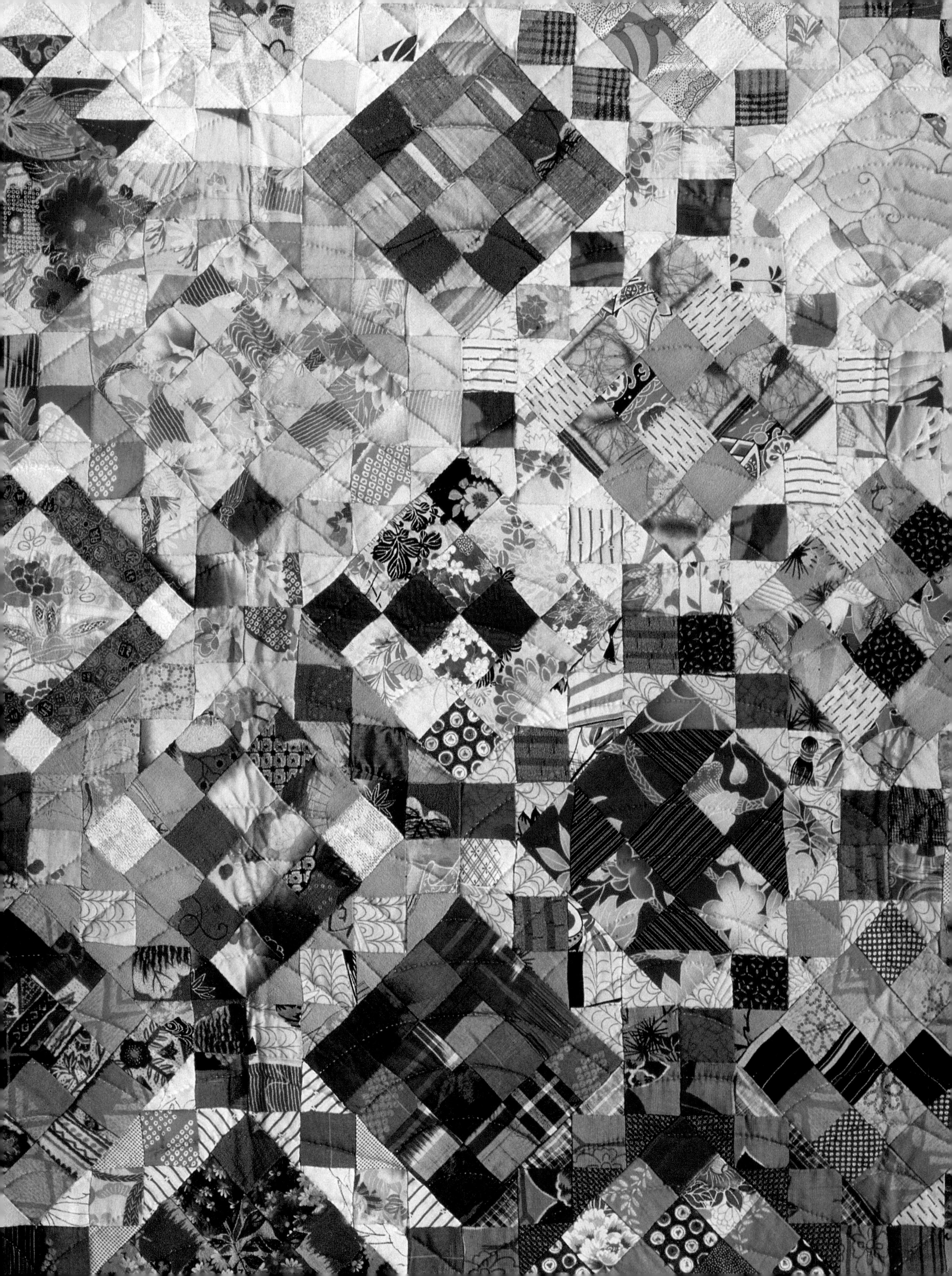

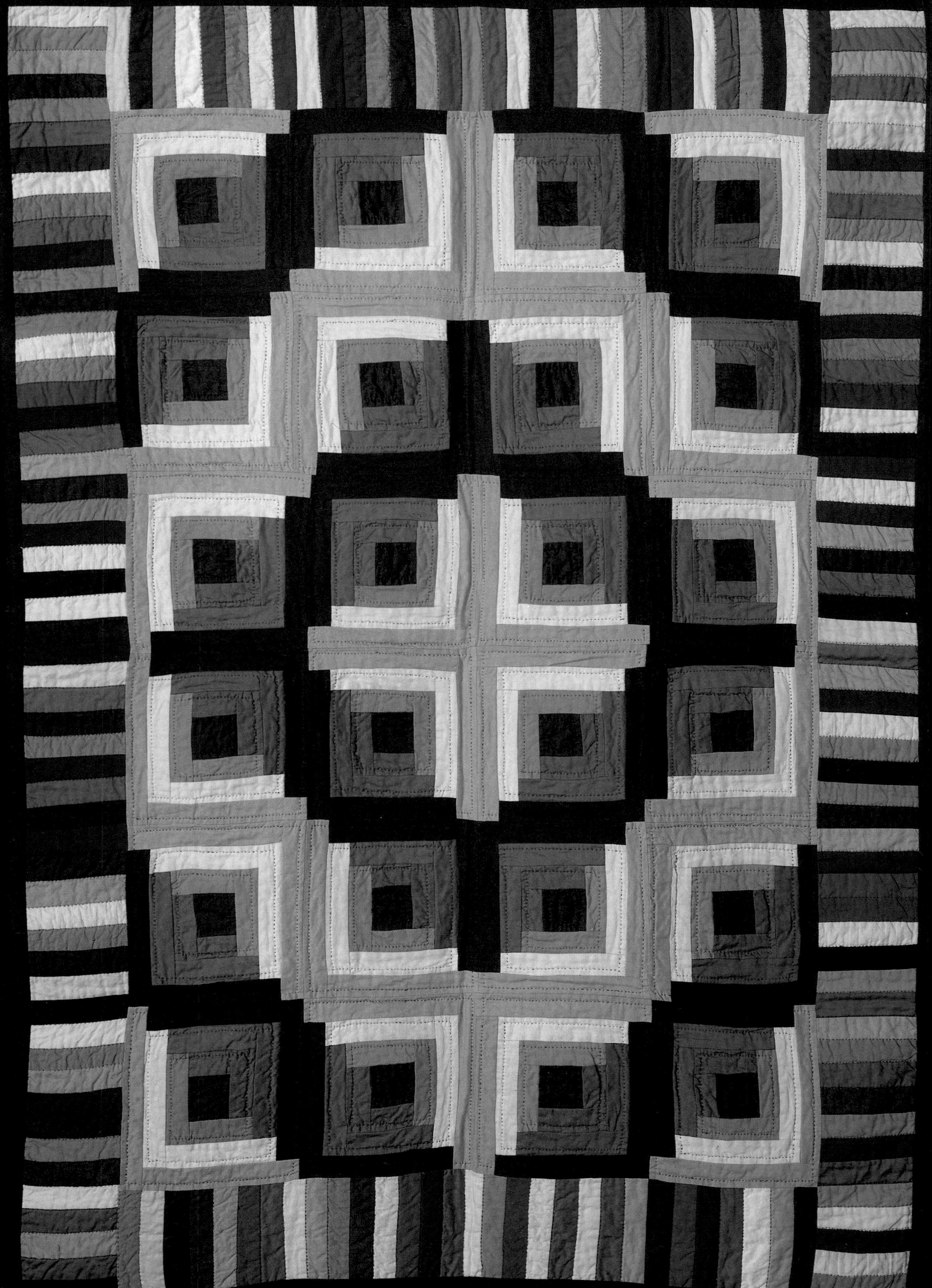

Other Ethnic and Cultural Traditions

Amish Quilts

From a purely aesthetic point of view, Amish quilts probably represent the most significant group of quilts made by American women. Amish quilts are justly renowned for their extraordinarily imaginative and expressive use of color manipulated within a simple and rigid universe of nonrepresentational geometric patterns such as Center Diamond, Diamond in the Square, Four-Patch, Nine-Patch, Bars, Ocean Waves, Tumbling Blocks, Sunshine and Shadow, Log Cabin, and Rob Peter to Pay Paul.

Amish quilts were almost invariably made of solid-colored rather than printed fabric, and often displayed deeply saturated colors. Amish quiltmakers employed color in painterly ways, juxtaposing large or small squares, diamonds, bars or triangles of similar value or intensity to create powerful visual rhythms. It is readily apparent to even the untrained eye that Amish quilts reveal an understanding of color unique to the sect and completely foreign to the sensibilities and traditions of non-Amish quilters. One might also be surprised by the unconventional symbolism of color in Amish quilts. While most of us see black as the color of mourning, for example, the Amish consider black, which is the dominant color of their clothing, to be the color of joy. Similarly, while many commentators have pointed out the "modern," minimalist qualities of Amish quilts, comparing them with the canvases of modern painters, these fabric works were actually made within an extremely conservative Christian fundamentalist culture that has steadfastly rejected virtually everything associated with the modern world. Modern artists such as Kenneth Noland, Brice Marden, and Mark Rothko have consciously sought to reduce their own work to its most basic elements, eliminating representational context and allowing color and form to speak for themselves. But Amish quilts proceed from the place modern artists seek to find. We should, therefore, be careful and mindful about project-

◀ **Log Cabin—Barn Raising Crib Quilt**

A member of the Yoder family. c. 1985. Holmes County, Ohio. Cottons; machine pieced and hand quilted. 48 x 34 in. Collection of Ardis and Robert James.

In this vibrant little quilt, a classic Log Cabin pattern is surrounded by a piano keys border to create an effect reminiscent of a tile mosaic.

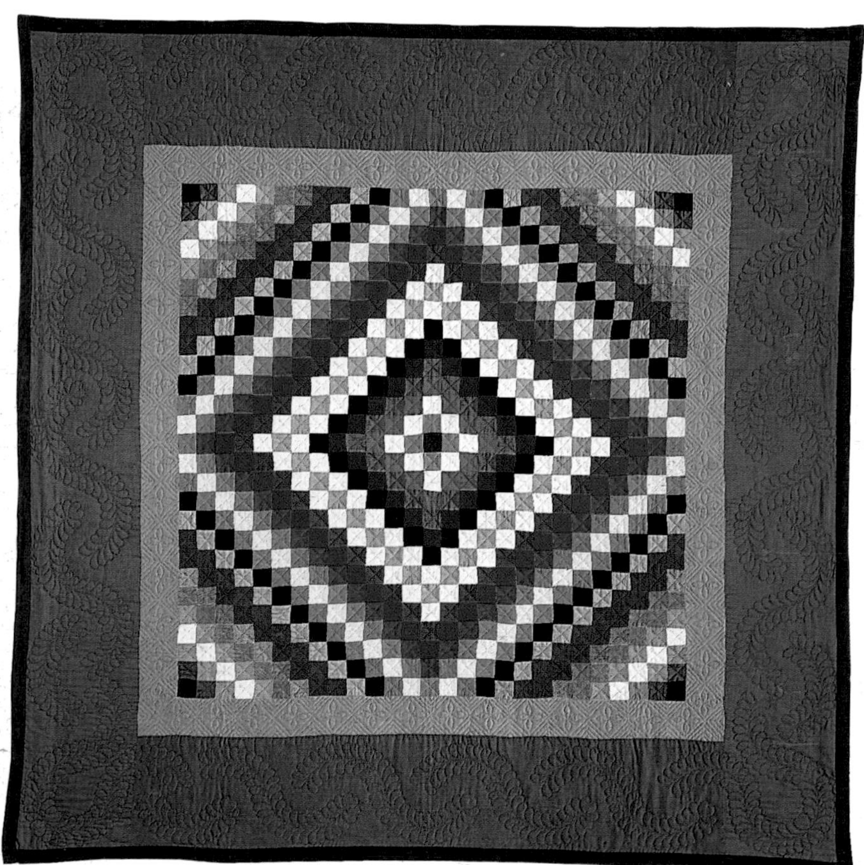

◄ **Sunshine and Shadow**

Unknown Amish artist. c. 1910. Lancaster County, Pennsylvania. Wools; hand pieced and quilted. 80 x 80 in. Collection of Douglas Tompkins.

This early example of the Sunshine and Shadow pattern employs a dozen fabric colors, carefully chosen, precisely manipulated, and strikingly juxtaposed.

ing our own meanings onto the quilts and attempt instead to understand the culture that produced them.

The content of an Amish quilt stands in marked contrast to the prevailing concerns of the greater American society and clearly represents the Amish desire to remain apart from the distracting temptations and complexities of the "English" world. Amish quilts belong to a different world, a world reduced to essentials and infused with constant worship and spiritual reflection, where matters of the spirit are an integral part of everyday life, and word and deed are one and the same. Amish quilts reflect the Amish culture's integration of the spiritual into daily life by their inseparable fusion of function and beauty. The Amish tend to place little value on art, considering it frivolous because it serves no practical purpose. Instead of hanging works of art on their walls, they choose instead to make everyday things beautiful. The Amish choose not to separate beauty from function, commerce from community, or worship from work. Their quilts, most often made from wool, are warm and comforting; at the same time, they are beautiful and reflective of the spiritual values of the Amish communities and of its deeply reverential people.

The Amish are members of a religious order that had its origins in the Protestant Reformation movement of the early 1500s. Although Martin Luther is the most well-known figure to break from the Catholic church at the time, many other reformers and reform groups were also active during this time of religious upheaval. In 1536 a Dutch Anabaptist priest named Menno Simons founded a new church. Like all Anabaptists, Menno Simons believed in voluntary adult baptism at the time of confession of faith. His church also espoused complete separation of church and state, as well as pacifism and nonresistance, which translated into a refusal to participate in the military or to bring law suits against others. Menno Simons's followers, still known today as Mennonites, looked to God's representatives, the elders of the church, for guidance in all facets of their daily lives and adhered to a strict set of church imposed doctrines. Although widely persecuted, the Mennonite church grew and spread throughout Holland, Switzerland, and Germany over the next 150 years.

In the 1690s a zealous Swiss Mennonite bishop named Jacob Amman and his followers founded the Amish religion when they broke from the mother church over the issue of church discipline. The Amish believed that the Mennonite church had grown lax in enforcing church

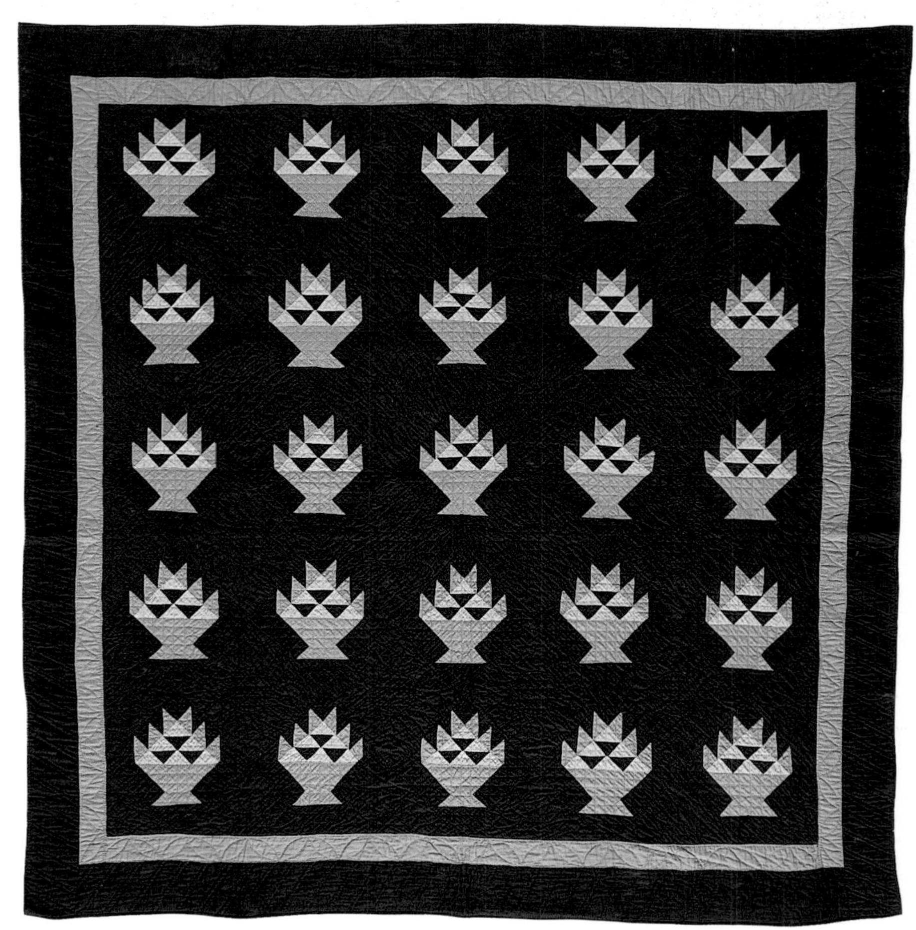

BASKETS ▸

Fannie Yoder. c. 1936. Emma, Indiana. Cottons; hand pieced and quilted. 76 x 76 in. Indiana State Museum, Indianapolis, Indiana.
This highly stylized *Baskets* quilt was made for Mrs. Yoder's daughter Elsie, who was born in 1915.

discipline among its members, and the new group of worshippers set up guidelines known as *Ordnung*, which dictated rules for behavior and their enforcement. To ensure compliance, members who did not adhere to strict church standards could be ostracized, or "shunned," by their family and friends, who were proscribed by elders from eating, drinking or socializing with the fallen.

The Amish came to America in the early 1700s, attracted by William Penn's promise of fruitful but inexpensive land and religious freedom. Some Amish families in Lancaster County, Pennsylvania, have farmed the same land for nearly three hundred years, land that is among the richest farmland on earth. Now as then, the Old Order Amish live simply, keeping to themselves and consciously avoiding the ways of "the world." They place community values above individual freedoms, practicing a strict and unadorned conformity in their clothing, grooming, and behavior. They distrust technology, eschew telephones and electricity in their homes, and rely on horses and mules to pull their plows, wagons, and carriages. Most Amish finish their formal schooling with the eighth grade, believing that too much education engenders individual pride, which is disdained. Advanced formal education is seen as unnecessary or even counter to the purposefully simple, rural, and agrarian way of life chosen by the Amish.

Over the years, groups of Amish have broken from the rigid Old Order to form new, less conservative sects. Today, the Amish are not a monolithic group with uniform beliefs, but, rather, a number of related sects with slightly different codes of behavior. Midwestern Amish sects such as the Beachy Amish have been greatly influenced by the comparatively liberal Mennonites with whom they have lived and interacted for decades. Members of some of these more liberal sects are allowed to wear adorned clothing, attend school beyond the eighth grade, and even drive cars, all of which are forbidden by the Old Order.

The Amish began to make quilts in the late nineteenth century. The earliest Amish quilts date from mid-century, but few were made prior to the 1880s. True to their conservatism, the Amish rejected the busy patterns favored by contemporary society and instead modeled their designs after the long outdated and unfashionable central medallion style popular a hundred years earlier. Early Amish quilts were made exclusively from wool, another throwback to earlier times. The Lancaster area Old Order Amish were the most conservative of all the various sects of the religion, and their quilts reflect the society's restraint. Lancaster Amish quilts were made of solid-colored cloth and were arranged in strict geometric patterns. Printed fabric was never used: it would have broken the simple and intense rhythms of the pieced geometry and disturbed the pure color of the top. The two favorite patterns of the Lancaster Amish were the Center Diamond, an upended square set within angular borders and often accented with or augmented by smaller squares and diamonds, and the Bars, strips of color laid down vertically. The simplicity of the patterns allowed large segments of pure, saturated color to resonate against each other to vibrant and dazzling effect. Lancaster Amish quilts are also known for the fine quality of their needlework, which complements the quilts by filling the large blocks and bars of solid color with finely worked vines, diamonds, and other motifs, adding richly patterned surface detail to the quilts' starkly powerful overall impression.

Midwestern Amish quilts, made in less conservative enclaves, often have more small pieces arranged in busier patterns than do Lancaster area quilts. They also tend to employ a lighter and brighter overall color palette. In addition, many midwestern Amish quilts use black, a color not usually found in Pennsylvania quilts, as a background field against which brighter colors are played. While midwestern Amish stitching is as fine as that of the Pennsylvania Amish, it tends to be less detailed, partly because the more complex pieced patterns of the Midwest leave less open room for quilting.

Most of the finest Amish quilts were made between 1880 and 1940, at which time influences from outside the Amish community began to seriously dilute the purity of the tradition. The Amish tradition is largely moribund today, its days of glorious accomplishment past. The early Amish made quilts simply for their own use; the world largely ignored their work since it was so far outside the mainstream. The tremendous burst of interest in Amish quilting and the Amish way of life over the past thirty years has paradoxically contributed to the demise of the tradition. Particularly in Lancaster County, tourism has exerted enormous pressure on the Amish and their stubbornly isolated existence. A complex tourist industry has developed around the Amish in Lancaster County, promoting and sometimes exploiting the perceived quaintness of their way of life. Over six million people a year now come to see the Amish communities outside of Lancaster, to drive past the Amish farms and watch "them" turning their fields or haying with horse-drawn equipment or to catch a glimpse as "they" drive along the side of the highway in simple black carriages. In Intercourse, the heart of the Lancaster area Old Order Amish community, A People's Place, an educational center dedicated to Amish and Mennonite arts, faith, and culture, offers films, books, craft and gift stores, as well as a quilt museum, where visitors can see exhibits of superb older Amish quilts and can purchase antique quilts and reproductions.

The fact that many of today's Amish women make quilts for sale to the world has inevitably affected the way these quilts look and the way they are made. The pressures of tourism and the marketplace have forced the great majority of these Amish quilters to work in generic pieced

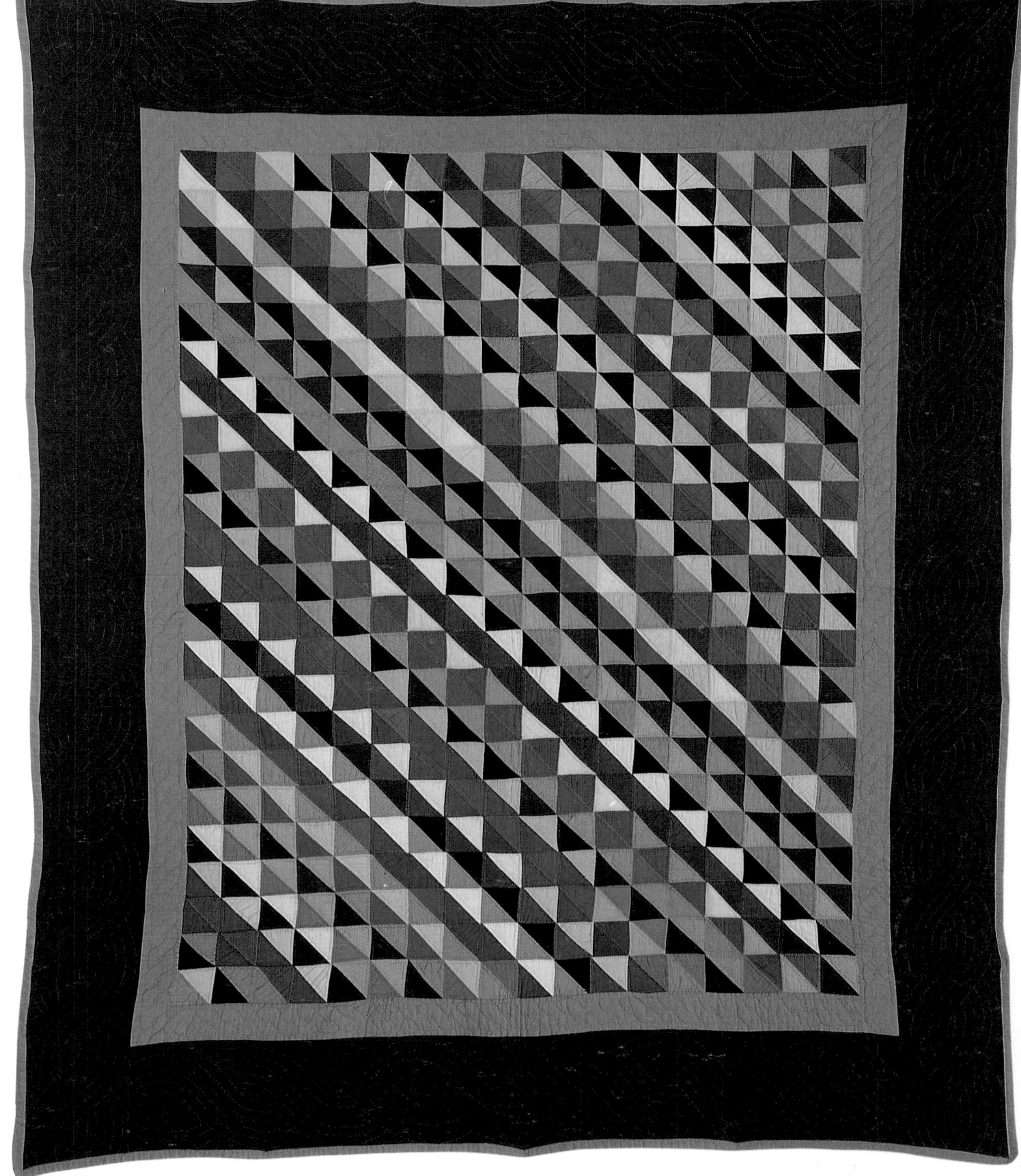

Geese in Flight ▶

Artist unknown. c. 1940. Holmes County, Ohio. Cottons; hand pieced and quilted. Private collection.

This carefully organized quilt is made up of diagonal rows of pieced triangles. Each row includes triangles of only two or three alternating colors. Some rows contrast light and dark colors; others place colors of similar value and hue side by side so that the eye sees these rows first as solid bars, pushing against the energy of the light and dark rows of "flying geese."

patterns and printed fabrics that have no connection to the Amish tradition. Fabrics and colors are chosen with an eye to the decidedly non-Amish tastes of the general marketplace, and the quilts often satisfy such worldly preferences as subdued pastels or small prints. Appliqué quilts, never a part of the Amish tradition, are preferred by tourists, and many Amish quiltmakers oblige with flowery patterns cut from calico. Because time is a factor when quilts are made for sale, few quilters bother or can afford to indulge in the time-consuming attention to detail that distinguishes traditional Amish stitching. The use of polyester fiberfill batting rather than traditional cotton has also compromised the intricacy of Amish needlework, since the polyester tends to retain its shape without finely applied stitchery.

Fortunately, a few talented Amish quiltmakers do continue to work within the narrow parameters of the classic Amish tradition, and they have produced quilts whose color and quality of stitching compare favorably with those made in the early decades of this century. The artistry of traditional Amish quilts has also had a profound and liberating influence on non-Amish quilters. Art quilter Michael James spoke for many when he said that he first realized that quilts could be art when he saw Amish work. Quilters around the world have studied and recreated traditional Amish patterns. Other modern quilters, such as Stan Book of California, have attempted to combine their admiration for traditional Amish quilting with their understanding of the color experiments of modern art. The great masterpieces of traditional Amish quiltmaking, many of them well known through publications and museum exhibitions, continue to elicit awe and respect for the focused intensity of their expression. They inspire quiltmakers around the world to reach for similar levels of artistic achievement and spritual concentration.

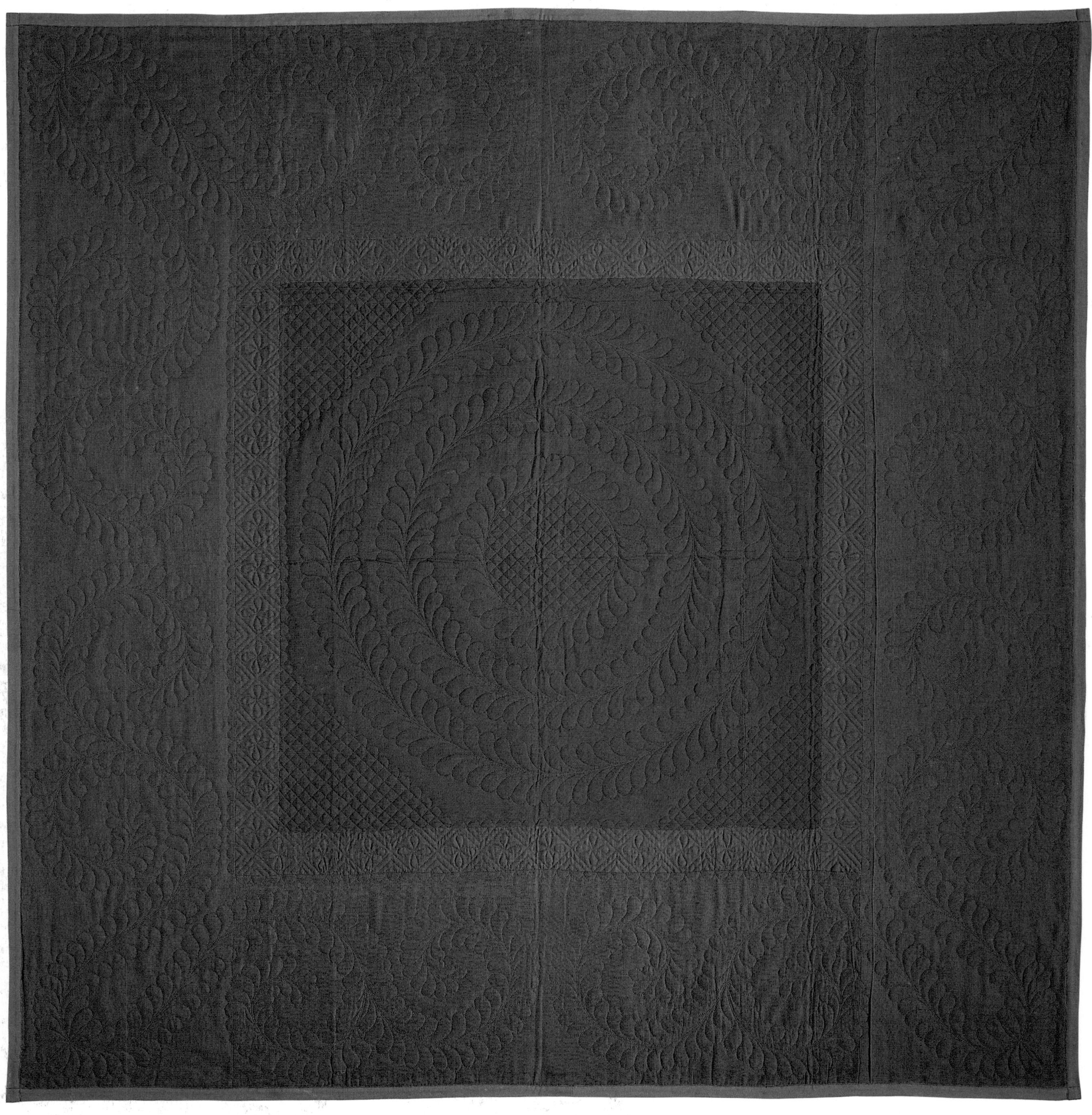

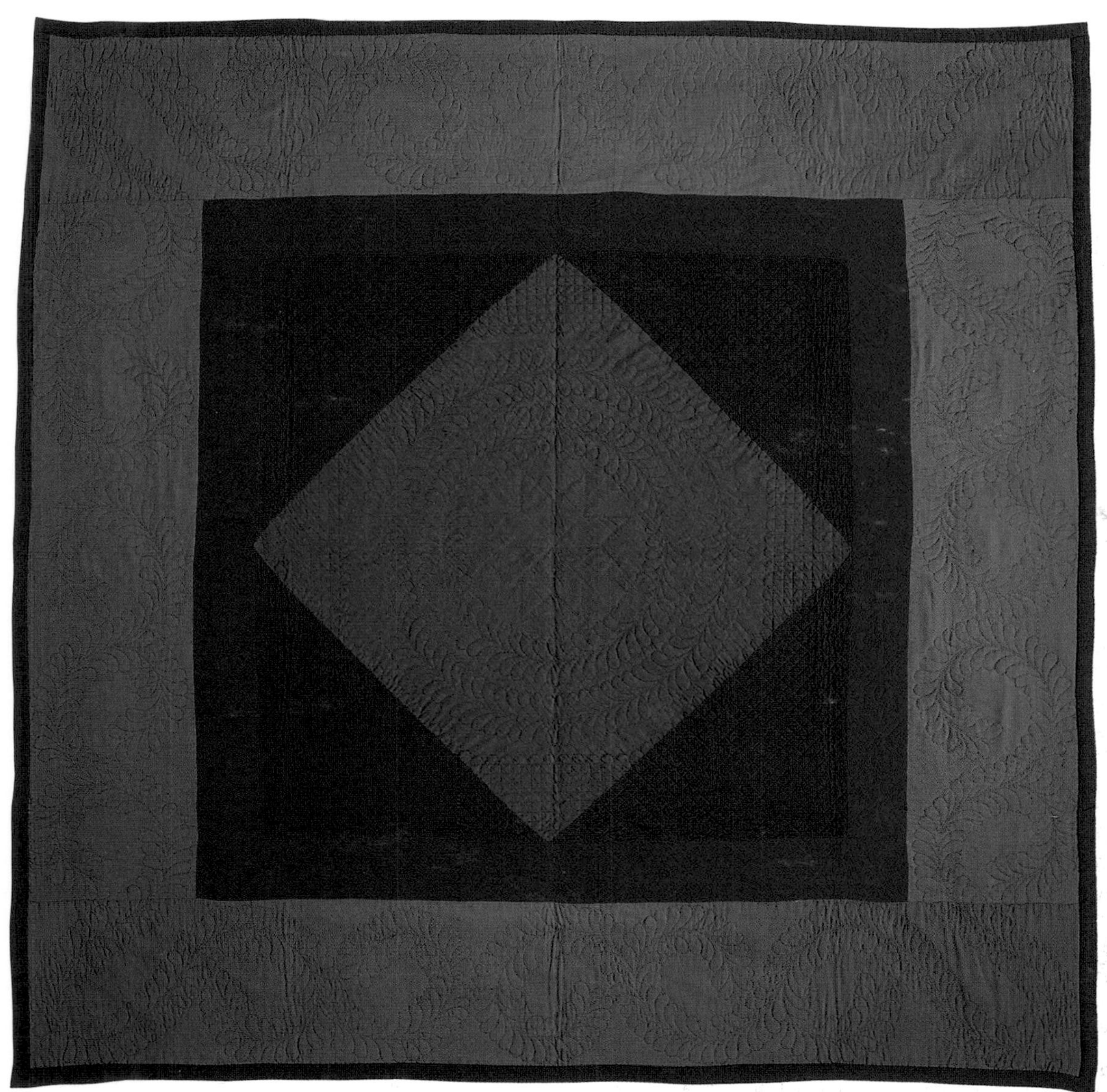

◄ DIAMOND IN THE SQUARE

Unknown Amish artist. c. 1920. Lancaster County, Pennsylvania. Wools; hand pieced and quilted. 78 x 78 in. Collection of Douglas Tompkins.

This astonishing exercise in pure color surrounds a central composition of intensely saturated blue, purple, and red with a wide field of cool brownish green and a thin purple border.

DIAMOND IN THE SQUARE ►

Unknown Amish artist. c. 1920. Lancaster, Pennsylvania. Wools; hand pieced and quilted. 78 x 78 in. Collection of Douglas Tompkins.

The combination of closely valued purples in the center diamond and the border is particularly effective in this classic Amish design. The light blue corner blocks keep the diamond tumbling in motion, while the black corner blocks in the square and the outside corners ground the rest of the quilt solidly.

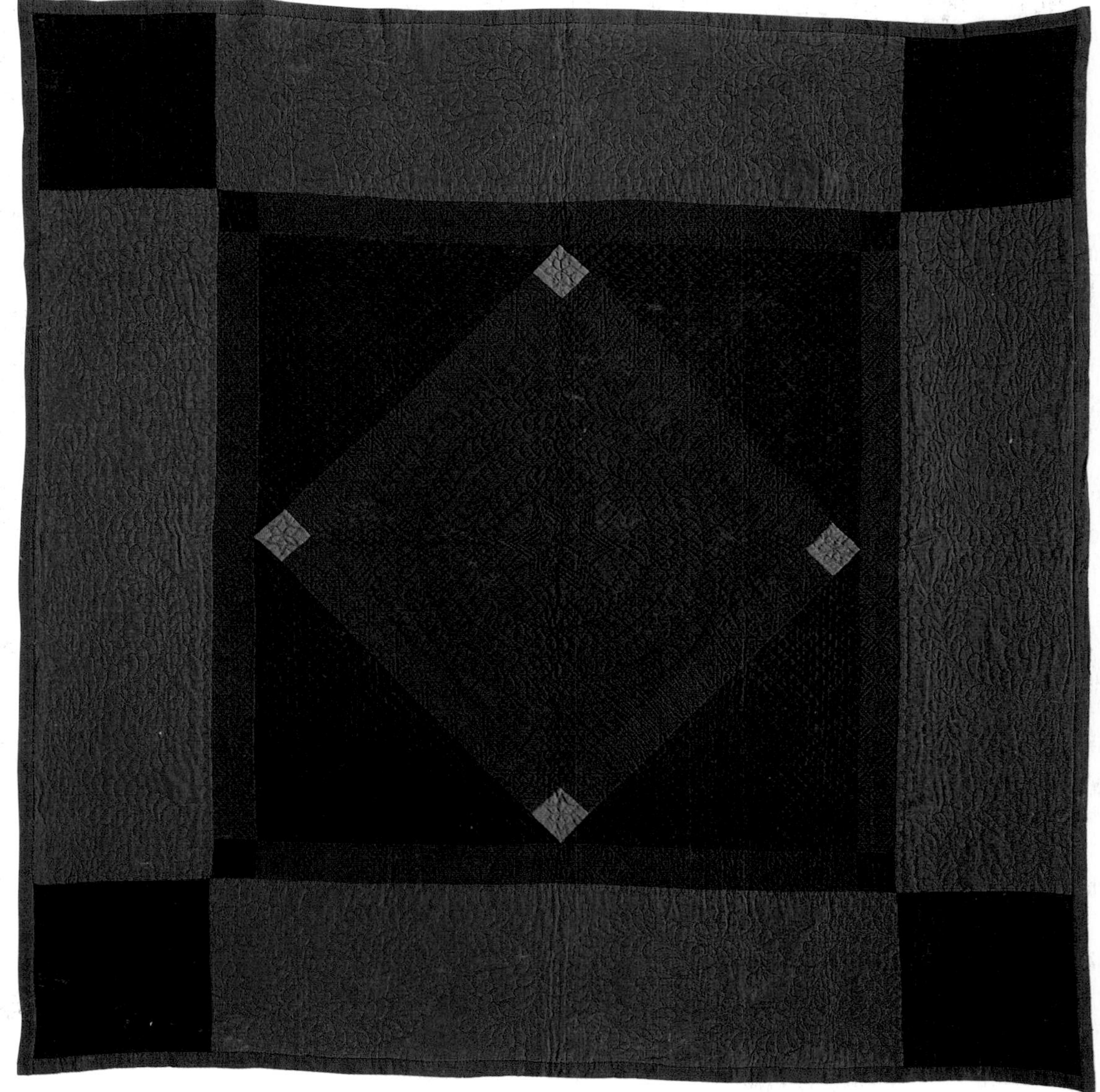

◄ CENTER SQUARE OR SQUARE WITHIN A SQUARE

Unknown Amish artist. c. 1895. Lancaster County, Pennsylvania. Wools; hand pieced and quilted. 79 x 78 in. Collection of Douglas Tompkins.

This early Amish quilt uses the simplest of patterns to brilliant effect, juxtaposing broad squares of solid-colored wools and covering them with a complex texture of intricate quilting.

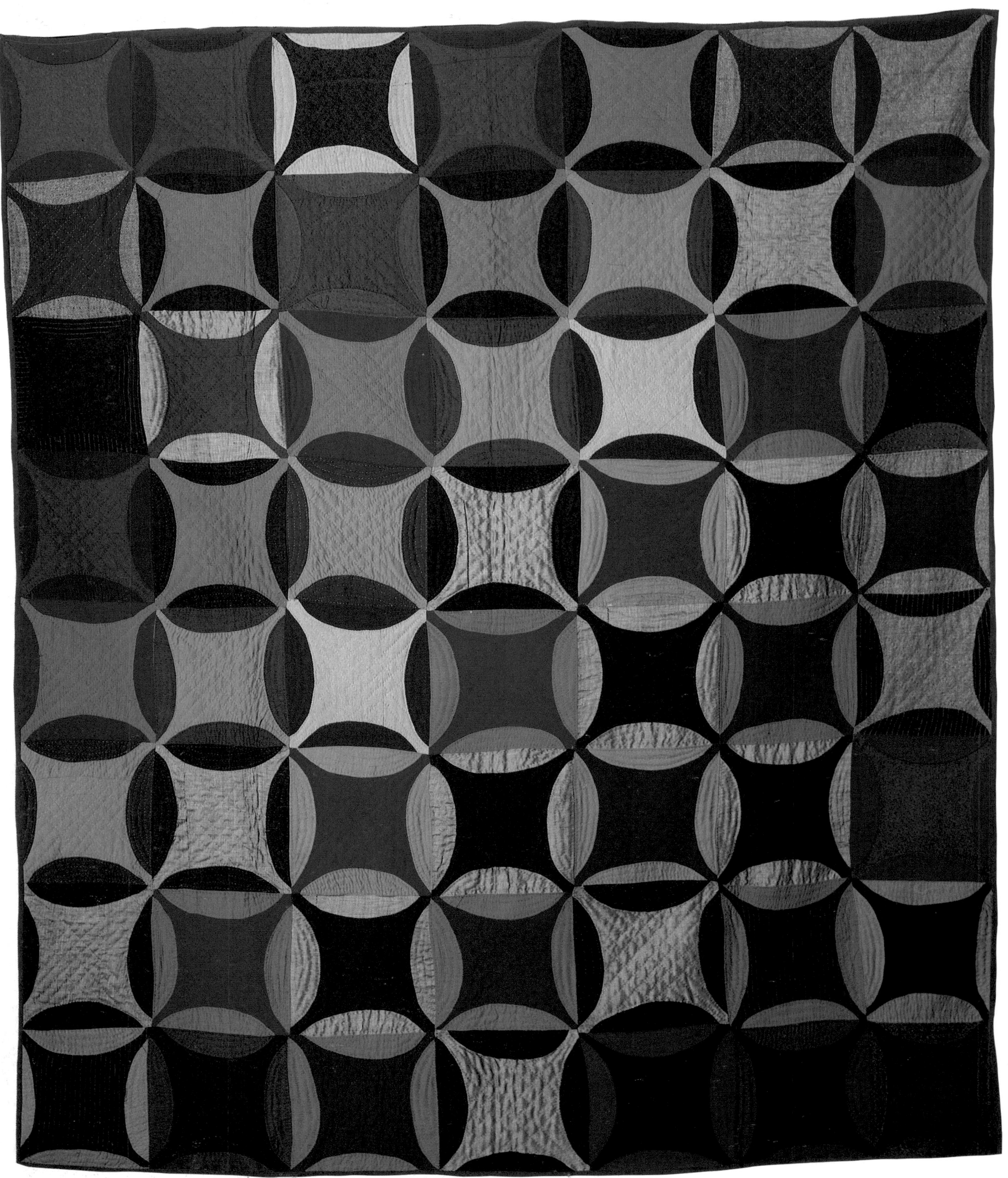

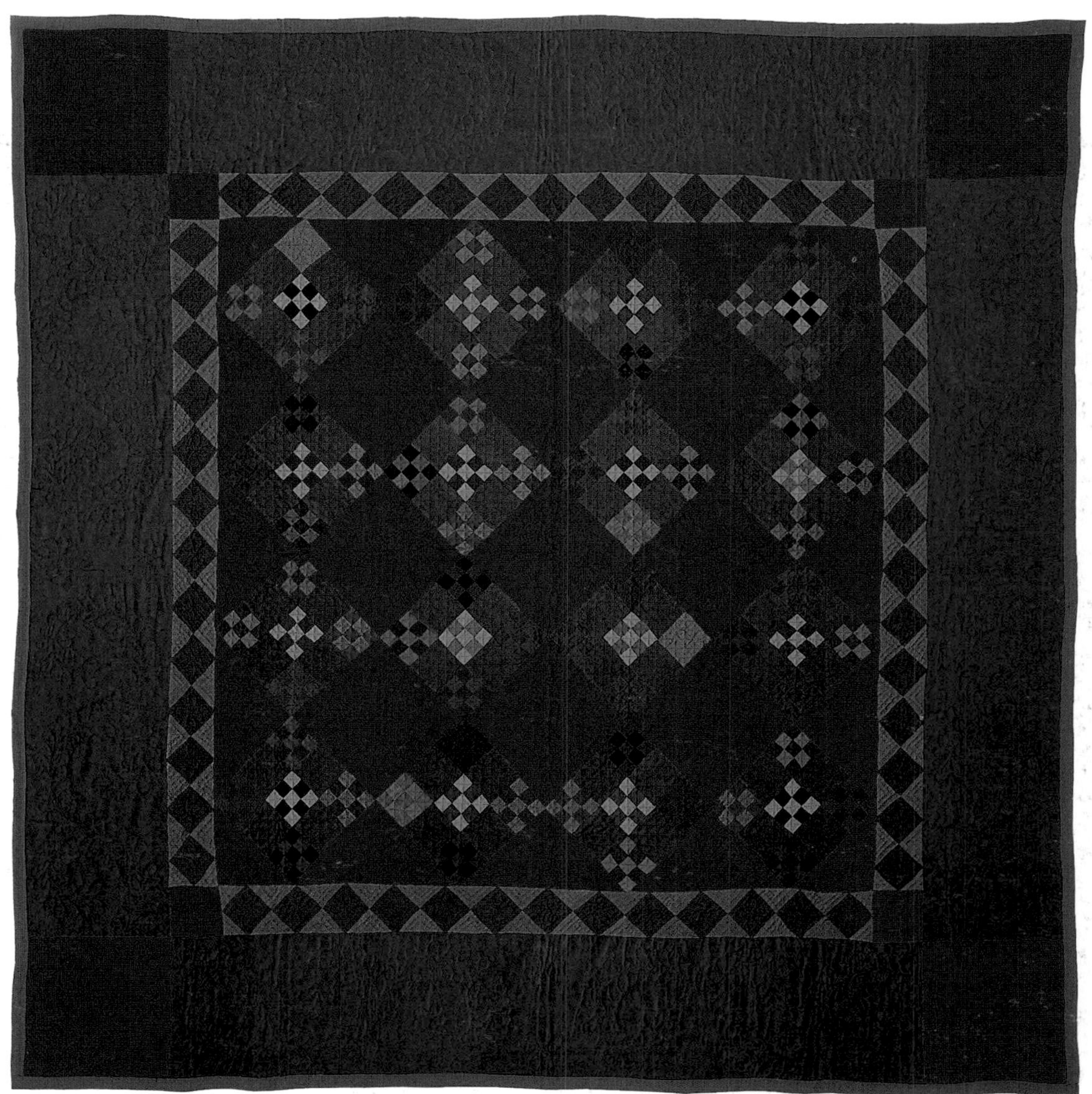

DOUBLE NINE-PATCH ▸

Unknown Amish artist. c. 1940. Lancaster County, Pennsylvania. Wools; hand pieced and quilted. 78 x 78 in. Collection of Douglas Tompkins.

Here, each one of the sixteen large diamonds in the central square is made up of nine small nine-patch blocks.

◂ ROB PETER TO PAY PAUL

Unknown Amish artist. c. 1880. Pennsylvania. Wools; hand pieced and quilted. 81 x 72 in. Collection of Ardis and Robert James.

This aptly named pattern is most commonly executed using only two colors. Here the quiltmaker has used a variety of brightly colored wools of different textures to create a constantly surprising composition.

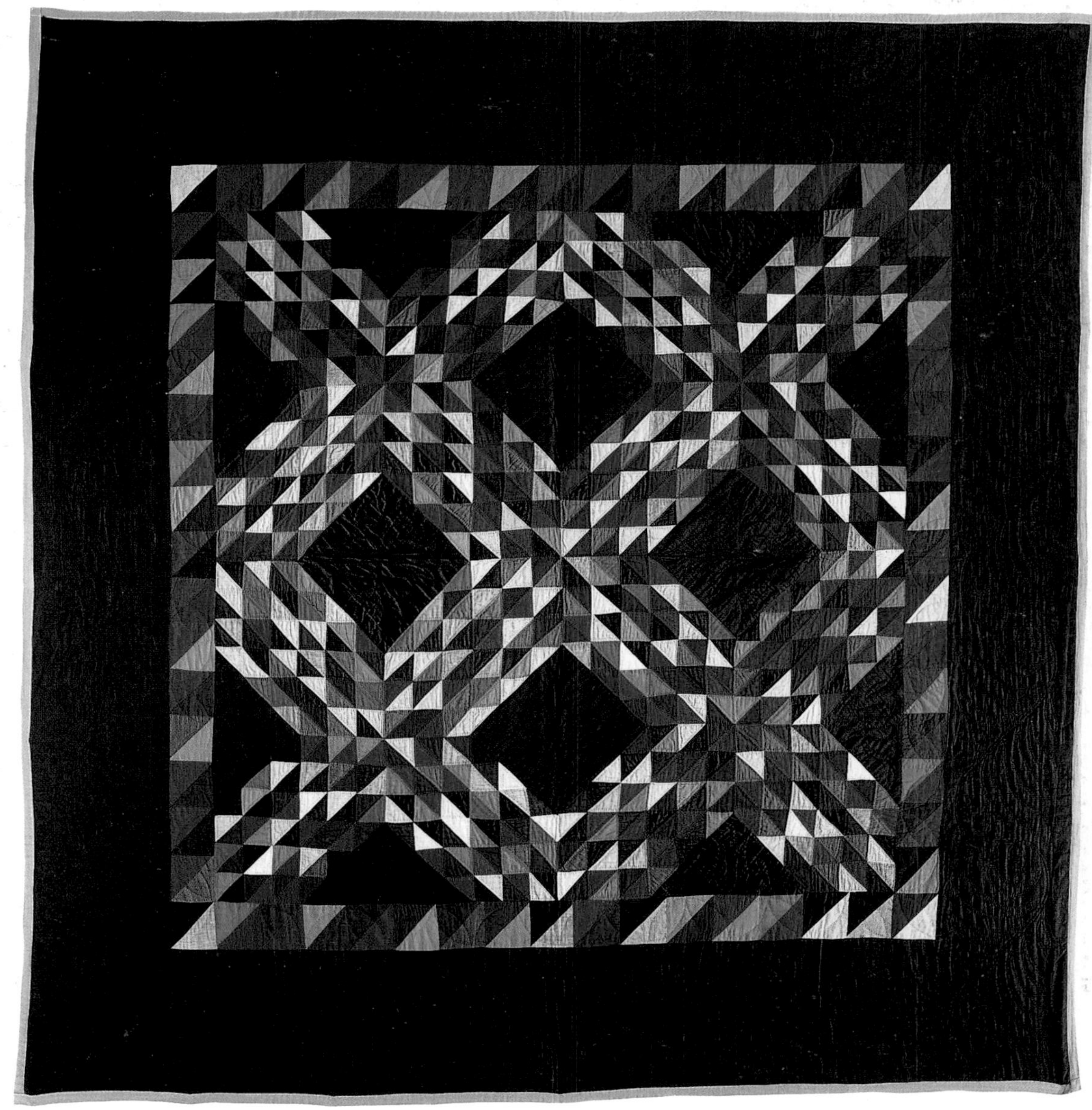

OCEAN WAVES ▸

Artist unknown. c. 1930. Holmes County, Ohio. Cottons; hand pieced and quilted. 79 x 79 in. Private collection.

Unlike most Amish quilts, which were carefully planned, the triangles of color in this Ocean Waves pattern were apparently organized intuitively. Equally random is the atypical sawtooth inner border.

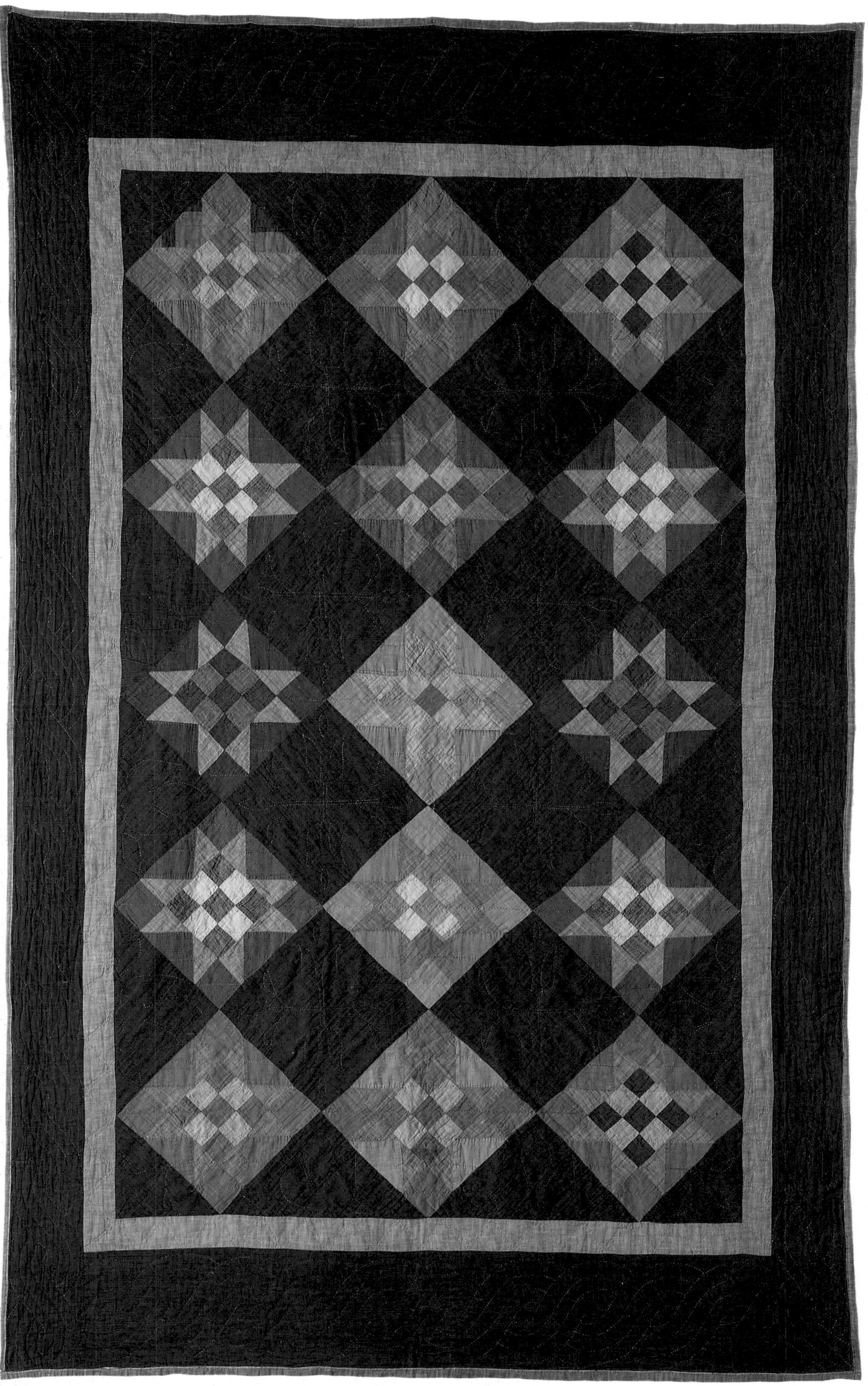

▲ **Nine-Patch in Star**

Artist unknown. c. 1930. Kansas. Cottons; hand pieced and quilted. Private collection.

The simple and relatively subdued midwestern quilt places a nine-patch at the center of a variable star pattern and plays a subtly varied palette of primary colors against a deeply saturated blue background.

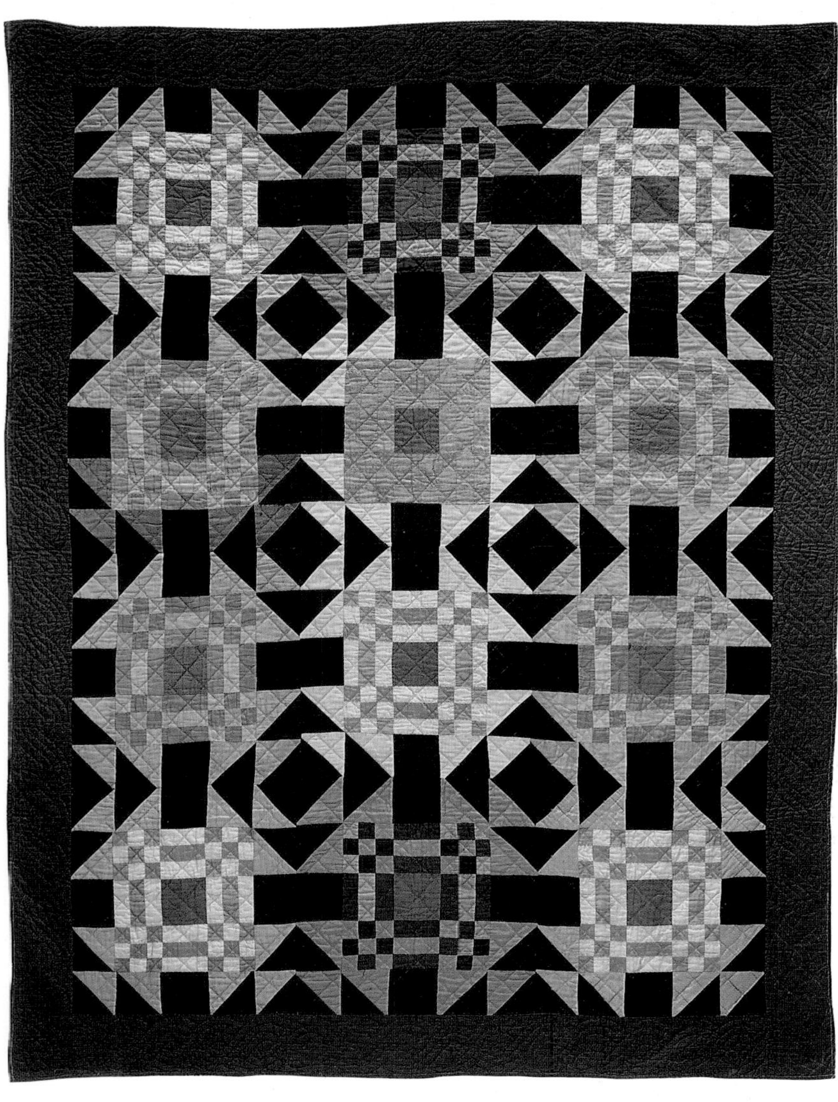

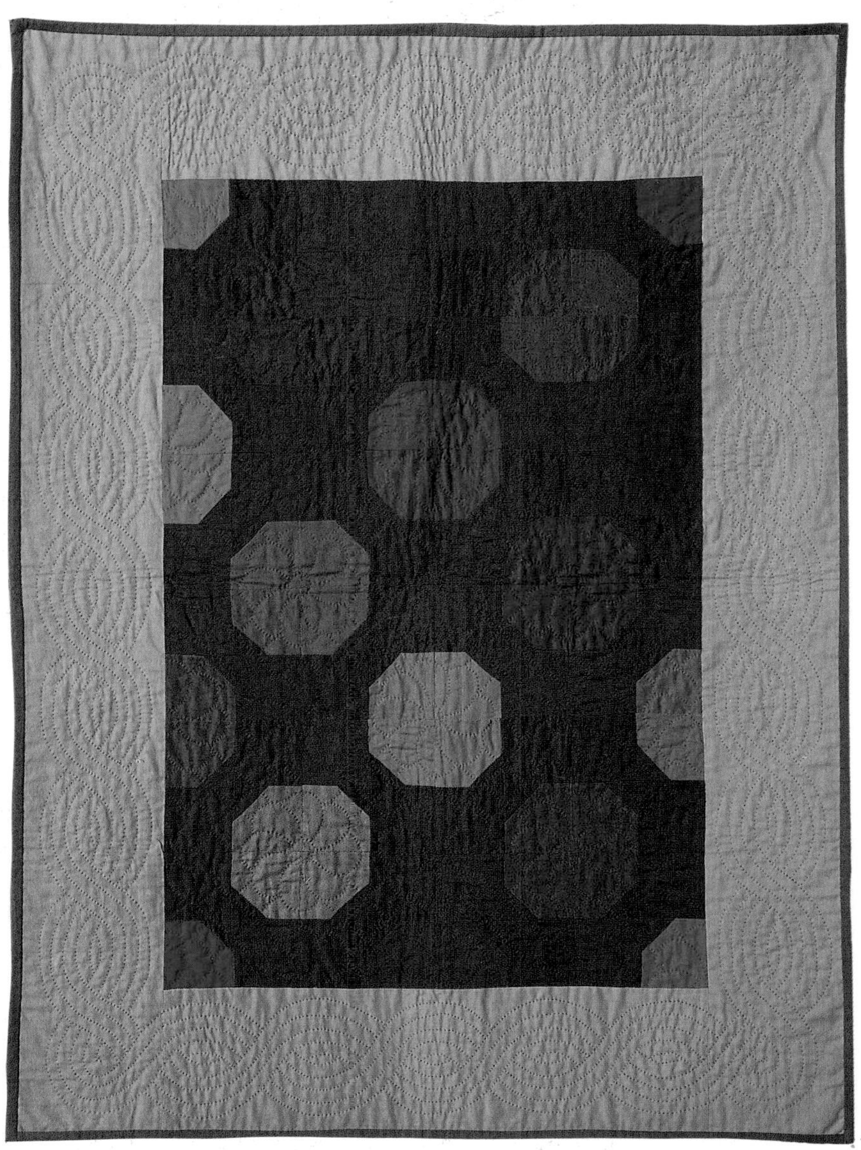

▲ Goose in the Pond

Lydia Schrock Yoder. c. 1920. Kansas. Cottons; hand pieced and quilted. 88 1/4 x 69 in. Indiana State Museum, Indianapolis, Indiana.

This corn-belt Amish quilt combines a subtly free palette with a large, boldly graphic pattern. Smaller units of nine-patches and bars, most of them in light pastel colors, are dominated by black diamonds in the square and vertically oriented rectangular pieces. The rich cocoa brown outer border provides a surprisingly coherent frame for the composition.

▲▶ Bow Tie Variation Crib Quilt

Lydia Miller. c. 1975–1978. Holmes County, Ohio. Cottons; hand pieced and quilted. 39 x 30 in. Collection of Ardis and Robert James.

In this variation on a simple but classic pattern, bow ties in two subtly different browns are set off by octagons of varying colors. The central composition is framed with a five-inch-wide curry yellow border and completed with fine overall quilting.

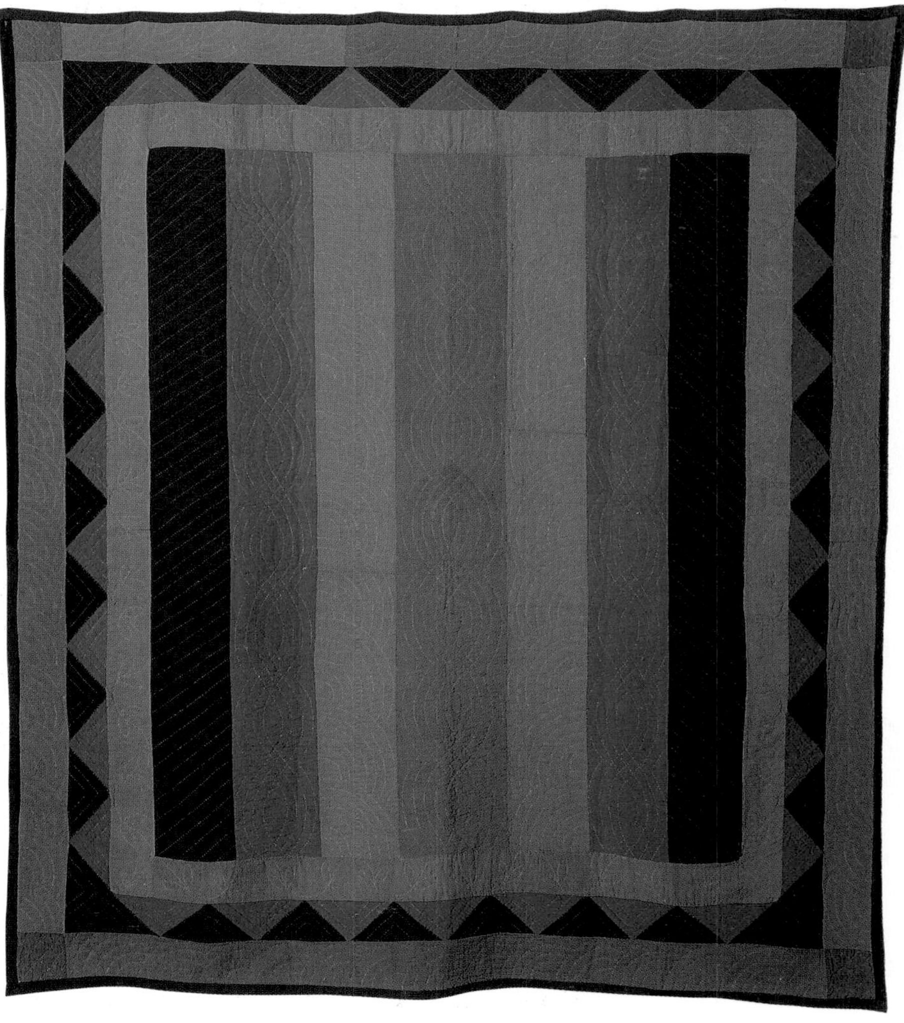

Bars ▶

Unknown Amish artist. c. 1920. Ontario, Canada. Wools; hand pieced and quilted. 73 x 67 in. Collection of Ardis and Robert James.

Although the better known Amish settlements are in Pennsylvania and the Midwest, there are also Amish communities in southern Ontario and other western Canadian provinces. This example of the simple Bars pattern combines hot orange and orange-yellow with cool blue and black to produce a vibrant effect.

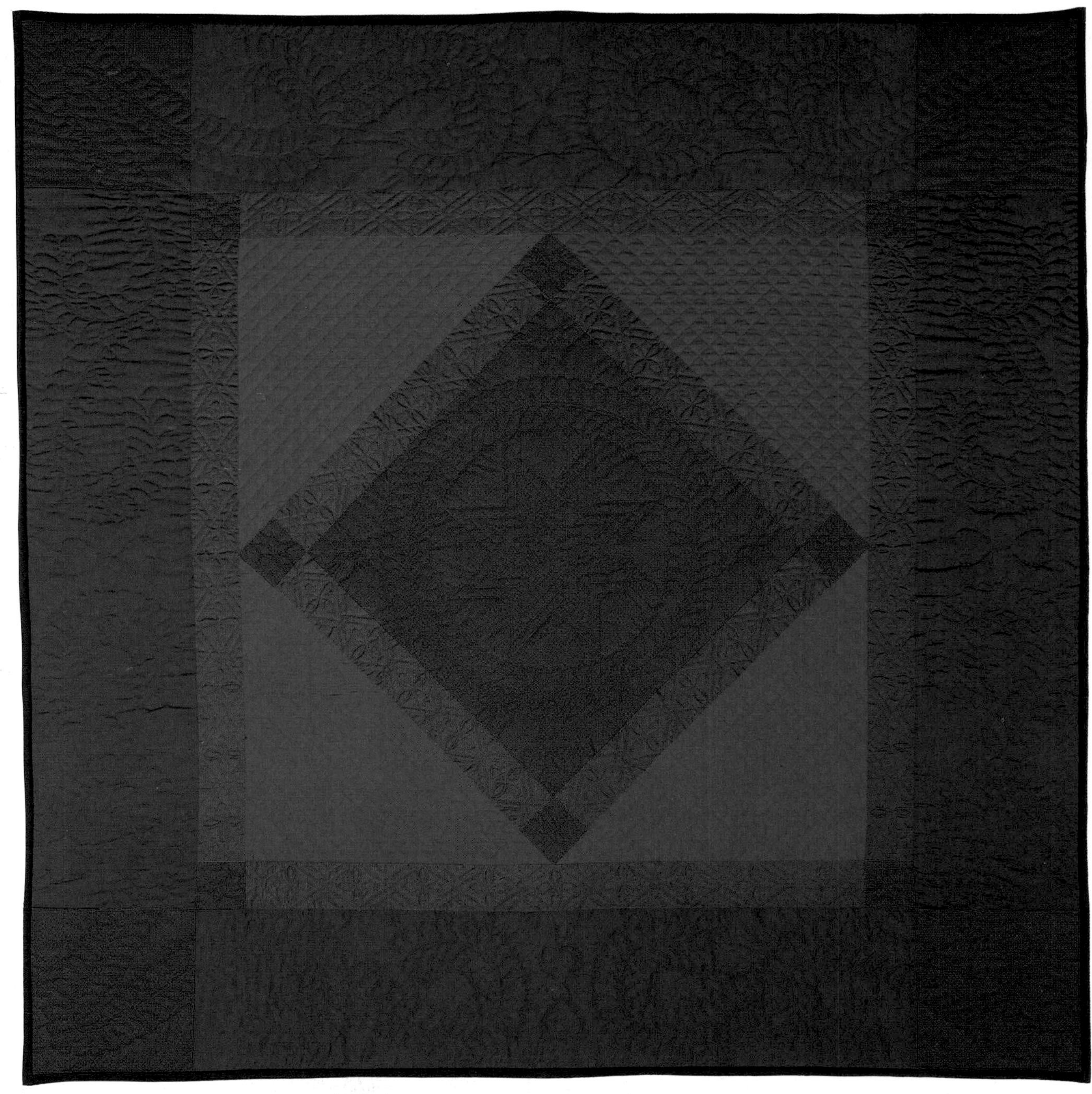

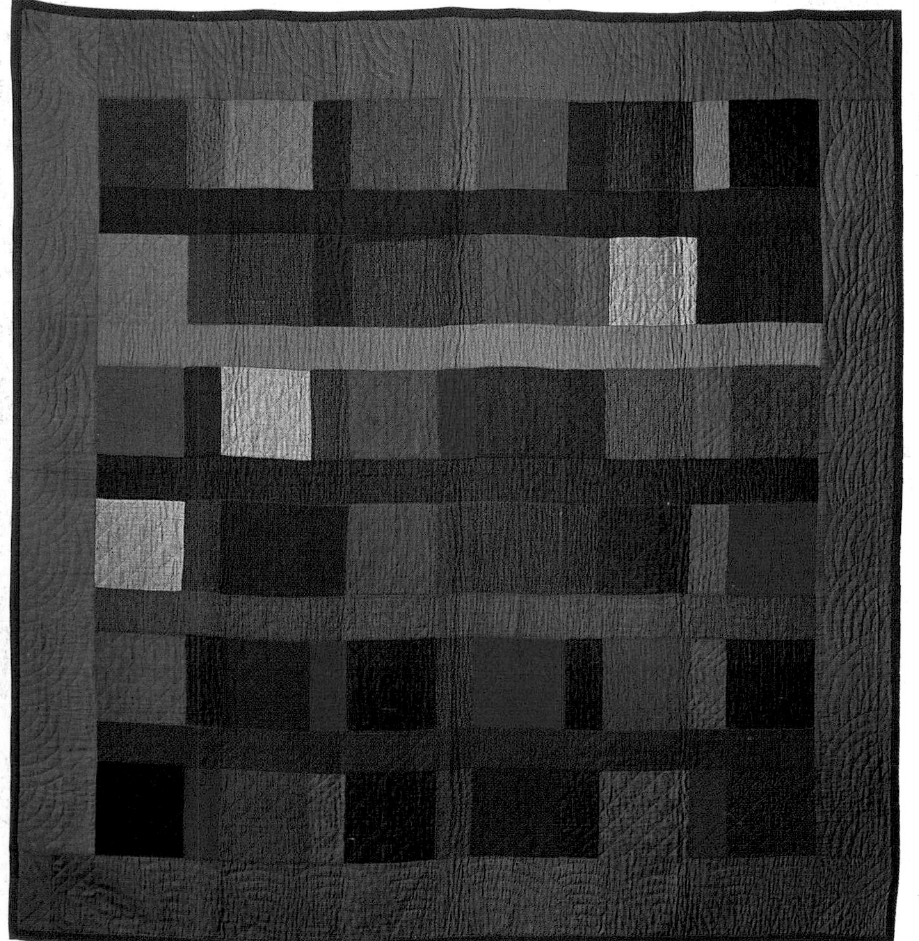

▲ Diamond in the Square (Detail ▶)

Daniel and Emma Stoltzfus. c.1982. Lancaster, Pennsylvania. Cotton/polyester blends; machine pieced and hand quilted. 88 x 88 in. Witte Museum, San Antonio, Texas.

The large expanses of solid color in this recent traditional Amish quilt are covered with intricate hand quilting. The central red diamond is quilted in a large concentric eight-pointed star that is set within a feather circle or crown. There are simple six-pointed stars within each corner of the diamond as well as within each of the corner blocks. The green strips are quilted in continuous double diamonds centered with four-petaled flowers.

◀ Blocks and Bars

Artist unknown. c. 1910. Mifflin County, Pennsylvania. Wools; hand pieced and quilted. 82 x 80 in. Private collection.

This unique quilt's pattern falls somewhere between the simpler Bars pattern common to Lancaster County, Pennsylvania, and the more complex Chinese Coins, often worked by Holmes County, Ohio, Amish quiltmakers.

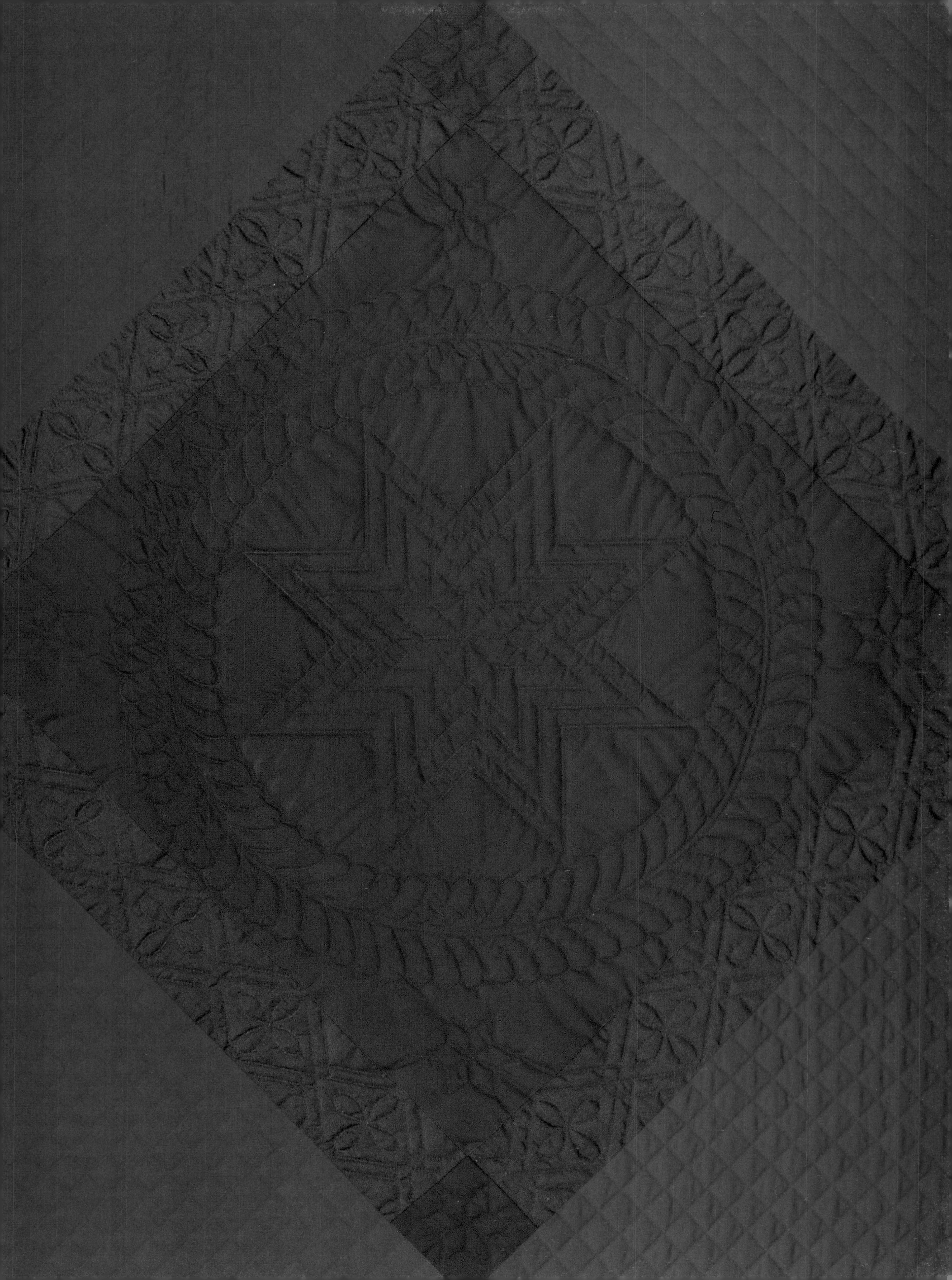

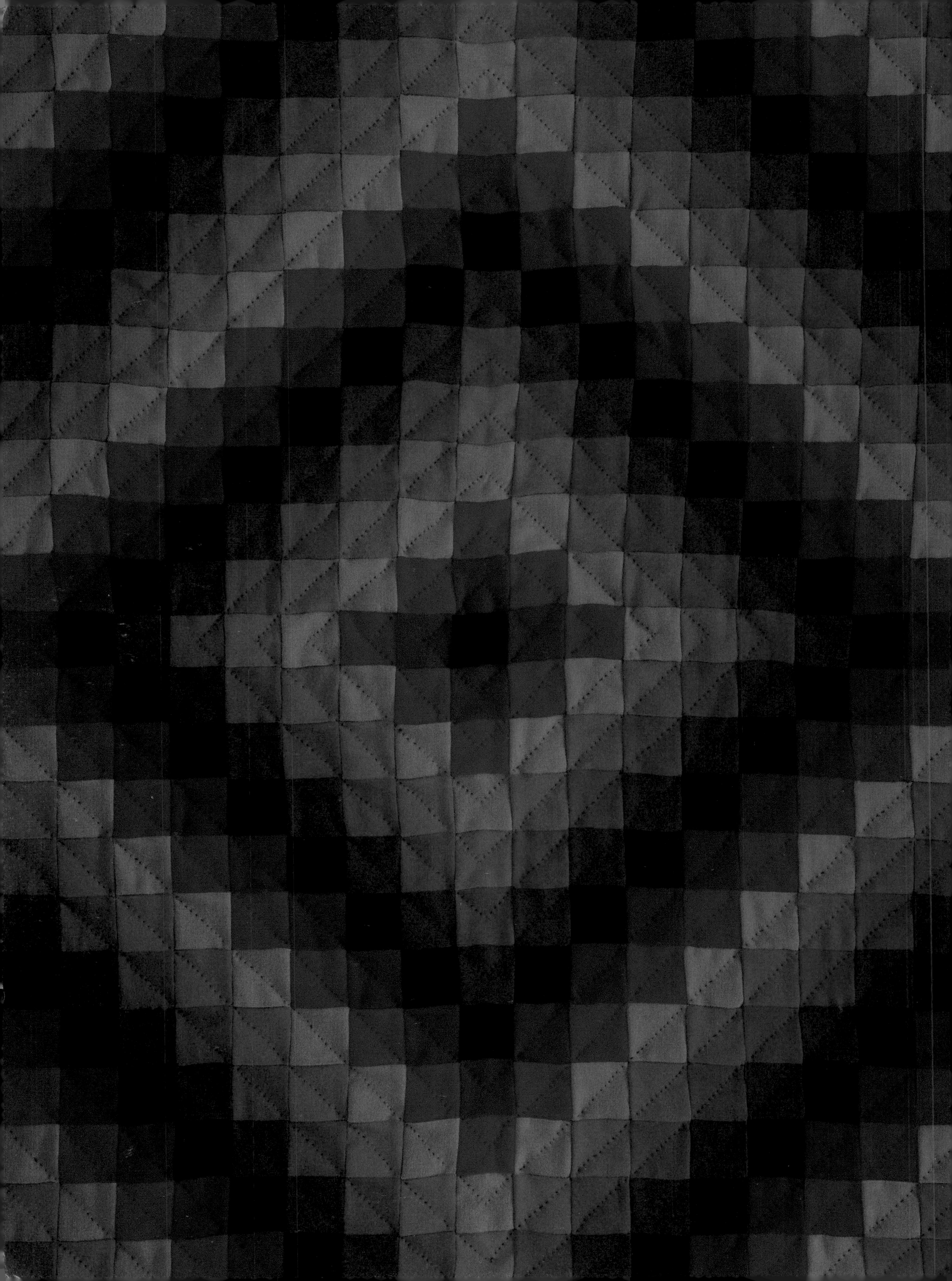

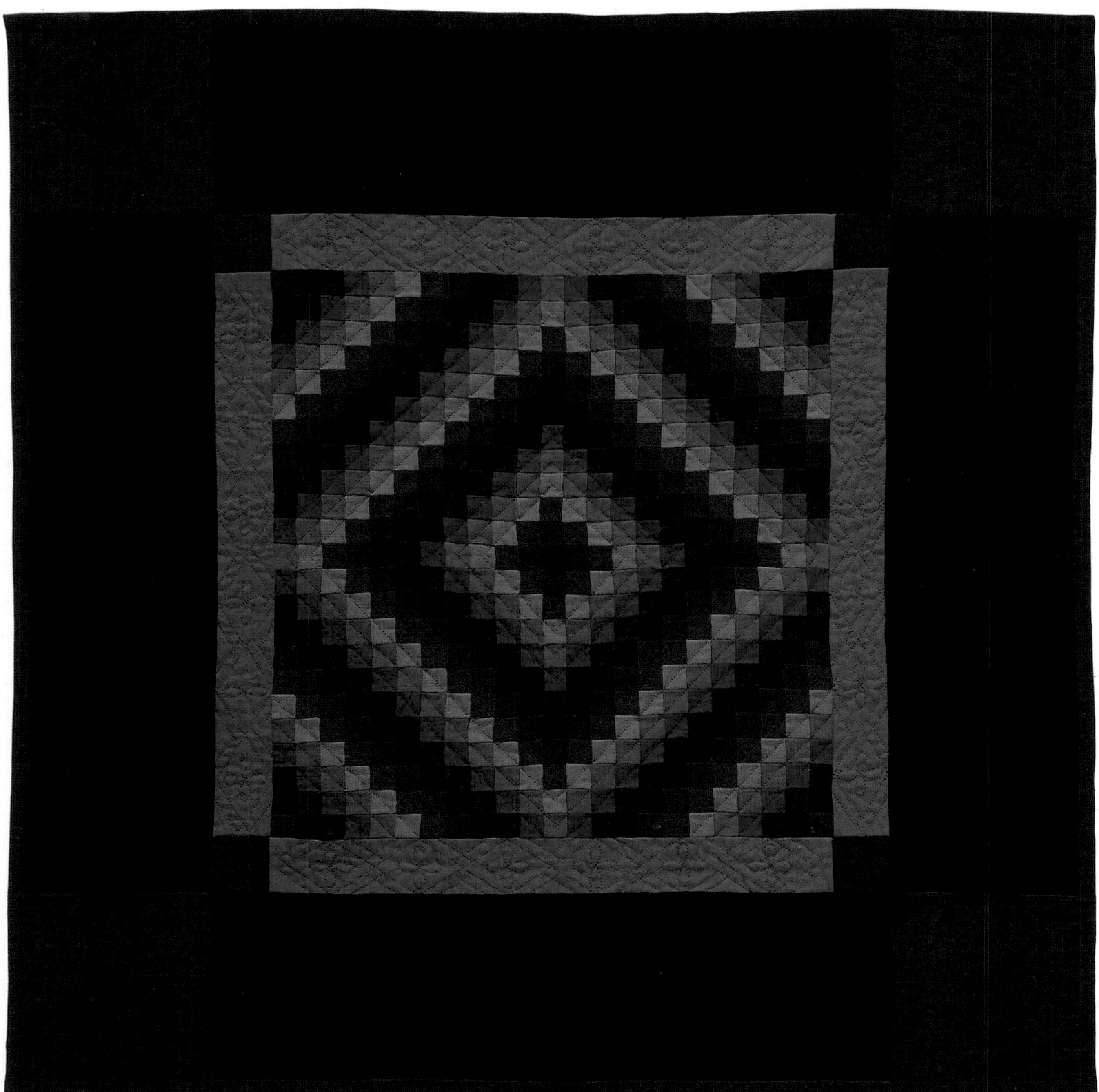

▲ TRIP AROUND THE WORLD (◄ DETAIL)

Mary Glick. 1992. Quarryville, Pennsylvania. Wools; hand pieced and quilted. 49 x 49 in. Collection of Linda Reuther.

Unlike many Amish women, Mary Glick did not take up quiltmaking until she was an adult. She creates wall hangings and bed quilts based on traditional Lancaster County Amish patterns and works in wool as well as cotton, making her an anachronism among contemporary Amish quiltmakers.

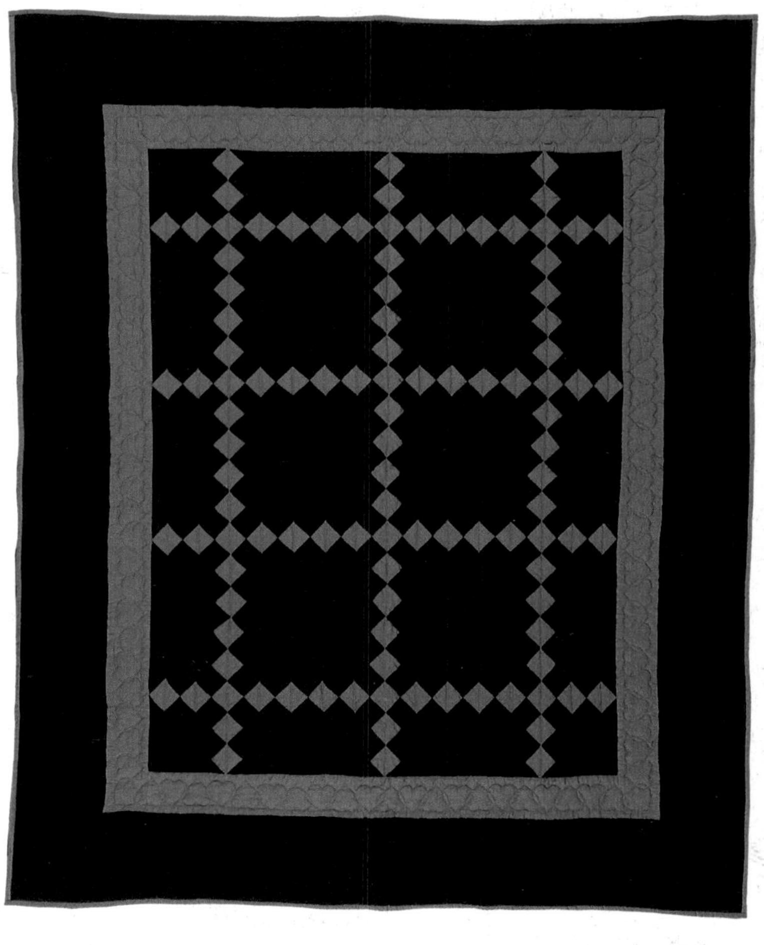

DOUBLE NINE-PATCH OR SINGLE IRISH CHAIN ►

Lena E. Miller. 1986. Preston, Minnesota. Cotton/polyester blends; hand pieced and quilted. 82 x 67 3/4 in. Minnesota Historical Society, Saint Paul.

The Double Nine-Patch and Single Irish Chain are constructed in exactly the same manner. The visual effect of the chain is created by using only two colors placed so that one color forms an unbroken line both horizontally and vertically. In this example, the intense blue chain glows brightly against the dark blue and black background.

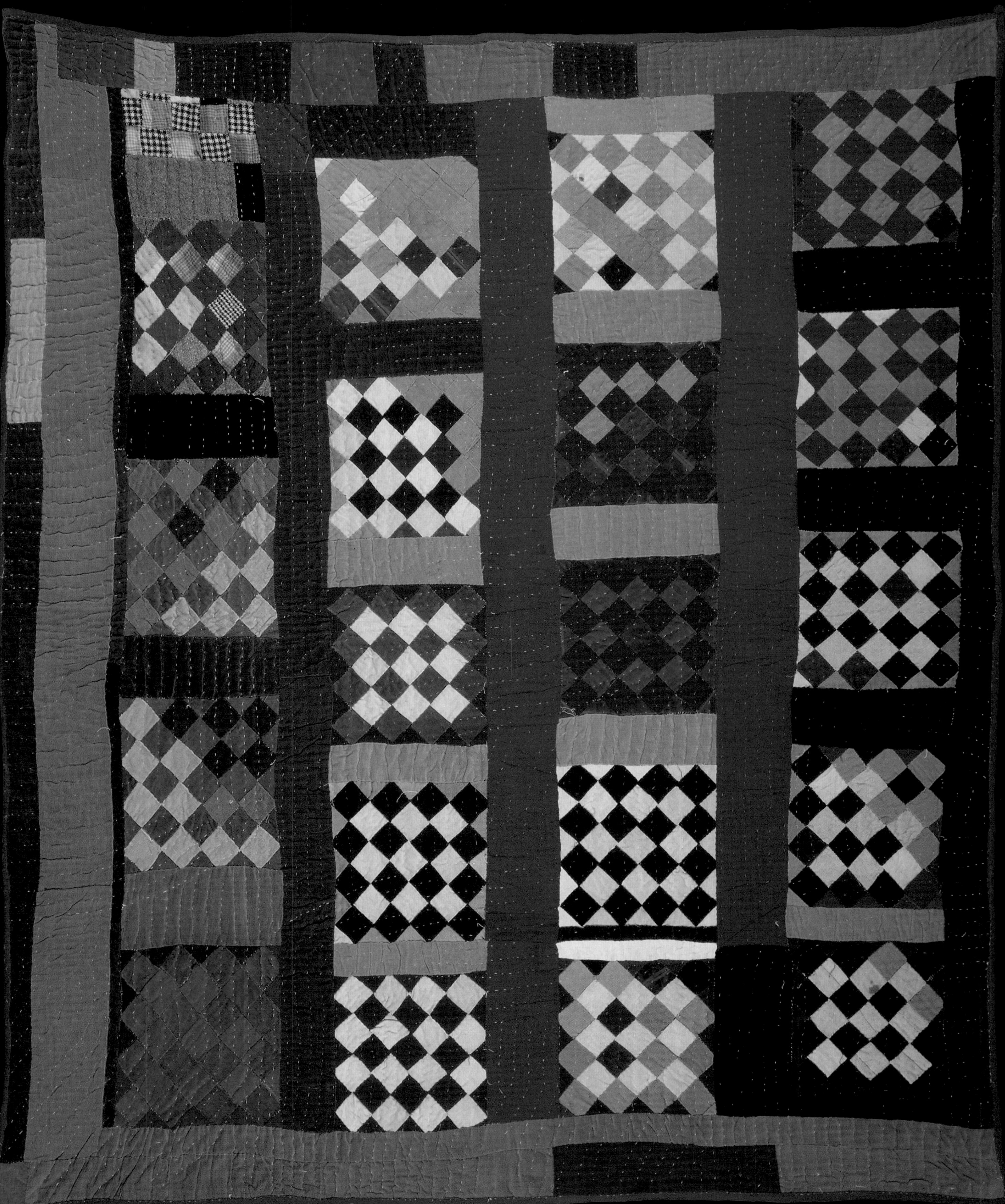

African-American Quilts

Quilts made by African-American women tell the rich and complex story of the black experience in America over the past two hundred years. Unlike Amish quiltmaking, which is defined by the unique religious separatism of the Amish people, African-American quiltmaking is not the work of a community of people working from a single, shared experience, but, rather, the work of many different people living in many different situations. African-American quilts naturally reflect, therefore, the wide variety of experiences in the lives of their creators. Efforts to stereotype African-American quiltmakers lose sight of the fact that the "American" element is central to their work. Blacks did not bring quiltmaking with them from Africa; rather, African-American quiltmaking has European-American origins which place it firmly within the mainstream of quilting history. A look at African-American quilts, is, therefore, a look at the imprint of the lives of black Americans on the traditional American quilt.

Slave women, many of whom were highly skilled needleworkers, sometimes sewed for their masters and are known to have made quilts that are indistinguishable from antebellum European-American quilts. Even the few surviving quilts made by slaves for their own use do not display a separate, parallel aesthetic, but instead follow traditional pieced or appliqué patterns. Like their white masters and peers, nineteenth-century African-American women, slave and free, made block-style pieced quilts, central medallion quilts, and block and overall appliqué quilts. By the late Victorian Age, African-Americans joined in the making of popular crazy quilts and other decorative silk pieced quilts. African-Americans have continued to make traditional pieced and appliqué quilts throughout this century and have developed distinctive approaches to the art that reflect the rich cultural heritage of black America.

Undoubtedly the best known of all African-American quilts, which also stand among the great treasures of American quilting, are the two powerful and evocative pictorial Bible quilts completed in 1886 and 1898 by Harriet Powers, an illiterate former slave from Athens, Georgia. The earlier quilt, now owned by the National Museum of History and Technology, Smithsonian Institution, and the later, currently in the collection of the Museum of Fine Arts in Boston, were carefully documented, respectively, by Jennie Smith, an Athens art teacher, and

◄ **Diamonds**

Lucinda Toomer. c. 1980. Macon, Georgia. Cottons; hand pieced and quilted. 80 x 68 in. Museum of American Folk Art, New York, gift of William A. Arnett.

Lucinda Toomer (1890–1983) was named a National Heritage Fellow by the National Endowment for the Arts, Folk Arts Program, in 1983. Her mother taught her to quilt when she was twelve, and she continued to make quilts throughout her long life.

an anonymous contemporary writer. Smith came upon the earlier quilt at an agricultural fair and immediately recognized its importance. She eventually was able to buy it from Powers, who was extremely reluctant to part with what she called "the darling child of my brain." Smith and the anonymous reporter recorded Mrs. Powers's own explanation of the various pictorial blocks in the two quilts, thereby providing a fascinating historical document of the quiltmaker's intentions and deep religious conviction.

Unfortunately, relatively few nineteenth- and early twentieth-century African-American quilts have been positively identified, and fewer still possess any substantial documentation. The Powers quilts are the leading exceptions to this rule and now stand alone. We may never know if Harriet Powers's quilts represent the tip of a lost iceberg of African-American pictorial quiltmaking, or are, indeed, the isolated and extraordinary anomalies they appear to be. Until recently the quilts of European-American women were dismissed as relatively unimportant domestic needlework; the quilts of African-American women were considered doubly unimportant (if in fact they were considered at all), and few can be documented with real certainty. The names, works, and possessions of slaves were rarely recorded by their owners, and even after emancipation and the Civil War, blacks were often overlooked by census and other official recordkeepers for a host of practical and political reasons. Although other primary sources such as diaries and narratives of abolitionists and former slave owners occasionally mention quilts and quiltmaking, too few reliable documents exist for any firmly grounded scholarly analysis. The historical evidence remains frustratingly sketchy and therefore open to theory, a ground upon which conservative scholars tread lightly and with trepidation, waiting and searching for more conclusive information.

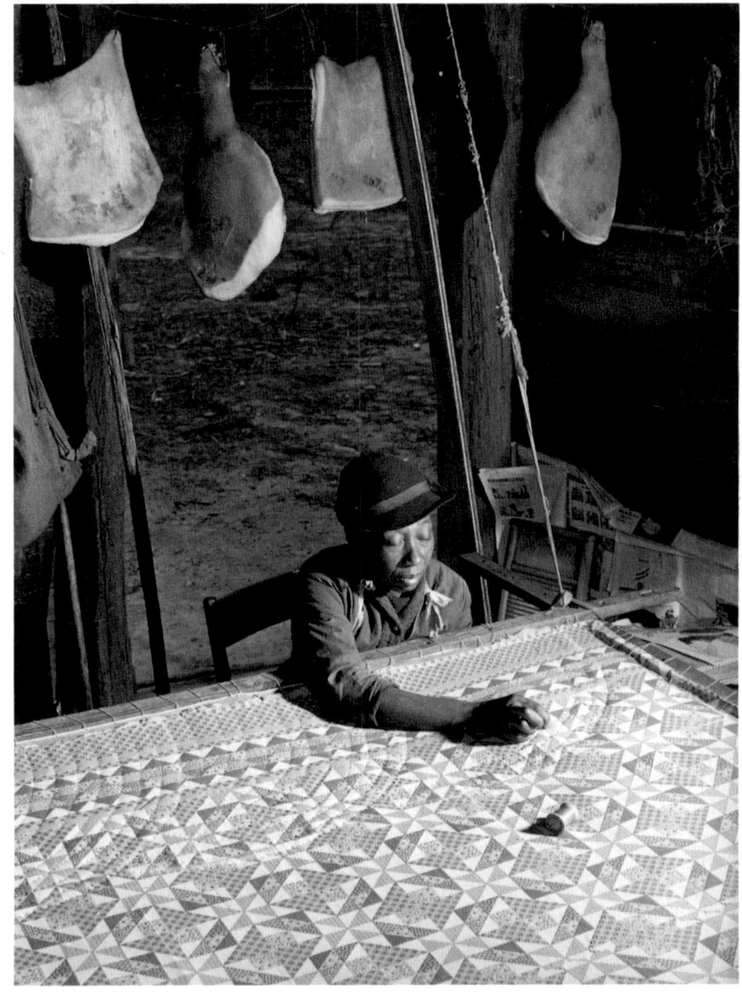

◄ *This intent quilter was photographed at work in a smokehouse near Hinesville, Georgia, in April 1941. Her carefully pieced geometric quilt, which includes a double pinwheel, is entirely regular in design. Courtesy of the Farm Security Administration Collection, Prints and Photographs division, Library of Congress.*

▼ *Women and children pose on a washday in front of their home near Thomasville, Georgia, in this c. 1890 photograph. An appliquéd block-style quilt, presumably made by one of the women, is seen at left. Collection of the Hargrett Rare Book and Manuscript Library, University of Georgia Libraries.*

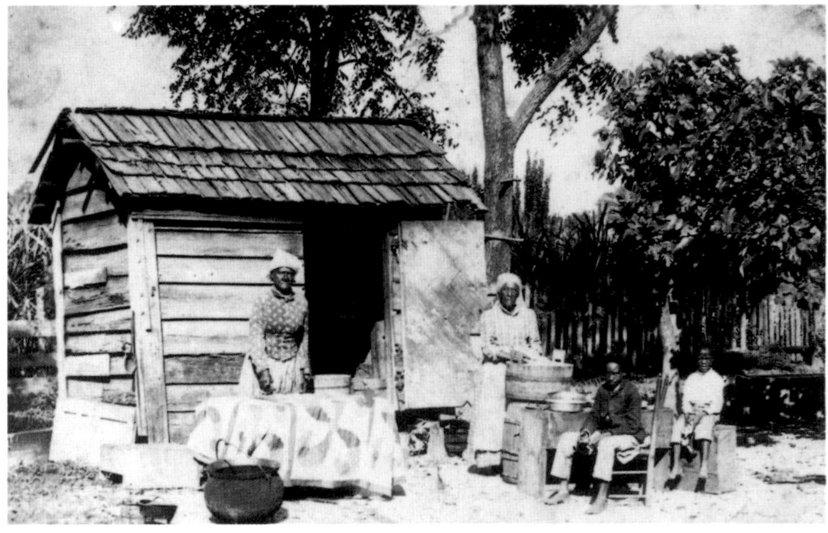

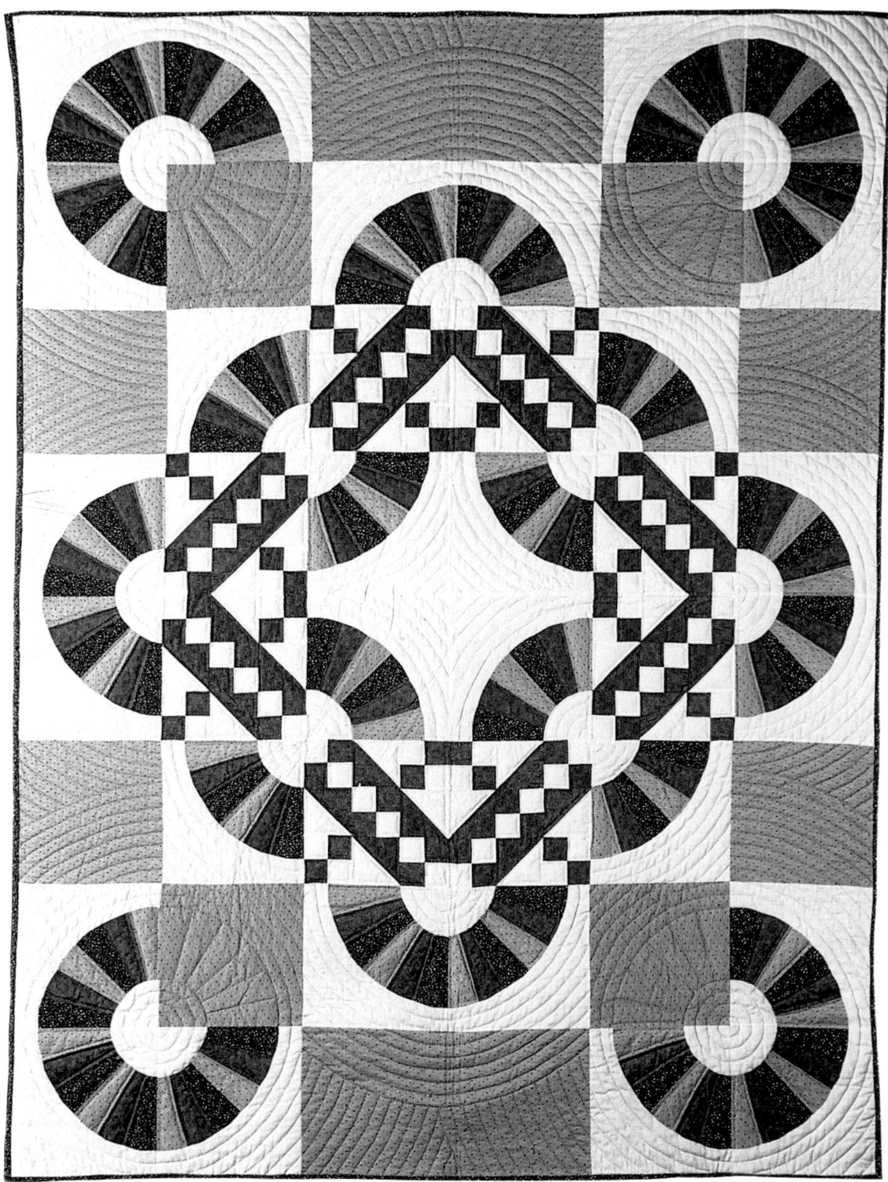

Underground Railroad and Grandmother's Fan ▶

Myla Perkins. 1984. Detroit, Michigan. Cotton/polyester blends; hand pieced and quilted. 90 x 69 in. Collection of the artist.

The Underground Railroad pattern, originally called Jacob's Ladder, was renamed by some women with abolitionist sympathies before the Civil War. The subdued palette of this quilt gives it a somber and powerfully dignified feel.

The civil rights movement of the 1960s stimulated increased interest in African-American culture among whites and blacks alike, and as a result much more attention has been paid to African-American quilts made since that time. The civil rights movement also empowered African-American quiltmakers by helping to release them from the pressure to conform to white society's norms and expectations and by encouraging them to seek their own history. Like artists and craftspeople working in other media, many African-American quilters began to search for culturally distinct ways to express themselves. In addition, historians and collectors began to seek out and embolden previously neglected quilters and traditions, eventually bringing them and their work to the attention of a marketplace suddenly keenly interested in folk art and ethnic diversity. The marketplace has, unfortunately, often responded by distorting and oversimplifying African-American quilting, emphasizing certain types of work perceived as peculiar to black quilters, while overlooking other types of African-American quilting.

Among later twentieth-century quilts made by African-Americans, the best-known and perhaps most misunderstood form is the strip quilt. Pieces of material are sewn together into long narrow strips which are then joined to form the quilt top. The strips are often made up of fabric pieces of different sizes, colors, and patterns, and usually run the full length or width of the textile. The craftsmanship of strip quilters is often casual and improvisatory; instead of using paper templates to guide the cutting of material into pieces of exactly the same size, strip quilters often cut the cloth directly, by eye, a method that results in slight variations from piece to piece. Strip quilts are typically full of asymmetrical patterns and wild color rhythms, and they can be visually refreshing and exciting to eyes that are used to seeing the geometric regularity and balanced color of European-American pieced quilts.

Strip quilts are now made by African-Americans throughout the Southeast. Lower class women who often cannot afford to buy much new fabric and must use whatever is available in the household find that strip quilts are particularly suited to their needs. Strip quilts have received much attention and have been the subject of several museum exhibitions and publica-

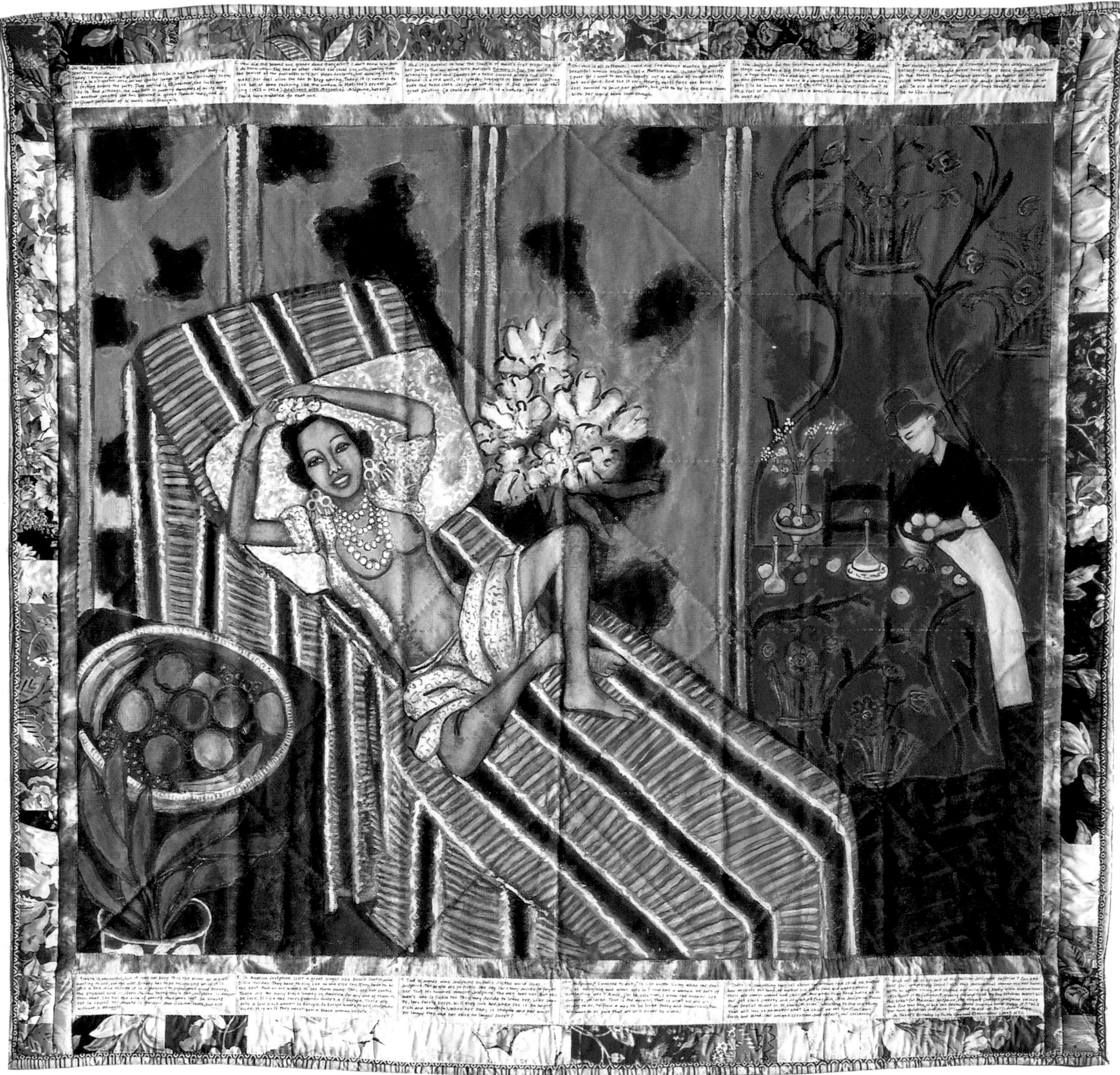

▲ **Jo Baker's Birthday**

Faith Ringgold. 1993. New York, New York. Acrylic on canvas, cotton frame; hand pieced and quilted. 72 x 72 in. St. Louis Museum of Art.
The black American vaudeville star Josephine Baker was the toast of Paris in the 1920s, where her openly sexual dancing and costumes created a sensation. This portrait of Baker was commissioned by the St. Louis Museum of Art.

tions in recent years. They have also become very popular among folk art collectors. However, historical precedents of this now common tradition are as hard to trace as those of the earliest African-American quilts. The first firmly documented examples of the style, which are few and far between, date from the 1920s and 1930s; there are no known direct nineteenth-century antecedents of the style.

While a number of scholars have noted similarities between woven West African textiles and African-American strip quilting, the evidence is purely visual and therefore must remain speculative and inconclusive. The relationship, while provocative, sometimes striking, and always intriguing, might conceivably be as coincidental as the connection between abstract nineteenth-century geometric quilts and modern painting. In other words, just because African-American strip quilts and West African textiles sometimes look similar, it does not necessarily follow that they share similar aesthetic roots. In fact, many strip quilts that could be mistaken for African-American work have been made by white women who typically are of the same lower economic class as some black strip quilters, and who are also seeking to make functional quilts from materials at hand. It appears the strip quilt may have more to do with class than it does with race. Ironically, like a self-fulfilling prophecy, the strip quilt style has been embraced by many contemporary black quilters who, in looking for their cultural roots, have learned from "experts" that strip quilting represents the true African-American quilting style; in fact, strip quilting represents just one of many traditions.

The African roots of other African-American folk arts, such as blues, seagrass basketry, and stoneware pottery, have been clearly documented. However, quilting differs from these other crafts in one significant respect. African-Americans learned the craft of quilting in America; Africa had no parallel quilting tradition that could directly impact on the work of slave quilters and their progeny. Indeed, American quilting was brought to the West African republic of Liberia in the early nineteenth century by freed slaves from America. The idea was passed down to their descendants, and a strong and decidedly mainstream American quilting tradition continues to this day in Liberia, a fact that clearly refutes any notion of underlying African cultural influence. Nothing about these Liberian quilts is demonstrably African or even African-American, except for the racial and cultural heritage of their makers.

Whatever their sources, we can say with real certainty that late twentieth-century African-American strip quilts, with their asymmetry and unusual color and pattern combinations, do proceed from a radically different aesthetic sensibility than most European-American quilts. Strip quilting represents an alternative to the block-style method of organizing and piecing together a quilt top. The make-do ease of organizing material in strips lends itself to utilitarian scrap piecing and explains the popularity of the technique among poorer women. However, strip piecing can also be rigorously organized. It has been adopted and explored to very different effect by such masterful art quilters as Nancy Crow and Michael James. Both James and Crow are colorists interested in working with many gradations of color in a single quilt; Crow once stated that her artistic goal was to put as many colors as possible in a single quilt. James has expressed great interest in contemporary African-American strip quilting, and Crow has been strongly influenced in recent years by the work of the recently discovered African-American strip quilter Anna Williams. Among Crow's most recent works are series of asymmetrical quilts made from solid-colored, often hand-dyed fabric and based on the One-Patch and Bowtie patterns.

Another popular idiom among contemporary African-American quilters is the pictorial story quilt. Harriet Powers's Bible quilts remain the supreme examples of this form in all of American quilting, but many other outstanding examples have been made over the past one hundred years. Recently, quilters from backgrounds as diverse as those of Faith Ringgold, Yvonne Wells, and Sarah Mary Taylor have expanded the genre, creating quilts based on historical and contemporary events, personal experiences and observations, dreams and visions, religious texts, and even cartoon characters. Faith Ringgold, who grew up in Harlem, is one of the best

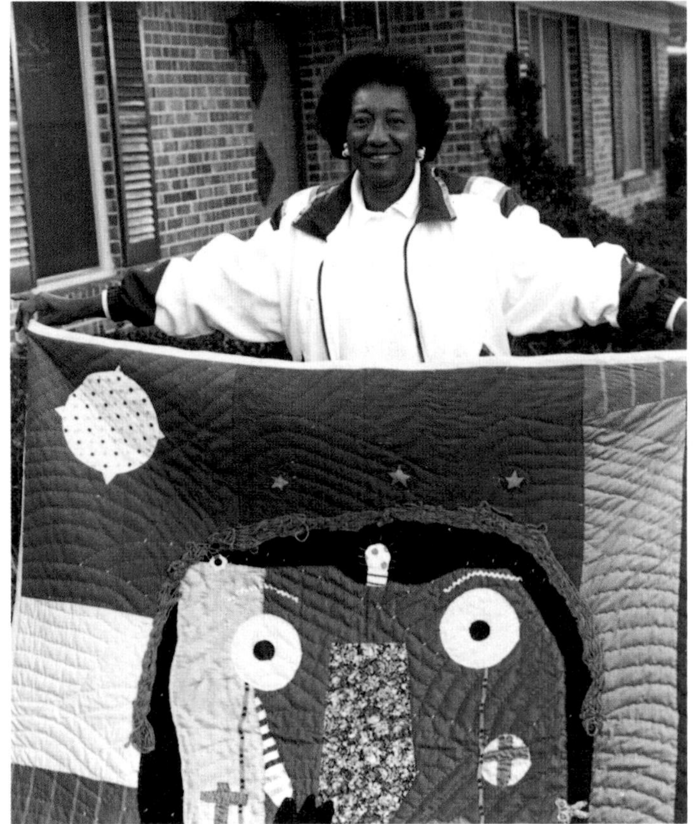

◀ *Yvonne Wells of Tuscaloosa, Alabama, is a former school teacher and a self-taught quilt artist. She poses here with her quilt "Me Masked."*

known of all art quilters. Ringgold was well known for her paintings, dolls, and masks before she began making quilts in the early 1980s. Her textile work, which combines painting and quilting to produce resonant images of black life, is represented in the collections of a number of major American museums, including the Metropolitan Museum of Art in New York, the St. Louis Art Museum, and the High Museum in Atlanta. Ringgold often includes African fabrics in her quilts, bordering her pictures of African-American life with pieces of cloth imported from her ancestral homeland. Other black art quilters such as Carole Harris, Michael Cummings, and Carole Yvette Lyles also use African-made cloth and build abstract designs with the richly patterned textiles.

Southern folk artists Yvonne Wells, a former schoolteacher, and Sarah Mary Taylor, a former field worker and domestic whose mother was also a quilter, sometimes take a more whimsical approach to their compositions. Wells, for example, has produced delightful Mickey and Minnie Mouse quilts that look wonderfully unlike Disney, and Taylor often fills her quilts with repeated images of prancing cats, dogs, watermelon slices, Coke bottles or other amusing figural designs. Taylor explains that the boldly contrasting colors typical of her work are personal and intuitive choices: "I match colors for my quilt covers like I match the clothes I wear. If I wear a black dress, I'd want red shoes and a red bag. If I was going to wear white, I'd prefer black shoes and a black bag." Both Taylor and Wells complement their fanciful compositions with serious and deeply felt work and have made many expressive quilts based on religious or civil rights themes.

Contemporary African-American quilters have often felt themselves either left out of the mainstream of American quilting as represented in the popular media or lumped stereotypically into a single, monolithic style. Two organizations have recently been formed to help remedy this situation by networking quilters and bringing enlightened attention to the breadth of their work as well as to historic quilts by black craftspeople. The Women of Color Quilter's Network, founded in 1985 by quiltmaker Dr. Carolyn Mazloomi of Cincinnati, has over one thousand members worldwide, publishes a widely read newsletter, and has sponsored several important exhibitions, including *Spirit of the Cloth*, which features a diverse range of works by twenty network members. Mazloomi, an aerospace engineer and self-taught quilter, says she started the network because she was angered by people who were taking advantage of unsuspecting black quilters and was also frustrated with feeling alone in her struggle. She describes the all too prevalent nature of the problem: "Traveling in the South, I'd meet African-American women quilters who literally were being robbed. They didn't understand the value of their work and would sell their quilts for $20 or $30. . . . The first ad I placed put me in contact with six other quiltmakers. At the time, we thought we were the only ones." The network is inclusive by definition, embracing folk artists and academically trained quilters, rural and urban women (and, despite its name, men), skilled and unskilled quilters alike. The National Association of African-American Quilters was coordinated by Baltimore quiltmaker Barbara Pietila in 1993 and is aimed at keeping knowledge about quiltmaking alive in the African-American community. To this end, the group's motto and admonition to its members is "Each One, Teach One." The organization's four-fold mission is: 1) To organize African-American quilters nationwide; 2) To support activities which promote the art of African-American quilts and quilters; 3) To preserve African-American quilts through conservation, documentation, and the establishment of an African-American quilt library for research and education; and 4) To keep the art of quilting alive in the African-American community by teaching, exhibiting, and quilting. Both the WCQN and the NAAAQ have done a great deal to correct the public's perception of African-American quilting. This has been a sometimes daunting task and would not have been achieved without the efforts of people like historian Cuesta Benberry, whose authoritative research, writings, exhibitions, and lectures have tried to show the continuing richness, complexity, and diversity of African-American work and its intimate relationship with the history of America and her quilting traditions.

The range and importance of African-American quiltmaking, both historic and contemporary, has yet to be fully understood or appreciated. While some types of African-American quilts are currently fashionable, other types are neglected because they do not seem to fit the popular and often stereotypical conceptions of African-

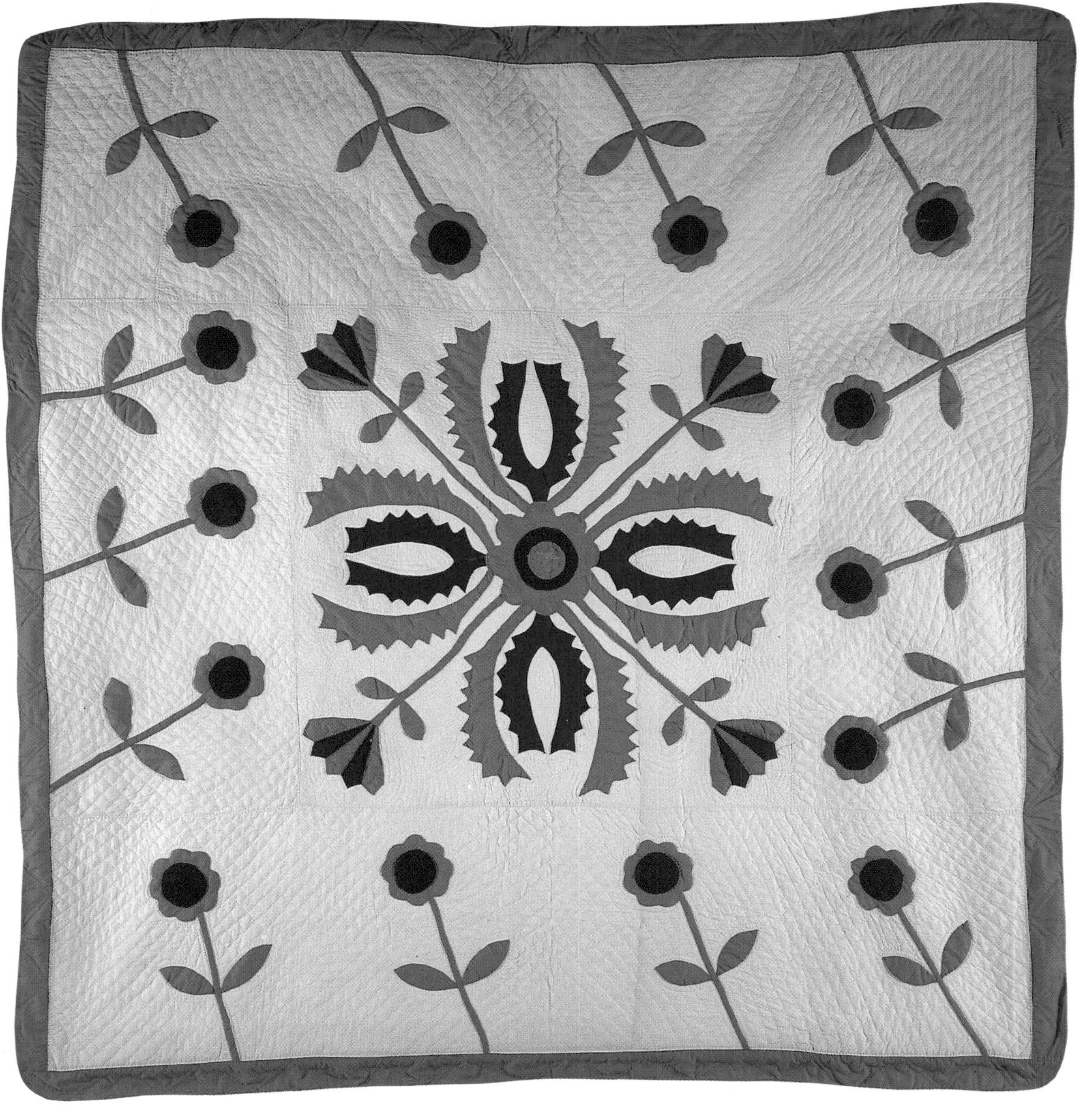

TULIPS ▸

Members of the Arthington Women's Self-Help Quilting Club. 1993. Arthington, Liberia, Africa. Cottons; hand appliquéd and quilted. 96 x 88 in. Collection of Kathleen Bishop.

In the 1820s, an abolitionist group called the American Colonization Society began repariating slaves to Liberia. Among the earliest settlers were women who had learned the craft of quiltmaking in the United States. Today their descendants continue to make quilts in the American style.

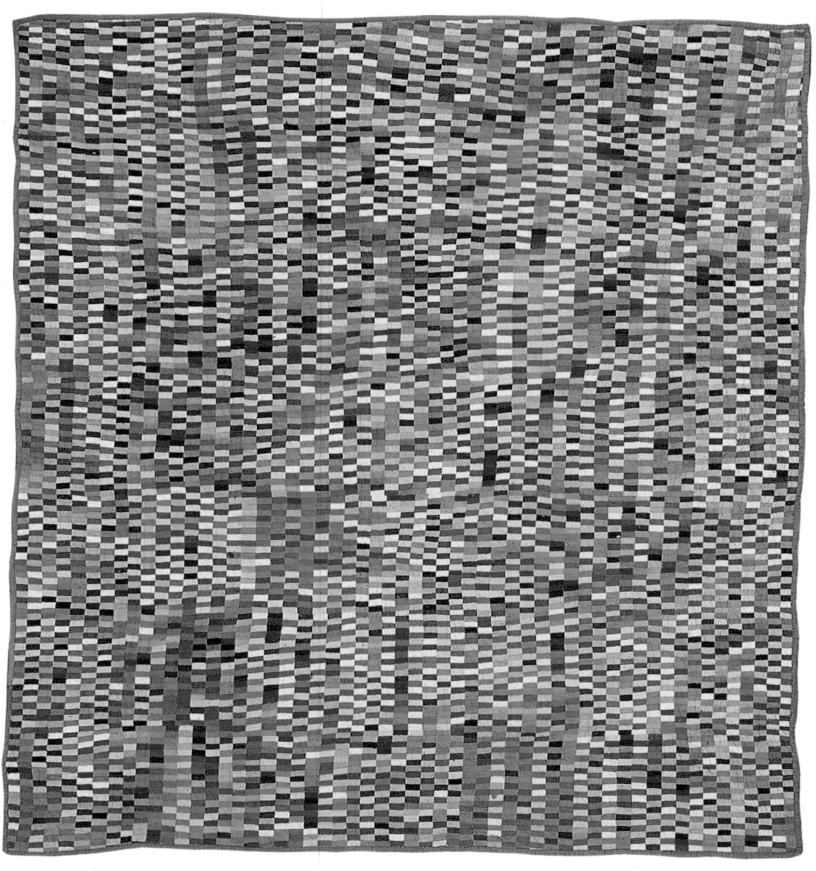

American work. Many researchers and groups are now working to correct the myths. Meanwhile, African-Americans continue to make quilts that reflect their own traditions, history, and culture. And these quilts are, of course, as diverse, imaginative, and individual as the people who create them.

PIECED STRIPS ▶

Josephine Elizabeth Water. c. 1930. Snow Hill, Maryland. Hand-pieced cottons. 83 x 90 in. M. Finkel and Daughter, Philadelphia, Pennsylvania.

Josephine Water used over 8,000 pieces to make up this vibrant quilt. The slight irregularities and the many fortuitous color alignments create a dazzling, active surface that leaves the eye no place to rest.

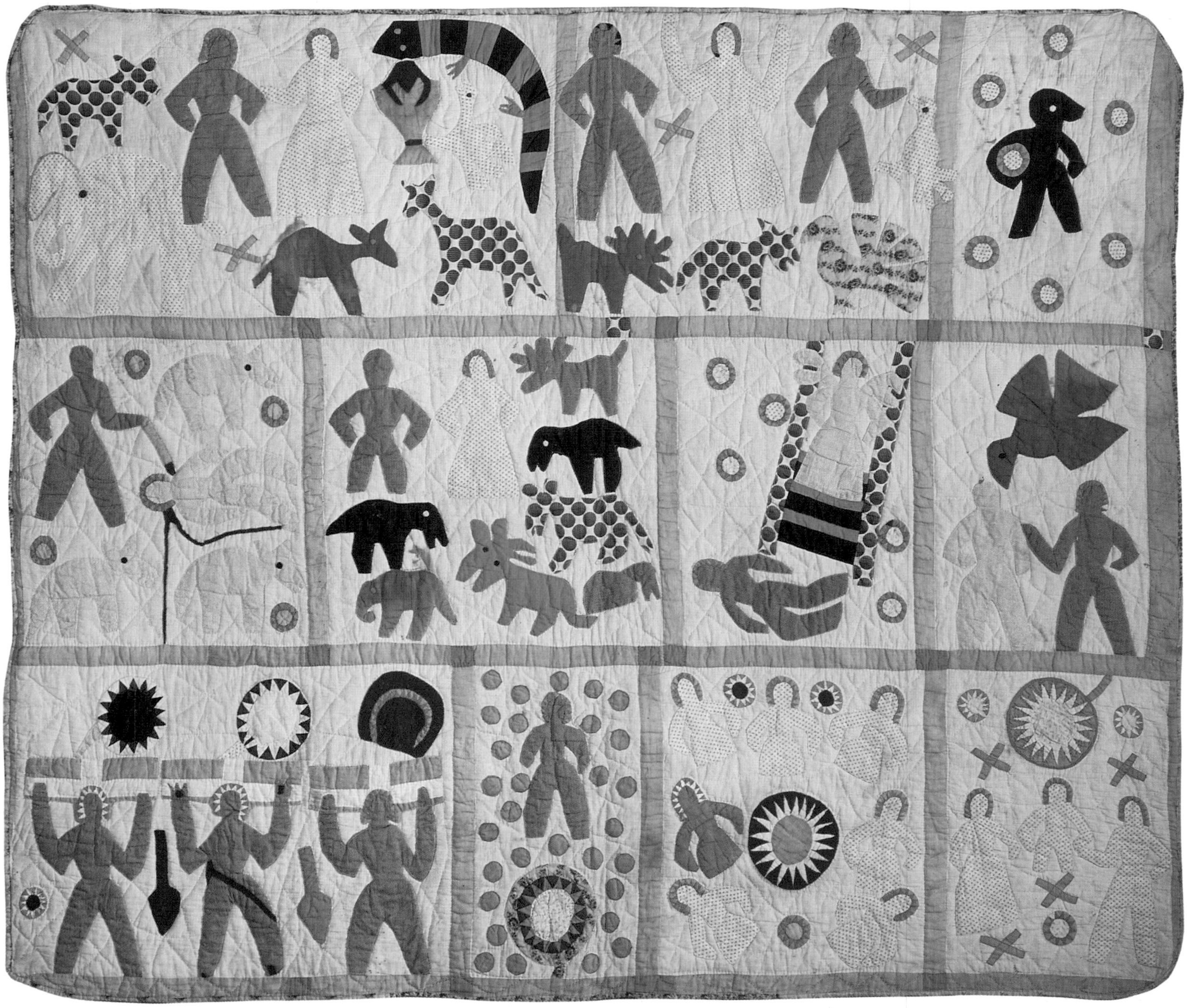

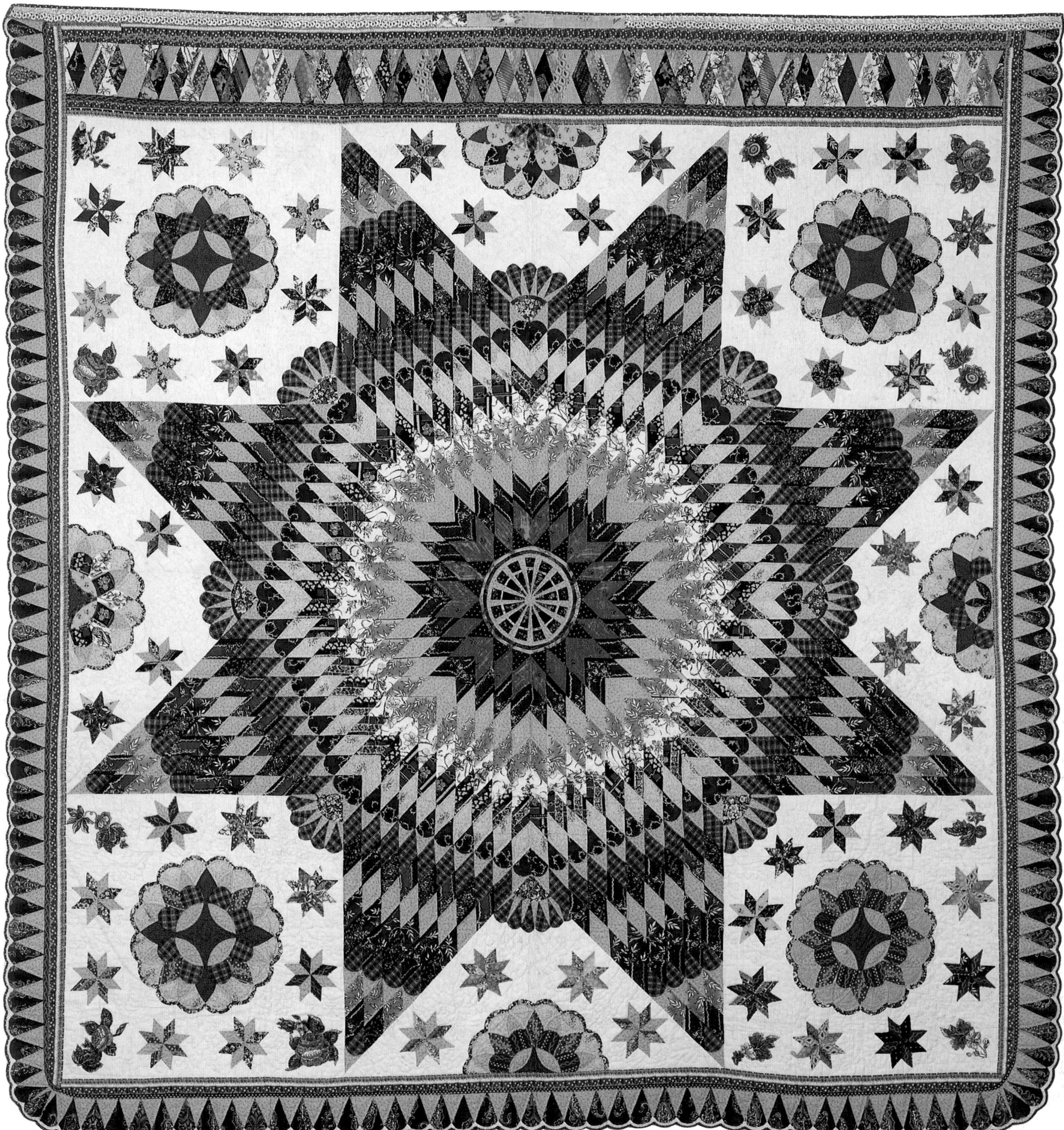

◄ THE BIBLE QUILT

Harriet Powers. c. 1886. Athens, Georgia. Cottons; machine appliquéd and hand quilted. 73 1/2 x 88 1/2 in. National Museum of American History, Smithsonian Institution, Washington, D.C.

Harriet Powers (1837–1911) worked as a seamstress for both black and white families in the Athens area. The odd size and horizontal format of her *Bible Quilt* suggest that it may have been intended as a visionary expression of its maker's deep religious faith rather than as a functional bedcover. The eleven unevenly sized squares depict biblical scenes. The quilt's colors have unfortunately faded considerably; the now light tan background was originally deep pink and the brown sashing between the squares was green.

▲ STARBURST

Artist unknown. c. 1850. Virginia. Cottons; hand pieced, appliquéd, and quilted. 102 x 96 in. The Valentine Museum, Richmond, Virginia, gift of Col. John Herbert Claiborne Mann.

This quilt descended in a former plantation owner's family. It is indisputably the work of a masterful quilter, who embellished the traditional Star of Bethlehem concept with her own design ideas. The dominant central star is bordered by four full and four half compasslike stars, set in circular fields of sky blue with scalloped edges. Forty-eight smaller stars sparkle against the quilt's light yellow background, while a number of small *broderie perse* flowers decorate the quilt's four corners.

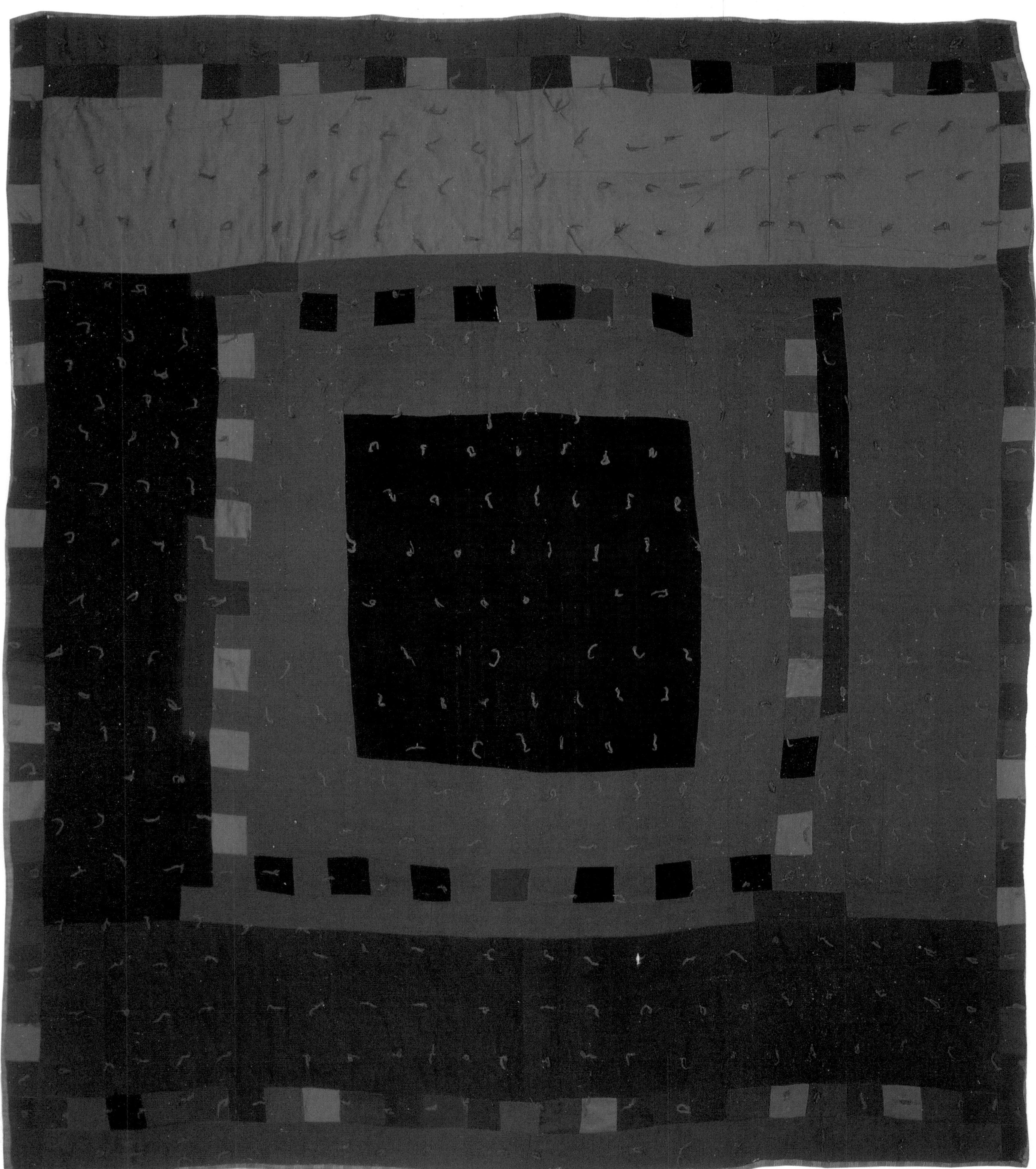

▲ **Tied Center Medallion**

Artist unknown. c. 1925. Southern United States. Wools; pieced and tied. 80 x 72 in. Private collection.

The green ties that hold the layers of this graphic quilt together provide a unifying element for its somewhat random design. Both blacks and whites in poor Southern communities are known to have made similar utilitarian quilts pieced from scrap materials in improvised patterns.

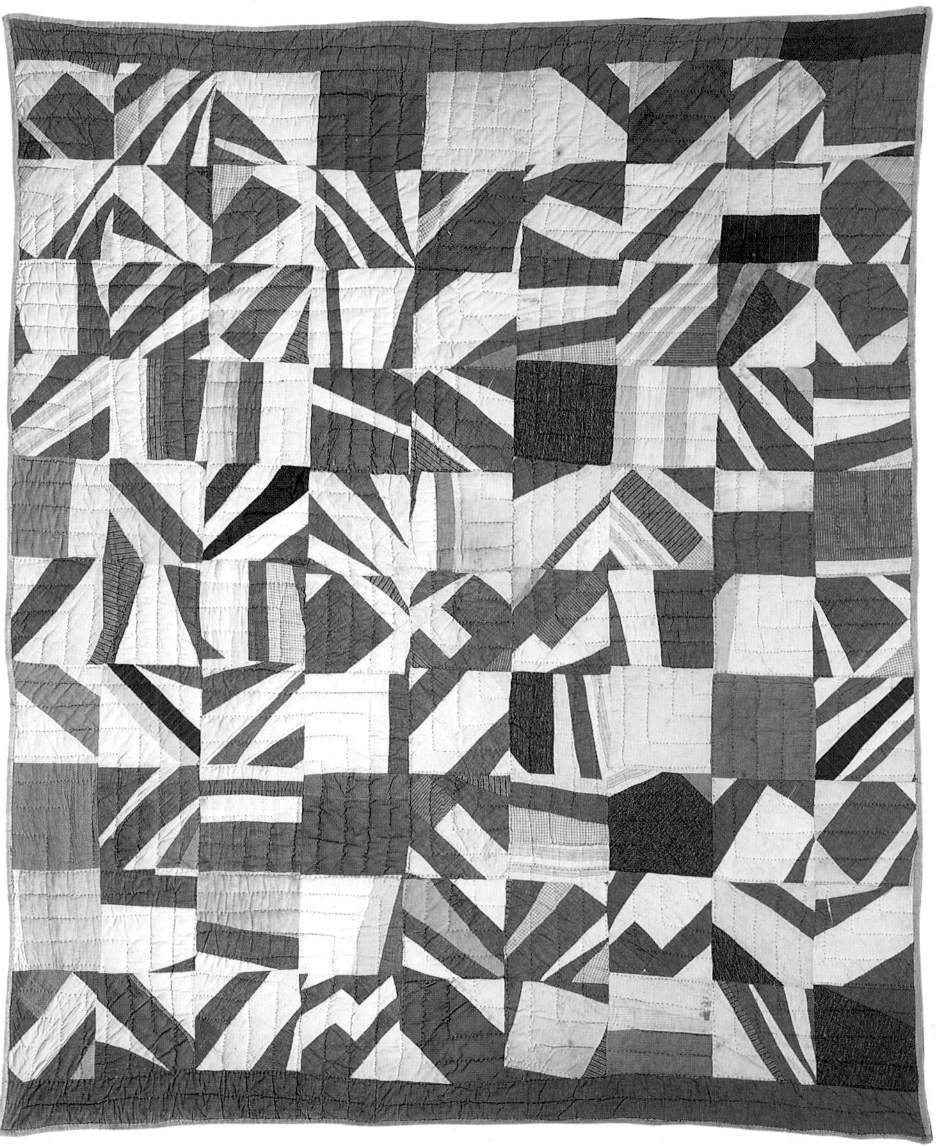

◄ Scrap Crazy

Artist unknown. c. 1920. Pickens County, Alabama. Cottons; hand pieced and quilted. 80 x 66 in. Collection of Robert Cargo.

Although at first the surface of this quilt appears random, it is actually quite deliberately constructed with nine vertical strips of ten blocks each. Ten of the blocks are single squares of solid-colored fabric, while the others are pieced. A few of the blocks are irregular in size, adding to the complexity of the quilt's visual rhythms.

Bow Tie Variation ►

Dora Gardner. c. 1955. Probably Muskegon, Muskegon County, Michigan. Cottons; hand pieced and quilted. 88 x 66 in. Collection of Blanche F. Cox.

Dora Gardner, born in Mississippi in 1891, learned to quilt from her grandmother. She moved to Michigan shortly before this quilt was made; the quilt thus represents a conservative Southern tradition. Gardner worked as a seamstress and is believed to have made more than 500 quilts. She recalled going to "October quilting bees" in Mississippi, which she remembered as "storytelling times, where there were enough women to make a quilt a day."

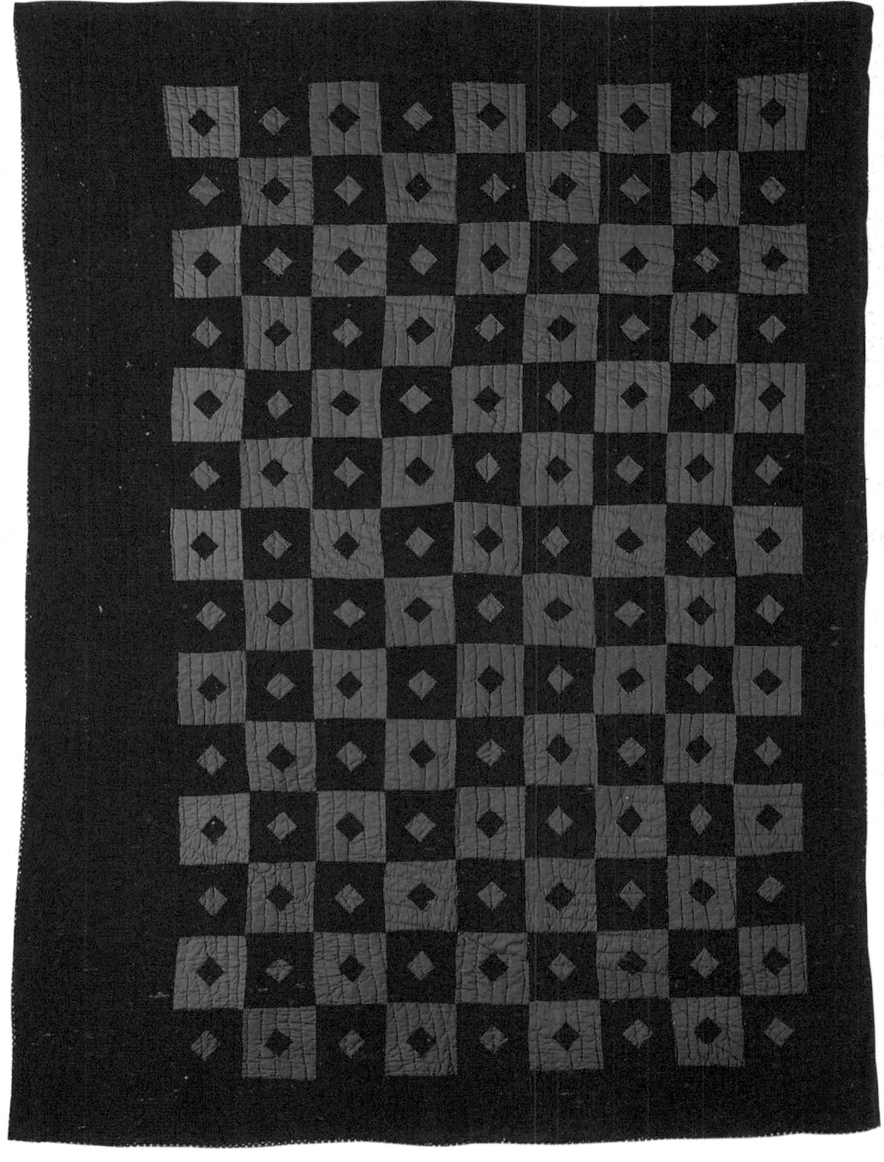

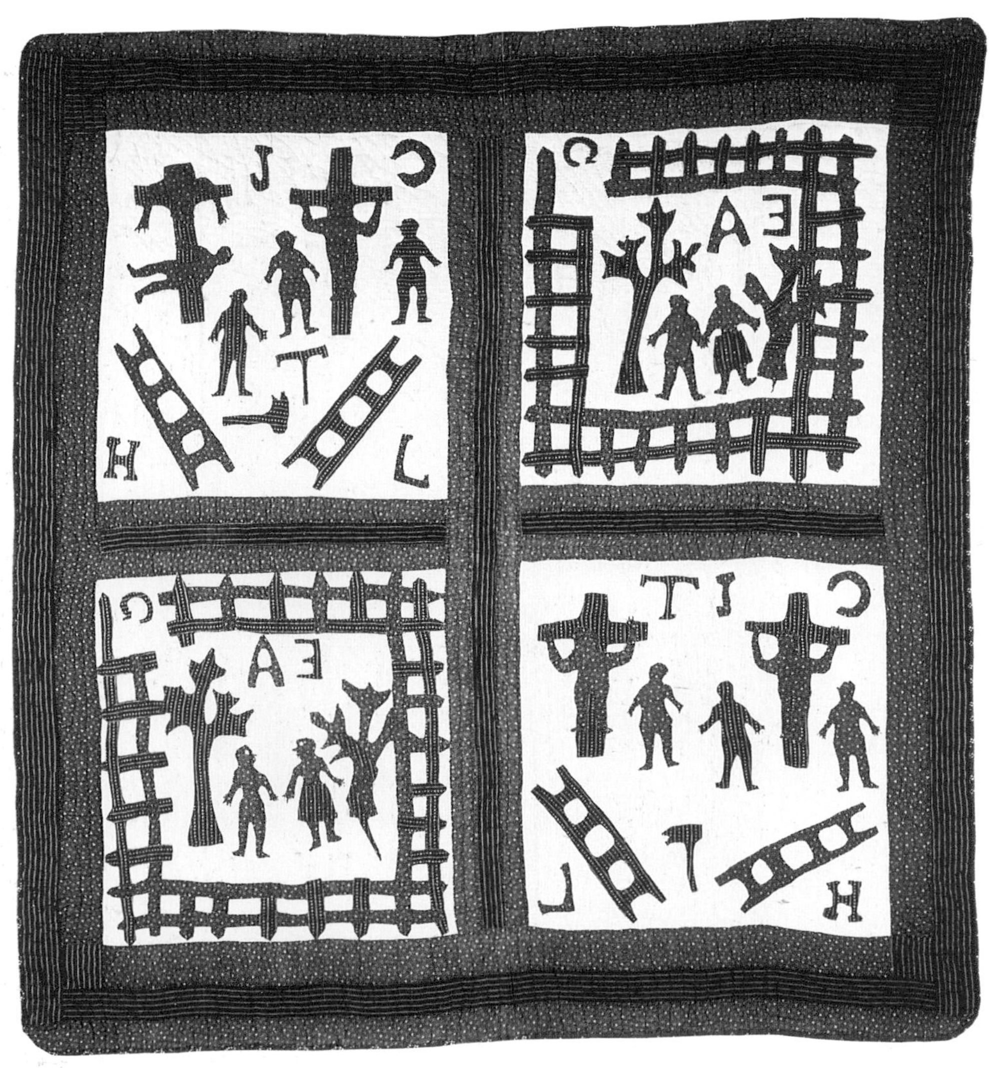

◄ Bible Scenes

A member of the Drake family. c. 1900. Thomaston, Georgia. Cottons; hand pieced and appliquéd. 76 1/2 x 71 in. Collection of Shelly Zegart.

This somewhat enigmatic work depicts Adam and Eve in the Garden and the Crucifixion; each image is represented twice with slight variations to make up the quilt's four blocks. Appliquéd letters, most of which seem to identify the scenes, are included in all four blocks, and cryptic images of ladders and what appears to be an axe are added to the two Crucifixion blocks.

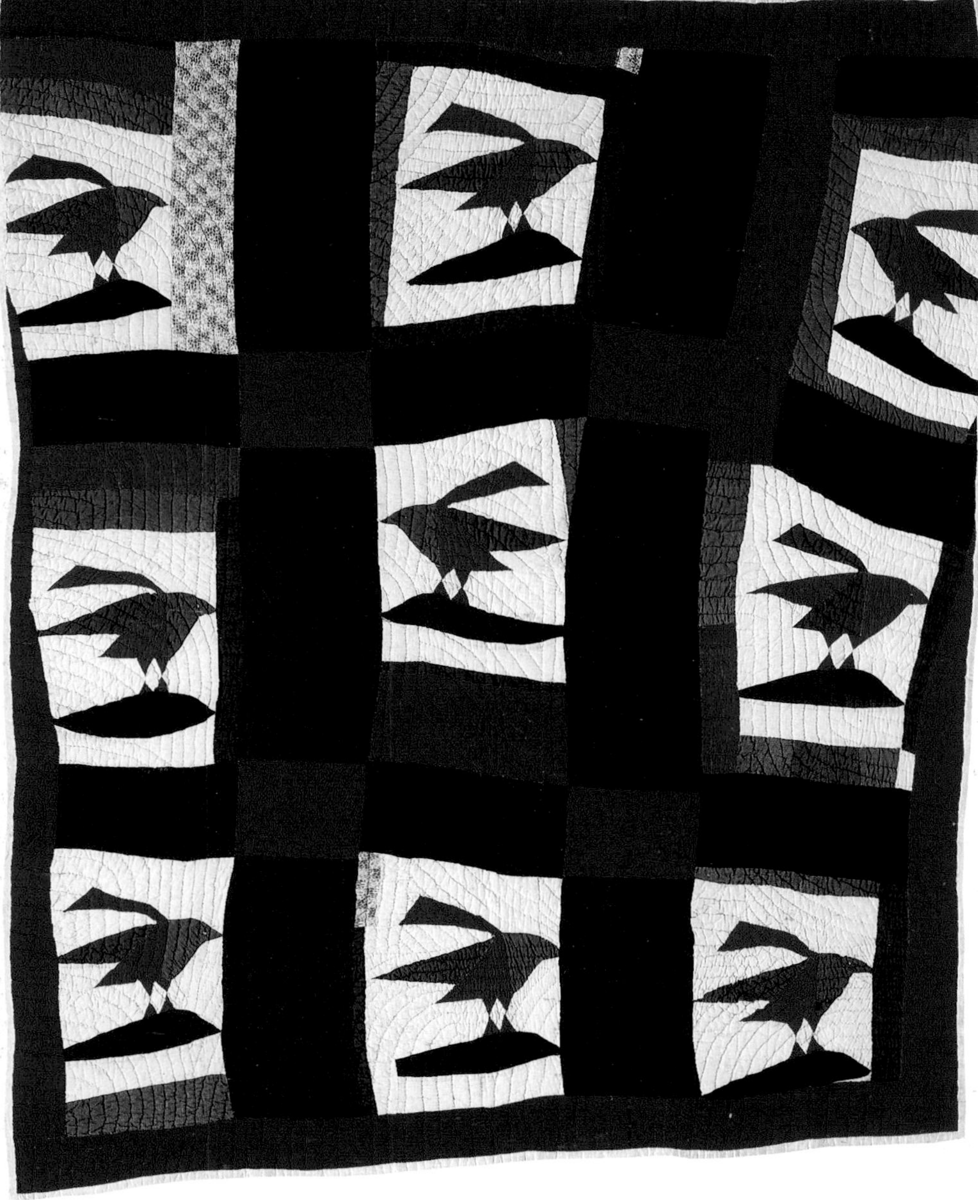

◄ Blackbirds

Blanche Ransome Parker. c. 1940. Carroll County, Tennessee. Cottons; hand pieced and quilted. 80 x 64 in. Esprit Quilt Collection, San Francisco, California.

Mrs. Parker was superintendent of Negro Schools in Carroll County at the time she made this remarkable quilt. The blocks are pieced, not appliquéd, a far more difficult technical approach that should have logically led to a more rigidly composed quilt. The odd-shaped blocks and strips of color accent the powerful, repeating rhythms of the blackbirds, while the two flopped birds set the whole top into flashing, dreamlike motion.

Lazy Man ►

Designed by Ruth Clement Bond, made by Grace Reynolds Tyler. 1934. Wheeler Dam Village, Alabama. Cottons; hand pieced, appliquéd, and quilted. 81 x 65 in. Collection of Grace Reynolds Tyler.

Ruth Clement Bond, who created the design for this quilt, was the wife of the highest ranking black official of the Tennessee Valley Authority, a rural electrification program that built hydroelectric dams during the depression years. This design is known to have been made by at least three other quiltmakers.

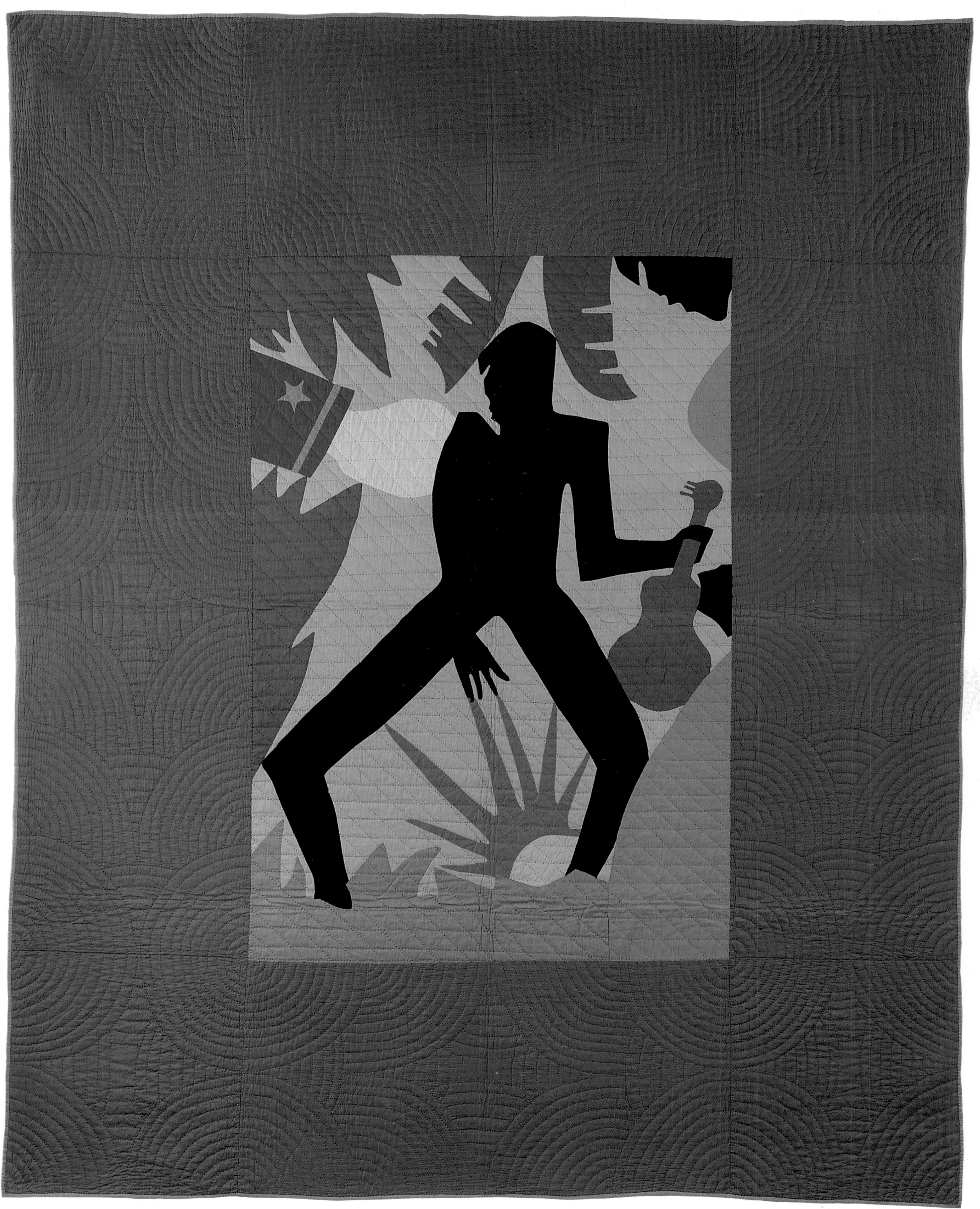

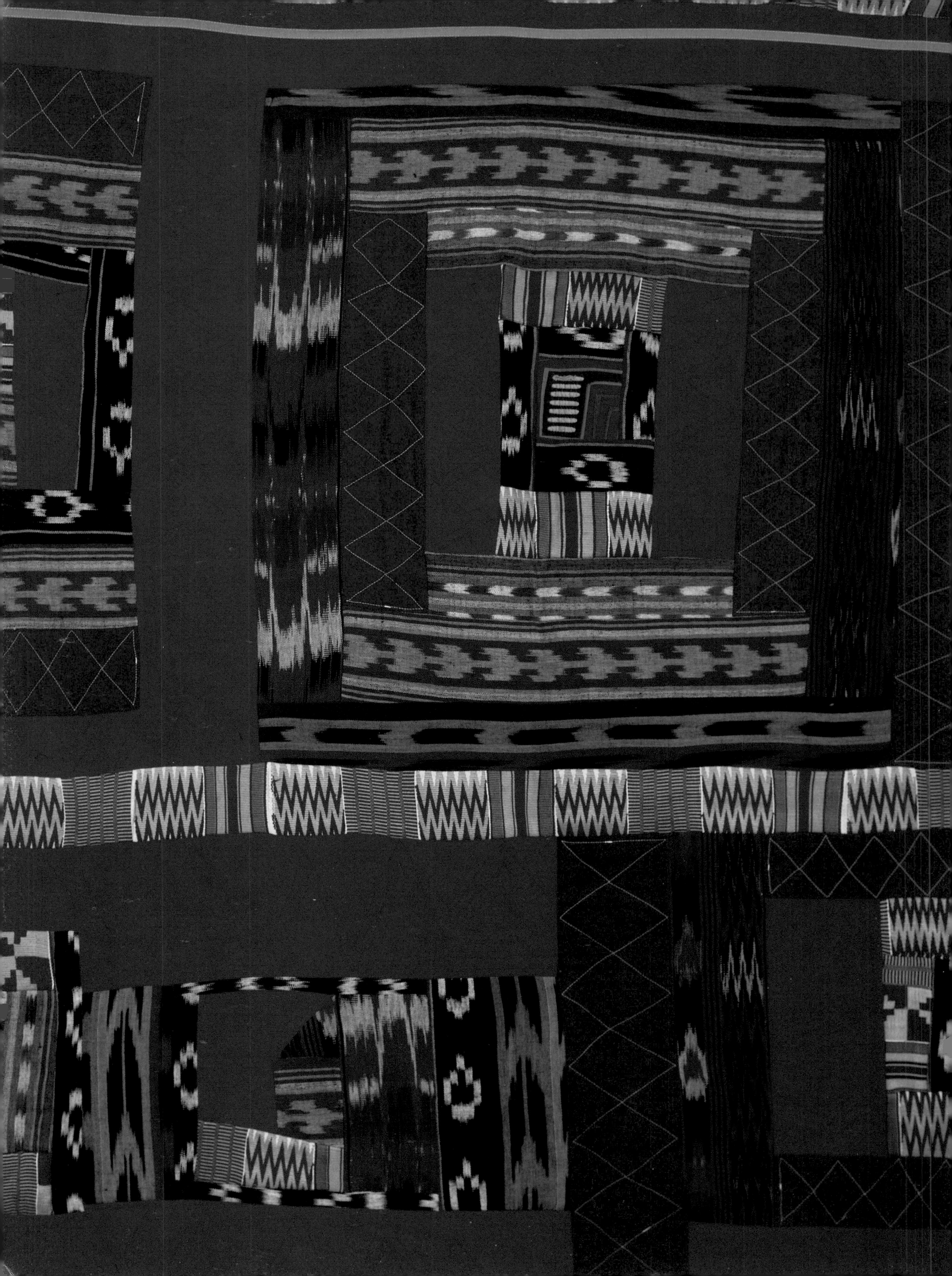

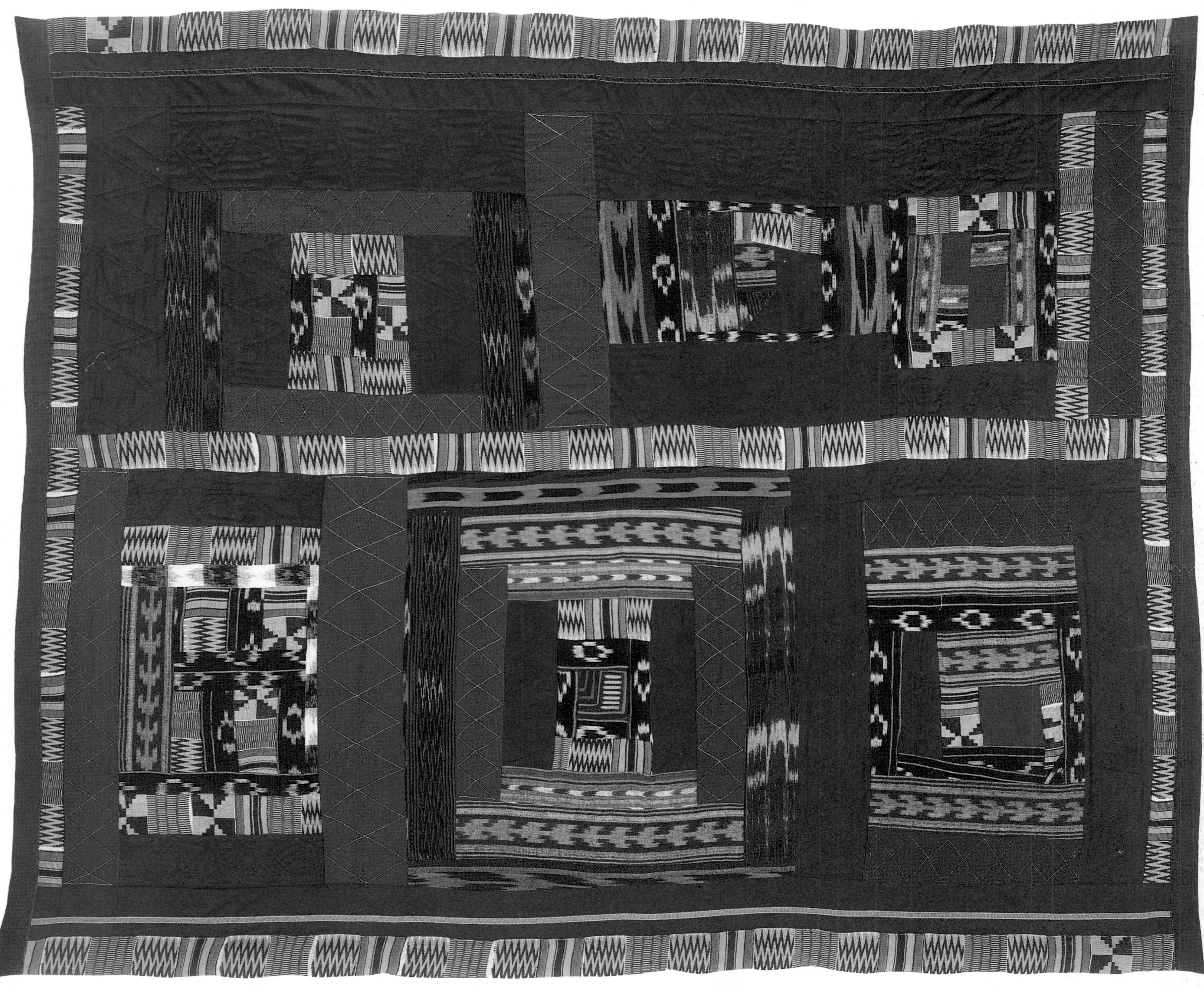

▲ **Shades and Colors for You** (◄ **detail**)

Ed Johnetta Miller. 1993. Hartford, Connecticut. Silk noil, African Kente cloth, South American molas; machine pieced and quilted. 70 x 86 3/4 *in. Collection of the artist.*

Ed Johnetta Miller is a textile artist who, in addition to quilts, also produces hand-painted silks, hand-dyed and handwoven fabric, and coats and jackets pieced from textiles from around the world. Although less eclectic than her clothing, Miller's quilts often combine fabrics from different continents in improvisational compositions.

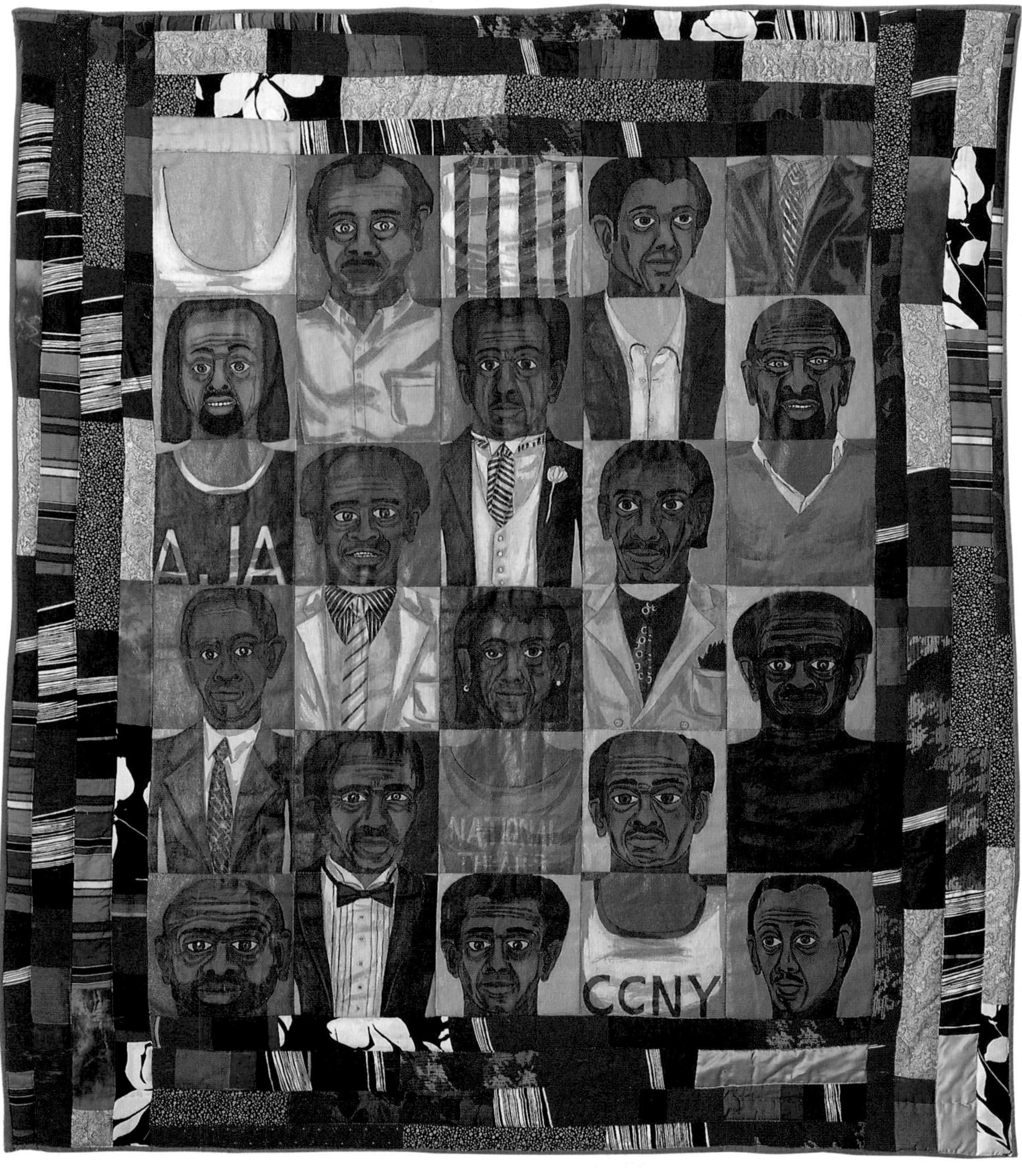

◄ **THE MEN: MASK FACE QUILT #2**

Faith Ringgold. 1986. New York, New York. Acrylic on canvas, cottons; pieced and quilted; sequin eyes. 70 x 62 in. Collection of Ardis and Robert James.

The painted faces of African-American men alternate here with seemingly interchangeable costumed torsos; three unmatched torsos fill the top row and three disembodied heads the bottom row. The twenty-five blocks of faces and torsos are surrounded by a framing border made of pieced African fabrics.

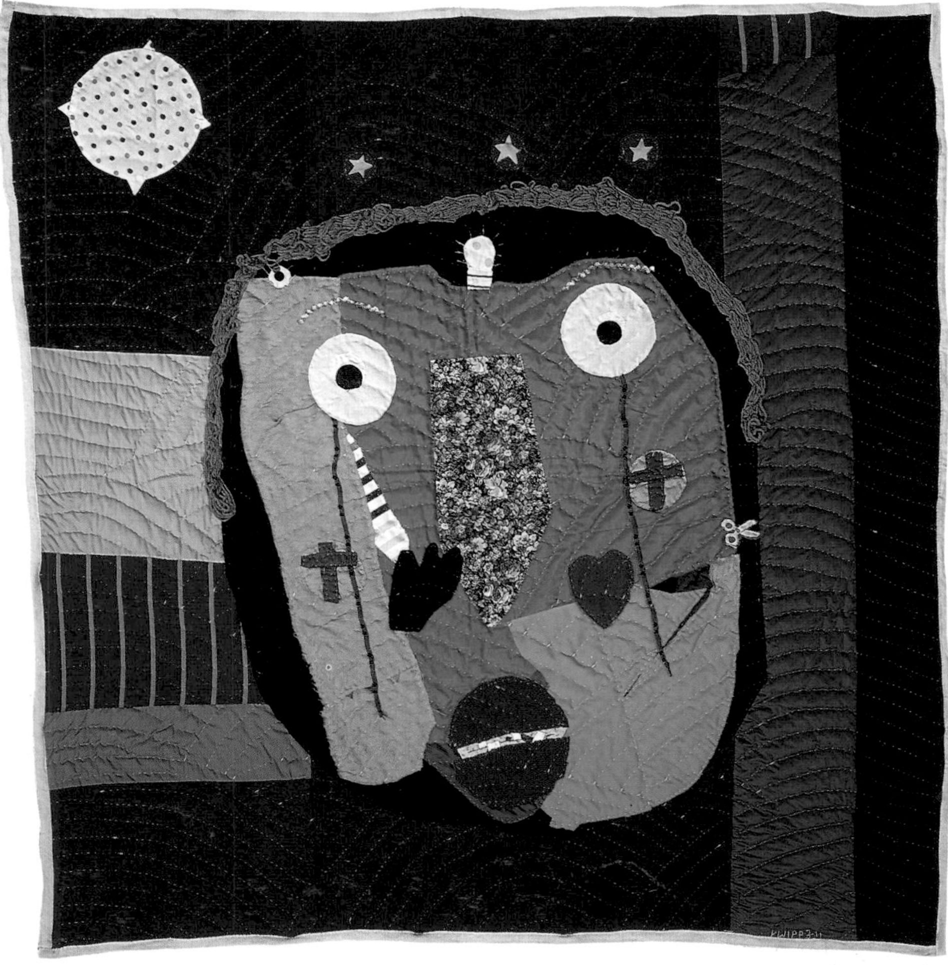

◄ **ME MASKED**

Yvonne Wells. 1993. Tuscaloosa, Alabama. Cottons and cotton blends, satin, velour, yarn, shoe lace. 60 x 58 1/2 in. Collection of Robert Cargo.

Yvonne Wells's quilts often manifest private visions, full of dreamlike images and fanciful juxtapositions. Here the artist offers an image of herself—masked and inscrutable, at once childlike and complex, amusing and unsettling.

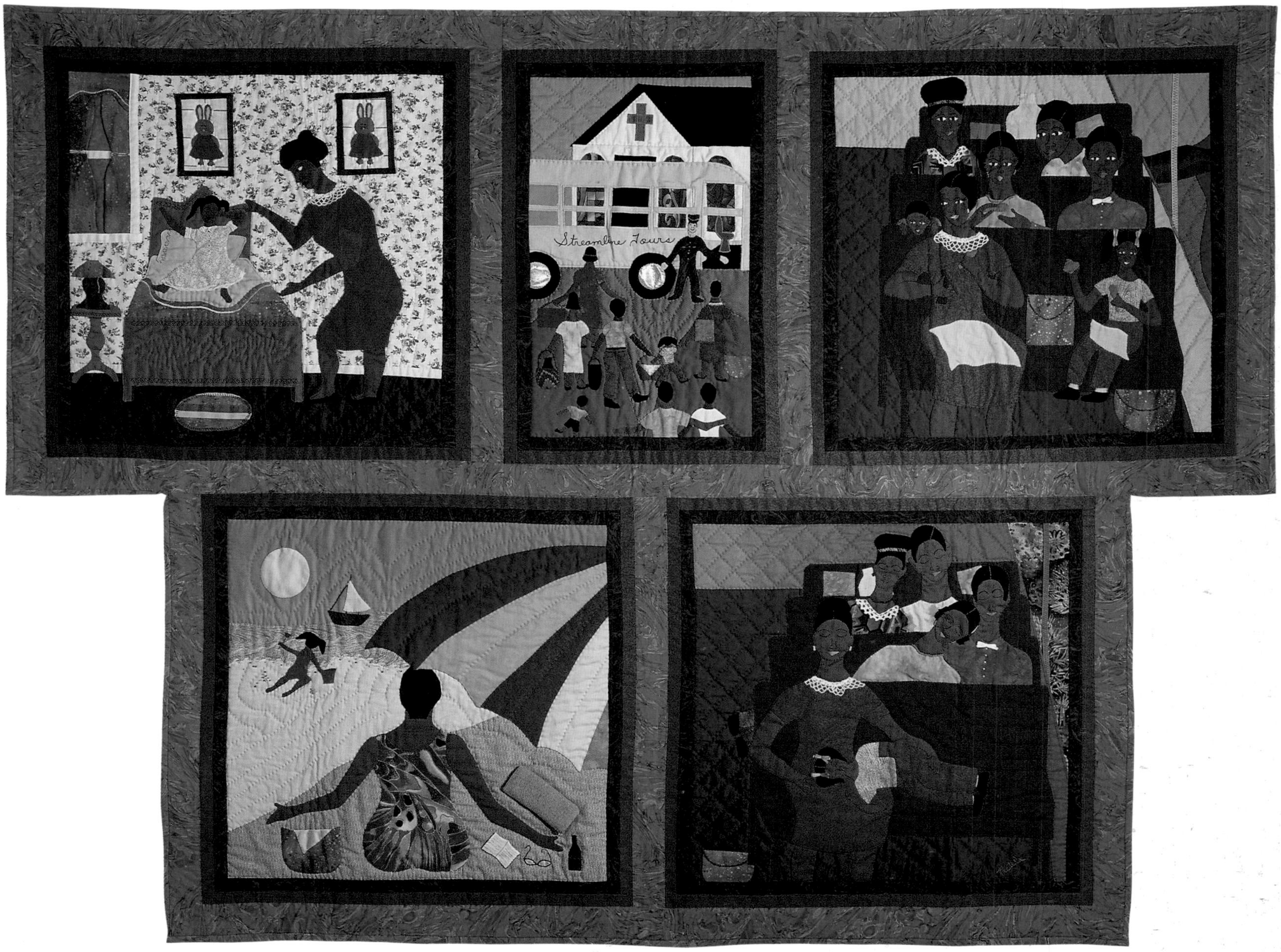

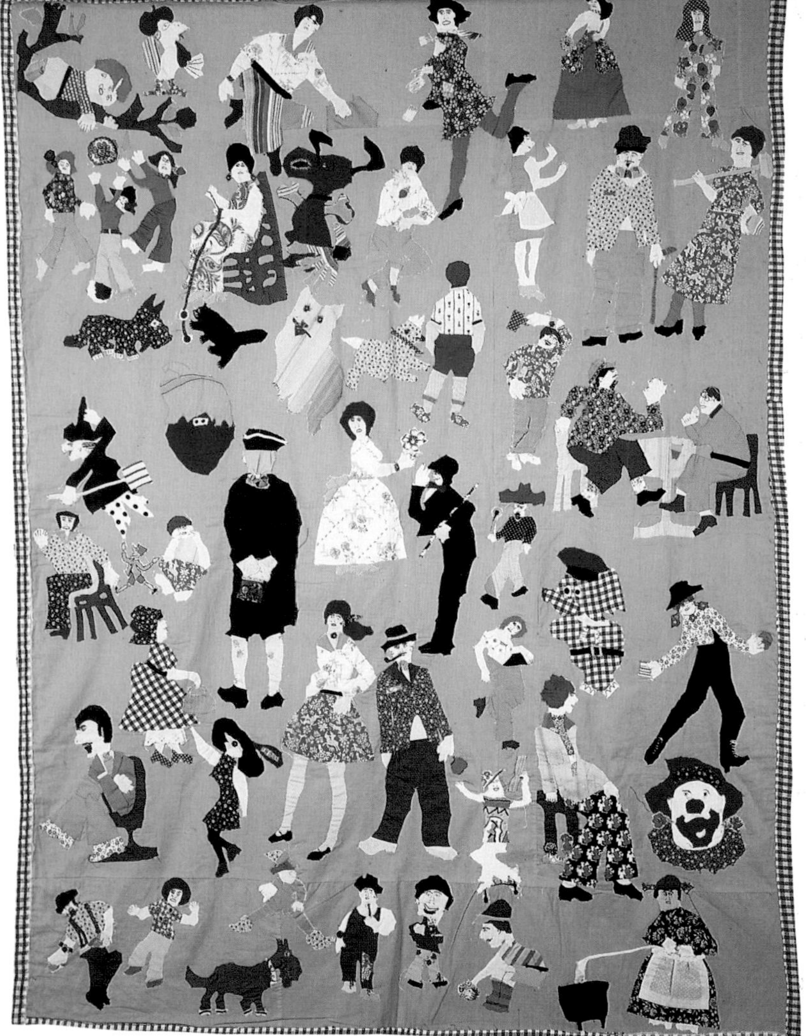

▲ Picnic Day for Barbara

Barbara Pietila. 1994. Baltimore, Maryland. Cottons; appliquéd. 47 1/2 x 65 1/2 in. Collection of the artist.

Barbara Pietila specializes in story quilts. Of this recent quilt she says: "One day on a fabric shopping spree my friend Barbara and I stopped at a KFC for lunch. My granddaughter was with us and Barbara told her a story of how she would go on bus trips with her grandmother when she was a little girl. She recalled how her grandmother would wake her at what seemed to be the middle of the night, they would go to the bus with their friends, eat her grandmother's biscuits on the bus, have their outing, and she would fall asleep on the return trip in her grandmother's big soft lap. I loved the story and made this quilt as a tribute to all happy childhood memories."

◄ People of the World

Lillian Beattie. 1979. Chattanooga, Tennessee. Cottons and cotton blends; appliquéd and embroidered. 71 1/2 x 54 1/2 in. Collection of Bets Ramsey.

Lillian Beattie, who died in 1988 at the age of 108, made several quilts on this theme. According to this quilt's owner, Bets Ramsey, "[Lillian Beattie] learned to piece quilts as a girl living in the household of a white family . . . [but] it was not until . . . she saw appliqué work [at the] . . . 1939 New York World's Fair . . . that she had any interest in quiltmaking. . . . Her daughter . . . says some days her mother got so carried away with her work that she forgot to eat lunch."

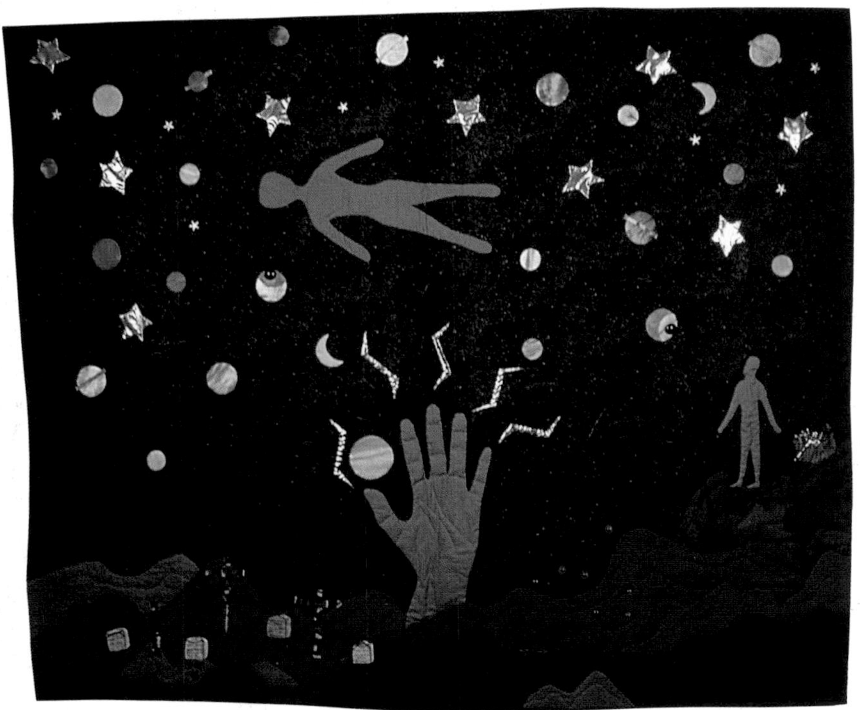

◄ **THE HOMECOMING**

Carolyn Mazloomi. 1992. Cincinnati, Ohio. Cottons and synthetics; hand appliquéd and quilted. 60 x 72 in. Collection of Sandra Joseph.

This deeply personal quilt depicts a soul in transition.

MEN OF THE TABOO ►

Carolyn Mazloomi. 1993. Cincinnati, Ohio. Cottons; embellished with cowrie shells, yarn, beads; hand appliquéd and quilted. 85 x 72 in. Collection of the artist.

Carolyn Mazloomi travels often to West Africa and traces the roots of her narrative impulse to the griots, the tribal storytellers of the land America ravaged for slaves.

Carolyn Mazloomi

Carolyn Mazloomi of Cincinnati, Ohio, is the founder of the Women of Color Quilter's Network, the first national attempt to network African-American quilters.

Mazloomi fell in love with quiltmaking after chancing on a folk art quilt in Dallas in the mid-1970s. She was so taken with what she saw that she decided to make a quilt of her own—and taught herself how. "There's no history of quilting in my family," she says. "My mom can't even sew. Neither could my grandmother." Mazloomi, a native of the Bahamas, actually grew up wanting to fly. She is now a licensed pilot and has a doctorate in aerospace engineering from the University of Southern California. In addition to her quiltmaking and teaching, she currently teaches part time in the engineering department at Ohio State University and is a FAA crash site investigator.

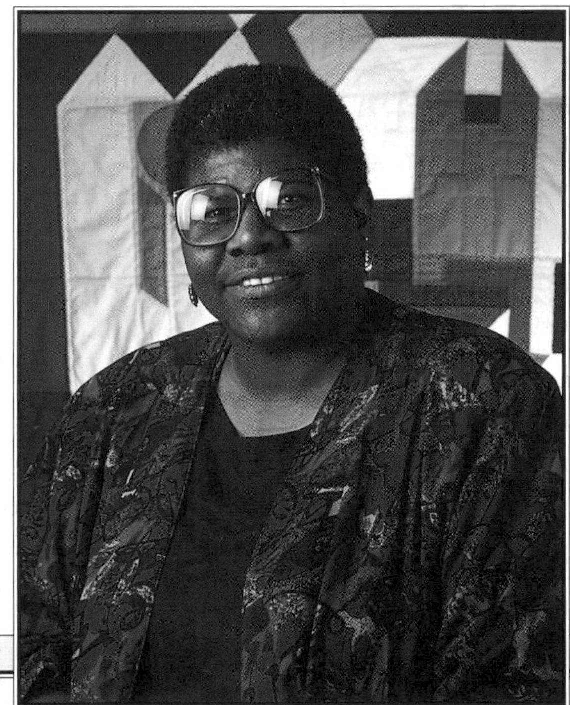

According to Mazloomi, "Studying African-American quilt history has helped me greatly in my teaching. Since I teach mostly African-Americans, they really get a sense first hand of the role their ancestors have played in quiltmaking in this country. Quiltmaking represents the creative legacy of ordinary black men and women, an artistic process that turns scraps of everyday life into works of functional and enduring beauty...Quilts are cultural documents. I would like it if one hundred years from now people can see these quilts and get a glimpse of how we lived our lives in this country as African-Americans."

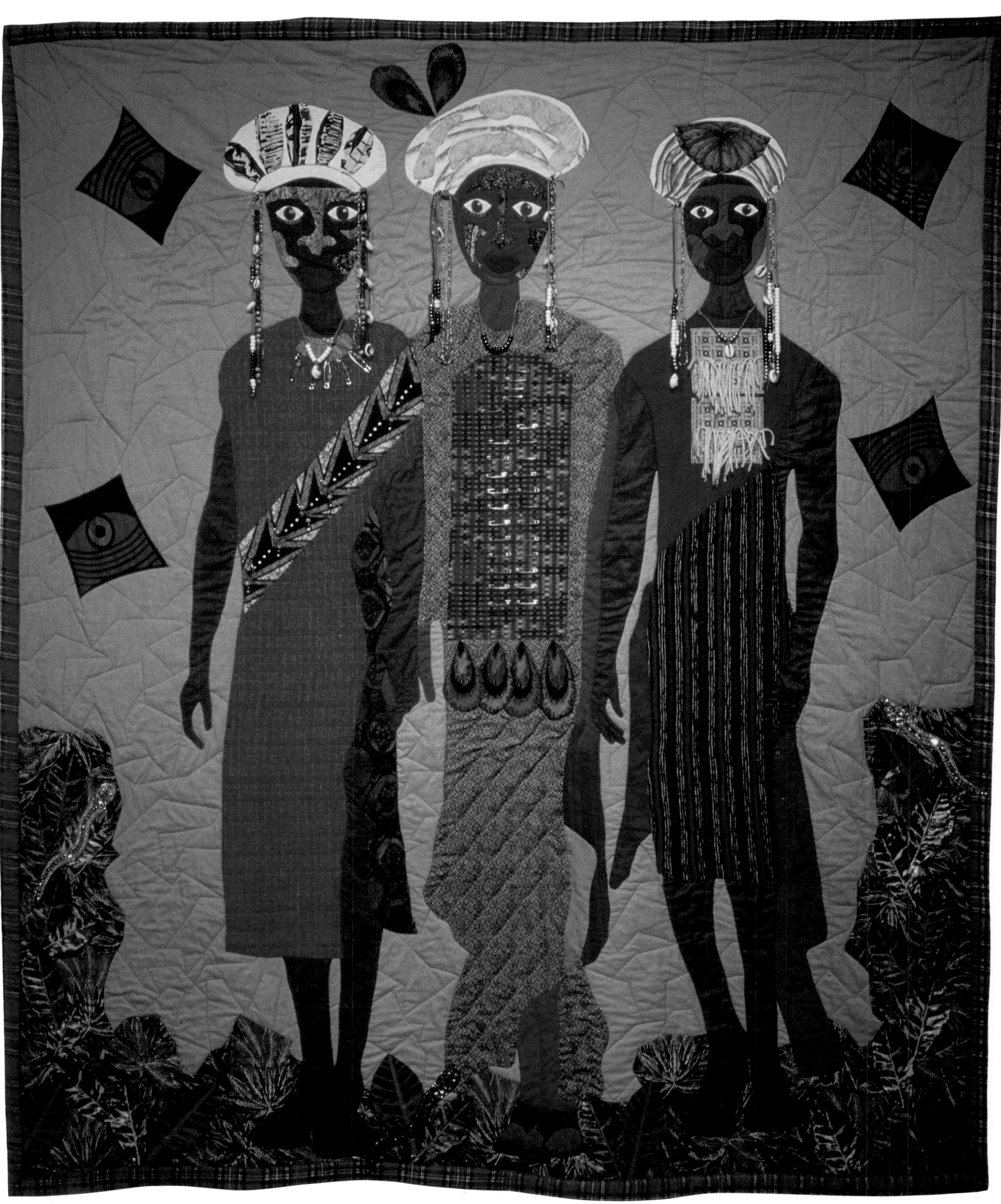

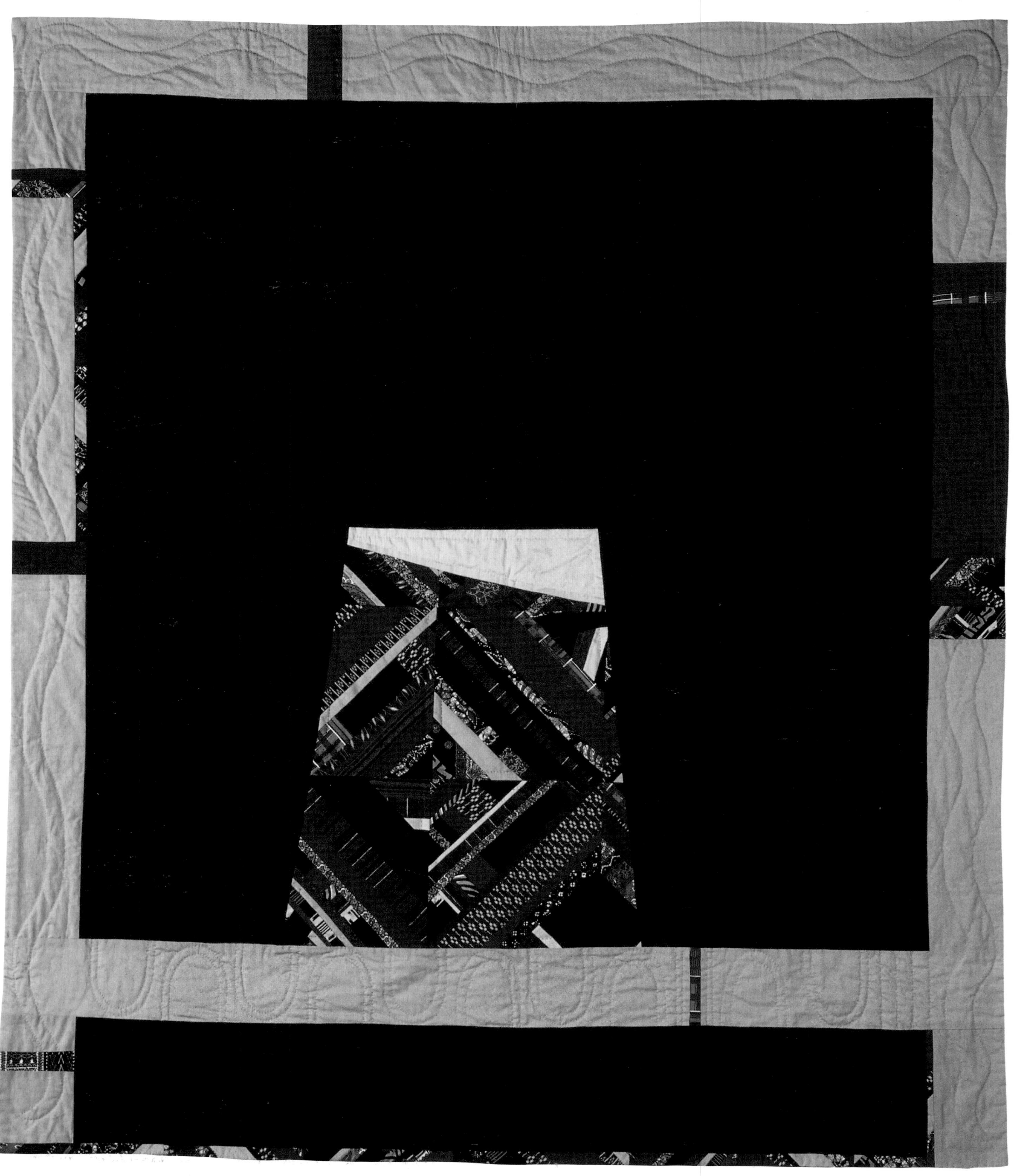

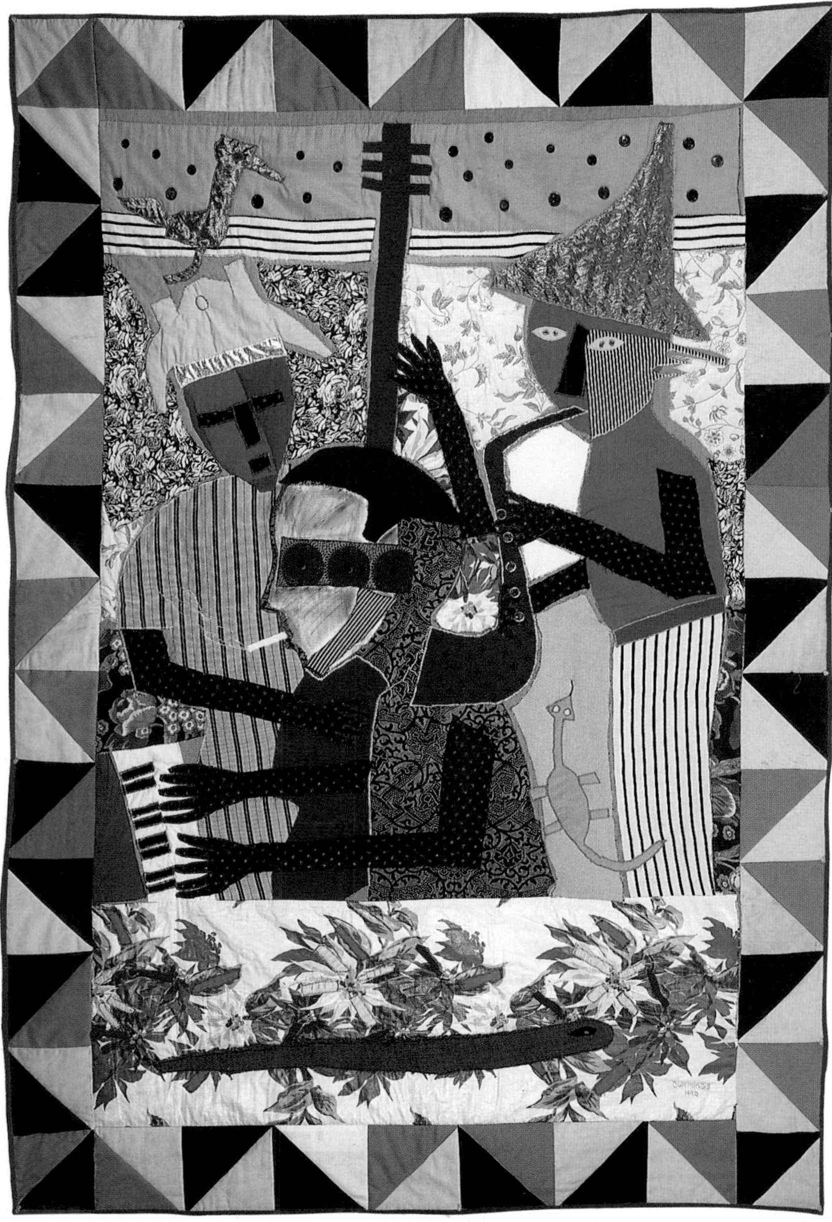

▲ AFRICAN JAZZ

Michael Cummings. 1993. New York, New York. Cotton blends, burlap, satin, metallic fabrics, beads; hand appliquéd. 108 x 72 in. Collection of the artist.

This quilt is one of a series inspired by an old poster of three black jazz musicians huddled in a smoke-filled room. Cummings has surrounded his trio—a bass player, pianist, and saxophonist—with a bright and jaunty border intended to replace the smoky atmosphere of the jazz club with a tropical African outdoor feeling, thereby suggesting the music's roots.

◄ APPROPRIATENESS OF YELLOW

Carole Harris. 1990. Detroit, Michigan. Cottons, hand pieced; hand quilted by Laura Rodin. 71 3/4 x 63 1/2 in. Collection of the artist.

Carole Harris took up quilting in 1966 because it seemed to her "a nonintimidating art form." Harris says, "The process of making a quilt is like the art of jazz musicians—they start with a melody and improvise from there. Both jazz and quiltmaking are spontaneous, putting little bits of things together to make a complete piece of art."

▼ MASKS #1

Carole Yvette Lyles. 1993. Columbia, Maryland. Cottons; machine pieced and quilted. 30 x 24 in. Collection of the artist.

Carole Lyles, an assistant professor of management at Loyola College in Maryland, made her first quilts in the summer of 1990 as presents for her nieces and nephews. She says: "[My] first quilt was crude, handmade and a truly liberating experience . . . I work from preliminary sketches that convey only the most essential aspects of a piece. The ideas come at all times of day and night and my workbook is full of sketches on scraps of paper, backs of envelopes, etc. . . . I work 'on the wall.' I have a studio with one wall that is a pin-up space. I usually work from the center out, building each level of the piece according to my sketch and my intuition. *Masks #1* is part of a series that explores the use of black and white fabrics . . . accented by a bold color or fabric such as the mask printed fabric used in this piece."

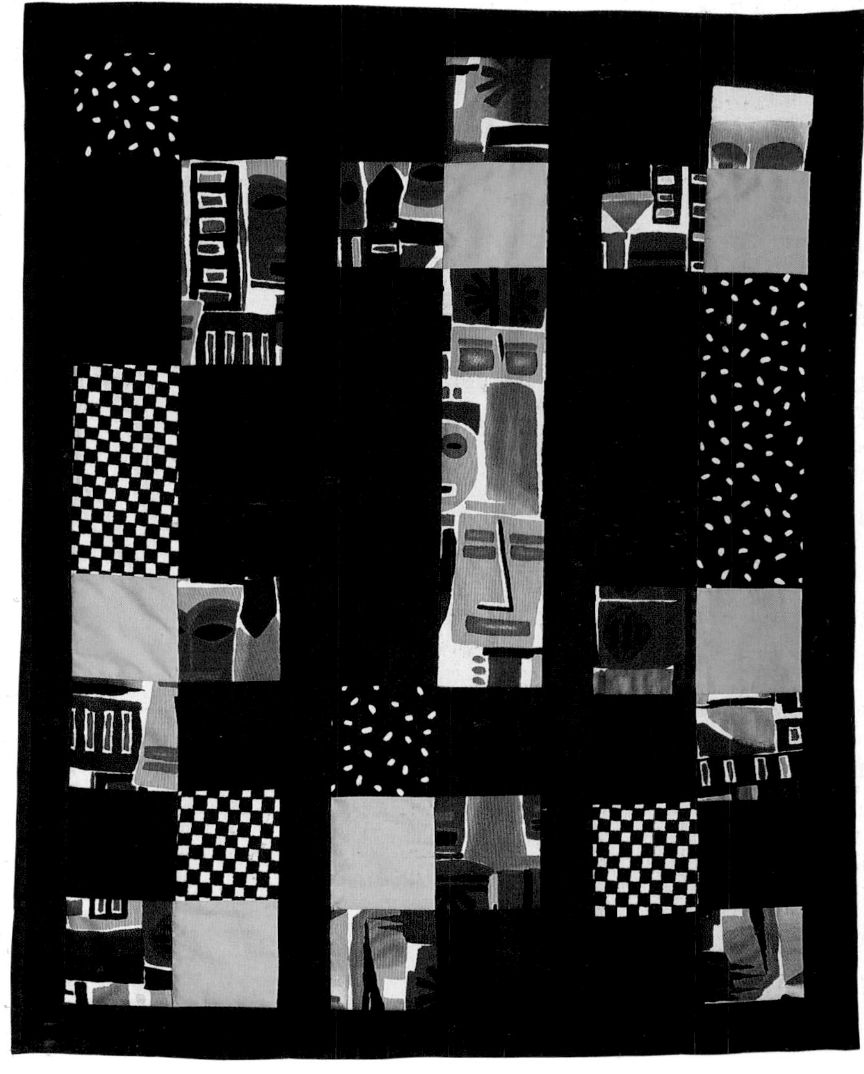

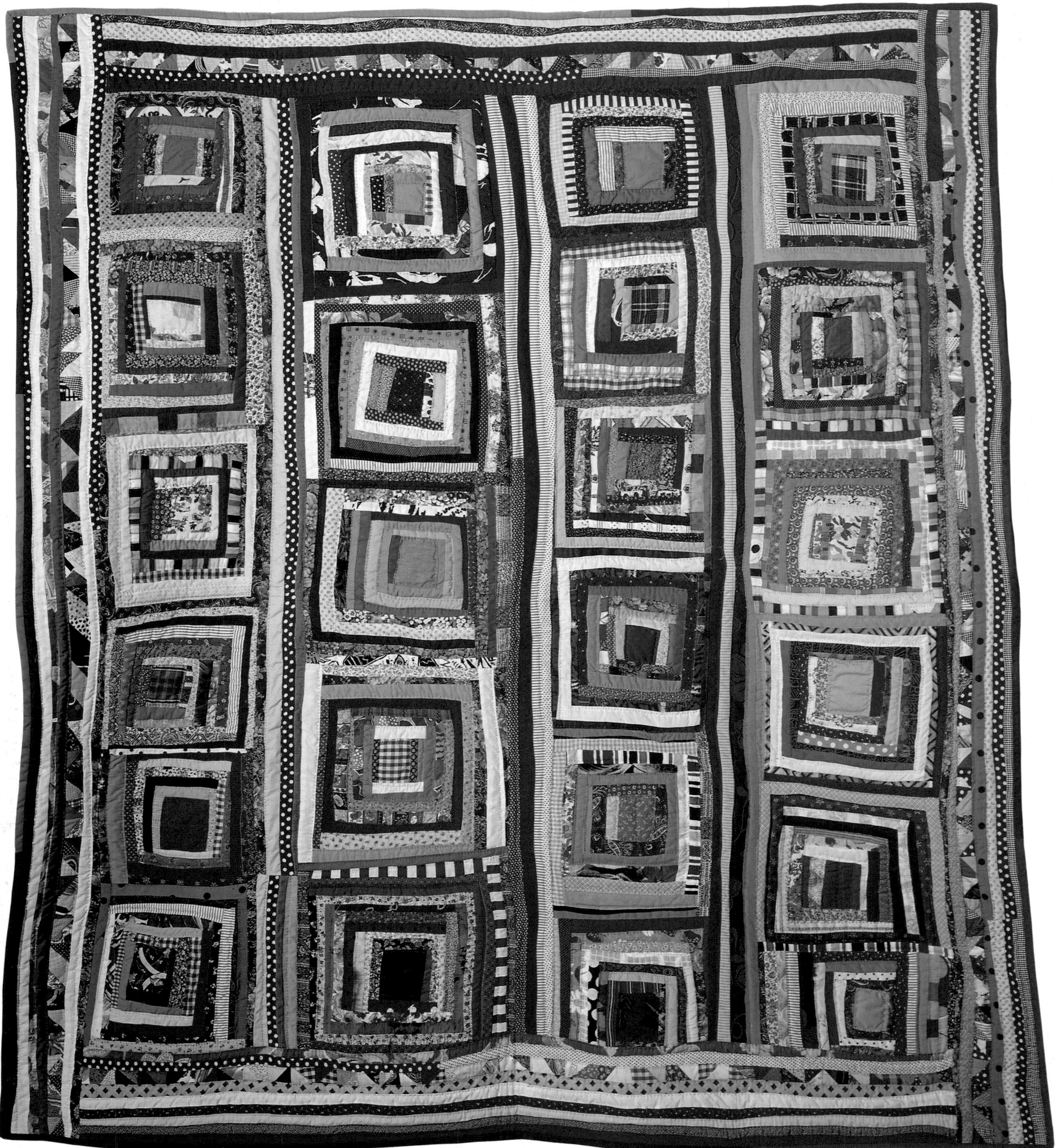

▲ LIX: LOG CABIN (DETAIL ►)

Anna Williams. 1993. Baton Rouge, Louisiana. Machine-pieced cottons; hand quilted by unknown artisan. 77 x 65 in. Collection of Ardis and Robert James.

This recent African-American interpretation of the traditional Log Cabin pattern is full of unexpected and asymmetrical color, fabric, and pattern rhythms. The twenty-three off-kilter Log Cabin blocks are set off with rows of thin vertical fabric strips and the whole composition is surrounded by a wide border of several strips. Anna Williams's work has had a liberating influence on many other quilters in recent years, including art quilters Liz Axford, Terrie Hancock Mangat, and Nancy Crow. Since first encountering Williams's work in 1990, Crow has made a number of freely composed quilts based on simple traditional patterns that are clearly inspired by her example.

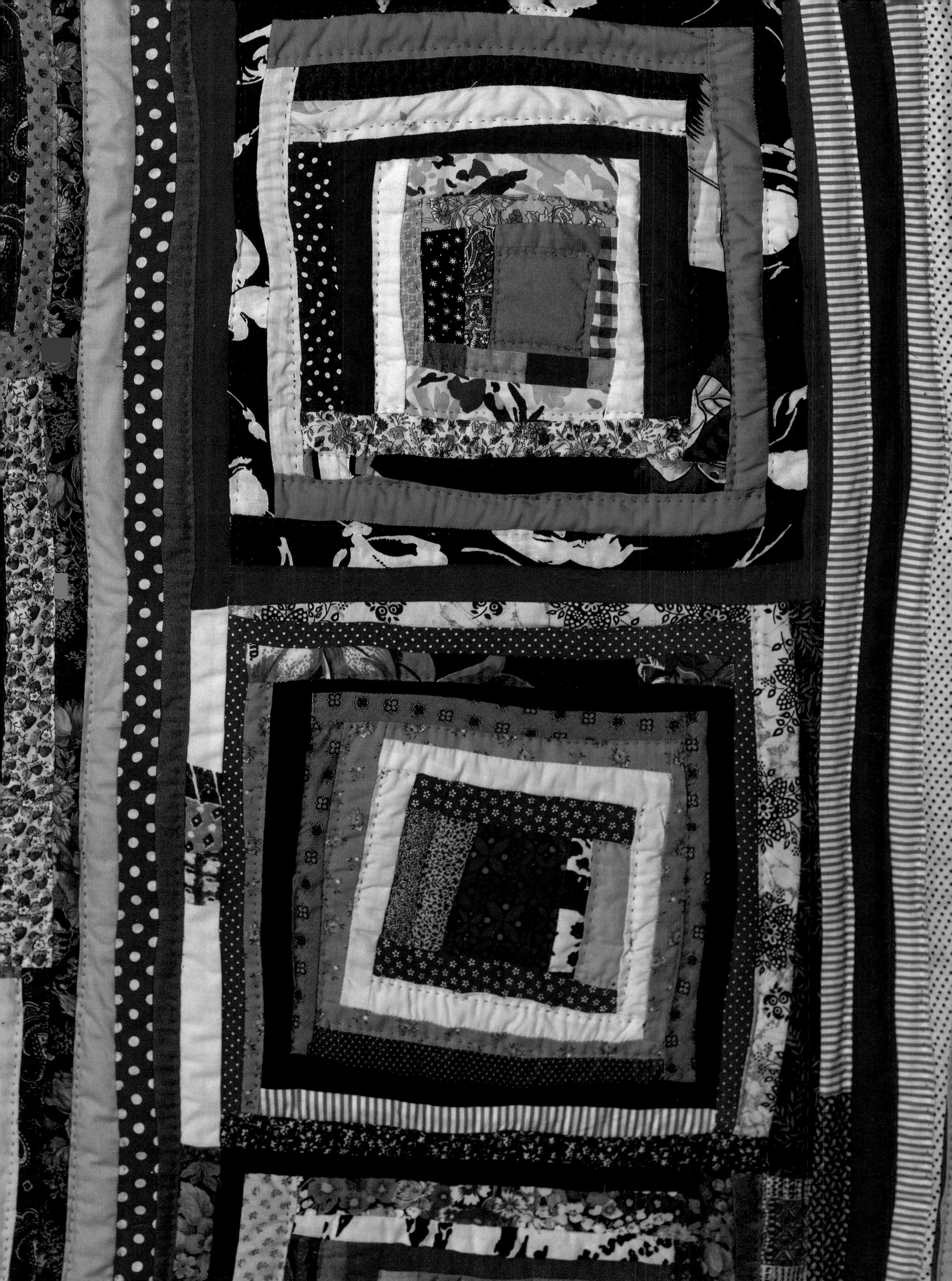

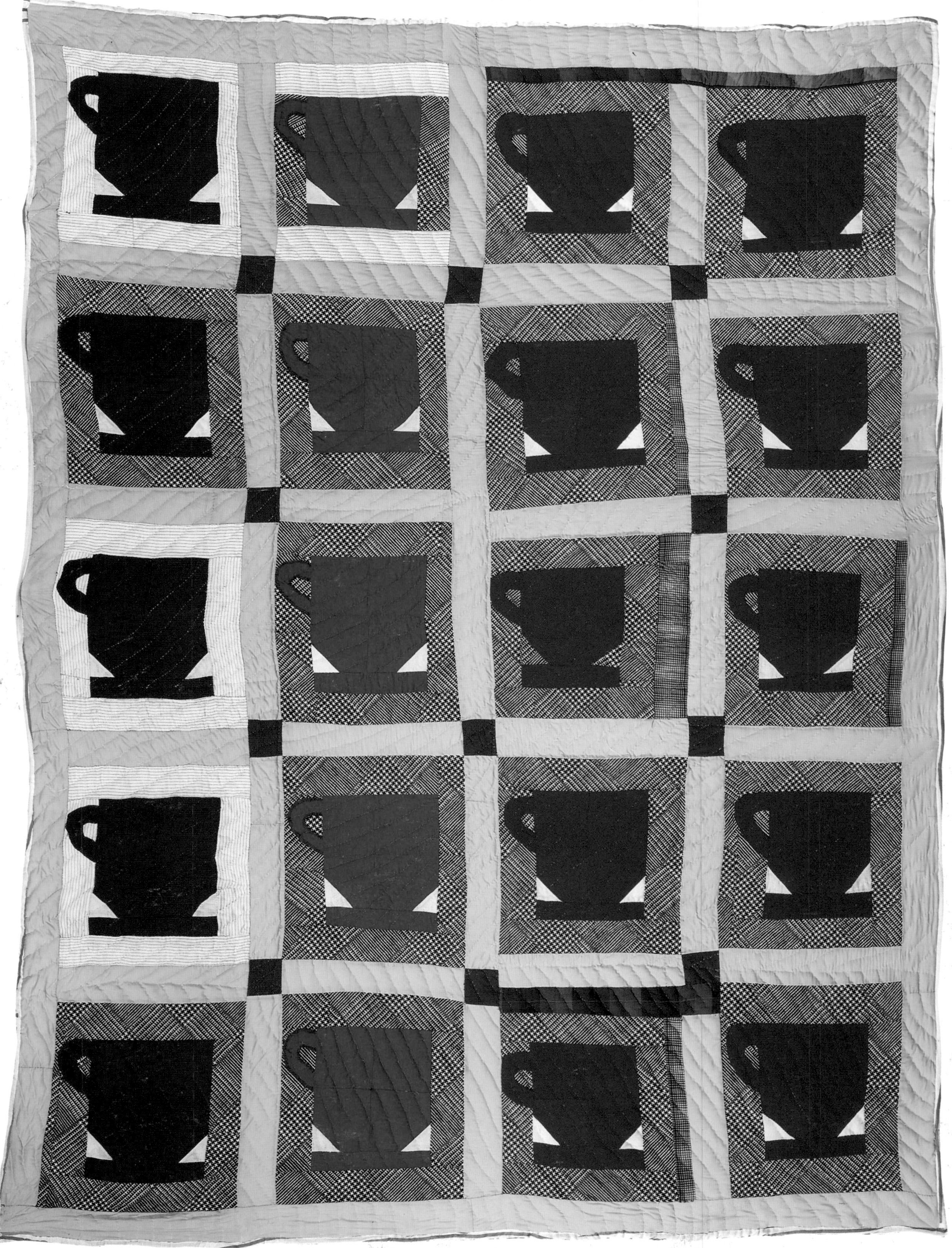

▲ **TEACUPS**

Lureca Outland. 1993–1994. Green County, Alabama. Cottons and cotton blends; hand appliquéd and quilted. 92 x 70 in. Collection of Robert Cargo.

Lureca Outland, who was born in 1904, learned to quilt from her mother. The variations of size and color of the freely cut teacups give this quilt an amusing exuberance that a more precise approach to craftsmanship would have stifled.

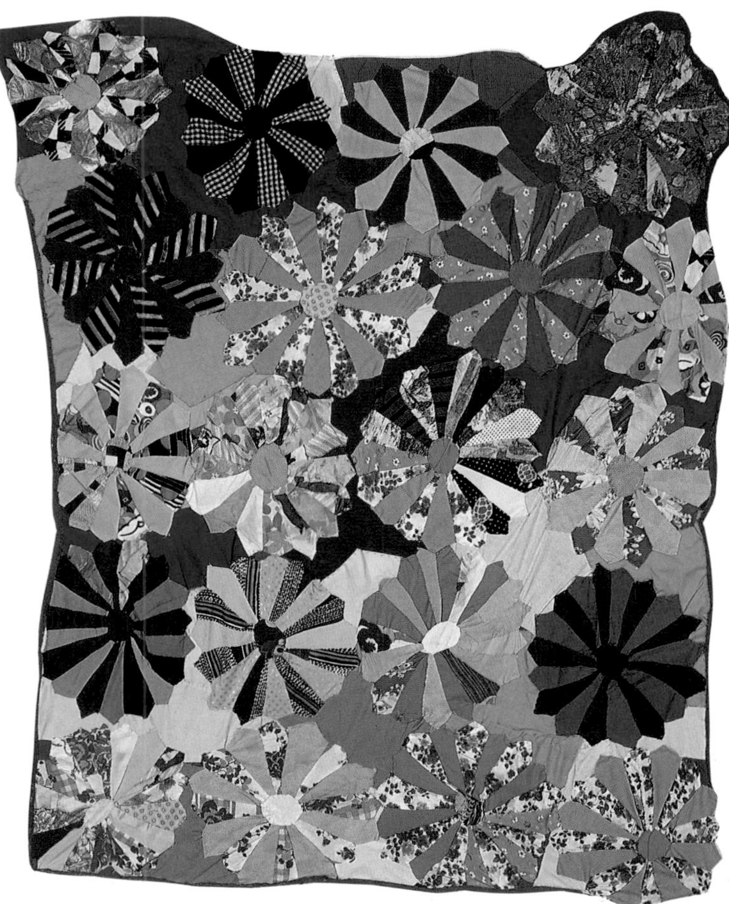

▲ **DRESDEN PLATE**

Arester Earl. 1979. Atlanta, Georgia. Natural and synthetic fabrics; hand pieced and quilted. Private collection.

Because of failing eyesight and poor health Arester Earl (1892–1988) created one block at a time and then sewed the blocks together loosely to form her often oddly shaped and unevenly stuffed quilts.

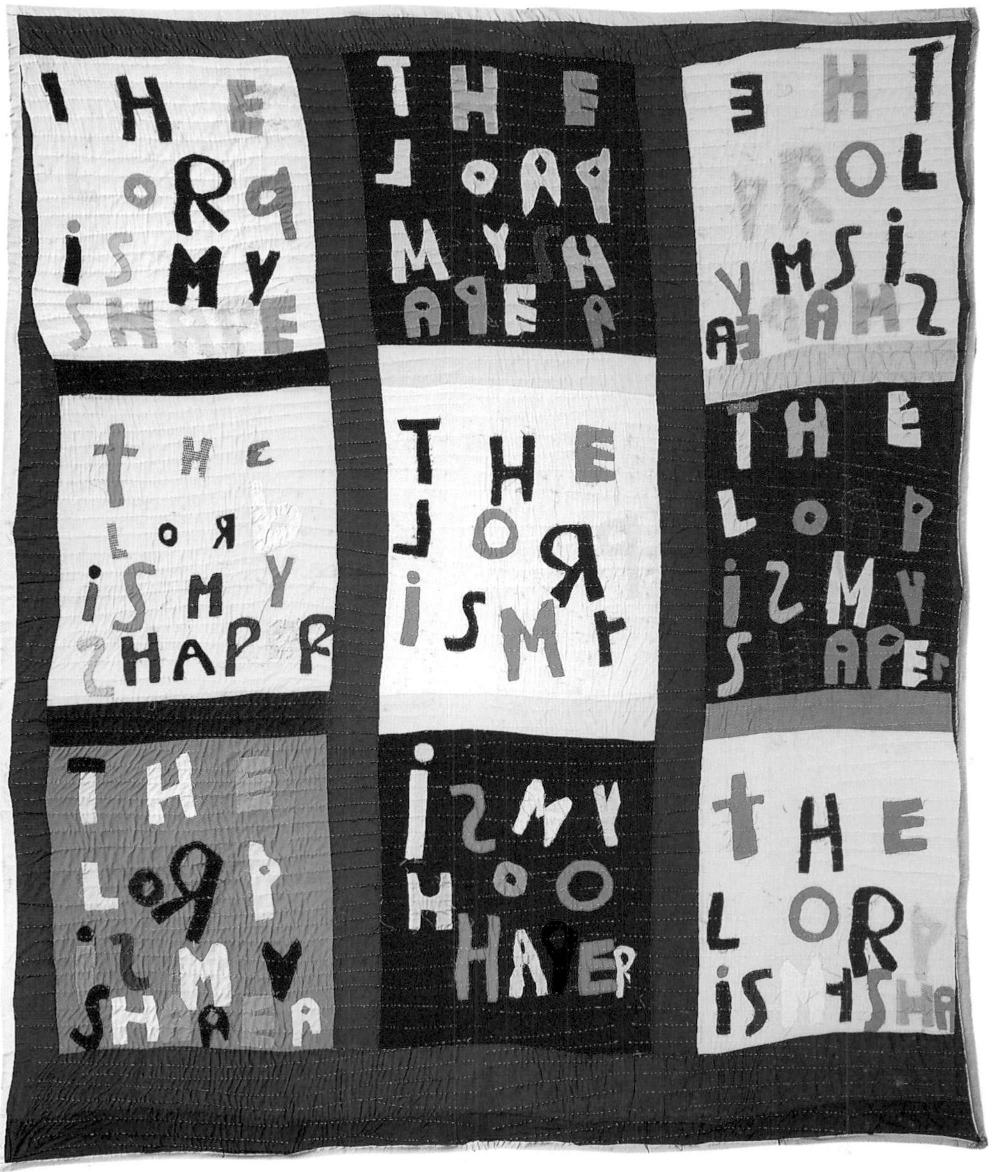

▲ **THE LORD IS MY SHAPER (SHEPHERD)**

Sarah Mary Taylor. c. 1987. Yazoo City, Mississippi. Cottons and cotton blends; hand appliquéd and quilted. 81 x 69 in. Collection of Robert Cargo.

Sarah Mary Taylor often builds her quilts out of repeated images or words. In this strangely powerful quilt, the provocatively misspelled first line of Psalm 23 is repeated nine times, creating an incantation in contrasting shades, sizes, and letter shapes.

◄ **LOG CABIN VARIATION**

Augusta Duncan. c. 1987. Alabama. Cottons and cotton blends; hand pieced and quilted. 94 x 90 in. Collection of Robert Cargo.

This patriotically colored Log Cabin variation puts the red square that normally appears in the center on the outside corner of the block. The logs are all cut freehand and thus vary slightly in size and spacing from block to block, giving the quilt a loose-limbed overall rhythm.

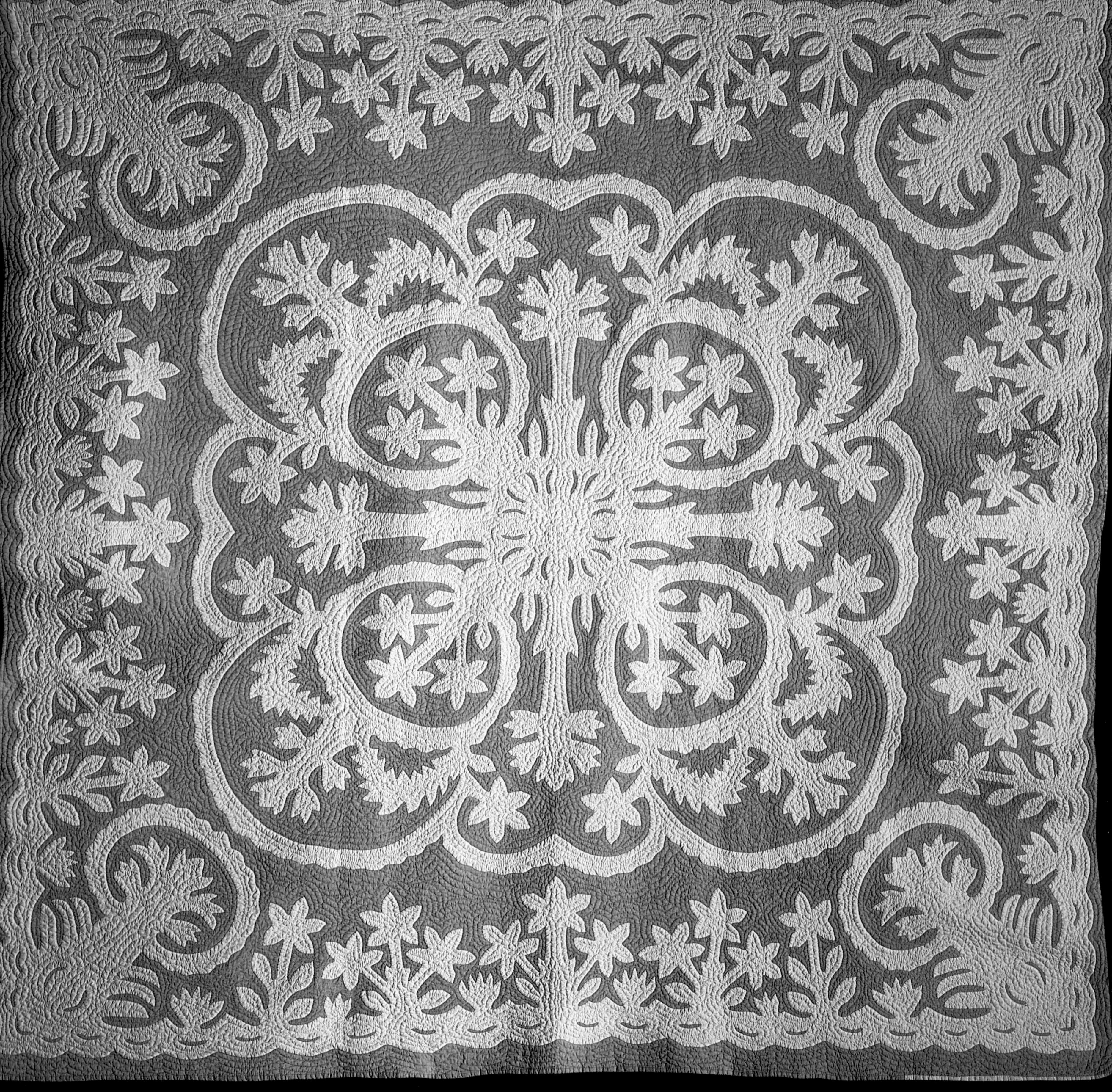

Hawaiian Quilts

The Europeans brought cotton and quiltmaking to Hawaii. Before contact, the people of Hawaii had fashioned clothing, bedding, and even sails from *tapa*, a fabric of varying textures and thicknesses made by soaking and pounding sheets of bark from the paper mulberry tree together. The resulting bark cloth was dyed with natural dyes and often decorated with free-hand or stamped designs. The wives of American missionaries introduced both cotton cloth and quilting to the ancient Polynesian culture of the Hawaiian islands soon after their arrival in the early decades of the nineteenth century. Sewing was an integral part of the missionaries' program to bring Western values and the Christian religion to the native islanders and was taught both informally and as part of the school curriculum as early as the 1830s.

The missionaries tried to introduce piecework to the native people, but apparently the idea did not make sense to the Hawaiians, to whom, as quilt historian Stella Jones speculates, the idea of cutting "new materials into bits to be sewn [back] together [again] seemed a futile waste of time." Instead, the Hawaiians seized on the idea of appliqué, which they observed in the relatively few quilts the Americans held back "for best," and made it their own. Unlike the missionaries, who came from New England where quilts were a necessity in the frigid winter months, Hawaiians quilted more for show than for practical, everyday use, and the more decorative appliqué technique suited this aesthetic emphasis.

By the end of the nineteenth century, two distinct appliqué traditions unique to Hawaii had resulted from the collision of British, American, and Hawaiian cultures. The first, Royal Hawaiian flag quilts, honored the short-lived Hawaiian Kingdom and its much admired kings and queens. Flag quilts were treasured above all others by their owners, who brought them out for show only to their most trusted and intimate friends and guests. Flag quilts remain to this day prized and hidden treasures within many island families. The quilts are known collectively by the name *Ku'u Hae Aloha*, an inscription often found on the quilts meaning "My Beloved Flag." Although this type of quilt may have been made as early as the 1840s, when the Hawaiian flag first took its standard eight-stripe shape with the official addition of Kauai to the kingdom, most were apparently made as memorial pieces after the greatly revered Queen Lili'uokalani ab-

◂ **Pikake and Tuberose**

Hannah Ku'umililani Cummings Baker. 1938. Island of Oahu, Hawaii. Plain woven cotton; hand appliquéd and contour quilted, machine stitched edging. 86 x 86 in. Bernice Pauahi Bishop Museum, Honolulu.

Hannah Cummings Baker (1906–1981) collected and shared many traditional patterns and taught thousands of students during a thirty-year career as a quilting instructor. Copies of the 213 patterns she designed and collected were donated to the Bishop Museum by her family after her death and are available to the public.

dicated in 1893 and the islands were annexed by the United States in 1898, never more to hold independent status or be ruled by monarchs. Flag quilts typically placed representations of four elongated Hawaiian flags, each usually consisting of eight alternating red, white, and blue stripes representing the eight major islands of Hawaii, and a Union Jack, representing the islands' close relationship with Great Britain. (Captain Cook had first discovered the Hawaiian islands in 1778.) The flags were set at right angles to each other around an appliquéd central medallion, which usually represented the Hawaiian coat of arms.

The second tradition, which is more widely practiced and varied, and which dominates Hawaiian quiltmaking to the present day, employs large but often delicate overall appliqué designs, many of them based on local vegetable and flower forms such as breadfruit, pineapple, or orchid. Legend suggests that the shadow of a tree seen cast on a large piece of cloth set outside to dry inspired the first such appliqué design. The cloth's owner thought the pattern so beautiful that she cut the branch and traced its design on the cloth. Whatever their origins, Hawaiian appliqué designs were typically made by cutting a single piece of solid-colored cloth that had been folded into eighths, thereby creating an intricate, radiating, symmetrical pattern. The idea is similar to the snowflakes cut from folded paper that many American children recall from grade school art classes. It may well have been influenced by popular paper cutting techniques of the early nineteenth century, including silhouettes and Pennsylvania Dutch *scherenschnitte*. Indeed, some researchers have speculated that missionaries may have taught paper cutting to the Hawaiians.

The large piece of carefully cut cloth, most commonly red or blue in early days, was then laid out and appliquéd onto a second solid-colored (usually white) background often made from a piece of sheeting, and was then intricately quilted all over with fine hand stitches. Some quilters included other smaller appliqué elements that echoed or elaborated on the central motif. Some designers simply added a repeating decorative element at each of the four corners of their quilt, while others made up complex borders that ran all the way around the quilt, sometimes covering most of the negative space of the quilt's background with elaborate designs. Some quilters cut their designs from light-colored cloth and set it against a contrasting dark background, or placed a light pink, green or blue against the

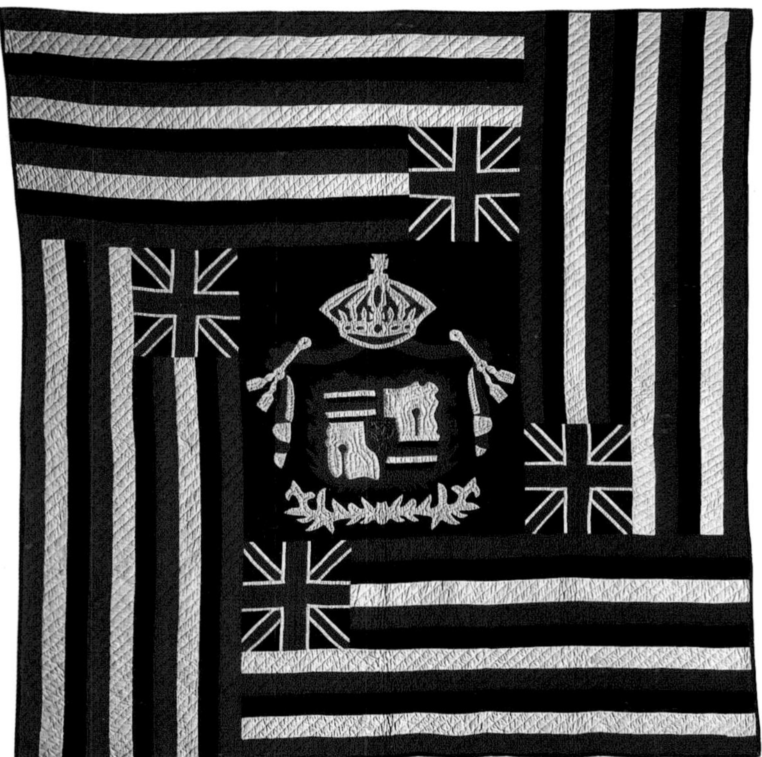

◄ **Ku'u Hae Aloha ("My Beloved Flag")**

Artist unknown. c. 1910. Waimea, Hawaii. Plain woven cotton; hand pieced, hand appliquéd, with hand contour and diagonal quilting. 90 x 90 1/2 in. Honolulu Academy of Arts, gift of Richard M. Cooke.

For Hawaiians, flag quilts symbolize the lost and deeply mourned kingdom of Hawaii, which came to an end with the U.S. annexation of the islands in 1898. In this typical example, four Hawaiian flags surround a stylized representation of the Hawaiian shield. The monarch's crown and ermine cape are appliquéd above the shield.

Recent interest in Hawaiian quiltmaking and quilt history has been fueled by the Hawaiian Quilt Research Project, which began in 1990. The group, which seeks to analyze quilts made prior to 1960, has held quilt days on all of the islands and has documented hundreds of historic quilts, recording them in photographs and transcribing stories and histories from owners and family members. The Research Project has also helped to make the public aware of the importance of the old quilts to Hawaii's cultural heritage, and has encouraged many people to become involved with preserving and continuing the tradition. Above all, the project has helped Hawaiians to feel proud of their rich and unique quilting traditions. A thirteen-part series on the history and techniques of Hawaiian quilting, produced by Hawaii Public Television in 1993, was taught by Elizabeth Akana and profiled many of the outstanding modern quilters of the islands, including Meali'i Kalama, Junedale Quinories, Annette Sumada, and Doris Nosaka. (Kalama, a legendary quilter and designer who died in 1992, was particularly influential in keeping the old traditions alive and taught a number of today's master quilters, including Akana. She was honored by the National Endowment for the Arts in 1985 as a National Heritage Fellow, the equivalent of Japan's Living National Treasures program.) Due largely to the efforts of the Hawaiian Quilt Research Project and the Hawaiian Public Television series, the Hawaiian quilt, a unique, distinctive, and still evolving folk art, is now being recognized for its cultural and historic value.

▼ COCONUT AND PINEAPPLE

Meali'i Kalama. 1973. Island of Oahu, Hawaii. Plain woven cotton/polyester; hand appliquéd and contour quilted. 108 x 108 in. Private collection.

Meali'i Kalama learned quiltmaking from her grandmother. Kalama is rightly considered one of the greatest of all Hawaiian designers; this quilt's beautiful original design demonstrates why her work is held in such high regard.

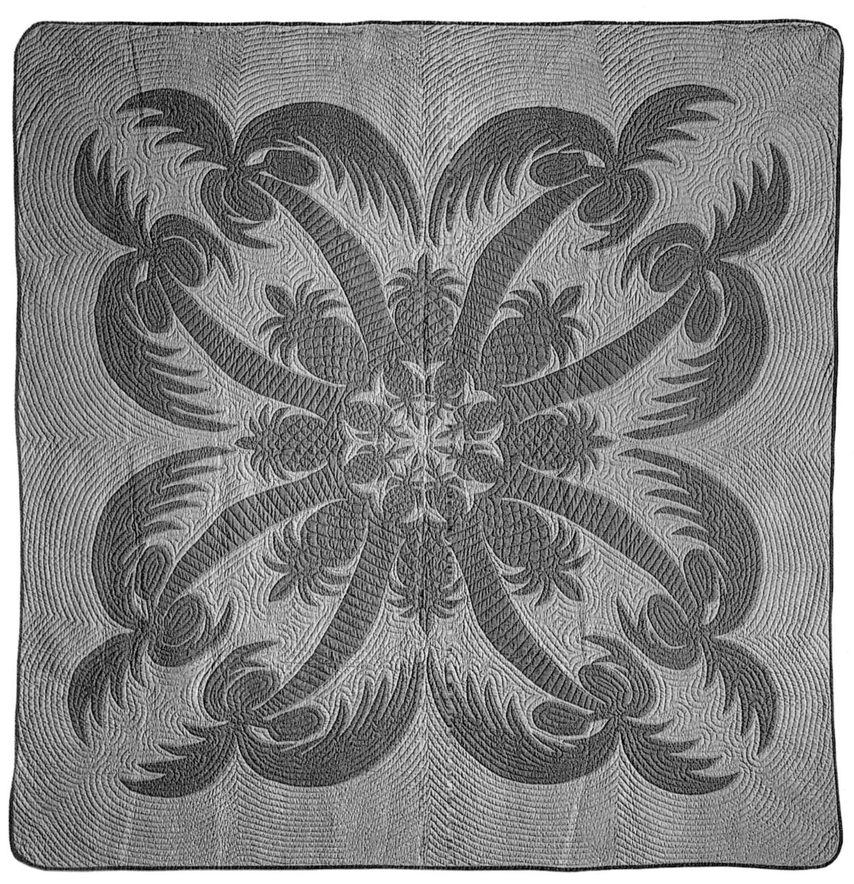

▼ KA HASU NANI O HALE'IWA ("THE BEAUTIFUL LOTUS OF HALE'IWA")

Doris Nosaka. 1984–1986. Island of Hawaii. Plain woven cotton; hand appliquéd and contour quilted. 101 x 103 in. Collection of the artist.

This unusual quilt employs three fabric colors to suggest flowering lotuses floating in a pond. The square, light-green inner border and small corner blocks are also atypical of Hawaiian design.

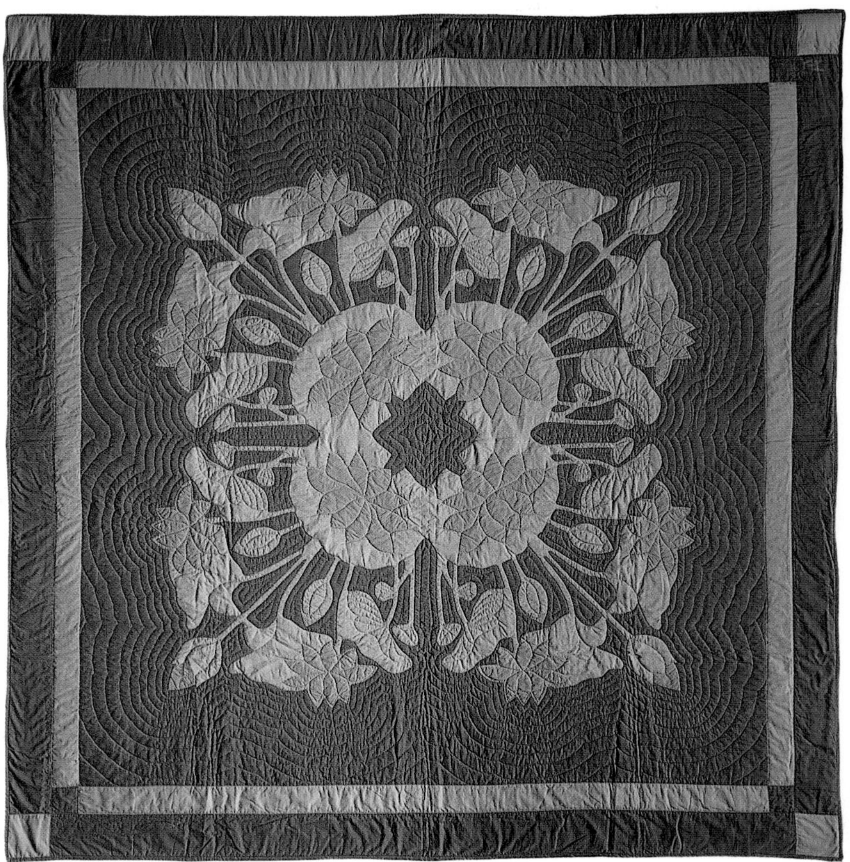

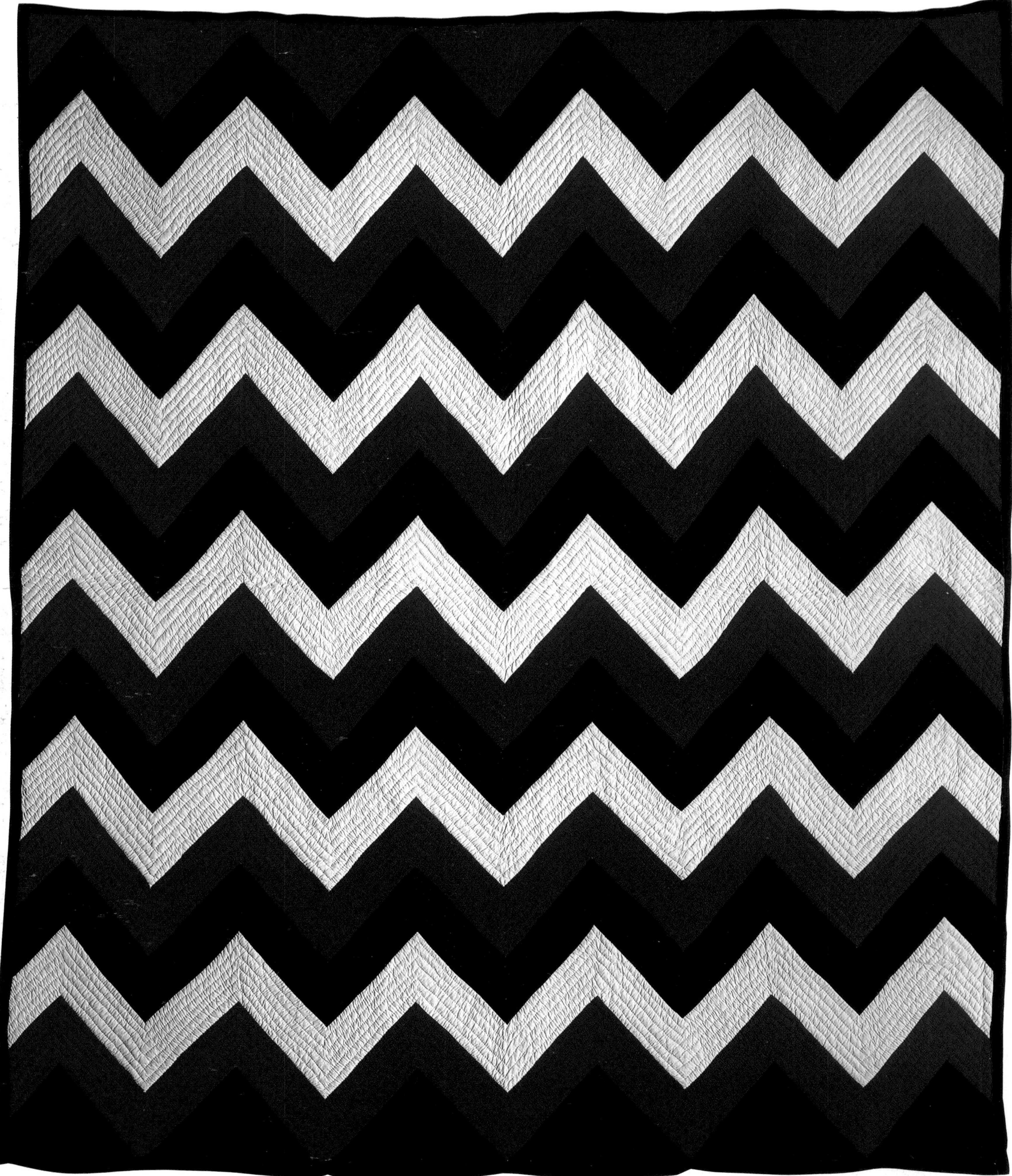

▲ **Kuli Pu'u**

Artist unknown. c. 1880–1910. Island of Kauai, Hawaii. Plain woven cotton; hand pieced, appliquéd, and quilted, machine stitched edging. 92 x 82 in. Honolulu Academy of Arts, gift of Mrs. Charles M. Cooke.

This powerful and atypical zigzag design explodes with energy. As in most Hawaiian quilts, the quilt stitching echoes the lines of the design, thereby subtly reinforcing the pattern on the quilt's surface.

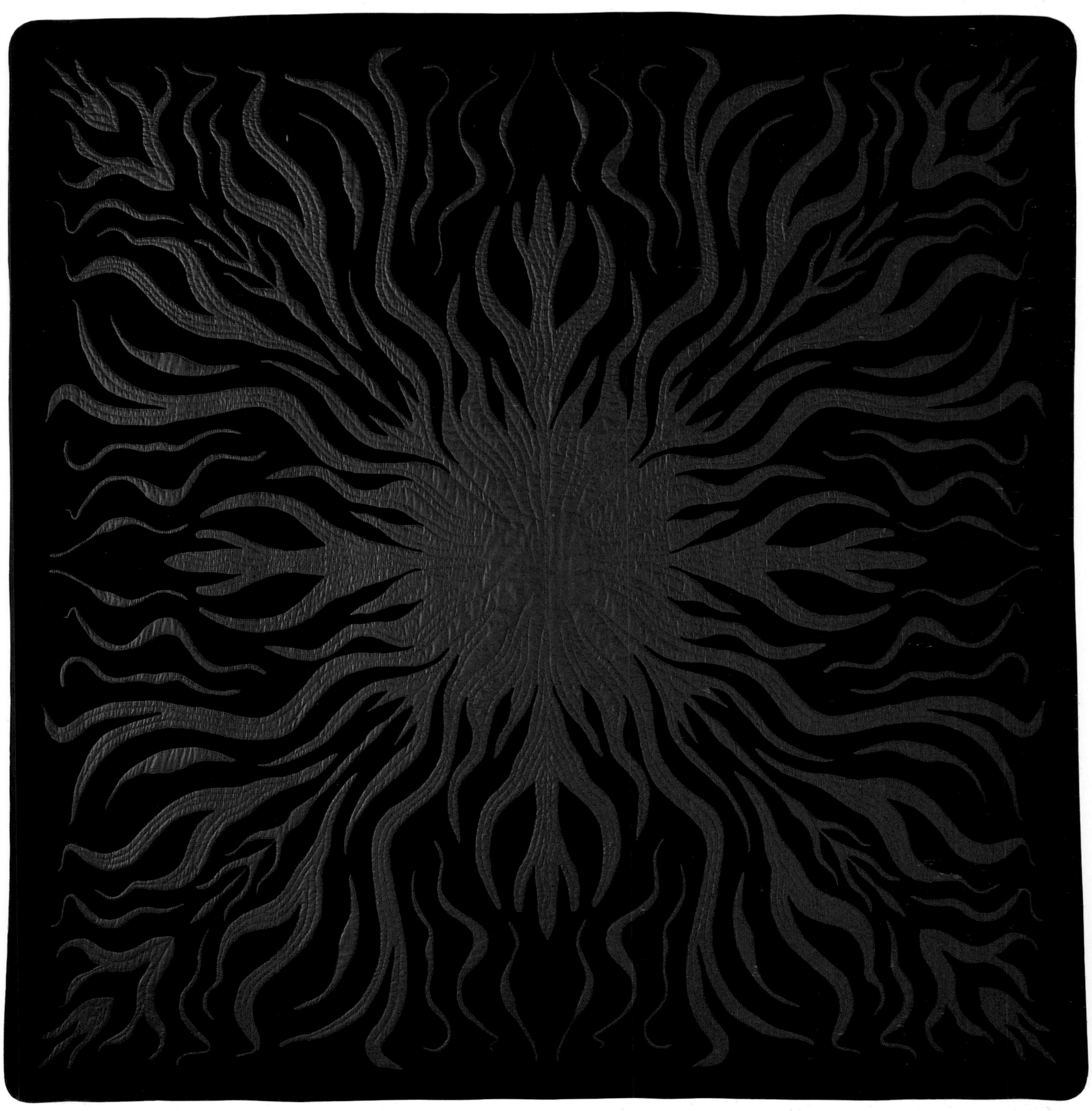

▲ **VOLCANO QUILT—I KA HO 'OKUMU ANA ("IN THE BEGINNING")**

Helen Friend. 1989. Honolulu, Hawaii. Cotton; reverse appliquéd and quilted. 96 x 96 in. Private collection.

Helen Friend's original design places the viewer above a volcano, looking down at an abstract pattern of flaming rivulets set off by black volcanic ash. Friend, who was born in England and emigrated to Hawaii in 1966, says, "I see [the volcano] as the birth of the island. This chain of islands is here because of the power of the volcano."

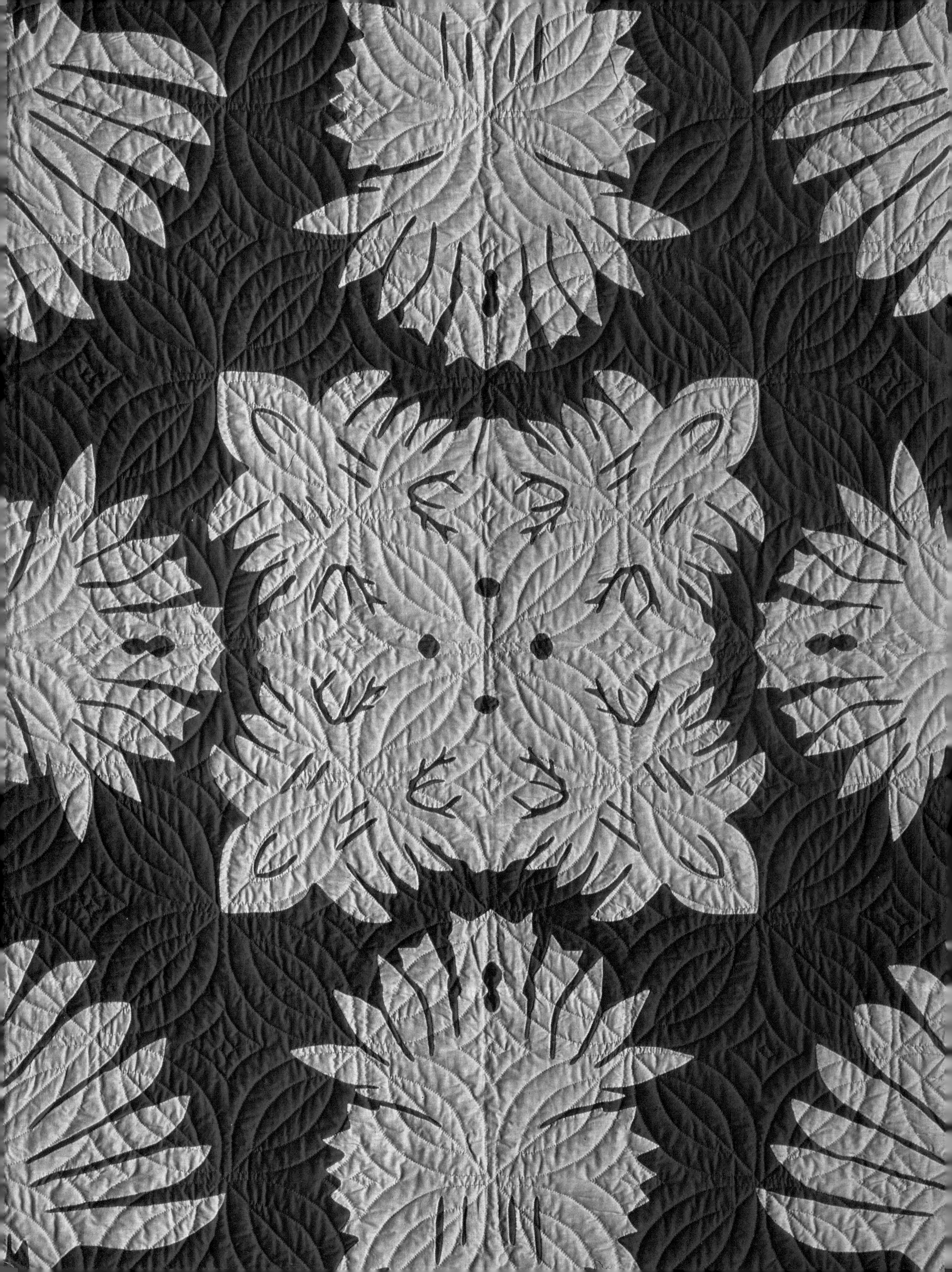

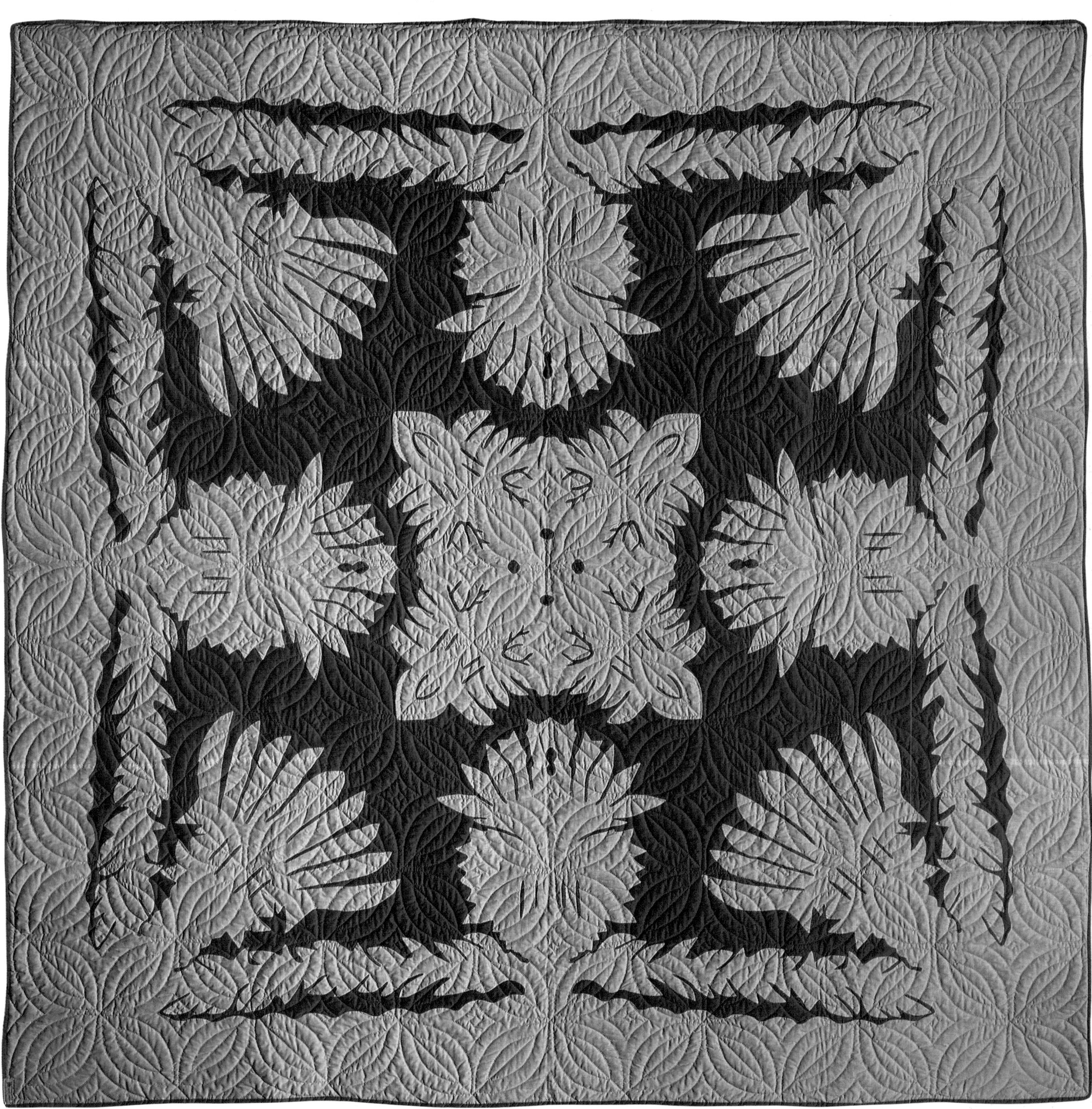

▲ **'AHINAHINA ("SILVERSWORD") (◄ DETAIL)**

Junedale Quinories. 1961. Island of Hawaii. Plain woven cotton; hand appliquéd with "kuahonu" (turtle's back) quilting. 97 x 97 in. Collection of the artist.

Silversword is an aptly named gray-green plant with dozens of thin leaves that form a round bushlike form. After nine to fourteen years of growth, the silversword produces a single spectacular tall flower spike and then dies. This quilt depicts the plant in its typical nonflowering state. Junedale Quinories learned quiltmaking from her mother, a professional quilter who also made quilts for her family's use.

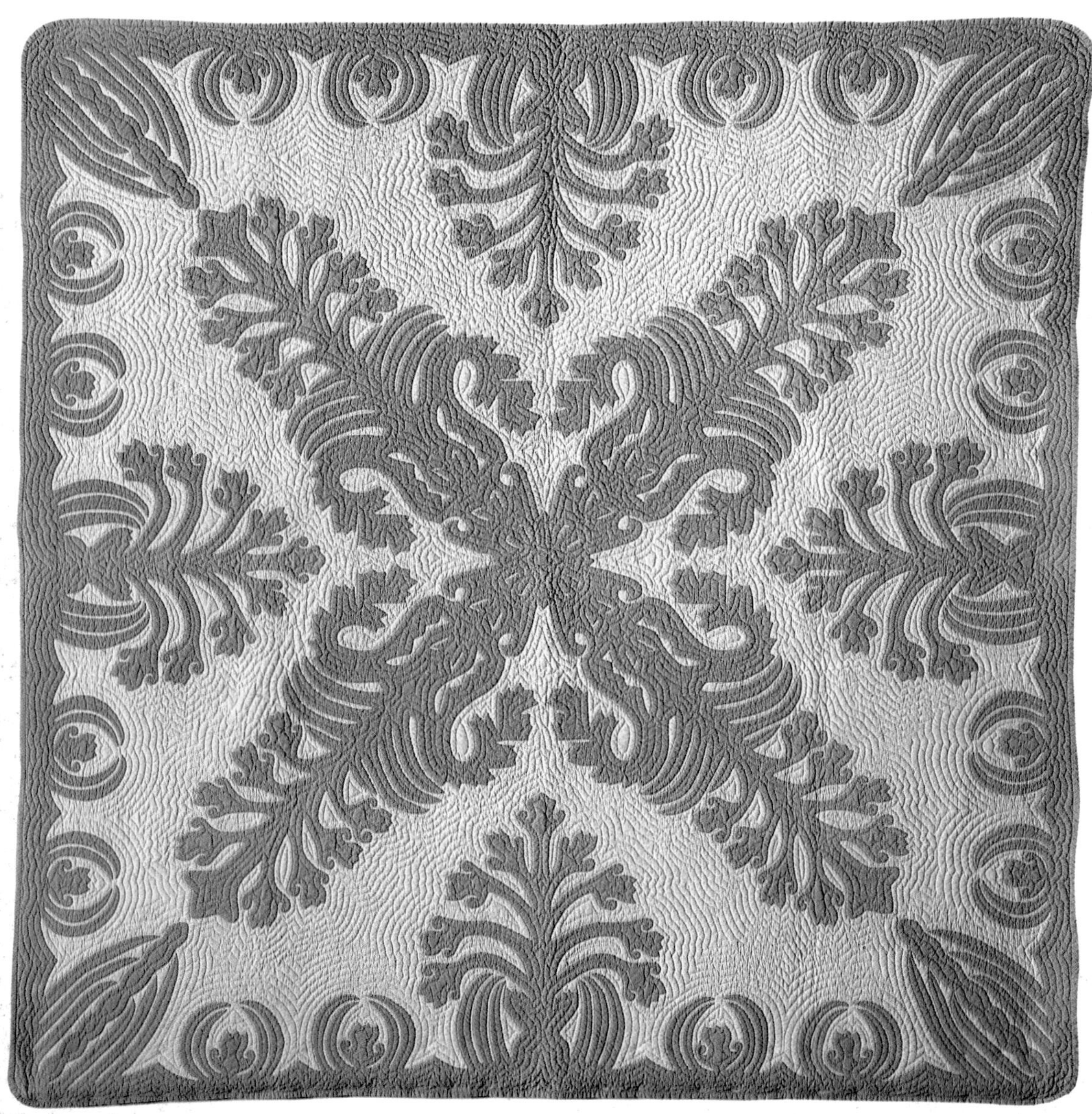

◄ **'AHINAHINA O HALEAKALA ("THE SILVERSWORD OF HALEAKALA")**

Annette Sumada. 1986. Island of Hawaii. Plain woven cotton; hand appliquéd and contour quilted. 110 x 110 in. Collection of Jiro Alan Sumada.

Silversword grows only in cinders on the sides of the volcanic Mount Haleakala on the island of Maui. The once common plant has become endangered in recent years. This quilt's central design depicts four intersecting silversword plants in bloom.

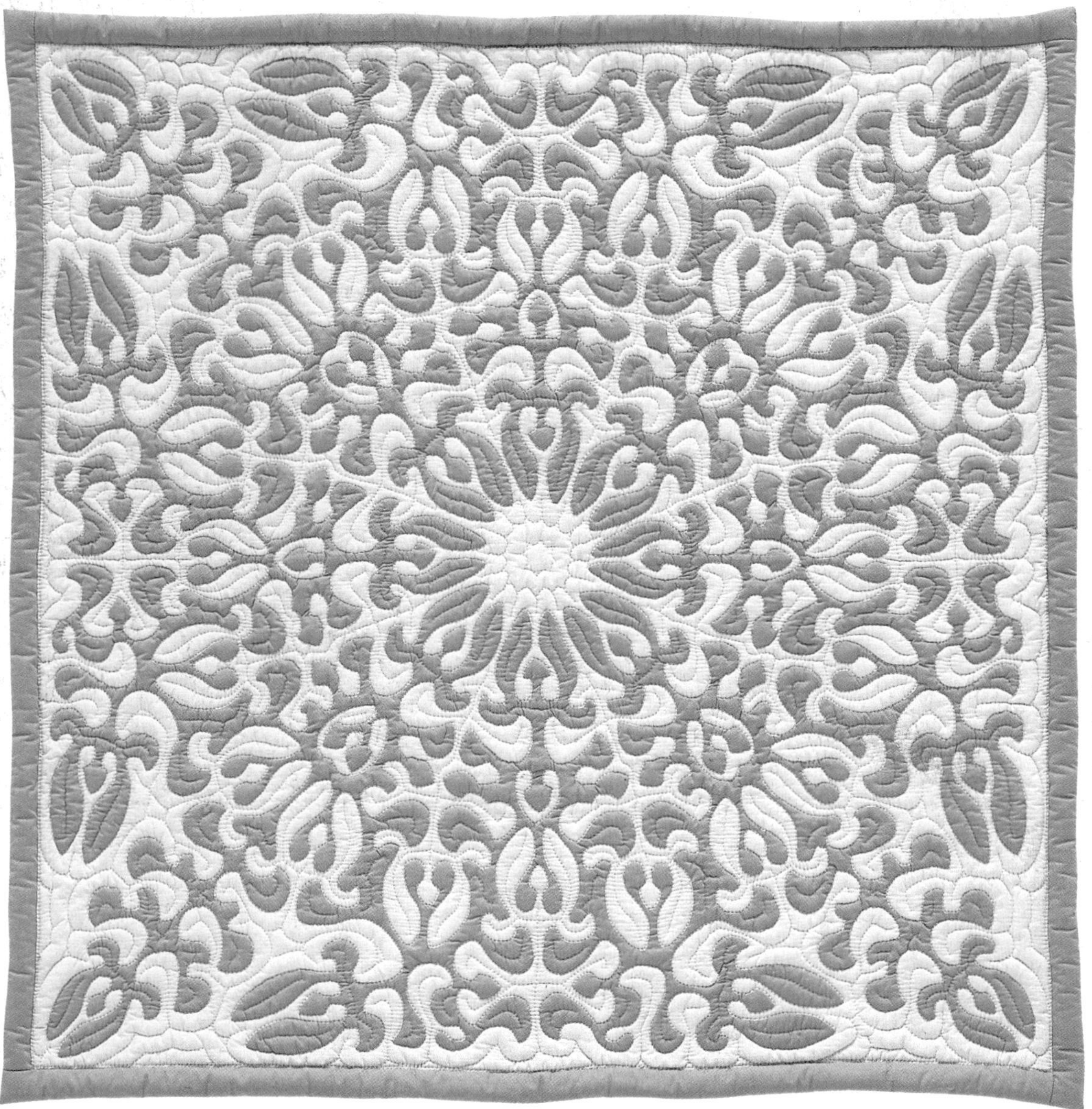

◄ **NA PUA E LIKO ANI-ANI ("FLOWERS AND BUDS MIRRORED")**

Stan Yates. 1994. Island of Kauai, Hawaii. Cotton; hand appliquéd and quilted. 44 x 44 in. Collection of Mr. and Mrs. Claire F. Story.

Stan Yates has applied his love of the complex geometric art of M.C. Escher to Hawaiian quilt design, developing what he calls "double designs," which are built of a single floral shape that repeats in both foreground and background. According to Yates, "The key aspect of the quilt design is that the symmetry of its unit cell can be shifted at its outer edge so that when outer edges of two unit cells are joined, the 'outside' becomes the 'inside.' The unit cell fits a 22 1/2 degree radial segment, so two unit cells comprise the standard 45 degree segment that yields the traditional eight-fold Hawaiian quilt design."

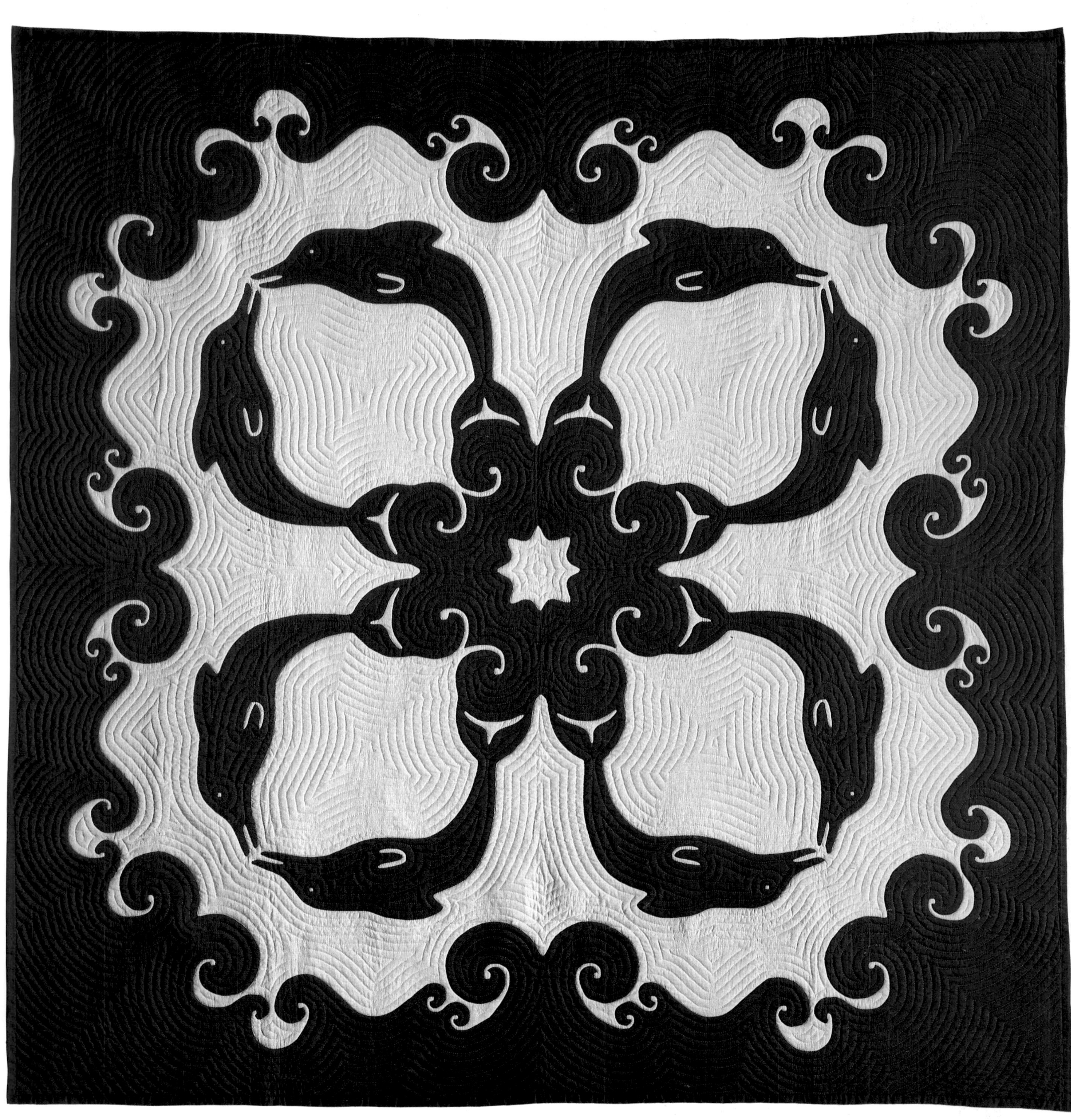

▲ **SINGING DOLPHINS**

Kathleen Puanani Nishida and Robin Keli'i Jensen. 1988. Island of Hawaii. Plain woven cotton; hand appliquéd and contour quilted. 92 x 92 in. Collection of Maua Kea Beach Hotel.

Animal motifs are far less common in Hawaiian quilt design than are images of flowers and vegetables. This original design captures the ebullient energy of dolphins playing among the ocean waves.

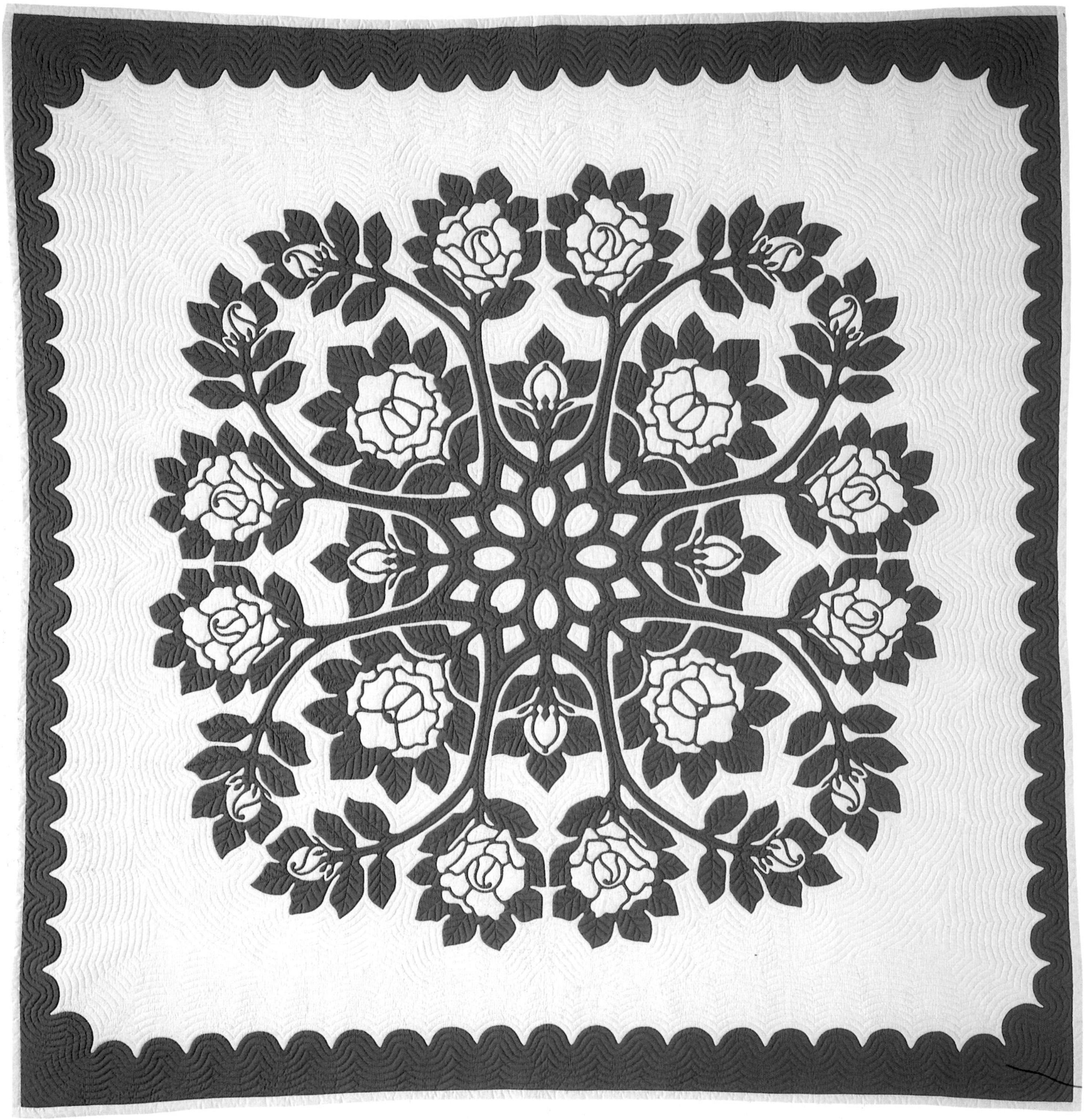

▲ Kiele Onaona ("Fragrant Gardenias") (Reverse ▶)

Sharon Balai. 1994. Kamuela, Hawaii. Cottons; hand appliquéd and quilted. 100 x 96 in. Collection of the artist.

Sharon Balai relates, "My home . . . is at about the 9000-foot elevation and the climate is cool and misty. The temperatures range from the upper 30s to the lower 80s. Gardenias . . . do especially well here and grow in profusion all around my home. *Kiele Onaona* . . . conveys my appreciation for the special way their fragrance surrounds and encompasses you into pleasant relaxation at the end of a day . . . Upon completion of this quilt, I was surprised to find that I actually prefer the appearance of the stitched design from the back." The reverse of *Fragrant Gardenias*, which stands by itself as a whole cloth quilt, makes explicit the importance of quilted design; we may well be looking at the wrong side of a quilt when we choose to view the pieced or appliquéd top only.

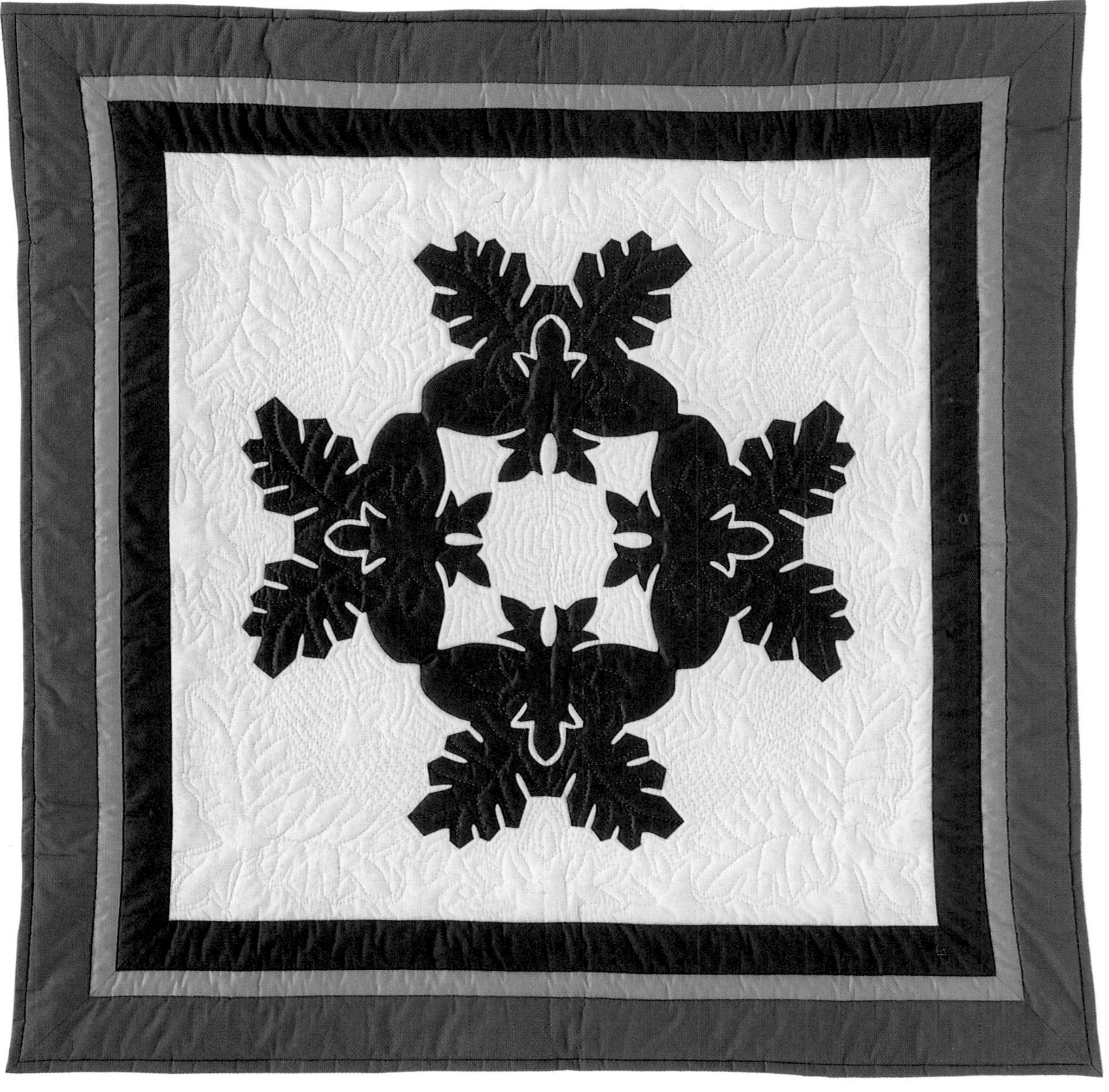

LEI OF LOVE (SIDE ONE) ►

Elizabeth Akana. 1993. Kaneohe, Hawaii. Cottons, hand appliquéd and quilted. 58 x 52 in. Collection of the quiltmaker.

On side one of this two-sided quilt, the love of the mountain and ocean Naupaka flowers are brought together in the beautiful lei worn by the prince.

◄ LEI OF LOVE (SIDE TWO)

Here, the princess seeks out the flowers of the mountain Naupaka to make her lei of love.

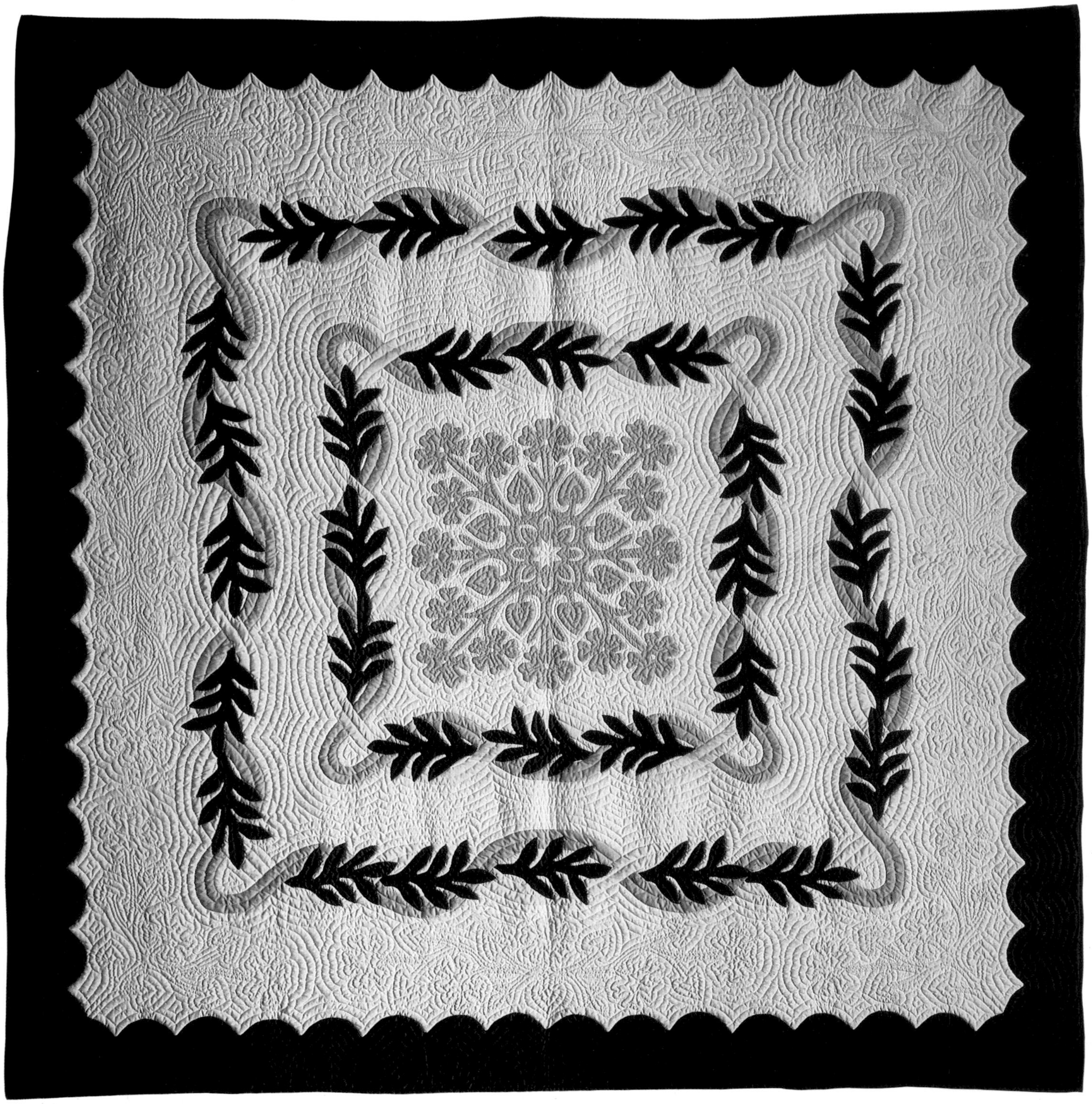

▲ Lei 'Ilima (detail ▶▶)

Designed by Deborah Kakalia, made by Charlotte Leimakani Cathcart. 1984. Island of Oahu, Hawaii. Plain woven cotton/polyester; hand appliquéd and contour quilted. 99 x 102 in. Collection of Charlotte Cathcart.

This quilt depicts a lei woven of yellow 'ilima flowers, the official flower of the island of Oahu. Charlotte Cathcart learned quilting from her grandmother and from Deborah Kakalia, who created the design from which this quilt was made.

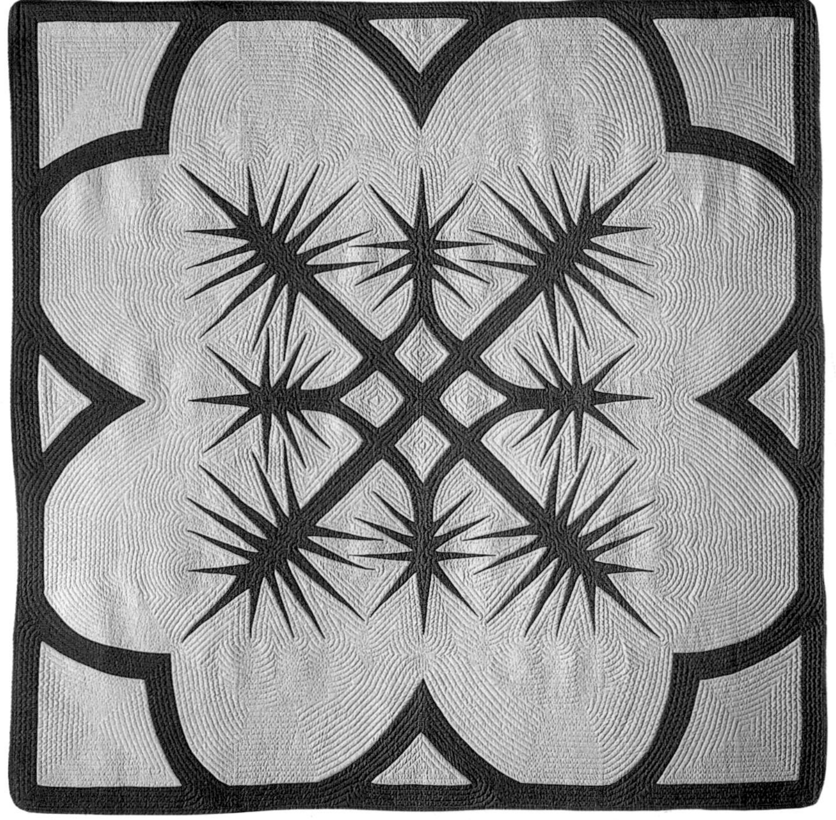

Chinese Money Tree ▶

Carol Downing Kamaile. 1981. Island of Oahu, Hawaii. Plain woven cotton/polyester; hand appliquéd and contour quilted. 100 x 100 in. Collection of the artist.

This original design was inspired by the long, spiky leaves of the Chinese money tree, which is a member of the *Dracaena* family.

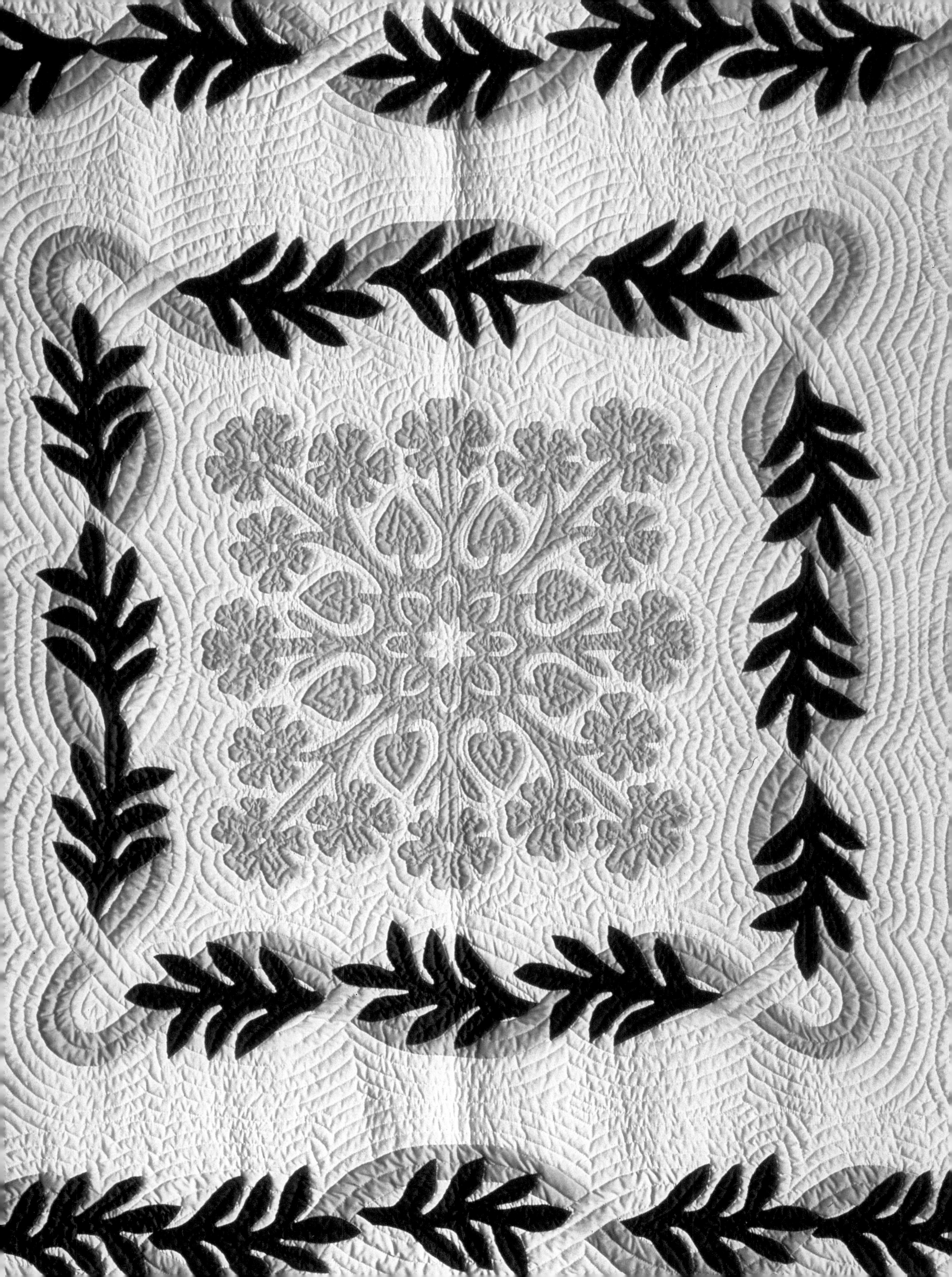

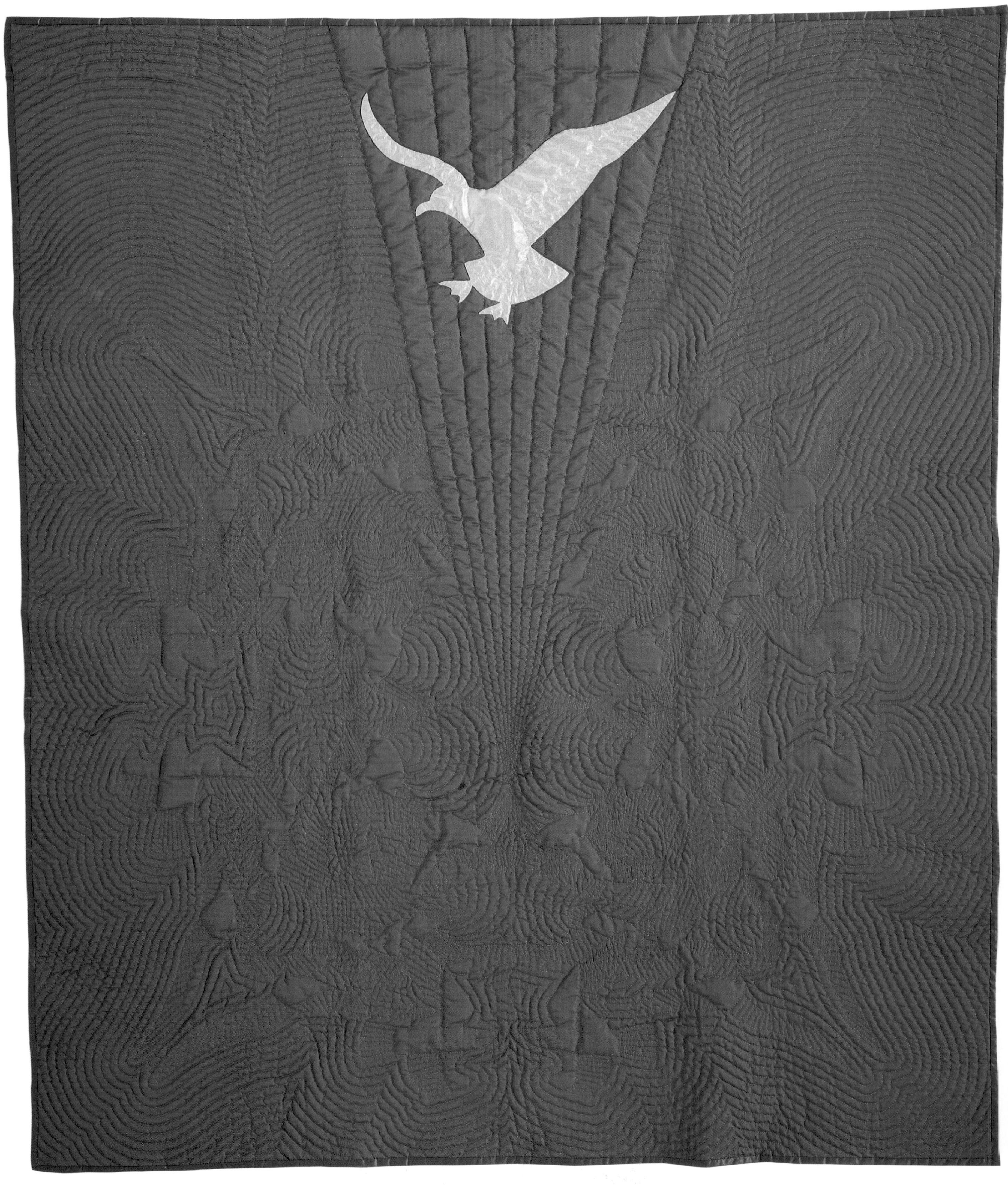

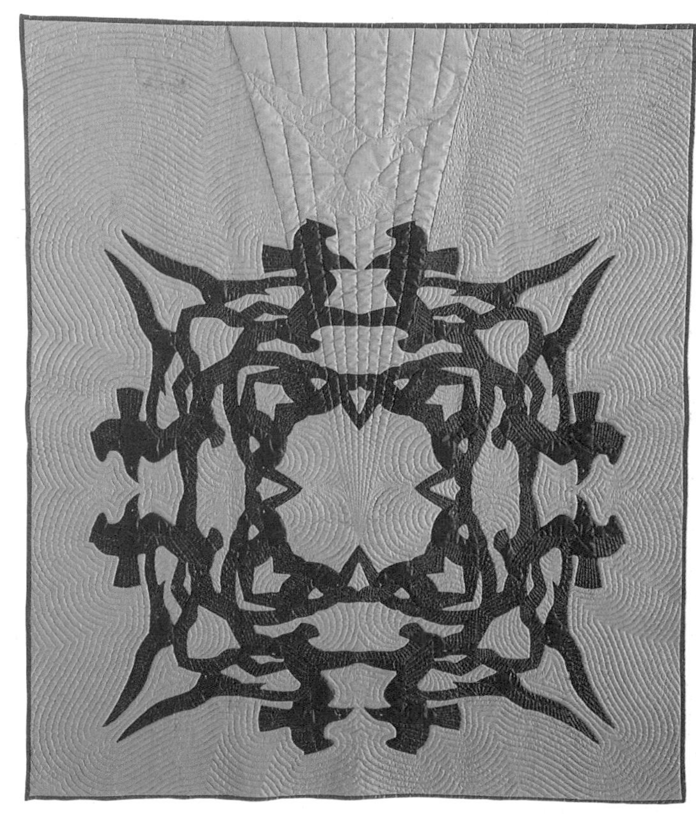

◀ Jonathan / My Way (reverse ▶)

Elizabeth Akana. 1992. Kaneohe, Hawaii. Appliquéd cottons; quilted by Kathie Dallas. 68 x 58 in. Collection of the quiltmaker.

The designs on both sides of Elizabeth Akana's two-sided quilts echo and interlock, thereby enhancing and reinforcing each other's meanings. Each side may be viewed separately, but the whole is more than the sum of the parts. This quilt, inspired by the book *Jonathan Livingston Seagull*, depicts on one side Jonathan proudly flying alone, while the reverse shows the flock of gulls from which he dared to stray. Akana says, "This quilt...reminds us all to be all that we can be, that indeed we do not have to fly with the flock but can instead be our own bird." The quilting on each side repeats the bird form (or forms) from the other.

Elizabeth Akana

Elizabeth Akana of Kaneohe, Oahu, is one of Hawaii's premier quilt historians as well as one of the state's most important and innovative quiltmakers. Although she was born in New Jersey and raised in Baltimore, Akana has lived in Hawaii since the early 1960s. She fell in love with the island quilting tradition through two quilts made by her husband's grandmother when he was a child. She studied both the history and practice of quiltmaking with the legendary Meali'i Kalama, who became her mentor. Elizabeth started her own quilt design business in 1969 while continuing to delve deeply into the history of quilting in the islands. Her 1981 book, *Hawaiian Quilting: A Fine Art,* distilled her extensive research on the subject.

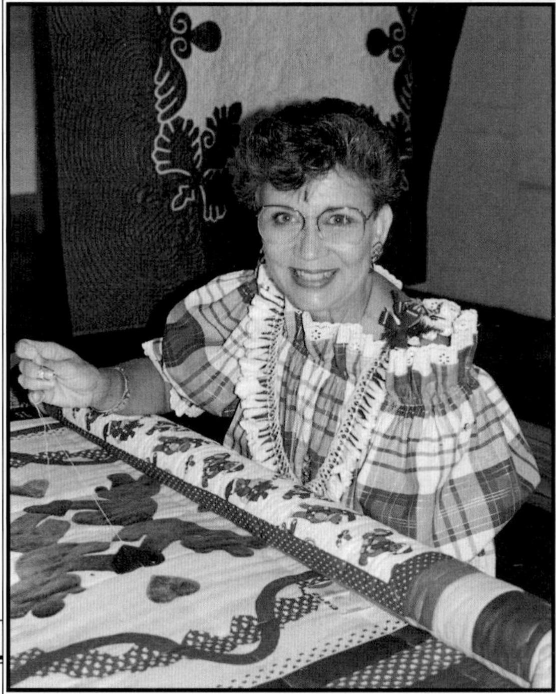

In recent years, Akana's quilting has brought her to television as part of a series on Hawaiian quilting produced by Hawaii Public Television. She has also been a guiding force behind the Hawaiian Quilt Research Project, which has documented hundreds of historic quilts throughout the islands. She has organized several exhibitions of Hawaiian quilts and exhibited her own quilts in Japan and on the U.S. mainland. Among her newest projects is a commission by the Honolulu Police Department for its new headquarters building. The quilt will have a traditional wide Union Jack flag border and will tell the history of law enforcement in Hawaii through a central medallion design composed of six appliquéd representations of police badges.

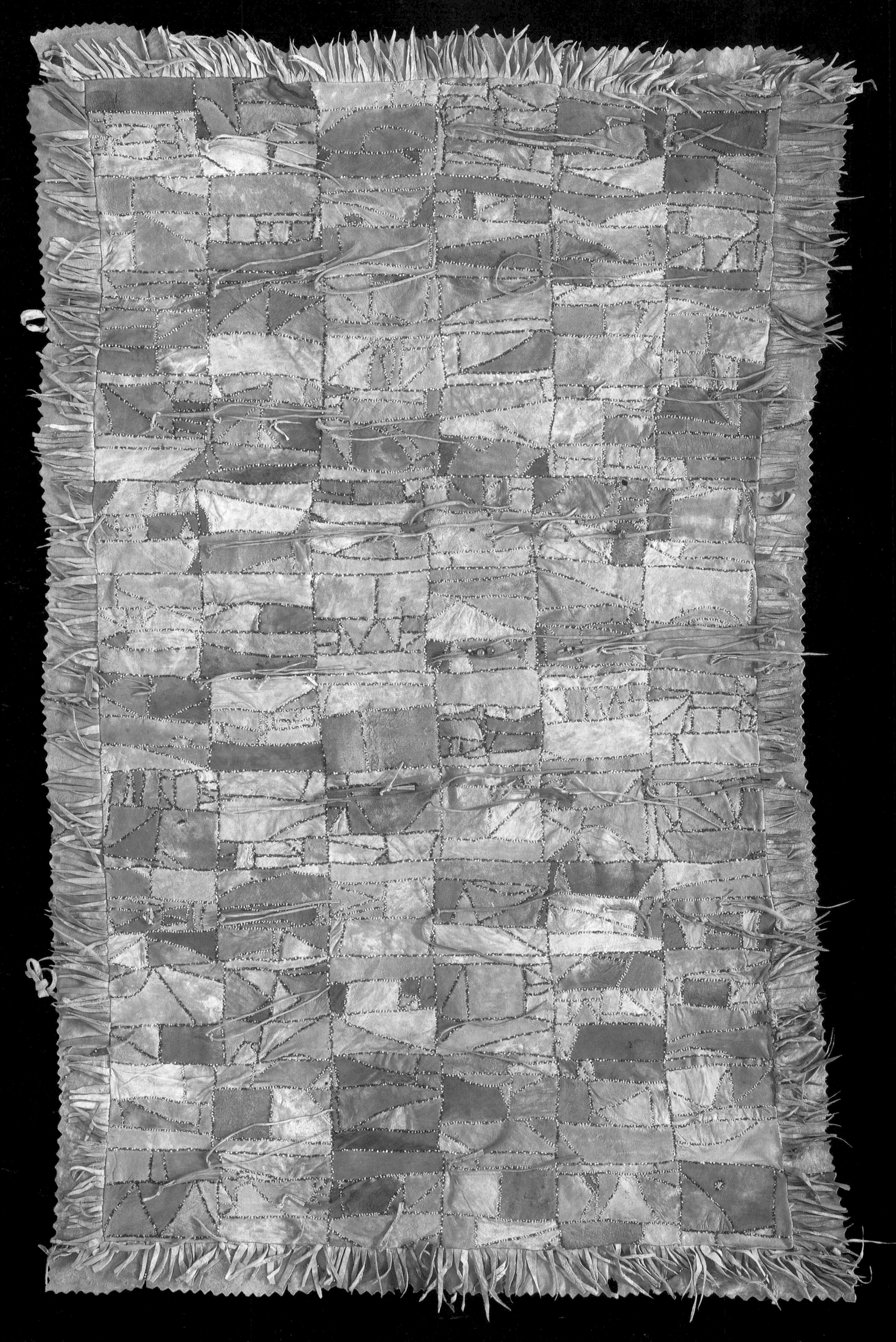

Native American Quilts

Quilts and quiltmaking were not a part of traditional precontact Native American culture. Most Native Americans used animal skins and furs to warm themselves at night. Woodland tribes used the skins of plentiful deer, while buffalo robes were used as bedcovers by the Plains tribes. In the early nineteenth century, tightly woven blankets decorated with abstract, geometric designs were a specialty of the Navajo in the Southwest; these extremely warm, durable, and handsome weavings were coveted by many other tribes and became known as "chief's blankets" because of their high value. Blankets were also a staple of the European-American fur traders, who exchanged them for beaver pelts taken by members of the Woodland tribes of the northern United States and Canada. Indians readily accepted Hudson's Bay blankets; they valued them both for personal use and, often more importantly, for use as ceremonial gifts.

Like African-Americans and Hawaiians, Native Americans learned quiltmaking from European-Americans. Tribes all over the West were conquered and resettled on reservations in the later years of the nineteenth century, and this constant contact with white culture inevitably resulted in the adoption of some of its ways. White soldiers and settlers carried their quilts west. Soldiers' wives in the forts not only used but undoubtedly made quilts and were carefully observed by Indian women. Missionaries and church groups seeking to convert heathen Indians to Christianity taught quilting and other traditional European homemaking skills to Indian women, and quilting was one of the domestic arts taught to Indian children in boarding school home economics classes.

Although Native Americans were taught traditional European-American patterns and techniques, they, like the Hawaiians, quickly found ways to incorporate their own cultural heritage into their quilts. In the late 1800s and early 1900s, for example, Plains Indian women adopted the traditional Lone Star, or Star of Bethlehem, design. This large star pattern reminded Indians of their own highly symbolic Morning Star motif, which was commonly painted or beaded on clothing, hides, bags, and shields. Indians, particularly the nomadic tribes of the northern regions of the West, were keen observers of the heavens, which not

◂ **Beaded Leather Crazy**

Unknown Sioux artist. c. 1880–1900. South Dakota. Suede, leather fringe, trade beads; hand pieced and beaded. 64 x 41 in. Collection of the Roger J. Bounds Foundation, Inc.

This unique, small quilt embodies the collision of Native American and Victorian cultural traditions in the late 1800s. Made from oddly shaped pieces of leather, it is the size and shape of a pony blanket. Instead of employing the embroidery stitching typical of Victorian crazies, the pieces of suede are sewn and decorated with rows of tiny trade beads. Long strips of rawhide are tied randomly to the quilt top, while an evenly cut rawhide fringe borders the outside edge.

only measured time for them, but also carried great symbolic significance. Except for the sun and the moon, Venus, the Morning Star, is often the brightest object in the sky and can be seen clearly in the hours just after sunset or before dawn. In the northern hemisphere the Morning Star rises before dawn in the east early in the spring and travels across the sky to the west as the year progresses. To the Indians the progress of the Morning Star represented the path that the spirits of the dead travel to earth and provided a symbolic link between themselves and their predecessors, forebears, and departed relatives. The Morning Star quilt pattern is dominated by a large, pieced eight-pointed center star that fills the entire quilt top. The pattern also attracted the attention of Great Lakes tribes, who added repeating appliquéd floral motifs traditional to their culture between the points of the star. The Morning Star remains by far the most favored pattern among Native American quilters and, because of its highly charged symbolism, has become an important part of many of their funeral and burial rites.

Another unique Indian quilting tradition developed among the Seminole people of the Florida Everglades region. When the hand-cranked sewing machine reached the Everglades in the 1880s, the Seminoles used it to sew narrow strips of cloth together. The resulting strips of banded fabric could then be cut into segments and cleverly reassembled to create new patterns, which the Seminoles used to decorate their clothing. The strips were left unquilted to emphasize their graphic, two-dimensional designs.

Without the sewing machine the Seminole strip technique would have been impossible since its tiny patterns could not have been practically worked by hand. After strips of cloth of contrasting colors were sewn together, the segments could be assembled in a variety of ways. Some were cut at a 90-degree angle and either reassembled side by side or offset; others were cut at an angle other than 90 degrees and then reassembled. Repeating rhythms or medallion patterns could be achieved by joining segments from different strips. The Seminole strip quilting technique is practiced by a number of contemporary quilters, most notably the art quiltmakers Judith Larzelere and Michael James, both of whom have used unquilted strips to create highly expressive and original quilts for many years.

Although Native American quilts were inherently symbolic objects, they certainly had many practical uses as well. Primarily used as warm bedcoverings, they also served to decorate walls or cover doors, to wrap seekers on vision quests, to help heal sickness, or were given in gift exchanges at powwows or other ceremonies within and outside of the community. These and other symbolic and ceremonial uses continue to dominate Indian quiltmaking today. Most Native Americans do not sell their work, but instead make quilts as gifts. As Richard White explains in *The Native Americans*, "In Indian society . . . material goods introduced by Europeans transcended their immediate utilitarian ends. Repeatedly Indian peoples put such goods at the service of honor. Indians honored other human beings . . . by making them gifts. Indians honored those with spiritual powers whose aid they needed by making them gifts. Many Indian peoples honored the dead by burying valued goods with them or by distributing goods to mourners at the time of burial."

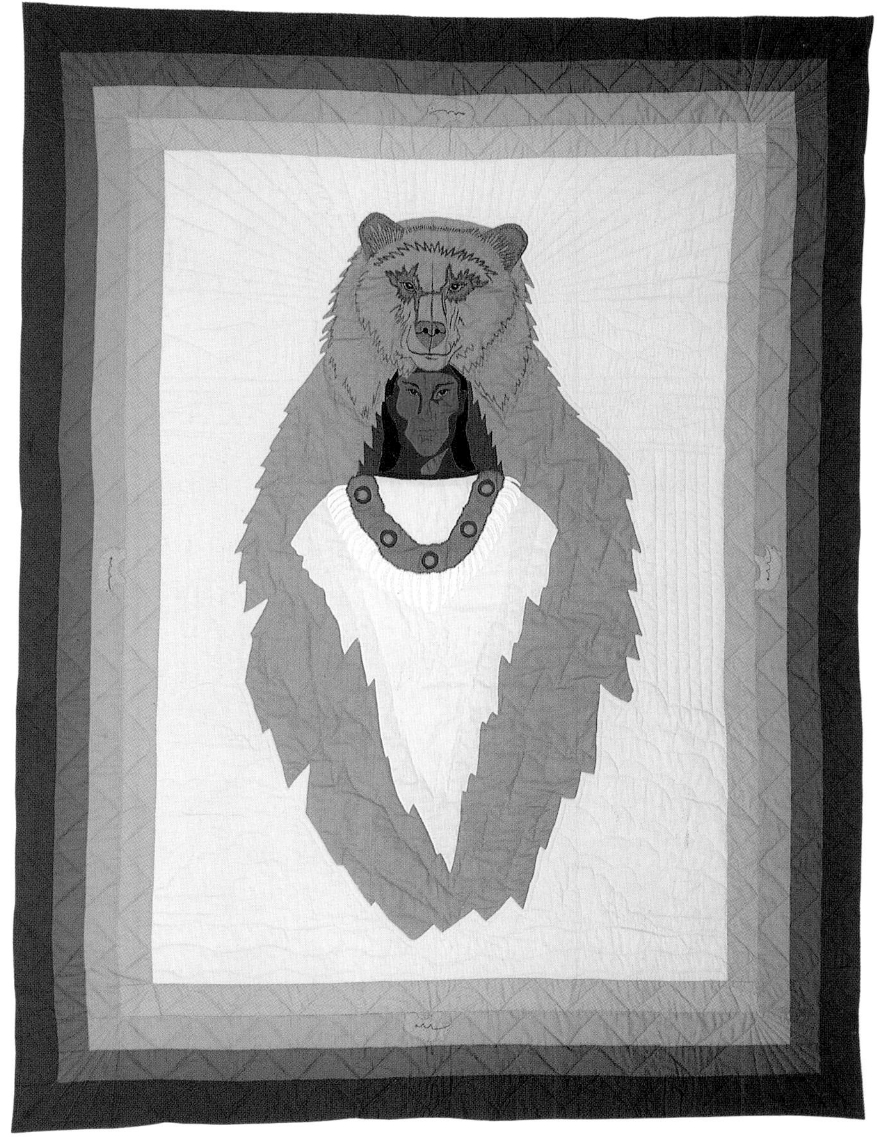

BEARMAN ▶

Nancy Naranjo. 1993. Fairview, New Mexico. Cottons; hand appliquéd, embroidered, and quilted. 85 x 64 in. Collection of Jean Berube.

Women on both the Eastern Cherokee and French sides of Nancy Naranjo's family made quilts. She and her Cherokee grandmother made a scrap quilt together when she was a child. Naranjo says, "I like to make pictorial quilts (I also paint) about traditional stories, about special moments in life, about times when the concrete world and the spiritual world become one." *Bearman* captures such a moment.

Gift exchanges have always held a central place in Native American societies, which are in attitude and tradition far more communal than those brought to America by European settlers. White settlers and traders were completely baffled by Indian attitudes toward property and invented the familiar phrase "Indian giver" in response to the Indians' peculiar expectation that gifts be returned or reciprocated equally. The Indians for their part were perplexed by the white man's reluctance to part with their gifts. In his book *The Gift*, Lewis Hyde explains, "The opposite of 'Indian giver' would be something like 'white man keeper' (or maybe 'capitalist'), that is, a person whose instinct is to remove property from circulation, to put it in a warehouse or museum (or more to the point for capitalism, to lay it aside to be used for production)...Tribal peoples [on the other hand] usually distinguish between gifts and capital. Commonly they have a law that repeats the sensibility implicit in the idea of an Indian gift. 'One man's gift,' they say, 'must not be another man's capital.'" Although Native Americans inevitably adopted many aspects of the individualistic, impersonal, commodity-based culture brought by the Europeans, they have retained the communal gift exchange or potlatch to the present day, and quilts have become one of the most common gifts made for exchange during these ceremonies.

Of course, some Native American quiltmakers do make quilts that are intended for sale outside the community. Because the medium is readily understood by outsiders, it is very attractive to the marketplace interested in contemporary Indian arts. Native American artists who have chosen the quilt as their medium, such as Margaret Wood and Nancy Naranjo, are now making quilts eagerly sought by collectors around the world. These and other contemporary Native American quilters from different tribal cultures have drawn from their own cultural traditions and adapted distinctive design motifs to the quilt. Hopi sandpaintings, Pueblo pottery, Navajo blankets, Sioux painted parfleches, Woodland beaded leggings and moccasins, and other traditional models have inspired some truly singular fabric work. Some quiltmakers work strictly within their own tribal design heritage, while others include a wide range of traditional Indian design motifs.

Despite its origins outside the Indian community, quiltmaking has become an increasingly important Indian craft and is practiced by members of many tribes. From the beginning, quiltmaking seems to have been assimilated readily by these highly creative people. Perhaps it satisfied their traditional affinity for fine handwork as well as being quickly recognized as an artistic way to express their spiritualism. Whatever the case, today's Native American quiltmakers give eloquent voice to dearly held cultural values and beliefs.

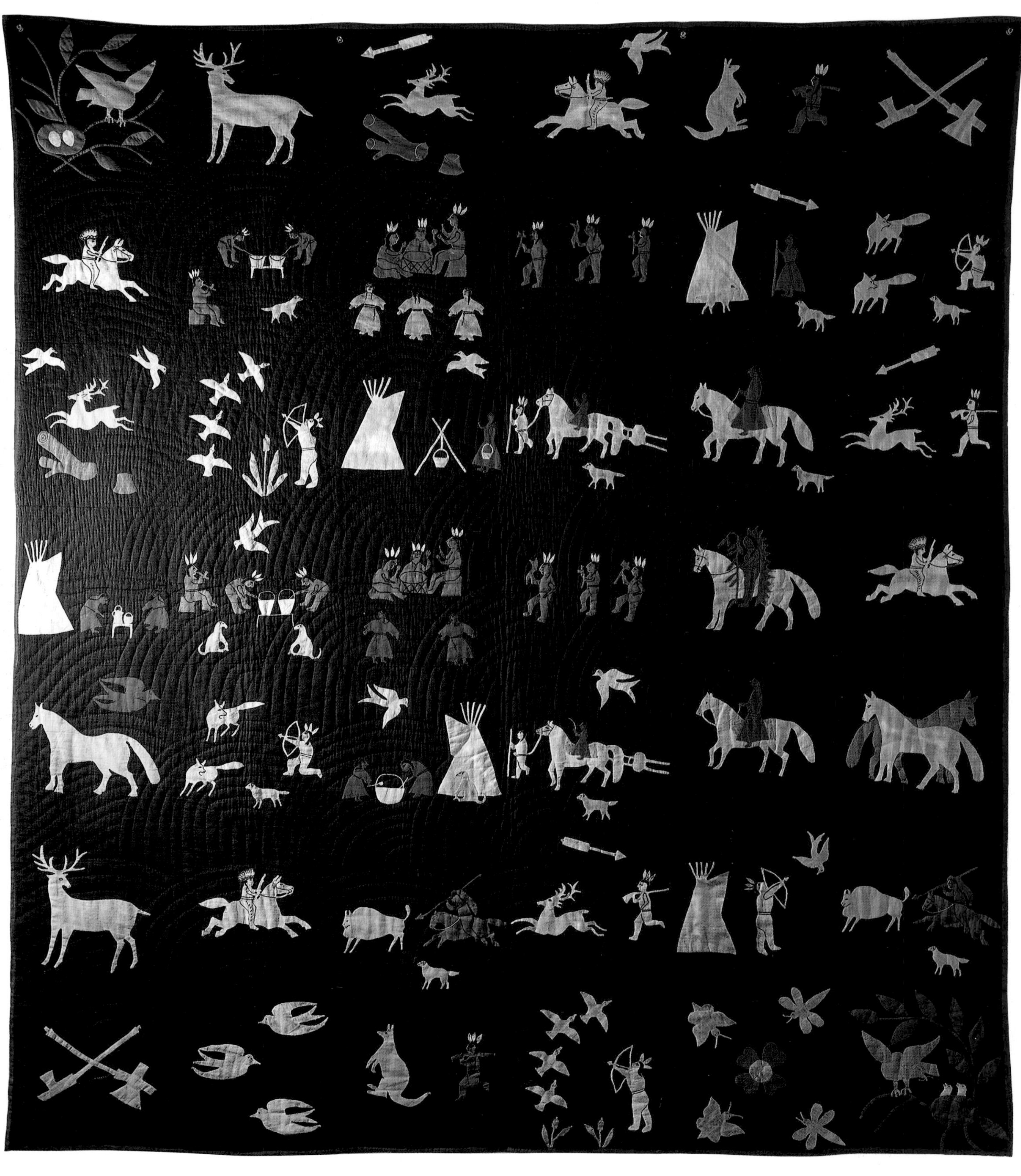

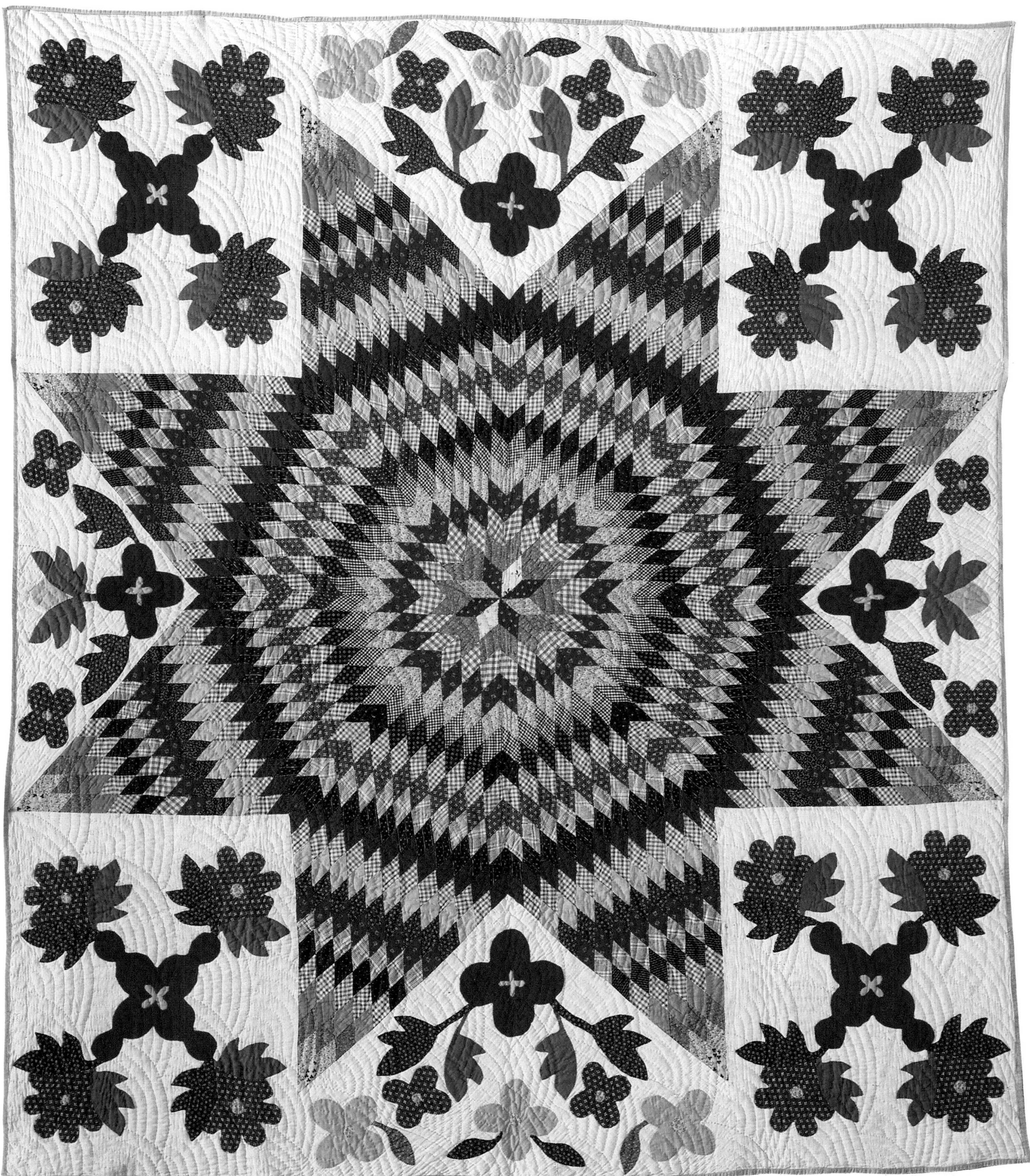

◄ PICTOGRAPH QUILT

Unknown Sioux Indian artist. c. 1900. Crow Creek Reservation, South Dakota. Cottons; hand appliquéd and quilted. 78 x 70 in. Private collection..

This unique piece includes a variety of appliquéd representations of Native American life. The white, tan, blue, and red pictographs of horses, hunters, women, dogs, deer, birds, buffalo, tepees, arrows, crossed peace pipes, and tomahawks, etc., are organized into seven rows and set against a solid black, contour-quilted background.

▲ LONE OR MORNING STAR

Unknown Sioux Indian artist. c. 1890–1910. North Dakota. Cottons; hand pieced, appliquéd, and quilted. 78 x 70 in. The Shelburne Museum, Shelburne, Vermont, gift of John Wilmerding.

Indian quiltmakers of the Plains and upper mid-West adopted the traditional Anglo-American Star of Bethlehem or Lone Star pattern in the late 1800s because it closely resembled their own Morning Star motif, widely used on clothing and ceremonial objects. Star quilts have become part of many Indian funeral and burial ceremonies.

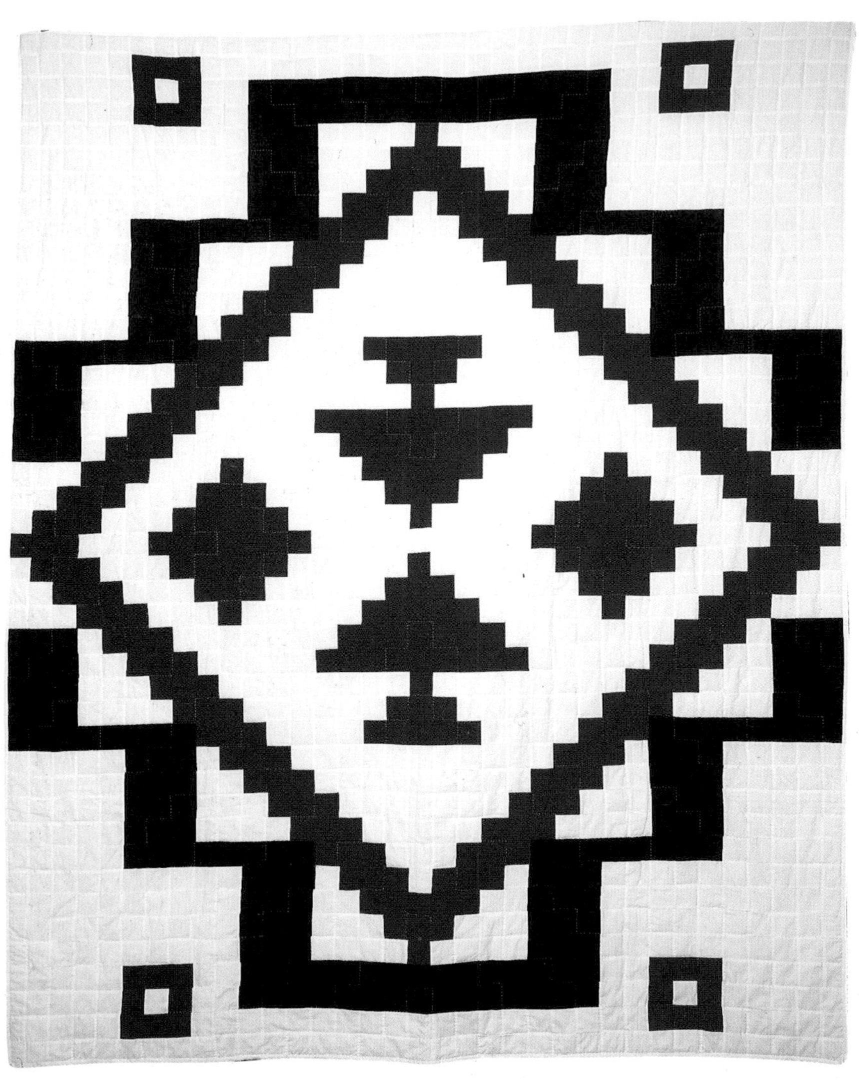

◄ TONY'S QUILT

Mary Henio. 1993. Thoreau, New Mexico. Cottons; machine pieced and hand quilted. 96 x 88 in. Collection of the artist.

Mary Henio is a member of the Navajo Women's Sewing Co-Op, a combination day care center and cottage industry which was formed in 1988 to offer local women with small children an income-producing opportunity. Members of the Co-Op create traditional quilts as well as Native American quilts which reflect the rich rug weaving tradition of the Navajo people. They try to copy the colors of the land and mesas surrounding Thoreau. This quilt was named in honor of Mary Henio's late husband, who helped design it.

▼ NAVAJO RUG

Conrad House. 1993. St. Michaels, Arizona. Cottons; machine pieced. Collection of the artist.

Conrad House is an accomplished multimedia artist who was recently inspired to work with fabric after viewing some historic Navajo chief's blankets at the National Museum of the American Indian in New York. The rich Southwestern tradition of woven blankets has inspired a number of Native American quilters who find a special challenge in translating the woven designs to pieced fabrics.

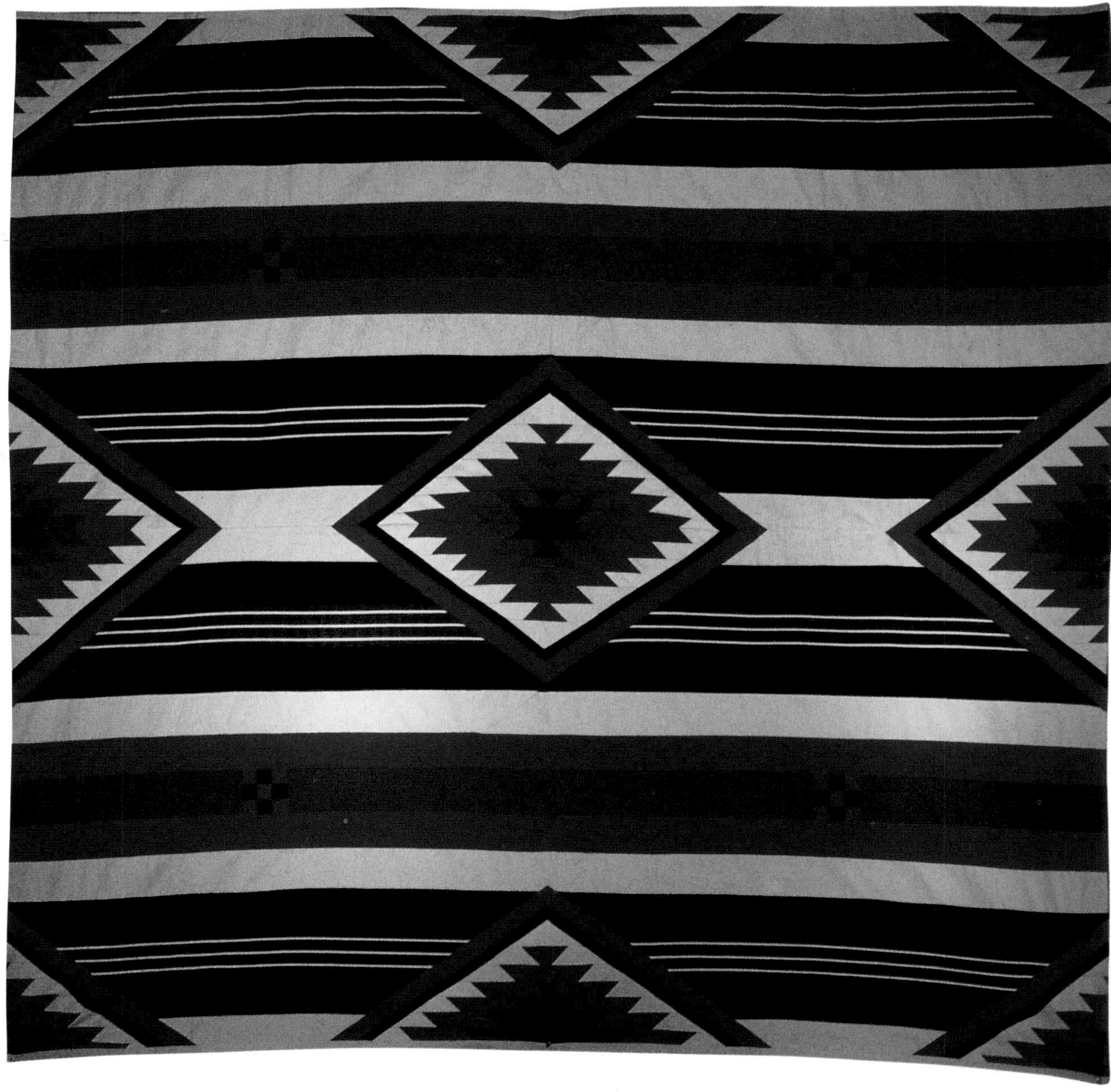

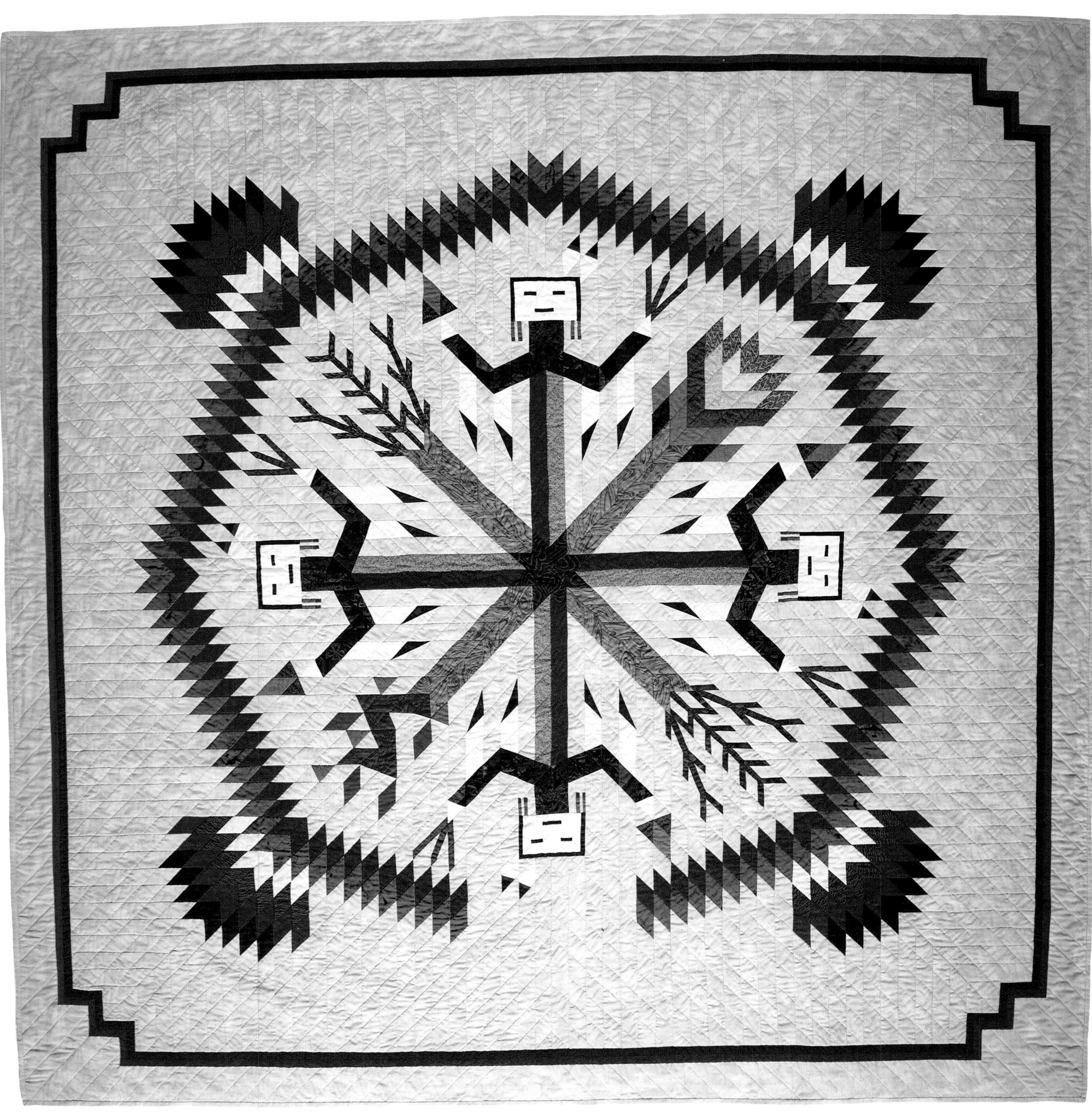

▲ **SANDPAINTING**

Dri Brown. 1993. Pasadena, California. Cottons; machine and hand pieced, machine and hand appliquéd, machine quilted. 84 x 84 in. Collection of the artist.

Dri Brown's interpretation of a traditional Southwestern Indian design includes over 2,600 pieces and took over a year and a half to complete.

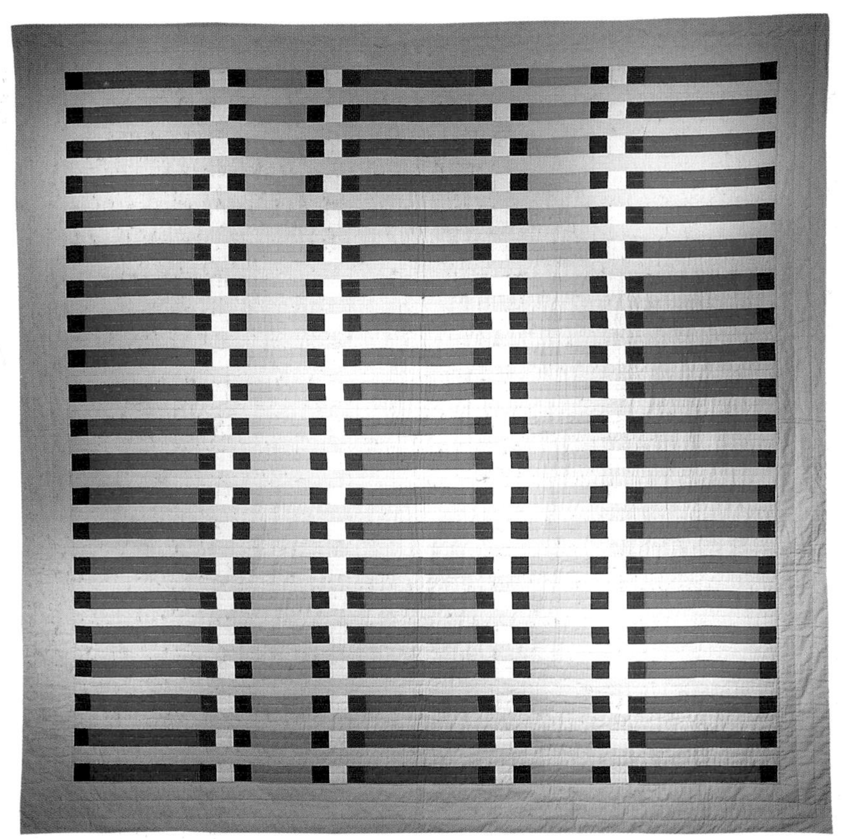

◀ **BEADED STRIP QUILT**

Margaret Wood. 1987. Phoenix, Arizona. Cottons; machine pieced and hand quilted. 95 x 95 in. Collection of the artist.

This design of colorful horizontal stripes alternating with tan strips was inspired by a Sioux girl's beaded hide robe.

SPIRIT #1 ▶

Margaret Wood. 1992. Phoenix, Arizona. Cottons with ultraseude, polyester satin ribbons, turquoise, onyx, abalone shell, and mother-of-pearl; machine pieced, appliquéd, and quilted. 73 1/4 x 53 1/2 in. Collection of the artist.

This quilt presents images drawn from Southwest tribes, especially the Navajo and Hopi: plus signs for stars, the zigzag for lightning, gray stairsteps for clouds. The number four, for Native Americans a spiritual reference to the four cardinal directions, is repeated often. The brown handprints are those of Margaret Wood's two children.

Margaret Wood

Margaret Wood of Phoenix, Arizona, is a Native American quilter of Seminole and Navajo heritage. Wood, who has a masters in library science from the University of Denver, began making quilts and clothing inspired by traditional Native American designs in the late 1970s. She says, "My work in quilts and clothing is based upon centuries of Native American...tradition. [Indians have] a long history of embracing new materials and decorative ideas. I consider my work a continuation of the evolution of Native American fashion and decorative work."

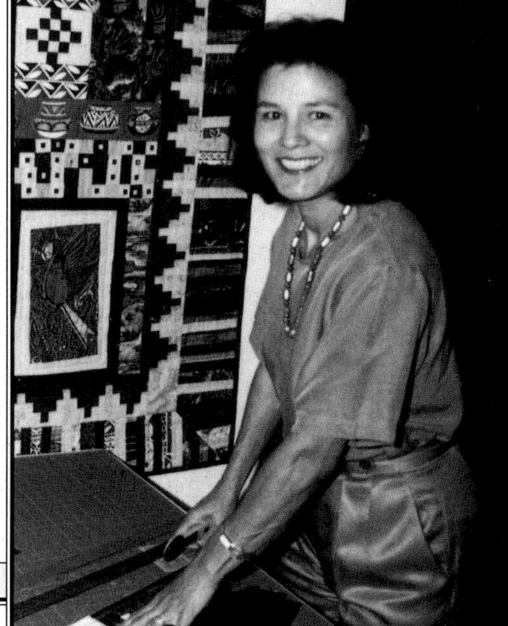

Wood's work has drawn on a wide variety of objects such as Hopi jewelry, Navajo chief's blankets, Southwestern pottery, and Plains Indian beadwork. Her *Bag Series* is based on Native American containers. After attempting to adapt colors and design elements from a Hidatsa pipe bag into a medallion quilt format, Wood decided "to just make the bag and produce [the designs] using Seminole patchwork." All the quilts in the series are functional bags that echo, in greatly oversized form, the decidedly unquiltlike shapes of their inspirations. The Hidatsa pipe bag quilt, for example, measures 112 x 29 inches.

Wood is currently assisting Marsha MacDowell of Michigan State University with a Native American quilt documentation project. Thus far the two women have held "American Indian Quilt Discovery Days" in Phoenix, Arizona, New York, and other sites around the country. The research project, which is co-directed by MacDowell and C. Kurt Dewhurst and conducted in collaboration with the Smithsonian's National Museum of the American Indian, will result in a special exhibition and publication of Native American and Hawaiian quilts in late 1996 or early 1997.

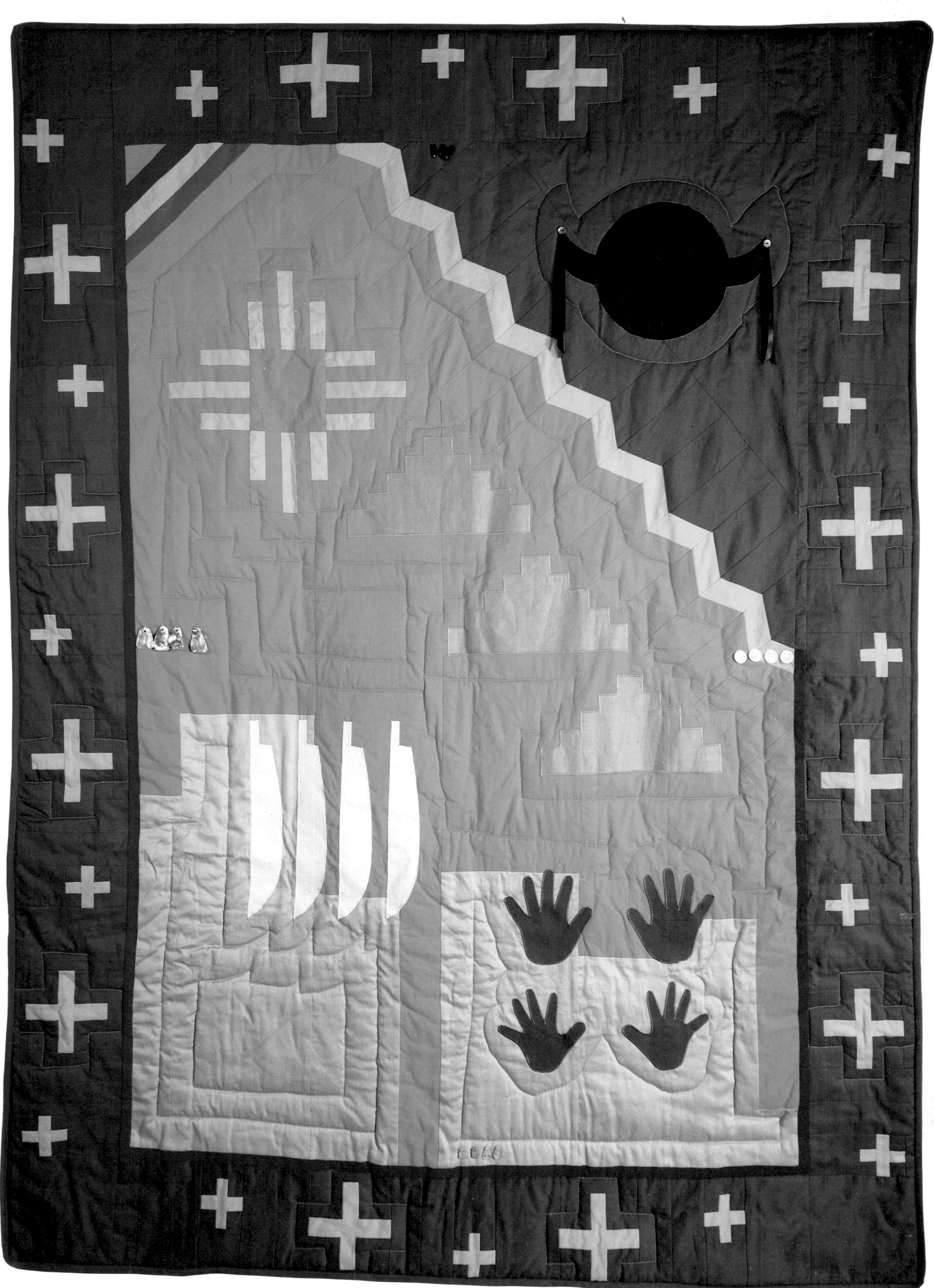

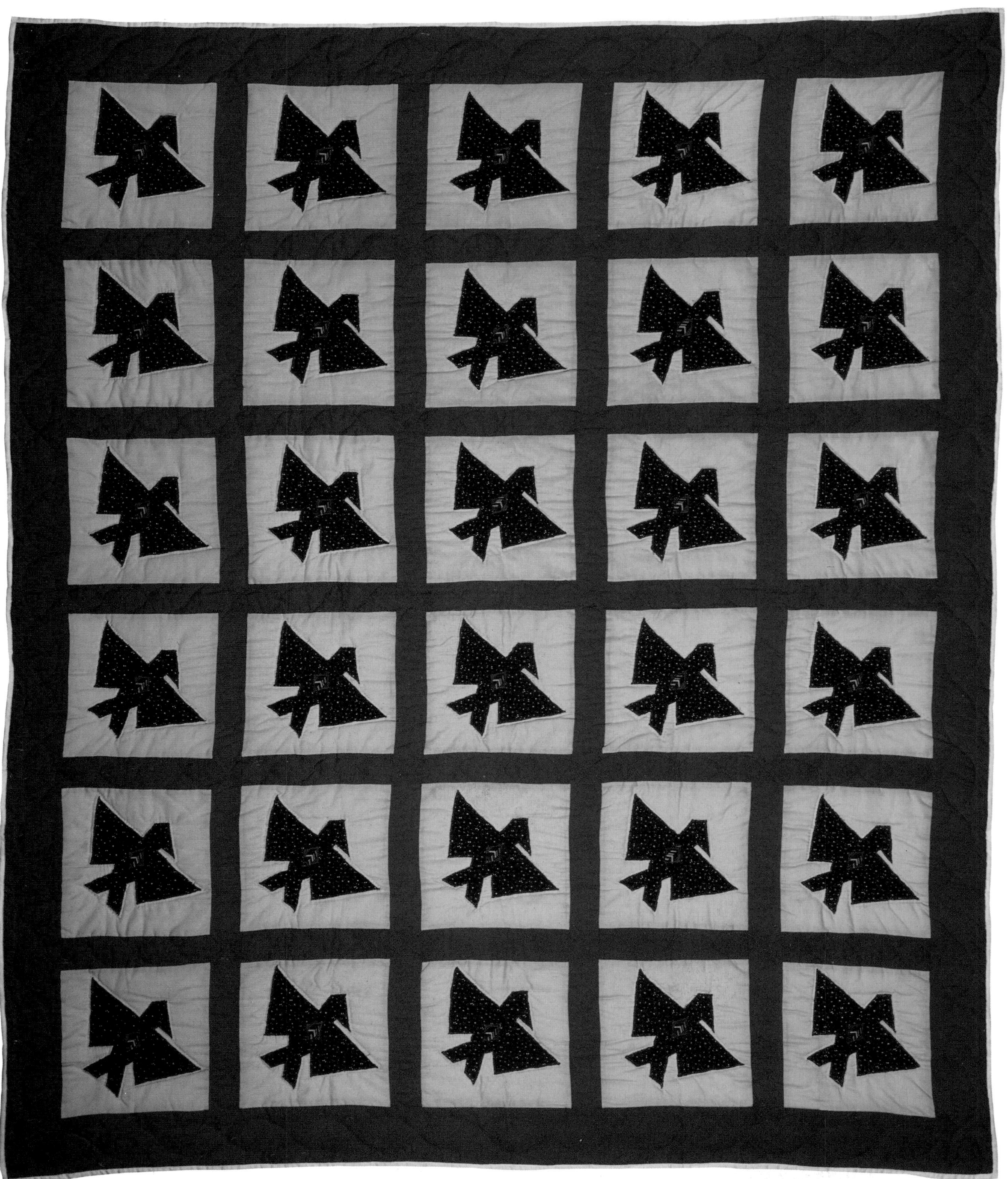

▲ **THUNDERBIRDS**

Alice and Floyd Fox. 1987. Sault Ste. Marie, Michigan. Cotton/polyester blends; machine pieced and appliquéd, hand quilted. 87 x 74 in. Michigan State University Museum, Michigan Traditional Arts Research Collection, East Lansing, Michigan, gift of Alice Fox and Rita Corbiere.

Alice Fox is an Ottawa/Ojibway storyteller and black ash basket maker. Each of the thunderbirds has a striped multicolored diamond-shaped appliqué on its breast.

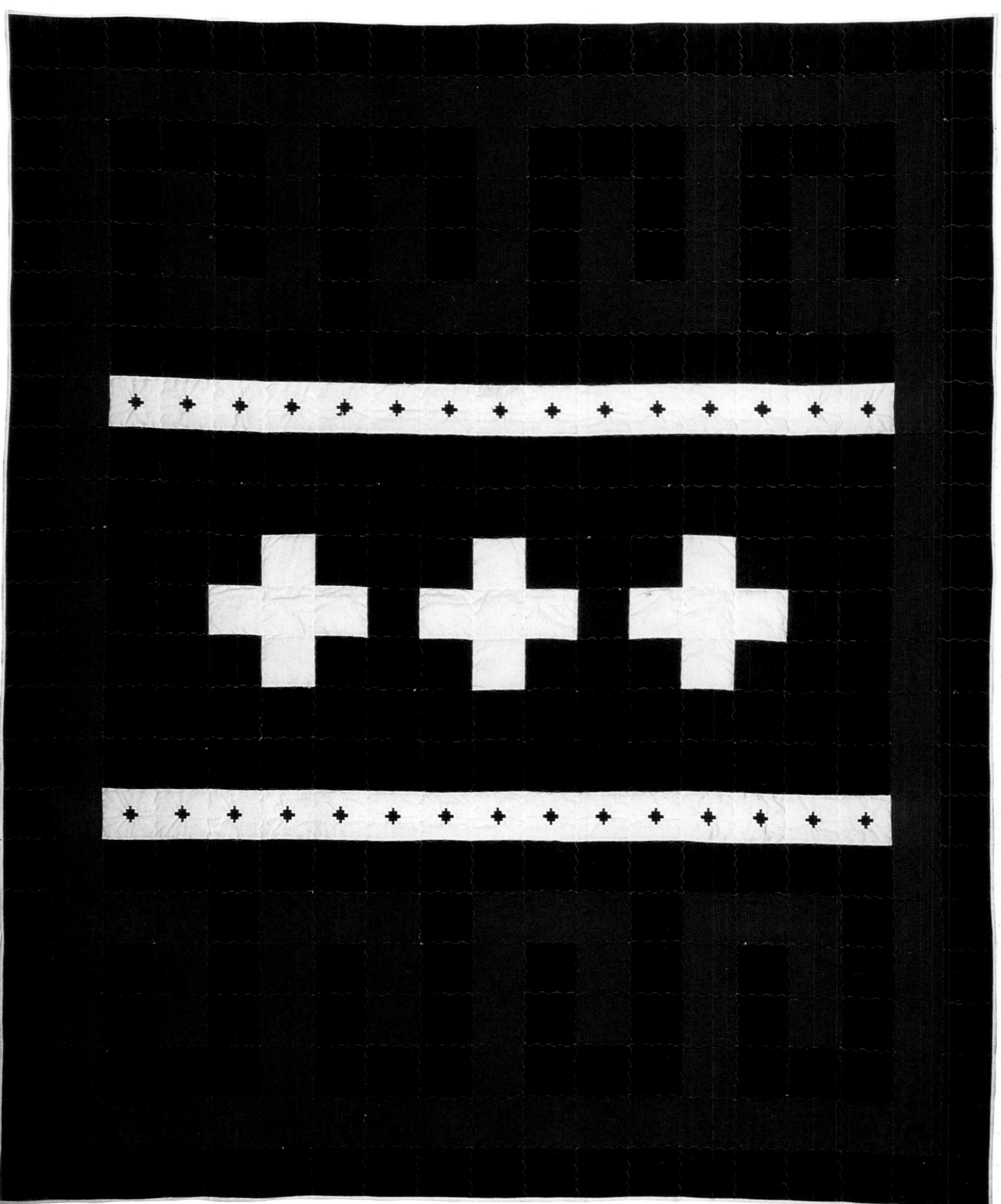

▲ **CHIEF'S BLANKET**

Alberta Lewis. c. 1993. Leupp, Arizona. Cotton/polyester blends; machine pieced and quilted, embroidered. 81 x 68 in. Michigan State University Museum, Michigan Traditional Arts Research Collection, East Lansing, Michigan.

Alberta Lewis is a Navajo quiltmaker who here has adapted a traditional blanket pattern. The quilt has a central medallion of three white crosses on a black ground. The white bands above and below the center have a black embroidered design.

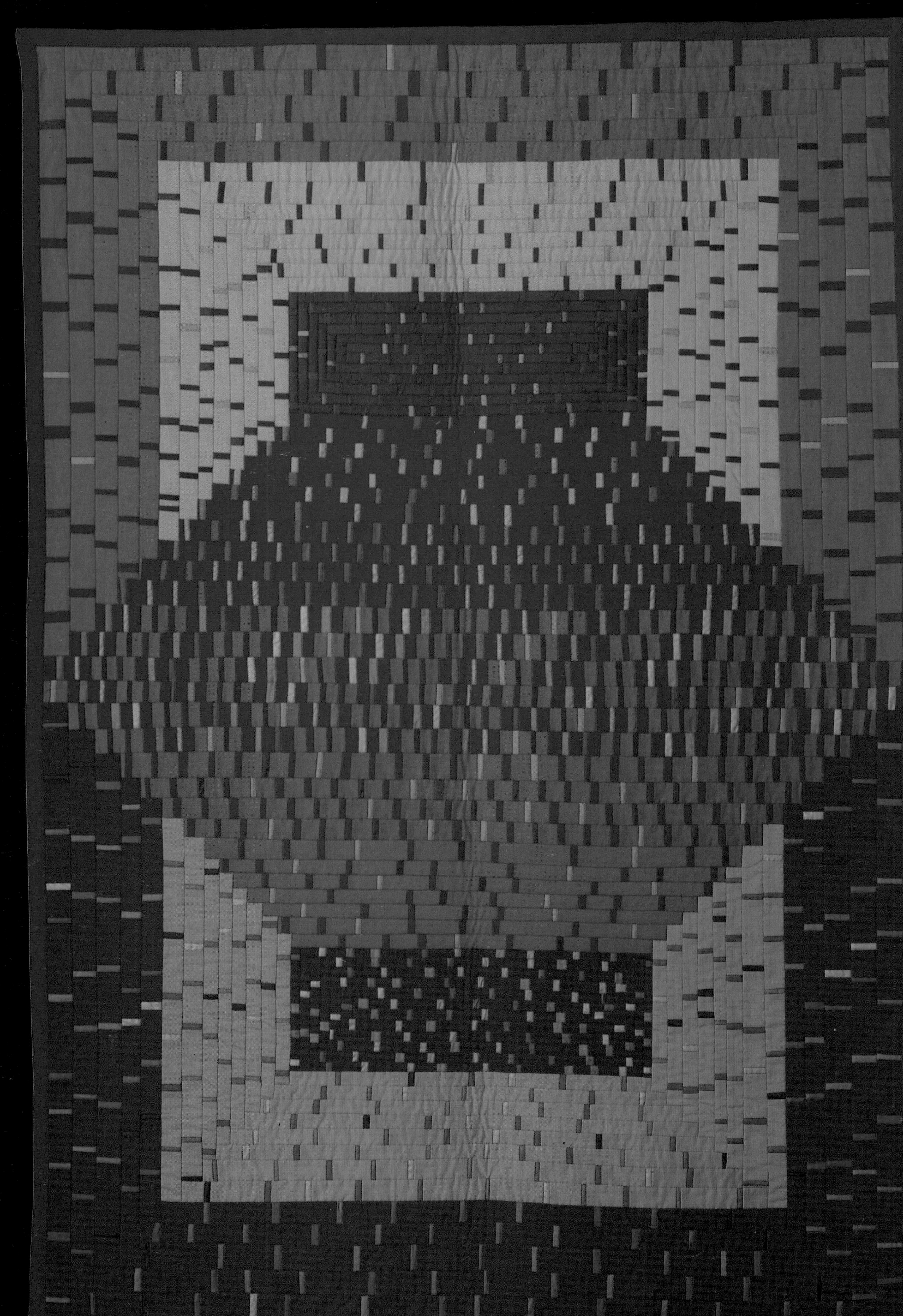

The Art Quilt

Beyond Function: A New Approach

Over the past twenty-five years, a number of studio artists, most of them academically trained, have chosen the quilt as their preferred medium, producing works intended to be hung like paintings rather than used as bedcovers. By completely separating the expressive and decorative from the functional aspects of the quilt, these artists have freed themselves from a host of formal and technical expectations and limitations and opened up broad new avenues for experimentation. Many of these quiltmakers have brought techniques from the fine arts to their work, incorporating collage, painting, printmaking, photographic transfer, complex fabric dyeing, and other nontraditional methods. Others choose to work within the technical parameters of the traditional pieced and appliqué quilt, but with the addition of innovative designs and unconventional subject matter that explores new and sometimes uncharted aesthetic territory. As in any developing field, the results of all this experimentation have been mixed, but the most successful art quilts represent a vibrant, diverse, challenging, and stimulating body of work that promises to help keep quiltmaking alive and growing for generations to come.

What exactly is an art quilt, and what makes it different from a traditional bed quilt? Studio Art Quilt Associates, a leading nonprofit advocacy group, defines the art quilt as, "A contemporary art work exploring and expressing aesthetic concerns common to the whole range of visual arts, painting, printing, photography, graphic design, assemblage and sculpture, which retains, however, through material or technique a clear relationship to the folk art quilt from which it descends." Quilt National, the leading juried exhibition of art quilts, is necessarily more specific about the technical distinctions that define the medium: "All work [considered

◂ **Red and Blue Jar**

Judith Larzelere. 1985. Dedham, Massachusetts. Cottons; machine pieced. 63 x 44 in. Collection of Ardis and Robert James.

Judith Larzelere assembles her quilts using a machine strip-piecing method developed by the Seminole Indians in the late nineteenth century. She places unevenly spaced flecks of color into the pieced strips of cloth, which are then cut and reassembled to create compositions that dance and sparkle with light and color. Like the Seminoles, she leaves her work unquilted. The resulting flat surface allows color rather than texture to dominate. This quilt is made of two immense Log Cabin—Courthouse Steps blocks, assembled back to back to form a jar shape.

by the judges] . . . must possess the basic structural characteristics of a quilt. It must be predominantly fabric or 'fabric-like' material (to which other materials may be added) and must be composed of two distinct layers— a face layer (which may be pieced, appliquéd, and/or painted) and a backing layer. The face and backing layer must be bound together by hand or machine-made functional quilting stitches or tied embellishments that pierce all layers and are distributed throughout the surface of the work."

Art quilts, then, attempt to bring artistic approaches and concerns to the forefront of quiltmaking. Like all works of art, they are intended to be beautiful and/or expressive, and to elicit a response from the viewer. Art quilts are often content driven, made to explore and in some way make manifest their makers' subjective ideas or feelings about a particular concept, situation, or experience. Although most are not strictly representational and many are not even remotely so, they often carry titles that suggest their makers' inspirations and/or intentions. Many are accompanied by detailed, written "artist's statements," which attempt to explain the nexus of motivating forces and the meaning behind the work. Others are presented as pure abstractions, and viewers are left to project their own interpretations onto the work.

Although art quilts reflect decidedly modern ideas about design, intention, and function, they also retain clear ties to the traditional and often utilitarian quilts that preceded them. The so-called art quilt movement dates its own beginnings to around 1970, but, as the definitions above suggest, the movement is deeply rooted in America's quilting traditions. Some types of quilts have always emphasized the decorative or expressive aspects of the medium over the practical and functional. As early as the late 1700s, talented quiltmakers sometimes made unique appliqué quilts "for best," or simply to satisfy their own creative urges. These quilts, which typically featured original designs and carefully chosen fabrics, were brought out only for company or other special occasions. They were made to be seen, to decorate beds rather than provide warmth, and were often unlined and unbacked. Similarly, the highly complex appliqué quilts of the 1840s known as Baltimore albums were made largely for show and were entered regularly in local competitions. The vast array of fabric available in what was then the center of the American textile industry and the country's leading port city allowed these quiltmakers to showcase their highly developed technical skills through complicated appliqué constructions that could employ dozens of different fabrics and intricate quilt stitchery that bound the quilts' thin layers and decorated their tops.

The crazy quilt, the most direct ancestor of the art quilt, was never intended to be functional, but, rather, gave the quiltmaker free reign to express herself and show off her sense of humor, love of fantasy, and talent for design as well as her facility for fancy embroidery stitches and other decorative elements. Crazy quilts embraced the Victorian fascination with busy design, creating asymmetrical (but usually well-planned) mosaics made up of many unevenly shaped pieces or scraps of fabric. The more detailed visual information the quiltmaker could pack into her design the better. Quiltmakers sought out and purchased special fabric for use in their crazies, and were particularly fond of the fancy dress silks currently in fashion. Some crazies were embellished with pieces of hand-painted fabric, scraps of relatives' clothing, fabric printed with historical and other scenes, lace or tasseled borders, miniature costumed figures, stuffed work or other special elements as part of the overall collage. Ribbons, bangles, beads, sequins, fancy buttons, embroidered pictures, and metallic threads also appeared on some crazies. All these materials have been rediscovered in recent years and used to great advantage by art quilters such as Susan Shie, Terrie Hancock Mangat, and Jane Burch Cochran.

The art quilt also has roots in the English-born Arts and Crafts Movement of the late nineteenth and early twentieth centuries that reacted against the dehumanizing effects of the Industrial Revolution and its soulless products and elevated handcrafts to equal standing with fine arts. The Arts and Crafts Movement emphasized the intimate connection between use and beauty, rejecting unnecessary decoration and anticipating the Bauhaus dictum that "form follows function." In an effort to bring art, quality, and meaning into every aspect of their daily lives, fine artists were inspired to design everyday household objects from furniture to tea kettles, stripping forms to their essences. The artist/craftsmen of the Arts and Crafts Movement revered the work of earlier handcraftspeople, especially the Shakers, but they avoided nostalgia by encouraging experimentation and by placing their new and original designs on a par with the best of the past.

The blurring of lines between craft and art that began with the Arts and Crafts Movement continues to the present day and informs the entire contemporary craft movement. After World War II a number of studio craftspeople began to make ceramics, weavings, furniture, and other objects that reflected the influence of contemporary art; at the same time they continued the work of their Arts and Crafts predecessors by honoring the traditions of fine handwork and craftsmanship. The American Craft Council and its affiliated American Craft Museum, founded in 1956, provided a forum and showcase for the work of such seminal artist/craftspeople as textile artists Mariska Karasz and Katherine Westphal. The American Craft Museum has mounted numerous exhibitions of quilts, ranging from an early 1960s solo exhibition by Jean Ray Laury to *Nancy Crow: Work in Transition* in 1994.

In the 1960s, artist/craftspeople looked increasingly to the fine arts for inspiration, creating works that, unlike those of traditional craftspeople, separated form and content from function. They experimented with new techniques and materials, many of them derived from the fine arts or the crafts of other cultures around the world. The seminal exhibition *Objects USA*, which included early art quilts in addition to cutting-edge furniture, ceramics, and several other fine crafts, traveled throughout the United States and around the world from 1969 through the early 1970s and opened many eyes to the new world of American crafts. Throughout the 1970s and 1980s, galleries and museums paid increasing attention to the work of contemporary craftspeople as the American public gained respect for fine crafts and recognized their aesthetic and expressive value.

The art quilt movement began in the 1960s with the renewed interest in handcrafts. Many of today's leading art quilters are children of the '60s who studied art in college and were drawn to handcrafts both as a means of expression and as a way to make a living. During the 1960s antique American quilts, particularly those made by the Amish, first caught the attention of art critics and collectors who were struck by their sometimes powerful graphic qualities. Artists and craftspeople recognized the expressive power latent in the quilt and decided to experiment with the medium. Like most Americans, many of them had been familiar with quilts and/or needlework since childhood, but had never viewed quilts as art. The transition to quiltmaking for some artists seemed, therefore, like a homecoming, and they progressed quickly in mastering the techniques of working with their newly chosen medium.

Jonathan Holstein's 1971 Whitney Museum exhibition *Abstract Design in American Quilts* changed forever the way quilts were seen and understood, opening the door for both the antique and contemporary quilt to become part of the world of art. The quilt's relationship with the art world is, however, complicated by deep historical prejudices. Through their choice of medium, quilt artists enjoy an access and liberty denied to most modern artists. People who have never heard of Klee, Mondrian, Albers, Noland, or Rothko, or people who would never consider visiting an art museum, especially not a museum of "that modern art," often have no difficulty responding to (or even creating) the art of a colorful geometric quilt top. Thousands of Americans have slept peacefully under wild and powerful abstractions they would probably never even consider hanging on the walls of their home. Ironically, if the same image were presented to them within a frame or within the context of an art gallery rather than a domestic setting, many would react negatively. But the original, functional bases of quiltmaking can often obscure the notion of the art of the piece, allowing people to appreciate a quilt for one or many reasons. Depending on the viewer, a single quilt can be seen as artistic, purely decorative or simply functional, or all of the above.

Unfortunately, the broad appeal of the quilt has also worked against its acceptance as a medium for art. As Studio Art Quilt Associates points out, "While useful distinction can no longer be made in the studio between the Art Quilt and any other large two-dimensional work of art, a distinction continues to exist in the marketplace." Some gallery owners have resisted accepting the quilt as art, and some quilt artists now avoid the use of the word "quilt" when describing or promoting their work. Some have settled on "fabric collage" as an artsier alternative. Regrettably, some quiltmakers have compounded the difficulty of the situation

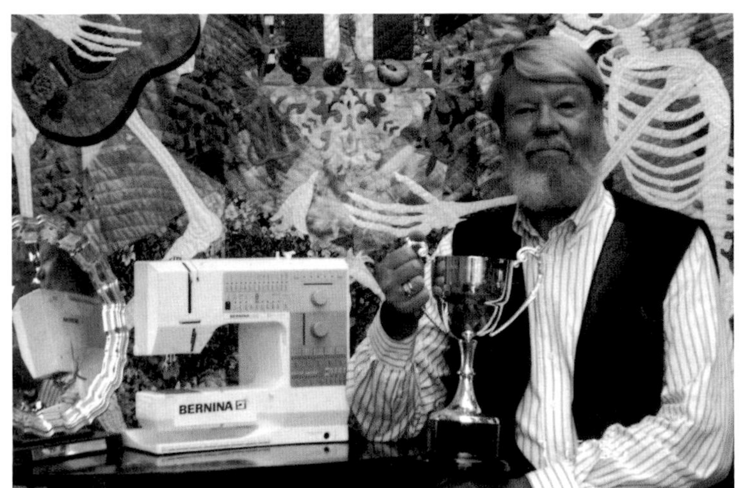

◀ *Jonathan Shannon poses here with his controversial quilt "Amigos Muertos" ("Dead Friends"). The quilt's subject matter has disturbed some viewers, but it has also won several awards.*

by harboring unrealistic notions about the value of their work, which, if it is to be truly indistinct from other studio art, needs to be competitively priced. For these and other reasons, the market for art quilts remains limited and supply far exceeds demand.

The question of content in this traditionally safe and comforting medium can also be contentious, especially in more conservative circles. Many people have strongly held notions of what a quilt should look like and what subject matter is appropriate. Jonathan Shannon's quilt *Amigos Muertos* ("Dead Friends") has been at the center of debate in the quilt community since it was barred from the American Quilter's Society 1994 competition by sponsors who felt uncomfortable with its imagery, because "it might upset our viewers." The bittersweet quilt, made as a memorial to the many artists who have died of AIDS and cancer, depicts a pair of dancing skeletons and is based on the traditional Mexican "Day of the Dead" celebration, held annually on All Souls Day. Throughout the world of traditional quiltmaking, Shannon's controversial quilt has raised provocative questions about expectations, judging standards, context, censorship, and propriety, and has inspired spirited exchanges between quilters. Quilt historians have established the quilt's precedents in the long-standing traditions of mourning and memorial quilts and among such profound historic examples as the solemn and grimly fatalistic graveyard quilt made in 1839 by Elizabeth Roseberry Mitchell of Lewis County, Kentucky, now owned by the Kentucky Historical Society. The majority of quilters, whether they like Shannon's quilt or not, have defended his right to exhibit his choice of subject matter and to let viewers decide its legitimacy.

Like contemporary artists in other media, art quilters feel free to address a wide range of social and personal issues through their work. Nancy Crow's powerful series of memorial quilts called *Chinese Souls* was inspired by her visit to the Chinese city of Xian, where she witnessed two truckloads of bound teenaged prisoners being driven off to be executed. Meiny Vermass-van der Heide and Susan Shie have both subtitled some of their works "green quilts" in order to draw attention to environmental problems, and other quiltmakers have produced works that focus on environmental issues such as the depletion of the rain forest and the extinction of the spotted owl. Such timely and varied subjects as the Los Angeles riots, Hurricane Andrew, and international terrorism have all elicited quilts, while titles such as *Frenzy, High School Graduation, Two Solitudes,* and *The Healing Heart* suggest the range of personal issues being approached by today's quiltmakers.

Quilts and quiltmakers are not alone in their struggle for acceptance. *Art That Works*, a recent exhibition and catalog of functional American decorative arts, points out that " the oft-heard refrain that the crafts are now accepted as art is overstated. Not all collectors or curators will pigeonhole expressive objects according to the materials from which they are made, but there still exists a definite collector-curatorial bias against objects that have evolved from craft materials and techniques." The often confusing historical division between quilt as craft (or folk art) and quilt as art is widely reflected in museum exhibitions and collections. The types of antique quilts that made up Jonathan Holstein's *Abstract Design* exhibition at the Whitney Museum are, ironically, not part of any museum's art department. The Newark Museum's department of

American decorative arts, for example, has long maintained an outstanding collection of antique quilts, and the museum was one of the first institutions to mount exhibitions that pointed out the artistic qualities of quilts. In 1985 the department of American decorative arts commissioned art quilter Michael James to make a quilt for the collection. The same year, completely unbeknownst to curator Ulysses Dietz, the museum's department of American art bought a quilt by painter Faith Ringgold. Similarly, the Boston Museum of Fine Arts has a small group of antique quilts as part of its American decorative arts collection, but its one art quilt, also by Ringgold, is part of the contemporary art department. To further confuse the picture, the MFA also actively collects contemporary pottery, silver, furniture, and other fine crafts, which are segregated by medium as part of the decorative arts collection.

Like artists or craftspeople working in any other medium, the best of today's studio art quilters have created bodies of work that can be identified by an immediately recognizable and original visual style. The works of such dedicated, long-time art quilters as Therese May, Joan Lintault, Yvonne Porcella, and Terrie Hancock Mangat are distinguished by each artist's personal vocabulary of visual ideas and techniques, developed over many years of experimentation, trial, and error, and dozens, if not hundreds, of quilts.

Many art quilters find inspiration in nature. Pauline Burbidge has made a number of shimmering quilts, including *Nottingham Reflections*, that explore the themes of fish, water, and movement. Michael James's series *Sky/Wind Variations* suggests the ever-changing interplay of sunlight on shifting cloud forms, while such works as Yvonne Porcella's *Morning Mist*, Jan Myers-Newberry's *Birch Eyes*, and Emily Richardson's *Sky Scape* offer impressionistic glimpses of other closely observed but ephemeral natural phenomena. Other quilt artists are more literal in their depictions of nature. Joan Lintault's *In the Grass* "bring[s] perpetual summer indoors" through its intricately detailed renderings of plants, flowers, insects, and even "the nasty things waiting in the grass," and Nancy Whittington's *Opening Palm* pulls the quilt's viewer into intimate contact with part of a vastly oversized palm leaf. Tafi Brown prints ethereal cyanotype (blueprint) photographs of tree branches, plants, and flowers on cloth and incorporates them in compositions such as *Wood Spirit Woods*.

Other quiltmakers prefer to make purely abstract works, extending the parameters and vocabulary of the traditional geometric pieced quilt. Liz Axford, for example, has recently made several vividly colored Log Cabin–inspired quilts constructed of myriad lopsided squares of different sizes. Both the piecing and quilting of her *Freehand 8:Torn* were unplanned improvisations. Ellen Oppenheimer has developed a method of piecing inlays of jagged shapes that allows her to create fabulously complex linear puzzles such as *Neon Maze*, and Pam Studstill builds intricate abstract landscapes out of carefully prepainted fabric. Studstill is the ultimate quilt serialist: she avoids pinning specific titular references to her endlessly inventive geometric quilts by simply assigning them chronological numbers, i.e., *Quilt #43*, *Quilt #92*, etc. Painting the fabric allows Studstill to substantially increase the amount of pattern at play in her work. To add more pattern to her quilts, which are constructed only of solid-colored cloth,

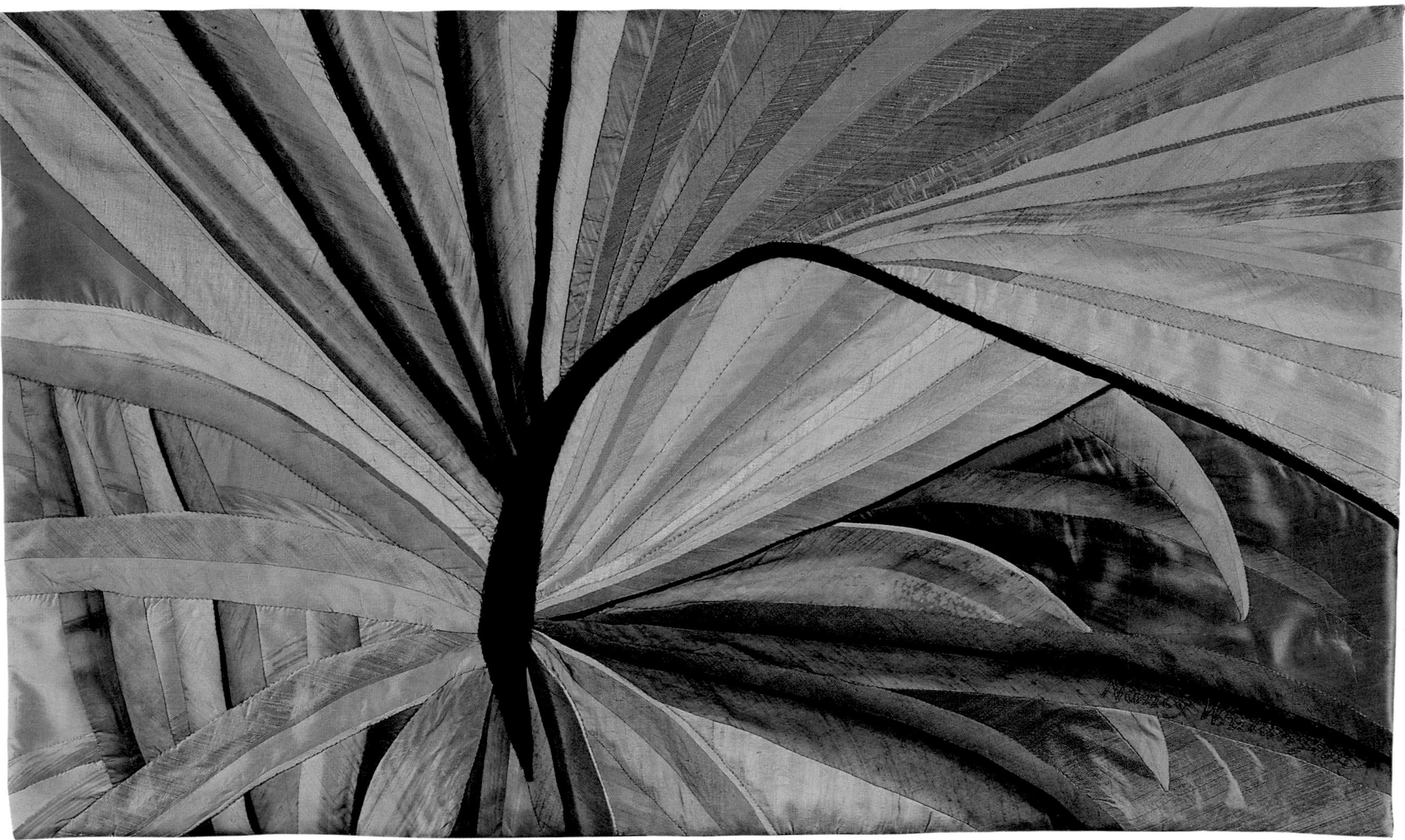

▲ **Opening Palm**

Nancy Whittington. 1993. Carrboro, North Carolina. Dyed, painted, and appliquéd silk. 32 x 51 in. Collection of the artist.

The artist says of her approach to quiltmaking: "Like many traditional folk quilters, I use color and pattern to express emotions and connections to life all around me. Although I paint and draw extensively, I particularly like the decorative quality of the quilt surface, which has its own very rich effect, so different from painting. This decorative quality is reflected everywhere in nature."

Judy Larzelere creates strips of Seminole pieced cloth full of tiny stripes of color. She has made a number of quilts based on greatly oversized Log Cabin squares; her *Red and Blue Jar* is built from two huge, pyramid-shaped Courthouse Step blocks.

Storytellers such as Therese May, Terrie Hancock Mangat, and Jane Burch Cochran take a more or less narrative approach, filling their quilts with ambiguous representational images that often suggest more than they explicitly depict. May's often amusing work, which combines thick paint and machine stitching, presents familiar domestic objects in unfamiliar, dreamlike settings. In her *For All the World to See*, for example, a huge fishbowl "flies" through space on a magic braided rug "carpet," surrounded by small and purposefully naive representations of a chair, a dress, a cat, and a child in nightcap and pajamas. Mangat's *American Heritage Flea Market* juxtaposes representations of such quintessential American symbols as Uncle Sam, a Coca-Cola sign, the American flag, Elvis Presley, and the Statue of Liberty, while Cochran's *The Last Dance* places an old cheesecloth dress she found in a bag of rags at the center of a composition that also includes a red mask, four blackbirds, and a "found" pair of evening gloves, all of which are set against a background of patchwork embellished with buttons and beads. And

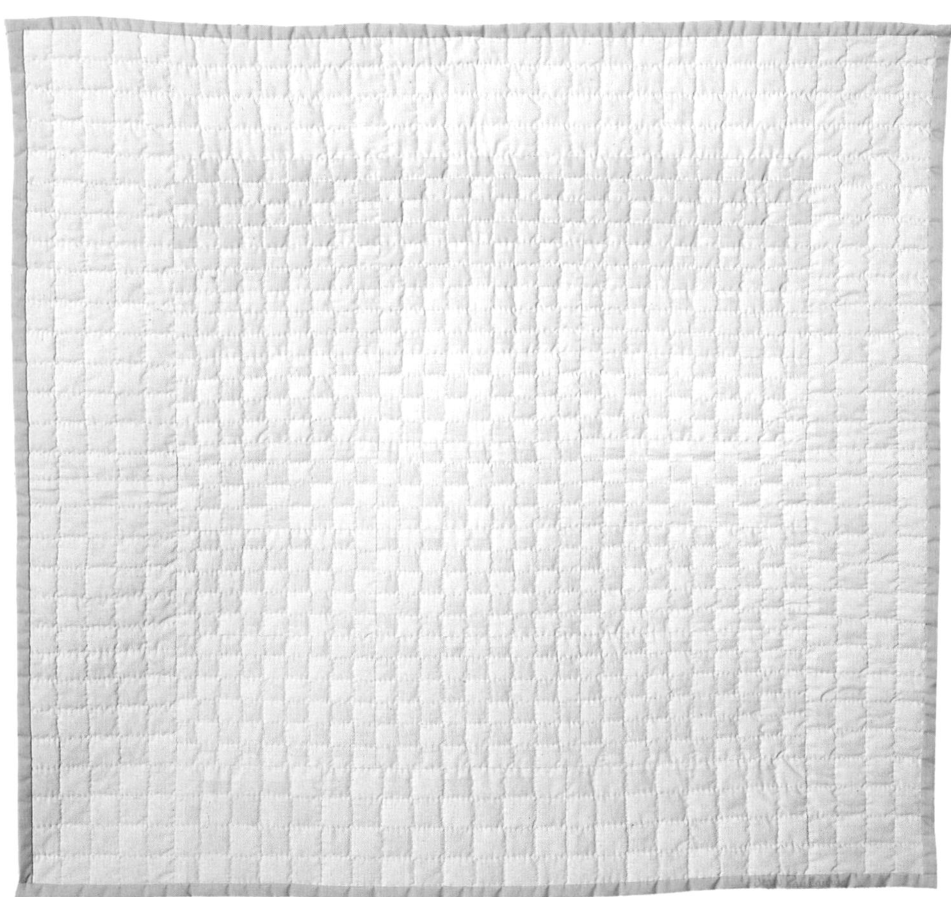

◄ **LIGHT SHOWER**

Jean Ray Laury. 1984. Clovis, California. Pieced cotton and cotton muslin. 30 x 28 in. Collection of Ardis and Robert James.

Jean Ray Laury's numerous and influential books, magazine articles, lectures, and workshops have made her a leading figure in the contemporary quilt world since the early 1960s. She has encouraged thousands of people to design their own quilts, incorporating ideas drawn from their experiences, observations, and surroundings. This small quilt, made up of uniformly sized squares of dyed fabric, explores the quality of light through subtle gradations in color.

many of Yvonne Porcella's recent quilts, such as *Keep Both Feet on the Floor*, have added playful figures to her own boldly colored geometric compositions.

One of the first textile artists to concentrate on quiltmaking was Jean Ray Laury, an Iowa native who has lived in California for many years. Laury, who was trained as both an art educator and designer and holds a Master of Fine Arts degree from Stanford University, began making nontraditional quilts in the mid-1950s. In the 1960s she designed and wrote about quilts for a number of widely read women's magazines, including *Family Circle*, *House Beautiful*, *Better Homes and Gardens*, and *Cosmopolitan*, enabling her to reach millions of readers throughout the country. Through her many magazine articles, her books *Appliqué Stitchery* (1966), *Quilts and Coverlets: A Contemporary Approach* (1970), and *The Creative Woman's Getting It All Together at Home Handbook* (1977), as well as numerous lectures and classes, Laury exerted a tremendous influence on countless other quilters. She encouraged those of all skill levels, from novice to expert, and her simple, modern-looking designs were widely copied. In *Quilts and Coverlets: A Contemporary Approach*, Laury offered a host of design methods, showed quilters how to incorporate seemingly mundane objects from their daily lives into their designs, and introduced work by such other early quilt artists as Therese May and Joan Lintault. She wrote:

> *Anyone can make a quilt. The process may take time, but it is not difficult. Whatever your sewing skills, drawing ability, or designing talents, they can be adapted to quilt making. . . . At its best, a quilt is a personal expression—not a mimic of the ideas or designs or color preferences set down by someone else. Original design is not beyond the capacity of any homemaker or student or quilt maker . . . Traditional designs no longer meet our needs. Creativity and inventiveness make it possible to modify and rejuvenate the old approaches and techniques. . . . If we can retain the structural integrity of the traditional quilt, and add to it a contemporary approach in color and design, we will achieve a quilt which merges past and present.*

Without question, the two most influential and, perhaps, the artists who best represent the development of the quilt as art have been Nancy Crow and Michael James. Both are academically trained artists who have created outstanding and much admired quilts since the mid-1970s, and both have had enormous impact on other quilters as teachers. They are dedicated promoters of the art form and, as spokespeople for the art quilt, have been instrumental in shaping public and critical debate on the subject. The consistently high quality of their work, their tireless search for new solutions, and their ongoing evolution as creative artists represent the careers of the best of today's art quilters.

Before turning to quilts in the mid-1970s, Nancy Crow, who has a masters in fine arts from Ohio State University, was a ceramist and weaver. She began making quilts seriously in 1976 and turned to quiltmaking full time in 1979. Her quilts are known for their use of intense and wide-ranging color palettes in complex and intricate geometric design structures. Many of her designs have been based on traditional pieced patterns such as the Log Cabin, Jacob's Ladder, or Double Wedding Ring. Like many other studio quilters, she works in series, exploring a particular design motif through as many as twenty or more variations. Crow's series called *Bittersweet* (1980–1982), *Lady of Guadalupe* (1988), and *Mexican Wedding Rings* (1988–1990) have probably had the most im-

COLOR BLOCKS #41 ▶

Nancy Crow. 1993–1994. Baltimore, Ohio. Pima cottons; hand dyed and hand pieced; hand quilted by Marla Hattabaugh. 41 x 51 in. Collection of the artist. © 1994 by Nancy Crow.

This example of Crow's most recent work was cut directly, without the use of templates, as though drawing with a pencil and paper. *Color Blocks #41* is part of a large body of improvisational quilts made in preparation for Crow's solo show at the prestigious Renwick Gallery of the Smithsonian in the fall of 1995.

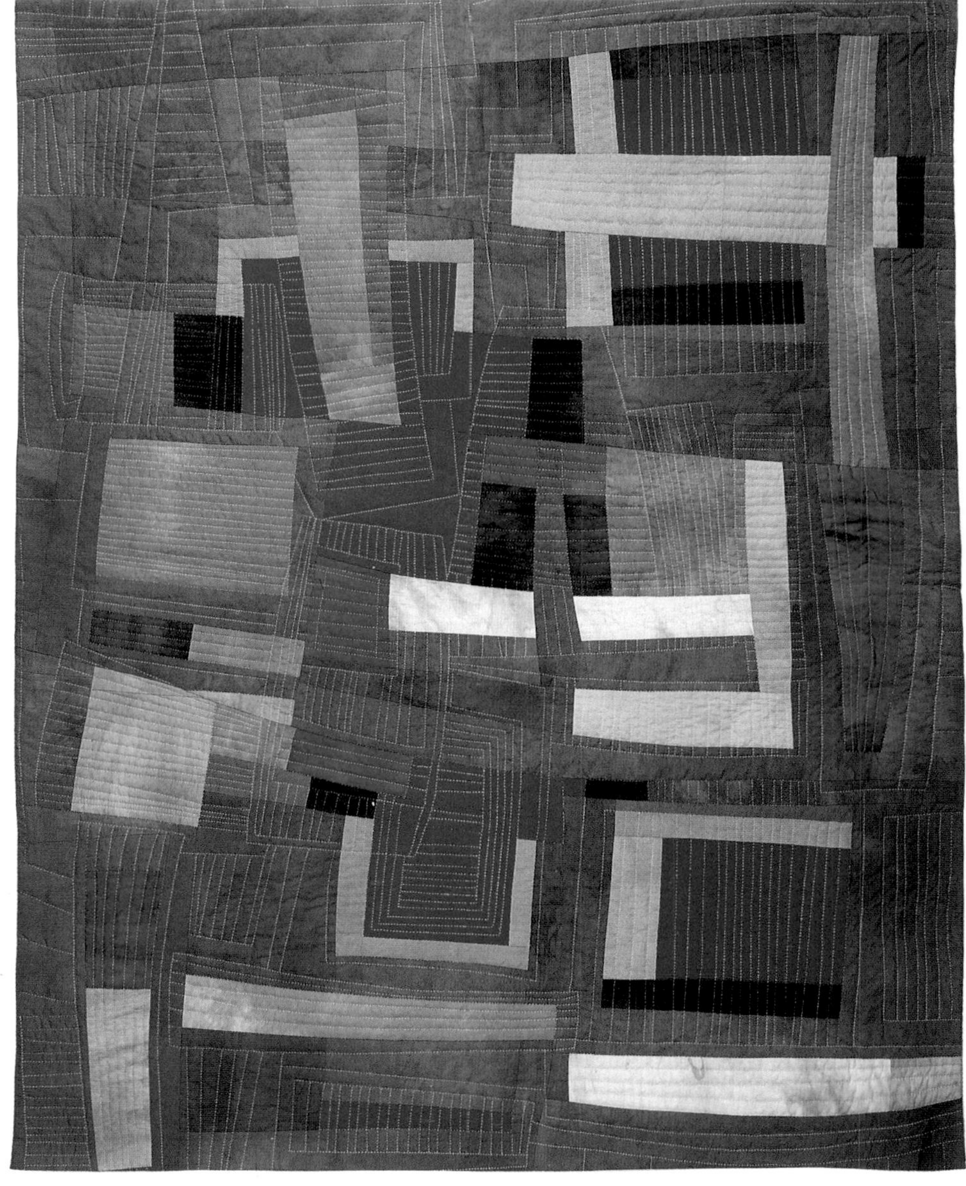

▼ *Nancy Crow has been a leader in the art quilt movement since the late 1970s, both through her teaching and her own consistently challenging work.*

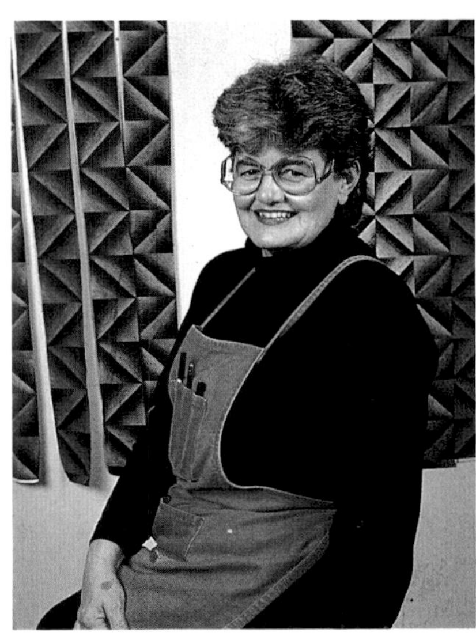

pact on other quiltmakers. Quilts from the twenty-two-piece *Bittersweet* series appear in New York's collections of the Museum of American Folk Art and the American Craft Museum.

Crow has used strip piecing in many of her works, assembling long, narrow strips of contrasting fabric that are sewn together and can then be cut and reassembled as she works on the overall design of the quilt. All of Crow's quilts are hand quilted, although she assigns this time-consuming work to skilled needleworkers who follow her instructions. In several instances she has turned her quilts over to Amish quilters in nearby Holmes County, Ohio. A number of other art quilters who are interested in making the rich surface texture of hand quilting part of their work follow the same practice, acting as artist/designers and leaving the highly skilled and labor intensive craftsmanship of the hand quilting to others.

Many of Crow's most recent quilts have been made without templates, which frees up their design and avoids the tediously mechanical nature of much of her previous construction work. She is now cutting fabric directly, a practice which she compares to drawing. She has also been using hand-dyed fabric, some of it of her own making, to give a wider range of rich and deeply saturated color. Using the very simple and basic traditional One-Patch and Bowtie patterns as her point of departure, she has created a number of extraordinarily complex designs, full of brilliant and unexpected color combinations, off-center rhythms, and painterly gradations of hand-dyed cottons. Paradoxically, some of these quilts, although based on the simplest of traditional patterns, are, in their conceptual complexity and visual impact, farther removed from tradition than any of Crow's previous work.

Throughout the late 1970s and the 1980s, Crow devoted as much energy to teaching and promoting the art quilt as she did to her own work. She has probably done more than any other single individual to advance the cause of the quilt as art. In 1979 she helped create the first Quilt National, a juried exhibition whose mission is "to promote the contemporary quilt as an art form." It has been held every other year since 1979 at the Dairy Barn Southeastern Ohio Cultural Arts Center in Athens, Ohio. Quilters from all over the world submit entries for consideration; the most recent exhibition, Quilt National 1993, for example, drew 1,100 entries from over a dozen countries, of which only 84 were chosen as finalists. Each exhibition is now available in a published catalog, and selected quilts travel from the Dairy Barn to venues around the United States and Japan for two years after their presentation at Quilt National. Quilt National's influence on the movement has been enormous. It has brought worldwide public and critical recognition to the art quilt and to the works of many individual quilters who have become its leading exponents, including such major figures as Yvonne Porcella, Michael James, Pamela Studstill, Therese May, Judith Larzelere, Jan Myers-Newbury, Jane Burch Cochran, and, of course, Nancy Crow herself.

Michael James, like many art quilters, is a formally trained painter and printmaker who obtained a Master of Fine Arts degree from Rochester Institute of Technology, one of the country's most highly regarded art schools. As a painter, he found himself leaving larger and larger areas of his canvases blank to show the texture of the stretched linen. In 1973 he began to work entirely in fabric, a logical step considering his natural affinity for cloth. In his typically meticulous fashion, James started by teaching himself hands-on about the history and techniques of the medium, making many copies of traditional patterns. As he worked his way through the basics of designing and constructing quilts, he became frustrated with the instructional texts that were then available and set out to write the book that would have helped him when he was a novice quiltmaker. James's two highly technical books on the craft of quiltmaking, *The Quiltmaker's Handbook: A Guide to Design and Construction*, published in 1978, and *The Second Quiltmaker's Handbook: Creative Approaches to Contemporary Quilt Design*, published in 1981, gave aspiring quilters the most carefully detailed blueprint available to date, and offered a host of new design ideas to those interested in moving beyond traditional patterns. In his preface for a new edition of *The Quiltmaker's Handbook*, published in 1993, he wrote, "While much innovation has gone on since its first publication, the fact remains that the quiltmaker needs to know the ins and outs of hand piecing and quilting, of blocks and borders and sets, and of the range of traditional techniques that have proven adaptable to contemporary needs. This book provides that basic body of solid information."

In the 1970s James worked extensively with curved seam blocks, then turned his attention in the 1980s to strip piecing methods derived from Seminole Indian quilting. He searches continually for new approaches, abandoning particular design methods when they begin to seem too facile. His most recent quilts explore ways to design without relying on an underlying grid structure as he attempts to achieve coherent overall designs that cannot be broken down into

SPIRIT DANCE ▶

Michael James. 1994. Somerset Village, Massachusetts. Cottons and silks; machine pieced and quilted. 49 1/2 x 49 1/2 in. Collection of the artist.

This quilt represents part of the artist's recent attempt to break out of a grid system of organization. James notes, "Freeing myself from the geometry of [the grid structure] has allowed me to open up my work to exaggerations of linear movement and distortions of free-form figures that had seemed impossible before."

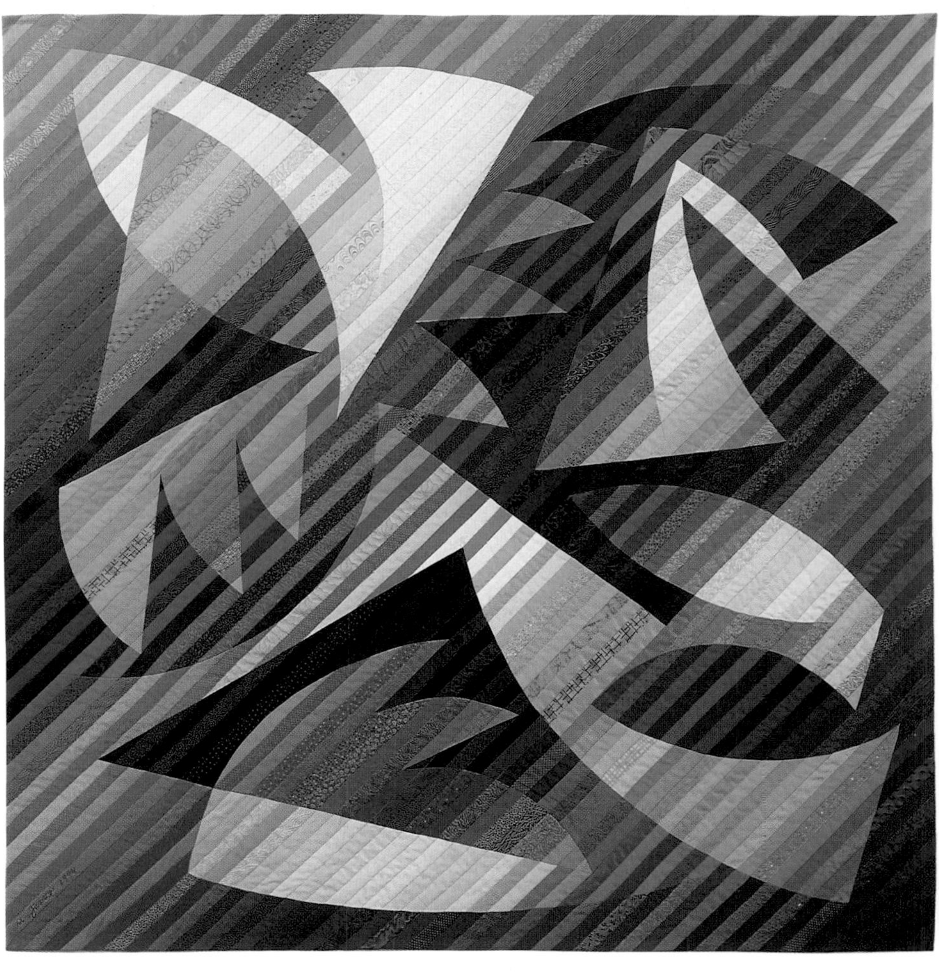

▼ *The influential art quiltmaker Michael James is seen here with his quilt "Intersections," completed in late 1994.*

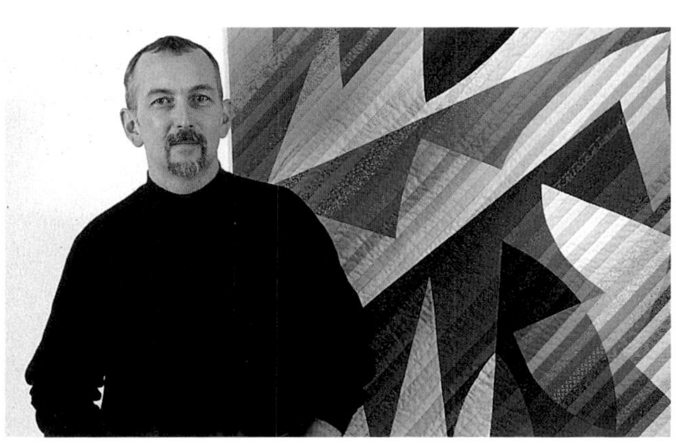

smaller organizing units. Some of these quilts are full of jagged, interlocking, dancing forms that have the "spontaneity of graffiti," as he described his 1992 quilt *Suspended Animation*, while others seem to reflect the influence of the cool colors and soft undulating forms of traditional Japanese landscape painting.

While most art quilters choose to test the limits of quiltmaking while still remaining within the traditional media of textile and thread, some newer quilt artists are expanding the very definition of what constitutes a quilt by introducing new materials to their constructions. Mimi Holmes's recent *Compost Quilt*, for example, is designed as a biodegradable shroud for her grandmother, and includes such decidedly nontraditional materials as leather, wood, egg shells, dryer lint, dried coffee grounds, orange rinds, banana skins, and artificial horsehair upholstery stuffing. Other artists are stretching boundaries by making quilts that take new shapes or perform new functions. Many art quilts are considerably larger than bed size, and some depart from the traditional square or rectangular format of the bed quilt. Terrie Hancock Mangat's *Dashboard Saints* measures 99 x 123 inches, and Jan Myers-Newberry's *Depth of Field III: Plane View* is 84 x 131 1/2 inches. Both of these monumental quilts are intended to be oriented horizontally, like paintings, rather than vertically like a functional bed quilt. Nancy Erickson has made a series of oddly shaped quilts that portray a pair of playful and inquisitive lion cubs interacting with various natural phenomena or human artifacts, the contour of the quilts being dictated by the shapes of the cubs and their surroundings rather than by a prescribed "frame" for the "picture" as is found in conventional appliqué quilts or paintings. Yvonne Porcella has made immense, three-dimensional kimono-shaped "quilts" (one measures 132 x 86 x 14 inches), Gayle Fraas and Duncan Slade have made three-dimensional folding screens, and Michael James has recently made several round quilts as part of his effort to escape from grid-based designs. Susan Shie's *The Calendar Fetish* includes over one hundred moveable pieces, and Arturo Alonzo Sandoval's *Millennium Portal No. 1* is a round, kinetic "satellite window" made of painted canvas, mylar, Cibachrome photographs, mirrored Plexiglass, and other high-tech materials on a motorized mount that spins around at one revolution per minute.

Others are making quilt art, if not art quilts, by using the quilt as a reference point. The well-known modern artist Robert Rauschenberg probably lead the way in his 1955 "combine painting" *Bed*, in which he used his old Log Cabin quilt, sheet, and pillow as a canvas. (The work is now in the collection of the Museum of Modern Art in New York.) Several other multimedia artists have incorporated quilts or quilting into their works, and, conversely, some quiltmakers are occasionally working in

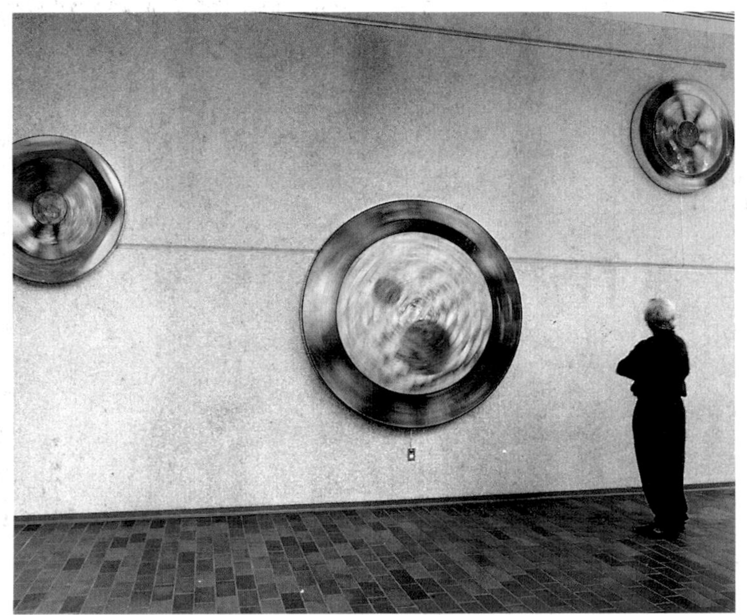

◄ *Quilts from the innovative "Millennium Series" by Arturo Alonzo Sandoval are seen here on exhibit at the University of Kentucky. The circular quilts, intended to evoke views from satellite windows, rotate on motorized mounts at one rpm.*

the other direction, expanding their approach by significantly varying their media. Fraas and Slade, whose painted quilts combine landscape images with trompe l'oeil pieced surfaces, often confer with architects to site commissioned pieces in public and corporate spaces. "As artists concerned with ideas first, the work doesn't always manifest itself as a quilt. When fabric surfaces aren't applicable [because of space and light conditions], we use a similar visual approach using enamels, painted and screen-printed on aluminum." To cite another more radical example, when Terrie Hancock Mangat retired the old Singer sewing machine given to her by her mother, she turned it into a sort of memorial to her own quiltmaking by encrusting every inch of it with mementos, including her trademark beads, bits of patchwork, and a host of small, personal objects from her recently deceased mother's jewelry drawers.

In its early stages, the evolution of the art quilt in no way intersected or interacted with the traditional bed quilt. Many traditional quiltmakers, quilt collectors, and quilt enthusiasts initially felt threatened by the innovations of art quilters, convinced that the two forms were mutually exclusive or perhaps that the art quilt's experimentation might somehow invalidate traditional approaches. However, through the continuing efforts of Jean Ray Laury, Nancy Crow, Michael James, Yvonne Porcella, and other masterful teachers, the art quilt has enriched traditional quiltmaking in recent years, challenging and inspiring many traditionalists to experiment with new techniques, color combinations, and original design approaches. In turn, most art quilters were initially drawn to the form by traditional quiltmaking and continue to look back to earlier designs as a source of inspiration. As the British quiltmaker Pauline Burbidge has put it, "I don't want to just throw off the traditions of quiltmaking, because I am close to that tradition and love being inspired by it. I am certainly inspired by the old quilts and I like to show that inspiration through my work." This mutual exchange of ideas and techniques has helped to keep traditional quilting fresh and forward-looking and promises to continue to keep it vital in years to come. It has also helped many art quilters to open a dialogue with quilters of all persuasions and, at the same time, to supplement their incomes while continuing to pursue their chosen medium. Traditional quilters and aspir-

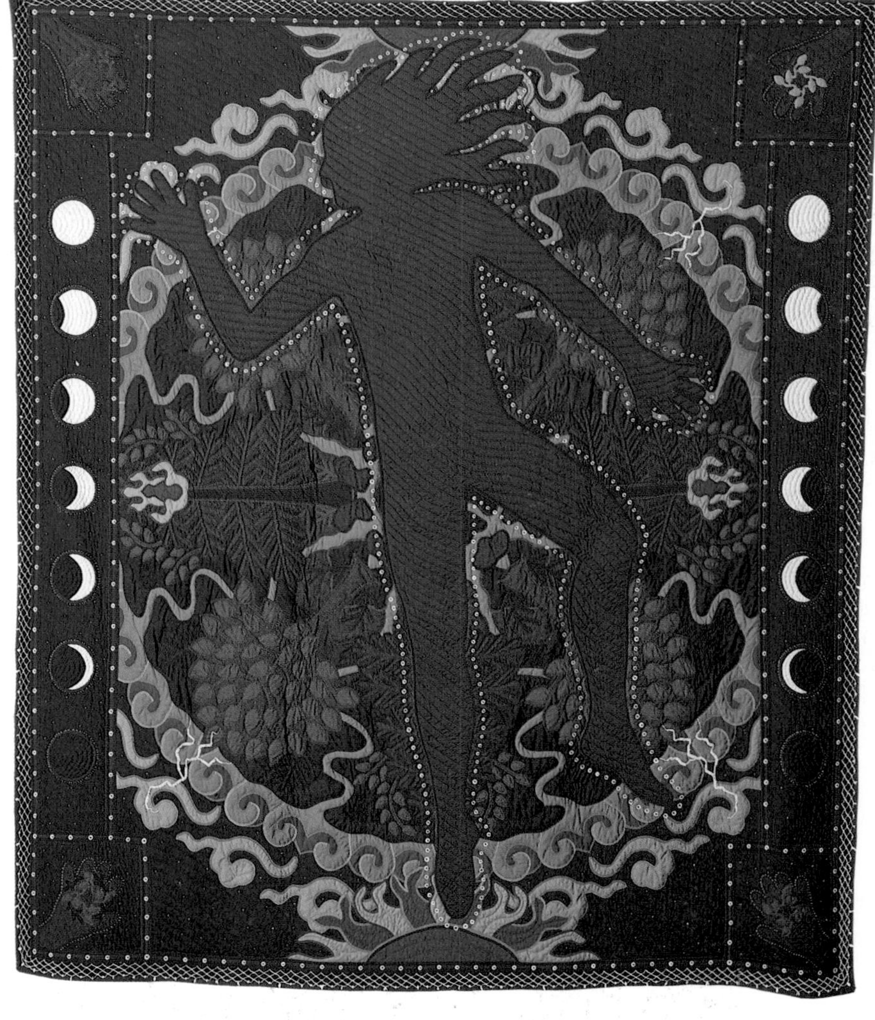

REVELATION ▶

Patrick Dorman. 1987. Seattle, Washington. Cottons, mother-of-pearl buttons, glass buttons and beads; hand appliquéd, hand quilted, with spot stitch beading. 92 x 83 in. Collection of Ardis and Robert James.

According to Dorman, "The [central] mandala of Earth, Air, Fire, and Water is surrounded by images which mark the passage of time: rising and setting sun, seasons of the year, cycles of the moon. My . . . [life-sized] shadow floats within this place and time." *Revelation* received an Award of Excellence at Quilt National 1987.

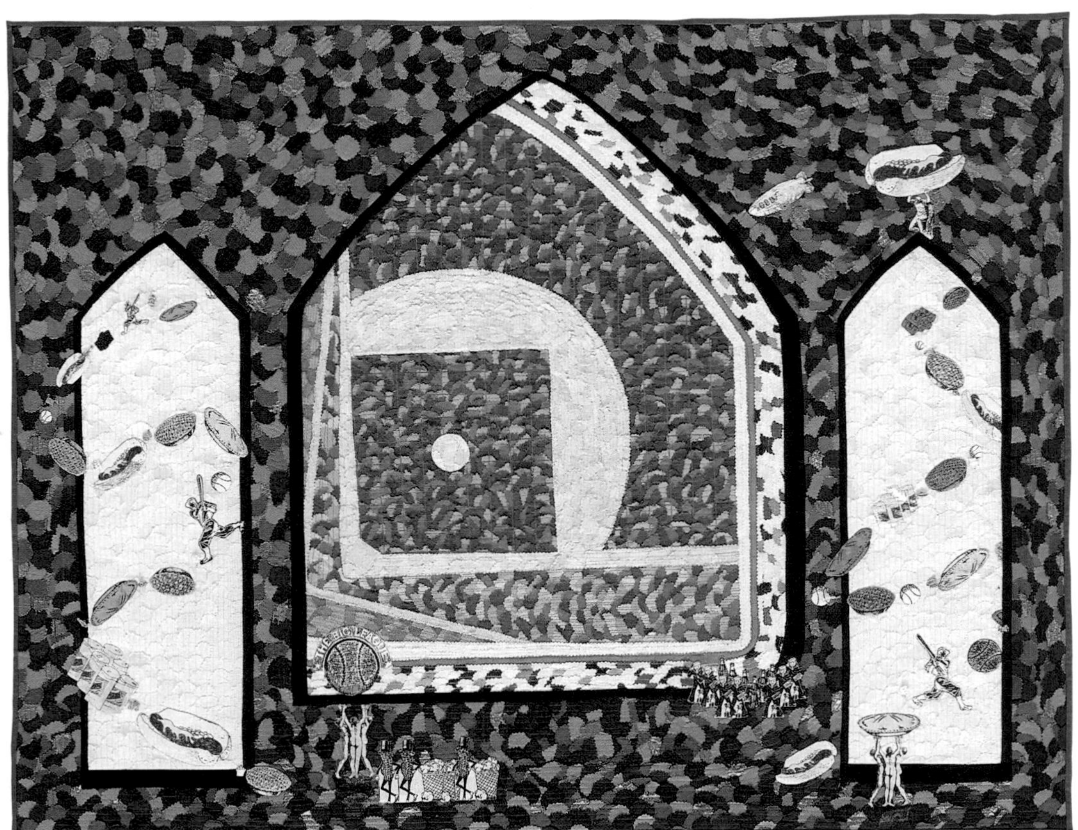

◄ **BASEBALL: AS AMERICAN AS APPLE PIE AND QUILTS**

Holly Junker. 1989. Sacramento, California. Cottons, xerox transfer, metal embellishments; hand cut, machine stitched, hand tied. 43 x 55 1/2 in. Collection of Yvonne Porcella.

Holly Junker uses pinked and frayed edged fabrics to blend color and form and to blur the traditionally hard edges of the pieced quilt. Many of her quilts try to suggest the appearance of aerial landscapes or distant vistas, where colors blend, edges merge, and dimensions flatten.

ing art quilters alike attend classes given by those major figures already mentioned as well as many other leaders of the art quilt world such as Nancy Halpern, Risë Nagin, Susan Shie, Elizabeth Busch, and Judy Larzelere. These artists offer inspiration, encouragement, and fresh ideas to thousands of quiltmakers, and have helped to break down the walls of prejudice that too often divide the old from the new.

A number of recent exhibitions and symposia have also narrowed the gap between art and traditional quilts by encouraging dialogue. In 1989 quilt historian Sandi Fox contributed an essay, "The Unbroken Thread," to the catalog of an invitational exhibition of art quilts called *America Enshrined*, shown at the Great American Gallery in Atlanta. In her essay, Fox noted that, "The artists in *America Enshrined* [Yvonne Porcella, Therese May, Susan Shie, Nancy Crow, Jane Burch Cochran, Holly Junker, Nancy Erickson, and Ed Larson among them] present innovative work that is both redefinition and reaffirmation." From November 1991 to May 1992, the Kentucky Quilt Project again helped lead the way by presenting *Louisville Celebrates the American Quilt*. This interrelated series of exhibitions and symposia included a twentieth-anniversary rehanging of Holstein's 1971 exhibition *Abstract Design in American Quilts*. Four of the event's other exhibitions included contemporary quilts: *Always There: The African-American Presence in American Quilts* presented a powerful overview of African-American quilts from slave-made pieces to art quilts by Michael Cummings and Carole Harris; *Narrations: The Quilts of Yvonne Wells and Carolyn Mazloomi* offered a selection of recent work by two of the leading contemporary African-American quiltmakers; *Quilts Now* showed the work of twenty-five art quilters; and *Quilt Conceptions: Designs in Other Media* featured quilt-inspired works in paper, wood, ceramics, glass, and various fiber constructions, as well as a full-sized Log Cabin "quilt" made of cigarette packages.

In late 1993 the Museum of the American Quilter's Society presented its first exhibition of art quilts, Nancy Crow's *Work in Transition*. Always considered to be traditionally oriented, the museum also exhibited selected art quilts from the collection of Ardis and Robert James in 1995. The

Jameses, who own an extraordinary collection of antique quilts, were also the first major collectors of art quilts, and have insisted that their art quilts stand side by side with their antique pieces. Nancy Crow was the keynote speaker at the American Quilt Study Group's 1994 seminar, and the 1995 inaugural session of *Quilts in Santa Fe,* a biennial symposium that was directed by Sandi Fox, offered an integrated, "multi-disciplinary and cross-cultural" program that included presentations by quiltmakers Yvonne Porcella, Jonathan Shannon, and Jean Ray Laury, as well as by Fox and several other prominent quilt historians.

These types of events, exhibitions, and inquiries hold great promise for the future of both quilt study and quiltmaking by attempting to tie the disparate threads of the quilt's meanings—past, present, and future—together. By exploring ground common to all quilts and quilters, today's quiltmakers and historians can support and learn from each other, broadening their perspectives and at the same time recognizing their unifying interests. The traditional quilt and the art quilt are equally valid means of expression, and both will remain vital as long as their creators continue to experiment and innovate.

We can only guess which of today's quilts will have lasting value, and which will, ultimately, belong only to their own time. Such contemporary labels as art and traditional may prove meaningless in the long run. History has often shown that what may be wild experiment today can appear to be conservative tomorrow. All fashions ultimately fade, revealing the wheat obscured by the chaff. Perhaps the best measure of lasting quality is proposed in Eliza Calvert Hall's *Aunt Jane of Kentucky*: "Did you ever think how much piecin' a quilt's like livin' a life? . . . The Lord sends us the pieces, but we can cut 'em out and put 'em together pretty much to suit ourselves, and there's a heap more in the cuttin' out and the sewin' than there is in the caliker." The most lasting quilts are those that, through whatever technical means and artistic approaches they employ, most fully embody the lives of their makers in all their roiling complexity, and thereby speak to us all of our shared humanity. Paradoxically, the quilts that delve most deeply into the self are often the most universal. As Aunt Jane put it, "Patchwork? Ah, no! It was memory, imagination, history, biography, joy, sorrow, philosophy, religion, romance, realism, life, love and death; and over all . . . the love of the artist for her work and the soul's longing for immortality." The best quilts, whether traditional or art, are fully capable of carrying all of these essential human meanings across the generations.

A manifesto issued by Walter Gropius, first director of the Bauhaus School of Design, speaks eloquently of the synergy that may result from dialogue and interaction between craftspeople and artists, and, by implication, between artists and their audiences:

> *Architects, sculptors, painters, we must all turn to the crafts. Art is not a "profession," there is no essential difference between the artist and the craftsman. The artist is an exalted craftsman. In rare moments of inspiration, moments beyond the control of his will, the grace of heaven may cause his*

work to blossom into art. But proficiency in his craft is essential to every artist. Therein lies a source of creative imagination.

Let us create a new guild of craftsmen, without the class distinctions which raise an arrogant barrier between craftsman and artist. Together let us conceive and create the new building of the future, which will embrace architecture and sculpture and painting in one unity and which will rise one day towards heaven from the hands of a million workers like the crystal symbol of a new faith.

Gropius's admonitions and his powerfully hopeful vision are as pertinent today as they were when the manifesto was first issued in 1919. It is to be hoped that quilters will succeed where others have failed, by honoring tradition and innovation, craft and art, process and product, in equal measure. Quilts have always been as diverse as the people who have crafted them, reflecting and representing the lives and creativity of women and men of every stripe. But quilts are also uniquely democratic and democratizing objects, with a proven ability to cut across boundaries of all kinds and unite people of disparate beliefs, classes, and cultures. As such, quilts may also hold the power to break down the traditional, if artificial, barriers that separate high from low, art from life, soul from work, and meaning from context. These are all indeed "arrogant" barriers, which ultimately serve only to divide us from each other. The quilt has always been an art form and an artifact that binds us together at the same time that it reflects our differences. It is, perhaps, then up to us to recognize that we alone can limit the quilt's potential to express who we are or deny the many meanings it can bring to our lives. The future of the quilt rests in our hands, in the development of our own understanding of its immense possibilities. The quilt is America's art form, a medium that has already shown itself to be large and flexible enough to represent this country in all its racial, ethnic, and cultural diversity. Given the chance, it may prove large and democratic enough to represent the global village as well.

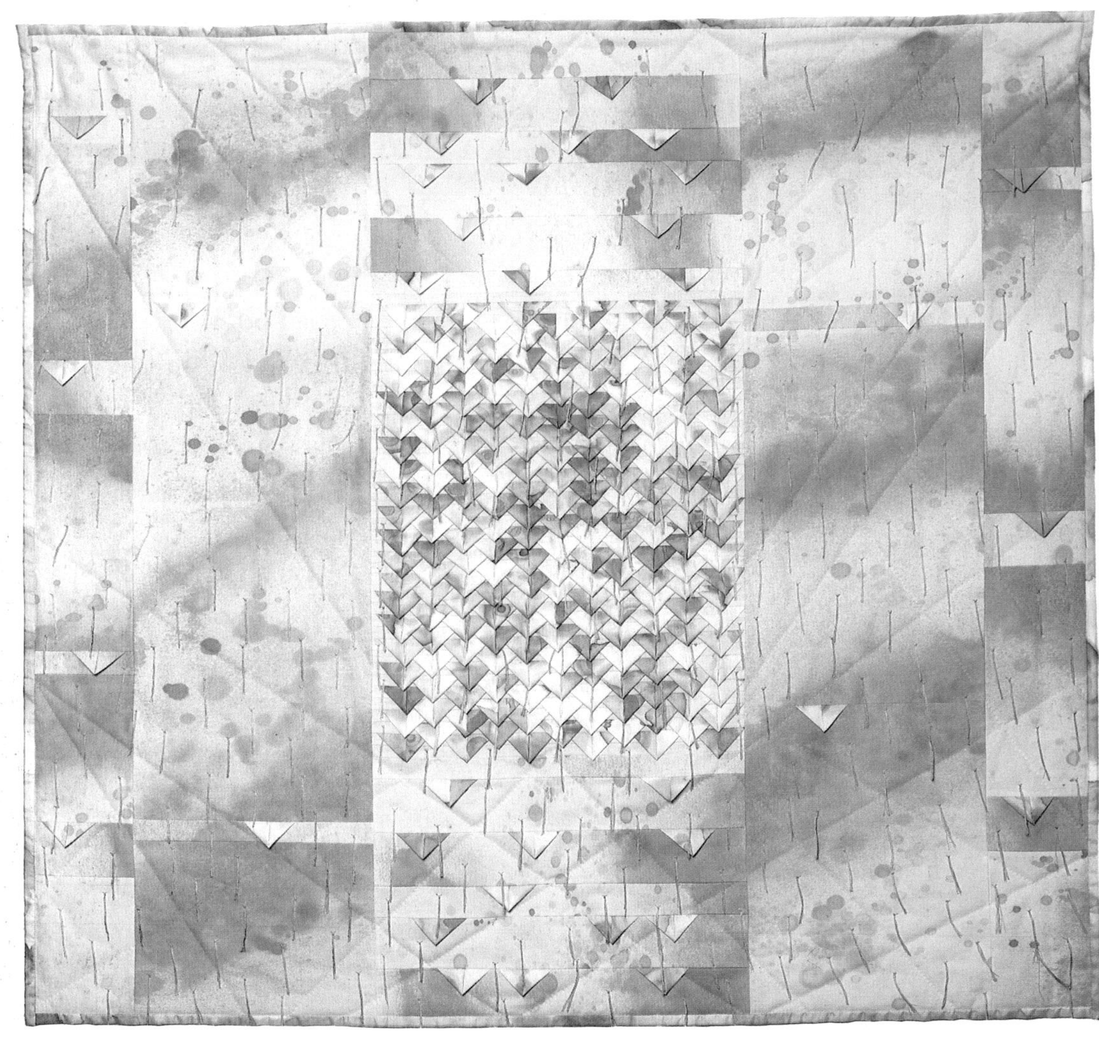

MORNING MIST ▶

Yvonne Porcella. 1984. Modesto, California. Hand-painted cotton and silk; machine pieced, hand quilted, hand tied. 50 1/2 x 47 in. Collection of Fairfield Processing Corp. (Roy Young, President).

This evanescent, monochromatic work captures the beauty and magic of an early morning landscape before the sun has had time to clear the mist.

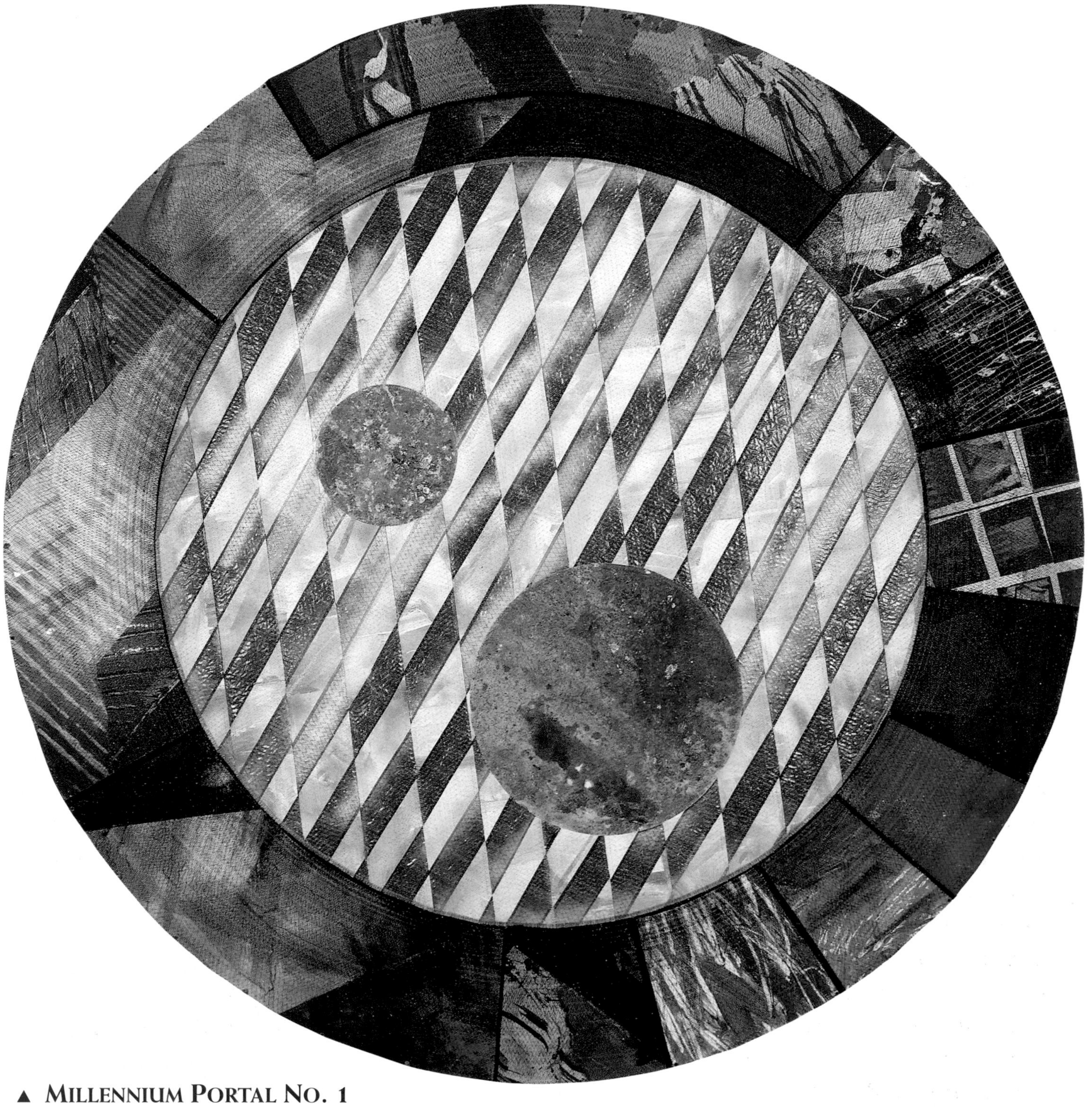

▲ MILLENNIUM PORTAL NO. 1

Arturo Alonzo Sandoval. 1993. Lexington, Kentucky. Mylar, paint, canvas, colored and metallic threads, Cibachrome, mirrored Plexiglass; interlaced and stitched on motorized mount. Diameter: 77 in. Collection of the artist.

This kinetic "quilt" is part of a series representing visions of the post-millennial universe. The quilt, which depicts planets seen from the window of a satellite, is set in a motorized mount that turns at one rpm to suggest the very slow rotation of satellites in outer space. According to the artist, who is a professor of art at the University of Kentucky, "The fiber artworks in *The Millennium Series* . . . carry my message of Hope for humankind. They depict the universe, not as black and empty, but filled with intense color, light, pattern, and texture."

THERE'S NO PLACE LIKE . . . ▶

Lynne Sward. 1992. Virginia Beach, Virginia. Cotton and blended fabrics, fusible web; machine and hand appliquéd, machine quilted. 38 x 41 in. Collection of the artist.

Lynne Sward is also known for her quilted clothing. In this recent small quilt, she bonded with fusible web and did most of the sewing and quilting by machine.

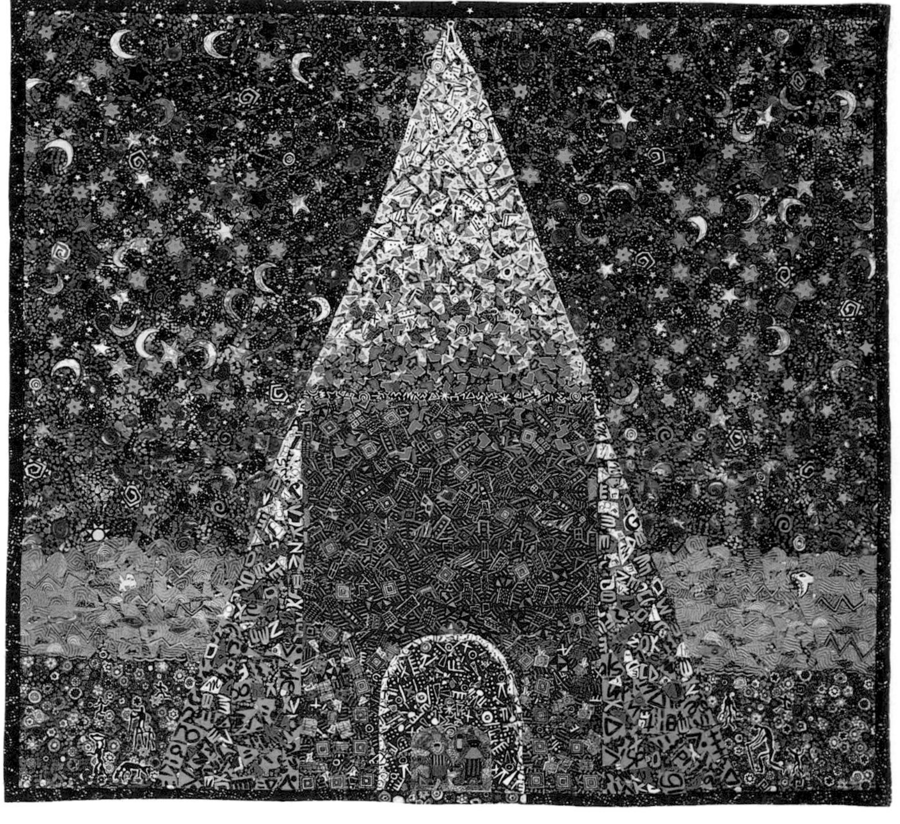

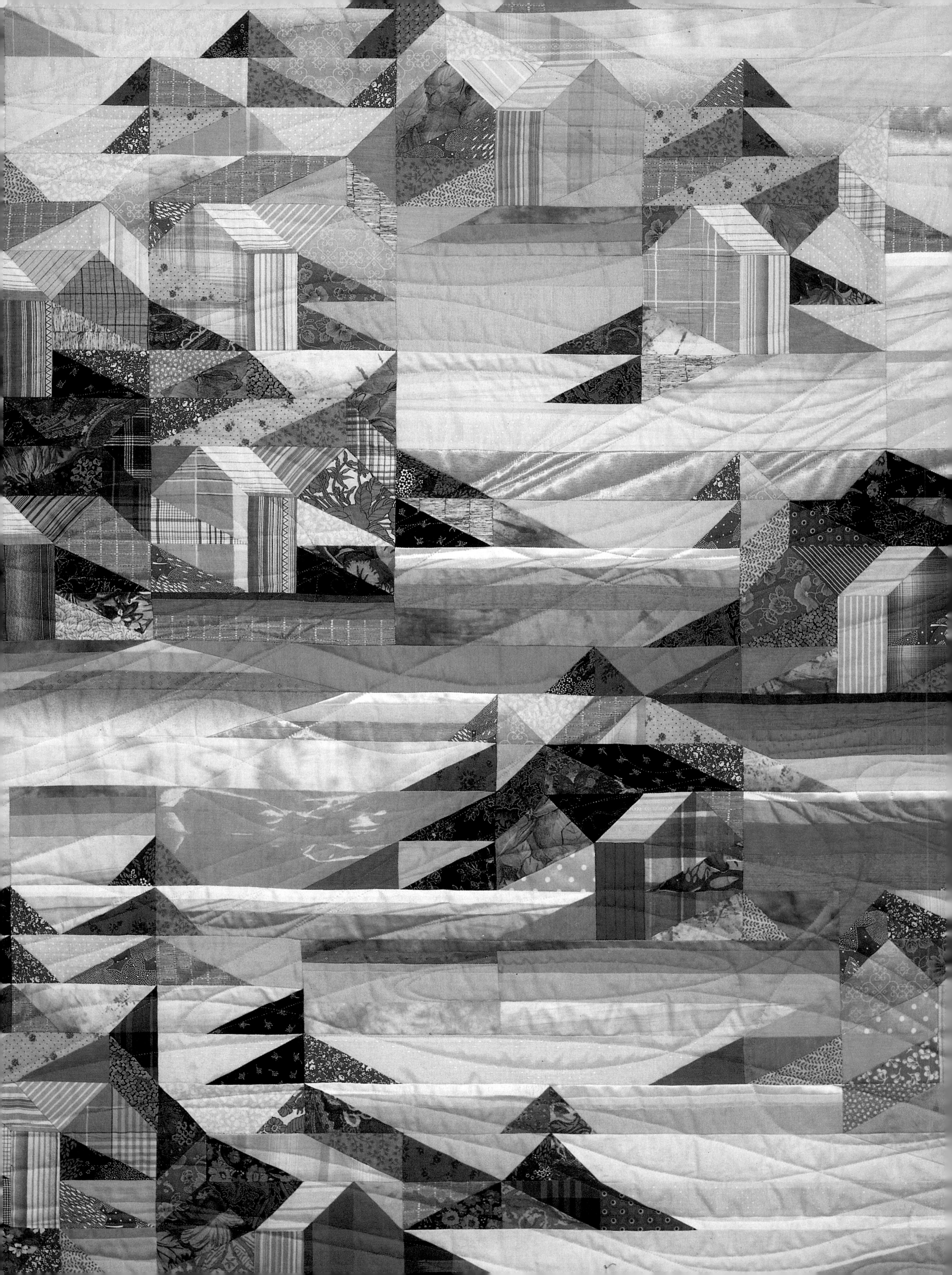

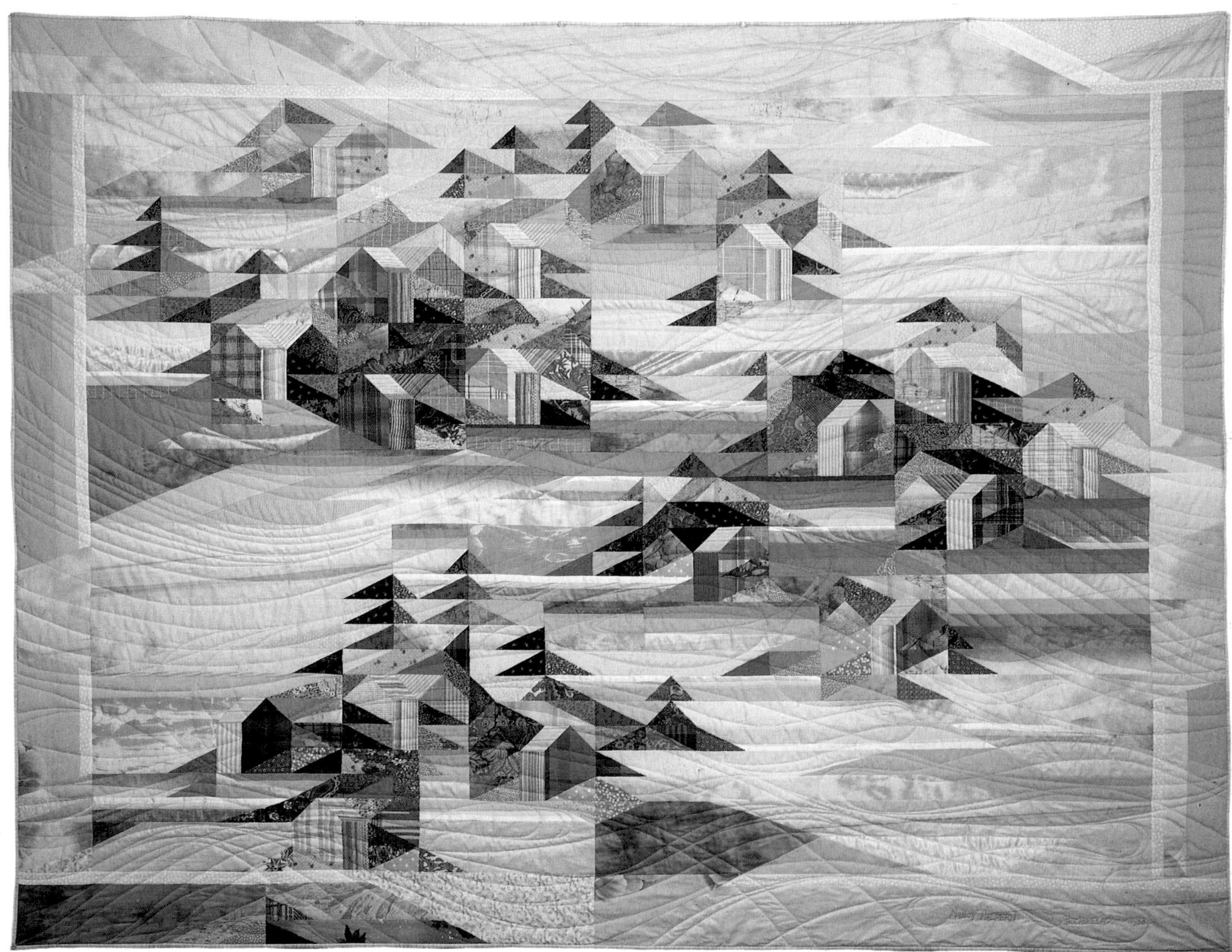

▲ ARCHIPELAGO (◄ DETAIL)

Nancy Halpern. 1983. Natick, Massachusetts. Cottons and synthetic fabrics; hand and machine pieced, hand appliquéd and quilted. 72 x 96 in. Collection of the New England Quilt Museum, Lowell, Massachusetts.

Nancy Halpern's distinctive abstract landscape quilts have influenced many other quilters. This piece was commissioned by the New England Quilter's Guild for its new museum. Wanting to make a quilt that represented her New England background and her entire community of fellow quiltmakers, craftspeople, and musicians, Halpern pictured herself standing on the rocks of Deer Isle, Maine, looking out to the many small, spruce-covered islands that dot the bay, and added houses for herself and her friends. She "used plaid fabrics for the houses because they looked like an architectural x-ray, allowing you to see past studs and beams into each interior . . . many houses became personalized: I would 'give' them to friends as birthday presents, and one was made form the scraps of a shirt of a friend who was temporarily homeless. In many ways, the sense of community was strengthened by using fabric donated by friends. When I finished, I counted contributions from twenty-two different people."

DEPTH OF FIELD III: PLANE VIEW ►

Jan Myers. 1985. Minneapolis, Minnesota. Procion-dyed cotton muslin; machine pieced and quilted with the assistance of Joanne Olson of Richfield, Michigan. 84 x 131 1/2 in. Collection of Ardis and Robert James.

The interlocking rectangles and grids on this huge quilt appear to be superimposed, thereby creating a powerful illusion of three-dimensional space.

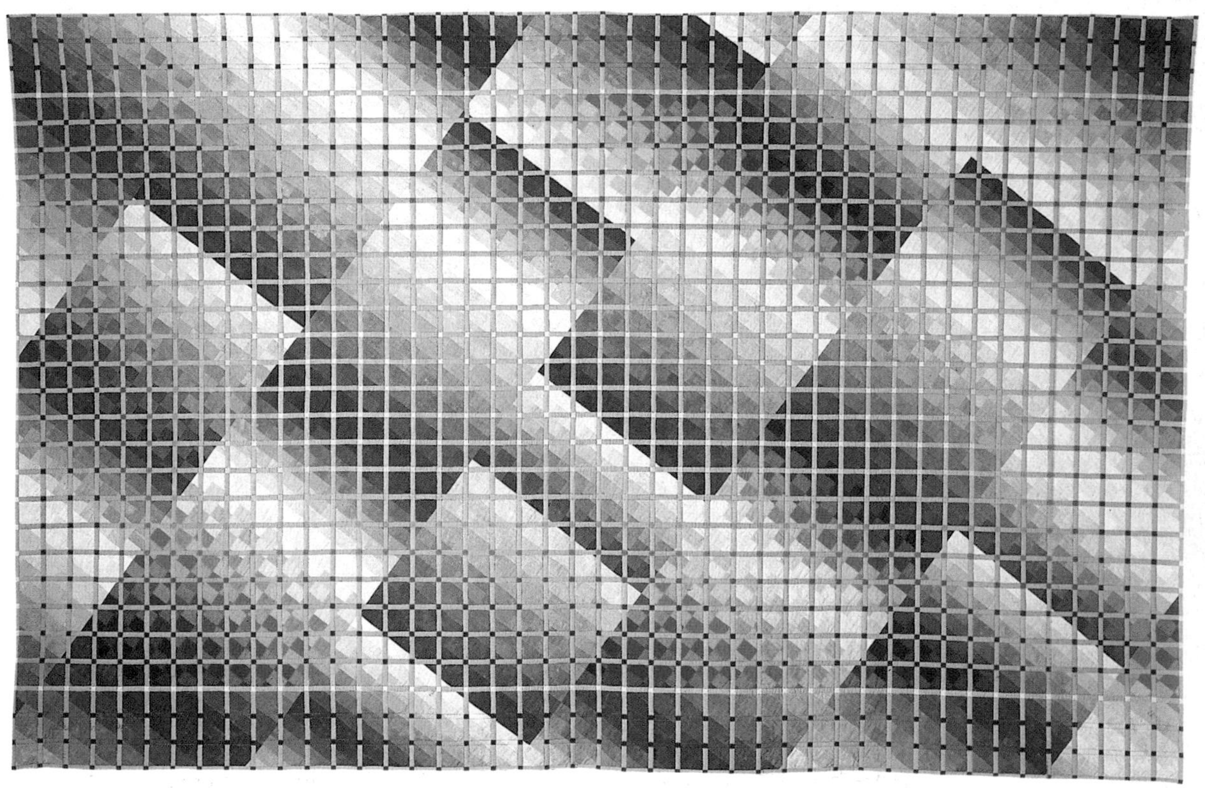

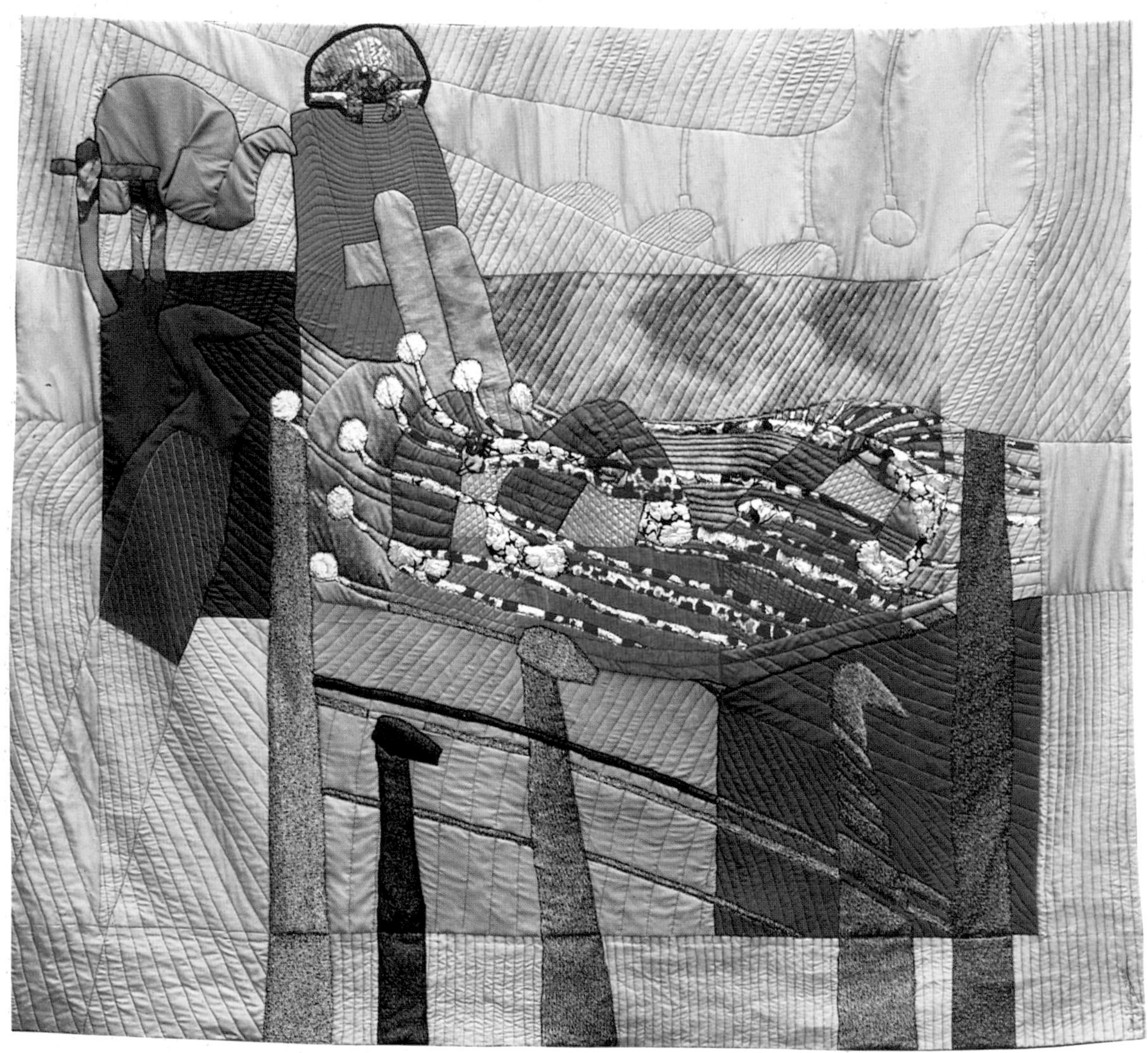

◄ **PILLARS**

Jean Hewes. 1983. Los Gatos, California. Cotton, rayon, silk, polyester, brocades; machine appliquéd. 92 x 95 in. Collection of the artist.

Pillars won the Domini McCarthy Award for Exceptional Craftsmanship at the 1983 Quilt National competition. Its background cloth was pinned and assembled from different pieces of fabric, and then the ambiguous design was layered and pinned on the background before all were machine stitched together.

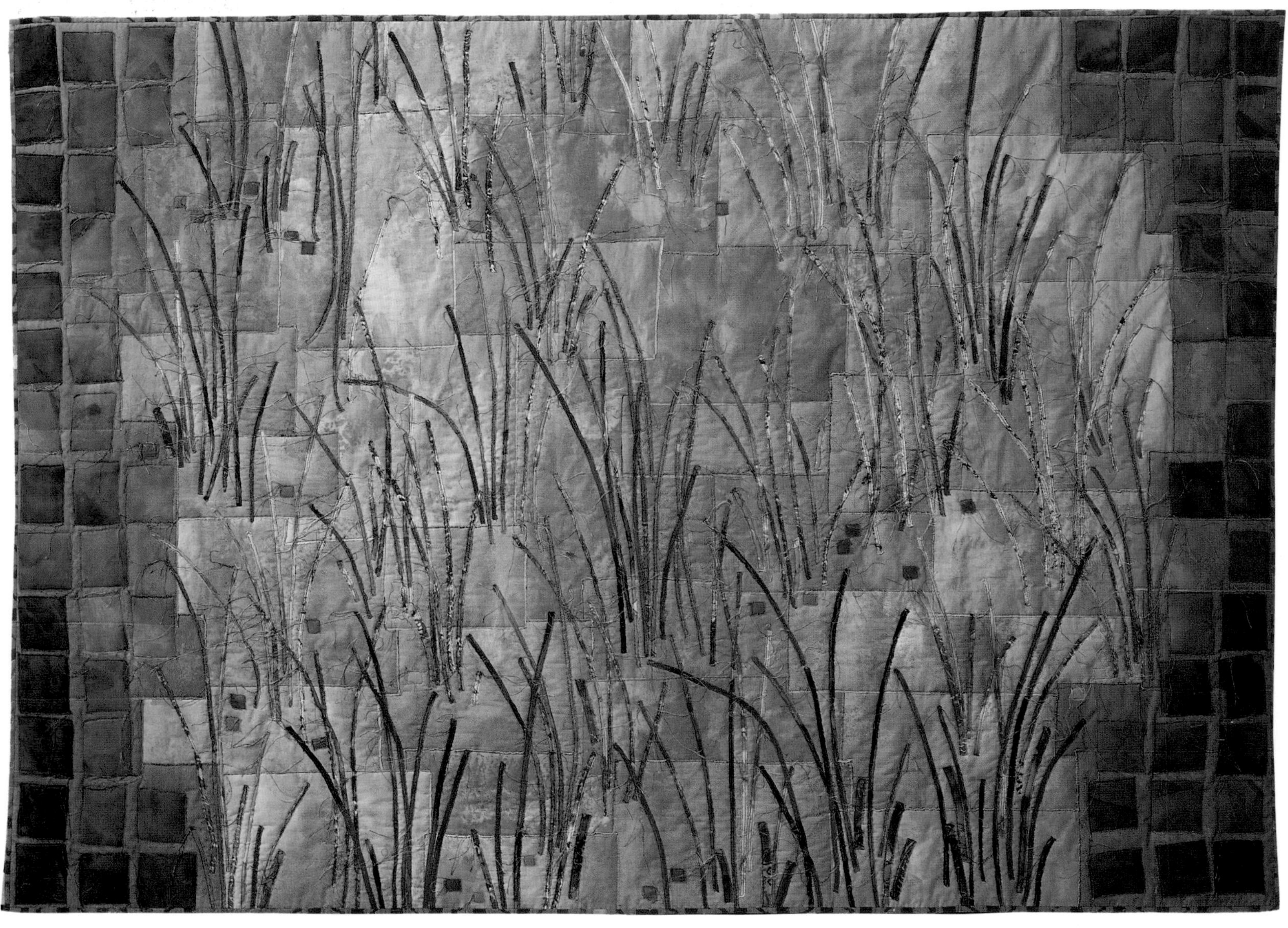

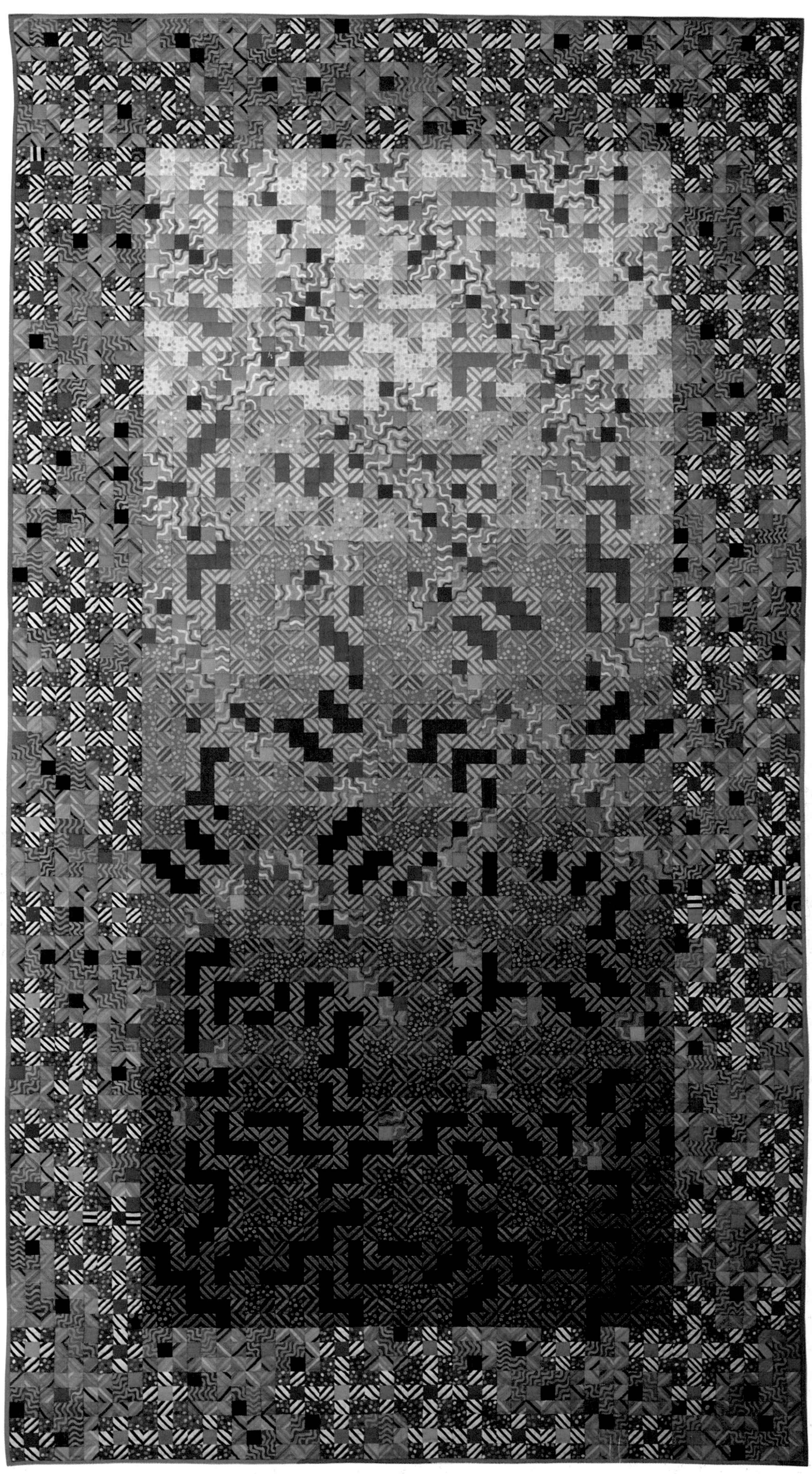

Quilt #107 ►

Pamela Studstill. 1993. Pipe Creek, Texas. Cottons, fabric paint; machine pieced, hand quilted. 99 x 54 in. Collection of John Walsh III.

The long central panel of this recent Studstill quilt is graduated from light to dark, while the wide border maintains an evenly distributed palette.

◄ Parameters

Erika Carter. 1993. Bellevue, Washington. Hand-painted cottons and silk organza, commercial cottons; machine appliquéd and quilted. 45 x 65 in. Private collection.

Parameters is part of a new series by Erika Carter that addresses boundaries and definitions of self. She says, "The grasses are metaphors for the success and growth one can experience working within defined parameters as suggested by the silk organza squares." The success of this design thus reflects in technical terms the spiritual journey it explores.

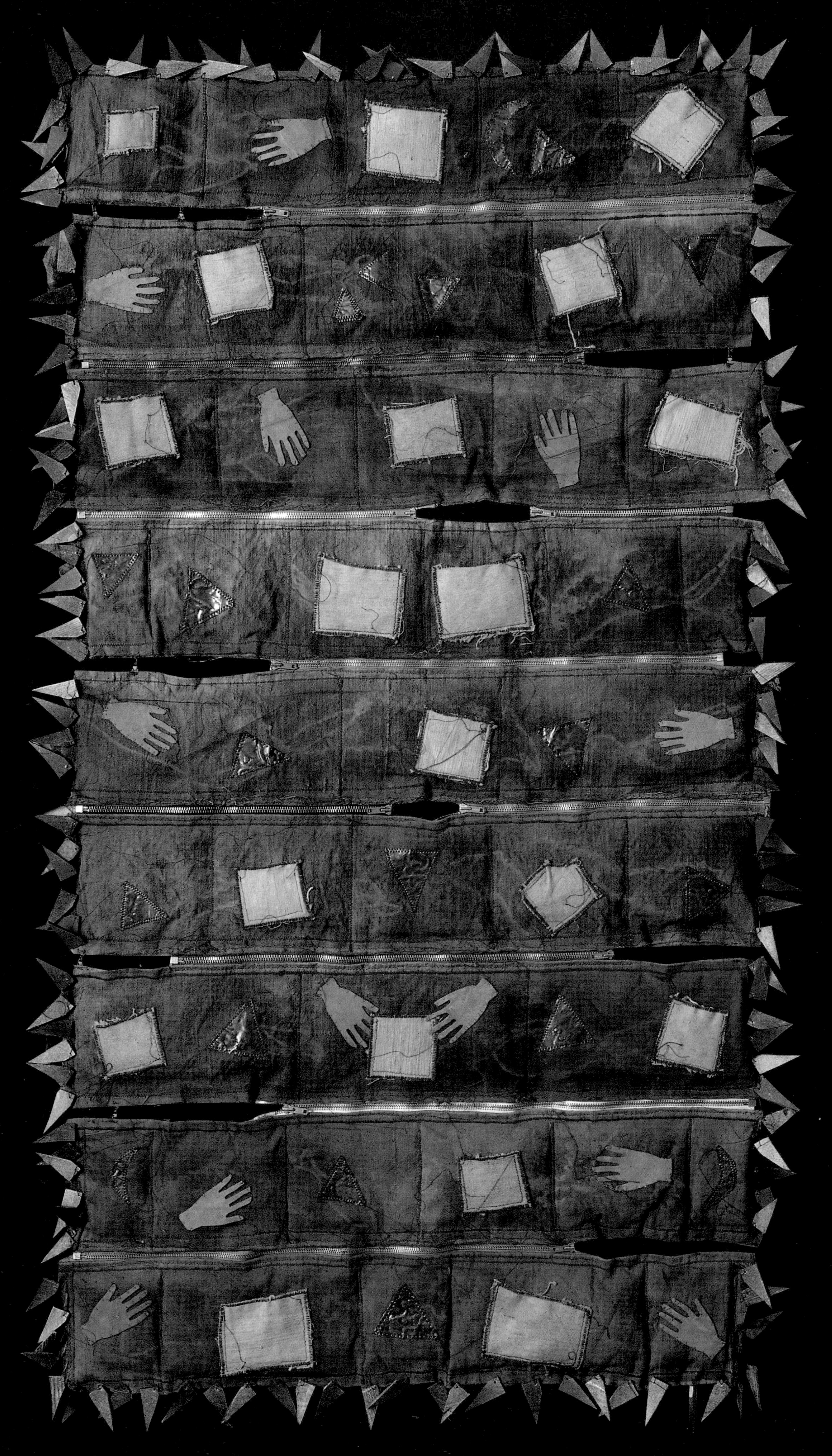

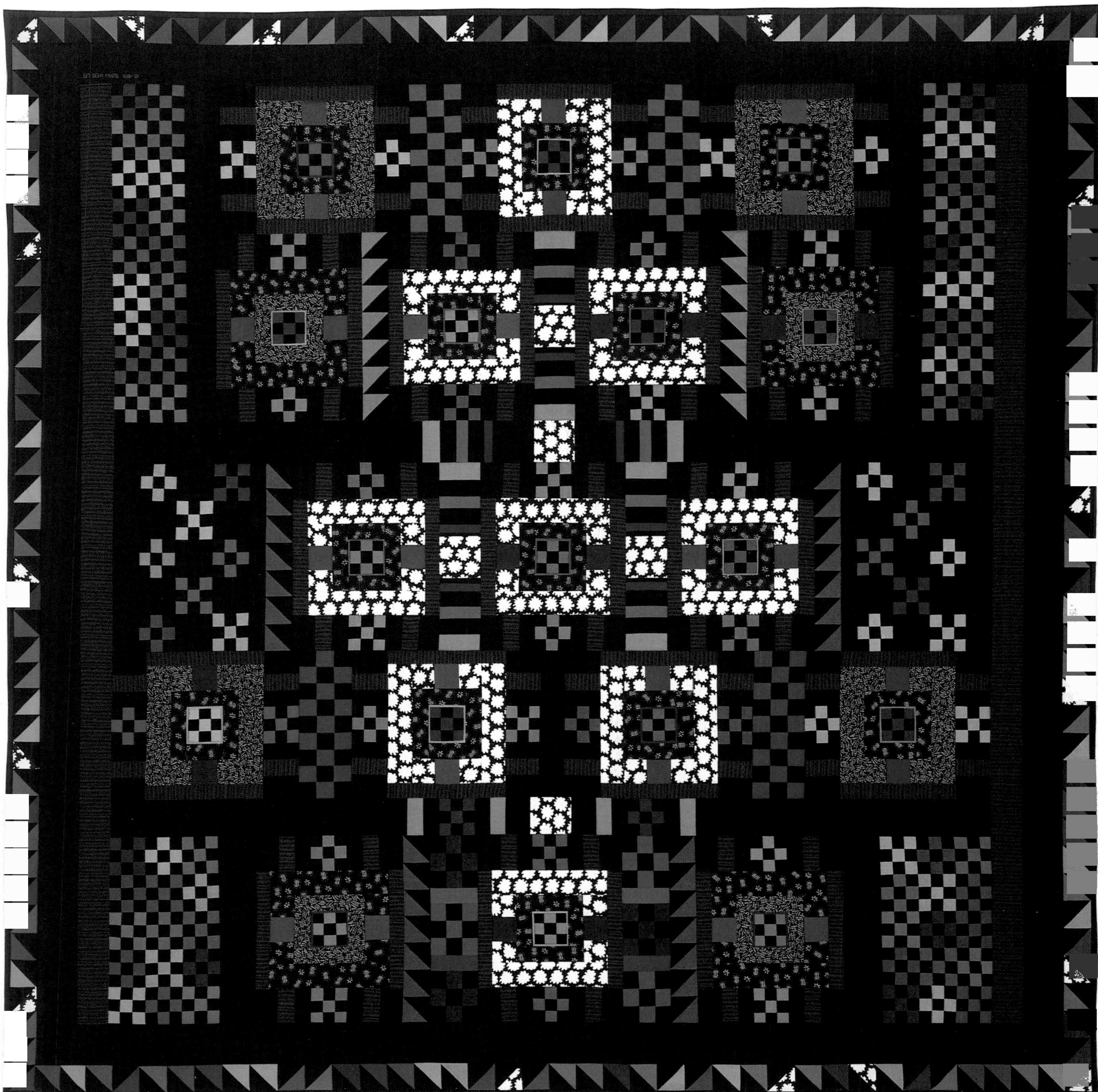

◄ QUILT FOR THE DEATH OF ONE I LOVE(D) (COMPOST QUILT)

Mimi Holmes. 1993. Minneapolis, Minnesota. Obi stiffener fabric, netting, leather, wood, paint, zippers, thread, egg shells, dryer lint, vermiculite, dried coffee grounds, orange rinds, banana skins, grapefruit rind, fake horsehair (upholstery material), spray paint, copper; fabric-dyed, machine embroidered, machine stitched, hand stitched, hand appliquéd. 60 x 34 in. Collection of the artist.

Made up almost entirely of biodegradable materials, this genre-bending quilt, at once amusing, poignant, and unsettling, was conceived as a burial shroud to be draped over the coffin of the artist's grandmother.

▲ CALABASH

Susan Webb Lee. 1989. Weddington, North Carolina. Cottons; machine pieced and quilted. 65 x 66 in. Collection of the artist.

Calabash is made from a combination of both solid-colored and printed fabrics. The complicated geometric pattern, which includes dozens of tiny nine-patch units, appears symmetrical at first glance, but a closer look reveals subtle quirks that keep the eye off balance and moving from place to place.

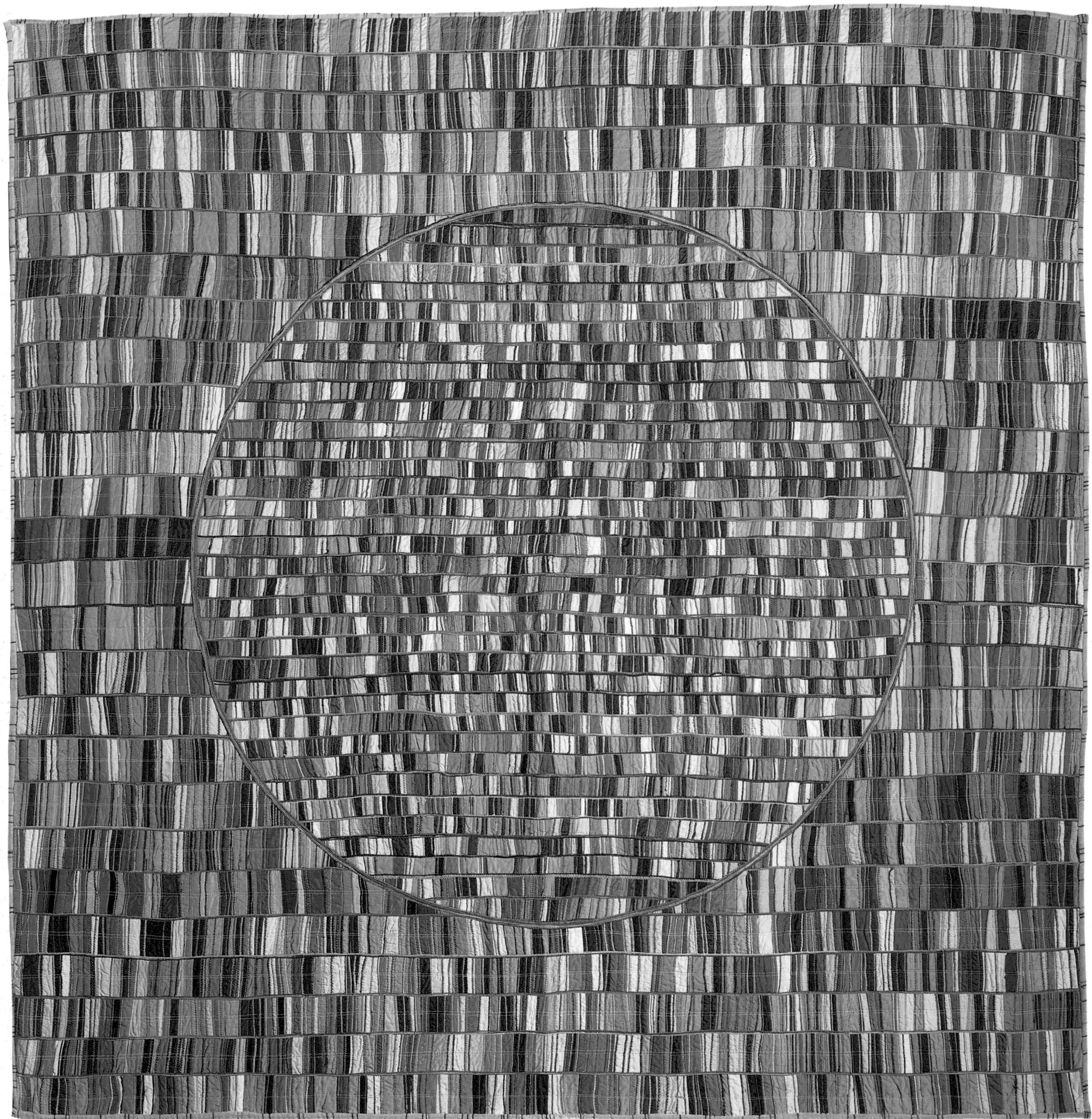

▲ CIRCLE ON SQUARE 1 (DETAIL ►)

Lucy Wallis. 1984. Somerset, England. Taffeta overlaid with wool stitching, cotton backed and tied, bound with velvet. 108 x 108 in. Collection of Ardis and Robert James.

Lucy Wallis is an English jeweler and sculptor who has made relatively few quilts. This large and meticulously worked example of her work is pieced from hundreds of strips of taffeta to create a shimmering and highly complex surface.

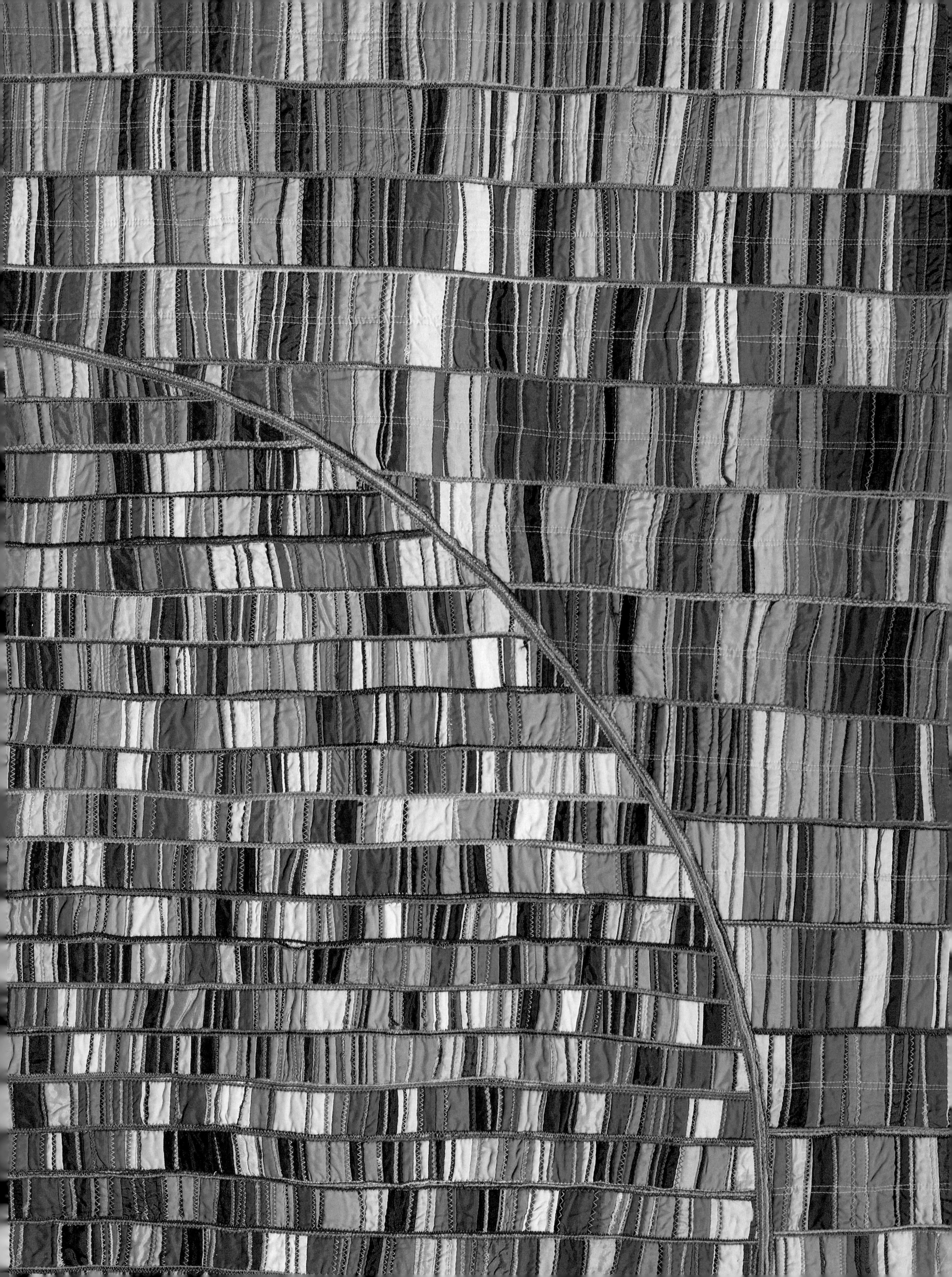

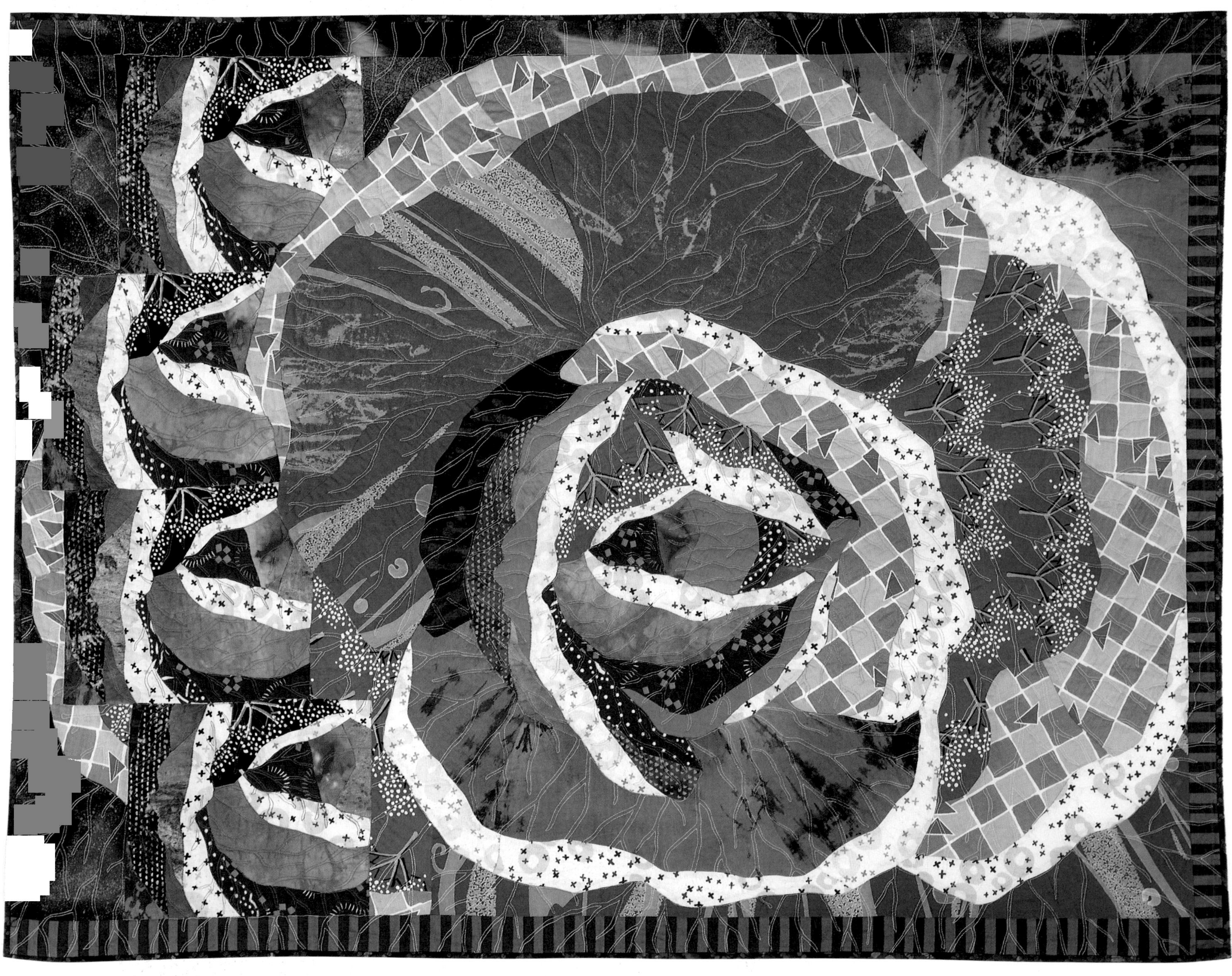

▲ **CABBAGE**

Ruth McDowell. 1993. Winchester, Massachusetts. Cottons; machine pieced and hand quilted. 53 x 41 in. Collection of the artist.

Ruth McDowell's pieced quilts present flowers, trees, and vegetables using the broken, mottled appearance of the pieced work to abstract the object(s) being portrayed, thereby simulating the effects of light in a painterly way. McDowell's work is firmly grounded in traditional quiltmaking; she uses only commercial fabrics and stitches her quilts entirely by hand.

FOR ALL THE WORLD TO SEE ▶

Therese May. 1984. San Jose, California. Cottons, satins and velvets, acrylic paint; machine pieced and appliquéd. 85 x 89 in. Collection of John Walsh III.

With its cryptic title, eclectic juxtaposed imagery, and deliberately naive workmanship, this quilt is typical of Therese May's best work. As in many of her quilts, the surprisingly potent combination of visual and intellectual elements continues to resonate in unexpected ways, becoming richer with each viewing.

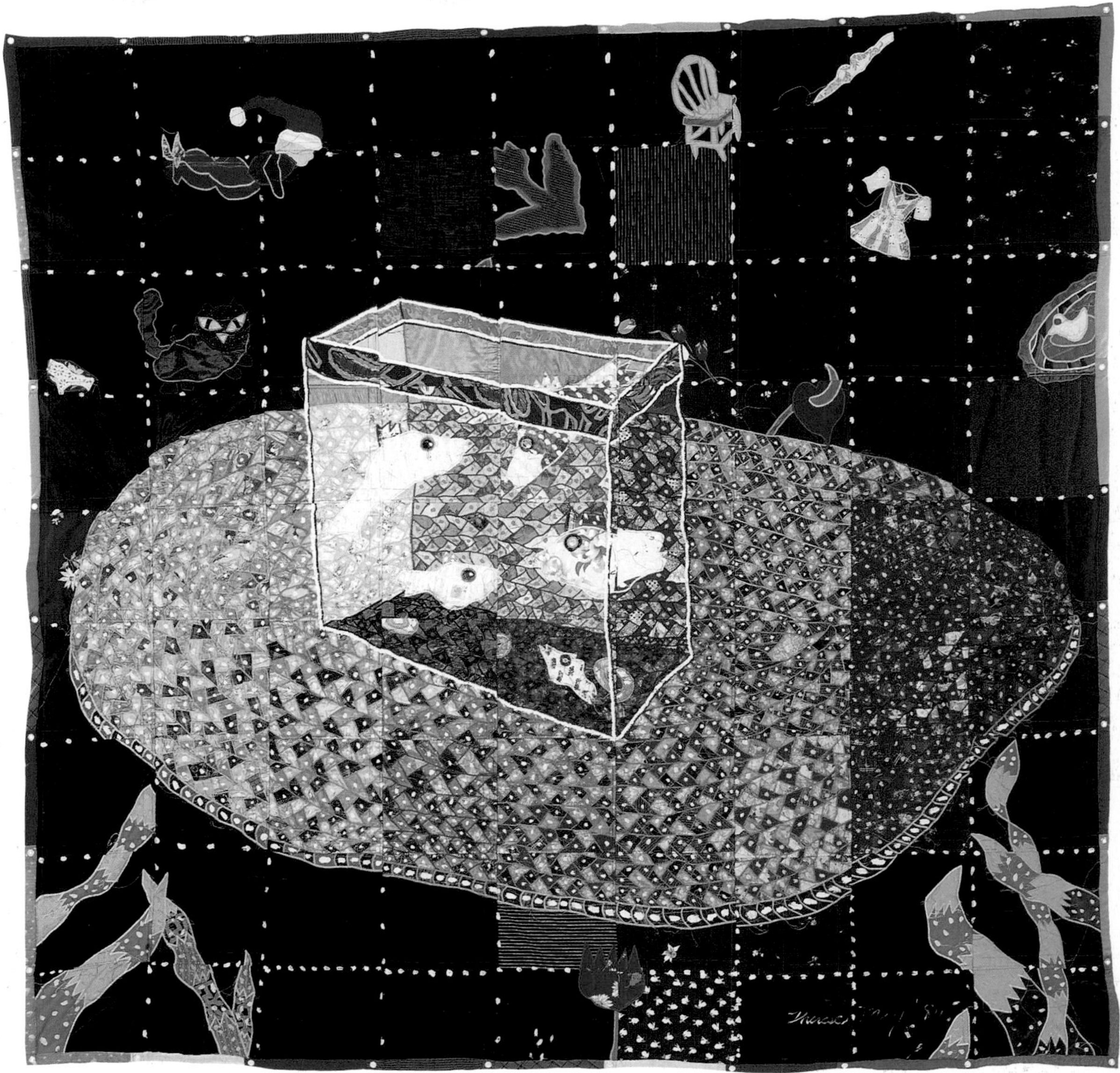

SAWBLADE ▶

Therese May. 1985. San Jose, California. Cottons; machine appliquéd on cotton canvas; acrylic paint. 69 x 78 in. Collection of Ardis and Robert James.

This swirling design was inspired by a giant sawblade May saw at a country fair. The painted pattern of the blade, background, and inner border resembles a braided rug. The quilt was awarded Most Innovative Use of the Medium at the 1985 Quilt National competition.

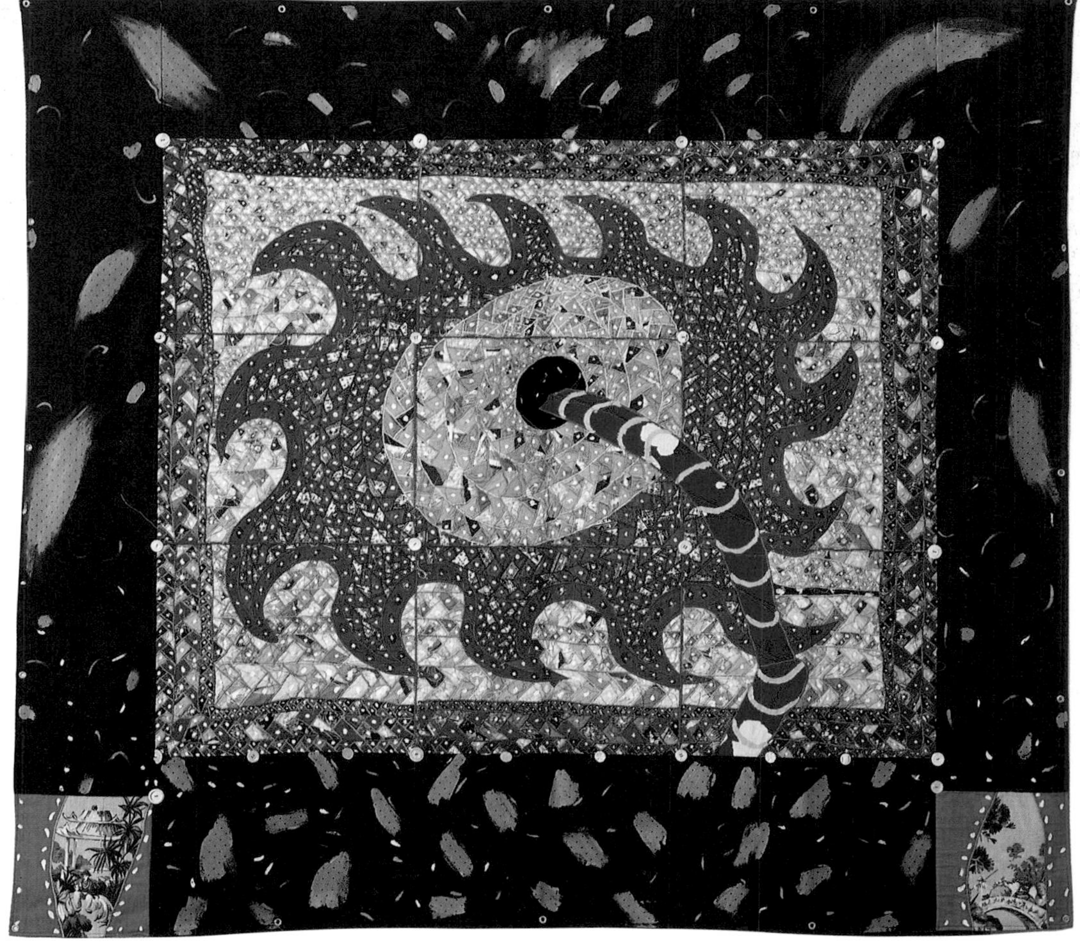

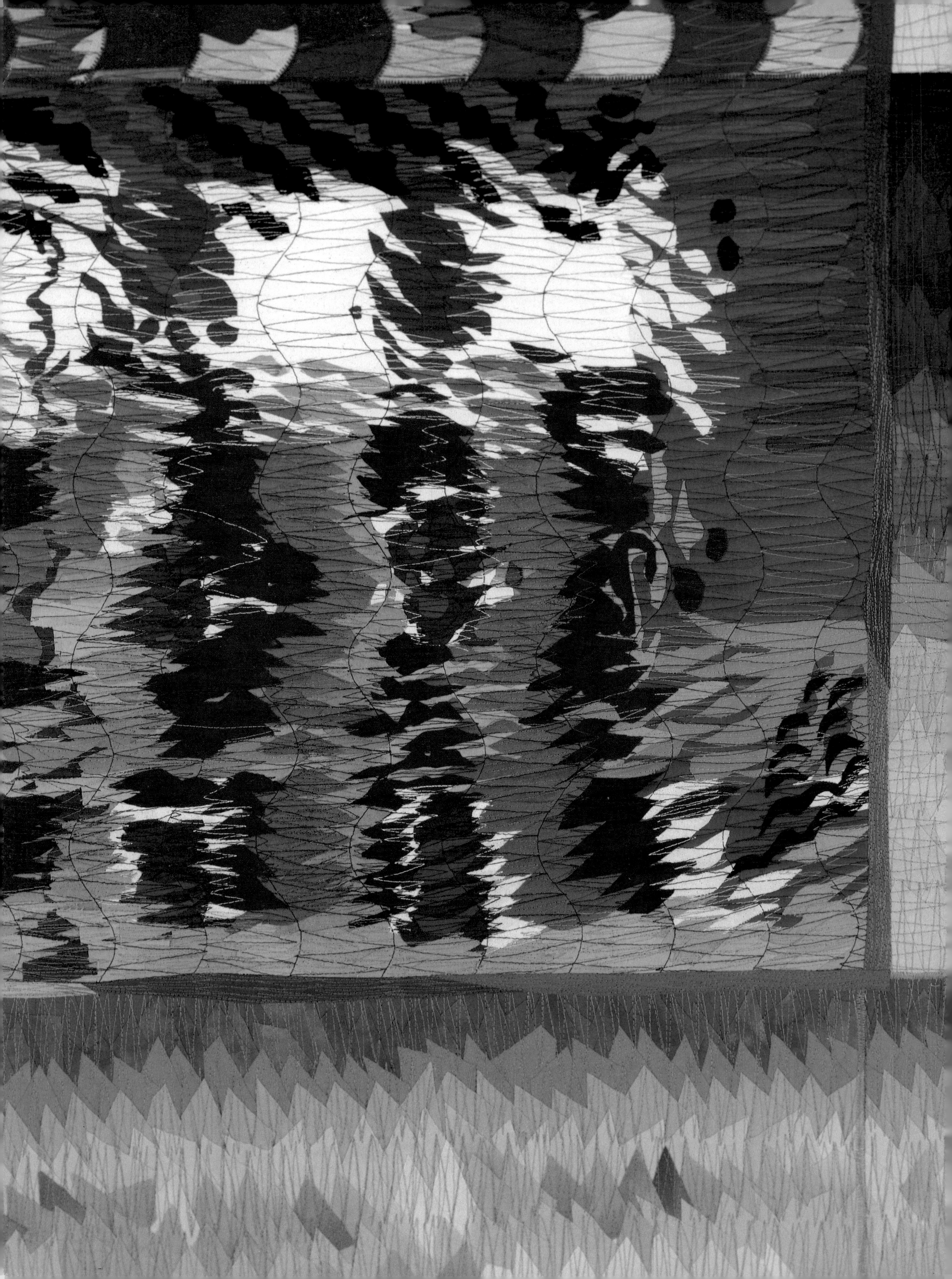

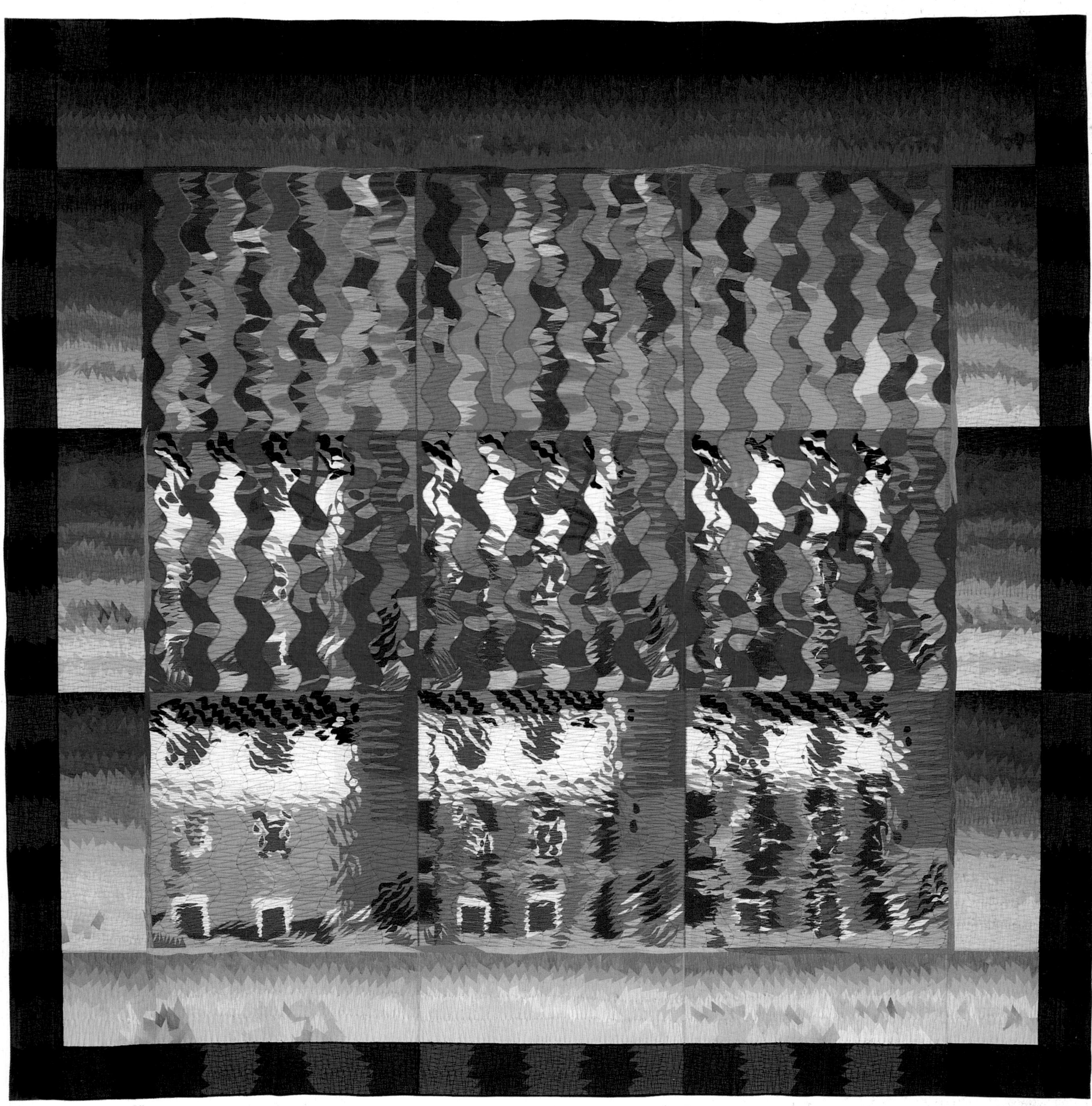

▲ **Nottingham Reflections (◄ detail)**

Pauline Burbidge. 1993. Nottingham, England. Cottons, some hand-dyed; machine pieced, appliquéd, and quilted. 80 x 80 in. Collection of John Walsh III.

This impressionistic quilt is part of a recent series by Burbidge that explores water and movement. The illusionistic, painterly effects, which seem to capture reflections in water, are achieved entirely through skillful manipulation of the fabrics.

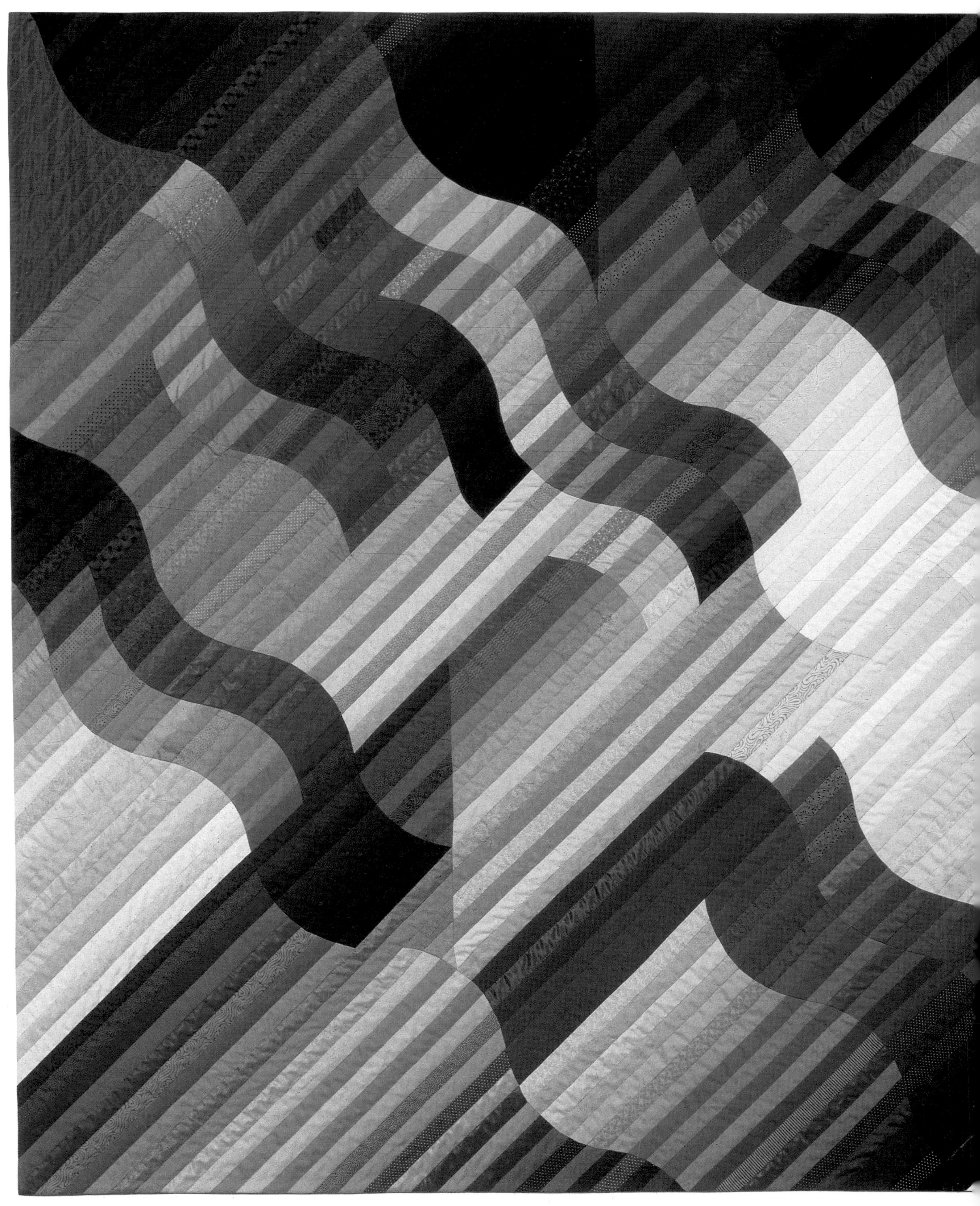

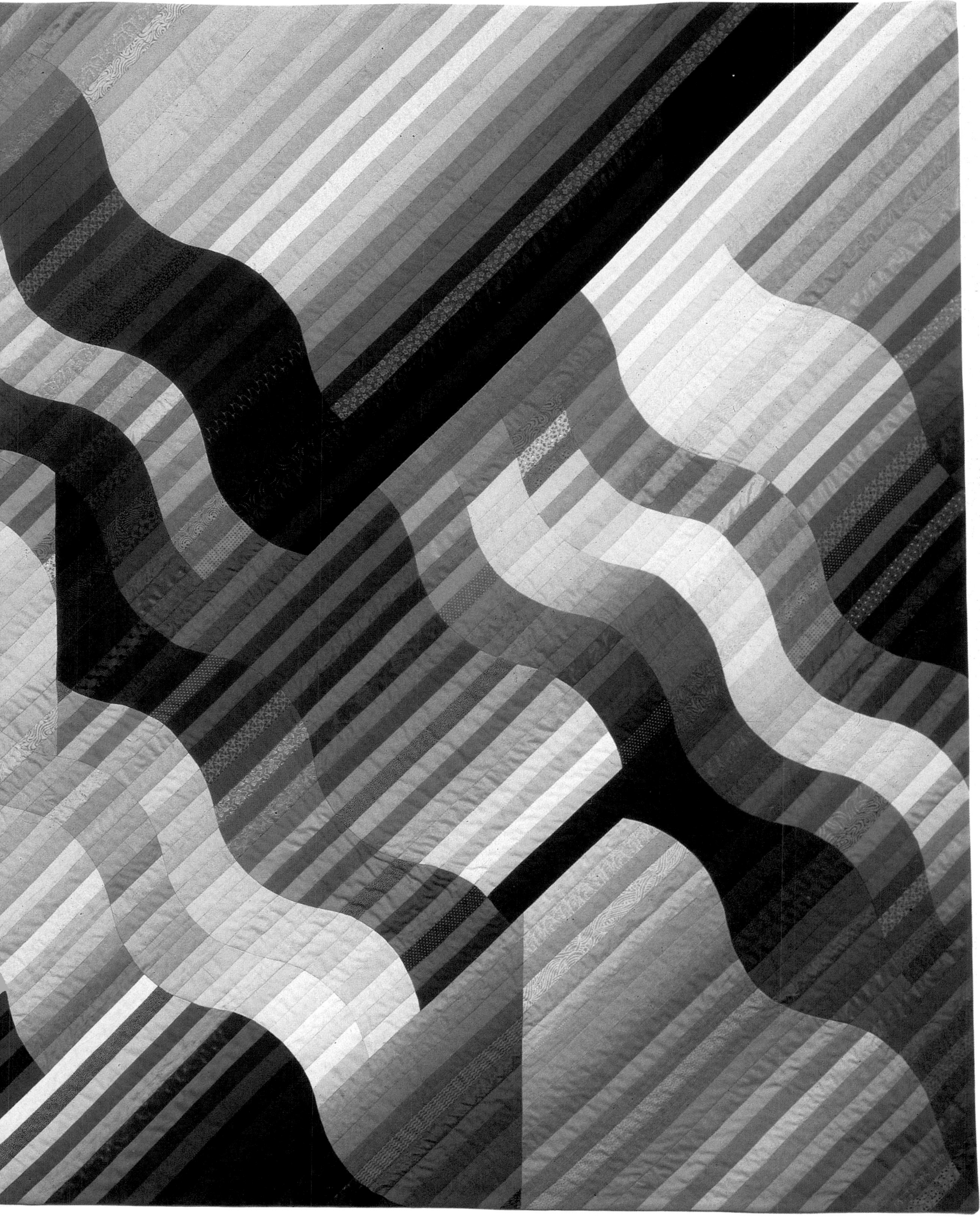

▲ **Sky/Wind Variations II**

Michael James. 1990. Somerset Village, Massachusetts. Cotton, silk taffeta; machine pieced and quilted. 51 x 86 1/2 in. Collection of the artist.

Like many of Michael James's quilts, this impressionistic work explores the visual and emotional effects of carefully juxtaposed strip-pieced fabric, suggesting the rhythmic play of color and light in a wind-tossed skyscape.

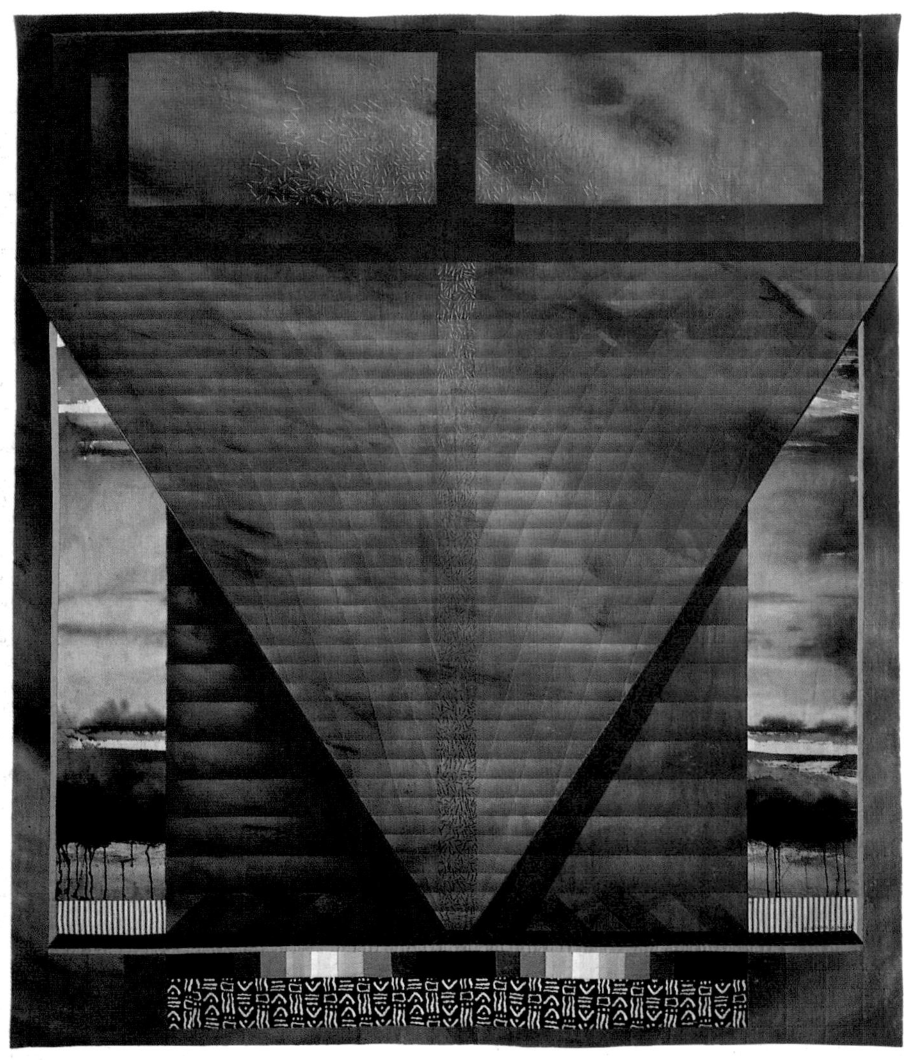

◄ **When We Were Young**

Elizabeth A. Busch. 1990. Bangor, Maine. Acrylic paint on raw cotton canvas treated with colored pencils, commercial fabric, embroidery floss; handbrushed and airbrushed, machine pieced, hand appliquéd, embroidered, and quilted. 80 x 69 in. Collection of the artist.

This quilt is one of a series by the artist exploring spatial and geometric illusions within unfamiliar color palettes.

Drawn to Edges . . . Cape Newagen ►

Gayle Fraas and Duncan Slade. 1994. Edgecomb, Maine. Cotton broadcloth; screen-printed with "pieced" pattern, all else hand painted with fiber-reactive dyes; machine and hand quilted. 60 x 60 in. Collection of Dr. David Becker and Lois Lunin.

This piece was commissioned for a specific residential site; the size and compositional scale of the work were determined after review of the architectural plans. A scaled gouache study preceded the quilt. The Maine coastline reflects the artists' interest in landscapes. Although from a distance the screen-printed pattern seems to have been pieced, the artists actually printed and painted on a single surface and quilted by both hand and machine.

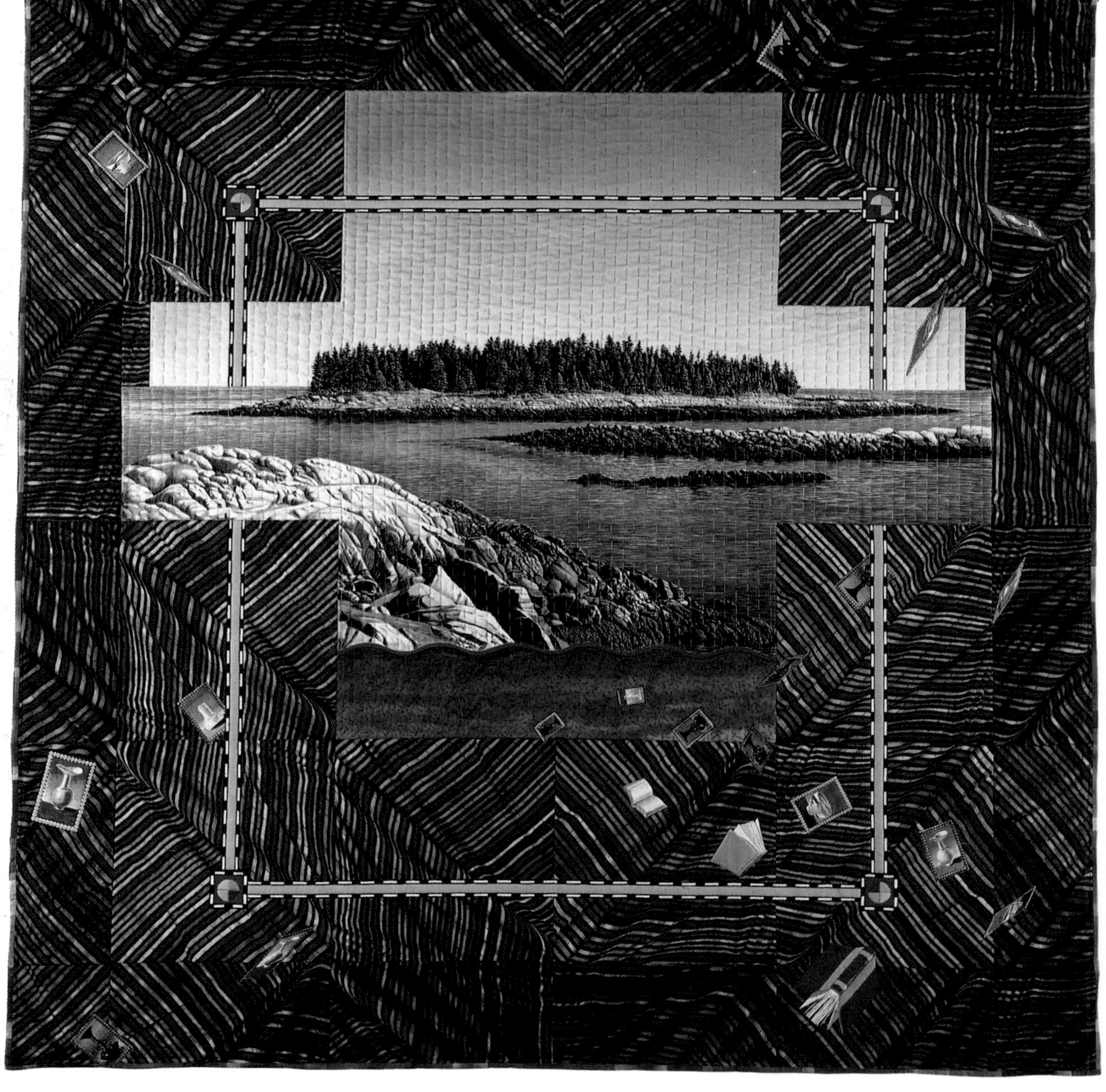

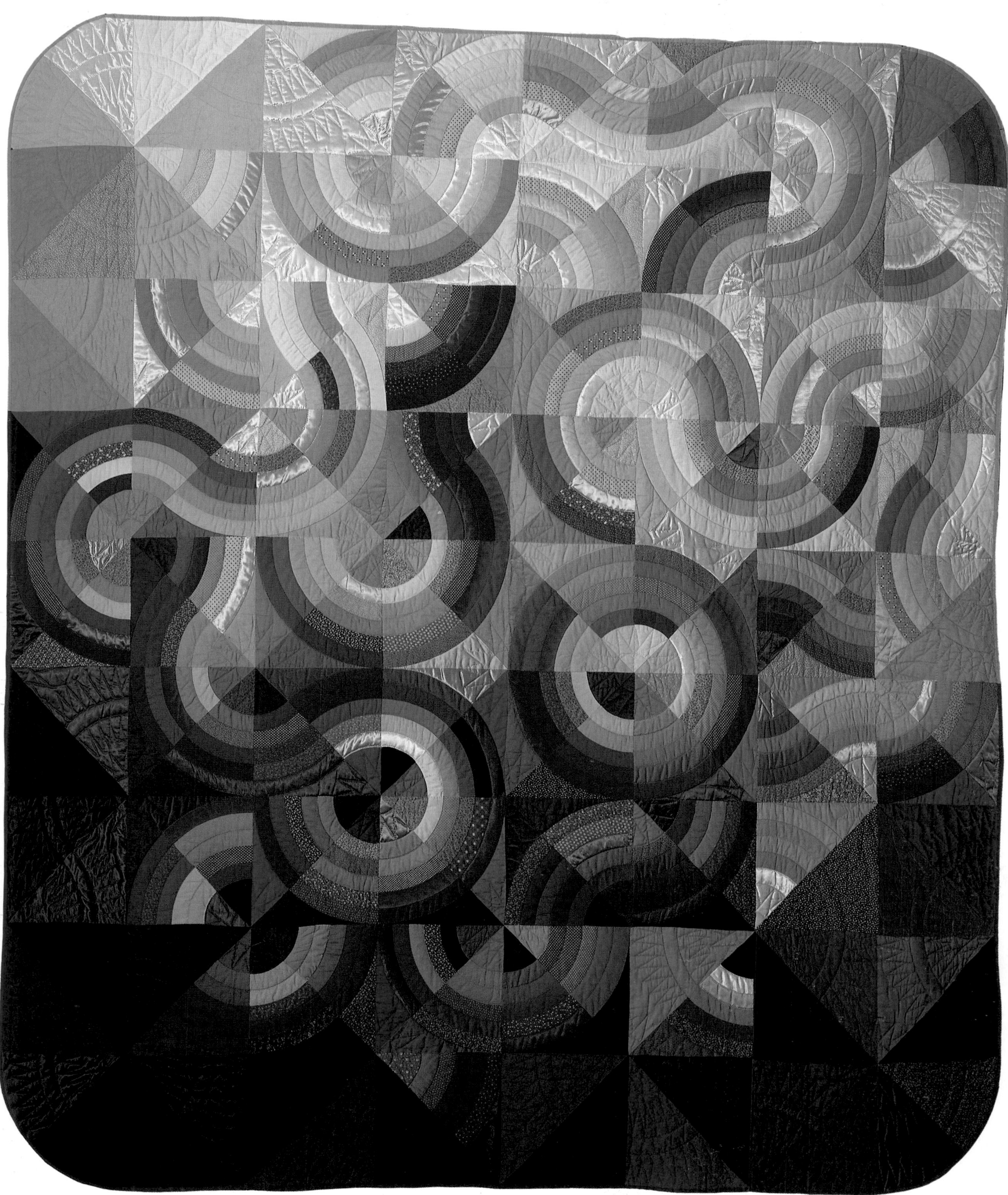

▲ **AURORA**

Michael James. 1978. Somerset Village, Massachusetts. Cottons; hand pieced and quilted. 108 x 96 in. Collection of Ardis and Robert James.

This early quilt by James is a prime example of his use of curved seams as a central design element, resulting in a composition full of swirling, refracted, repeating patterns.

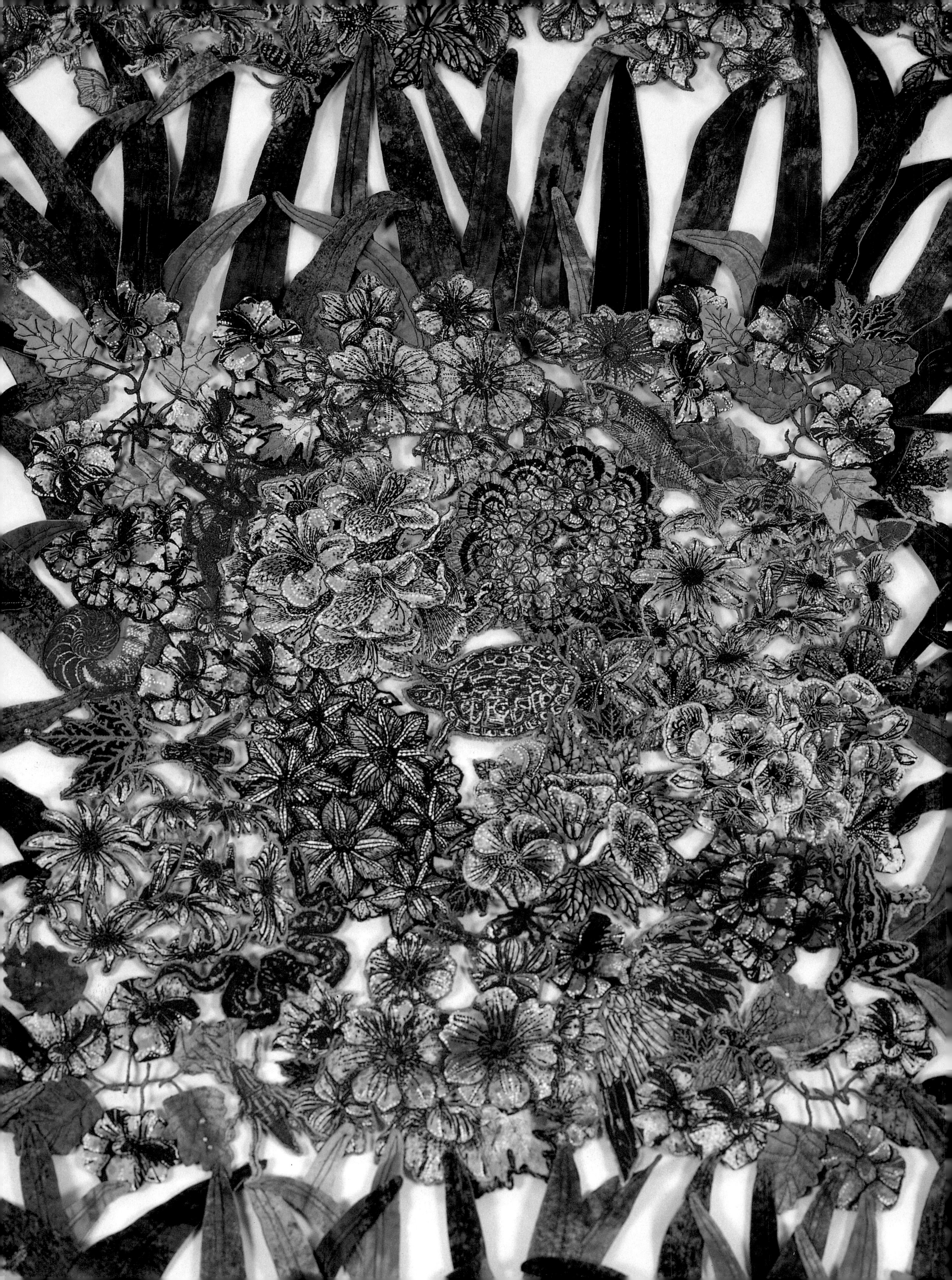

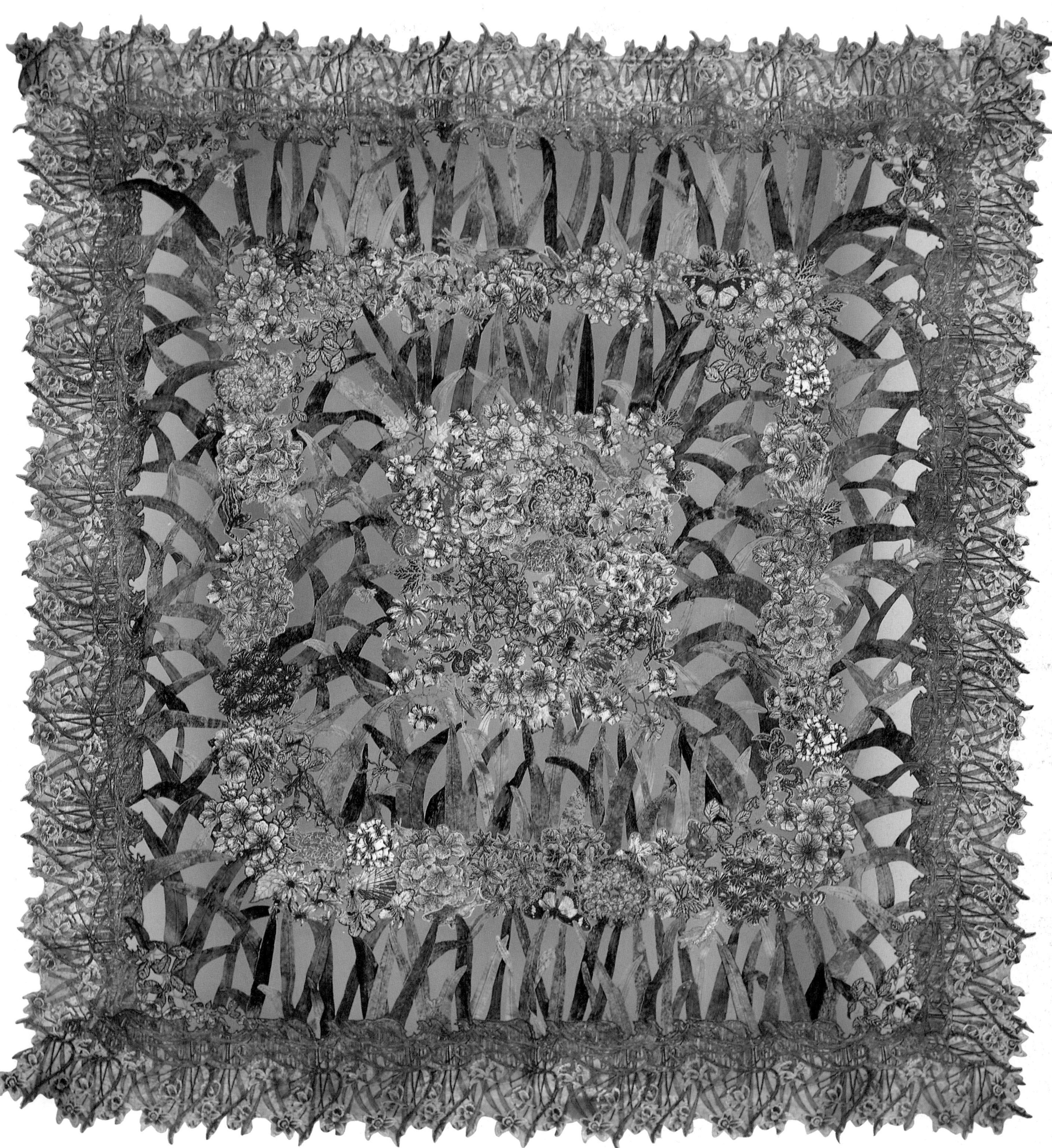

▲ IN THE GRASS (◄ DETAIL)

M. Joan Lintault. 1993. Carbondale, Illinois. Cottons, hand-dyed, screen-printed, and painted; machine pieced and quilted; hand embellished with beads. 98 x 91 in. Collection of John Walsh III.

The viewer looks through as well as at this innovative quilt, in which myriad images of flowers and insects are separated by two inner borders of plant forms and open space.

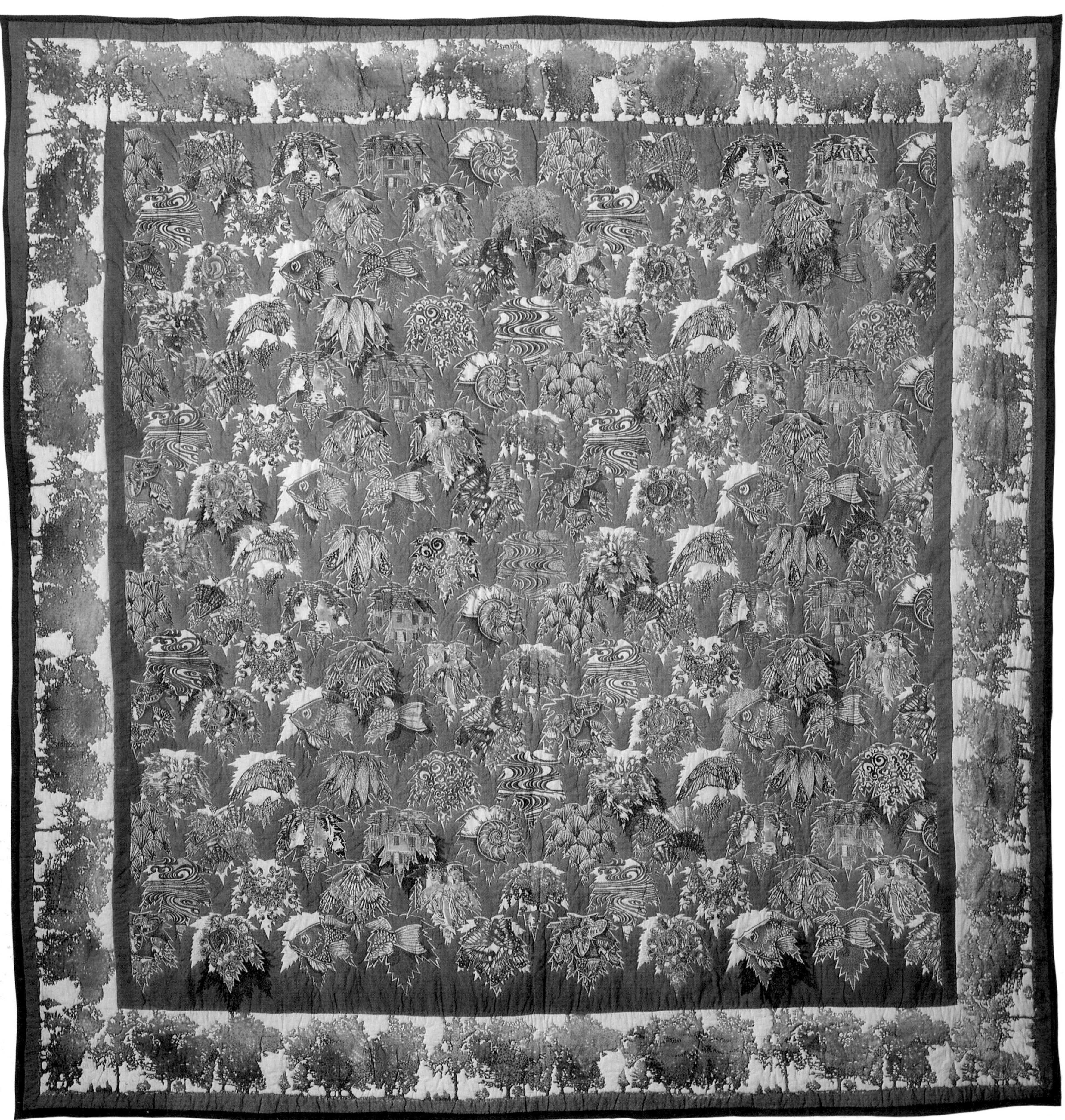

▲ **Gaia (detail ▶)**

M. Joan Lintault. 1992. Carbondale, Illinois. Cotton with rice-paper resist stencil printing, dye painting, and drawing; machine quilted. 90 x 86 in. Collection of Ardis and Robert James.

This quilt was named for the Gaia hypothesis formulated by Lynn Margulis and James Lovelock, which posits that the earth and all living things are a single interconnected organism. The quilt is symbolically made of whole cloth. According to the artist, 'The entire design is painted onto one piece of fabric and is neither appliquéd nor pieced. The primary motif . . . is the leaf. Within the many leaves are animals, bugs, trees, and various other things, including my cat, my house, my sister, and myself."

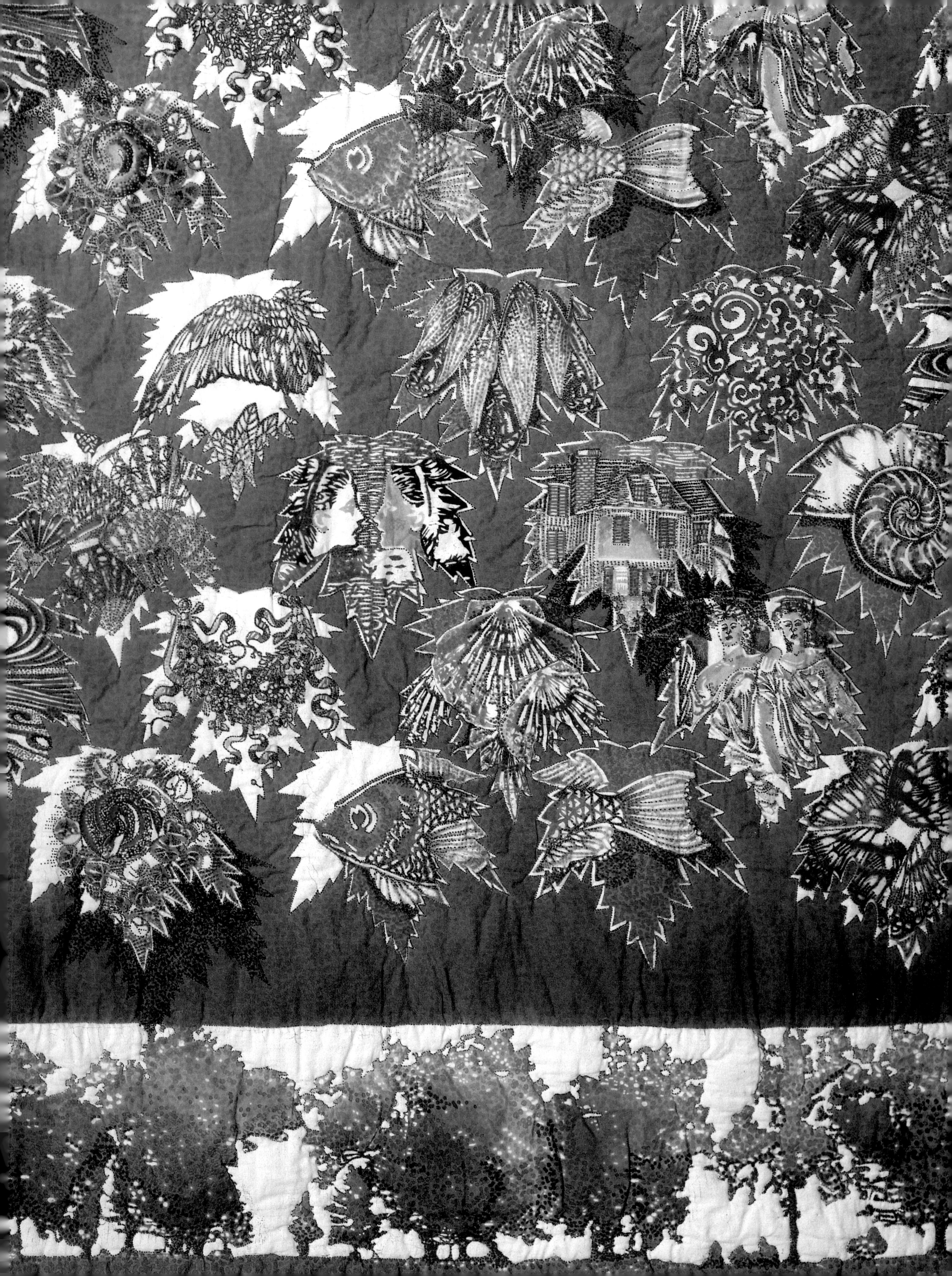

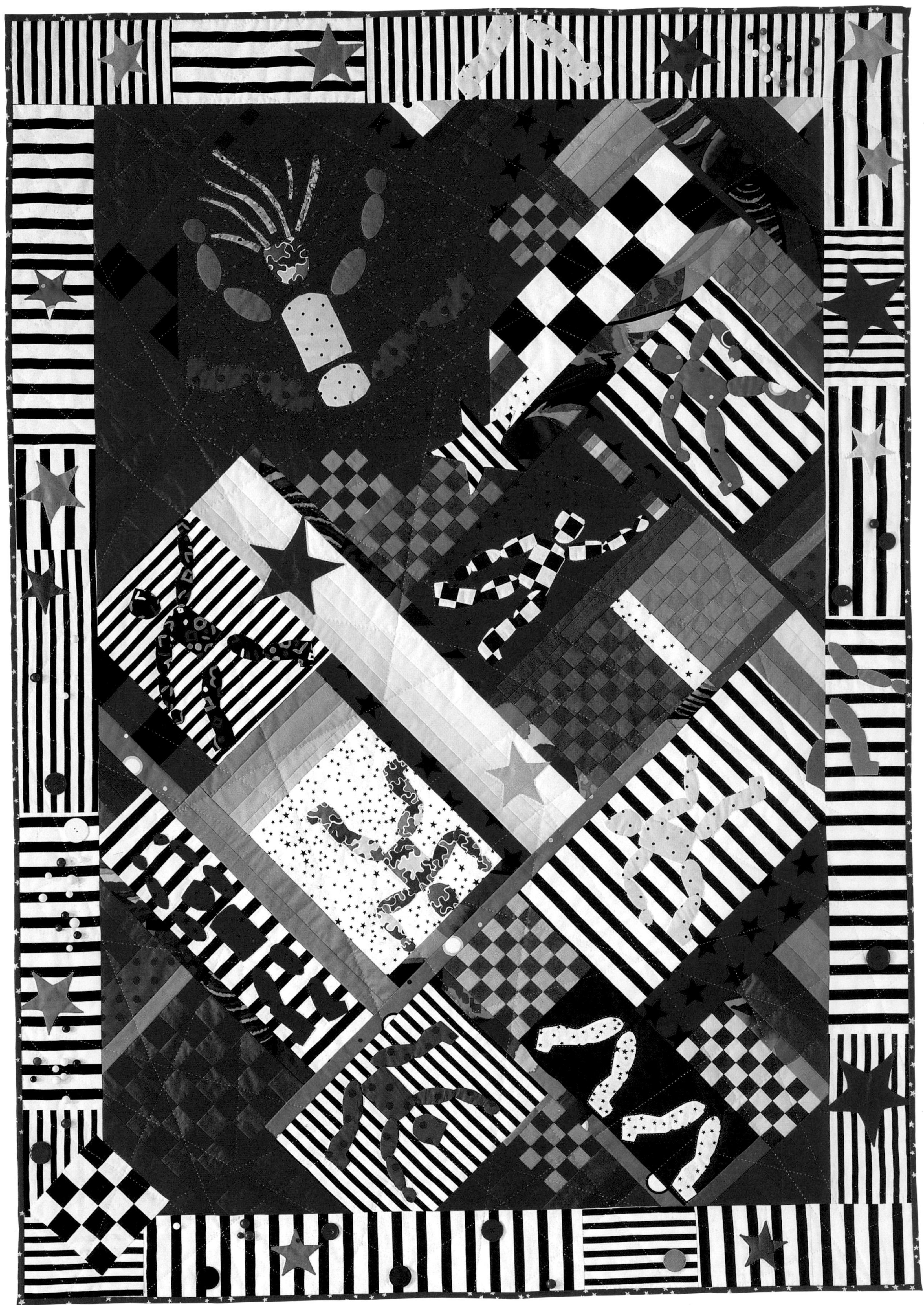

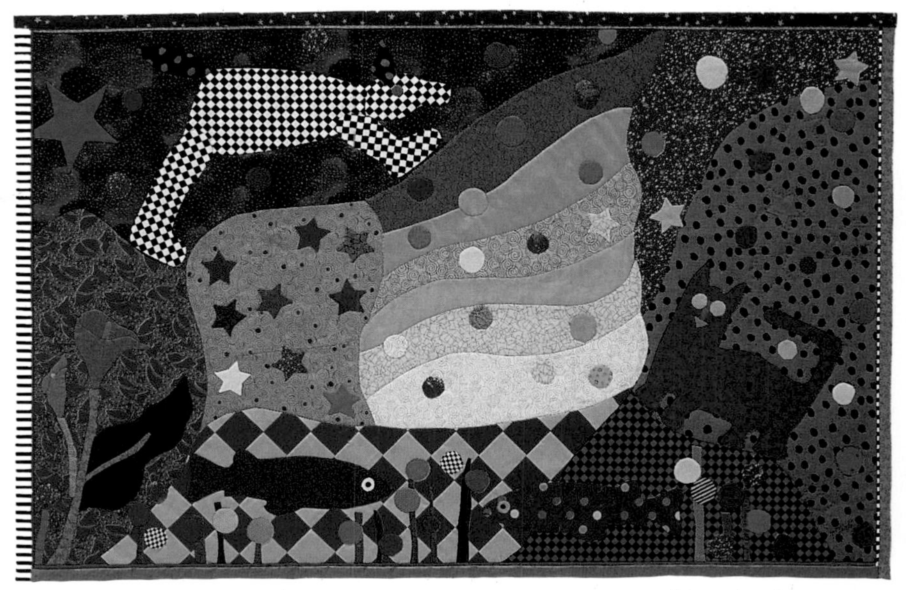

If I Could Make A Glass Dog Bark ▸

Yvonne Porcella. 1994. Modesto, California. Cottons; machine pieced, hand appliquéd and quilted. 34 x 52 in. Collection of the artist.

This cheerful quilt embodies Porcella's fantasy vision: "If I could make a glass dog bark, I could make a bright colored flag mountain, and fish swim in a checkerboard sea." Porcella used appliqué to join the different surface fabrics to the batting and backing. Then came secondary layers of pictorial forms, such as animals and flowers. Finally, she added small circles "as if some giant paint brush were spashing polka dots."

◂ Keep Both Feet on the Floor

Yvonne Porcella. 1991. Modesto, California. Cottons; machine pieced, hand appliquéd and quilted with hand-embellished and hand-painted backing fabrics. 77 x 54 in. Collection of the artist.

Yvonne Porcella's daringly free and wide ranging palette has been extremely influential. The title for this vibrant work came from a trolley driver at Dollywood amusement park in Tennessee who refused to leave the parking lot until all passengers had "both feet on the floor and all body parts inside."

Yvonne Porcella

Yvonne Porcella of Modesto, California, is one of the most important and influential of art quilters. She has exhibited, lectured, and taught quiltmaking widely in the United States, Europe, Japan, and Australia, and has inspired thousands of quilters worldwide through her teaching. The peripatetic Porcella is also the founder and president of Studio Art Quilt Associates, a national nonprofit corporation dedicated to the promotion of art quilts.

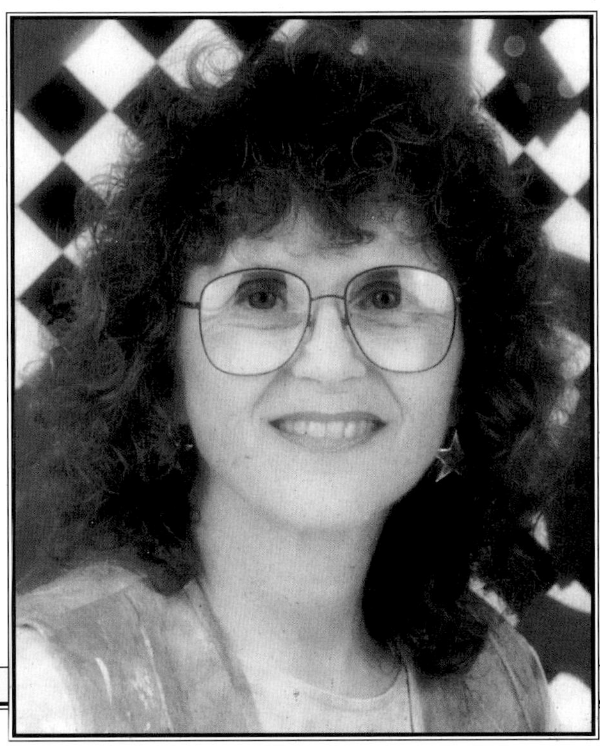

Unlike most quiltmakers, Porcella has no formal artistic training. She spent nineteen years as an operating room nurse, an experience which she says taught her discipline and precision. Before taking up quiltmaking, Porcella earned a reputation for her pieced clothing, and she published four books on the subject. After encountering a kimono-shaped Japanese bedcover in a museum exhibition, she was inspired to make similarly shaped quilts. When two of her piecework kimonos were juried into Quilt National in 1981, the transition to quiltmaking was complete.

Porcella is best known for her innovative use of color. Her wide ranging work includes both dazzling quilts that abound with wild color juxtapositions, playful energy, and good humor, and peaceful quilts awash in soft, serene pastels. She uses a wide variety of commercial fabrics but also hand paints her own fabrics. Her most recent book, *Colors Changing Hue*, is an instruction book on fabric painting for quilters and fiber artists of all levels.

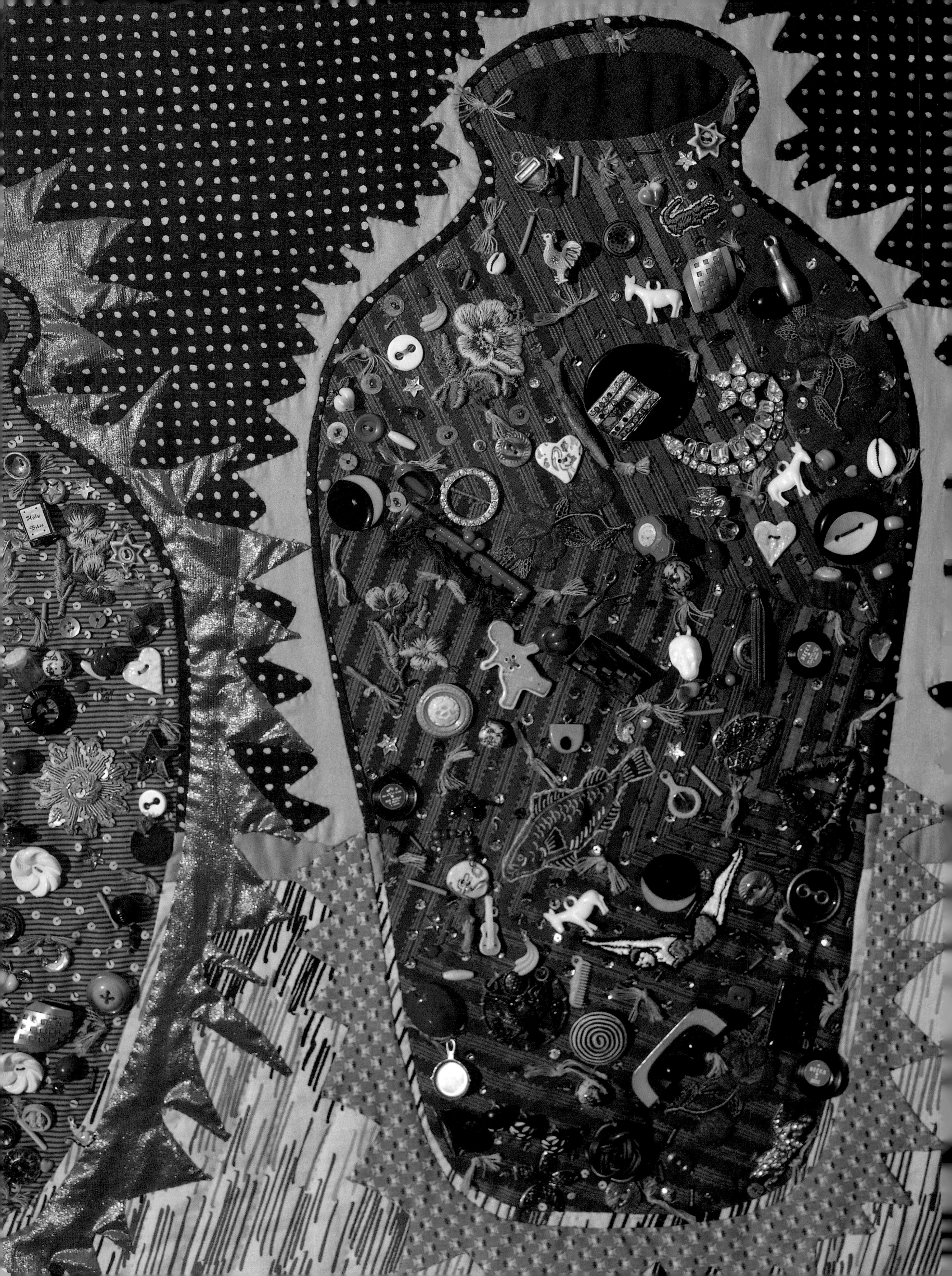
Holy Bible

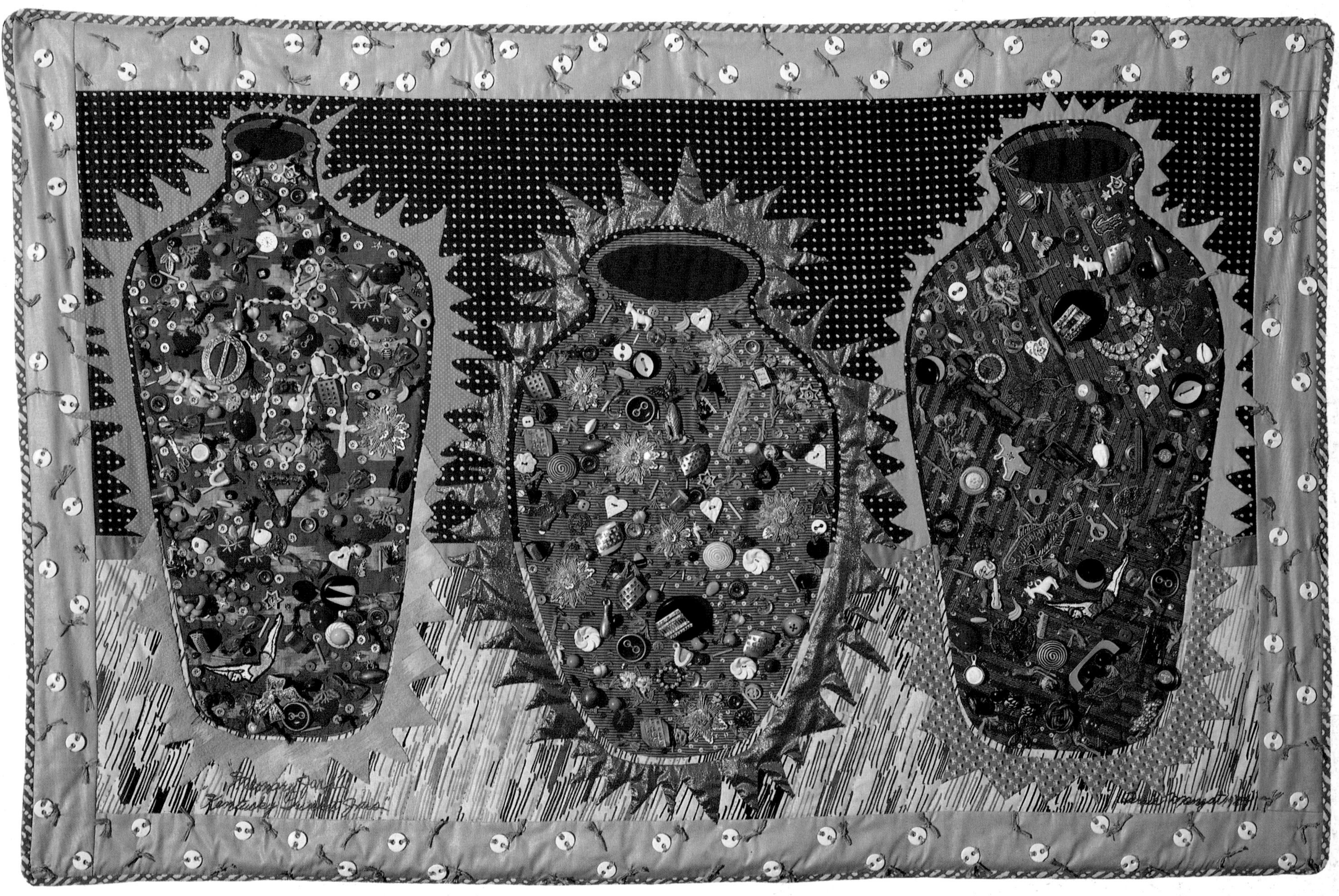

▲ **MEMORY JARS (◀ DETAIL)**

Terrie Hancock Mangat. 1984. Cincinnati, Ohio. Cotton blends and novelty fabrics; tied, reverse appliquéd, embroidered. 33 x 50 in. Collection of Ardis and Robert James.

This heavily embellished quilt, inspired by a memory jar belonging to the artist's grandmother, translates three-dimensional objects into a two-dimensional medium. Like the ceramic memory jars it depicts, the quilt is encrusted with hundreds of tiny personal mementos.

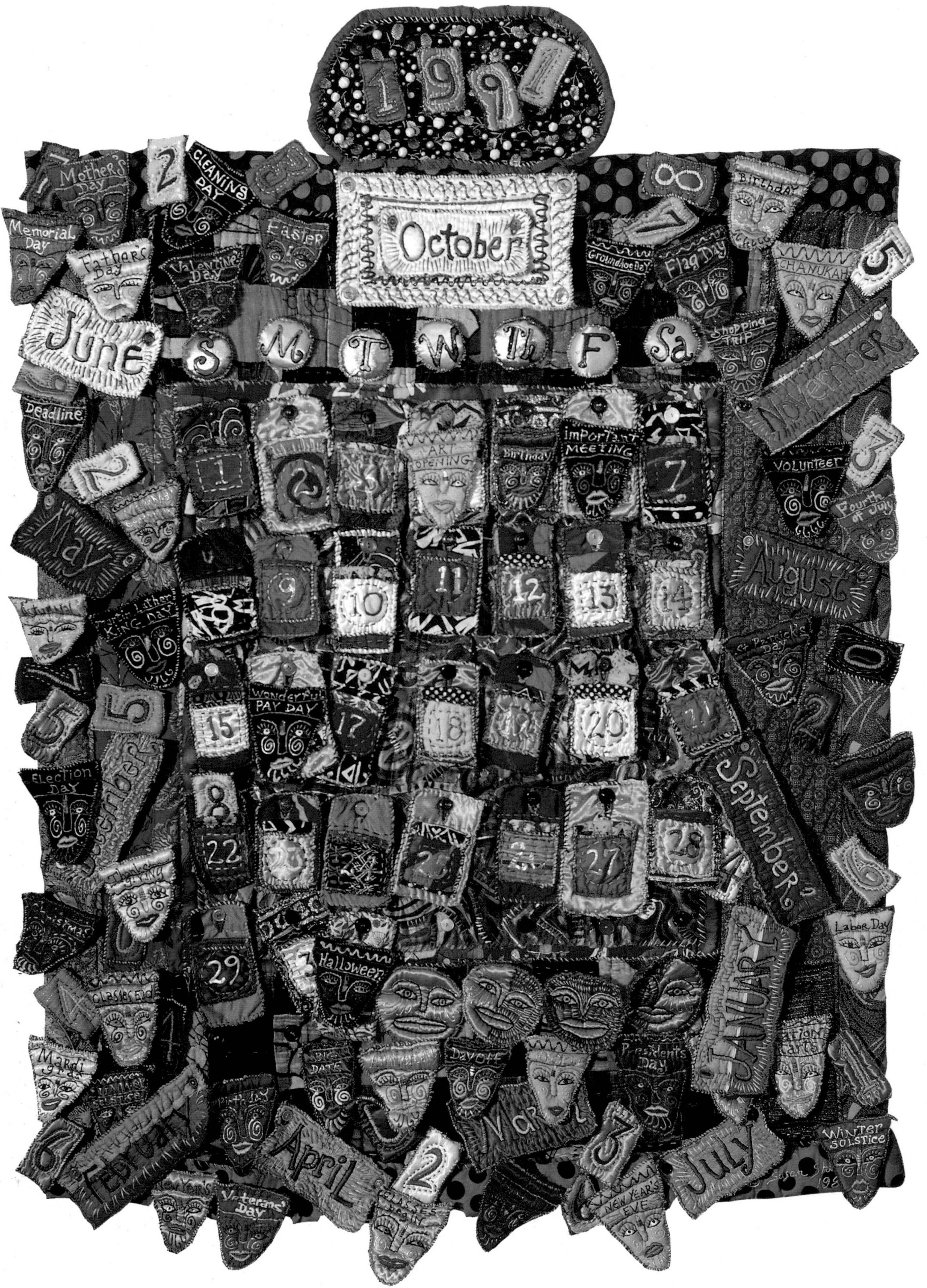

▲ THE CALENDAR FETISH: AN ALTAR TO TIME (DETAIL ►)

Susan Shie. 1989. Wooster, Ohio. Cottons, satins, metallics, textile paint, quartz crystals, buttons, pins; hand sewn, hand quilted and embroidered. 72 x 60 x 3 in. Collection of Ardis and Robert James.

This incredible interactive wall quilt includes at least 125 moveable pieces and will tell time month by month through the year 3332. There are thirty-one day pockets which move on five rows of seven buttons and hold pieces of cardboard for important messages and events. The phases of the moon are pins that can be moved from the border to the central five-by-seven-row grid. The holidays float in the "asteroid zone" outside the calendar grid.

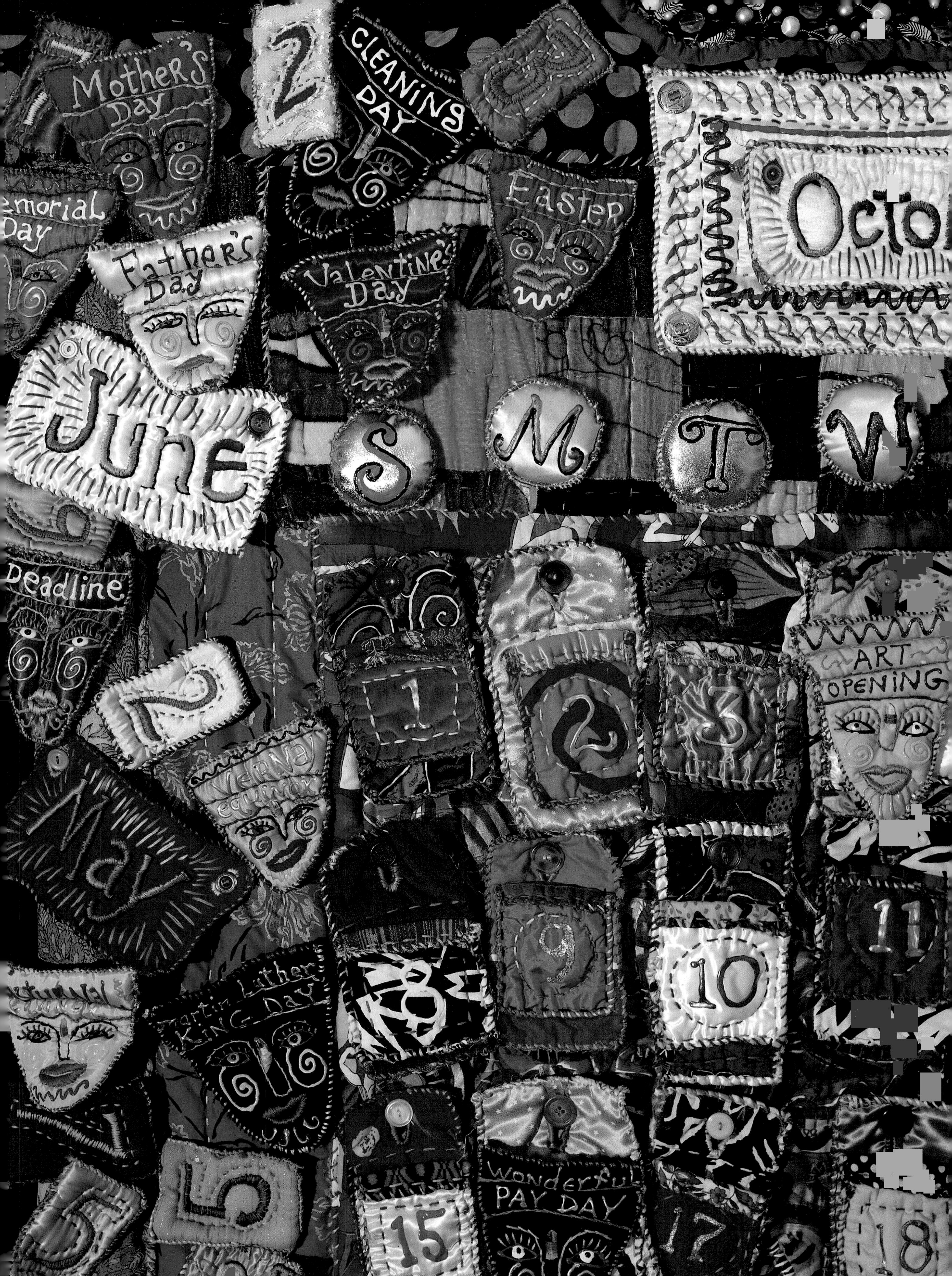

Mother's Day
2
CLEANING DAY
emorial Day
Easter
Octo
Father's Day
Valentine's Day
June
S
M
T
W
Deadline
ART OPENING
1
2
3
Vernal equinox
May
9
10
11
8
KING DAY
Wonderful PAY DAY
5
5
15
17
18

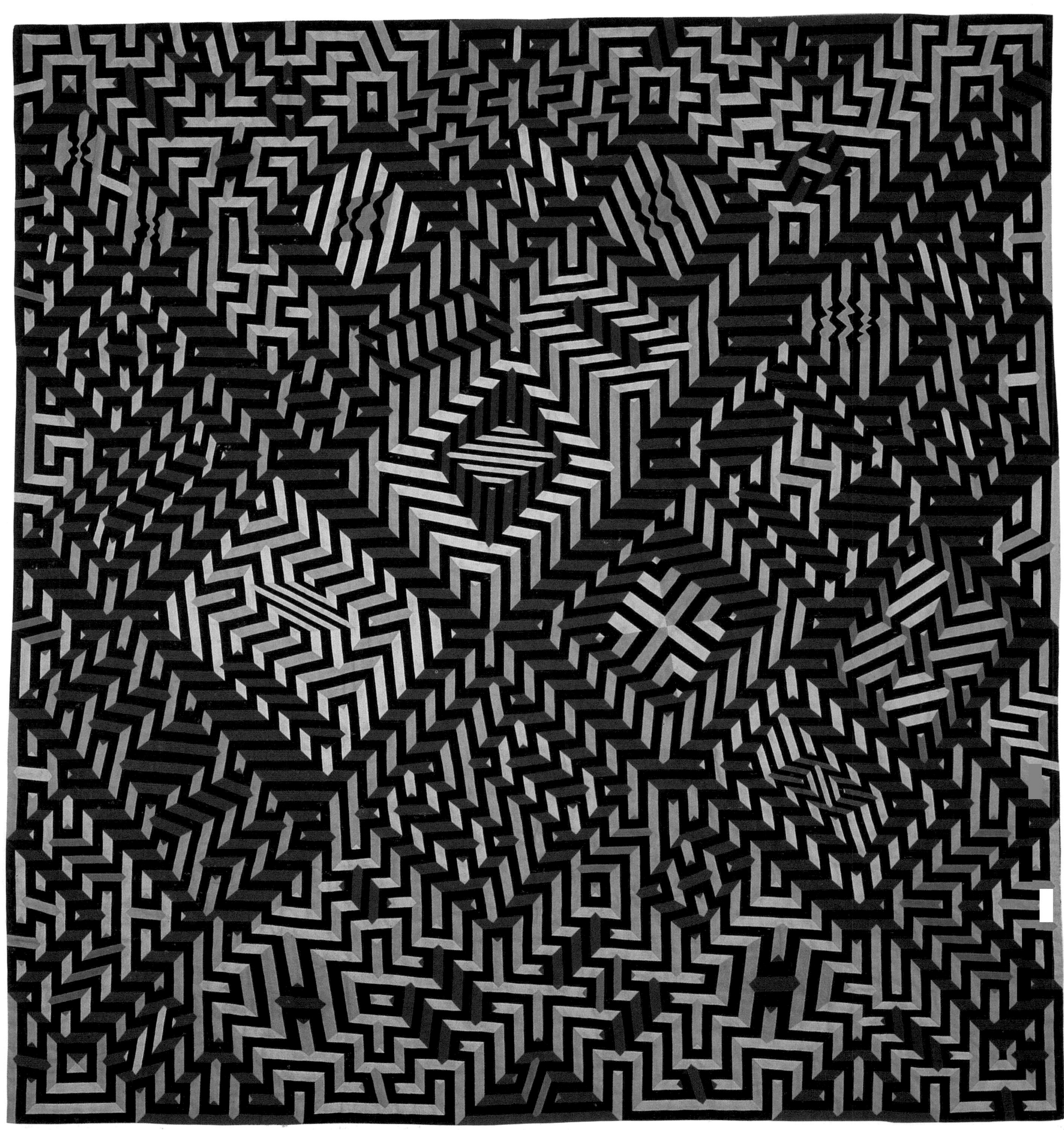

▲ **NEON MAZE**

Ellen Oppenheimer. 1993. Oakland, California. Silk-screened and hand-dyed fabrics including some over-dyed commercial prints; machine pieced and hand quilted. 50 x 48 in. Collection of the artist.

In addition to her intricate art quilts, Ellen Oppenheimer also designs neon signs. Her *Neon Maze* is part of a series employing a unique technique of inlaid machine piecing which allows a line or lines to take a wildly convoluted path through the quilt. This quilt won the Domini McCarthy Memorial Award for Exceptional Craftsmanship at Quilt National 1993.

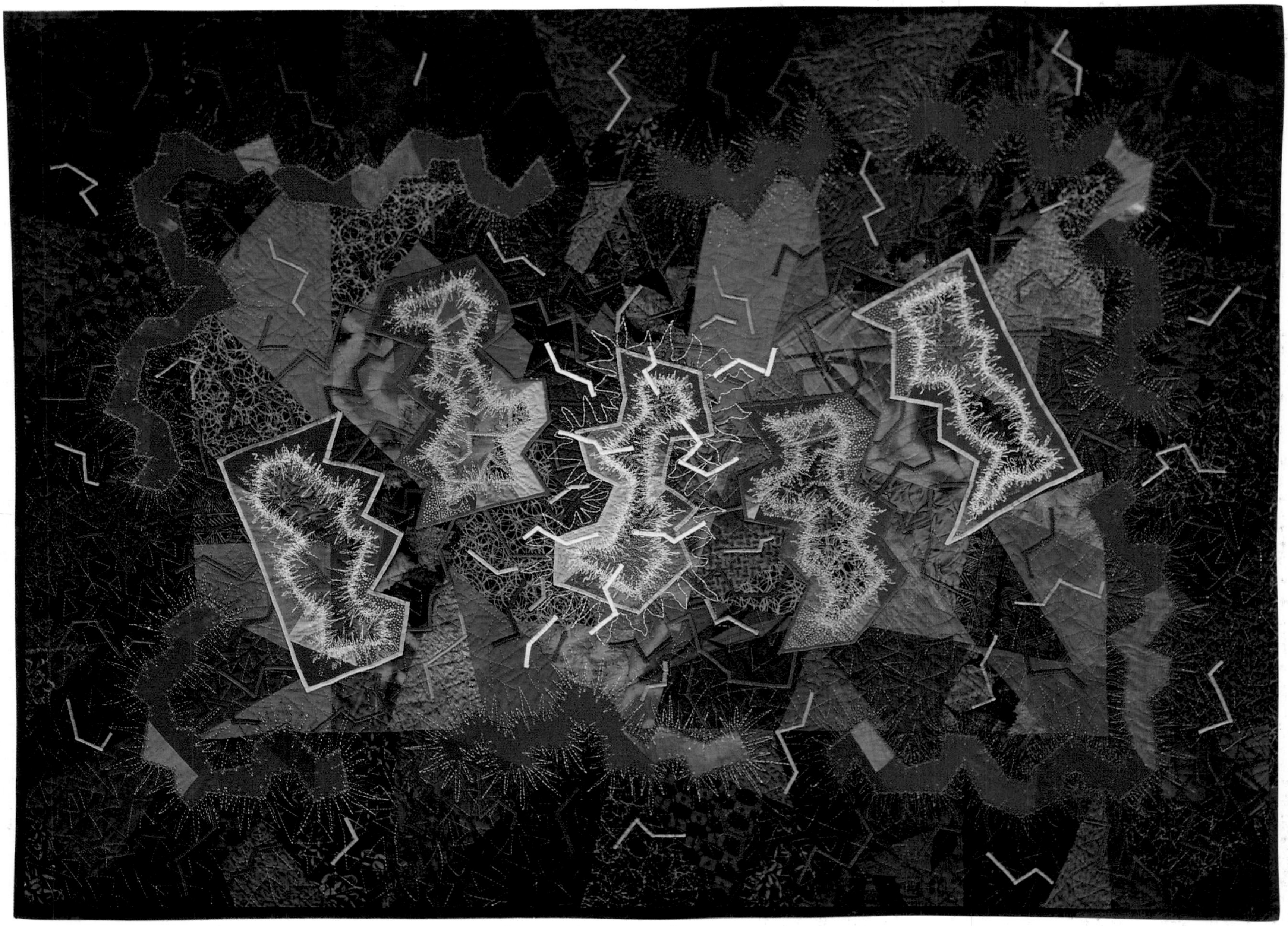

▲ AFTERSHOCKS

Libby Lehman. 1993. Houston, Texas. Commercial and hand-dyed cottons, rayon and metallic threads; machine pieced, appliquéd, reverse appliquéd, embroidered, and quilted. Collection of the artist.

Libby Lehman's suggestively titled quilts often use explosive form and color to portray intense states of emotion. This quilt was made in response to the recent San Francisco earthquake.

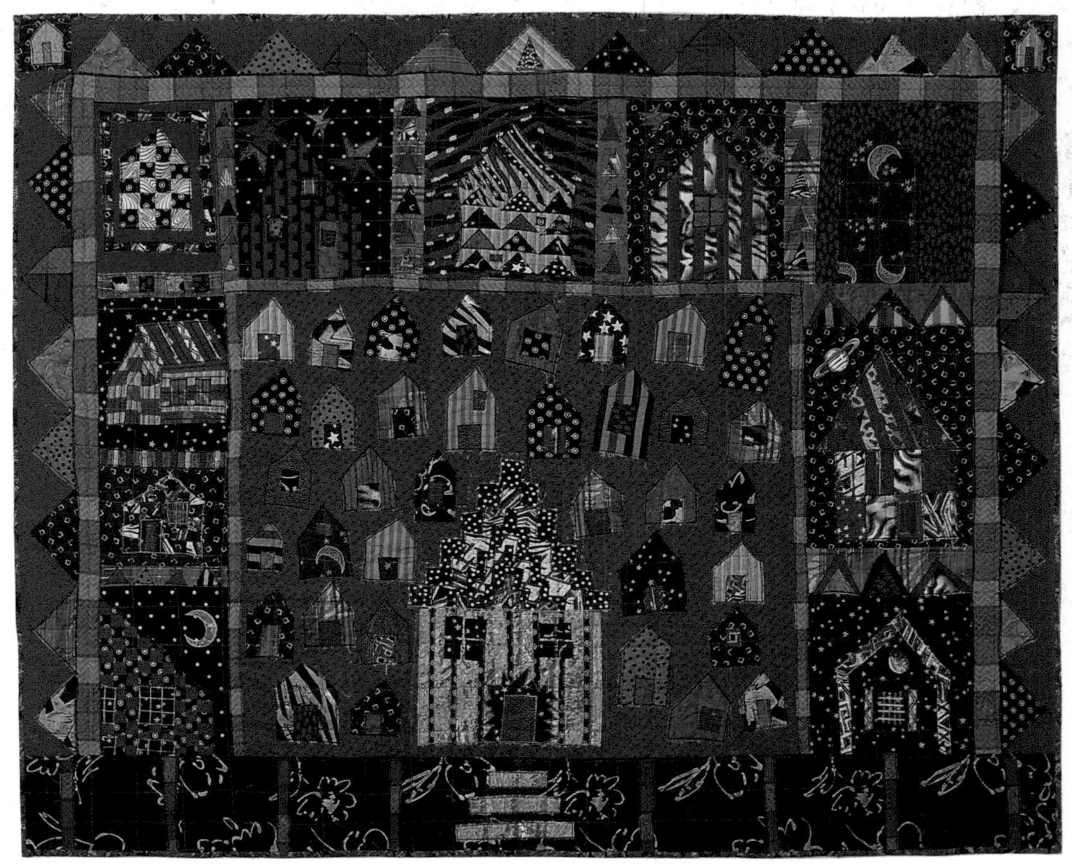

THE NEIGHBORHOOD ▶

Sally A. Sellers. 1993. Vancouver, Washington. Cottons and synthetic fabrics; machine appliquéd, machine pieced, machine quilted. 51 1/2 x 64 in. Collection of the artist.

This quilt is one of a series inspired by young children's drawings of houses, which Sally Sellers describes as composed of "joyful, uneven triangles and squares and rectangles."

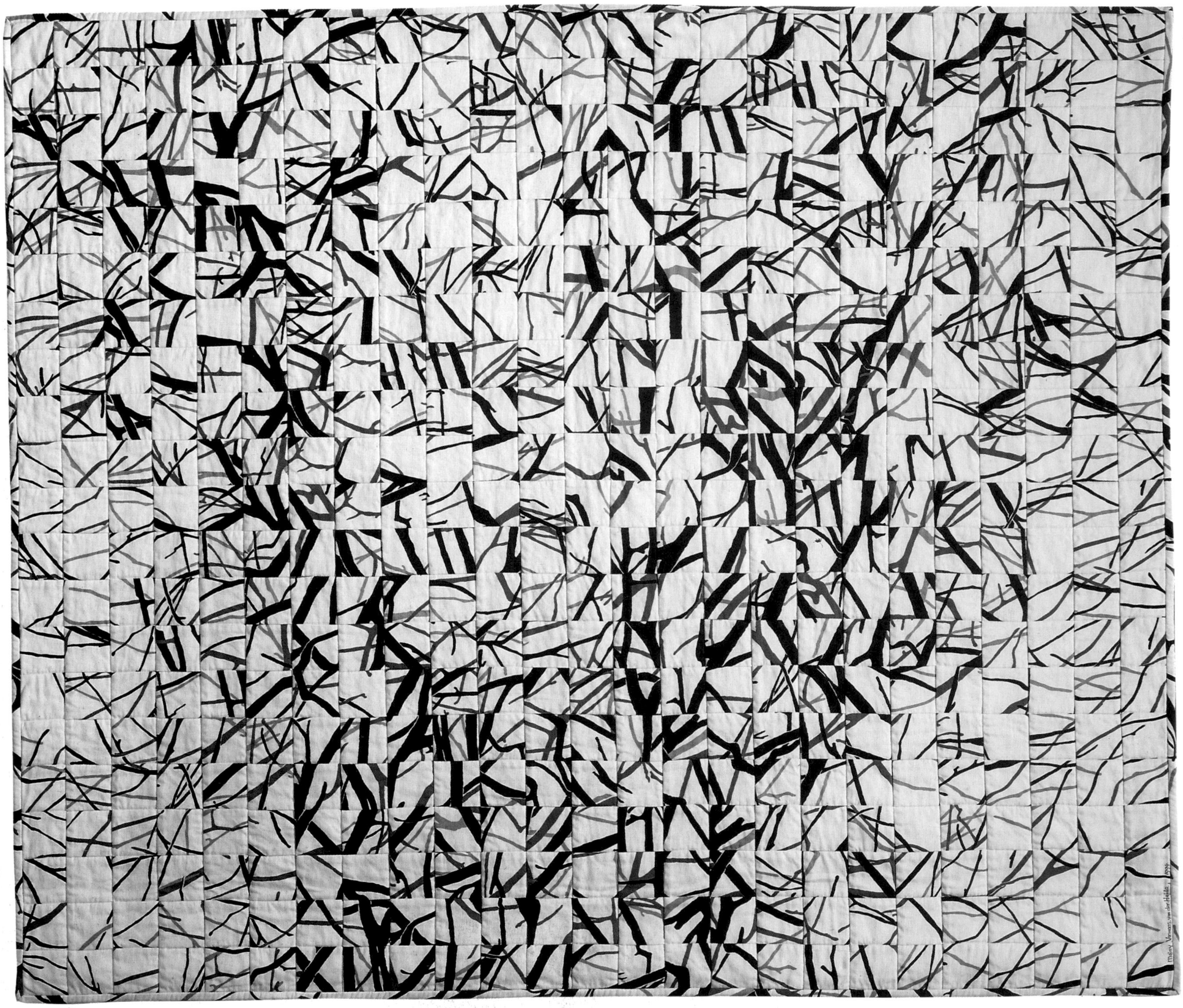

▲ EARTH QUILT #44: LINES V

Meiny Vermaas-van der Heide. 1994. Tempe, Arizona. Cottons; machine pieced and quilted. 58 x 48 1/2 in. Collection of the artist.

This quilt was inspired by a trip into Lapland, beyond the Arctic Circle in Sweden. According to the artist, "The landscape . . . was awesome, pristine white with black lines of the bare tree branches as the only accents. The 'Lind' Design [fabric] by Lena Boije [purchased in Stockholm] reminded me of this trip . . . The design idea for *Earth Quilt #44: Lines V* was to exaggerate the above impression by doing a close-up of the black lines against the pristine white snow landscape, basically by strip-piecing and re-piecing of the ['Lind' Design] fabric."

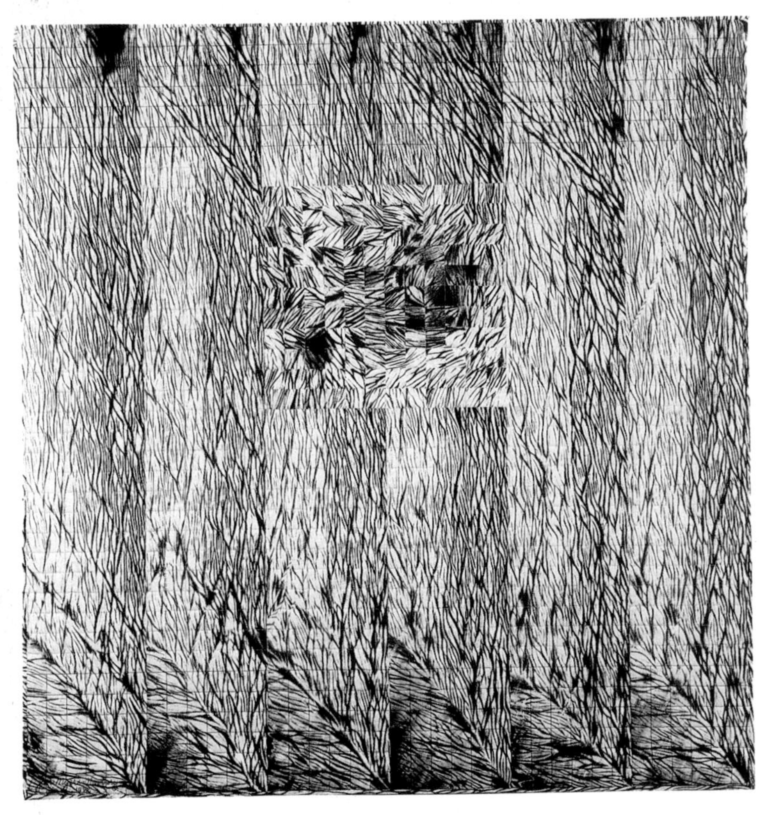

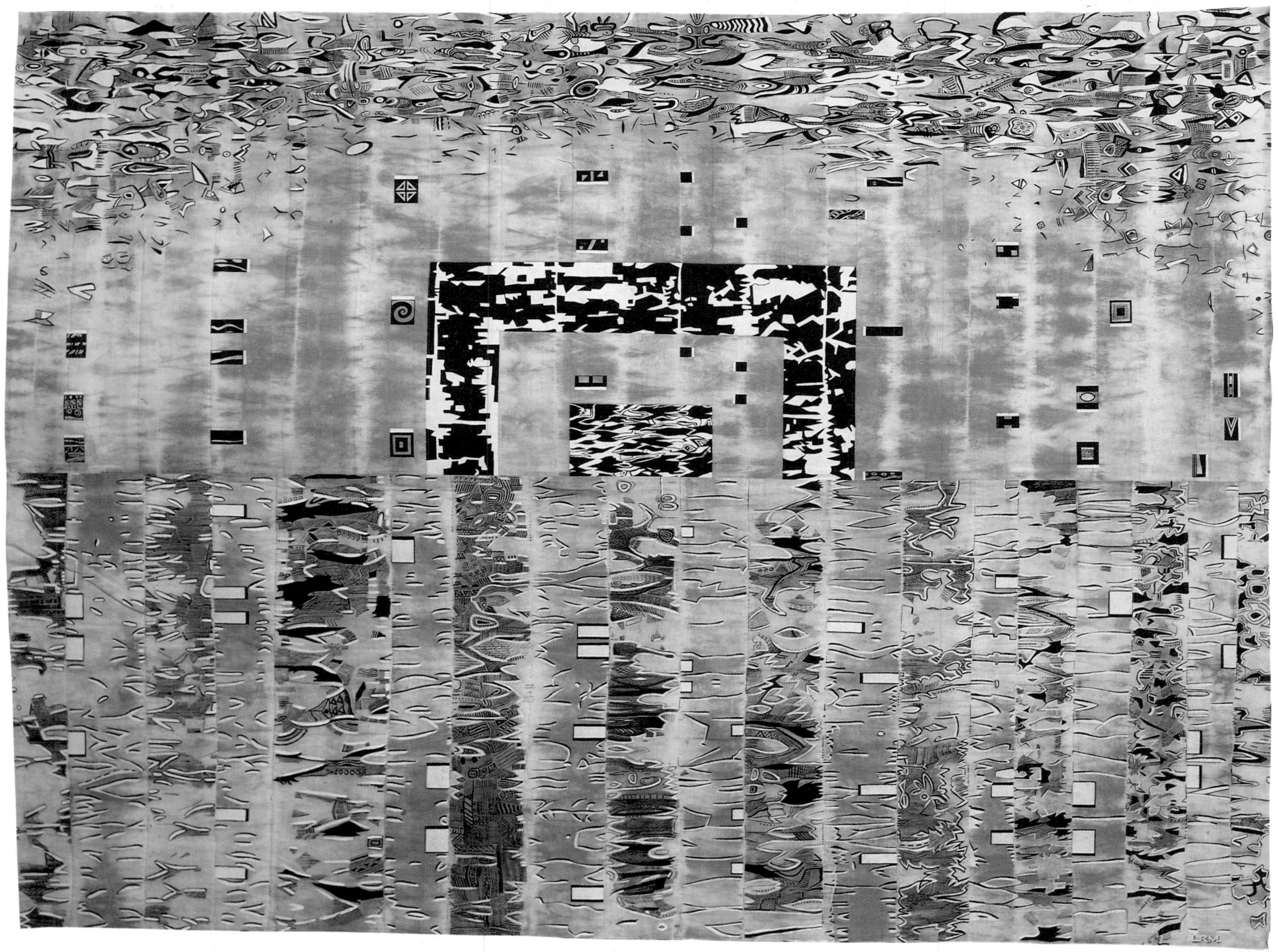

◄ **BIRCH EYES**

Jan Myers-Newberry. 1992. Pittsburgh, Pennsylvania. Hand-dyed cotton fabric; machine pieced and quilted. 54 x 57 in. Collection of the artist.

This tie-dyed quilt, made up of large *shibori* panels, emphasizes pattern over color. *Birch Eyes* won Best of Show at Quilt National 1993.

▲ **OPENING MOVES**

Linda MacDonald. 1991. Willits, California. Cotton, Procion resist-dyed and discharged; hand painted. 52 x 71 in. Collection of Ardis and Robert James.

The artist relates, "This quilt is made from fabric that has been resisted, dyed twice, and discharged twice. Discharge is a chemical that removes some but not all of the dye. The resulting fabric has a distressed look, . . . the look of a fabric that has a history. I then painted with black and white fabric paint and responded to images that had appeared because of the fabric treatment." The title refers to the inverted U shape or gate at top center.

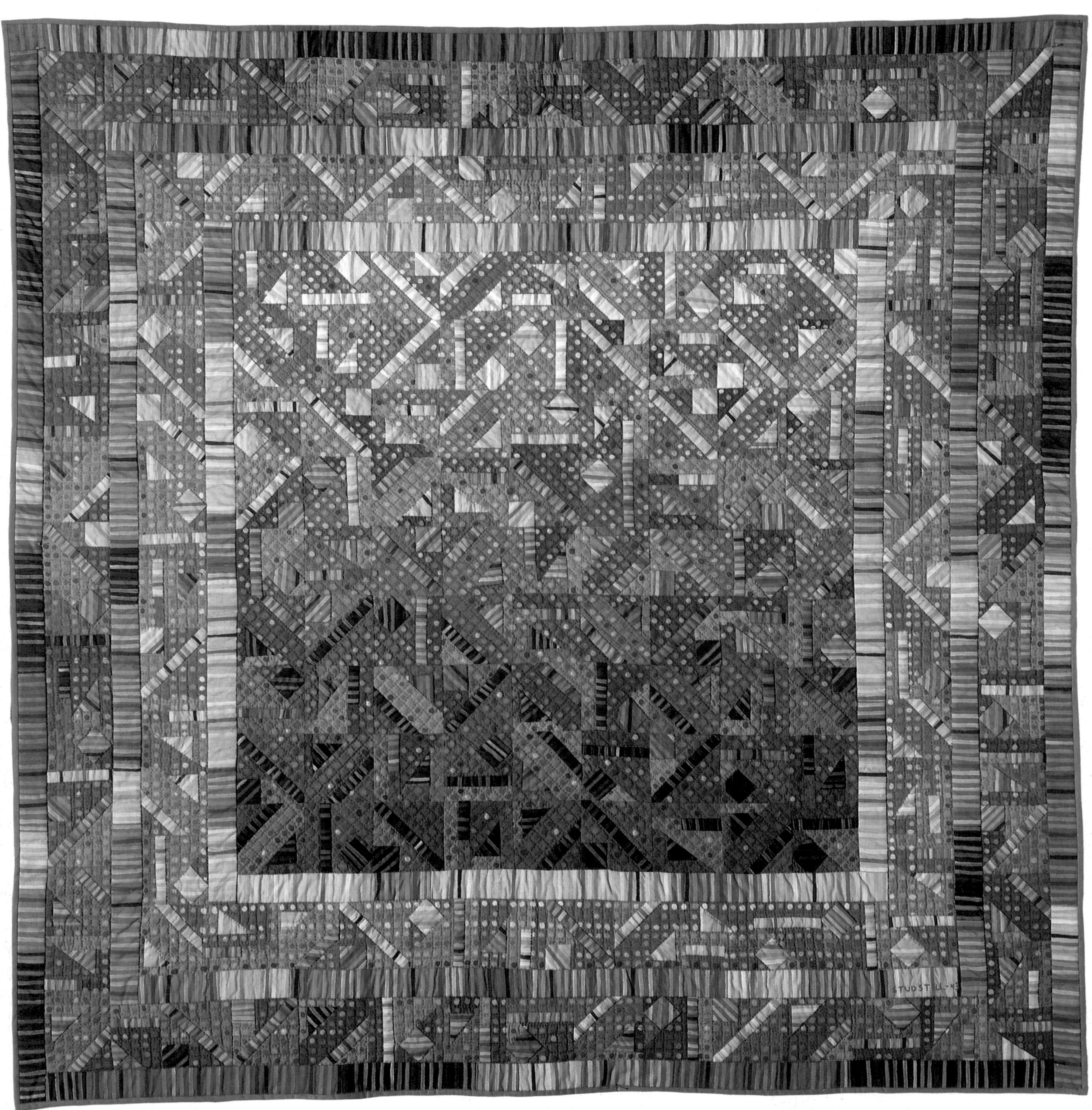

▲ QUILT #43 (DETAIL ►)

Pamela Studstill. 1984. Pipe Creek, Texas. Cottons and cotton blends, fabric paint; machine pieced, hand quilted. 55 x 55 in. Collection of Ardis and Robert James.

This early example of Pamela Studstill's work is typical of her endlessly inventive pieced quilts, which explore large and small patterns of light and dark within a fabulously complex surface design that is full of color, pattern, and texture.

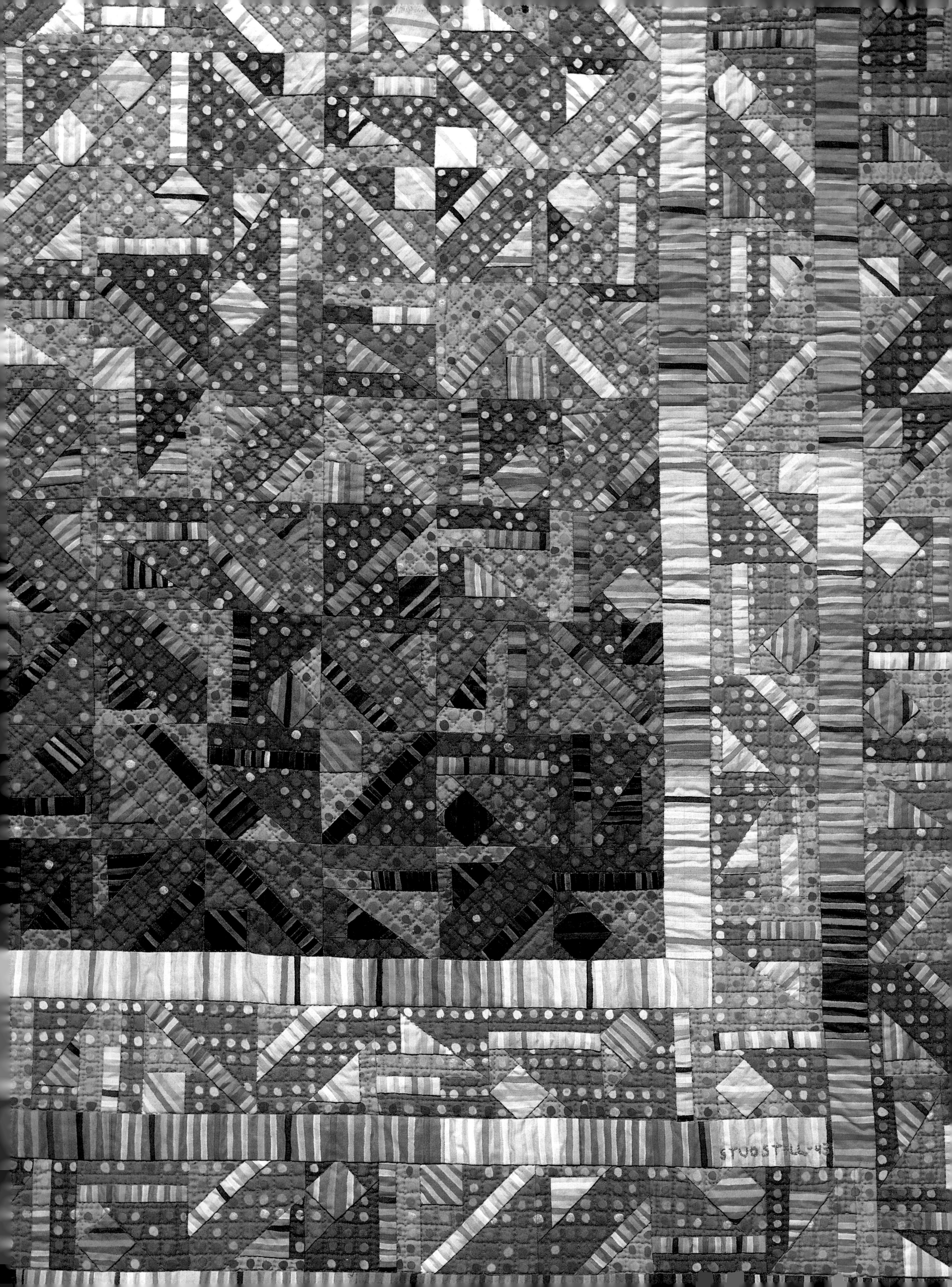

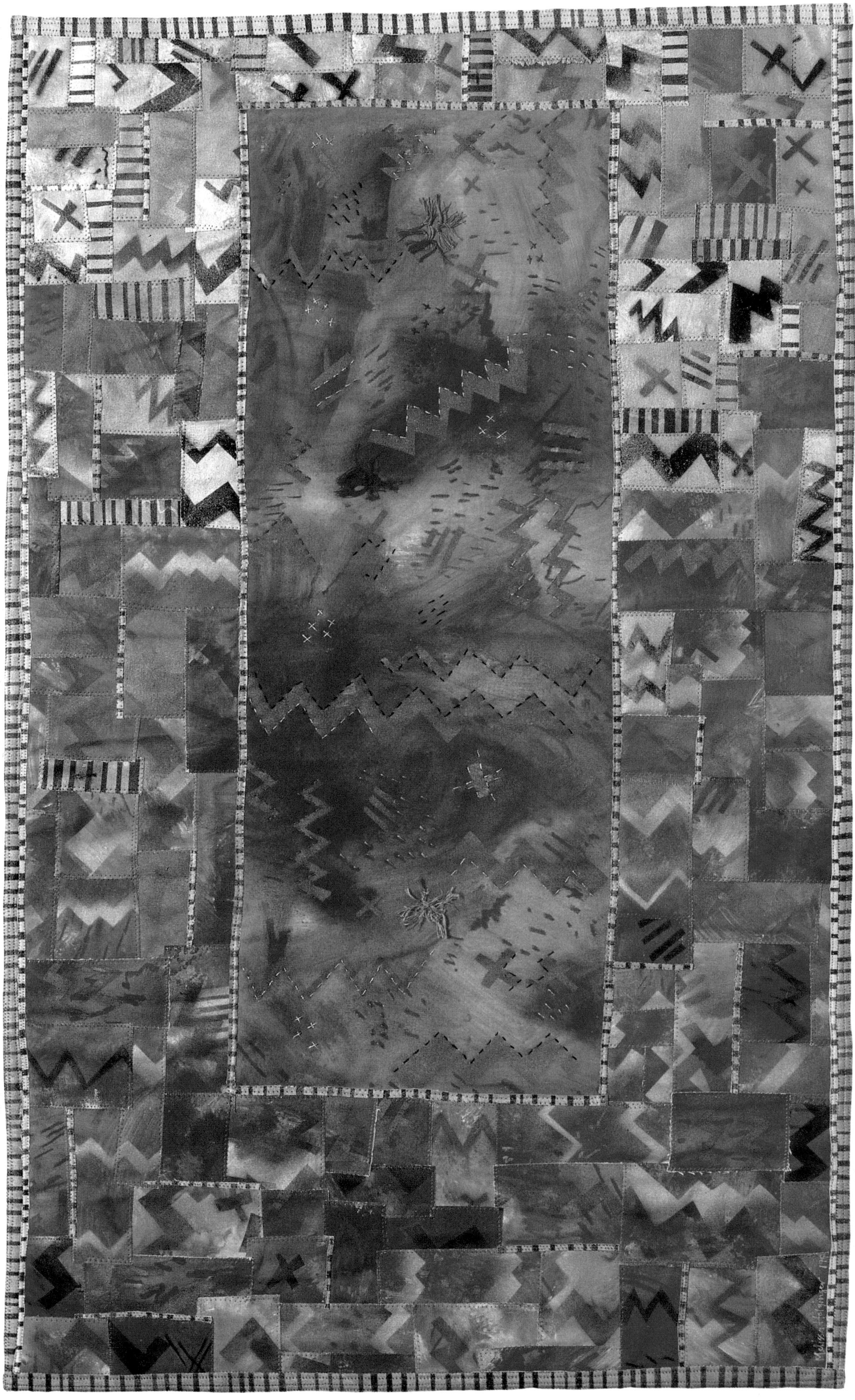

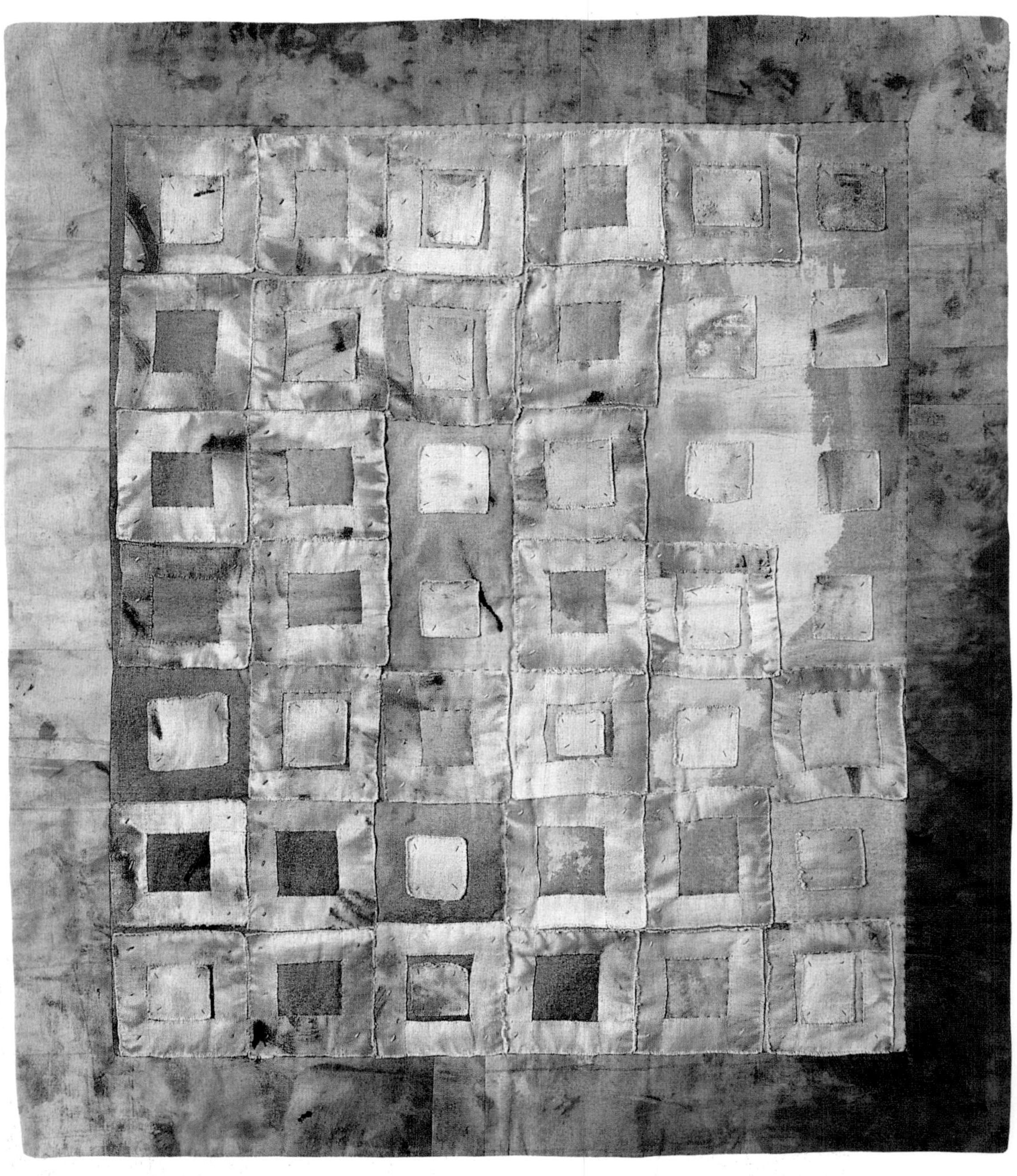

SKY SCAPE ▸

Emily Richardson. 1993. Philadelphia, Pennsylvania. Acrylic and textile paint on canvas, muslin, string; hand appliquéd, machine pieced, hand quilted. 35 x 30 in. Collection of the artist.

Sky Scape uses a grid pattern made from raw-edged painted canvas to suggest the play of color and texture in a changing sky full of windblown clouds and dappled sun.

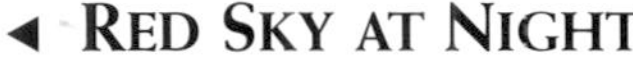

◂ RED SKY AT NIGHT

Melissa Holzinger. 1993. Arlington, Washington. Cotton duck, acrylic paint, pastels, embroidery floss; hand painted, airbrushed, machine embroidered, machine pieced, machine quilted. 48 x 29 1/2 in. Collection of the artist.

"Red sky at night/Sailor's delight" runs the old adage that informs this quilt. Melissa Holzinger remembered it from her childhood, a time which for most of us is one of absolute "certainty and clarity" when "the glory of a fiery sky was simply that."

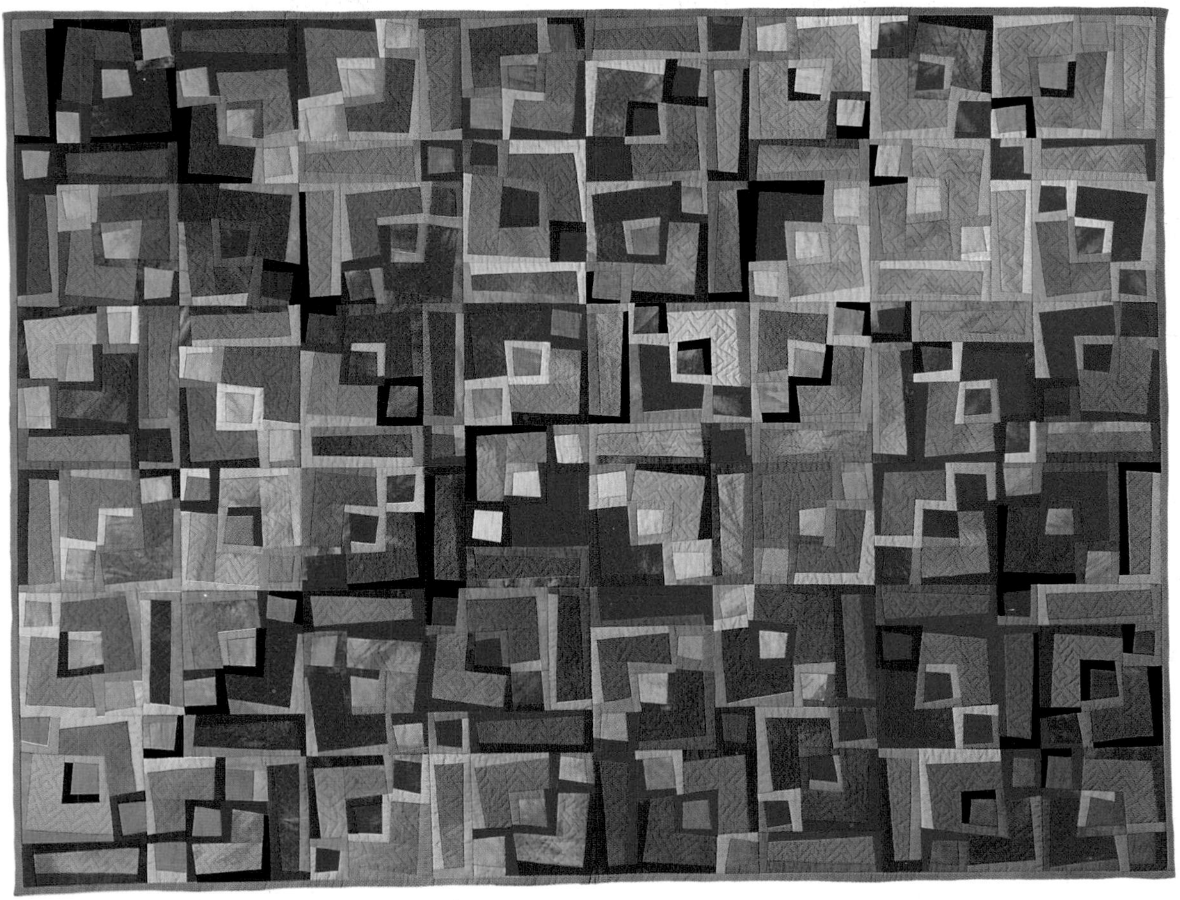

◂ FREEHAND 8: TORN

Liz Axford. 1993. Houston, Texas. Commercial and hand-dyed cottons; improvisationally pieced, machine quilted. 53 x 70 in. Collection of the artist.

Liz Axford's spontaneously composed quilts reflect the influence of contemporary African-American quiltmakers such as Anna Williams. *Freehand 8: Torn* uses an original variation of a Log Cabin block as its basic design element. The quilting design was also improvised.

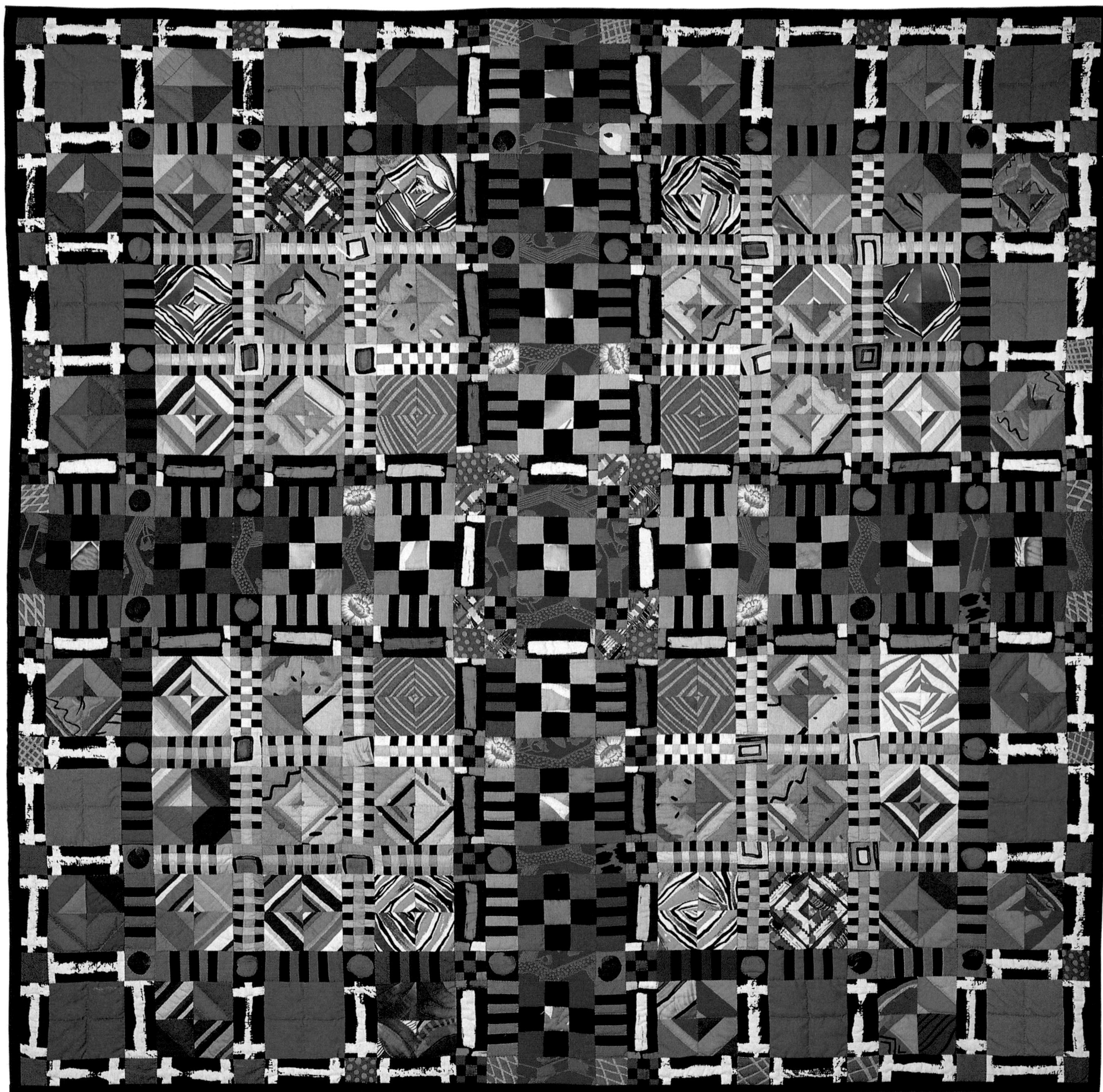

▲ COLOR BLOCKS #1

Nancy Crow. 1988. Baltimore, Ohio. Cottons; hand pieced; hand quilted by Elizabeth Miller. 62 x 62 in. Collection of the artist. © 1988 by Nancy Crow.

Crow's ongoing *Color Blocks* series, which now includes over sixty quilts of varying sizes, began in the late 1980s as a means of exploring color through the use of simple, uncomplicated forms. When starting the series Crow said, "I want the simplest of means to achieve the most glorious results." *Color Blocks #1* is built of only three template pieces—two differently sized squares and a rectangle.

LADY OF GUADALUPE II ▶

Nancy Crow. 1986–1987. Baltimore, Ohio. Machine-pieced cottons and cotton blends; hand quilted by Marla Hattabaugh. 80 x 64 in. Collection of Ardis and Robert James.

This extremely complex quilt is one of a series on the Lady of Guadalupe theme that Nancy Crow began in 1985. She says, "At age nineteen, I lived in Mexico City and studied art at Mexico City College. While there, I became familiar with this Saint and her symbolism. I was fascinated by the idea of 'goodness' radiating out from and around the form of Our Lady. In 1985, I felt a real need to produce quilts that reflected a sense of 'goodness.'"

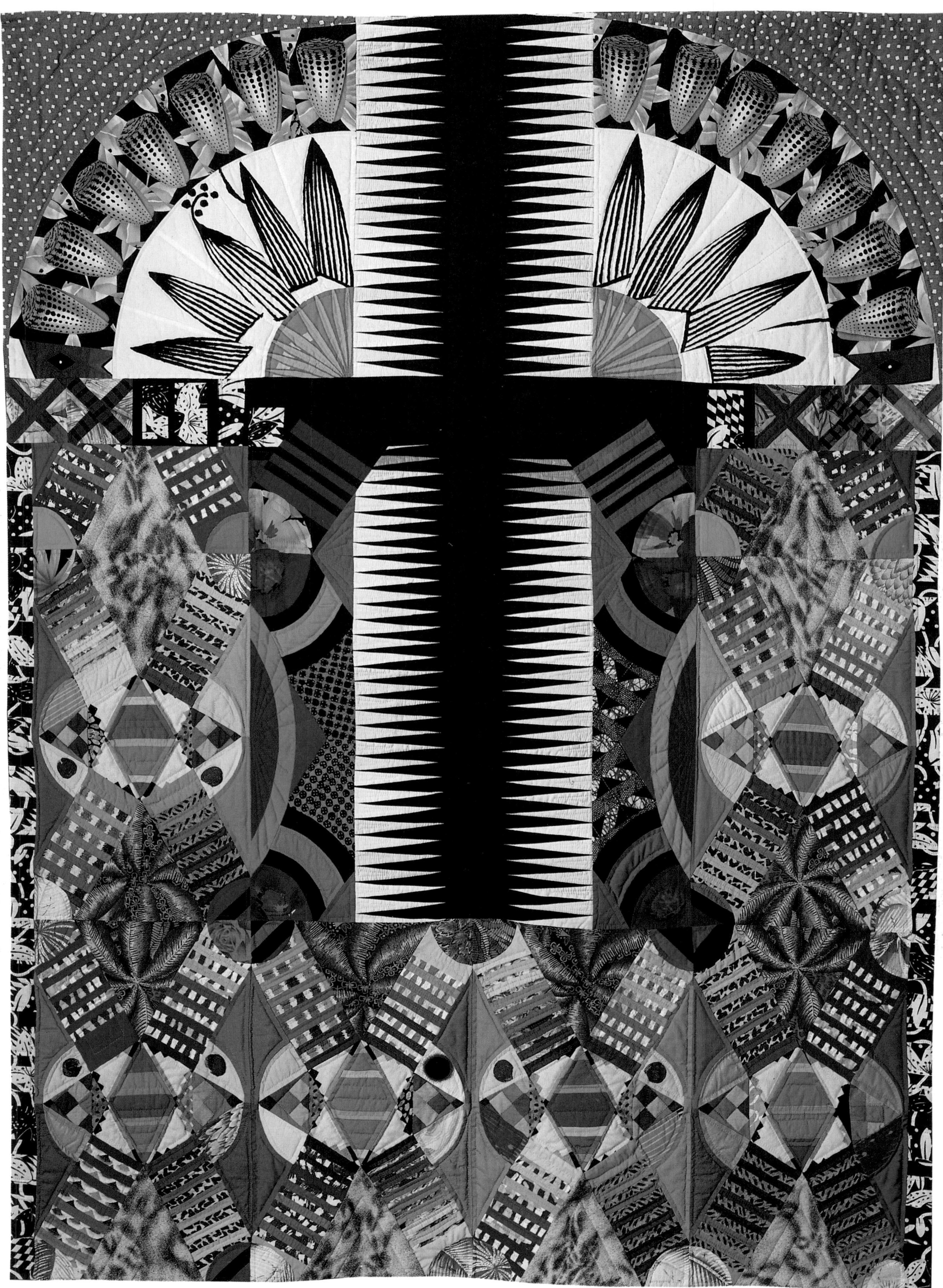

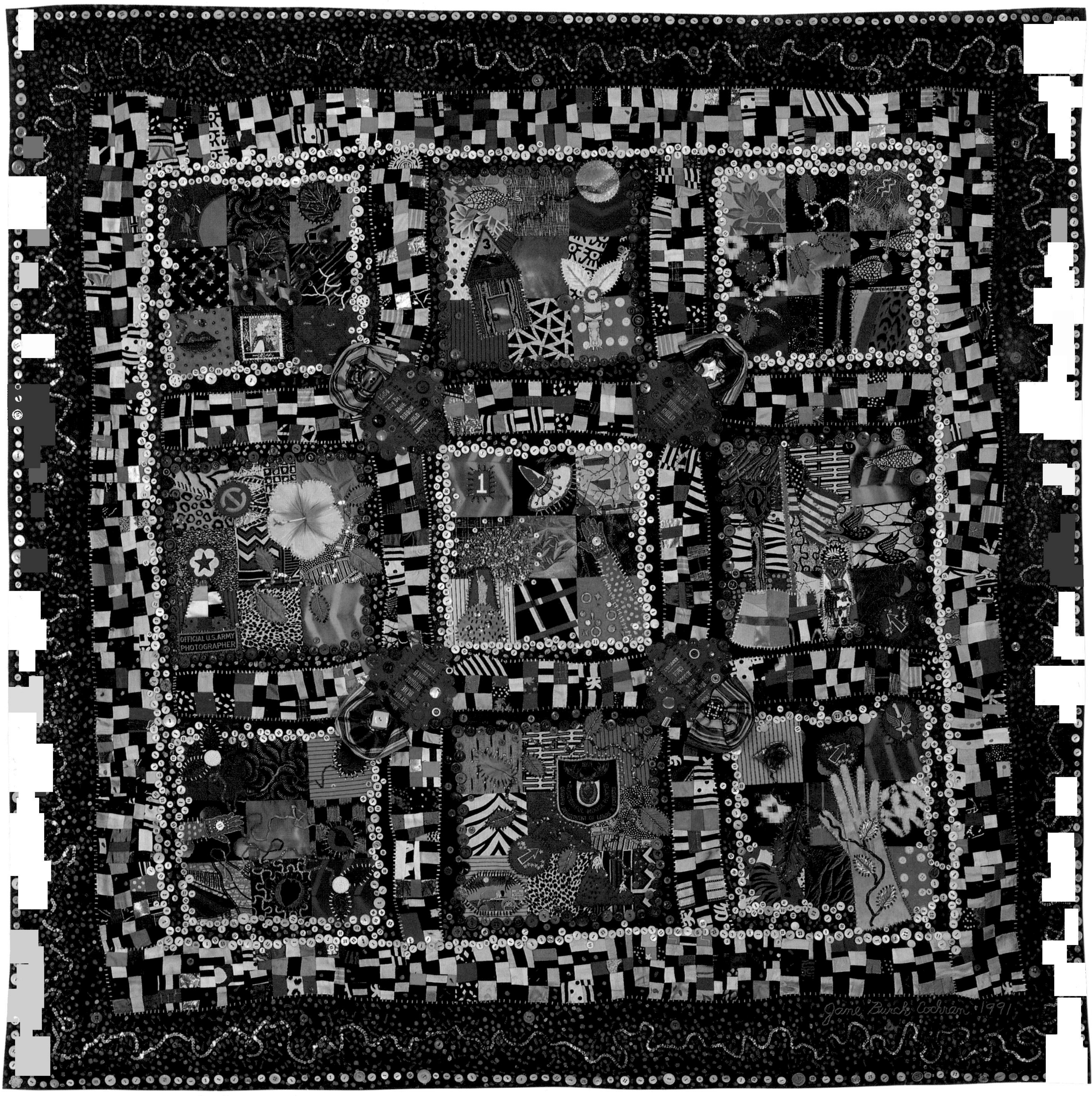

▲ **LIFE STARTS OUT SO SIMPLE**

Jane Burch Cochran. 1991. Rabbit Hash, Kentucky. Various fabrics, artificial flowers, kid glove, military and other patches, ribbon, beads, buttons, sequins, paint; machine pieced, hand appliquéd, hand embellished. 68 x 68 in. Collection of Fidelity Investments, Covington, Kentucky.

Jane Burch Cochran says, "*Life Starts Out So Simple* began as an exercise to use in teaching to embellish a nine-patch square. I then just started experimenting and playing with embellishment. I used some of the treasures people gave me or I collected . . . [including] ribbons, scout patches, [and] WWII patches which belonged to my husband and his father. The awards we win start out so innocent such as 'Kentucky Blue Ribbon Child' and become more serious as we grow up. The title also refers to the simple format of the nine-patch square, which can become rather intricate when attacked by an embellisher."

THE LAST DANCE ▸

Jane Burch Cochran. 1990. Rabbit Hash, Kentucky. Assorted fabrics, old dress, gloves, buttons, beads, paint; machine pieced, hand appliquéd, hand embellished. 79 x 69 in. Private collection.

According to the quiltmaker, "*The Last Dance* was conceived when I found an old dress made of cheesecloth in a bag of rags. I attached the dress to the canvas background using a thin coat of gesso. I painted and embellished the dress, then added the gloves, mask, and blackbirds. The quilt seems to tell a story, but the narrative developed on its own and is for the viewer to determine."

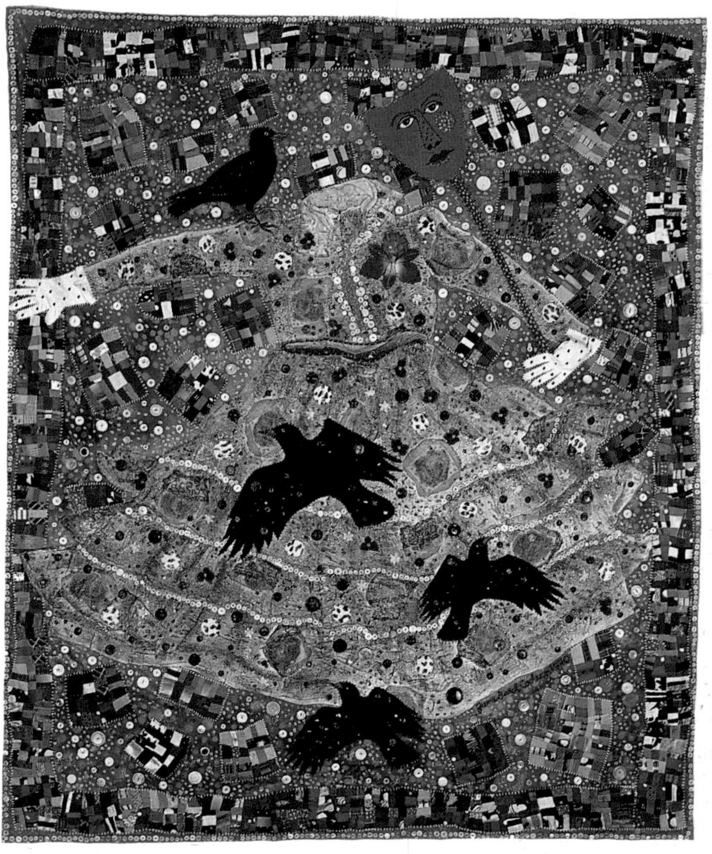

Jane Burch Cochran

Jane Burch Cochran, who lives in an old log cabin on the Ohio River in Rabbit Hash, Kentucky, with her husband, dogs, and cats, is an academically trained painter who began making full-sized quilts in 1985. She says, "In my quilts, I try to combine my art training in painting, my love of fabric, and the tradition of American quilting. Although my work has its roots in Victorian crazy quilts and Native American beadwork, the nostalgia is set off by my interpretations as an artist living today. I unconsciously combine the loose, free feeling of abstract painting with the time-consuming and controlled techniques of sewing and beading. I continue to use common symbols and quilt patterns and to recycle old gloves and other materials to create a new narrative. The gloves (hands) are reaching and searching for both questions and answers about race, the environment, and the human psyche. My quilts are highly embellished with beads, buttons, and paint to enhance the narrative with a unique and personal texture."

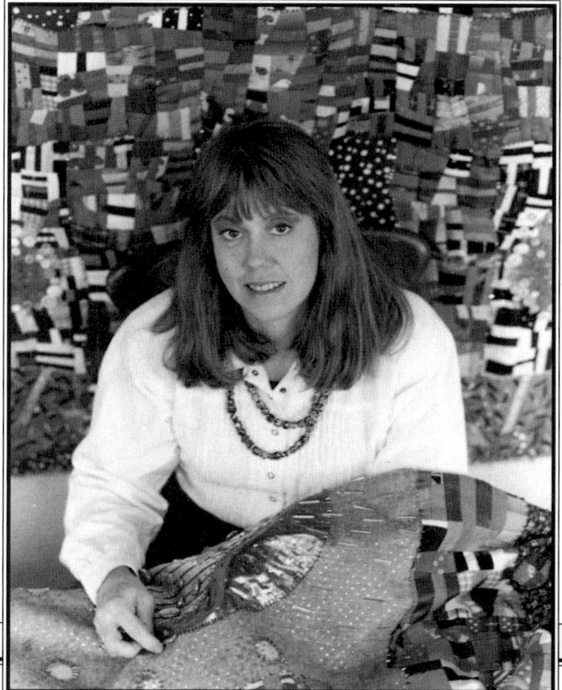

Describing her working technique, Cochran continues, "I use strip piecing to make my patchwork. I do not measure but just start cutting and sewing strips, usually in combinations of three strips. I then cut these apart into smaller pieces and just keep sewing and adding until it grows into large enough patches to use. I love to create the patchwork. It's like making lots of small paintings. I then appliqué the patchwork and other pieces to a background using bugle beads or seed beads."

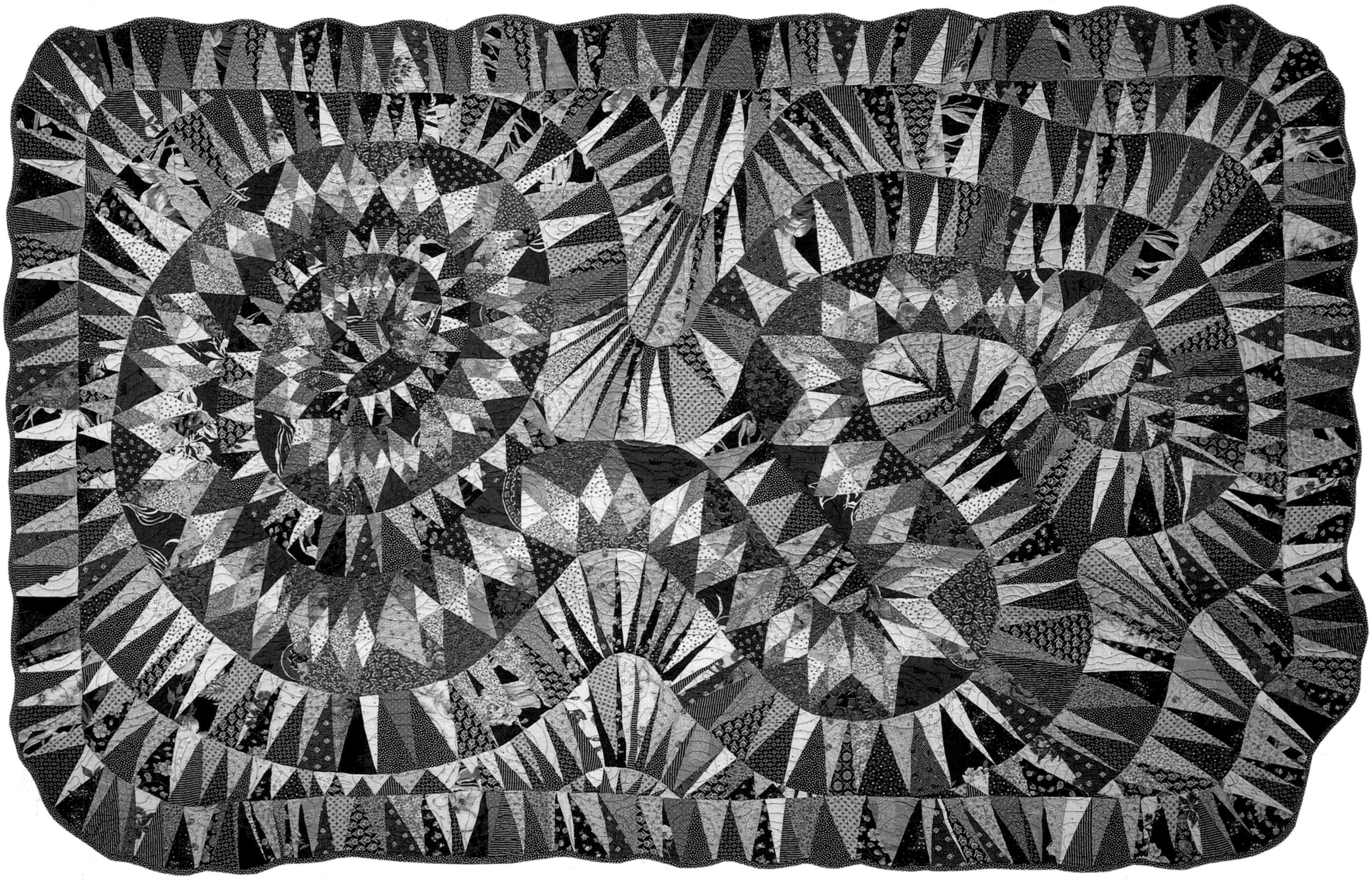

▲ **SNAKE**

Helen Giddens. 1989. Mesquite, Texas. Cottons; machine pieced and quilted. 70 x 110 in. Collection of Ardis and Robert James.

A complex design of triangles and diamonds tightly contained with coiling lines gives this quilt both its name and the impression that it is ready to explode at any second. All of Helen Giddens's quilts are made solely of scraps.

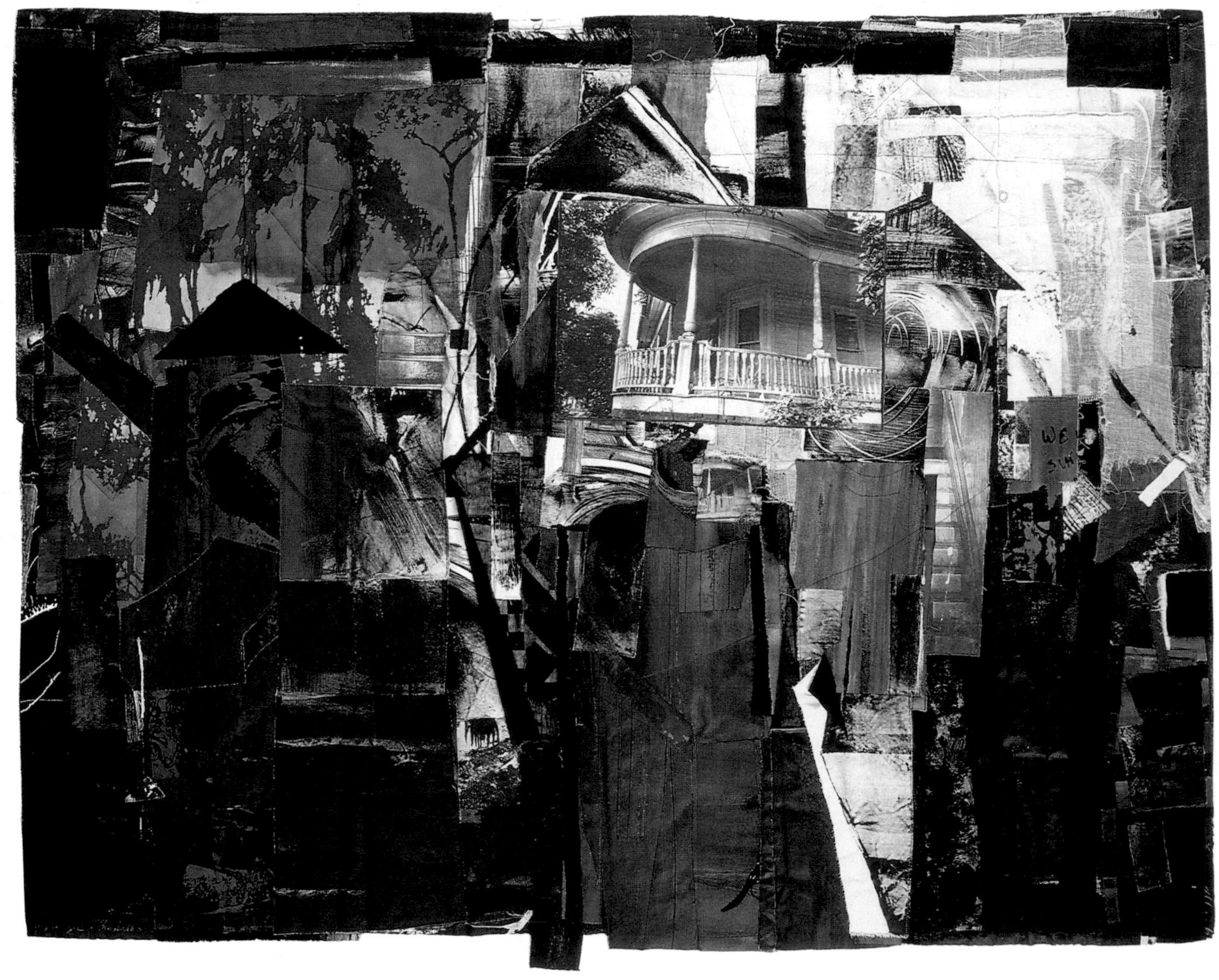

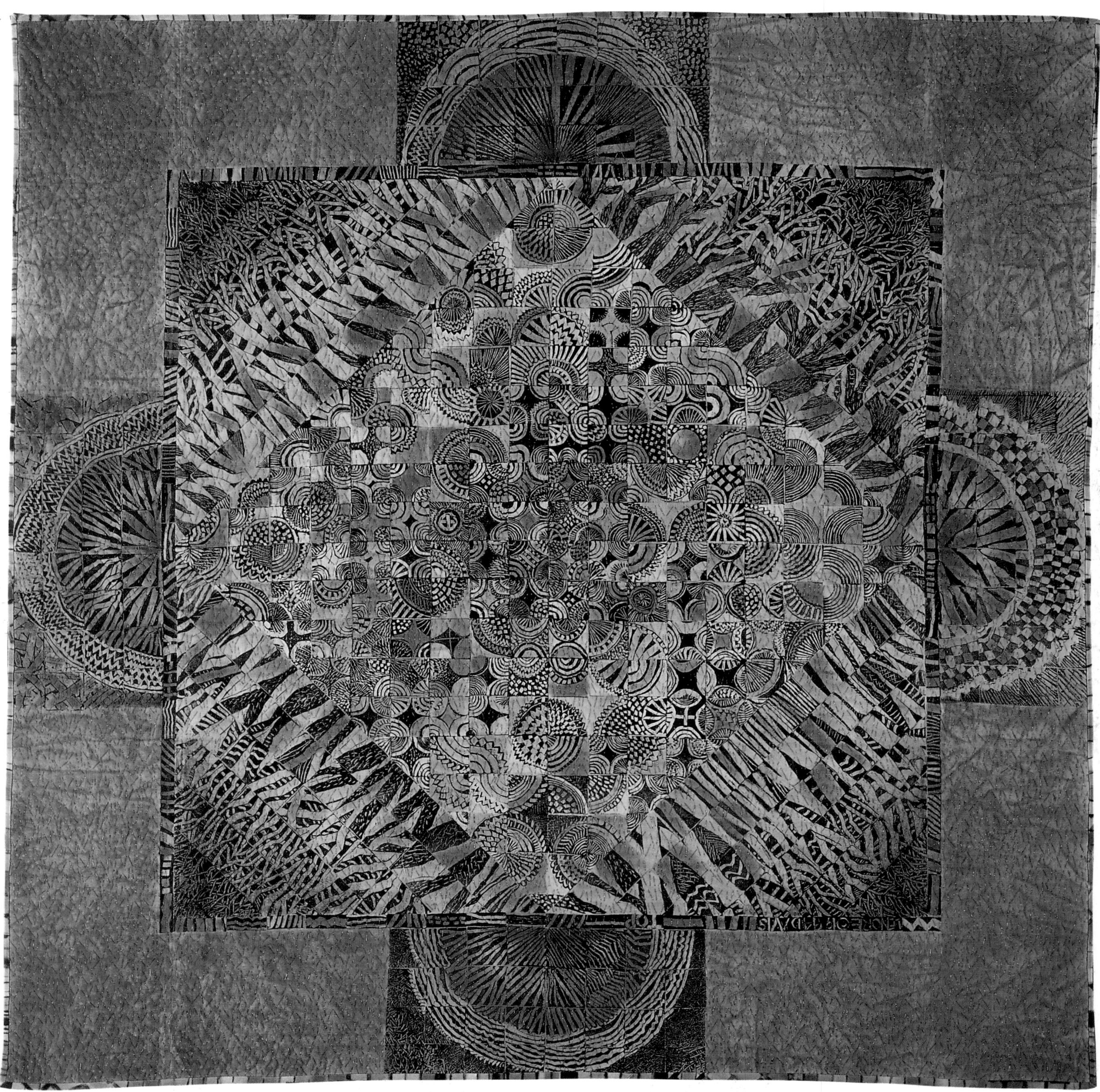

◂ **Work Ahead**

Fran Skiles. 1993. Plantation, Florida. Cotton duck, silk screen, photo transfer, Polaroid print, fabric paint; machine pieced and quilted. 55 x 53 in. Collection of the artist.

This quilt was executed in response to 1993's Hurricane Andrew and depicts the destruction and chaos left in the wake of that devastating storm. The photo of the house, which was actually taken before the hurricane struck, was transferred to cotton duck using a color laser copier. Fran Skiles says, "I have been working in brown and black colors for the past few years. The hurricane quilt is not all that different from my current palette, perhaps a bit more somber."

▲ **The Yellow Diamond**

Lenore Davis. 1994. Newport, Kentucky. Cotton velveteen, metallic thread, textile paint, and dye; monotyped, painted, and hand quilted. 60 x 60 in. Collection of the artist.

This is one of a series of whole cloth quilts by Davis that use printing techniques to simulate the effects of patchwork.

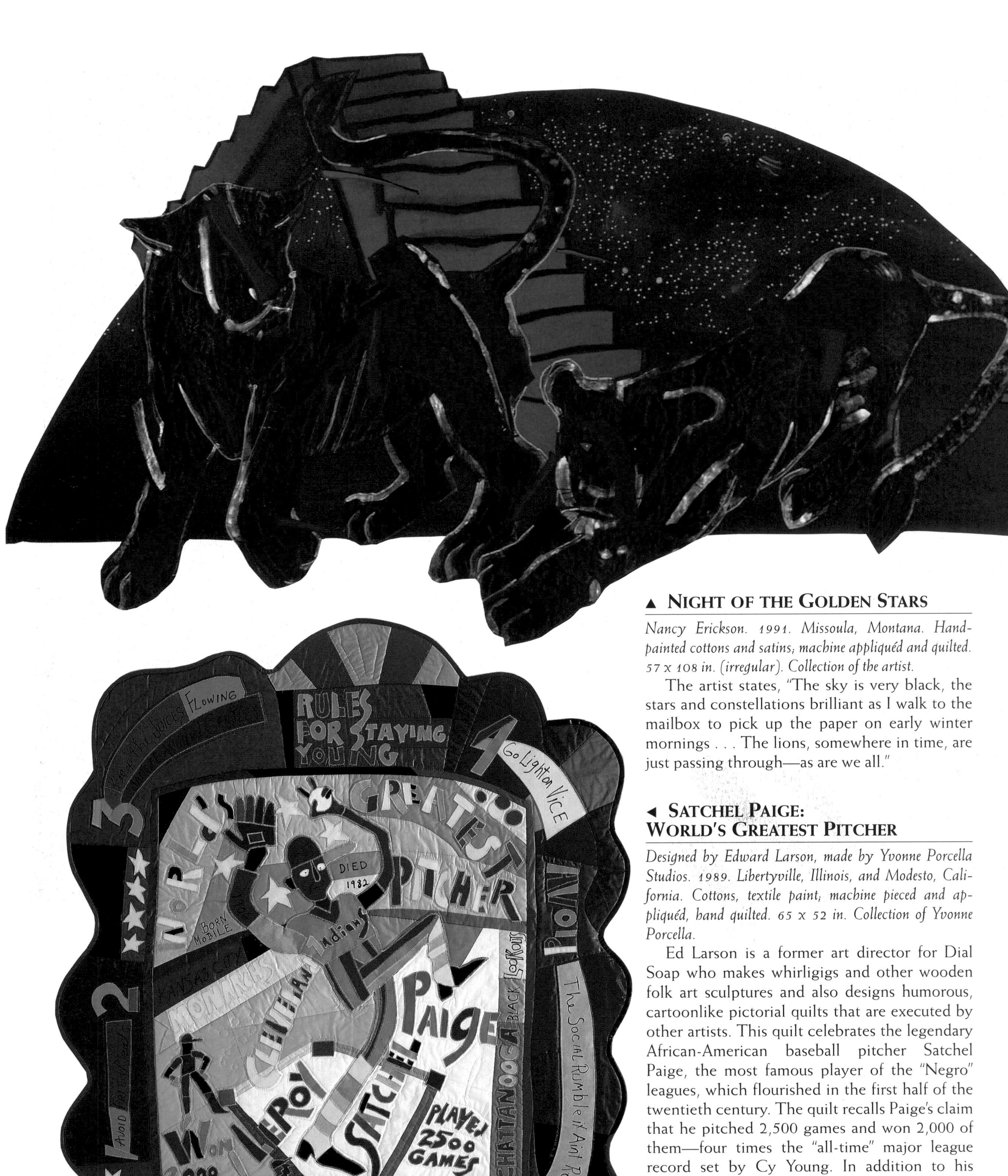

▲ NIGHT OF THE GOLDEN STARS

Nancy Erickson. 1991. Missoula, Montana. Hand-painted cottons and satins; machine appliquéd and quilted. 57 x 108 in. (irregular). Collection of the artist.

The artist states, "The sky is very black, the stars and constellations brilliant as I walk to the mailbox to pick up the paper on early winter mornings . . . The lions, somewhere in time, are just passing through—as are we all."

◄ SATCHEL PAIGE: WORLD'S GREATEST PITCHER

Designed by Edward Larson, made by Yvonne Porcella Studios. 1989. Libertyville, Illinois, and Modesto, California. Cottons, textile paint; machine pieced and appliquéd, hand quilted. 65 x 52 in. Collection of Yvonne Porcella.

Ed Larson is a former art director for Dial Soap who makes whirligigs and other wooden folk art sculptures and also designs humorous, cartoonlike pictorial quilts that are executed by other artists. This quilt celebrates the legendary African-American baseball pitcher Satchel Paige, the most famous player of the "Negro" leagues, which flourished in the first half of the twentieth century. The quilt recalls Paige's claim that he pitched 2,500 games and won 2,000 of them—four times the "all-time" major league record set by Cy Young. In addition to his prowess as a player, Paige was known for his amusing "Rules for Staying Young," which included such homespun homilies as "Avoid running at all times" and "Never look back—something might be gaining on you."

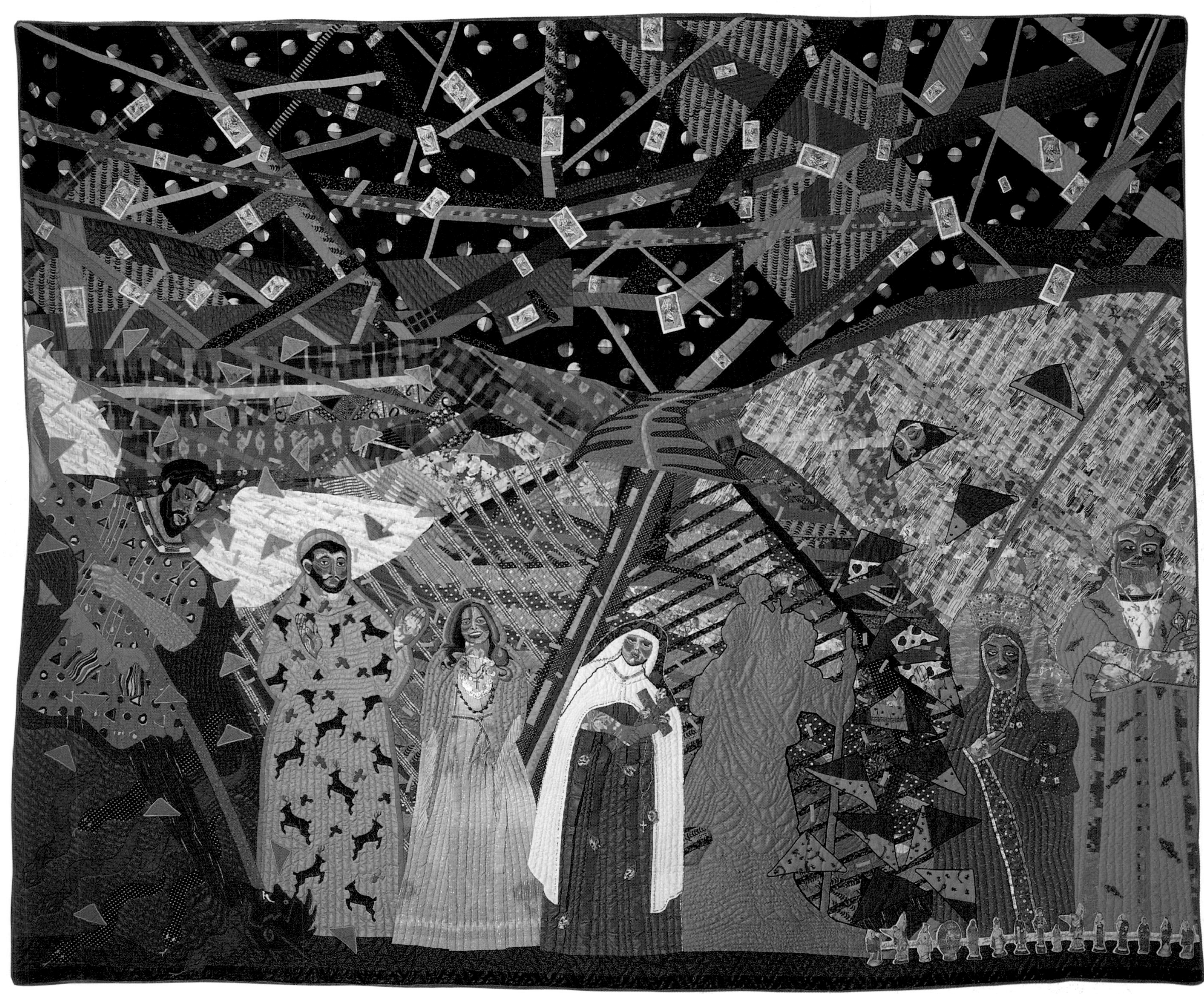

▲ **DASHBOARD SAINTS: IN MEMORY OF ST. CHRISTOPHER (WHO LOST HIS MAGNETISM . . .)**

Terrie Hancock Mangat. 1985. Cincinnati, Ohio. Cottons and cotton blends; hand appliquéd and machine pieced; reverse appliqué, embroidery, beadwork, color photocopying; hand quilted by Sue Rule, Carlisle, Kentucky. 99 x 123 in. Collection of Ardis and Robert James.

The artist has oriented this quilt so the viewer seems to be in the driver's seat of some obsessively devout Catholic's car, looking over a dashboard laden with plastic figurines of saints. From left the figures represent St. Michael casting out the Devil, St. Francis, Mary Magdalene, St. Theresa, St. Christopher, St. Valentine, the Virgin Mary, and St. Peter. St. Christopher, seen as a ghost, and St. Valentine, who has been cut up and floats into space, were desanctified by the Catholic church and are being mourned by the other figures. Terrie Mangat comments, "I've often wondered what happened to all the prayers offered to saints who, the church now tells us, were never able to receive them."

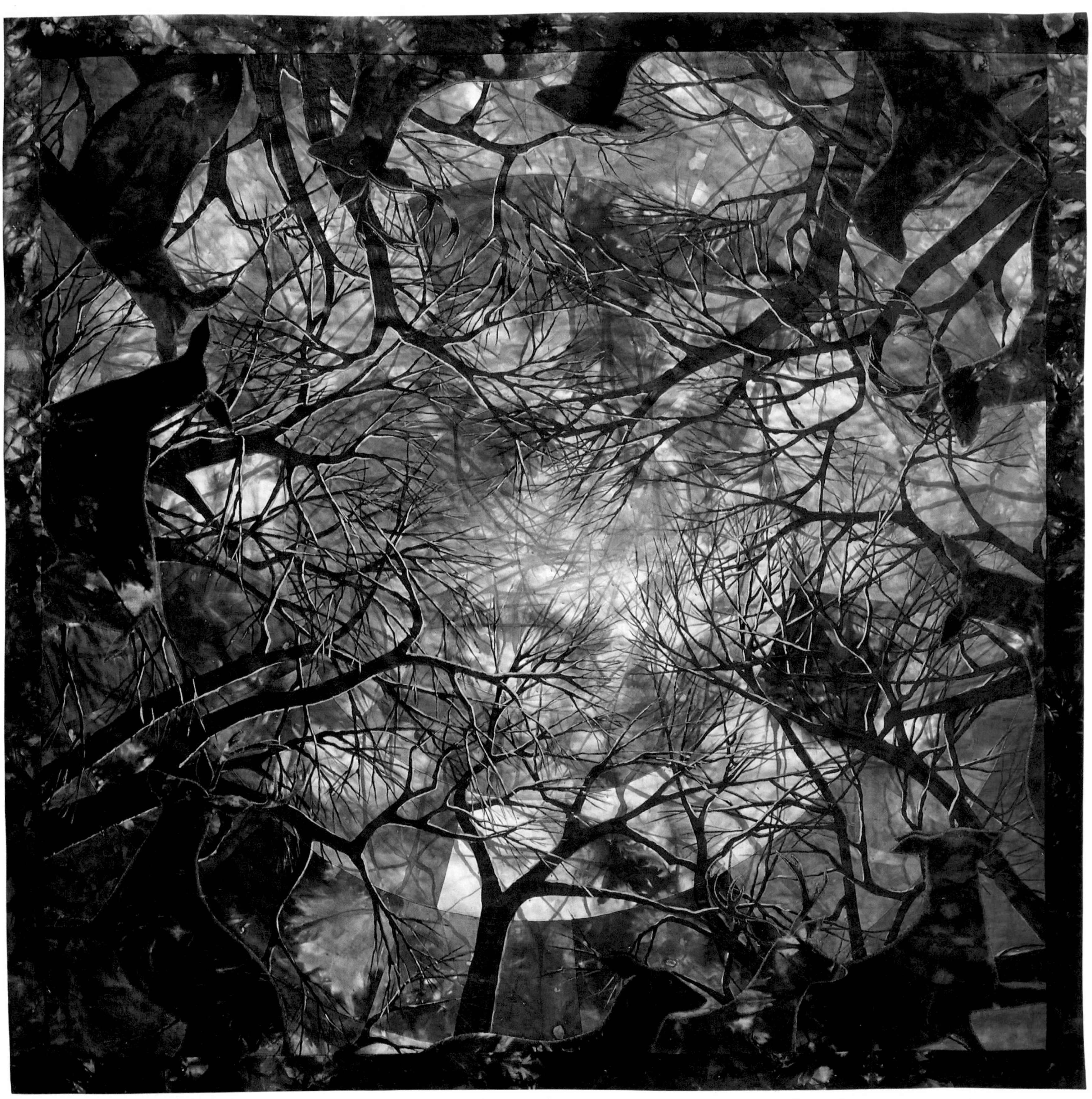

▲ BETWEEN THE SPIRIT AND THE DUST

Roxanna Bartlett. 1993. Boulder, Colorado. Dyed and painted cotton sateen, cotton velvet, and perle cotton; machine pieced, appliquéd, tied. 69 x 69 in. Collection of the artist.

Roxanna Bartlett's quilts attempt to capture what James Joyce called epiphanies—fleeting moments of intense spiritual and emotional insight. Joyce described an epiphany as "a sudden spiritual manifestation . . . a revelation of the whatness of a thing . . . [in which] the soul of the commonest object . . . seems to us radiant."

WOOD SPIRIT WOODS ▶

Tafi Brown. 1993. Alstead, New Hampshire. Cottons, cyanotype prints and photograms; hand pieced and quilted. 70 x 50 in. Collection of the artist.

In addition to making quilts and teaching elementary school art, Tafi Brown designs timber frame houses. This quilt celebrates her own house, which she designed and helped build. According to Brown, "I've tried to keep my life as simple as possible . . . I've always felt, and teach, that 'with discipline comes freedom.'"

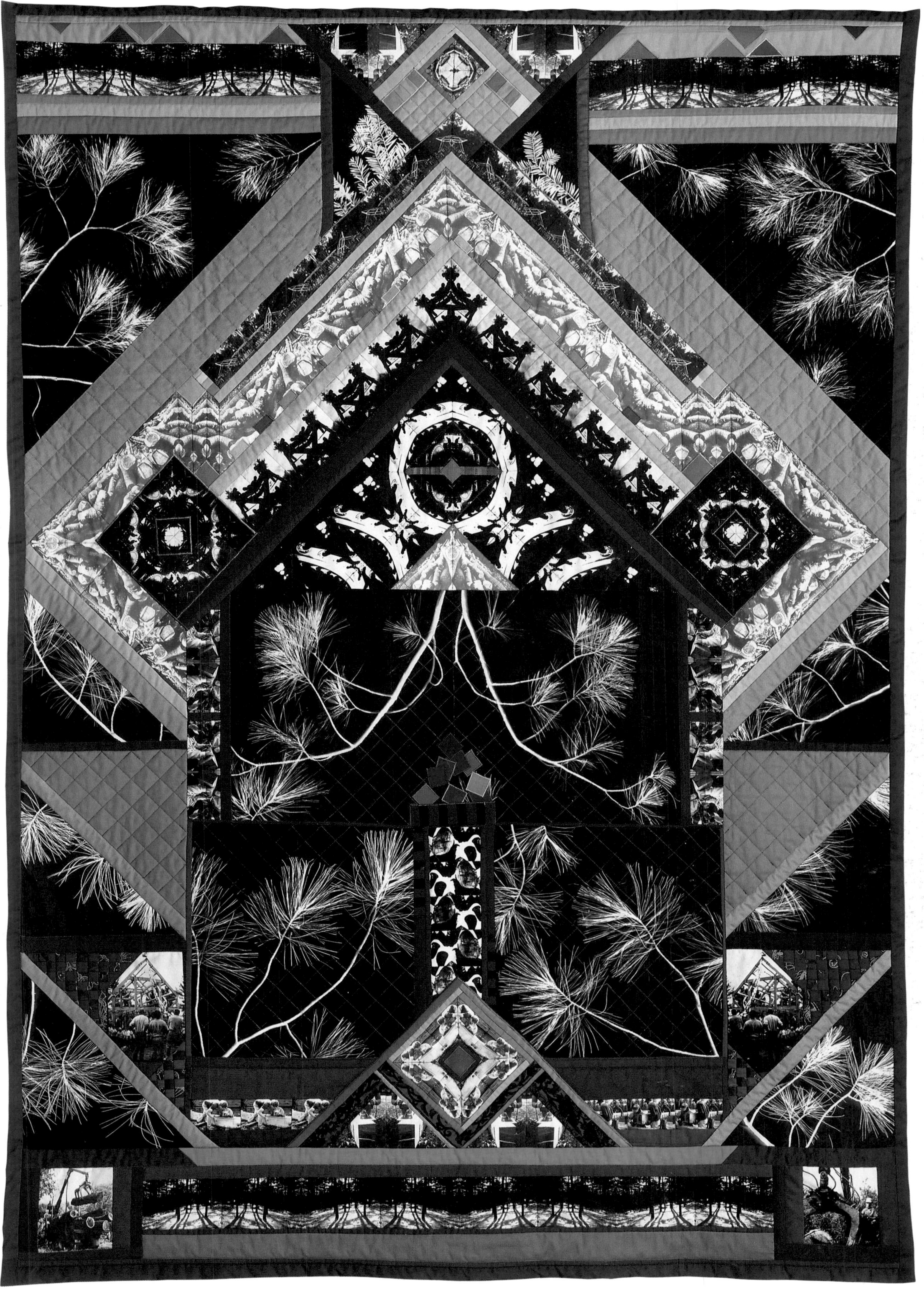

Selected Resources

Museums and Public Exhibitions

Abby Aldrich Rockefeller Folk Art Center
Box C
Williamsburg, VA 23187
(804) 229-1000
Antique quilts on rotating exhibit; daily 11–7.

Baltimore Museum of Art
Jean and Allen Berman Textile Gallery
Art Museum Drive
Baltimore, MD 21218
(301) 396-6266
Over 200 antique quilts, including Baltimore albums, often on exhibit; call ahead for information.

Daughters of the American Revolution Museum
1776 D Street NW
Washington, D.C. 20006
(202) 879-3241
Collection of nearly 200 eighteenth- and nineteenth-century quilts; call ahead for information.

Denver Art Museum
100 West 14th Avenue Parkway
Denver, CO 80204
(303) 575-2196
Over 200 antique and contemporary quilts; call ahead for information.

Esprit de Corp
900 Minnesota Street
San Francisco, CA 94107
(415) 648-6900
Changing exhibition of maverick quilts; by appointment only.

Henry Ford Museum
Box 1970
Dearborn, MI 48121
(313) 271-1620
Collection of over 200 quilts; call ahead for information.

Honolulu Academy of Arts
900 South Beretania Street
Honolulu, HI 96822
(808) 538-3693
Largest public collection of antique Hawaiian quilts; call ahead for information.

Indiana State Museum
202 North Alabama
Indianapolis, IN 46304
(317) 232-1637
Large collection of Indiana Amish quilts; call ahead for information.

Metropolitan Museum of Art
American Decorative Arts Department
Fifth Avenue at 82nd Street
New York, NY 10028
(212) 879-5500
Highly refined small permanent collection; quilts always on exhibit Tues.–Sun. 9:30–5:15.

Museum of American Folk Art
Two Lincoln Square
New York, NY 10023
(212) 496-2966
Frequent exhibitions including quilts; call ahead for information.

Museum of the American Quilter's Society
Box 3290
Paducah, KY 42002-3290
(502) 442-8856
Changing exhibitions of antique, contemporary, and art quilts; annual contest; call for information on current exhibitions.

Museum of Early Southern Decorative Arts
924 South Main Street
Winston-Salem, NC 27108
(919) 722-6148
Early Southern quilts always on exhibit; daily 10:30–5.

Museum of International Folk Art
Museum of New Mexico
Box 2087
Santa Fe, NM 87504-2087
(505) 827-8350
Eclectic collection of antique and contemporary quilts includes examples by NEA National Heritage Fellows; call ahead for information.

National Museum of American History
Smithsonian Institution
Division of Textiles
Constitution Avenue between 12th and 14th Streets
Washington, D.C. 20560
(202) 357-7889
Collection of 275 quilts, including Harriet Powers's *Bible Quilt*; call ahead for information.

National Museum of Man
Canadian Centre for Folklife Studies
Metcalfe and McLeod Streets
Ottawa, ON K1A OM8
(613) 993-2497
Over 300 antique and contemporary Canadian quilts; call ahead for information.

New England Quilt Museum
18 Shattuck Street
Lowell, MA 01852-7076
(508) 452-4207
Changing exhibitions of antique, contemporary, and art quilts. Mon.–Sat. 10–5, Sun. 12–5.

Old Sturbridge Village
Sturbridge, MA 01566
(617) 347-3362
Collection of 150 predominantly New England antique quilts, some always on exhibit; April–October, daily 9–5; call ahead for information on winter hours.

Quilt National
Dairy Barn Cultural Arts Center
Athens, OH
(614) 592-4981
Biennial juried traveling exhibition of art quilts; call for information and venues.

Quilt San Diego
9747 Business Park Avenue #228
San Diego, CA 92131-1653
(619) 695-2822
International arts organization dedicated to the promotion and appreciation of the quilt as art. Organizes *Visions*, biennial juried traveling exhibition of art quilts; call for information on venues.

A People's Place
Intercourse, PA 17534
Changing exhibitions of antique Amish quilts.

Royal Ontario Museum
100 Queen's Park
Toronto, ON M5S 2C6
(416) 978-3655
Over 100 antique quilts from England, Canada, the U.S., and other countries; call ahead for information.

The Shelburne Museum
Box 10
Shelburne, VT 05482
(802) 985-3346
Approximately 100 antique quilts and other bedcovers from collection of over 700 on rotating exhibit. Late May–late October, daily 10–5; call ahead for winter hours and availability.

Upper Canada Village
Box 740
Morrisburg, ON K0C 1X0
(613) 543-2911
Ontario quilts on rotating exhibit. May–October, daily 8:15–4:30; call ahead for winter hours.

The Valentine Museum
1015 West Clay Street
Richmond, VA 23219
(804) 649-0711
Important collection of over 100 predominantly Virginia quilts; call ahead for information.

Henry Francis du Pont Winterthur Museum
Winterthur, DE 19735
(302) 656-8591
Over 100 early quilts, some always on exhibit; call ahead for information.

QUILT ASSOCIATIONS AND STUDY GROUPS

American Quilt Study Group
660 Mission Street, Suite 400
San Francisco, CA 94105-4007
(415) 495-0163

Canadian Quilt Study Group
1109-160A Street
White Rock, BC V4A 7G9

Friends of Fiber Art International
Box 468
Western Springs, IL 60558
Advocacy group for contemporary fiber art, including quilts.

The Kentucky Quilt Project, Inc.
635 West Main Street
Louisville, KY 40202
Sponsor of Kentucky documentation project, special exhibitions, and forums; publisher of exhibition catalogs and *The Quilt Journal: An International Review*.

National Association of African-American Quilters
Box 20617
Baltimore, MD 21223

National Quilting Association
Box 62
Greenbelt, MD 20770

Studio Art Quilt Associates
Box 287
Salida, CA 95368
Advocacy group for quilt artists. Clearing house for information on art quilts and quiltmakers.

Women of Color Quilters Network
556 Bessinger Drive
Cincinnati, OH 45240

QUILT DEALERS

America Hurrah
766 Madison Avenue
New York, NY 10021
(212) 535-1930
Joel and Kate Kopp
Antiques.

The Margaret Cavigga Quilt Collection
8648 Melrose Avenue,
Los Angeles, CA 90069
(213) 659-3020
Antique and contemporary.

Robert Cargo Folk Art Gallery
2314 Sixth Street
Tuscaloosa, AL 35401
Antique and contemporary Southern, esp. African-American.

Connell Gallery
333 Buckhead Avenue
Atlanta, GA 30305
(404) 261-1712
Martha Connell
Art quilts; represents many leading artists.

Darwin D. Bearley
98 Beck Avenue
Akron, OH 44302
(216) 376-4965
Antiques, esp. Amish; by appointment.

M. Finkel and Daughter
936 Pine Street
Philadelphia, PA 19107
(215) 627-7797
Antiques.

Laura Fisher
1950 Second Avenue
Gallery 84
New York, NY 10022
(212) 838-2596
Antiques.

Great Expectations
14520 Memorial Drive, Suite 54
Houston, TX 77079
(713) 496-1366
Karey Bresenhan
Antique and contemporary.

Mid-West Quilt Exchange
495 South Third Street
Columbus, OH 43215
(614) 221-8400
Sandra Mitchell
Antiques; by appointment.

Judith and James Milne
506 East 74th Street
New York, NY 10021
(212) 472-0107
Antiques; by appointment.

Quilts Unlimited, Inc.
440A Duke of Gloucester Street
Williamsburg, VA 23185
(804) 253-8700
Antique and contemporary.

Stella Rubin Quilts and Antiques
12300 Glen Road
Potomac, MD 20854
(301) 958-4187
Antiques; by appointment.

Thomas K. Woodard
799 Madison Avenue
New York, NY 10021
(212) 988-2906
Antiques.

Shelly Zegart
12-Z River Hill Road
Louisville, KY 40207
(502) 897-7566
Antiques, esp. maverick quilts; by appointment.

QUILT CONSERVATION CENTERS

Conservation/Collections Care Center
New York State Parks and Recreation Division for Historic Preservation
Pebles Island
Box 219
Waterford, NY 12188
(518) 237-8643

The Textile Conservation Workshop
Main Street
South Salem, NY 10590
(914) 763-5805

Textile Conservation Center
Museum of American Textile History
80 Massachusetts Avenue
North Andover, MA 08145
(508) 686-0191

Index

Page numbers in **bold** indicate illustrations.

INDEX

Photography Credits

Photo courtesy America Hurrah, New York City: pp. 27, 32–33, 35, 36, 38 (bottom), 58, 59, 175, 179 (bottom), 180, 182 (bottom), 196.

Photo courtesy American International Quilt Association: Gary Bankhead, photographer: p. 122.

Photo Art and Image, Baltimore, Maryland: Huguette May, photographer: p. 207 (bottom).

Photo by Gavin Ashworth: pp. 151, 186.

Photo courtesy Joshua Baer & Co., Santa Fe, New Mexico: All reproduction rights reserved by Joshua Baer & Co.: p. 234.

Baltimore Museum of Art, BMA 1984.323: p. 48 (bottom).

Photo by Gary Bankhead, Houston, Texas: p. 120 (bottom).

Photo by Karen Bell: pp. 135, 142 (top left), 150 (top).

Photo by Brian Blauser, Athens, Ohio: p. 274 (top).

Quilt © Tafi Brown: p. 303.

Photo by Deloye Burrell: p. 263.

Photo by Ken Burris: frontispiece, pp. 34 (top), 65, 71, 84, 116 (bottom), 122–23, 139 (bottom), 235.

Canadian Museum of Civilization, negative no. 579-4315: p. 19.

Photo by David Caras: pp. 253 (left), 253 (right), 261 (top), 272–73 (copyright 1990 Michael James); photo copyright David Caras: p. 268.

Photo by Robert Cargo: p. 192.

Photo by Randy Cochran: pp. 296, 297 (top), 297 (bottom).

Photo by Taylor Dabney: pp. 152 (top), 153: © 1989 Taylor Dabney: p. 152 (bottom)

Photo by Peter Dreyer: pp. 140–41.

Photo by DSI Studios: pp. 129, 134.

Photo by Red Elf: p. 137.

Photo by Nancy Erickson: © 1989 Nancy Erickson: p. 300 (top)

Photo by Exhibit Touring Services of Eastern Washington University: p. 239.

Photo courtesy M. Finkel and Daughter Antiques: p. 194 (top).

Photo by J. Kevin Fitzsimons: pp. 251 (left), 251 (right), 294.

Photo courtesy Cora Ginsberg, Inc.: p. 20.

Collection of the Hargrett Rare Book and Manuscripts, University of Georgia Libraries, negative number UW539: p. 188 (right).

Transparency courtesy Hearts and Hands Media Arts: p. 230.

Photo by Gary Heatherly: p. 199.

Photo by Cathy Henkel, *Seattle Times*: quilt © Conrad House: p. 236 (bottom).

Photo by Matt Hoebermann: pp. 8, 166 (top).

Quilt © 1993 Mimi Holmes: p. 264.

Photo by Michael Honer, Upland, California: p. 150 (bottom).

Photo courtesy Ardis and Robert James: photo by Myron Miller: pp. 90–91.

Photo by Phil Jones: p. 145 (bottom).

Photo by Brent Kane: p. 96.

Photo by Elaine F. Keenan: p. 281 (bottom).

Photo courtesy the Kentucky Quilt Project, Inc.: p. 95.

Photo courtesy Kei Kobayashi: From the exhibition *Made in Japan: American Influence on Japanese Quilts*, photo by Takayuki Ogawa: pp. 154, 158, 159, 161 (top), 161 (bottom), 163, 166 (bottom).

Photo by Paul K. Kodama, Honolulu, Hawaii: p. 219.

Photo courtesy Kokusai Art: pp. 10, 15, 157, 160, 162 (top), 167, 168–69, 173, 181 (top left), 212, 214, 215, 217 (left), 217 (right), 218, 220–21, 222 (top), 223, 226 (bottom), 226 (top)–227.

Quilt © Susan Webb Lee: p. 265.

Photo by Bill Le Lemore: copyright Bill Le Lemore: p. 238 (top).

Photo courtesy Les Golding, Tyne & Wear Museums, England: p. 117

Photo Light Impressions: Mark Renken, photographer: p. 237.

Photo by Clark Marten: p. 139 (top).

Photo by Jack Mathieson: p. 237.

The Metropolitan Museum of Art, New York: accession no. 58.41: John Bigelow Taylor, photographer: p. 24.

Photo courtesy Michigan State University, Traditional Arts Research Collection: pp. 189, 197 (bottom), 206.

Photo by Myron Miller: pp. 13, 17, 30, 46, 47, 53, 54, 55, 57, 61, 62, 64 (top), 66–67, 69 (top), 69 (bottom), 74, 75 (top), 76 (top), 76 (bottom), 78–79, 81, 82–83, 88 (top) 89, 98 (left), 98 (right), 107, 114, 128 (top), 165 (bottom), 170, 178, 181 (bottom), 181 (top right), 202 (top), 208–209, 242, 250, 255, 261 (botom), 266–67, 269 (bottom), 275, 278–79, 282–83, 284–85, 289, 290-91, 295, 298 (top), 301.

Minnesota Historical Society Museums Collection: accession no. 1987.43.1: p. 185 (bottom).

Photo by Michel Monteaux: p. 115 (bottom).

Collection of the Museum of American Folk Art, New York: accession no. 1984.33.1, p. 8; gift of Dr. Robert Bishop, accession no. 1985.37.9, p. 48 (top); accession no. 1986.20.1, p. 80; accession no. 1990.7.1, p. 186.

Photo courtesy the NAMES project, Smithsonian Institution: photo by Mark Theissen: p. 109 (top); photo by Jeff Tinsley: p.109 (bottom).

Reprinted from *Nebraska Quilts and Quiltmakers*, by Crews and Naugle. By permission of Lincoln Quilters Guild, Lincoln, Nebraska, copyright 1991 by University of Nebraska Press: p. 121.

Photo by Andrew Neuhart: p. 92.

Photo courtesy Nihon Vogue: pp. 162 (bottom), 164–65 (top).

Oregon Historical Society, Portland, negative no. 21876: p. 52 (right).

Photo by John Peelle: p. 288 (top).

Transparency property of Quilt San Diego: photo by Carina Woolrich, San Diego: quilt © 1993 Sally A. Sellers: p. 287 (bottom); quilt © 1993 Melissa Holzinger: p. 292; quilt © 1992 Emily Richardson: p. 293 (top); quilt © 1993 Liz Axford: p. 293 (bottom); quilt © 1993 Roxanna Bartlett: p. 302.

Photo courtesy Yvonne Porcella: p. 258.

Photo by Mary S. Rezny: pp. 254, 259 (top).

Photo by Sharon Risedorph: pp. 87 (top), 112 (top right), 113, 119 (bottom), 127, 132 (top), 132 (bottom), 144, 145 (top), 146 (top), 172, 176, 177 (top), 177 (bottom), 179 (top), 198 (bottom), 222 (bottom), 224 (top), 224 (bottom), 225 (top), 225 (bottom), 228 (top), 229, 281 (top), 300 (bottom); courtesy Connell Gallery, Atlanta, Georgia: p. 256; quilt © 1990 Yvonne Porcella: p. 280.

Photo by John Ryan: pp. 200–201.

Photo by J.D. Schwalm: p. 128 (bottom).

Photo courtesy the Shelburne Museum, Shelburne, Vermont: photo by Ken Burris: p. 63.

Photo by Shutterbug, Inc., Bowling Green, Kentucky: pp. 72–3.

St. Louis Museum Purchase: Museum Minority Artists Purchase Fund: The Honorable Carol E. Jackson, Mr. and Mrs. Steven M. Cousins, Mr. and Mrs. Lester R. Crancer, Jr., Mr. and Mrs. Solon Gershman, Mr. Sidney Goldstein in memory of Chip Goldstein, The Links, Inc., Gateway Chapter, The Honorable and Mrs. Charles A. Shaw, Donald M. Suggs,Casually Off-Grain Quilters of Chesterfield, Thimble & Thread Quild Guild, and funds given in honor of Questa Benberry: p. 190.

Photo by Greg Staley: pp. 130–31, 193.

"The 3rd Exhibition of Quilt Nihon": p. 162 (bottom).

Photo © 1993 Steven J. Titus: p. 9.

Photo courtesy The Vermont Quilt Festival: pp. 40–41.

Photo by Ken Wagner, Seattle, Washington: p. 97.

Photo © Maude Wahlman: p. 211 (top left).

Photo by Richard Walker: pp. 106, 125.

Photo courtesy Thomas K. Woodward American Antiques and Quilts, New York: p. 49.

Photo by Carina Woolrich, San Diego: p. 264.